Stephen Spender

Stephen Spender

A Literary Life

JOHN SUTHERLAND

OXFORD
UNIVERSITY PRESS
2005

OXFORD
UNIVERSITY PRESS

Oxford   New York
Auckland Bangkok Buenos Aires
Cape Town Chennai Dar es Salaam Delhi Hong Kong Istanbul
Karachi Kolkata Kuala Lumpur Madrid Melbourne Mexico City Mumbai
Nairobi São Paulo Shanghai Taipei Tokyo Toronto

Published by Oxford University Press, Inc., 2005
198 Madison Avenue, New York, New York 10016
www.oup.com

Library of Congress Cataloging-in-Publication Data
Sutherland, John, 1938–
Stephen Spender : a literary life / John Sutherland.
p. cm.
Includes bibliographical references and index.
ISBN 0-19-517816-5–
1. Spender, Stephen, 1909–
2. Poets, English—20th century—Biography.
3. Critics—Great Britain—Biography.
I. Title.
PR6037.P47Z87 2005
821'.912—dc22
2004009727

1 3 5 7 9 10 8 6 4 2
Printed in the United States of America
on acid-free paper

I suppose that he [Stephen Spender] and Maurice [Bowra] between them have had a more decisive effect on me than anyone else; Maurice by knocking a great deal of nonsense with which one came up from school out of one, and making a man of one in an almost Kiplingy sense; Stephen by being very naive and morally impressive and shrewd at the same time; in those days, the early twenties, the moral vocabulary of the Victorians had become too discredited; words like good and bad, right and wrong, kind and cruel were scarcely allowed at all among the intelligentsia [. . .] Stephen was rather as Shelley must have been, evidently he did not know about this ban, and used the old words with great simplicity and full values and restored the moral currency . . .

(Isaiah Berlin to Alice James, 31 December 1949)

Contents

List of Illustrations

Picture credits

Preface

No British poet of the twentieth century has provoked a more perplexing response among his contemporaries than Stephen Spender. His name is as familiar to those who claim to know poetry as that of his great friend, W. H. Auden. Such things are hard to gauge but Spender probably remains better known than the other leading poets of the 1930s quartet, Louis MacNeice or C. Day-Lewis. Certainly more so than George Barker, Roy Campbell or Edith Sitwell – all famous in their day, now gone, or on their way, into literary oblivion.

Spender's early success, as a twenty-four-year-old poet praised (and published) by T. S. Eliot, was, in the event, a cross he bore all his life. He himself good-naturedly saw the attacks he sustained over the years as some kind of 'tax' he must pay for the huge applause that *Poems, 1933* had received. Posterity was, it seemed, determined to take him down a peg or two. They never quite succeeded and they never stopped trying. But somehow his quality (and, I would argue, his literary greatness) weathered the assault.

None the less, few poets of the twentieth century have been more attacked: less for his poetry than for what it is supposed 'Stephen Spender' stands for as a poet. Much of the opprobrium against Spender can be traced back to F. R. Leavis and the 'Scrutineers' of Downing College, for whose stern generations he was the incarnation of that modern Gomorrah, the London Literary World.

Spender outlived most of his contemporaries but not, alas, his critics. Over six decades of literary and professional life his output was extraordinarily varied: he was a novelist, playwright, essayist, lecturer, broadcaster and prolific reviewer. His extra-literary activities were equally varied. Steeped from birth in Edwardian liberalism, throughout his life Spender participated in good causes. He helped preserve works of art from destruction in the Spanish Civil War; he helped advance the civic education of firemen during the Second World War; he participated in the de-Nazification of post-war German libraries; he helped get UNESCO off the ground; he helped found and went on to co-edit two of the most successful journals of ideas in the twentieth century (*Horizon* and

Encounter); he founded *Index on Censorship* and originated the idea of the Poetry Book Society.

More than anyone of his time Spender understood the importance of cultural milieu. Behind literature, art or music (or even good conversation) there must be what he liked to call 'community'. He cultivated the society of literary and artistic people. Many successful careers were nurtured by his early patronage. Not the least of his achievements was to bridge American and British post-war culture during periods of great political tension between the two countries. It is appropriate that he should have been both knighted for his services to English Literature and appointed the poet laureate of America (Poetry Consultant to Congress).

My own acquaintance with Spender was in one of his smaller parts, as a tenured professor of literature. I was, for three years, his colleague at UCL in the early 1970s. Given the difference in our ages, I was more conscious of him than he of me. But two things were clear to me. He was a very good teacher. And all those who knew Stephen at all well either liked him immensely or loved him.

No one knows better than a biographer the impossibility of trapping a whole life on paper. Biographies can be long but they are never complete. In this book I have tried to get as much down as possible while the trails are still warm. It will be supplemented by the personal recollections and memoirs of those who knew him much better than I: primarily his wife Natasha (a main source for the second part of this book). Spender's marriage to Natasha Litvin in April 1941 represented a distinct new phase in his life. There were a number of such phases – not least his turn away from the life which he lived in the early 1930s, in Germany. Spender was disarmingly frank – courageously so – in dealing with his formative sexual experiences in books such as *World within World*. Unfortunately, however, his frankness, far from disarming critics, has given some of them ammunition with which to attack him. Unfairly. Spender, I would maintain, can only be understood as a creative writer forever 'making himself'. And one's judgement should be reserved for what – in his years of (relative) maturity – he succeeded in becoming. This is something that he quite reasonably claimed in opening so much of his private life up for public inspection.

Literary biographies typically skip over the subject's early years. Often this is because little documentary evidence remains. Often, too, the biographer wants to get on to 'achievement'. Stephen Spender was fascinated

by his own early life and wrote extensively about it. In order to understand himself, he felt, he must first understand his childhood and youth.
Fortunately there survive both literary remains and oral testimony about
the first thirty years of his life. Young Spender occupies (disproportion-
ately) half the following narrative.

Spender is a poet inextricably associated with a decade: the 1930s.
That period too occupies a disproportionate space in the following pages.
My aim has been to describe a man of many (and often perplexing)
parts and to convey the admiration I have come to feel for him, the
more I have learned about his remarkable life and his distinguished body
of literary work.

Ambitious Son, Failed Father: 1909–30

My parents' sin was to sin
My mother's sin was to conceive in sorrow:
I was not born from the laughter
But from the dry lust, the dry falling
Through the dust and death of my father.
(Stephen Spender: ms poem to
Gabriel Carritt, c. 1930)

My father thought he was a VIP, and he wasn't.
(Humphrey Spender, 1997)

My father had his children too late.
(Christine Spender, 1998)

Stephen Spender, long after he had been orphaned, viewed himself in direct relation to his father. He was, as his titles put it, a 'backward *son*', an 'ambitious *son*', 'the public *son* of a public man'. So it was with the other Spender offspring (although they did not, like Stephen, write about it). Harold Spender dominated his four children's lives, in death as in life. None more so than Stephen, for whom his father was the epitome of 'failure'.

Edward Harold Spender (always known as 'Harold') was born in Bath, 22 June 1864, the son of a remarkable mother and a less remarkable father. John Kent Spender was a physician catering to the valetudinarian clientele of the spa town. The Spenders were a medical family on both sides, and had been established in the Avon area for 300 years. On this side, Stephen Spender's English roots run deep and straight.

Although its great days were past, nineteenth-century Bath was a literary as well as a health resort. The Spender family was cultivated and the women, particularly, were creative and politically enlightened. In his later years J. K. Spender was Physician to Bath's Mineral Water Hospital (as had been his father before him). He had a 'free' as well as a fee-paying surgery and did not, his eldest son wryly records, 'make a fortune out of medicine'. But Dr Spender was comfortably off. Philanthropy was an ingrained family trait. So too was bookishness. The Spenders had a circle of literary friends. Walter Savage Landor was the most famous; Henry Crabb Robinson − Wordsworth's friend − was a cousin.

Following legislation in the nineteenth century, doctors were increasingly prosperous and 'gentlemanly'. J. K. Spender rose with his profession. He was able to marry well in 1858 and by 1870 took up residence at 17 The Circle, one of Bath's desirable addresses. His wife, Lily Kent Spender (1835–95), was another doctor's child. Her father, Edward Headland, had been a fashionable physician in practice at Portland Place in London. Mrs Headland, Lily's mother, was a daughter of Ferdinand de Medina. (Humphrey Spender sees this ancestry as significant; there was Jewish blood on both sides of his family.) Well educated, cultivated, fluent in French and German, and good-looking, Lily was a catch for the provincial Bath doctor.

Despite having eight children (four of each) – occupation enough for a Victorian physician's wife – Lily was a woman of indefatigable intellectual aspiration. In her youth she had taught herself Greek, rising early in the morning to do so. 'A born hostess and social magnet', she was, her son J. A. Spender records, 'a devoted public worker'. But her main work was devoted to the welfare of her family. Fanatically methodical, she had each of her eight children taught a different musical instrument. She gave them a flying start with her programme of nursery education: 'Writing came to us as naturally as walking,' Harold recalled – and at about the same toddling period of life.

Lily was a staunch believer in educational achievement. Three of her children (one a girl at Somerville) were undergraduates at Oxford simultaneously in the early 1880s. Shortly after her marriage she began writing for money to provide her young ones with the higher necessities of life – such as Oxford University. She graduated from 'heavy' essays on the German poets to 'three decker' novels for the circulating libraries. 'For twenty years,' her son records, 'she wrote without ceasing in the intervals between housekeeping, bringing children into the world, and cultivating a wide circle of friends.' As a novelist, Lily K. Spender established herself as a lesser George Eliot – a writer who wisely did not encumber herself with children and housekeeping.

The bulk of Lily's literary earnings (some £1,600) was set aside for her children's university education. None of her children became doctors. J. K. Spender himself 'never pretended' to like the profession, his elder son records; 'the whole bent of his mind was literary'. And it was towards the writing professions (and 'doing good') that the boys' sense of vocation was also bent. It was not all work. Lily resourcefully created small funds for the family's annual holidays. A further sum was put aside for her husband's eventual retirement. It was a retirement she was not destined to share. She died early of cancer, at the age of sixty.

The two highest achievers among the eight Spender children were J. A. Spender (1862–1942) and Harold. Another brother, Hugh, was to make a smaller name for himself as a novelist and journalist. 'J. A.' (as he was to be known) was 'ugly'. Freckled and with red hair, he was, inevitably, nicknamed 'Carrots'. Harold by contrast had inherited the family good looks. The Spender brothers, divided by two years in age, were lucky to attend Bath College as 'day-boarders'. It was a period when it was establishing itself on Arnoldian lines as 'the best classical school in the country' under its dynamic head, T. W. Dunn.

In an environment where high achievement was routine, Harold excelled. No one that Dunn judged incapable of winning a scholarship to Oxford or Cambridge was admitted into his sixth form. Among this élite Harold Spender was head boy in his final year at the school, 1882–3. Both J. A. Spender (also, in his time, head boy) and Harold won the expected scholarships to Oxford. The elder brother went up in 1881. Harold followed in 1883. J. A. Spender was an Exhibitioner at fashionable Balliol. Harold was an Exhibitioner at less fashionable University College. These were, as Harold fondly recalled, Oxford's 'great days', and he was now part of that greatness.

The Spender brothers did Dunn proud: J. A. Spender got a first in Part I of the classical schools. Struck down by 'a mild attack of pleurisy' which dulled his mind, he had to make do with a second in finals ('I wondered how I could ever talk to my parents or set foot in Balliol again'). Harold Spender graduated in 1887 with a double first. A perfect performance.

More than J. A. Spender, Harold was imbued with the spirit of Oxford high-mindedness, epitomized in the examples of J. R. Green and Arnold Toynbee. These saintly men had taken the ideals of Christian Oxford into the East End – 'darkest London', as it was called. As a star graduate Harold could have remained at the university with the prospect of a fulfilling life as a fellow. Dons had recently been allowed to marry and the life was in every sense amenable. But Harold Spender had resolved, like Toynbee, to do something 'worthwhile' with his gifts.

Resolving was one thing. Choosing the right profession another. For a while Harold drifted. Shortly after coming down from Oxford, in late 1887 to early 1888, he filled in as tutor to the novelist Mrs Humphry Ward's son Arnold. The Wards were currently living at 61 Russell Square. The young man was in the house when the advance copies of *Robert Elsmere* were delivered in January 1888. Mrs Ward's novel of 'faith and doubt' (whose hero was based on Toynbee) became the bestseller of the century. Through Mrs Ward and the Oxford network Harold met the Barnetts, Canon Samuel and Henrietta, current custodians of Toynbee Hall. Before taking over from the martyred Toynbee (who died early of consumption), Barnett had been vicar of the slum parish of St Jude's. The Barnetts were to become lifelong friends and patrons of both Spender brothers. At one of Mrs Ward's famous 'Thursdays' Harold also met her particular friend Henry James, who was evidently much taken by the handsome tutor.

Personal accounts of Harold stress a number of features. Dominant was what Henrietta Barnett (supposed at one time to have been in love with him) called his 'exceptional physical beauty'. He was tall, open-faced, broad-shouldered, 'with a mass of fair hair, and very fine, very blue, very shy eyes'. He was athletic, without being obnoxiously 'hearty'. He wore a moustache, trimmed in youth, shaggy in age. Facially Harold was compared, in later life, both to Nansen, the Scandinavian explorer, and to Lloyd George. Friends sometimes noted an air of 'vagueness and distraction' in the young man's fine features. He was famously absent-minded. This abstraction alternated with a bubbling talkativeness which friends found endearing in the highest degree. He was 'flamboyant' in conversation – often 'overbearing' and 'absurd'. But, as a contemporary recalled, 'Spender was a "charmer", and people laughed at him, while respecting and liking him.' Friends agreed that if Harold had a fault it was 'impulsiveness'.

Both the Spender brothers had a flying start and a clear vocational path laid out before them. Oxford laurels and powerful relations opened the way to a career in journalism and eventually politics. Two uncles, Edward Spender and William Saunders, were magnates of provincial journalism. Saunders, who married J. K. Spender's sister, had founded the *Eastern Morning News* in 1864 and was, for a period in the 1880s, MP for Hull. He had also founded the country's first press agency. Saunders had taken the trouble to come to Oxford in person to entice the brilliant Spender boys into working for him after graduation.

J. A. Spender duly came under his uncle Saunders's wing, and – after the briefest of apprenticeships – was made editor of the family paper at the precocious age of twenty-three, in 1886. There was a core of steadiness in J. A. Spender, lacking in the mercurial Harold, who was, even at this stage, temperamentally a crusading journalist rather than a managing editor. The elder brother's career unfolded with the precision of a Napoleonic campaign. Having served a five-year apprenticeship as an editor in the provinces, in 1892 J. A. Spender (after a quarrel with his uncle) moved to London, where after a brief interval on the *Pall Mall Gazette* he joined Newnes's newly established Liberal organ, the *Westminister Gazette*, under the legendary editor Edward T. Cooke. 'J. A.' duly became editor in 1896, when Cooke left for the *Daily News*. Barely thirty years old, J. A. Spender had made it to the top of his tree in three well-calculated moves. Under his editorship the *Westminster* (whose circulation never rose above 25,000) became the most politically influential paper in the kingdom. The daily leaders, which embellished the pea-green front-page, gave J. A. Spender the status of an unofficial Cabinet minister.

J. A. Spender married May Rawlinson in 1892 – a beautiful girl, an artist's daughter, and, as family legend had it, a former flame of Robert Louis Stevenson. Blissful as the union was, the couple were to have what the family called a 'g.s.' – a great sorrow. There were no children. Sorrowful it may have been, but it allowed J. A. Spender to devote his formidable energies to the demanding business of daily journalism.

Harold was markedly less steady than his elder brother. He was also more incendiary in his politics. His liberalism (which would eventually crystallize into allegiance to Lloyd George, rather than to J. A. Spender's cynosure, Asquith) was 'radical'. For a while, immediately after coming down from Oxford in summer 1887, he too took up work with his uncle, William Saunders, editing for him 'a little paper known as *The Democrat*, devoted to land taxation'. But he disliked this 'drilling'. Harold eventually prevailed on his uncle William to introduce him to Passmore Edwards, editor-proprietor of the first halfpenny London evening paper, the *Echo*. Young Spender was duly taken on as a 'cub' reporter in 1888.

Passmore Edwards's paper was congenially Liberal and it was at the metropolitan heart of things. It was an exciting time to be in London, still reeling from the near-revolution of 'Bloody Sunday' – the Trafalgar Square riot by the unemployed in November 1887. But work on the *Echo* was gruelling. 'The old man' was bad-tempered, high-handed, 'satanically' sarcastic and proverbially mean. For three years Harold barely survived on three guineas a week living in lodgings in Thanet Street. He encountered prejudice from his fellow hacks. 'Fleet Street hated the universities', Harold discovered; 'they despised our degrees'. Nor was he one to hide the Spender light under a bushel.

Edwards's fortune – which he was later to apply (like Andrew Carnegie) to the founding of grim public libraries bearing his name – would be made by ruthless skinflintery. As Harold discovered, it was Edwards's practice to recruit clever young men, 'suck their brains' and discard them at the point where they might think themselves worth more than three guineas a week.

According to Harold's autobiography, *The Fire of Life* (1926), 'Passmore Edwards had fully emptied my brains by 1891, and . . . we parted company.' Writing in 1924, it suited him to throw a veil over the episode. The break with Edwards in fact took place rather earlier and was precipitated by

Harold's throwing himself into the ranks with the East End dockers in their great strike of August 1889. In this action 10,000 workers, under Ben Tillett, came out for five weeks, demanding the 'tanner an hour' rate. Their victory was formative in the emergence of the Trades Union movement and through it the Labour Party.

This activist interlude ended with Harold himself unemployed. There intervened one of the periods of restlessness that punctuate his career. He fell back on the Liberal journalists' network. Edward T. Cooke secured him the temporary headmastership of a prep school at East Sheen. This berth lasted three months. But schoolmastering did not serve. Like Hull, it was too quiet. In what looks like desperation, Harold turned to his alma mater, where his former tutor Michael Sadler (later Master of University College in Stephen's time) found him a position in extra-mural teaching.

For the next few months, in the service of Oxford and London universities, Harold travelled all over the country lecturing to audiences of self-improving provincials on history and literature. He was a good lecturer (his children thought he never did anything else). He loved the theatricality of it – the fulsome introductions, the gown, getting the audience 'in the palm of his hand', and, above all, the ringing applause. He was soon promoted to Staff Lecturer. Had he stuck to the work, with his academic record, a fellowship might well have followed and thereafter a distinguished university career. But – as he put it – 'the larger world called me'.

In early 1892, Edward T. Cooke (possibly encouraged by his new assistant, J. A. Spender) invited Harold to join the *Pall Mall Gazette* as a 'Parliamentary Sketch Writer'. He was again on his way. Harold none the less remained loyally committed to the East End and his 'settler' mission among the natives. For a couple of years, after his return to London, he lodged in Toynbee Hall with the Barnetts. On leaving the settlement he took a small house in nearby Newark Street, Stepney, behind the London Hospital, where he was to live for six years. Here, still in the depths of 'Darkest London', he formed what was to be a life-long friendship with his Oxford contemporary, Hubert (later Sir Hubert) Llewellyn Smith (1864–1945).

Another young idealist (and Double First), Smith lived in Mile End. For the best part of a decade the two young men enjoyed one of those 'manly' relationships that later generations invariably assume to have been homosexual. As Smith recalled, 'we constantly met, and for a series of

years we always spent our summer holiday together – glorious mountaineering or sightseeing tours in Switzerland, the Tirol, Pyrenees, or
Italy'. The holidays came to an end when Smith married, in 1901.

In Stepney Harold threw himself into good works. He had a small
billiard table which served as a focus for the working men and boys
who used his Newark Street house as an informal meeting house. He
ran the Shakespeare Club in Walter Besant's People's Palace and chaired
a weekly debate at Toynbee Hall. He was a member, with Llewellyn
Smith, of the Mile End Vestry. He organized help for Jewish refugees
fleeing the European pogroms, teaching them English in an evening
school. He fought the growing anti-immigrant movement in England,
a movement which would culminate in the obnoxious Aliens Bill of
1905. He opposed the Christian conversion campaigns (only the 'greedy'
among the Jews succumbed, he observed). He stood, unsuccessfully, for
local elections on a pro-immigration plank, demanding the free entry
of persecuted Jews to the country.

These 'radical' years were the most fulfilling time of Harold's life.
Professionally things went well, if a little bumpily. Together with his
brother he resigned from the *Pall Mall Gazette* when it switched political horses in November 1892. The Astors generously gave the young
Liberals six months' severance pay. Harold used his bonus to take his
mother on holiday to Rome, repaying some of the debt he owed her
for putting him through Oxford. Lily had only a couple of years to live,
and the maternal pen was flowing over the page no longer. The cannier
J. A. Spender remained in London to set things up with the magnate
George Newnes, who had agreed to found a new Liberal paper.

On his return from Rome in January 1893, Harold joined his brother
and Cooke on the just-launched *Westminster Gazette*, the 'sea-green
incorruptible' as it was called for its distinctively coloured paper. Harold
was engaged to write his sharp sketches and gossipy reports from the
gallery and the lobby of the House of Commons. It was as correspondent for the *Westminster* in 1893 that Harold saw Gladstone making his
last (and futile) Home Rule speeches, with 'the powers of human oratory
carried to their highest point). If he had stuck with 'J.A.', Harold would,
with his elder brother, have risen to the top of journalism's slippery pole.
But in 1896 there came a break, never to be mended. Harold does not
go into detail in his autobiography, but the cause can be reconstructed.
It revolved, once more, around his loyalty to the East End and his addiction to street politics and Home Rule.

Now a trusted tribune of the people, Harold had been asked by disgruntled workers to organize a bus strike in 1896. By his own account, he marshalled the campaign brilliantly:

I had no sleep for a week. I organized the pickets at all the East London yards. Whenever a vehicle was got out of a yard I crowded it with busmen, whose fares I paid, and told them to stick on until the bus returned to the yard. The General Omnibus Company gradually tired of these operations and came to terms. The men's hours were reduced from fourteen to twelve.

Strikes were becoming increasingly widespread and ugly. Soldiers were called out in miners' actions in 1893 and 1898, and strikers were shot dead. Harold's political activism evidently forced a rupture with the sedate *Westminster* (just taken over by its new editor, J. A. Spender). The brothers were never to work as colleagues again. It seems, too, that until Harold's death personal relations were distant and somewhat strained. Harold moved on to become the 'House and Lobby' correspondent of the *Daily Chronicle*. Its sharp line on Home Rule was more congenial to him than the *Westminster*'s.

Over the next couple of years there were some profound changes in Harold's life. He was no longer, at thirty-five, a very young man. It was time to settle down, or at least slow down. His vigour was legendary, but scarcely sustainable (or even dignified) in middle age. For six years, he had worked in Fleet Street, dined regularly at the National Liberal Club, while living and doing good works in the East End. Doubtless there were other activities we shall never know about. Humphrey Spender overheard his father in old age talking remorsefully about certain 'wild oats' scattered around in the days of his young manhood. Humphrey assumes some kind of sexual delinquency. Although it is not impossible that Harold kept himself pure until his forty-first year, it would not have been unusual for a strikingly handsome man of the world, living the semi-Bohemian life of a London journalist, to have lapsed.

Whatever Harold's wild oats were, they cannot have been expensive and he can have had little time to sow them. He was always pressed for time and money. Often he would walk the four miles back along the Embankment to his small house in Stepney after a night's work at his paper. A cost was paid in his health, splendid athlete that he was. As a result of 'foolish overwork' he was on at least one occasion taken into the nearby London Hospital, where he was visited by a flower-bearing Henry James.

The *Daily Chronicle* position lasted until 1899 when Harold – as was now his pattern – resigned 'at a moment's notice' on a point of principle. He would not follow the paper's pro-war, anti-Boer line. Infused with pro-Boer sympathy, Harold stood as an anti-Imperialist candidate at Bow and Bromley (Tower Hamlets) in the by-election of October 1899. Britain in late 1899 was gripped by jingoism, sanctioned by the two main political parties and whipped up by their Fleet Street satraps. Harold's criticism of Joseph Chamberlain's war party was uncompromising. The contest was spectacularly dirty. Harold was portrayed as a Communist in Liberal clothing. He wrote in protest to *The Times*, citing the noble example of Burke in 1774. It was a forlorn plea. Harold was deserted, as the papers noted, by the leaders of his party. They were nervous of his 'radicalism'.

Harold lost his by-election. The Conservative candidate polled 4,238 and the Radicals a respectable, but hopeless, 2,123. Almost immediately, C. P. Scott offered Harold a job on the (then radical) *Manchester Guardian*. It was a sympathetic act and witnessed to the regard in which Harold Spender was now held as a journalist. He was dispatched by his new employer to North America to cover the 1900 Canadian General Election. An inveterate explorer, Harold took the opportunity to forage deep into the US. On his return, he would live in Manchester for a year, writing leaders. Scott's paper and its anti-war line suited Harold. The rainy northern city didn't.

In 1901, Harold returned to his old London stamping grounds as Gallery reporter for the *Manchester Guardian*. It was a step down from the editorial desk, but what he wanted. He took a flat in Victoria Street, near the House. He was now a force in the gathering anti-war movement. And over his years in the Commons he had become personally associated with the politician who, above all others, was to form and deform his later career, David Lloyd George.

In 1901 Lloyd George was in the process of persuading George Cadbury to acquire the *Daily News* as his (Lloyd George's) organ. Harold was recruited as co-editor – the highest rank he had hitherto attained in journalism (or would ever attain, as it turned out). Cadbury's Christian evangelicalism was no problem for Harold, who had been inured to virtuous abstinence by his East End years. But the proprietor's quixotic insistence that the *News* should publish no racing news and accept no drink advertising 'practically sentenced our enterprise to financial death from the start'.

Work on the *Daily News* brought Harold into contact with two of the paper's literary luminaries, G. K. Chesterton and Hilaire Belloc. Both were visitors at the Victoria Street flat. Here, over 'tobacco parliaments', the *News*-men devised their campaign. Their paper was steadfastly anti-war, and propagandized against the iniquity of British concentration camps, set up by Kitchener (with the approval of the Liberal government) in November 1900. The *News* published Emily Hobhouse's first-hand accounts of atrocities in the camps. The paper fed Lloyd George material for denunciatory anti-war speeches in the House and splashed those speeches in its columns. Predictably the *News*'s circulation plummeted.

The campaign against the South African concentration camps was noble. But professionally it was risky. Another risk was 'going the whole way' with Lloyd George. None the less, for the moment, the risks seemed to be paying off. In 1903 Harold bustled round the country as a special correspondent, putting together a series of articles under the rousing and characteristic title, 'Wake up, Liberals!' As always, however, Harold could never stay in one place long enough to consolidate his achievements. He resigned his editorial position on the *Daily News* in 1904, on the usual grounds of 'principle'. He felt his 'independence' was being curtailed. It was now his invariable pattern.

This last resignation was overshadowed by another, more significant change in Harold's life. In January 1904 he married Violet Hilda Schuster. The twenty-six-year-old only daughter of Ernest and Hilda Schuster, Violet was Oxford-educated, cultivated (an artist and published poet) and beautiful. Miss Schuster was also very rich – or, at least, her family were. Her father, Ernest Joseph Schuster, was a distinguished barrister and already a public figure (he would, fourteen years later, play a key role in carrying through the Treaty of Versailles). The Schusters were, for many generations past, a banking family (their business was eventually, in 1919, to become the National Provincial). The founder of the English line of the family, Francis Joseph Schuster, had come with his family from Frankfurt-am-Main in 1866, on the annexation of the territory by Prussia. They set up the firm of Schuster Brothers in Manchester, where they promptly naturalized, having slightly earlier converted from Judaism to Christianity.

As they put down roots in their new homeland, the family became

more English than the English. The Schusters were soon Anglican, public
school and Oxbridge – very 'establishment'. They acquired country houses
where Schuster men could hunt, shoot and fish. None the less, overlaid
as it was by their adoptive country, the racial heritage of Schusters would
be significant for Stephen Spender, and would endow him with a sense
of difference from his father.

That we [the children] were of Jewish as well as German origin was passed
over in silence or with slight embarrassment by my family . . . When we were
children it was not mentioned to us that we were at least a quarter Jewish, and
from the conversation of nurses and governesses I gathered that the Jews were
a strange race with hooked noses (I imagined them to be like fish-hooks) and
avaricious manners, with whom I certainly had no reason to imagine I had
any connection. When, at the age of sixteen, I became aware of our Jewish
blood, I began to *feel* Jewish.

For all their adaptation to English ways, the Schusters had retained
the closeness of a clan. They were also, all of them, extraordinarily high
achievers in a number of fields. Francis's son Felix was one of the
country's leading bankers. Felix's brother, Arthur, was to be a world-
famous mathematical physicist. Ernest was in law – and at the top of
that pole. Violet Schuster's mother, Hilda (née Weber, Ernest's wife),
represented another rich strand of other-than-Englishness. Her father,
Sir Hermann Weber, was a doctor from the Catholic Rhineland who
came to England because he wished to live in the country of Shakespeare's
tongue, and who stayed there because his patients loved him and peti-
tioned him to do so. On Hilda's side of the family there was the Danish
blood of the Gruenings.

The marriage settlement between Harold and Violet Schuster, drawn
up by the bride's lawyers, runs to eighteen pages. It settles £20,000 on
her (the sum translates to around a million in today's values). The bride's
family undertook to set up and maintain a fund, administered by Ernest
Schuster and untouchable by Harold, which would guarantee the couple,
and eventually their offspring, £600 a year. It was a generous document,
but unusual in its precise safeguards.

What the forty-year-old Harold brought to the marriage was good
looks, intelligence, high principles, and proven ability as a political journalist. But from the first the Schusters were suspicious about his financial prospects (hence the eighteen pages). It was, for Harold, a magnificent

match, marked by an appropriately grand wedding and showers of lavish gifts. But Violet's dowry brought with it more wifely power than was comfortable for an Edwardian gentleman. The prenuptial contract made clear that the money on which they would set themselves up was hers, not his. In the long term Harold was putting himself into the hands of the Schusters, unless he could earn substantially more than he had hitherto. They were benevolent but firm hands.

Violet immediately made her views felt. The life of a parliamentary reporter was wholly unsuited to that of a family man. 'My wife,' Harold recorded, 'who possessed great literary gifts, constantly urged me to turn to novel writing.' Violet's urgings were, of course, supported by 20,000 strong arguments. Reading between the lines, it is evident that it was expected Harold would soon go into Parliament – now that he was rich. In the meanwhile, Violet suggested, he might do foreign correspondent work. It was a happy compromise. He loved travel.

The Spenders took their honeymoon belatedly, in Egypt, from November 1904 to January 1905. The trip was to be enshrined in family lore. When he was a little boy, as Stephen writes in *World within World*,

My mother would describe a honeymoon journey she and my father had taken to Egypt – the pyramids – thence to Florence – Giotto's Tower – in days when 'we were rich'. There were photographs of my father with a pyramid behind him, arms folded, sepia moustache trailing on each side like fox brushes, in the faded brown print; of my mother with her motoring veil, seated in the corner of a car which looked like a minute church.

The couple lived at 18 Pembridge Gardens until 1907, when their first child was born. They then moved into 47 Campden Court, a more spacious house in Kensington. It was conveniently near the Ernest Schusters, who lived alongside the Albert Hall. Nor was it too far from Fleet Street and Westminster. Here, in Kensington, three more children were born. In his new home Harold dutifully turned his hand to writing novels. The first fruit of his new career was an Egyptian romance, *The Call of the Siren* (1905). He followed with a political novel, *The Arena* (Constable, 1906). It is dedicated to 'my wife who inspired all and wrote some of this book'. The narrative opens in the High Alps. Two young Englishmen are intrepidly scaling the heights, in treacherous ice and snow. The leading figure is lean, bronzed, handsome and aristocratic. The other is Sancho Panza to his companion's Quixote (Llewellyn Smith must not have liked this) – stout and very much second in command. They save a beautiful girl stranded in the storm on a glacier. She is profoundly grateful to these gallant 'cavaliers' – especially the thin handsome one with the moustache.

A year later, Lucy Arnett discovers that her rescuer was none other than Lord Alfred Markham, a Marquess's elder son. Spurning aristocratic comforts, he has devoted his life to living with the poor in South London, and lives in a settlement run by Canon Barnard (Canon Barnett must have had a jolt when he read this page). Lucy is the daughter of a famous philosopher: one of the new breed of woman produced by 'hockey, bicycling, and the motor car'. Their relationship renewed, the couple fall headlong in love.

At the same moment, the young lord is summoned to the House of Commons where the chief whip of the Liberal Party tells him: 'We don't want politicians; we want men like yourself, who really know the poor.' The 'Arena' – Parliament, that is – calls; the poor of the London slums also need the young nobleman; he wishes to marry Lucy (who has succumbed, without resistance, to 'the man – the master – the primeval conqueror'). What will Alfred do?

To cut a long (and amazingly bad) story short, he does it all. He scrapes into Parliament as a Radical candidate – uniting the liberals and the socialists; he marries the pliant Lucy; he saves the country and raises the working classes to lower-middle-class decency. *The Arena* is an embarrassingly incompetent novel. But it articulates Harold's dilemmas and hints at his dearest ambitions. He hoped that the Liberal Party would come through with a seat for him. And then – who knew?

Buoyant with their Schuster thousands, the Spenders enjoyed the Edwardian golden years – the crushes (with the obligatory 'high' handshake), the country weekends, the soirées, the cornucopias of the great London department stores, the institutionalized gluttony, the cheap servants, the continental travel, the permeating sense of British imperial greatness. 'These were the *great* days,' Harold nostalgically recalled in 1925, 'those days of the long dinners and the comfortable two party system, the gas lamps, the hansom cabs and the smoky underground.'

They were also family years. The children had come in rapid succession: Michael in 1907, Christine in 1908, Stephen in 1909, and Humphrey in 1910. It is likely that this rapid sequence of childbearing (there was also at least one miscarriage and a clumsily performed hysterectomy) ruined Violet's health. Invalidism meant that there was kindness and civility but no intimate closeness between mother and children. The servants were always intervening, 'distancing' them. Humphrey remembers that when he was taken in to see his mother for their daily encounter, both of them would be prepared by their respective maids to look their best. Knowing his love of bright objects, Violet's jewel-box would be out on the coverlet for him to play with. When time was up, the servant would take him out. The jewels would be put away.

Stephen's recollections of his mother are limited to a mental snap-shot album: her lying on a chaise-longue, for example, complaining of debts; her coldly correcting him for a childish slip of the tongue; some strangely romantic brief encounters:

I remember a still earlier time when before a dinner party she would bend over me, as I lay in bed, to say good night, and the amethysts round her white neck, the stiff satin of her golden dress, her scent, were a splendour such as today I would find in a Titian or some Venetian beauty.

The children confirm that, when they were old enough to register such things, there was friction between their parents. Christine, seventy years later, remembered them bickering 'over my head, if you know what I mean', as a very little girl. 'They quarrelled a lot,' she recalled. Stephen published in the 1930s a powerful poem: 'My Parents Quarrel in the Neighbour Room'. An underlying and persistent cause for rows was Harold's sense of having had his wings clipped. It might have been different if his books had enjoyed a great success, but they did not. It would certainly have been different if he were Harold Spender, MP. Obviously the Spenders were comfortably off, 'rich' even in the early years. But that was because of Schuster money, not Spender achievement.

Harold had thrown himself into foreign travel – now without Violet, who was either bearing children or recovering (with increasing diffi-culty) from the serial ordeal. In 1906 he made his first visit to Greece with his old friends the Barnetts and was converted to the 'Greek Cause'. For the rest of his life he would be a passionate philhellenist. He was forever forming aid committees, and firing off memoranda to the authori-ties about crises in the Balkans and the plight of refugees.

In 1909, as Harold says with his usual grandiloquence, he was 'drawn back to the storm'. That is to say, he accepted a post as Gallery corre-spondent for the *Manchester Guardian*. It was, in career terms, exactly where he had been ten years earlier. But now he was manifestly closer

to the centre of political power. He was not just reporting, he was partic-
ipating. In 1909 he acted as one of Lloyd George's secretaries on the
campaign for the 'People's Budget'. If he played his cards right, and did
nothing 'impulsive', he might reasonably expect to enter Parliament on
his patron's coat-tails.

Restless as ever, in 1910 Harold moved from the *Guardian* to the
Morning Leader, which was absorbed by the *Daily News* in 1912. By this
whirligig, he found himself back with his old employer, doing his old
job. But his standing was no longer what it had once been. As a Gallery
reporter, Harold was haunted by a reputation for indiscretion. On at
least three occasions he was publicly accused of a breach of professional
confidence. In 1908 he was alleged to have divulged to the *Daily Telegraph*
private discussions between Lloyd George and the Kaiser. In 1911 he
was denounced by Balfour, no less, in the Commons for having prematurely divulged the King's pledge on Lord's reform. And, towards the
end of his life in 1924, Lloyd George would destroy him utterly by
publicly (and falsely) branding him a liar for having 'invented' an interview and sold it to an American paper for money.

In 1912, Harold turned his hand to foreign articles for the *Daily News*.
At this period, he was furiously active in Balkan relief work and on
Anglo-Hellenic committees, working for Greek refugees. He was also
regularly spending some months a year in France. His travelling had
become frenetic. Over the period 1913–14, he made no fewer than three
trips abroad. They combined pleasure and business to an almost comic
degree. In January 1914, for example, he undertook a long ski-tour in
the high Norway mountains. Having swept down from the snowy peaks,
he interviewed the King for his paper, having brought with him, among
his skiing-gear, a top hat and frock coat.

In late 1913 the Spender family had moved from Kensington to a
furnished house in Sheringham, on the Norfolk coast, for what Harold
terms 'domestic reasons'. Presumably Violet's health was a principal consideration. She was now a confirmed invalid. Stephen Spender's image of
his mother over the Sheringham years is of a reclining invalid, 'perpetually grieving over I know not what'.

There was a doctor at Sheringham, Dr Knyvet Gordon, in whom
Harold had particular confidence (it was this physician who, when Violet
fell chronically ill, persuaded her to have all her teeth out – the children never forgave him). Gordon may have influenced him in his choice
of residence. It is also likely that the family was experiencing what would

be the first of many cash crises. And, of course, with the outbreak of world war, it was felt prudent for the family to reside out of London. A sea-front house, the Bluff, was to be the Spender home for six years and here it was that Stephen came to consciousness in an atmosphere of 'austere comfort against a background of calamity'.

On the face of it, Sheringham was an odd choice of wartime refuge. Placed as it was on the North Sea, 'looking almost into the face of the enemy', it would be in the front line of any naval invasion – were the enemy reckless enough to try such a thing. It was also the point of coastal entry for Zeppelins. According to Harold, there were veritable 'armadas' of these bomb-bearing airships silently cruising their way over the Bluff. He would, he claims, regularly return from air-raids in London to Zeppelin raids in Sheringham. The first bomb dropped on England, Harold proudly records, landed in the garden next door to the Bluff. On their part, Humphrey, Christine and Stephen remembered only one Zeppelin and lots of false alarms (Christine recalled the children being bundled off to Cambridge on more than one occasion, to be out of the 'firing line'). Humphrey remembers waving to the German crew of the machine, and Fritz cheerfully waving back.

These raids and alarms supplied Stephen with what seems to have been a formative experience. In 1916, a mine was discovered on the cliff, beneath the house, and had to be detonated. They were all conducted or carried to the shelter by soldiers, clad in 'tickly rough uniforms', as Humphrey vividly remembers. The experience stayed with Stephen and inspired one of the poems ('A First War Childhood') in the series of childhood recollections in the poet's last collection, *Dolphins*, published in 1994, when he was eighty-five:

> Then a bomb exploded –
> The night went up
> In flame that shook
> The shrubbery leaves,
> And soldiers came
> Out of dark speared with flame,
> And carried us children
> Into their dugout
> Below the earth.
>   Ear pressed against
> The khaki uniform

> Of mine, in his arms,
> I could hear his heart beat –
> With the blood of all England.

Harold, one suspects, rarely picked up his children for a cuddle.

Stephen was four when the family went to Sheringham. Unlike Christine, he had no conscious recollection of his natal Kensington. The rural upbringing was, as Stephen described it in later life, lyrically Wordsworthian:

My childhood was the nature I remember: the thickness of the grass amongst whose roots were to be found heartsease (the small pansies which are the colour of the iris in a golden eye) ... At evening, floating above the flat Norfolk landscape, there appeared range upon range of mountains with gulfs and valleys between high peaks, which stayed motionless, sculptured on the sky out of clouds. Sometimes, also, at midday, in the sky whose blue was as solid and opaque as the flushed green of a field of young corn, perfect white pictures would appear, as on a screen. 'Look, milk jug, a white milk jug. It is exactly like a milk jug,' I would cry. 'No, silly,' my sister would say. 'It's a cat, a white cat, can't you see that?'

Christine remembered her brother's sometimes going off happily by himself in the woods and fields. It was at this period that Stephen conceived the desire to become a naturalist: 'an old man with a long white beard, like a photograph I had seen of Charles Darwin'.

At Sheringham the different characters of the four Spender children emerged. Michael, the firstborn, was his father's firm favourite. 'If Humphrey,' Christine wrote, 'was the pet of the Spender family, Michael, the oldest, was the adored. His parents gave him an extraordinarily reverent consideration in almost everything and the younger children looked up to him as to a demi-god.' Shortly after his birth, Violet composed a poem – 'My Son (After Burger)' – applauding Michael's demi-divine pre-eminence among babies:

> Look upon my lovely child,
> With his curls, a golden splendour,
> Rosy cheeks, eyes blue and tender!
> Neighbours, have you such a one?
> All the neighbours answer, 'None!'

The tribute would echo throughout his life (a tragically short life: he would die aged thirty-five). Machinery fascinated Michael. As a child he developed an obsessive interest in trains (particularly making them run on time, Humphrey tartly recalls, just like the Fascists). In the first instance, it was the Hornby toy train set that preoccupied him. He moved on from toys to the larger world of trainspotting. As a young teenager it was Michael's driving ambition to get a photograph on the cover of the leading spotters' magazine. He set up a tripod to catch trains steaming dramatically around a bend at speed. Humphrey was recruited to help in a menial capacity. Michael duly got his picture, had it published, took his glory and went on to other even more ambitious feats. His humble assistant, Humphrey, caught the photographic virus from Michael and would go on to be one of the distinguished photo-journalists of his generation. Tellingly, it was not Michael who gave Humphrey his first camera, but his kind uncle Hugh (Spender) – one of the family's 'failures'. Michael seems, on principle, never to have helped his siblings – using his superior abilities always to maintain his superiority over them.

He was a difficult brother for supposedly 'backward' brothers like Stephen, or those who were struggling with handicaps, like Humphrey (whose eye problems, until they were rectified, retarded his early education), or 'a mere girl' like Christine. He was less a role model to emulate than living conclusive proof that they could never succeed as Michael succeeded – so there was no point in even trying. Stephen's relationship with Michael was, from their earliest days, fraught. As he records in *World within World*, their first nanny:

related a story which illustrates vividly the earliest relationship of Michael and me. When we were aged he five and I three, apparently I was always victorious in our nursery brawls. But, one day, when Michael lay recumbent under my puny feet, nanny said: 'Get up, Michael, and knock Stephen down' – which Michael promptly did. And for ever after this, to the joy of nanny and all her successors, he always did.

As his formidable mind developed, Michael no longer needed the older child's physical might in order to 'knock Stephen down', although as Christine observed, Stephen was always 'inclined to quarrel' with his elder brother and evidently stood up to him – with invariably humiliating consequences. There are many recollections of Michael's using his

firstborn status and 'scientific' intellect to slash and cut his siblings (particularly Stephen) down to size. Literally. 'I was very tall,' Stephen says of
himself as a youth:

One morning when I came down to breakfast, Michael looked closely at my
ankles and said, 'Of course Stephen could be expected to wear socks with
vertical stripes which emphasize his verticality rather than horizontal ones to
subdue it.' When I was thirteen, he analysed a spot of my blood and gravely
announced that it must be classified in a very inferior category. A year later he
produced an even more depressing report on my skull, which, he declared,
reverted to the Neanderthal.

These putdowns were eerily humourless (Stephen inoculates himself
against their cruelty by injecting sly wit into the narration). According
to Humphrey, Michael '*never* saw the funny side of things', until a few
months before his death in 1945. The solemnity made him seem inhuman.
All that mattered to Michael was excelling.

After he had read around in psychoanalysis, Stephen came to think
that Michael was entirely lacking in 'subjectivity' – he could only see
the objective, or scientific aspect of things. He, Stephen, was by contrast
'hyper-subjective', with a corresponding blind-spot. 'Often Michael
seemed to me,' Stephen felt, 'like a person who had neglected to
develop one of his faculties' – a well-meaning, but not entirely harmless, psychopath. In later life, worried by this apparent disability, Michael
subjected himself to a course of Jungian psychoanalysis. Bizarrely, he
claimed to be able to remember absolutely nothing of his childhood,
and Stephen had to accompany him, to supply the necessary memories
for the therapist to work on. It confirms Stephen's sense that, mysteriously, he and Michael had polarized out elements of their genetic inheritance: hyper-objectivity and hyper-subjectivity; scientist and poet;
machine and human.

It was Michael who most faithfully fulfilled his father's exaggerated
aspirations. Harold Spender, as Humphrey sarcastically noted, 'gave us a
sense of mountains to climb'. But it was Michael who would undertake an actual expedition to conquer Everest. Stephen, meanwhile,
suffered from nosebleeds and an astigmatic fear of heights. Humphrey
could never see the point of following his father's crazed admonitions
to reach for the stars. Michael won prizes, from his Norfolk schooldays
onward, through his glittering years at Balliol (Stephen, like his father,

was to go to lowlier University College and spectacularly did *not* win prizes, or even a degree). Michael's academic over-achievement had a chilling effect on Stephen, who developed an invincible distaste for exams, tests, and any course of professional life that required 'training'. It was a symptom of his 'hyper-subjectivity'.

Christine, the girl in the family, was overshadowed not just by her elder brother Michael but by all her brothers. By her own self-punitive account, she was as a little girl 'naughty', wilful, 'not pretty', 'stupid', and 'horribly interfering'. Christine was closest, in childhood, to Michael and particularly close to her father in the months leading up to his death. Immediately after Harold's death she was close to Stephen as she had been in the early Sheringham years. One concludes that the girl in the family was neglected because she was a girl and that as such it was her destiny to be neglected.

The baby of the four, Humphrey, was the darling of the household. He remembers Sheringham as a 'kissing and cuddling sort of place' – but the kisses and cuddles came from the servants, not his parents. Humphrey was well suited to play the part of family darling. He was, in early childhood, strikingly beautiful in a 'Bubbles' kind of way (his analogy). Normally the sweetest of children, Humphrey had a fierce temper which could be roused under extreme provocation. On one occasion he was about to take a croquet mallet to Christine's head (she had 'nagged' him about his missing shots) and was only restrained by Michael with the cold prohibition, 'you'll be hanged if you kill her.'

Not until he was seven was it diagnosed (as a result of Christine's ceaseless 'nagging, nagging' of her parents) that Humphrey had acutely short sight. He was taken to a London specialist. Twice, in his hearing, he heard his parents being told that 'the boy will be blind in six months'. There ensued what Humphrey ruefully calls his 'mutilation'. His flowing curls were cut. He was dosed with arsenic (on the grotesque misapprehension, apparently, that his eye problems were a symptom of congenital syphilis); he was obliged to wear triplex wire-frame glasses. Most damagingly, he was under strict doctor's orders not to strain his eyes by reading. He was consequently kept from books for long periods (initially a year), and for many years forbidden to read after 4.30 p.m., it being thought that artificial light would exacerbate his weakness. Predictably, Humphrey became extraordinarily visual. Even more than Stephen he cultivated his mother's artistic gifts – although he despised her arts-and-crafts taste. Trained as an architect, he would go on to become a gifted news-photographer in the 1930s. If Stephen was overshadowed by Michael, Humphrey was overshadowed by Stephen. The oxygen, he says, would be sucked out of the room when his older brother was present. Stephen, he felt, was 'incapable of joining in *ordinary* conversations'.

The regime to which the quartet of Spender children was subjected in their early years is described by Stephen as one of 'Puritan decadence' – a condition incarnated in Harold. 'The Puritan Decadents,' *World within World* explains (none too clearly),

have unseeing, rhetorical faces, faces of immature boys who are prematurely aged, faces of those upon whose mind some operation has been performed removing those centres which were conscious of the body. To the son of the Puritan decadent, his body is a nameless horror of nameless desires which isolate him within a world of his own. He is divided between a longing to become like the others who walk about in their clothes without desires and as though they had no bodies, and a sense that nevertheless for him his guilt gives him back his body.

Escaping from this condition would be the main struggle of Spender's early years.

It was at Sheringham that Spender received his first formal education. The children were taught to read almost as soon as they could talk by nurse-governesses. They were all literate before they left home for kindergarten. Violet herself gave them art classes and made the boys do embroidery. Stephen's school career started cheerfully enough at Miss Harcourt's little establishment, in nearby East Runton. Michael meanwhile was at a proper boys' school, Miss Bolding's in Sheringham. It was at Miss Harcourt's that Stephen Spender fell in love with the seven-year-old Penelope: his first affair of the heart. Christine remembered her distinctly as a pretty little girl called Penelope Waterfield. Stephen was not the only boy to be captivated by her 'milk and rose complexion'.

The path to East Runton ran along the railway line and the three children, walking the two miles to school, would gaily wave to their father as he whizzed by on the Monday morning train 'to town'. Humphrey's recollections are less decorous. He claims that he and Stephen would unbutton their trousers and 'point our willies' at their proud, but apparently shortsighted, daddy. When Harold was staying at Sheringham through the week, he would himself take the children to school; sometimes in the donkey cart which was the family's principal means of transport. Stephen recalls such occasions in *World within World* as red–letter days:

My father would take my sister and me to Miss Harcourt's school at East Runton. On the way he would tell us stories. There was the story of the Rubber Man who could climb any building and stretch his neck to see over any wall. This I liked even more than the ones about the parrot my father owned when he was a boy.

Christine confirmed what Stephen claimed in *World within World* and in such poems as 'My parents kept me from children who were rough'. As she said, 'we were never allowed to play with poor children because my mother regarded them as not only rough, but also as perpetual carriers of infectious diseases'. The Spender children were chronically overprotected. None the less, there was some rough and tumble at Miss Harcourt's. Schoolboys always remember their playground fights, and in *World within World* Stephen describes a boy called Forbes:

with whom I used to fight. Forbes had black wiry hair and flashing black eyes behind his steel–rimmed spectacles. One day, when we were rolling over one another on the ground, he got into a passionate rage . . . The will of Forbes was breaking against my body as though against a gate. Suddenly afraid, I lay on top of him and held him very closely in my arms, and at that moment I experienced a sensation like the taste of a strong, sweet honey, but not upon my tongue, and spreading wave upon wave, throughout my whole body.

Over the Sheringham years, Harold Spender's life was dominated by the war, as was that of every middle-class male, serving or civilian. He still wrote the odd piece for the newspapers and was getting down to his life of Asquith (an unpalatable subject for him). It was rational for him to be able to do research and keep up his contacts in London without the distractions of a raucous family and ailing wife. In town he would stay at one of his clubs. He could keep in touch with political affairs. He still had a Press pass. His secretary, the faithful Captain Devoto, would spend the weekdays at Sheringham writing up Harold's dictation.

Captain Devoto's commission was in the non-combatant Salvation Army. He had a family in North America and avoided conscription 'somehow', Christine recalled. While Harold was in town, he was the only adult male in the Sheringham household. Humphrey remembers him as a 'big fat man', with a queer sense of humour – 'A piece of meat about as large as a bee's knee', he would slyly request at lunch, crippling the children with mirth. It would have been logical to have had a female secretary, but as Christine observed, 'I don't think my mother would have stood for that.'

Harold would normally leave Sheringham on weekdays by the early morning train for London. He would come back at the end of the week; or, if it was a day trip, by 9.30 at night – although trains were often delayed during the war. Doubtless Harold had a separate life in London, in which his wife now played no part. An invalid, Violet must sometimes have been poor company. Perhaps as a kind of genteel protest against her husband's middle-of-the-road Victorianism, she cultivated a passion for 1890s art – 'advanced' in the 1890s, now somewhat *passé* – Rackham, Dulac and Kate Greenaway figured high among her preferred artists. Violet's paintings, mainly pictures of flowers, her embroidery, and her poetry (a volume, *The Path to Caister*, was privately published after her death in 1922) had a 'sacred' status for the children.

In the six years they were at Sheringham, Harold Spender complacently calculates, he wrote five books – two novels and three chatty biographies of Prime Ministers. The war was not, however, a good time for sales. Harold now earned only a pittance from journalism. In a period of censorship ('gagging', as he contemptuously called it), Harold may not have been considered trustworthy. Nor could he trust himself to work in a censored Fleet Street – he loathed the dishonesty of it. Pacifist and outspokenly anti-war since his Boer War days, he felt that if only the 'facts' were published by the papers, peace might come before Britain and Germany bled each other to death.

Increasingly the Spenders depended on Schuster money, something that had an insidiously puncturing effect on Harold's self-esteem. They had evidently run through Violet's dowry, and now relied on her father Ernest discreetly topping up their bank account (to which, as a bank director, he had confidential access). Even in Norfolk, the household was extensive. There were two, sometimes more, live-in servants, nurses and governesses, a male secretary and Violet's medical treatment to pay for. Michael was, by the age of eight, at boarding school at Gresham's, which meant fees. And there was Harold's weekly travel to London, and his overnight expenses there. Stephen pictures in *World within World* 'my mother lying on a chaise-longue in Sheringham complaining about debts, and telling me in a taxi in London that she was five pounds overdrawn'. 'I reckon we were pretty well always in debt,' Christine recalled.

Towards the end of the war Harold found an occupation for himself propagandizing for the War Savings effort. The scheme was devised by Lloyd George; now Britain's Prime Minister and at last at the top of the slippery pole. It entailed Harold going round the country persuading the population to part with their money as freely as they did their sons. The War Savings propaganda required the kind of platform rhetoric that came naturally to Harold. It seems that he did the work voluntarily. He was repaid, in kind, by Lloyd George, who sanctioned a biography (grandly called *The Prime Minister*), a book which was to be Harold's magnum opus.

This exciting interlude supplies an irreverent anecdote in *World within World*:

My father did not actually see much of Lloyd George except at one period, after 1918, when he was writing his biography . . . On one of these occasions he took me in a taxi with him. It was a memorable journey for me at the age of ten, because it was not only a visit to the shrine of a living and reigning deity, but also the first time I had been to the centre of London after dark . . . When we reached 10 Downing Street, my father told the taxi driver to wait and me to stay in the taxi, while he went into the door beyond which there was Lloyd George. I waited in the damp down-pouring darkness for what seemed an infinite time, at the end of which I became more and more conscious of a physical need which, in the childhood of a boy taught to be ashamed of his body, can be so memorably agonizing . . . I noticed then that the fog had thickened, providing me with a kind of smoke-screen, while at the same time the noise of the rain caused a diversion. So I let down the window of the cab very softly and relieved myself out of the window. I had scarcely finished, and, trembling, was crouching on the back seat, when the driver poked his head through the window and asked: 'Did you see what I see?' 'What?' 'Just now. Didn't you see him go by?' 'Who?' 'The Prime Minister.'

In Sheringham Harold served his King in the office of Special Constable. The blue-uniformed constables – reinforced by a cohort of Sea Scouts – would keep a wary lookout for invading Germans and any infringement of the blackout. In nearby Norwich, it was said, you could be arrested for lighting a match at night. Harold also helped raise 'Volunteers' – a 'Home Guard', or 'Dad's Army'. There were some 5,000 such weekend soldiers in the Sheringham area. They drilled, kitted out in khaki, on the local golf links when it wasn't raining, learned to shoot at targets improvised from motor-car tyres, and waited for the call which, happily, never came. As enthusiastic as he was in everything he did, Harold organized talks and sing-songs for the volunteers and for troops billeted in the area. The moral tone was high.

Soldiering apart, Harold did not have a good war. His prospects of entry into Parliament had fallen through. He was in the wilderness until Lloyd George's triumph in 1916. And then the Prime Minister had younger, more vigorous (and possibly more reliable) aides than the fifty-two-year-old Liberal warhorse Harold. There was no eminent place for him in Fleet Street. His pro-Boer reputation hung round his neck like an albatross in these warmongering times. The atmosphere at Sheringham was darkened by the death of Violet's favourite brother, Alfred, in Flanders in 1916. It was the occasion of a poem, and in the extremity of grief she sacrificed the forced rhymes that mar her other verse:

> And first they told her of the way he died:
> A noble death – and meet for one so brave.
> And then they told her of his life – a saint!

But, the poem continues, Lear-like, 'he will never come again, never'. As Christine recalled, the children wore black bands on their coat sleeves and she 'tied black ribbons on her pigtails instead of blue, as a sign of mourning'. The black bands were never off for long. There were other more or less distant relatives killed in the fighting and the maids lost their lovers one by one.

During the war years at Sheringham Harold came under the gaze of his children. The boys, at least Humphrey and Stephen, were put off by their father's unrelenting tone of Victorian 'manliness' – the 'old chap' mode of address, the 'Excelsior!' admonitions that they must climb to the top (of what? Stephen would wonder). Michael, the favourite and an honorary adult, was less disgusted than the other boys – although he despised his father's 'unscientific' intellect. Christine charitably put the growing alienation with his offspring down to her father's advanced age.

Following Christine's apologetic explanation, one may plausibly see Harold Spender as a Victorian paterfamilias out of his time. He would, for example, read Dickens and Tennyson aloud to his 'flock', with florid emotionalism. Humphrey remembers Christmas holidays at Sheringham, even the jolliest of them, as an annual ordeal: 'Dad used to dress up as Santa – totally unconvincing.' There would be a ritual distribution of presents at 6 p.m. 'sharp' on Christmas Day, before supper. The old coachman, Mr Carter, was brought in to share the festivity – it not being right for Dives to exclude Lazarus – but Lazarus was quickly shunted into the kitchen when the meal itself was served. As the highpoint of the later evening, Harold would read aloud *A Christmas Carol*, the tears streaming down his cheeks.

It was Harold's habit to tell his sons long serial stories of his own invention on the walks that he felt were good for their growing bodies. He would invoke an atmosphere of 'manly' comradeship ('Away from the women at last'). 'He would pretend,' Stephen recalled, 'that we were climbing with him on the Alps, traversing glaciers, attached to one another by a rope, with the clink of an ice-axe hacking steps on the face of the ice. At such times he seemed, with his blue eyes, his sandy hair and moustache, and his chiselled nose, like a Viking.' In early childhood, Stephen Spender loved this charade. As he grew older, he good-naturedly tolerated it. When it threatened to continue into adolescence, he came to despise this play-acting habit of his father's and his 'ignorant windbaggery'. Nor did Harold admire aspects of his second son. He nagged Stephen from his earliest years for being 'round shouldered', 'flabby', and generally 'unmanly'. Intending only robust encouragement of the sergeant-major kind that worked so well with the Sheringham Volunteers, he inflicted festering wounds. Humphrey – by now a natural athlete and well coordinated – ached for his older brother.

Christine, the most indulgent of the children, concluded charitably that Harold's tale-telling and game-playing 'was what TV is nowadays'. On his part, Stephen less generously came to see his father's play-acting as evidence that, underneath, he was 'afraid of life'. It was all a masquerade, a 'cowardly' evasion. His mother, he thought, was the braver of the two, for all her invalidism and hysterical outbursts. Harold inhabited 'a world of rhetorical situations'. 'It is no exaggeration,' Stephen later wrote, 'to say that in the end his unreality terrified me. Just as Midas turned everything he touched to gold, so my father turned everything to rhetorical abstraction.'

There is a surviving letter, written by Harold at this period, apparently to the Schusters. He was ill and thought (mistakenly) he was going to die. His deathbed instructions catch his tendency to melodramatic gesture, his 'rhetorical abstraction' and his desperate paternal anxiety to do the right thing:

On the guidance of their [the children's] lives I should like to say one or two things. (1) I should like each of the boys to be brought up to a *profession*. I should like one to take up Medicine and another Law. If one of them shows early enough a very strong liking for the Navy send him to Osborne and Dartmouth – but *not* unless there is a strong preference. I have a strong desire that *one* should shine in public life, but I leave it to you to direct this matter. I feel from my own experience that it is useless for a young man to enter public life in England unless he has some endowment behind him. But I think it is well worth while for a family to set aside a deliberate income for a boy who exhibits talent and industry in public affairs. But that income must only be continued as long as the talent and industry are maintained in full vigour. If you can manage to reduce these considerations to a practicable plan, you would be carrying out my wishes. Yours sincerely, Harold Spender.

PS If Michael exhibits a strong passion for a musical training and calling, then I leave it to your discretion to let him follow this. Harold.

It's a remarkable letter, not least in its willingness to spend the Schusters' money for them, and the fact that his daughter gets no mention whatsoever.

Violet was more perceptive, and her mother's eye evidently saw into the characters of her children more accurately. But in her actual day-to-day dealings with her children, as Stephen remembers:

She was hysterical, and given to showing violent loves and hates, enthusiasms and disappointments which made us feel that our family life was acted out before a screen dividing us from an outer darkness of weeping and gnashing of teeth, immense rewards and fearful punishments. Cooks, governesses, relations, friends, were forever entering our lives, sunning themselves in radiant favours, only to commit some act which caused them never to be mentioned again, unless with an air of tragic disapproval.

It was Violet's belief that 'one becomes a positive slave to one's servants if one is kind to them'.

There may have been some jealousy on Violet's part when servants became too attached to her children or her husband. To the end of his life, susceptible young women were in the habit of falling in love with

Harold, who in middle-age, as in youth, was strikingly handsome. Taking their cue from their mother, the Spender children would make life 'hell' for servants they took against. As the children grew up, nurses and nannies were replaced by 'nursery-governesses' – so described because, in addition to tuition, they were expected to undertake the humbler tasks of childminding. One of these nursery-governesses, seventeen years old when he was seven, 'sexually abused' – that is, fondled – Humphrey. He found the assault 'interesting and educative'. His parents were apparently oblivious.

From this passing parade of servants and live-in helpers, three survived: 'Berthella' and Captain Devoto. It was 'the luckiest chance ever', as Humphrey puts it, that while at Sheringham the Spenders took on a pair of sisters, Bertha and Ella Mills. They were collectively nicknamed 'Berthella' by Violet. The nickname stuck and they, apparently, tolerated being called it. Berthella were twenty-five and twenty-three respectively when the Spenders took them on at the Bluff (in 1916, as one can best determine). They were inherited from a family who were on their way to India. As boarding servants, they each received £25 a year and keep.

As they are portrayed in *World within World*, 'Ella was mild and patient, smiling always with an air of waiting. Bertha, her elder sister, was reckless and opinionated, a leader and example and judge.' Bertha took charge of the kitchen, as head cook; Ella was, while Violet lived, the mistress's maid. For the children Berthella became 'our mother, for ages' as Humphrey puts it. They were still on the scene and still motherly in the 1940s, when Natasha Litvin married Stephen. These Norfolk servants enjoyed a level of intimacy with the children which went far beyond that of their parents. Ella, the gentler of the duo, was still bathing a naked Humphrey at the age of twelve, until an appalled Harold found out about it. (Humphrey promptly broke his arm, and so still had to be bathed by her – he liked it immensely, as he mischievously recalls, 'and so did she'.)

'We loved them,' Humphrey remembers, 'although we mocked them.' Berthella were a source of hilarious malapropisms. They would refer darkly to the 'male seck' and the 'female seck' (thinking, presumably, of the 'war of the seckses'). They were a fund of comical rural saws such as: 'It's a bad back door that don't let through no draughts.' Their Norfolk folk usages ('getting ariddy of it') never ceased to tickle the cosmopolitan Spenders. Berthella were themselves stoical and long-suffering and expected the same of their charges. When Stephen contracted jaundice during the Second World War, Natasha Spender remembers Bertha saying 'sometimes Ella's eyes get as yellow as kingcups but she never complains of *jaundice*'. On one occasion Stephen complained about a headache, only to be bleakly informed by Bertha, 'we *often* has headaches in the kitchen'. Bertha, particularly, took particular offence when the children were 'sickistic'.

Over the years they became a family institution. They 'looked over' both Humphrey's prospective wife, Pauline, and Natasha Litvin. They declared themselves satisfied with Stephen's pianist fiancée, making no comment on the young woman's striking beauty and talent but noting approvingly that 'she's illegitimate and don't care who knows it'. They admired women with the courage to take on all-comers. By a nice symmetry, Captain Devoto married Bertha after he was widowed. Violet wrote poems on Berthella. The poem to Bertha takes the form of a jaunty, mock epitaph:

> Here lieth Bertha, killed by work.
> She never would consent to shirk.

'Ella with a Hairbrush', dated 1921, a year before Violet's death, takes the form of a New Year's Greeting accompanying a gift:

> With so much sorrow far and near
> It seems a foolish thing, I fear,
> To wish you joy this coming year.

Even in wartime, the Spenders always contrived to have their traditional summer holidays. One such annual event was particularly momentous for Stephen. Readers of *World within World* will be struck by the epochal stress the author puts on the family holiday in the Lake District, 'when I was nine years old'. In his mid-life memoir Spender consciously alludes to Wordsworth's 'fair seed-time had my soul' in his description of the episode. It was during this summer vacation, in Wordsworth's own 'native mountains', that 'the seed of poetry was planted in me'. The poet was born. In his *Desert Island Discs* broadcast Spender recalled, and recited, his first Wordsworthian effusion in verse as dating from this moment in his childhood.

Although he remembered details of the holiday 'vividly', Spender was chronically, and typically, vague about the date. In fact, the Wordsworthian holiday took place in August and September of 1917. It was the blackest year of the war in Britain. There was rationing, huge casualty lists (which had hit home at the Bluff), wounded soldiers in all the towns, and the strong apprehension that the Germans, as a result of their latest 'push', might even win.

The description Stephen gives of the holiday in *World within World* is beautiful, self-analytic and – at crucial moments – self-deprecating. On their way north the family spent a night in a hotel in Leeds, 'the first I had ever stayed in'. Maladroit as ever, young Stephen disgraced himself 'by allowing the large yellow-striped hairy caterpillars, which I always carried about in a box with me, to escape in the lift, where they got on the clothes of our fellow guests'.

The family duly arrived at Skelgill Farm, 'below the side of a mountain called Catbells', and immediately 'we four children scrambled up the side of the mountain with my father to view the lake [Derwentwater]'. With a conscious echo of Hood's 'I remember, I remember', Spender recalls the formative impression the landscape made on him:

I remember the rainy lakeside days, and how, after the rain, great raindrops would cling on to the serrated leaves of brambles like hundreds of minute lenses, through which the sun, emerging in a rinsed sky, would gleam with a new-seeming whiteness. I remember the long black slugs on paths wrinkled by many torrential downpours, and the smell of the earth, and how on our walks we found rock crystals on the stones like enjewelled caskets.

The pragmatic Humphrey stole one of the crystals which was being used as a doorstop in a nearby cottage.

'The countryside is fused in my mind', Spender writes in *World within World*,

with my first sustained experience of poetry: For here my father used to read to me the simple ballad poems of Wordsworth, 'We are Seven', 'A Lesson to Fathers', 'The Lesser Celandine'. The words of these poems dropped into my mind like cool pebbles, so shining and so pure, and they brought with them the atmosphere of rain and sunsets, and a sense of the sacred cloaked vocation of the poet. In the warm evening while I lay in bed at Skelgill Farm, I heard the murmuring of my father's voice as he read the Longer Poems of Wordsworth to my mother.

The holiday had a more prosaic and this-worldly aspect for Violet Spender, who conscientiously kept a diary of the event. Her account opens on 1 August 1917 with quartermaster's precision:

Left Sheringham at 8:13. Party consisting of Daddy Mummy Michael Christine Stephen Humphrey and Miss Cox 2 suitcases. 2 large ruck sacks containing lunch and tea. A huge stone bottle full of lemonade (2 gallons) large hold all, five satchels, one camera, 2 despatch cases, Miss Cox's attaché bag, Daddy's little bag, Christine brought her doll and toy dog and Humphrey had his little china mouse in his pocket.

After lunch on the first day the privileged son, Michael, went off to Keswick with his father by boat. It was 'Michael's first row', his mother proudly recorded. In the town Harold bought a butterfly net for Stephen. It was a luxury that the boy had a 'low-ceilinged bedroom' of his own. At home he was obliged to share with Humphrey. Stephen's room was soon 'full of caterpillars – in tooth brush jars, tumblers, boxes, every-thing he can lay hands on. They are fed copiously and carefully guarded from cold, etc.' As the diary records, he watched their health day by day and solemnly informed his mother when 'one has a bilious attack, another a wound, another is in difficulties over changing its skin'. In morning prayers, conducted by Harold, while the rest of the family were patriotically praying for the dead and dying in France and that God might punish their 'cruel foe', Stephen (as Violet discovered) was piously interceding with his Maker for the well-being of the less robust of his larvae.

The holiday was idyllic for the adults as a brief return to the distant luxuries of pre-war life: 'No one seems paying much attention to rations,' Violet records. 'One sees no soldiers, hears no guns. It is difficult to believe there is a war going on.' It was all a world away from Sheringham, 'where we have guns firing all day – big guns, machine guns, bombing; every sort and kind of gun practice'.

The Edenic location brought husband and wife together in second honeymoon intimacy. After the children were in bed they would sit tran-quilly on the farm porch watching the sun go down over the Buttermere mountains or they would wander, hand in hand, over the lower slopes of Catbells. If the evening were dull, they would play chess. It was prob-ably the last unalloyed happy episode of the marriage.

Already the mother's keen eye had picked out the details that marked her children's differently evolving personalities. On 5 August, after going to the little church at Newlands (where the metropolitan Spenders were amused to see the vicar accompanying himself on the harmonium like a nightclub singer), they went off to pick bilberries on Catbells.

The children thoroughly enjoyed themselves about the mountain slopes. Their remarks were amusing. Humphrey, hearing a grasshopper: 'Daddy! what's that noise like a motor bike in the bracken?' Stephen when his hands had become stained with bilberry juice: 'Look how ripe my hands are getting!' The slopes of Catbells are very slippery without nailed boots. Michael has adopted a rather swaggering slangy schoolboy way of speaking and behaving but he has rather a remarkable appreciation of nature. He made us stop climbing and turn round to look at a broad beam of light breaking through a cloud making a wide bright band right down the flank of a mountain and striking a point in the valley where a little group of farm buildings lie among trees, making them gleam with a shining whiteness. Got home rather late.

Humphrey was 'mad' about cars and motor cycles as a little boy. Stephen Spender, prophetically, has Auden's 'dyer's hand'. Michael takes charge of the family and lectures them on optics. Christine is invisible.

It is painfully clear from Violet's journal how effectively Michael eclipses his siblings. It is Michael who goes off with his father when there are important letters to post. It is he, alone of the children, who rows on their expeditions by lake to Keswick; he who goes fishing with his father and catches a five-pound pike ('They seem to have had a tough fight with him'); he who goes to get the photographs developed – photographs for which he has grouped the family with the usual imperious commands ('Smile!').

The drenching rain set in a week after the family's arrival, on 10 August. Up to that point the weather was blissful. Thereafter it was relentlessly wet, cold and windy. The onset of the bad weather was evidently a trial for Harold. On 20 August he discovered that he had important things to do in London. He left with his secretary by the 7.40 from Keswick. The family mood palpably relaxed with the departure of Daddy. There were fewer 'expeditions', 'drills' and 'parades'. But the sole responsibility of caring for the Spender household bore heavily on Violet. The weather got even worse. Walks were only possible in oilskins. Fires were kept going all day – August though it was. Crouched round the fire, she helped Stephen with his butterflies, killing bottle and display boards.

On 31 August, a dank and misty Friday, Michael dragged his mother to the extreme end of the Pass of Newland valley. Looking down from the shrouded peak he came out with the characteristic comment: 'I'm *not* going to give up hope of a view nor yet of Daddy coming home on Saturday.' He asked 'endless questions', as Violet wearily noted ('supposing the earth were flat instead of round, would there be a horizon?')

The strain was too much for Violet. She collapsed. On Friday 7 September Miss Cox telegrammed to Harold, who rushed back from London, dramatically motoring in from Penrith. It was a serious breakdown. Violet was confined to bed for a week on doctor's orders. Harold, meanwhile, returned to Sheringham with Michael, his aide-de-camp, on 18 September. For the other Spenders, the holiday dragged on until the 20th.

The following day Stephen, Christine and Humphrey set off for Norfolk under Miss Cox's superintendence. Violet followed by herself a week later – travelling first class, one supposes. It was, none the less, a difficult journey. She was upset by drunken Scotch soldiers 'rather desperate' about going back to the front. As the much-delayed train drew into London, there was an air-raid in progress: 'Star shells and shrapnel were bursting over the train and there were flashes from the guns. Brilliant searchlights like sparks of giant wheels rolled swiftly across the sky.'

Violet was met at Euston by Harold, 'who had been taking refuge in the Tube Station'. The railway station was blacked out. There were, of course, no porters, and reclaiming the bags from the luggage van was a nightmare. They stayed the night at the Schusters' town house, 12 Harrington Gardens. On the 25th, Violet was 'in bed all day. Too tired to read or do anything.' Harold's physician friend, Dr Knyvet Gordon, ordered 'several days rest'. Harold and Violet returned to Sheringham on the Friday of that week. The annual holiday was over and the family returned to its former Norfolk and London routines.

As Spender records in *World within World*, 'when I was nine I took one of the most important decisions of my life. I decided to go to boarding school.' Stephen's ninth birthday would have been in February 1918. In fact he did not go to boarding school until January 1919, when he was almost ten. The 'important decision' on Stephen's part was evidently

inspired by the sight of Michael returning from Gresham's (a public
school, at Holt in Norfolk) in summer 1918. He cut a fine figure, and
Stephen cites a desire to emulate his older brother as what motivated
him to leave home: 'I felt that if only I went to boarding school, wore
a uniform, and had my hair close-cropped like Michael's, I would become
sure and efficient like him.' He wryly recalls, in *World within World*, that
'my parents looked at Michael and looked at me, and agreed that such
a change was desirable'.

It was at this stage that Stephen suffered most painfully from his
father's low opinion of him, and what Christine called the 'bullying' –
he was 'round shouldered', indefinably a 'sneak' and, that most wounding
of accusations for a sensitive boy, 'unmanly'. Following their father's cue
the children also began to see Stephen as 'the family fool'. Violet, alone,
seems to have protected him – perceiving him as the most sensitive of
her four children. He was in their eyes, one assumes, his mother's
'pampered' favourite and something of a battleground between his parents.
It must have been emotionally confusing. There was also a lot of physical upheaval at the time. Armistice in November 1918 changed the larger
world and, with peace, the Spenders could return 'home' to London in
safety.

One of the reasons for letting Stephen leave home was, doubtless,
that he should be conveniently out of the way while house-removal
plans were made. He was duly dispatched to the Old School House
(OSH – the preparatory department of Gresham's). Unfortunately for
young Spender, the blazer and cropped haircut did not transform him
into a facsimile of Michael. He recalls in some detail his dispiriting and
traumatic experiences in *World within World*. A first blow was the instruction that he must not expect any fraternal support in the struggles to
come. Michael was, as Stephen was firmly informed, not his brother but
'Spender One' – a higher order of creation, and as indifferent to his
sufferings as a Greek god.

Stephen's sufferings at OSH are Promethean in the telling – but tinged
with the comedy which typically colours his anecdotes. Once a General
Knowledge paper was set for the whole school. At the top of a chart
recording the results there stood (inevitably) the name 'Spender One'
with 90 per cent correct answers: at the bottom was 'Spender Two' with
0.5 per cent.

Spender Two soon lost interest in his caterpillars, which, touchingly,
he had brought with him in a box almost as large as the trunk containing

his personal effects. There were no substitute hobbies. So wretched was he at OSH that his only comfort was flight into an 'inner world' in which he would picture himself as a Saint Stephen, or a 'Christ on the Cross'. In *World within World* Spender records that, among other things, the boarding-school indifference about personal modesty was disturbing to him:

On my second morning at school I was told to go and take a cold shower. I entered a room where I saw a number of boys, some of them pubescent, completely naked. It was the first time I had ever seen any nakedness, outside my own family, and it made a strong impression on me.

Many boys are unhappy at school. Was Stephen Spender more so than most, or did he – the hyper-subjective child – just feel it more? Whether typical or atypical, about one thing Spender was very sure. His school-days between the ages of nine and twelve were the unhappiest of his life. He recalls in *World within World* that whenever horrible things happened in later years he would console himself with the thought, 'This isn't nearly as bad as the beginning of term at the OSH.'

One assumes that Michael did not protect Spender Two as he easily could (and should) have done. Perhaps he tacitly condoned or even actively participated in the bullying. The most abject humiliation was heaped on Stephen when, having taken more than their fair share of bread (a commodity still rationed in the post-war years), he and some fellow offenders were handed over for condign punishment by the master (Mr Wynne Wilson) with the verdict: 'These boys are worse than Huns, they're FOOD HOGS.'

The day boys at OSH were Stephen's particular enemies. In the spirit of a lynch mob they fell on Spender Two – the indicted Food Hog. According to his later account, 'some boys tied pieces of rope round my arms and legs and pulled in opposite directions. I was flung down a hole at the back of the platform of the school dining-room, called the Kipper Hole, because heads of kippers were thrown there.' Evidently it was where scraps were stored in bins after meals. The school would have had pigs and other livestock to supplement its ration allowances.

This punishment had happened before – 'unceasingly'. But on this occasion it was particularly traumatic. Spender recounted it twice in print, and on *Desert Island Discs* as marking a threshold point in his child-hood. In the extremity of his wretchedness young Stephen did not, as would seem normal, turn to his older brother. He cycled off to the house of the piano teacher where he had a private lesson. Walter Greatorex was a gifted instrumentalist. The piano teacher was 'a man whom all the boys loved' (with the exception of the young virtuoso Benjamin Britten, who disliked him intensely). Like Stephen, young Auden (another pupil at Gresham's, a couple of years further ahead) found Walter Greatorex extraordinarily sympathetic. 'My first friendship with a grown up person, with all that means . . . if the whole of the rest of my schooldays had been hateful, which they weren't, his existence alone would make me recall them with pleasure.'

Greatorex apparently had no inflated estimate of Stephen's musical talents and predicted, correctly, that he would never be any good on the piano (although, like Humphrey, he was to be 'mad' about music all his life). But after his experience in the kipper hole the boy could not play a single note or even talk coherently. He broke down. Greatorex listened to what had happened. There must have been a lot that tumbled out – possibly about Stephen's sense of feeling 'different' from the other boys. Greatorex offered eerily prophetic consolation: 'You may go on being unhappy until you are twenty or so, and a year comes when you are very free and only waiting to go up to the University. You will probably travel abroad and then that will perhaps be the happiest time of your life.'

At this distance it is not clear what Stephen learned at OSH (certainly not keyboard technique), beyond a visceral hatred of public school fascism; an only slightly less visceral dislike of classwork, and formal examinations; and a sensation of unease about the unclothed bodies of his fellow pubescent schoolboys.

With peace the Spenders' family life was changing into what would be its final domestic form. While Stephen was at school, the household moved from Sheringham to establish itself at 10 Frognal, in Hampstead. They found their new establishment, according to Christine (who was at home at this point), after looking around 'for ages'. The house was rented on lease. It was a great red brick structure ('ugly', Stephen always thought, and 'owl-like' with its two hooded front windows), big enough for Harold to set up his Victorian household with its six family members and five live-in servants (Berthella, two housemaids, Ivy and Violet, and Captain Devoto). It was near to the Heath; a tonic, presumably, for Mrs Spender's health.

Violet superintended the decoration of the new house (it was a happy interlude in her now generally unhappy life, as Christine remembers). The children were 'parked' at Sheringham and Harold in the National Liberal Club. The furniture, put away in 1913, was taken out of store. The house was done up in the familiar mixture of mid-Victorian (Harold's) and late-Victorian (Violet's) style. Prominent on the wall of the living-room was Hunt's *The Light of the World* and there were Rossettis everywhere ('my mother was mad about Rossetti'). Morris patterns covered the walls and draped the windows. Violet had a little dressing-room ornamented with her beloved Rackham and Dulac drawings. There was lots of art nouveau furniture in the house, and wedding presents dating back to 1904. Brass screens and brass coal-scuttles and examples of Harold's beloved Balkan peasant art (Humphrey's detested 'little boxes') were 'all over the place'. It was, however, one of the advantages of Harold's being a journalist that the family always had the latest gadgetry. They had been on the telephone from their earliest days in Kensington. Michael introduced wireless into the household, with all the apparatus of 'cat's crystal, valves, and condensers'. The Spenders were, Humphrey recalls, 'one of the first families in England to listen in, each with our headphones'. Frognal was among the first domestic houses to have big horned gramophones. It was, if gloomily Victorian in ambience, an efficient, well-located, comfortable establishment for a growing family.

Middle-class families like the Spenders had been damagingly hit by wartime taxation. Harold had evidently earned little from his books over the past few years, and the Schuster funds regularly ran low. And, as Harold was never allowed to forget, it *was* Schuster money. Christine saw her father being sent off to the National Liberal Club by her mother, 'without money, because he would only spend it'. The Schusters were increasingly scornful of the man whom Violet had married, who had so signally *not* come up in the world. The epithet 'spendthrift' was muttered (it is still uttered by surviving members of the family when Harold's name comes up). 'My Schuster uncles thought my father was a fool,' Christine recalled.

There was one great consolation. After the war, travel was again possible. In June 1921, the *Daily Telegraph* sent Harold to Ireland, to report on the opening of the Ulster Parliament by the King. He made further trips to Ireland in September 1921 and 1922 and had some thrilling brushes with 'Sinn Feiners'. He was still an ardent Home Ruler, if more discreetly so nowadays. Harold visited America in 1921 and 1923. On the first

American trip, a speaking tour, Violet went with him. She also collected, belatedly, her degree from Somerville.

By 1919–20 Stephen, having spent a year at OSH, was well into his tenth year. In the normal course of things he would have graduated to the Big School at 'eleven plus', in October 1920. Evidently Gresham's did not want Spender Two. A report was sent to Stephen's parents indicating that their boy was 'backward' – a euphemism for 'educationally subnormal'. The shameful epithet etched itself on his mind. On his return from Gresham's as an unwanted, *backward* boy, Stephen was subjected to more of his father's wounding ('namby-pamby') belittlement. It was not intended cruelly, but as a kind of man-to-man, 'pull yourself together' brusqueness. The parents must, however, have been in something of a quandary. What to do with Stephen? It would be awkward for him to be at home just at the moment in the still new house at Frognal. Harold, as he often (and fatally) did in such dilemmas, took advice from his friend, Dr Knyvet Gordon. What was the right course of action for his 'backward' son? As it happened, the doctor himself had a son at Charlcote boarding-school in Worthing. It was a small 'crammer', specializing in preparing boys for Common Entrance. It was a no-nonsense establishment – the rod was not spared. The two men evidently agreed that it would be just right for Stephen.

Spender memorialized his experiences at Charlcote in his novel *The Backward Son* (1940) and in his later essay, 'Day Boy'. Humphrey certifies their account as photographically accurate. Charlcote is described in 'Day Boy' as 'a school run in the most dishonest way'. It lures middle-class parents with brochures showing facilities (swimming-pools, well-stocked libraries, tennis courts) that have been fabricated specially for the prospectus like so many Potemkin villages. As Stephen scornfully discovered, the school made up its numbers with 'sons of shopkeepers', and employed the poorest kind of staff. Stephen discovered that one of the masters lived in a bed-sitting-room, and he was 'overwhelmed with horror at my first contact with the truly sordid'.

The worst horror at Charlcote was that 'the head master loved caning'. There had been no corporal punishment at Gresham's. The subtler punishment of the 'Honour System' replaced the cane. At home Harold had a principled aversion to beating his children. Charlcote was by contrast a 'brothel for flagellants'. Humphrey (who joined Stephen a couple of terms later) reckons he was flogged every week, usually for 'stupidity' (his weak eyes meant he had been kept from reading for several years), or 'insolence'. In his first term Stephen seems not to have been beaten (thanks to a letter, from his mother, to the headmaster explaining that he was 'delicate'; it got him no credit with his much flogged school-fellows).

Humphrey was just ten when he too was bundled off to Charlcote. In later life he could never bring himself to talk to Stephen about their shared Charlcote memories, because 'mine were so awful'. Humphrey was bound to stand out and get into trouble in a prep school environment. His warmth of character was an affront to the frigid regimentalism of Charlcote. Soon after arrival he was discovered kissing one of the school's maids. 'Do you do that kind of thing at home?' he was sternly asked – that favourite schoolmaster's reprimand. 'Yes, I do,' Humphrey innocently replied (he was forever canoodling with the maids at Frognal). A beating ensued – the first of many. Cuddles may have been prohibited but there was, as Humphrey calls it, 'furtive sex' in the dormitories. He recalls, in particular, penis-measuring sessions after lights out, with tape measures and much stifled giggling. Stephen, as he remembers, did not take part. But, as *The Backward Son* records, there was smut and bawdy talk, some of which eleven-year-old Geoffrey Brand (i.e. Stephen) finds strangely exciting.

As he records in *The Backward Son*, Stephen put himself out to protect his younger brother (as, pointedly, Michael had not protected him, Stephen, at Gresham's). It was some consolation that his misery was now shared. The persecution of the Spender brothers at Charlcote climaxed in the second term with the discovery that their maternal name was 'Schuster' ('Schroeder' in the novel). This led to their being 'sent to Coventry'.

The brothers' persecution as 'Huns' makes up the bulk of *The Backward Son*'s narrative. It climaxes with a great fight, described at epic length. A more trenchant description is given in 'Day Boy':

One day I came to realize that the person I should attack was not my brother, but the ringleader of the boys who were persecuting us. I therefore challenged him to a fight. I do not remember who won, but I do remember that while we were fighting a small and cowardly boy called Wallace, whom I had often protected, sneered at me and shouted, 'Yah, Hun!' When we had finished fighting I addressed myself to him. I remember him looking very terrified and I remember that he was leaning against the window. I raised my arm, and I do not remember whether I struck him, but I must have looked cruel. He fell back against the window, which was smashed, although he was not hurt. There was an awed exuberant fall of silence on the boys in the changing room as they looked forward to the prodigious punishment that would doubtless fall on me.

Humphrey's recollection is that Stephen won this fight. And he was, for the first time, caned.

The brothers' misery ended on 5 December 1921, during school rehearsals for a performance of *Hamlet* (Humphrey recalls that it was, precisely, during the opening battlement scene). The boys were summoned to the head's study to be informed that 'your mother is seriously ill'. In fact she had died during a surgical operation on the 4th. Perversely the brothers' first reaction on hearing of their grievous loss was one of 'glistening joy'. Joy because in his letter to the headmaster, their father had also told him that they were to be withdrawn from Charlcote.

It is not entirely clear what killed Violet, just forty-four years old. It seems to have been a botched operation for adhesions to repair the effects of an earlier botched hysterectomy. Significantly her dying words were not delivered to her husband or her children, but to the servant, Ella, the gentler component of Berthella. Spender makes his mother's last words, as relayed through Ella to the family, the conclusion of his autobiography, *World within World:* 'I remembered how my mother, the night before she died, said to Ella, who was lighting the little gas fire in her bedroom, "Tell them I have had a very happy life".'

It seems that poor doctoring was, at least partly, the cause of Violet's unhappy death. The operation was performed at home, as was common at this period. Harold's loyalty to his Sheringham friend, Dr Knyvet Gordon, was – Humphrey thinks – a misjudgement which was fatal to his mother's health (all the children 'hated' Gordon). It is said also that the anaesthetist at the operation was drunk. He was a neighbour of whom Harold (mistakenly) had a high professional opinion. One will never know. But it is clear that after Violet's death, Harold was prostrated with self-flagellating grief.

At the time, in December 1921, it was less grief than embarrassment that overwhelmed the children. The boys were 'rushed home' to Frognal to be met by the melodramatic scene described in *World within World:*

I remember entering a room and seeing my father seated on a chair with his head in his hands. When he saw us he raised his arms, embraced us and exclaimed: 'My little ones. You are all your old father has left.' He was genuinely stricken and there was certainly no falsity in his voice or his expression. His usual expression, indeed, was deleted with grief, like a clownish white grease paint which had smoothed out the characteristic lines. Yet he communicated a situation which put him outside us by dramatizing that we were all he had.

For the next couple of years, Harold would gather his 'little people' around him as his shelter from the cruel world. This meant no more boarding-school, at least for a year or two. But, of course, schooling there would have to be. For a short interval Stephen and Humphrey went to the Hall, the local prep school in Hampstead. Christine evidently went to King Alfred's as a day-girl. The nearly adult Michael remained at Gresham's.

There ensued a period in which Harold conscientiously devoted himself to his children, spending much time at home. He worked hard at making family holidays a success, and devised any number of home projects of an educational and improving kind. As part of this new domesticity, Stephen and Humphrey were 'day boys'. They spent the last two terms of the 1921–2 year (January to July 1922) at the Hall, sleeping at home. Technically, the thirteen-year-old Stephen Spender was already old enough to go to 'big school' but he was still too 'backward' academically to cope. He would need to be brought forward, 'crammed', if necessary. Spender describes in *World within World* the interview in which he was placed at the Hall:

A few days after the death of my mother, my father took me to see the headmaster of the day school in Hampstead where it was proposed that I should be sent, in order to be (together with my sister Christine, who was also brought home) a companion to him in his widowhood. The headmaster said something to the effect that it was a loss to children to have no mother. 'Fortunately at his age, they do not realize it,' my father said. This remark had a complex effect on me. I recognized its justice. If I felt the death of my mother at all, it was as the lightening of a burden and as a stimulating excitement. Yet I was humiliated at his demonstration of my own lack of feeling. I longed to be stricken again in order to prove that next time I would be really tragic. But the only loss which I could imagine affecting me greatly was my father himself. For this could make me that pathetic figure, an orphan. Thus I longed for my father to die in order that I might demonstrate my grief to him, as he watched me from the grave.

The new school was a merciful release from the horrors of Charlcote. At the Hall Stephen encountered the kindness under which he always bloomed. He attracted the attention of a particularly gentle and cultured teacher called Mr Gladstone, who, among other treats, took his music-loving pupil to see the opera *Hansel and Gretel*. Mr Gladstone, Humphrey thinks (uncensoriously), 'fell in love with Stephen a bit'.

Under this kinder regime Stephen Spender's intellectual abilities at last showed themselves. He was promoted quickly into a higher class and even featured creditably in the Swimming Sports Day, at the end of his short career at the Hall (Stephen was never a *good* swimmer, according to Humphrey, who was). At this period of his life Stephen was already talking about being a poet and play-acting the part. The family made a trip to Switzerland, where Humphrey watched his brother striking a romantic pose at Chillon while reciting Byron's poem. At this period, as Humphrey recalls, Stephen thought 'Humbert Wolfe was marvellous' (Wolfe's influence is clearly evident in Stephen's school magazine poetry of the 1920s). Stephen Spender was faithful to this Georgian versifier until Auden, with one cutting remark in his Oxford rooms, damned Wolfe, together with 'Siggy' Sassoon, as 'no good' – verdicts which Stephen humbly accepted.

If Stephen Spender had found his future vocation, Harold Spender was still floundering. After the war – drawing on his old university extension skills – he marketed himself as a 'popular lecturer'. He was never happier than when he was on a platform basking in an audience's rapt attention. Whatever solace to their father's punctured self-esteem, Harold's 'popular lectures' were agony for the Spender boys if, as occasionally happened, they were unlucky enough to be in that audience. Humphrey disgustedly remembers his father coming to Gresham's, while he and Michael were at that school, 'in a Daimler, wearing plus fours', his secretary in attendance. On such occasions, his sons would listen, writhing, to a windy lecture on some such subject as 'tramping through the High Pyrenees', knowing, all the while, that their father was doing it for a huckster's fee or simply to show off.

In *World within World*, Stephen records his particular mortification at being dragged along (as he often was) to his father's lectures in connection with his social work in Hampstead:

After the death of my mother, he liked taking me to small pietistic gatherings of Nonconformist Youths, which took place in the drawing-rooms of certain members of the congregation of Lyndhurst Road Congregational Church. One evening . . . when my father was delivering a homily to some gathering of devout youths, in the darkness of the chair-crowded room I suddenly realized that they were all sniggering at him . . . I felt outraged and indignant and at the same time I experienced a sense of pity. But my attitude towards his public appearances, which until then I had regarded as spectacular successes, was for ever changed.

Harold's non-conformist tendencies, after his wife's death, hardened into something like mania. He became a regular attender at the Revd Dr R. F. Horton's Lyndhurst Road church, adopting a Lloyd-George-style chapel moralism. He worked 'zealously' with Horton's St George's Young Men's Club (little to the young men's edification, as Stephen Spender testifies above). When, however, Horton, in his sixties, took to wife a nineteen-year-old chorister, the Spender family attendance at Lyndhurst suddenly ceased. According to family legend, the young woman rebounded into the arms of the minister from a hopeless affection for the impregnably virtuous Harold.

Harold's devotion to his children's welfare, suffocating as it may have seemed, was well motivated and, in its way, imaginative. He helped his 'little people' organize a 'Frognal Museum Society', which assembled a cabinet of scientific and natural 'curios', all carefully labelled and described. He encouraged them to produce (as their own work) a family newspaper, the 'Frognal Gazette'. Launched in September 1919, it ran to twenty pages and there were a dozen or so irregular issues, costing a nominal 1s. per copy, run off on the paternal Gestetner (Captain Devoto assisting). Stephen was the 'literary editor'. Christine did a gossip column in the character of the family canary, Dicky Dicks (the bird was 'bald', she recalled). Humphrey did the art. Michael wrote the occasional scientific treatise.

The grandly titled Frognal Museum Society recruited some grand speakers to address it. They included Frederic Harrison and Arnold Bennett, as Humphrey remembers. It is clear that Harold was doing well by his children, providing them with an enviably high level of intellectual stimulus. Of course, he was turning them, in his mind, into little journalists and public debaters just like himself.

Humphrey and Stephen shared a bedroom in the square tower which rose over the slate roof of 10 Frognal. Stephen recited poetry as they lay in bed. Humphrey remembers conversations in the bedroom after 'lights out' (his father's terminology) in which Stephen confessed his intention of being a poet. Eighty years later Humphrey would say he 'can hear him today', in his mind's ear rolling off Swinburne's sonorously alliterative lines. A close description of the boys' bedroom is given in *The Backward Son*:

The two beds with their iron frames enamelled a rich black, the green carpet, the rug by the side of each bed, the satin wallpaper, the reproduction of two royal portraits by Holbein on the wall, the mantelpiece with an imitation boot covered with hyacinths in china on it. The wine-red curtains were drawn, and the whole room glowed in electric light which dazzled the whitewash above so that it slightly blurred the join of wall and ceiling seen from where he lay.

This interlude – what one might call the Frognal Museum Society years – lasted from Violet's death in December 1921 until 1923. It was, for Harold, a period of mourning and partial reconstruction. Insidiously, however, his old lust for travel and political adventure reasserted itself. Michael was by now in the sixth form at Gresham's and preparing for Oxford. Christine was attending a day school in the Hampstead area, St Christopher's. Humphrey had been packed off to join Michael. Stephen was kept at home to go to nearby University College School as a day boy.

Living continually at home, Stephen felt the full brunt of his father's possessiveness, something that had grown to neurotic proportions in the years following Violet's death. As Stephen observed, his 'character changed. He became anxious and concerned ... My sister and I were not allowed out of the house unaccompanied, and every moment of our day was watched and worried over.' At the age of sixteen, Stephen and his seventeen-year old sister 'were only allowed sixpence a week pocket money, so that if ever we went out of the house and wished to take a bus ride, we had to go to my father and ask for leave'.

As they grew up into stormy adolescence, Harold, the paterfamilias, became ever more embarrassing to his children, especially his two younger sons. Victorian to the core, he never, of course, talked about sex. Humphrey got his first glimmerings about 'the facts of life' from a copy of *Gray's Anatomy*, on a solitary and otherwise grim visit to his great-aunt Constance in Bath, aided with recollections of the furtive after-lights sessions at Charlcote. 'My father,' Stephen bleakly recalls, 'never discussed sexual matters with me, or even mentioned that sex existed. I became so afraid of coarse talk that I used to walk out of the room if I ever heard any of the boys [at University College School] using it.' Sex was taboo, but Harold had a Victorian obsession with bowels. The children were dosed, to toxic levels, with 'Virol, Scott's emulsion, Kruschen Salts, Syrup of Figs, and castor oil' – all designed to produce 'regularity'. Harold would ask the children daily if they had done 'their little duty'. Even on birthdays, they were not allowed to open their presents till they had 'done their little duty'.

The effect was to make Stephen, at least, morbidly conscious of his bodily functions. As a schoolboy at University College School 'it became impossible for me to use the lavatory during the eleven o'clock break, when all the other boys went to relieve themselves: the lack of concealment in such an act was an inconsistency that I could not understand, since I had learned that the whole of civilization was based on the concealment of physical acts'.

Some physical acts were not concealed. Stephen remembered as 'the most dreaded of experiences'

the daily bristly kiss which my father publicly planted on my face each morning at ten minutes to nine, at our garden gate and in front of a long procession of boys who trailed up to school. In order to avoid the full disgrace of this I took to going very early to school. I found I was happier there than at home, so I also would stay as long there in the evening as was possible.

Anything more than temporary escape from the domestic oppression was, however, impossible. Once, when he was sixteen, Stephen

tried to win back his long-lost faith in me, by telling him about some books I was reading. I told him that I had just read a book by Bernard Shaw. My father stopped still in the path where we were walking and said: 'I have heard of other people having children like that, but I have always prayed God I might be spared.'

One would like to think it ironic, but evidently it was not. Harold did indeed implore his Maker to spare his son from the defiling touch of Modern Literature. He tried vainly to instil 'proper' Victorian taste into his children. According to Humphrey, 'He used to drag us round the galleries', rushing them past Renoir's nude ladies, with the command

'Boiled lobsters, don't look!', stopping to admire at length the G. F. Watts.

Above all, Harold was obsessed with being 'straight'. When Humphrey approached his father's friendly secretary, Captain Devoto, to get some paltry concession at school, the request provoked a twelve-page letter on 'not being a sneak' from Harold. 'The revenge we took on him,' Stephen recalled, 'was never to laugh at his stories. At meals we would listen acidly to his conversation about politics, and if ever we could detect any inaccuracy in what he said, we would hasten to correct it.'

From 1924 to Harold's death in 1926, the Schusters (notably Stephen's grandmother, Hilda Schuster), took effective charge of the Spender family finances. Until his death, in 1924, Ernest Schuster (Hilda's husband) had been a dutiful and giving, if stern, grandfather. He walked with the children every Sunday, and evidently took an interest in their religious and moral upbringing. Harold may have hoped that the death of his father-in-law would release some money, in the form of a bequest. It did not. They would, of course, be maintained, but in the former way, as abject pensioners. As Stephen remembered, 'on a 31 bus, on the black-ened route that leads from Earls Court to Swiss Cottage . . . my father told me (with the crowds standing outside the pubs of Kilburn) that my grandfather in his will had left us "just enough money to keep us out of the workhouse"'.

There was a growing rift between the Harold Spenders and the rest of the family. J. A. Spender was in a different political camp and in his mind had written Harold off. Humphrey remembers the humiliation of playing tennis with the Schusters (at which he was good and Stephen 'hopeless'), wearing shabby whites. 'They always made us feel inferior,' he recalls. The Schusters enjoyed (when away from their offices) an ultra-English country house existence at Nether Worton, in Oxfordshire. They had risen far above their immigrant Jewishness. Not that they were ashamed of their origins, or frightened of prejudice (they gallantly declined to shed their German name during the war). They had just decided to be English and did it, as they did everything, efficiently. When one of the family, Arthur Schuster, was slandered as a German spy he won £100 in damages and passed it on to the Red Cross.

Stephen's feelings about his Schuster relatives and his Schuster heritage were complex – sometimes he was emulous and proud of the connec-tion. On other occasions, he rejected what they stood for and was affronted by their exaggeratedly crusty Englishness. He was much less uncertain about his grandmother, Hilda Schuster, now widowed and the Spenders' family paymaster. She was, he records, 'one of the most important influences of my life'.

Hilda survives in family lore in numerous, much repeated, comic anecdotes. Her personality was a strange compound of philanthropy and pathological meanness. Her tongue was sharp. Nor did she mellow or weaken with age. In her nineties (and one of the wealthier women in London) she could be seen running for buses. After the death of her son, Alfred, in Flanders in 1916, she became a Quaker, a form of religion which put a firm line of separation between herself and her husband's Jewishness and high Anglicanism. The pro-German sympathies which she had inherited from her Catholic father were sustained during the war and after. Much of her philanthropy during the 1920s was directed to aiding German suffering and refugees. In her huge double flat by the Albert Hall, she would sit bolt upright at her desk, alongside her a large pile of banknotes for 'ladies in khaki coloured dresses'. The flat would be freezing, one lump of coal glowing dully in the grate, the furniture under shrouds.

After her husband Ernest's death, Hilda took control of her son-in-law's finances with an iron grip. It aggravated Harold's 'deep and humiliating sense of obligation', as Christine calls it. The humiliations were not without their comic side. As Christine remembered, on one family holiday in Salcombe, Devon, in summer 1925:

Granny rang up to say, 'the books have just come through' – she kept these books, you know, and she said, 'You're spending too much.' My father said, 'You see children, we're spending far too much. We must feed on mackerel for the rest of the week.' And for the rest of the week we had soused, rolled, boiled mackerel. We couldn't stand it any more. After a week my father said – 'I think we'll go down to town and buy a nice chicken, and some cream and some strawberries.'

Strawberry rebellions apart, the shame must have been unbearable for Harold. As Christine perceived, 'he felt he should be earning for us all. But in the background Granny was supplying *all* the money.' Harold had no regular source of income nowadays at all, except the small stipends he earned from lecturing. Christine found him in tears on one occasion when his voice failed and he had to cancel a lecture: 'It was because he couldn't earn his money, you see.'

In addition to drawing in the purse-strings, Hilda had other ways of emasculating Harold. 'My grandmother was really quite nasty sometimes,' Christine observed. 'She used to make fun of his books.' Harold's books, it must be said, were increasingly grandiose: *Men and Mansions* (1924), for example – a ramble through the great English country houses, written in the tone of an *habitué*. But, absurd as such productions were, Harold *had* written creditable, if not wonderful, books. Looking over the whole course of his life, he had been in his time a productive, honest and distinguished journalist more principled than the majority of his profession and his contemporaries.

In her grandson Stephen, Hilda encouraged intellectual rebellion against his father. Harold had a horror of 'modern' (i.e. post-Victorian) art. 'In our house at Frognal the names of Augustus John, Bernard Shaw, Lytton Strachey, Van Gogh, stood for a diabolic, cunning depravity, a plot of bearded demons against all which should be held sacred.' In the face of this paternal anathema Hilda 'used, when my father was away, to take me to the theatre. With her I saw plays of Chekhov, Ibsen and Strindberg, and experimental performances of Shakespeare.' Granny Schuster gave the sixteen-year-old Stephen a copy of Butler's *The Way of All Flesh* – that manifesto of filial rebellion against the generic Victorian father. Whatever her motives – and they were, from Stephen Spender's point of view, benign – Granny Schuster cannot have made Harold's last years of life easy for him. Nor, one suspects, did she want to.

After his two terms of the Hall's remedial treatment, Stephen was finally ready for a secondary school. Harold evidently felt that, although dramatic progress had been made, his son 'could not take' boarding school again. In what turned out to be an enlightened decision, it was decided that Stephen should attend University College School (UCS) as a day boy. The school was only a few hundred yards away from 10 Frognal. Its high intellectual tone and secular traditions suited Stephen. Also, UCS was 'the gentlest of schools'. He started out on the right foot: 'Guy Kendall, the headmaster, interviewed me and gave me such high marks for this interview that I started work in the fourth form.' What this meant was that Stephen had at last caught up with his 'year'. The promotion into the fourth form caused no difficulties: 'I soon settled down and did not find the work too hard.'

UCS was not a public school; 25 per cent of its intake were 'scholarship' boys, from the poorest classes. Hampstead was then, as it is to a certain extent now, inhabited by the clever classes of London society,

with a sizeable cosmopolitan component. Gifted working-class boys, Jews
and 'aliens' could get into UCS (as to the College it was attached to),
and have their fees paid, if they passed a competitive examination. The
'scholarship' boys opened up Stephen Spender's views on life, broadening the stultifying Victorian and Anglo-Saxon perspectives Harold had
laid on him, offering an antidote to the non-conformist narrowness of
10 Frognal and the bourgeois snobberies of Gresham's. By the most
circuitous of routes, Stephen ended up having the best school education of all the Spender children. As Stephen later discovered,

What I enjoyed most at UCS was the social life. There were any number of
societies, the chief of which was the debating society. I used to go to all the
debates, and I used to speak, very unsurely, from notes. My strong subjects were
the League of Nations and Free Trade.

The *Gower* (UCS's school magazine) records 'S.H.S.' as secretary of
the school's League of Nations Union (Junior Branch) in December
1924. It was the subject of his first recorded publication, in the same
magazine. The idealistic – and politicized – tone of this pacifist-inter-
nationalist society's discussions was characteristic of UCS, and left its
lifelong mark on Stephen. As he advanced up the school, Stephen eventually edited the *Gower*. He was able to consolidate a coterie of like-
minded friends. Since the school was only two minutes' walk from home,
in the same road, these friends could drop in or drift out as suited them.

Of course, the closeness meant that Harold could, conversely, drop in
at the school. On one awful occasion (when Stephen Spender was
studying for 'matric', around 1923–4) Harold 'came suddenly into the
classroom where I was working, and said to the Mathematics master,
"you must make my son Stephen work Harder"'. Stephen was 'considerably upset, and all the boys laughed':

Their amusement proved to be my salvation. My best friend, a boy called [John]
Cornforth, immediately said that my father should be known as 'The Man of
Wrath'. At first I was hurt, but soon I started to feel amused, and I told Cornforth
about my life at home, and this relieved me considerably. Cornforth and one
or two other boys used then quite often to invite me to their homes. I began
to realize that through the companionship of these boys I could create the
entirely humorous intimacy in my surroundings which I needed. My life
became intoxicated with companionship, and I wrote about my friends and

would lie awake thinking of my happiness with them. Although they were platonic, these friendships marked the end of adolescence for me.

He published his first poems in the *Gower* and the *Beanstalk* (the school's literary magazine) from 1925 onwards. His early efforts are signed 'S. H. Spender' or 'S.H.S'. 'Stephen Spender' would only emerge after his father's death. The earliest published poem is a homiletic verse called 'Procrastination' (a Haroldian theme, if there ever was one), published in the *Beanstalk*, December 1925:

> That I have wasted yesterday
>   Causes me great sorrow;
> For, though the sky was very gray,
> Eight hours I read, in the new hay;
> The sky is very blue to-day –
>   But I will work to-morrow!
> That I have wasted yesterday
>   Causes me great sorrow.

By March 1926, with a sonnet on spring, he had clearly advanced in his poetic craft:

> The rain drops from the mist endless and slow,
>   The trees are bare and black, the pavement gray,
>   The sky modestly hides . . . And yet they say
> Lightly that it is Spring in Salcombe now.

The world-weary (or perhaps just school-weary) piece ends: 'O God! . . . would I were there.'

In the *Gower*, March 1926, 'S.H.S.' turned out an 'official' poem celebrating the rigours of the school cadet's force annual 'Camp':

> Can'st thou remember all those miles we walked
>   O'er Salisbury Plain; and how we reached that din
> Of tourists called Stonehenge; and how we talked,
>   And drank weak, watered cider at an Inn?

After these unpromising interrogations, the poem becomes an interesting defence of the cadet corps ('we were taught fighting . . . so that others should not fight') and finishes with the militant sentiment that 'War' is a 'slut'. Privately, in his diary, Stephen observed more candidly that the OTC 'is a great benefit to world peace because it is so wretched'. In the same diary he records losing his religious faith in 1926.

Spender made close friends with masters at UCS, notably Geoffrey Thorp. Writing in *The Thirties and After* (1978), he remembered that Thorp 'influenced me greatly':

He was a member of the avant-garde, Bohemian, leftist 1917 Club, an ardent socialist, had progressive views about education, sex, art, health foods, etc, was an atheist, derided every conformism. He brought with him the gust of a new world which blew through the schoolroom when he entered it. As a result of his being there, three or four boys who were friends of mine became politically socialist and aesthetically avant-garde.

A few years later, in 1982, Spender wrote a short story (never published) about Thorp, called 'Mr Branch'. It offers a vivid vignette of Stephen, aged sixteen:

I had the most tormented adolescence anyone has ever had in the whole of history, I think. My self-consciousness was of such extreme degrees that sometimes when I walked along the street I seemed to be treading on spikes of fire and my head hailed on by splinters of ice. My body seemed skewered on the gaze of everyone I passed in the street – lanky, round-shouldered and spotty – I was revolved on a spit.

Thorp (Branch), to whom Spender enlisted as 'a kind of adjutant' was a necessary antidote. A veteran of the trenches and anti-school by nature, he was given to wenching, swearing, drinking, and the reading of dangerous books. In later life, Spender saw through his teacher. Like Harold, it was all 'rhetoric'. But he remained eternally grateful for the impressive range of extracurricular reading and culture (Joyce, Lawrence, Eliot) that Thorp put his way. Few other 'good' schools of the 1920s would have been willing to tolerate his heterodoxies (eventually, and inevitably, he was fired even from UCS).

Spender bloomed at UCS, partly because of its gentleness. It did not matter that he was no athlete, or that he was neurotic about bodily functions. It was a world away from Charlcote and also – as he would soon discover – from Oxford:

At the end of my time at UCS, when I was on the library committee, and was editor of the school magazine, and a sub-monitor, my opinions seemed to be taken quite seriously and I had no enemies. As soon as I got to Oxford, I found myself surrounded by public school boys who sneered at me because I was an aesthete, were indignant because I was a 'red', and who on occasions tried to break up my rooms. For this reason I felt far freer at UCS than I ever did in the snobbish environment of Oxford.

Paradoxically schooldays, which had begun by being the unhappiest of Stephen Spender's life, ended up by being among the most contented. He passed his 'Matric' in July 1925. He was admitted to the sixth form, and by 1927 he had won a place at University College, Oxford (presumably by interview, at which he usually did well). The Master of University College was Harold's old comrade from extramural lecturing days, Michael Sadler.

Serene and fulfilling as they were from the educational and growing-up point of view, Stephen Spender's years at UCS were complicated by Harold's final illness and the gradual disintegration of the Frognal ménage. After his wife's death, Harold had made one last desperate attempt to establish himself in public life. A by-election was called in Bath, in 1922. Bath was his home town, and the Spenders were a respected local family. This was to the good. Less good was the political fact that the Liberal Party was in the terminal stages of decay. Harold declared that he would stand as what he (optimistically) called a 'sane' Liberal.

In the event Harold performed very creditably, polling 8,699 against the Conservative candidate's 13,666, driving Labour into ignominious third place with 4,849 votes. Less memorable than the result was the electioneering. Harold made a sensation on local voters by recruiting the thirteen- and twelve-year-old Stephen and Humphrey for his canvassing. The boys:

were brought down by train from London, put on the platform beside my father who made a sweeping gesture towards us, exclaiming to the audience: 'I have brought up my reserves!' We were sent round the streets of Bath in a donkey cart. The donkey had hung round its neck a placard on which was written VOTE FOR DADDY.

Humphrey recalls the episode as mildly amusing and typical of his preposterous father. Commentators in Bath thought it was a clever gimmick. For Stephen the donkey cart and 'Vote for Daddy' was a humiliation he remembered all his life. It resurfaces in the opening quatrains of 'The Ambitious Son':

> Old man, with hair made of newspaper cutting
> A public platform voice,
> Tail coat and top hat strutting
> Before your constituents' applause –

Of course, they never would be his 'constituents'.

Stephen marks 22 October 1922 as the moment that he finally 'saw through' his father. He recalls, shortly before being called down to Bath, taking his regular Sunday walk with his grandfather Schuster:

On this walk I asked: 'Will Daddy win the Election?' and my grandfather said something abrupt to the effect that he hadn't a chance, and shrugged his shoulders with a movement of heavy impatience. There was something in this gesture which made me see that my bearded grandfather regarded my father's politics as a childish and profitless game.

Stephen saw his home life from 1921 to 1926 as a 'painful but necessary experience', forging his anti-Victorianism, making him a 'modern'. Filial rebellion was a key element. His father was Eminent Victorianism incarnate: what Leslie Stephen was to Virginia Woolf and General Gordon to Lytton Strachey. Life at Frognal may have been useful aversion therapy for his poet son, but for Harold the 1920s must have been unrelieved torment. 'I don't think he understood any of the boys', according to Christine. There were 'terrific rows . . . even with Michael. I was always trying to make peace in some way.' Stephen diagnosed in his father at this time a 'special kind of cowardice', a 'fear of discovery'. Exposure, that is, as a sham, a parasite, a 'failure'. He feared, like other fathers, his sons' harsh patronage.

Failing to make a mark either in British politics or with his surly and disaffected children, Harold turned to the only place on earth where he was appreciated – Greece. He made a second visit to the country in 1923 and a third in 1924. For the Byron anniversary he published with the assistance of Sir John Stavridi (an old friend, godfather to Stephen, and currently Greek consul in London) all the works of Byron relating to Greece. They came out in three volumes, as *Byron and Greece* (1924:

'an amazing achievement', Humphrey ironically observes; 'All those volumes and no mention of sex'). The 1924 trip produced Harold's last, and by no means his worst, book, *The Cauldron of Europe* (October 1925), an attractively light-hearted account of his most recent travels in the Balkans.

The University of Athens, through Stavridi's good offices, conferred an honorary doctorate on Harold in 1924. His fellow graduand at the ceremony in 1925 was the eminent classicist Gilbert Murray. The award was in recognition of Harold's long years of service for the Greek cause and for refugees in the turbulent period of the Civil War. The Greek government awarded him at the same time the Order of the Redeemer – a jewelled Tridema with sapphires. Harold Spender was, at last, a famous public man: but not, alas, in his own country. He did not make *Who's Who* in life nor the *DNB* after death.

The ceremony in Athens (at which none of his family were present) was probably the most gratifying moment of Harold's last decade of life. But 1924 also saw his most painful public humiliation. He had made a third trip to America in 1923, in the company of Sir Charles Wakefield and Sir Arthur Haworth, to present busts of 'conspicuous Englishmen' to 'our American cousins', as Harold liked to refer to them. On the trip, he made some useful journalistic contacts. In November 1924 he cabled to the *New York World* the report of an interview with Lloyd George. In it he quoted the former PM as complaining that Clemenceau and Wilson had worked out a 'secret compact' behind his back at the Peace Conference in 1919. American readers were naturally very interested in their President's cleverness. An infuriated Lloyd George peremptorily repudiated the 'interview', alleging flatly that it had never taken place. Harold was obliged to issue a grovelling statement: 'I was merely writing a sketch of Mr Lloyd George's home life. Mr Lloyd George did not authorize the statements, and if I have been indiscreet I take the whole of the blame.'

It was the end for Harold Spender as a 'Public Man'. His god had not merely failed him, he had turned his disciple away with Hal's brutal 'I know thee not old man.' Harold never lifted up his head again, and became progressively more ill. He 'saw himself as a failure', Christine recalled. Apart from some committee work as chair of the Hampstead Council of Social Welfare (a duty which he took seriously) his 'public life' was over.

Now seventeen, Christine had been withdrawn from school to nurse her father during his last illness on the Isle of Wight. They boarded with a 'dear old lady', Miss Howson, 'who drank'. Harold sank, inexorably. One of his final services to his daughter (ambiguous enough) was to arrange for her to attend a 'domestic science' college, on the grounds, presumably, that she would thus be trained to take care of other men, as she had him.

'My father's dying seems merged into this dreamlike period,' Stephen recalls:

He himself was unaccountably ill. The doctors thought at first there was something wrong with his teeth, then his feet. At one time he had an inflammation of the eyes, which caused him to have to lie in bed with leeches placed over them. During this period, in my merciless adolescence, I was at times contemptuous, triumphing over him; at times humiliated by his needs; at moments, only, sympathetic . . . once, when we were in a taxi going to a tea party, I noticed that there was a rust-coloured froth of saliva on his lips, and I very gently wiped his mouth.

An X-ray revealed that Harold's spleen was enlarged and would have to be removed. Stephen records that on his last meeting with his father, a 'trance-like' walk in Kew Gardens in April 1926, 'an understanding seemed to have been reached between us that he had to die'. He gave his son ten one-pound notes ('more money than I had ever had at any time before').

Stephen had told his father that he was going on a walking tour on Dartmoor, with his particular friend, John Cornforth. Much of Stephen's libido was sublimated into such 'walks'. On this occasion Stephen informed a bemused Cornforth 'that we must aim to arrive at a certain post office on a certain day, in order that I might receive the telegram to say that my father was dead'. This amazed his friend: 'as neither of us had any reason to think that the operation would prove fatal'. On this tramp through Hardy country both Stephen and Cornforth were 'traversing crises in our adolescence. We made frightful confessions to one another which left me shaken, as though with sobbing.' They reached the post office where the prophesied telegram announcing Harold's death was waiting for Stephen:

I took the train home. I was in such a calm, equable mood when I reached Paddington that my godfather [Sir John Stavridi], who met me, thought I could not have understood the significance of the telegram. When I said that I realized that my father was dead, he was shocked.

What killed Harold? He had, apparently, been diagnosed with Banti's disease (a disorder of the spleen) in early 1926. It is possible that after Lloyd George's rebuff he had lost his will to live. Whatever the precise nature of his ailment, he was admitted to Mountfield nursing home at Child's Hill, Hampstead, where he had an operation on his enlarged spleen on 14 April. He died at 7.45 a.m. on 15 April of a heart attack.

There followed the funeral. Stephen was not the only child to register anaesthetized numbness. Humphrey recalls that during this period (when the children were put up at the Stavridi home, in Regent's Park), 'I felt nothing, except the joy of riding in a Rolls Royce.' The funeral service was held on St George's Day at St Mildred's, Bread Street, just off Queen Victoria Road, near the Fleet Street haunts where Harold's best working years had been spent. The Revd Horton officiated. Lloyd George sent a Judas telegram of condolence from the House, dated 16 April, referring to the 'brilliant mind and great nobility of character' of 'one of my oldest and most trusted friends'. He did not, however, attend the funeral; nor did any representative of the Liberal Party. Apart from some loyal Greek diplomats, there were no dignitaries present (J. A. Spender barely made it, having to hurry back from India). The Schusters were thinly represented. Harold was, as Stephen would later put it, a certified 'failure'.

With the immediate family in attendance, the body was cremated in the morning at Golders Green and the ashes interred in the afternoon at Hampstead cemetery. The obituaries were many, respectful and muted. They noted the fact that Harold Spender's life had been lived in the shadow of a 'brilliant' brother. It was not expected that any of his books would last, but he was saluted as a battler for the Liberal causes that he had believed in.

The Spender children's verdicts were harsher. As Humphrey came to think, his father's life was composed of clichés, and 'such boring clichés'. Stephen's merciless epitaph is given in his poem, 'The Ambitious Son':

> Then you lay in your grave, for the first time alone.
> Devoured by worms, by newsprint forgotten,
> Superseded, pelted down,
> By our generation, still more rotten.

When I left your funeral, my face was hard
With my contempt for your failure still.
But, father, the hardness was a scabbard
For your resurrected will.

'Day Boy' ends with the cold, prosaic dismissal:

My father died whilst I was still at school, and after his death I had a very happy last year. I have no doubt it was only the conflict which was going on at home that prevented the other years from being as happy.

On his father's death Stephen gave the school library the copy of *The Way of All Flesh* which his grandmother had given *him*, to encourage filial rebellion. He had no further use for it, now there was no father to rebel against.

Harold Spender was laid to rest at the end of April 1926. Almost immediately, England was shaken to its roots by the cataclysm of the General Strike. The momentous seven days in May drove another wedge between Stephen and his elder brother. For Michael the Great Strike was a golden opportunity to do what he had most dearly wanted to do since childhood – be a train driver. As the country ground to a halt, in early May, Spender One rushed down from Balliol College, Oxford, to London, to offer his services to the government. Replacement ('scab') train drivers were desperately needed. In a letter to his college chum, Anthony Bull, Michael describes the thrill of being in sole charge of a goods vehicle: 'The smell of the hot oil, the feel of the controls, the responsibility and anxiety: the extraordinary motion.' Michael would stagger back after such stints to Frognal, caked in soot and sweat – to be told by a clucking Bertha to go off at once and have a bath.

   The fact that others might consider him a strike-breaker never troubled Michael. It was his nature to make machines work; and society was the largest machine of all. Meanwhile his fellow Greshamian, Auden, drove a car in London ('out of sheer contrariness') for the TUC – something that had him temporarily disowned by his irate relatives. What did Stephen Spender do in these stirring times? As Humphrey witnessed, his older brothers 'came to intellectual blows'. At the time, Humphrey admired Michael: 'I've since realized Michael's driving that train was a rather awful thing to do.' Stephen felt it was rather awful at the time.

There was perplexity among the guardian Schusters in summer 1926 as to what to do with the orphaned Spenders. Humphrey saw his grand-mother (Schuster) wringing her hands and melodramatically imploring, 'What shall I do with these darling children?' Darlings they may have been; the children were also a handful. Neither the Schusters nor the J. A. Spenders wanted to receive Harold's flock into their own houses at this stage of their adolescence. They cut an awkward figure in tidy households. Michael, now nineteen, had won an Exhibition at Balliol and had gone up in glory from Gresham's in October 1925 to read physics. He, at least, was on track to the stars – as directed by his father. Christine had been entered for a domestic science course at King's College London, as ordained by Harold, with a view that his daughter should acquire some wifely qualifications. She began her studies in October 1926. Stephen at the time of Harold's death was seventeen and a day boy at UCS. Humphrey, a year younger, was boarding at Greshams, and enjoying it – the games at least.

Immediately after his father's death Stephen suffered yet another serious illness. Tonsillitis was initially diagnosed by the family physician, Dr Berkeley Way. The diagnosis was subsequently corrected to one of rheumatic fever, by Stephen's eminent uncle, Parkes Weber. Eight weeks' bed-rest was prescribed. Confined to his bed in a strangely empty 10 Frognal, Stephen was looked after by Berthella. There were relapses. Paralysis set in. For a few tensely critical days in late September he was taken to the Hampstead Fever Hospital (where they whipped out the offending tonsils). His grandmother recalled his 'difficult moods' in her diary. When he was well enough to walk again, she brought him a stick (it cost £3 10s, as she noted punctiliously). This mysterious illness knocked on the head any thoughts that Stephen might be sent off to boarding school.

The long hours of illness, quiet rooms and convalescence produced a spate of poetry, which was duly published in the December 1926 issue of the *Beanstalk*. Most interesting is 'A Poem in the Meditative-Topical Style', reflecting on the newspaper report that 'A reproduction of Van Gogh's picture of some sunflowers has recently been obtained for an institution where fat people are starved.' The poem is an impressively witty performance for a seventeen-year-old, not least for its description of the painter's turbulent designs and the insight into Stephen's preco-cious aesthetic tastes:

An artist, loving poetry, in a vase
    Ranged some; an emerald background thickly shook
    Upon his rag; and then his colours took
And, being mad, he dared to paint the flowers.

About this time Stephen changed the printed attribution of his poems from 'S. H. Spender' to a defiant 'Stephen Spender'. Exit 'Harold'.

In the period following Harold's death, the J. A. Spenders took an interest in their gifted but wayward nephew Stephen. He was summoned to their house, Chantry Place, at Marden in Kent. 'Jasper' (as the Spender children irreverently called him) had noted, with avuncular alarm, his nephew's addiction to poetry. He was determined to divert the young man's ambitions to more profitable paths. 'J.A.' did not, of course, disapprove of poetry in the proper place – that place being at the foot of some column in a remote section of the *Westminster Gazette*.

Ever since the 1924 visit to Chillon, Stephen had made no secret of his Byronic ambitions. As part of his campaign of discouragement, J. A. Spender invited as a guest to his house in late summer 1926 the least prepossessing poet he could find for Stephen to meet, one Frank Kendon. Kendon was author of the just published verse epic *The Life and Death of Judas Iscariot*, a work which was currently creating no stir whatsoever. He was just thirty years old (but seemed ancient in Stephen's teenaged eyes), had a hangdog air, thin sandy hair, and was dressed in shabby tweed. He ate his cake, said nothing, and never looked at Stephen in his eagerness not to take his eyes off the great J. A. Spender. He was the perfect picture of the poetic dormouse. The lesson was crystal clear – go into public life, be a success like Uncle Alfred, own your fine house, drive your motor-cars. Or write poetry and pick up cake crumbs from great men's tables.

Ernest Schuster's death in 1924, followed by Harold's two years later, placed direct financial responsibility for the Spender children in the capable hands of a 'Committee' of senior Schusters and, more particularly, into the indefatigable hands of their grandmother, Mrs Hilda Schuster. It was initially intended that she would manage things until Michael was twenty-one (in 1928), when he could take over as guardian of his siblings. As it turned out, on graduating from Oxford, Michael shot off on an expedition to the Great Barrier Reef and Mrs Schuster was left in charge until well into the 1930s when the last of the children, Humphrey, came of age (and they had all come into their respective bequests). Meanwhile the under-age children were funded by the Schuster endowment to the extent of around £300 p.a. each. With some discreet topping up by the Committee, the combined income of the three younger children was sufficient to support a middle-class household in Hampstead. The Committee resolved that it was in the best interests of the children to keep on 10 Frognal. It would in the event remain their home for six years until February 1933, when the lease (which had been transferred to Sir John Stavridi) expired. The ménage retained the nucleus of the ever-loyal Berthella. Captain Devoto was also 'splendidly helpful' in the period after Harold Spender's death.

Treasures that they undoubtedly were, Berthella were of the servant class. A reliable housekeeper, of a higher social station, was required to oversee things. According to Stephen, his grandmother first thought of her friend 'Helen Alington' (i.e. Mrs Helen Paine) as the ideal house-keeper. But unfortunately 'being a contemporary of my grandmother she was now well over seventy'. Mrs Schuster then recalled that Mrs Alington had a young niece by marriage working at Lausanne in a temporary position with some relatives. The lady had taken tea with Mrs Schuster, in August 1926. This was Winifred Paine (called 'Caroline' in *World within World*). According to Humphrey, as soon as inspiration struck, Mrs Schuster dispatched a melodramatic telegram: 'Four dear children orphaned. Drop everything and look after them.'

Miss Paine duly came to London on 4 October 1926, to be met at Charing Cross by Mrs Schuster, who led her straight away to 10 Frognal. When she arrived Miss Paine was 'a mass of nerves' and phys-ically exhausted. On her part, Christine was 'almost ill with appre-hension and shyness'. It being October, Humphrey and Michael were away. Stephen – a gangling sixteen-year-old sixth-former, and still not entirely fit – was, pro tem, the man of the house. He gave Winifred 'the limpest of handshakes' while projecting an air of worldly ennui to cover his nervousness. Stephen and Christine were playing one of their board games on Winifred's arrival and continued playing, while revolving internally the great questions as to whether this young woman would 'do'. On her part the young woman was not sure she wanted this position. According to her own account, she was won over by Stephen's telling a hilarious and slightly malicious anecdote about the J. A. Spenders. The ice was broken. Mrs Schuster went off to confer with Bertha, before going home to Kensington, leaving Miss Paine in her new post.

The arrangement with Winifred Paine worked well. Her unusual personality, and a propensity to anarchy, encouraged the individuality of the Spender children – 'bringing them out'. Half-French on her mother's side, Winifred was bohemian and 'fast' by the standards of bourgeois, 1920s London. In her late thirties when she came to Frognal, she projected a European sophistication. 'Winifred smoked (cigarettes specially ordered in large quantities from Rothmans, cork-tipped, with filter). She had a cigarette lighter and her hand shook as she held it to the cigarette, saying something like "everybody seems to be getting pneumonia, boils, tonsillitis, tennis elbow, coughs, syphilis, etc., these days".' Ash would meanwhile be fluttering down from the cigarette loosely held between her lips on to the carpet (something that infuriated Bertha – who was otherwise wholly won over by the new mistress of Frognal).

Not only did Winifred's cigarette-holding hand shake, 'but her eyelids fluttered quite dramatically when she was expressing passionate opinions'. Her sexual aura was unenhanced by any subservience to the fashions of the day. As Humphrey notes, it was significant 'that she allowed her hair to go grey rather than dyeing it'. There was something mannish about Winifred Paine which added indefinably to her charm. She was, for example, knowledgeable about cars, 'her first having been a "touring" Rover, after which she became a Vauxhall fan'. She maintained the engine herself and always referered to her vehicle as 'she'. Winifred had a 'past'. She had served as a VAD nurse and had a fiancé killed in the Great War. Before taking up work in Switzerland she had, for a period, been matron at Stowe School. According to Humphrey, she had lost the position when she showed too much interest in the anatomy of a young boy who had developed a boil on his bottom.

Christine, Humphrey and Stephen 'simply fell in love' with Winifred. The attachment was particularly strong with Christine and Stephen, who were alone with her during term-time. As Stephen records, 'My sister and I began to like Winifred with an intensity which was perhaps rather dangerous.' Winifred Paine's views on sex were forthright and heterodox. She once informed Stephen 'that the idea of sharing a bedroom with a man, night after night, for her whole life was quite intolerable to her'. She had, as Stephen observed, a 'detached, almost amoral attitude on sexual habits'. Miss Paine never married. Humphrey believes that 'Winifred fell in love with all of us'. Once, when he was sick in bed, 'I had to fight her off.' 'I know she fell for Stephen,' he adds.

Stephen records his last year at school, 1926–7, as a happy interlude.

He had a coterie of congenial friends. He was reading voraciously, gobbling up modern literature (he had read *Ulysses* and possessed a copy before going up to university – some criminal teacher at UCS must have passed the banned book on to him; or possibly he bought it in Switzerland). His letters of the period are peppered with fragments of psychoanalytic jargon (*manie de persécution*, 'inferiority complex'), suggesting that someone had put Freud his way. His grandmother passed on to him André Maurois's *Ariel*, a florid biography of Shelley, which evidently influenced the young man's notion of what a poet should be.

On leaving Gresham's, it was decided by the Committee that Humphrey would go to architecture school. Stephen had won his place at University College, Oxford, to read history. He would go up in the autumn term, 1927. 'Won' is perhaps the wrong word. Unlike Michael, Stephen was not a good examinee. Indeed, it is difficult to find any examination he passed during the whole of his life – with the possible exception of his 'Matric' (equivalent to GCSE) and the British driving test (his friends who drove with him might well have thought he should have failed that).

Before going up Stephen needed to be 'finished'. A foreign language was required. The cosmopolitan Schusters were peremptory on this point. Mrs Schuster, of course, wanted her beloved grandson to go to her beloved Germany. He, perversely, wanted to go to France – about which the half-French Winifred had enthused him and where James Joyce was published. Mrs Schuster 'considered the French to be immoral'. This argument did not entirely dissuade Stephen, who longed for some immorality.

Nantes – the least Parisian of French cities – was settled on as a compromise. The more pliant Humphrey would meanwhile be bundled off to Freiburg for nine months, to study art at the university, German in a decent lodging-house (his grandmother was particularly keen that he should master the subjunctive tense) and skiing on the slopes (this last in honour of Harold). Then he would go off to the Architectural Association school, where he would study for four years. No plans seem to have been made for Christine after her domestic science course.

Lest Stephen be led into temptation *en route*, Humphrey and Mrs Schuster accompanied him to Nantes, where a suitably decent Protestant pastor's household had been secured for him to lodge in (it emerged that the family was desperate for the 300 francs a month which the arrangement brought them). The French visit took place in May 1927, with the expectation that Stephen would stay until late September. 'The Nantes thing was hilarious,' Humphrey recalls. As he remembers, the three of them were obliged to step over drunks in the streets, whom their grandmother, in the spirit of Nelson, resolutely declined to see, declaring (with an air of magisterial instruction), 'You are going to be happy here, Stephen.'

He wasn't happy. The weather was hot and stormy. The pastor's household was gloomy and oppressed by 'sordid' worries about money. The 'Nantanians' were unsociable. His French was stumbling and made him look 'stupid' in his own eyes. The countryside was banal and unromantic. He dreamed of young French women and men offering their bodies to him. None did. He was oppressed by 'an indescribable anguish of homesickness'. He wrote affectionate letters to Winifred. As he drily notes, 'By sending me to Nantes my grandmother had certainly triumphed. She had cured me of France for a great many years.'

He made bitter and eloquent pleas to be removed. His grandmother responded by sending him copies of the *Nation* (to keep him abreast of British political events) and bought him a bicycle. It was eventually conceded in early June that he might leave Nantes for Lausanne (about whose moral tone Winifred could reassure Mrs Schuster). He would go there via Geneva. An overjoyed but guilty Stephen offered to travel third class. 'In spite of the expensiveness of extras at Lausanne,' he reassured his grandmother, 'I do not think that *baths* at any rate can be dearer than here, which is 5 francs [each] time, when one has walked to the middle of the town!'

He would stay at Lausanne seven weeks, until 20 August, residing in a pension. It was handsomely situated looking down on Lake Geneva, and 'appallingly expensive'. Stephen had a room at the back, with a balcony looking over the mountains. In the pension – where there were a number of young men of different nationalities all 'broadening their minds' – Stephen had the romantic adventure he had so desperately longed for in Nantes. It was with a fellow lodger (and tennis partner). Stephen describes him as 'an English boy of my own age, well-bred and ignorant, delicate and uncultivated, beautiful and vapid'. The boy had, apparently, been at Gresham's about the same time as Stephen and was called David Maclean. They visited Chillon together – now a shrine for Stephen. In Stephen's bedroom the young men kissed, and almost went further before acute nervousness paralysed them into English decency.

Out of the frustrating experience, after much drafting, came Stephen's first significant work in prose, 'By the Lake'. In its printed version the story pivots on a scene in which the hero ('Richard') analyses his sexuality for the benefit of 'Donauld' (Maclean). 'The result of neglecting children and never telling them anything about sex,' Richard explains, 'is that they often get to know in a wrong way about it':

When I was nine my father sent me to a preparatory school at Worthing. At this school there was a boy who had come from Maida Vale, who was the son of a small shopkeeper there. He was a lewd boy who knew everything there is to know about the 'facts of life', although he was only ten. At any rate he used to teach us to make experiments with each other. I was rather more sensitive than the others, so I went further in consequence, I suppose . . . I think that as a result of this experimenting I got to fasten my sexual thoughts on men rather than on women . . . You see, I suppose I got what is called a 'complex'. Instead of falling in love with women, I started to do so with men.

The 'lewd boy' at Charlcote was John Knyvet Gordon, son of the doctor whom the brothers detested and Harold revered.

Injudiciously Stephen confided his powerful new sensations to Winifred. The Lausanne holiday was summarily cut short by an urgent letter from her saying that 'she was gravely ill and must have an operation'. The news that Winifred was at death's door provoked oddly mixed emotions in Stephen: 'What distressed me most was to realize that even when I cared most intensely for Winifred I was not released from my obsessive fascination for [Donauld].' He had discovered that he could experience two kinds of love, for two people of two sexes, simultaneously. By the time Stephen returned to London, 'Winifred was better.' Whether or not her 'grave illness' was a pulling of the domestic drawstrings is not clear. What is clear is that after Lausanne the 'intensity of my relationship with her [had] weakened'.

With his horizons broadened, Spender went up to university in October 1927. In his first year he was placed in college rooms over the High Street. They were noisy and uncomfortable. Stephen says little about his first term in *World within World*, other than that Oxford was not what he expected (presumably from his father's many anecdotes) and he was acutely lonely – the common experience of sensitive undergraduates. He came up with an income of £100 a term in his first year, raised to £115 in his second and third years. Since he was not yet of age, the disbursement of this Schuster money was supervised by his grandmother. He was brought up to Oxford by her on 6 October 1927. She inspected his rooms and 'fee-ed his scout', accompanying the tip with strict instruction as to her grandson's care.

Enough of UCS's classlessness was ingrained in Stephen for him to be disgusted by Oxford's public school ethos and its cult of crude masculinity. Public school boys came up in gangs, with contemporaries and networks already in place. And from university these young men tramped well-beaten tracks into the professions and commanding heights of British life. For them university was a hedonistic interlude between the discipline of school and the business of life. UCS did not operate in the same way, nor did Stephen Spender. Adjustment would not be easy.

Michael was, as earlier at Gresham's, little help. He had come up as a scholar to the top college, where he had read physics for a year. Then he had switched to engineering. When Stephen arrived, he was working with his usual superhuman 'efficiency' for finals – cramming three years' study into two. He serenely achieved his First. He was out of his brother's smaller orbit. In his less grand and 'claustrophobically' enclosed college Stephen could not rub along with the ruling élite of hearties, who cared only for 'games, drinking and girls'. Nor did he incline to the aesthetes. Weak fellows, as he thought, who burned incense in their rooms and called each other 'dear'. The exam-grubbing 'students' were likewise unappealing. Louis MacNeice – a Merton College poet who would share top spot in the pages of Oxford literary magazines with Stephen – had a similar dilemma, if with a slightly different Scylla and Charybdis. In Oxford, MacNeice discovered, 'homosexuality and "intelligence", heterosexuality and brawn, were almost inexorably paired. [This] left me out in the cold and I took to drink.'

Stephen (who was no drinker) took temporary refuge in gestures of protest. Craving society, he made himself flamboyantly anti-social. 'I became affected, wore a red tie, cultivated friends outside the college, was unpatriotic, declared myself a pacifist and a Socialist, a genius.' In the context of 1926 and the General Strike, Stephen Spender's red tie was provocative. Equally provocatively, Stephen hung his walls with reproductions from Gauguin, Van Gogh and Klee. He was not discreet in his small rebellions. 'On fine days', in his third term, he 'used to take a cushion into the quadrangle, and sitting down on it read poetry'.

Stephen made himself a target for the inevitable ragging. A bunch of freshman hearties came to smash up his rooms. 'They decided this not out of enthusiasm but on principle, because it was the correct thing to do,' Stephen wryly recalls. By his own account, he read aloud to the vandals a few lines of Blake which disarmed them. Despite his professed socialism, Stephen had (and would always have) a distaste for boozy *bonhomie*. His tastes were refined and still conditioned by his father's evangelical prejudices. 'Univ' was a heavy-drinking college, known collo-quially as 'the pub in the High'. Stephen smoked, of course. In the 1920s the elegantly dangling fag was part of the uniform, like the Oxford bags (loose wide cuffed trousers) and Fair Isle sweaters. Stephen would never, throughout his life, be a particularly well-dressed man. But socially his instincts drew him to cultivated society. It would take time and effort to discover and make a milieu for himself within – and in some sense *against* – Oxford.

Stephen's first weeks were excessively lonely ('I dislike being alone,' he once told his grandmother). He recalled waiting, 'uninterruptedly', for three days in his rooms hoping that his glamorous and 'gaily inac-cessible' cousin, John Schuster, would call. He did not. Stephen led an 'artificial existence', covering 'reams of paper with ungrammatical inco-herent sentences which I imagined to resemble the style of James Joyce in *Ulysses*. I read Shakespeare, the Elizabethans, the Romantics and the Moderns – little else. I used to go for long walks and bicycle rides into the hilly, tree-scattered river-winding country side.' It was Nantes all over again.

Stephen's problems were compounded by the subject he had chosen to study (or that his guardians had determined he should study). He ought to have enrolled for English – if nothing else it would have co-incided with his voracious programme of private reading. And if not English (which was still a new and suspect subject), Classics would have brought him sooner into intimate contact with contemporaries like Louis MacNeice and Cleere Parsons. Classics would also have brought him into the glittering circle of Maurice Bowra, Dean of Wadham College, with which he seems never to have coincided while at Oxford.

Instead Stephen elected to do History, changing after a couple of terms to PPE (Philosophy, Politics, and Economics). It may be that he thought that the politics would be *engagé* (which they weren't), and the philosophy to do with 'the meaning of life' (which it wasn't). The twentieth-century revivification of British philosophy (led by Moore, Russell and Wittgenstein) was some years off. There was, as yet, no tradition of teaching politics or social science. When Isaiah Berlin took PPE in 1931 there were no politics tutors in his college, Corpus, and 'he was grandly told to read *The Times* editorials to make up the deficit'.

The main advantage of PPE was that it brought Stephen into contact with the son of his tutor, the political philosopher and aesthetician Edgar Carritt. His son Gabriel (the 'Tristan' of *World within World*) was a freshman at Christ Church – 'college of the Bloods, the Rich and Aristocrats'. It was also Auden's college. Carritt and Stephen hit it off and embarked on what was to be a complicated and intense relationship. 'I was a little bit overwhelmed,' as Carritt later thought. He saw himself as a 'rough country boy' from Sedburgh – a private school which offered a ruggedly physical curriculum. Carritt's philosophy was that 'you could do anything if you were good at rugby football' – and he was, as it happened, a very good fly-half.

He represented a type which, at this period, fascinated Stephen: the superbly taciturn, well-bred, intelligent, manly Englishman. Carritt had regular good looks, deep-set eyes, and a snub nose over which W. H. Auden, an admirer, lyricized in his early poems. Carritt's lack of any intellectual pretension verged on arrant self-deprecation. Nor was he inclined to homosexual love affairs. One of Auden's privileged and exclusive set, he professed himself baffled by 'Wystan's great sounding nonsense'. Yet he continued seeing him. Carritt introduced Stephen to his parents, socially, at their house in Boars Hill. He stayed there over weekends and was a welcome guest. Stephen was not, of course, a good student, nor did he pretend to be, but 'father didn't worry about that'. Stephen got on particularly well with Gabriel's (very musical) mother, whom he would later extol to Virginia Woolf. Altogether Stephen had a higher opinion of the cultural milieu of the Carritts than did the son of the house.

At this period Carritt detected in Stephen what he calls a 'slight persecution mania . . . he thought people thought he was a bit soft'. Once they had become intimate, Stephen read his poems aloud to Carritt. He carried a sheaf about him, like identification papers in a hostile country, as he liked to put it. Carritt also wrote poems, but Stephen did not think much of them and 'Wystan' was 'very explicit' about their merits.

As Carritt good-naturedly recalls, 'people liked me – so I never worried about anything else'.

Stephen certainly liked him. And, as Isaiah Berlin noted, Stephen was mortified when Gabriel – as he did every three months (according to Berlin) – transferred his allegiance to Dick Crossman. The first poem in Stephen's first volume (the ill-fated *Nine Experiments*) is 'to G.C.'. Politics was not the basis of their affection. Although he would later become a Communist – and contemptuous of Stephen's left-liberalism – Carritt was at this stage of his life wholly apolitical. Nor did sex come into it. Hugh David's suggestion that there was an 'amorous' relationship between the two is, as Carritt pungently puts it, 'rubbish, absolute fabrication'. The two young men would go on long walks over the Berkshire downs discussing the book by Kafka or some psychoanalyst which they had just read. Or Stephen would recite the latest draft of his latest poem. On such matters they were of one mind. There was, however, a rift between them. Carritt's view of life was dominated by his sense of their cosmic insignificance: 'We're just piddling undergraduates,' he would tell Stephen. Carritt, as Stephen sardonically noted, 'inhabited the valley of the second-rate'. He had no intention of keeping 'Tristan' company there. Stephen's and Carritt's relationship was, as Stephen sums it up, 'of a tormenting and English kind – he liked me on condition that he might despise me'.

The emotional crisis of Stephen's first year at Oxford revolves around the enigmatic figure whom he calls 'Marston'. Gabriel Carritt identifies 'Marston' authoritatively: 'Stephen was [in 1927–8] very much in love with a chap called John Freeman (Dick Freeman's brother that was). He was a student at "Univ".' (This identification is borne out by references to Freeman in early letters to Isherwood.) Freeman was a 'superb boxer' (a blue), a runner and a skier. He was a pilot with the University Flying Club ('Helmeted', he 'drove through air', as one of Stephen's own favourite poems puts it). Marston had been to Yugoslavia, bringing back a pipe whose accidental breaking inspires one of the finest of Stephen's early poems, and one which he fondly chose to reprint in many collections during his lifetime:

> Marston, dropping it in the grate, broke his pipe.
> Nothing hung on this act, it was no symbol
> Ludicrous for calamity, but merely ludicrous.

That heavy-wrought briar with the great pine face
Now split across like a boxer's hanging dream
Of punishing a nigger, he brought from the continent;
It was his absurd relic, like bones,
Of stamping on the white-faced mountains,
Early beds in huts, and other journeys.

The poem, which was first printed in *Oxford Poetry* (1929), is a prime example of Spender's early-mature style. It is heavily dependent on private reference. It is a poem about a friend to be read by other friends. Marston excelled as a runner, like the boy in Housman's poem. He, too, was a 'balanced winner', but 'different from other athletes'. He was 'not talented, or intellectual or even strikingly intelligent'. What was extraordinary about him was, paradoxically, the 'purity of his ordinariness'. Marston was 'calm', 'English' and, as Carritt puts it, 'very good looking'.

The Marston poems make up the bulk of Stephen Spender's first significant volume of poetry (*Twenty Poems* – published calendrically when he was twenty years old). Marston also appears in the first paragraph of *The Temple*, the 1929 *Erziehungsroman* which Stephen rewrote in 1987. It opens: 'What Paul loved about Marston was his self-evident (so he passionately believed) innocence. He had noticed this quality the moment he first saw him, early in their first term together at Oxford.'

Friendship blossomed to intimacy. Marston agreed to go with Stephen on a five-day walking tour over the Easter Vac, along the river Wye to Tintern Abbey. Alas, the expedition with Marston was a 'depressing failure'. Stephen described it twice in print: in *World within World* and in *The Temple*. In both versions Stephen (having boned up on the relevant 'hearty' topics) tries too hard to interest his companion and is accused for his pains of fussing like 'an old woman'. The recitation of Wordsworth under the ruined arches of the abbey is a complete flop. Marston at one point says he has a stomach ache. Stephen twitters nervously like 'an old hen', only to be shut up by the blunt declaration, 'I think I'll do a shit under those trees.' The two men are obliged to share a bed overnight: 'Neither of them slept. Next morning, Marston got up saying: "Sharing that bed gave me a pretty grim idea of marriage, old son." They ate breakfast in silence.'

Out of the débâcle of the tour Stephen wrote what was one of his finest Marston poems (V in the sequence):

> Not to you I sighed. No, not a word.
> We climbed together. Any feeling was
> Formed with the hills. It was like trees' unheard
> And monumental sign of country peace.

Back in Oxford, at the beginning of the next term, Stephen sent Marston a frank letter 'stating my feelings towards him'. It was unwise. The word 'love' was used. Marston was alarmed. Stephen was alarmed by his alarm. The young men arranged to keep out of each other's way in college for the rest of the academic year – which, since 'Univ' is small, meant Stephen requesting permission from the Dean not to take meals in Hall – normally an inflexible obligation on undergraduates to keep them from sloping off to the fleshpots of London. The Dean is called 'Hugh Close' in *The Temple*. It is a pseudonym for John Maud, only twenty-five years old in 1928 and 'a spy sent by the old into the enemy territory of the young', as Stephen colourfully calls him.

A 'red-faced' Stephen confessed his love for Marston and the impossibility of their meeting in college. A reciprocally 'blushing' Maud agreed to make the necessary arrangements. He was sympathetic. According to *The Temple*, Stephen demonstrated the extremity of his plight by showing Maud one of his Marston poems ('Lying awake at night' – IX in the sequence, based apparently on their frustrating night in the bed and breakfast establishment). Embarrassment aside, Maud was impressed by Stephen's talent.

Oddly, the young men continued to meet from time to time in Oxford and London teashops for bleak conversations in which Marston would 'confide in me at length and with a certain effort all the worrying details of his life: his affairs with girls, his loneliness, his failures in his work, his fears when he boxed or flew'. It seems clear, despite what Stephen says, that Marston was emotionally involved and physically tempted. But he was disinclined to take involvement further than the teashop confessional. Finally, Stephen 'realized that the relationship could not develop, and I allowed it to lapse through neglect on my side'. Auden's verdict was characteristically trenchant: 'You want to be rejected, because you are afraid of physical relationships.'

It was all disappointment, sexual frustration, exquisite embarrassment and some danger. Yet, obscurely, it made Stephen (as he felt) into a poet. Looking back on the Marston affair in *World within World*, he records that it influenced my life. Immediately after the walking tour I began to write poems different from any others I had done. A concrete situation had suddenly crystallized feeling which until then had been diffused and found no object . . . Moreover, the friendship with Marston was one phase of a search for the identification of my own aims with those of another man. For, different as we were, there was a kind of innocence and integrity in him which was present also in my poetry.

Stephen's private verdict on the Marston affair to Carritt, in 1930, was stoical. There had been no physical gratification, nor even any expression of tenderness, on either side. But:

I don't think my love for Marston was unrequited, because I was never disappointed in him. I think that if after all my exaltation of him he had turned out to be a little shit, the whole affair would have been degraded. The point is that he really did respond to something that was one of the best things in myself, and he was complementary to it.

By the end of Stephen's first year, 'Oxford' meant a small group of close friends. Despite Carritt's attempts to corral him with the university's little people, Stephen's acquaintance was luminous and would grow more so as the century advanced: Richard Crossman (something of a 'fascist', as Isaiah Berlin thought, and destined to be a socialist minister), Humphry House (who would establish himself as the country's foremost Dickensian critic), Arthur Calder-Marshall (future man of letters and dabbler in prohibited literature), Rex Warner (soon to blaze as Britain's leading expressionist novelist), Louis MacNeice, and – closest of all – Isaiah Berlin and W. H. Auden, two men who represented the twin poles of philosophy and poetry.

The great event at Oxford was, of course, the meeting with Wystan Auden. Auden was, in 1928, a legend at the university. Born in 1907, the youngest of three sons of a Birmingham doctor (with unprofessional interests in classics and Freud), Auden had been at Gresham's big school while, unknown to either of them, Stephen was suffering in the kipper hole a few hundred yards away at OSH. Like Stephen, Wystan had resolved at the age of fifteen that he would be a poet. He had already a large body of striking poetry to his credit. In 1927, after much deliberation, T. S. Eliot had turned down a book of poems which Auden had submitted to Faber, with the moderately encouraging comment that 'I do not feel that any of the enclosed is quite right, but I should be interested to follow your work.' Eliot did not have long to wait. Auden's first published volume would appear (acquired by Eliot) under the Faber imprint in 1930.

The epochal encounter with Auden in summer 1928 was evoked by Stephen at least six times in print, many times in lectures and innumerably often in conversation. The most concise version is in the poem he wrote for Auden's sixtieth birthday in 1968:

> You – the young bow-tyed near-albino undergraduate
> With rooms on Peck Quad (blinds drawn down at midday
> To shut the sun out) – read your poems aloud
> In your voice that was so clinical
> I thought it held each word brilliant in forceps
> Up to your lamp.

Over the course of his first year at Oxford he had angled to meet Auden. He knew about him from his brother, who was a contemporary at Gresham's, and another old Greshamian, Christopher Bailey. Both were scientists and lovers of music. Carritt knew Auden as a fellow Christ Church man and had 'carried on with him some variation of the mildly tormenting and tormented relationship he had with me'. But 'Tristan' liked to keep his friends apart. He obstructed the persistent requests Stephen made to have an introduction (in recalling the episode sixty years later, Carritt admitted that, anyway, he did not think Stephen 'worthy' of Auden). In the 'snubbing' Oxford social atmosphere, Stephen complains, 'all these people talked to me of Auden, but none of them wanted us to meet'. Carritt least of all.

Time was running out if they ever *were* to meet. It was summer and Auden was a finalist. He was at another college and was studying another subject, English. Accidental collisions were unlikely. In the event, a lunch party, specifically designed to effect the introduction, was given by a mutual friend, Archie Campbell, at New College. There was no serious conversation between Stephen and Auden beyond a peremptory interrogation over coffee as to whom the younger man thought was the 'best poet writing'. Stephen injudiciously ventured Humbert Wolfe. 'If there's anyone who needs kicking in the pants,' Auden rejoined, 'it's that little ass.' Stephen did not, apparently, defend his deposed idol.

Despite the Wolfe gaffe, a summons to tea in Auden's rooms at Christ

Church duly arrived. Stephen's first impressions are famous from re-iteration: the reprimand for daring to arrive ten minutes late; the disori-enting entrance from blinding sunshine into the darkened, electrically lit room; the near albino pigmentation; the nicotine-stained fingers; the green eye-shade; the revolver in the desk drawer; the icy demeanour; the psychoanalytic smartness ('Repression leads to cancer'); the impe-rial edicts ('A poet can't make war stop', 'Germany's the only place for sex'). At their first meeting,

he asked me how often I wrote poetry. Without reflecting, I replied that I wrote about four poems a day. He was astonished and exclaimed: 'What energy!' I asked him how often he wrote a poem. He replied: 'I write about one in three weeks.' After this I started writing only one poem in three weeks.

From the first, Auden adopted the role of oracular master to a new and somewhat disordered disciple. On inspection of his manuscript poems, Stephen was instructed to 'drop the Shelley stunt'. The acceptable poets were indicated: Wilfred Owen, Hopkins, Edward Thomas, A. E. Housman and, of course, T. S. Eliot. The unacceptable poets were anathematized: Wolfe, Sassoon, de la Mare, and consigned to outer darkness. Edmund Blunden was in limbo ('not bad'). A pontiff where canonical poetry was concerned, Auden struck Stephen as being like a cabinet minister in his aim to set up a collective of new British modernist writing: 'his friend Isherwood was to be The Novelist. Upward was another of the Gang. Cecil Day-Lewis was a colleague.' As to himself, Auden's utterances were messianic: 'He thought that the literary scene in general offered an empty stage. "Evidently they are waiting for Someone," he said with the air of anticipating that he would be the centre of it.' Stephen's poems were scrutinized, and good lines very occasionally held up for approval.

Stephen evidently saw Auden regularly during what remained of the summer term, always in the role of humble acolyte. Usually the meet-ings were on Auden's territory (although a picnic on a glorious summer day on the Berkshire downs remained etched in Stephen's memory). So the term wore on, until:

After I had known him six weeks he must have approved of as many of my lines. Therefore it was rather surprising to discover that he considered me a member of 'the Gang'. Once I told him I wondered whether I ought to write prose, and he answered: 'You must write nothing but poetry, we do not want to lose you for poetry.' This remark produced in me a choking moment of hope mingled with despair, in which I cried: 'But do you really think I am any good?' 'Of course,' he replied frigidly. 'But why?' 'Because you are so infinitely capable of being humiliated. Art is born of humiliation,' he added in his icy voice.

After he had known Auden 'only a short while', Stephen showed him the short story 'By the Lake', which had come out of his Lausanne experience. It dealt with the love which still did not dare speak its name – in England, at least. Auden passed it on to his friend Isherwood, whose first novel *All the Conspirators* was published in mid-May. Stephen finally and belatedly met 'The Novelist of the Future' in Auden's rooms towards the end of term (on 9 June, as Peter Parker calculates). Auden had, as Stephen suspected, 'withheld the privilege' for obscure reasons.

When he arrived at the rooms in Christ Church, Stephen found Isherwood correcting a 'sulky' Auden's verse, in much the same schoolmasterly domineering way that Auden corrected Stephen's manuscripts. When they had finished, 'Isherwood made me a quite formal little speech saying he had read my manuscript, and that he regarded it as one of the most striking things he had read by a young writer for a long time, and so on.' In *The Temple*, Spender adds, 'he spoke as if he was infinitely old and mature'. On his part, Isherwood immortalized the encounter in his *roman-à-clef, Lions and Shadows* – begun in 1931, published in 1938 and written, evidently, at a period when he was inclined to be sarcastic. Stephen is made to seem young and immature, a six-foot-two baby:

A few weeks later, [Auden] arranged a meeting with the author [of 'David']. He burst in upon us, blushing, sniggering loudly, contriving to trip over the edge of the carpet – an immensely tall, shambling boy of nineteen, with a great scarlet poppy-face, wild frizzy hair, and eyes the violent colour of blue bells. His name was Stephen Savage.

'All Savage's friends betrayed him, in some minor degree, sooner or later,' the novel adds.

In terms of the cosmogony he offers in *World within World*, Stephen's universe revolves around the meeting with Auden in summer 1928. But a number of points should be made. It was a fearfully busy time for the older poet. This was his last term (he duly took his finals and got a gentleman's Third). Auden may have seen Stephen regularly during the summer term, but cannot – at this hectic period – have given the eager freshman from 'Univ' *all* of his time. There were so many other things to see to. Although he visited Stephen in Frognal during the long vacation, the twenty-one-year-old Auden would be off to Berlin ('the bugger's daydream', as he memorably called it) in October 1928. He would remain there until July 1929, when he would return to various teaching jobs (perhaps this was *his* 'humiliation'). The period at Oxford during which the two poets were in master-disciple relationship was probably no more than seven weeks.

The other point to make is that on the evidence of the Marston poems, the strongest of which precede Auden's irruption into his life, Stephen had already and independently, by May 1928, found his voice and a subject. These intimate poems would, over the next two years, be added to by the famous 'Pylon' exercises in materialist-expressionism, which may well have derived from the 'Drop the Shelley stunt' injunction, a growing interest in Socialism, and Auden's perverse observation that 'the most beautiful walk in Oxford was that along the canal, past the gasworks'. It is clear, however, that (even though they were dedicated to him) Auden had not seen before publication the four poems published by T. S. Eliot in the *Criterion* in October 1930 which were instrumental in establishing Stephen's reputation.

Clearly Auden had a terrific impact on Stephen, but direct influence on Spender's poetry is not easily found. The prosodic and metric freedom of Lawrence's verse (and behind it, Whitman) are, by contrast, very visible. One could also make the case that Eliot (particularly the Eliot of 'Gerontion' and 'Preludes') was more influential than Auden on the surge of poetry which would culminate in the finest of Stephen's early collections, *Poems, 1933* – which Eliot in fact published.

All this is to make the point that there was more than one powerful influence and source of patronage in the evolution of Stephen's early poetry. None the less, Auden's touch left an indelible mark – if not on the poetry then certainly on Stephen's idea of what it was to be a poet. Stephen was enthused to the point of fanaticism by the idea of the Pantisocratic commune, or 'Gang'. *The Temple*, substantially written in 1929, was a response to the communitarian spirit which Auden, in his term, expressed in *The Orators*. In a much-quoted letter to John Lehmann in 1931, Stephen wrote:

There are four or five friends who work together, although they are not all
known to each other. They are W. H. Auden, Christopher Isherwood, Edward
Upward and I . . . Whatever one of us does in writing or travelling or taking
jobs is a kind of exploration which may be taken up by the others.

The formation of the Gang led to a Gordian interchange of dedica-
tions. Auden's first volume of poems, printed by Spender, was dedicated
to Isherwood. Auden himself would reply with the long sequence *The
Orators*, dedicated to Stephen, and containing poems dedicated to Gabriel
Carritt, Rex Warner and Edward Upward. His *Poems 1927–1931* would
be dedicated to Isherwood. Isherwood's early novels were similarly inter-
dedicated. So the series would go on, the young men passing their works
to each other like rugby three-quarters, until it was broken in 1932 when
Stephen, as the result of his brief contretemps with Isherwood, would
withdraw the dedication of *Poems, 1933* (published in January), only to
reinsert it in the second edition of 1934.

As a general rule, Spender's published poetry is more reader-friendly
than that of Auden (or Eliot). One can glean enough to make sense of
the Marston poems, which are the most shrouded in privacy of his early
published works. It helps, but is not essential, to know that the route
which the train takes out of the station in 'The Express' (one of his most
anthologized pieces) is from Oxford, travelling east to London. Or that
in the poem 'Polar Exploration' he is drawing on a private joke with
Isherwood – whom he liked to picture in letters as another Scott of the
Antarctic.

Spender was always candid about how little he, even as a privileged
'gangster', understood Auden's extravagantly inward poetry, or Auden
himself, come to that. Writing to Harold Nicolson and Vita Sackville-
West, on the publication of Auden's first volume of poems in September
1930, he stresses that:

I am very fond of my friend without the least understanding him, and I think
that he is equally a mystery to his other friends . . . you feel that although he
is very fond of you when you are with him, you are never quite sure of him,
and that adds to his fascination . . . the poems are terribly obscure and I understand very little of them. But what I do understand I like very much . . . Auden
is very different from me: his attitude is much more clinical and perhaps obscu-
rantist.

Like the subsequent attempts at utopian living (at Cintra in 1931, for example), the experiment in gang-writing was a beautiful and doomed dream. But evidently Stephen subscribed to it in the late 1920s and for part of the 1930s. If nothing else, the gang-dream confirmed his belief that personal friendship mattered above all things. Certainly above getting degrees and pleasing one's rich and powerful relatives. The other imperative which he took from Auden was that poetry, to be done properly, required the whole of one's attention.

It was, if one followed the Auden line, a moot point as to whether one could combine poetry with marriage – or any kind of stable, emotionally demanding relationship. Boys were something else; as Auden saw it, one paid them not for sex, but to go away after sex and leave one in peace to the more important business of writing. In *World within World*, Stephen quotes J. C. Squire, whom he had invited, in his role as secretary, to speak at the University English Club:

at the end of a rather convivial evening [he] eyed me with a wavering severity to ask: 'What do you intend to do with your life, young man?' 'Write poetry.' 'Then you will be like me,' he sighed, as one of those ghosts warns before surrendering himself to the flames. 'You will write poetry until you are twenty or twenty-one. Then you will fall in love with a fair young girl and you will write more poetry. Then you will marry that girl and you will write reviews and journalism. Then you will have a fine young strapping baby and you will write more reviews and journalism. Then, when you are my age [43!], you will look back and think, "Well, perhaps after all, to have married that girl and had those children is worth more than to have written four hundred sonnets."'

That 'perhaps after all' would haunt Stephen's later life.

Auden and Isherwood were, when Spender first met them, sexually experienced and intermittent lovers. Stephen was inexperienced (a 'verger', in gang-speak) and, at this stage of his life, homosexually inclined. In his (very) unauthorized life of Auden, rushed out after the poet's death, Charles Osborne asserted that Auden initiated his disciple into sex. The assertion was indignantly repudiated by Spender in a letter to the *TLS*. In a private letter to another of Auden's unauthorized biographers, Humphrey Carpenter, he wrote in May 1980:

Despite the *TLS* and Mr Osborne, my relationship with Auden was entirely dissimilar from that of Isherwood with him. Auden was not attracted by 'stork-legged heaven reachers' like me. We were not sexual partners . . . I should think that Auden (and Isherwood for that matter) regarded me as sexually inhibited and inhibiting . . . In the 30s the idea of someone being sexually attractive was very strongly held. Although there were flattering references to my looks in *New Verse*, etc., very few of my friends found me attractive in that way . . . There was much choosiness and snobbery about looks.

What to do? The main business of the long vacation of 1928 was putting the communistic ideals of the Gang into practice. Stephen's admired Blake – the printer poet and radical – provided a model. Answering an advertisement, Stephen bought a small printing press, costing, as he later recalled, £5. 'It was a small hand press of a kind, I later learned, used sometimes for printing chemists' labels.' Drawing on the expertise which Harold had instilled into his children when publishing the *Frognal Gazette*, Stephen single-handedly and laboriously typeset two volumes. One was Auden's *Poems*; the other was his own small anthology, *Nine Experiments*. Both carry the imprint, '1928. Printed at No. 10 Frognal, Hampstead, N. W. 3'. The Auden volume is dedicated to Christopher Isherwood.

Both the Frognal pamphlets, as Stephen recorded sixty years later,

were in editions of 'about thirty copies' (my printing press could not cope with more than that number). Both editions are abominably printed, partly because I felt that it would be cheating if I damped the sheets of paper before printing. Therefore a lot of the typography has letters only half of which are printed. What adds to the value of the Auden pamphlet is that several copies contain corrections of these half-letters, and sometimes of words, in Auden's or my handwriting.

From the last comment, it is conceivable that Auden may have visited Frognal at some point after the edition was run off to proofread the virgin copies of his work. Or perhaps, as Auden's executor, Ed Mendelson, suspects, Spender sent copies to Auden for corrections around late October.

In *World within World* Stephen says (mistakenly) that he printed the Auden volume at the end of the long vacation of 1929, after his first Hamburg trip. He does not mention his own pamphlet, *Nine Experiments*, in *World within World*. The reason is that he was, even as late as 1951, deeply ashamed of it. Subtitled 'Being Poems written at the Age of Eighteen' (i.e. 1927–8, before and just after the epochal meeting in Peck Quad), *Nine Experiments* opens with a blaring 'Invocation':

> BRAY TRUMPETS,
> Blow for ever in my head!
> And ever let the violins, tempest-sworn,
> Lash out their hurricane;
> And let the Heavens splinter, and tear, and rage;
> Then let the exciting blood,
> The outrageous blood, & yet again the blood,
> Make heaven and music, and most self and savage.
> *Then let all burn beneath my printed page!*

There follows a less inflammatory dedicatory piece, 'for G. C.', followed by the Freudian-confessional, 'I must Repress'. Then comes an embarrassingly dutiful *hommage* to his new mentor, Auden, 'Come, Let us Praise the Gasworks', in honour of Oxford's finest view.

As Spender recalled in 1990:

When I wrote *Nine Experiments* I was still at the stage of putting my money on an appearance of madness in my poems . . . the attempt being exacerbated by the fact that I was an undergraduate at University College, Oxford – 'mad Shelley's' college.

Auden was evidently polite enough to Stephen's face, and could not but be flattered by the edition of his own verse. But he was scathing (and probably hilarious) about Stephen's efforts behind his back. Gabriel Carritt relayed Auden's sarcasms back to Stephen – possibly as clinching evidence that he was, after all, 'a little man'. Carritt's remarks 'had the effect of making me destroy every copy of *Nine Experiments* I could lay my hands on (sometimes stealing them from friends in order to do so). They also inhibited me from reading the poems again until 1990.' As a result of this massacre of his firstborn, the auction-room value of *Nine Experiments* has sky-rocketed. One of the surviving copies was sold in 1990 for $57,500. Stephen Spender, ironically, had no copy in his possession.

★

The academic year 1928–9 began well for Stephen. Isherwood was now a friend and kept a line open to Auden, who was in Germany. The Marston problem, if not solved, was under control. An enigmatic comment in the gossip column in the *Cherwell* to the effect that 'We take off our hat to Mr Stephen Spender (Univ. Coll.), for spending an afternoon watching every form of University sport in order to decide what game he should take up' may refer to his looking for new friends. The tone of the jest confirms that he was now a prominent and admired figure in university life.

Stephen again had rooms in college, as was usual for second-year students. Now more poised (and secure in his good looks and charm), he was forming what would be lifelong and emotionally sustaining friendships. A particular friend at this period was the poet Bernard Spencer. Jon Stallworthy describes him in a few vivid strokes:

Spencer, son of a High Court Judge in Madras, wore a bow tie and sidewhiskers – one wing of which was forcibly removed by hearties who raided his room. He refused to shave off the other, and continued to decorate his lampshade with 'surrealist, mildly obscene figures in pencil'.

In an interview in 1970, Stephen summed up his opinion of Spencer and his gifts: 'He was an extremely charming man, but I didn't really think he was talented. I thought he was rather hard working and sensitive and a bit ineffective. I'm afraid I slightly despised him in the way that one does despise one's contemporaries.'

Both Spender and Spencer published poems in the university literary magazine *Sir Galahad*, whose editor was Louis MacNeice. As Stephen recalled in 1970, 'I don't think I ever realized how good Louis was. He was a very intelligent, scholarly person, but I always thought he was a minor, whimsical talent.' The two poets were side by side in *Oxford 1928*, a collection edited by another friend, Cleere Parsons. As Stallworthy notes, Spender and MacNeice, who had come up a year earlier, in 1926, were 'slightly wary of each other'. In his memoir, *The Strings are False*, MacNeice noted, in a rather barbed way, that the undergraduate Spender 'was the nearest to the popular romantic conception of a poet – a towering angel not quite sure if he was fallen, thinking of himself as the poet always, moving in his own limelight'. MacNeice, 'the tall languid undergraduate from Merton', affected a more *ennuyé* pose than his lambently Shelleyan counterpart.

Elizabeth Harmon (later Elizabeth Longford) retained a vivid sense of her first sight of Stephen. She was a year ahead of him at Oxford, having gone up in 1926. As she recalled:

I can't remember meeting in the sense of being introduced. But I can remember first *seeing* him very clearly indeed. He did PPE. I did Greats. Both schools used to be sent to the same logic lectures. He must have just come up. I saw this startling sight. I couldn't believe my eyes, he looked so different *physically* from any other undergraduate there. He had this wonderful halo, this *aureole*, of hair. And his eyes were very very bright and looking round very restlessly. And a lot of people were looking round at *him* . . . There was only one other undergraduate who attracted my attention as looking interesting, and that was Douglas Jay. I was always rather in awe of him [Stephen].

The elegant Jay would become a close friend of Stephen's, and Elizabeth Harmon would, in their last year, be his co-chair on the Oxford Poetry Society (he did all the work, she concedes). Harmon saw Stephen as 'Shelley incarnate, at Shelley's college'.

Another friend at this formative period of Stephen's life was Arthur Calder-Marshall, an undergraduate at Hertford College. Calder-Marshall established what was to be a lifelong fascination for things forbidden by inviting the diabolist Aleister Crowley to speak at the university. The occasion ended in a legendary débâcle. Stephen formed another lasting relationship with the physically overwhelming Moore Crosthwaite. 'Immensely tall and immensely handsome', as Elizabeth Longford remembered: 'oddly enough, he looked like a Shakespearian "Moor", if you know what I mean – dark and beautiful'. He and Stephen would spend some time in lodgings together in Hamburg in the early 1930s, before Crosthwaite embarked on his career in the Foreign Office. In later life Stephen would find him grown rather 'stuffy' and 'conventional'.

During his second year Stephen began to form contacts in the London literary world. Commissions and contracts would follow. What Spender would resolutely *not* do over the year 1928–9 was work for his degree. This disinclination to study was causing irritation among his guardians. Stephen's battles with his family elders climaxed in the summer term of 1929. A suggestion that he might have some extra cash to go on a reading party with his Oxford friends during the long vacation of 1929 elicited a furious reaction from Aunt May (Mrs J. A. Spender), who 'seemed immediately to suspect that this was part of my colossal scheme to do no work all my life, and live a dissolute life on an inheritance'.

Stephen was summoned to Marden to be interrogated by Uncle Alfred in person. The young man protected himself, as he would through life, by throwing up an enigmatic façade. A formal report, written in the famous J. A. Spender 'balanced' style, resulted. 'Dear Mrs Schuster,' he began:

There is a sort of impenetrability about Stephen which is rather baffling. He is wonderfully good-mannered and takes everything that I say to him with greatest good-humour, and yet I somehow feel that I have made no impression on him, though he is too polite to say so. I did talk to him pretty plainly about his Oxford Schools [i.e. his degree examinations] . . . His gifts are literary and he is in the quite natural boyish stage of revolt from the elders. This is no harm except that it takes rather too much of his time and thought. He produces from time to time sophisticated little verses by his friend the genius, who takes infinite pains to find rhymes that grit the teeth and to express himself in symbols which only the élite understand, and I am afraid I sadly lose caste by my comments on them. But I risk that, for my main fear for Stephen is that he may settle down to being a dilettante on a small income and devote himself to writing minor poetry in what he calls the 'new manner'. If he can be laughed out of that and induced to use his talents in a simple and natural way I shall have no fear for him. I shall do all I can to keep in touch with him. Yours affectionately, J. A. Spender.

It's a kindly, astute, and wholly wrong-headed analysis.

In the event, quite other arrangements than undergraduate reading parties were made for the long vacation of 1929. John Maud was, as Stephen told his grandmother, 'very keen that I should go to Germany for a month, and learn to *read* rather than speak [German]. He says go to as many cinemas as possible, and read the newspapers. I think that ought to be all right.' It was, of course, his grandmother's dearest wish that he should learn to love the country to which her heart belonged (she may have been less convinced about the cinemas). It is likely that Stephen was excited by letters from Auden, who had been in Berlin since July 1928, and Isherwood, who had made his first eye-opening trip there in May 1928. Despite Uncle Alfred's strenuous objections, the German trip was approved and a budget allocated by Mrs Schuster.

The arrangement which was made through Maud is described in *The Temple*. The Dean, Hugh Close (i.e. John Maud), shows a young German,

Dr Ernst Stockmann (i.e. Erich Alport), one of Paul Schoner's (i.e. Stephen's) Marston poems. Stockmann, 'a pale intent young Jew', a homosexual Anglophile with a first-class degree in economics from Cambridge, invites the promising young poet to stay at his parents' house in Hamburg, over the summer. The name of the hero – 'Paul Schoner' – is ironic, combining the most puritanical and body-hating of the apostles with the German 'beautiful one'.

The night before leaving, Paul visits William Bradshaw (i.e. Christopher William Bradshaw Isherwood) in London. The two young men lament the censoriousness of England. Both resolve, eventually, to live in freedom in Germany as soon as they can escape. Meanwhile, for Paul, only a brief furlough is possible. Auden, Isherwood and Stephen clearly sought different things in Germany. For Auden it was the complex of sun, sex, new styles of architecture and the change of heart which he talks of in his much-anthologized poem of October 1929, 'Sir, no man's enemy'. Isherwood states frankly in *Christopher and his Kind* that 'Berlin meant boys'. This blunt motive has been questioned by Norman Page, who points out that Isherwood was careful to go to bed early in Berlin, so as to be fresh for writing the next morning. Page declines to 'take at face value the well publicized boasts by both Auden and Isherwood that they had gone [to Germany] purely and simply – well, simply – for sex'.

In his 1987 introduction to *The Temple* Stephen makes it clear that 'English Censorship' – and the crippling guilt that went with it – was what he wanted, primarily, to escape from. Germany 'was the front line in our war against censorship'. Censorship in England had reached almost totalitarian levels, under the Home Secretaryship of Sir William Joynson-Hicks. As 'the Policeman of the Lord', Joynson-Hicks had encouraged the London magistrates' prosecution of *The Well of Loneliness*, in summer 1928. The upshot was that Radclyffe Hall's publishers, Cape, withdrew the book.

Time for 'freedom', even in Germany, was short. In the 1987 retrospective essay affixed to *The Temple*, Stephen sums up Hamburg in 1929 as 'the last year of that strange Indian summer – the Weimar Republic'. The Wall Street Crash and Hitler would soon extinguish its glow. But for a twilight moment, 'Germany seemed a paradise where there was no censorship and young Germans enjoyed extraordinary freedom in their lives.' In *World within World* he describes his wonder at the young Germans he saw living 'the life of the senses [in] a sunlit garden from which sin was excluded'. His rhapsody on the *cultus* of sunbathing is Lawrentian:

The sun – symbol of the great wealth of nature within the poverty of man – was a primary social force in this Germany. Thousands of people went to the open-air swimming baths or lay down on the shores of the rivers and lakes, almost nude, and sometimes quite nude, and the boys who had turned the deepest mahogany walked amongst those people with paler skins, like kings among their courtiers.

As the lyrical tone of the above passage suggests, sex was an element in Germany's charm. There have been inevitable criticisms levelled at Auden, Isherwood and Spender for their 'sexual colonialism' of the young and vulnerable. In *Christopher and his Kind* Isherwood candidly admits that 'he couldn't relax sexually with a member of his own class or nation. He needed a working-class foreigner.' Exploitative as such a remark seems, there was a kind of mitigating idealism in it. In a 1987 interview, Spender remarked of this period that 'sex with the working class of course had political connotations. It was a way in which people with left-wing sympathies could feel they were really getting in contact with the working class.' The conjunction is immortalized in the first line of one of Stephen's 1931 poems, 'Oh young men, Oh young comrades'.

Spender seems to have imbibed less uncritically than Isherwood or Auden the Lane-Layard philosophy, dogmatically stated on the second page of *Christopher and his Kind*: 'There is only one sin: disobedience to the inner law of our own nature.' From the first, Stephen took the lead as the political conscience of the Gang. Although Auden's poems typically contain lines alluding to unemployment, Stephen regularly (after 1929) writes passionate poems on the subject – culminating in his 'dash at Harry Pollitt' (as Elizabeth Longford calls his brief membership of the Communist Party).

Auden and Isherwood were, by 1930, resolutely homosexual. Sexually less extremist, Spender was less exercised than Isherwood to reject the English bourgeoisie – in the form of middle-class family and social intercourse. One of the attractions of Berlin for Isherwood, and his diet of 'lung soup' and boys, was that it confirmed his utter repudiation of a background which, however hard he tried to scrub it off, was indelibly ingrained into his being. 'Wherever he was seemed to me to be the trenches,' Stephen observed. Fighting, that is. Spender was less at war with his background – between him and England it was less trench warfare than armed peace. Isherwood had, Stephen notes in *World within World*, a 'hatred' of 'English middle-class life' and all its institutions. On his part, Stephen was easy in either world: bohemian Germany, or the tea-parties in Bloomsbury, Rodmell, or country weekends at Garsington.

Unlike Auden and Isherwood, Stephen kept up friendly relations with his university and university friends (notably Isaiah Berlin) after leaving. He could lightly in September 1930 tell Isherwood (as Isherwood could never have told Spender, however jestingly) that he 'hoped, perhaps, to marry'. It seems that from the first Spender, unlike his closest friends, was keeping all his options open – social, sexual, residential, professional. This sense of difference (from Isherwood's rigidities particularly) may well have contributed to his choice of Hamburg (closer geographically to England) as his base.

Early versions of the novel which came out of the Hamburg experience were entitled 'Escaped' and 'The Liberal Cage'. *The Temple* was fixed on later, in allusion to the well-known stanza in Auden's *The Orators* which was eventually adopted as the novel's epigraph. Auden's reference is both to the apocalyptic destruction of the Temple in the Book of Revelation, and to the common use of the term for one's 'sacred' body (not to be polluted by sexual misconduct) in English public schools.

When did Spender write *The Temple*? It is not easy to say. In a letter to Harold Nicolson and Vita Sackville-West in September 1930 – when he was still close in time to the Hamburg trip – he says:

The novel is getting on slowly. In my first and second years at Oxford I wrote a novel which I sent to Cape. Cape didn't take it (very luckily) but Edward Garnett and Cape himself were very kind, so that I promised to send this novel to them. Indeed I told Garnett of the plot about a year ago, and he was keen on the whole idea though he said he doubted if I could ever write a book symbolizing the body. So I have taken a long time over it to prove that I am. It is now about a quarter written. I have been writing two months. Very sporadically.

Stephen alludes to this unpublished undergraduate novel in two letters to Isherwood, dated provisionally 'Spring 1930'. The first records that he has hopefully sent the manuscript off (despite his friend's thinking poorly of it) and the second gloomily reports that:

Cape wrote saying that 'it was not strong enough to fight its way through,' that he wanted very much to see anything else I might write as he had great confidence in my literary future, and advising me to put 'Escaped' aside for a year or two.

The title of this mysterious novel evokes Lawrence's 'scandalous' short story of 1929 'The Escaped Cock'. What seems most likely is that sections of 'Escaped' (predating the epiphanic Hamburg trip) were cannibalized into what became *The Temple*, whose manuscript at Texas is dated 'November 1929' (a date which he emended, in the 1987 printed version, to '1929–31').

Spender records in his 1987 introduction that:

I remember typing out several copies of a slightly later version of *The Temple* which I sent to friends, among them Auden, Isherwood, William Plomer certainly – to get their views about it – and a copy to Geoffrey Faber, my publisher.

Faber pointed out that there could be no question of publishing a novel which, besides being potentially libellous, was pornographic according to the law of the day. It is on the face of it odd that one publisher, Cape, should think the manuscript too tame, the other, Faber, too strong for publication – assuming that Geoffrey Faber and Jonathan Cape saw the same work. Not that the publishers were badly disposed to the young author. T. S. Eliot at Faber went to the trouble of consulting Erich Alport, who reported himself grossly libelled by the novel.

In 1931, continuing the round of publishers, Stephen showed the manuscript to John Lehmann, then working at the Hogarth Press, who urged Leonard and Virginia Woolf to take it on. He was unsuccessful. In 1933, Stephen passed a typescript of *The Temple* on to E. M. Forster, who gave him in return *Maurice* to read. The next year he began making notes for a revised version of the novel (perhaps inspired by the success of Isherwood's 'Mr Norris' stories, which he admired immensely). In winter 1934 he told Isherwood that he was 'going to completely rewrite *The Temple*. I have a really good idea of it now':

The point about *The Temple* is that it is a legend. The characters must have no nationality, the scene must be invented as the book goes along, because it is their dream. What I realized in my new vision of this book is that the walk down the river represents an attempt to return to their childhood. Obviously, this must be contrasted with some sort of an attempt to have sex with a woman in Parts One and Two. It is the reaction from that. The hero must be the kind of person who has invented some external standard of criticism which is so real that everything he does seems fantasy. Like the Marxist criticism of bourgeois art. He must end the book by violently rejecting the whole world of fantasy. I think he must decide to take a job, perhaps to be the assistant to a factory inspector. That really exactly suits his social position: it fits him into the machine of wealth, work and Happiness.

The proposed ending is so grotesque that one wonders whether Stephen is pulling his friend's leg, or clowning.

In January 1935, he wrote to tell Isherwood that 'I have started sketching the opening scenes of the *The Temple*, which I am going to call *The Liberal Cage* because it is an account of the completely free life possible in our time.' But, he adds, he intends to leave the novel in favour of the play (*Trial of a Judge*, as it was to be), 'which is far more necessary to me'. Stephen evidently left *The Temple* for many years. In 1945, he rewrote and expanded the Oxford sections, 'Young Poets', as a full-length novel entitled 'Instead of Death'. It was completed, typed up, but never saw print until it appeared in a further revised form in 1987.

The fullest account of Stephen Spender's 1929 Hamburg experiences is given in the first section of *The Temple*, 'The Children of the Sun', as rewritten in 1987. The novelist vouches for it as a 'truthful report'. As published in 1987, the novel concludes with the account of a walk along the Rhine with Joachim (Herbert List) and his boyfriend, Heinrich, a passionate but not very sensible, although extremely beautiful, Communist. The actual walk with List took place from the first to the ninth of September. Out of this autumnal *Ausflug* came the fine poem 'In 1929' (called 'Written Whilst Walking Down the Rhine' in *Twenty Poems*):

> A whim of Time, the general arbiter,
> Proclaims the love instead of death of friends.
> Under the domed sky and athletic sun
> The three stand naked: the new, bronzed German,
> The young communist, and myself, being English.
>
> Yet to unwind the travelled sphere twelve years
> Then two take arms, spring to a ghostly posture.
> Or else roll on the thing further ten

And this poor clerk with world-offended eyes
Builds with red hands his heaven; makes our bones
The necessary scaffolding to peace.

The poem was first published in the *Oxford Outlook* in May 1930. Stephen sent a copy to his grandmother, apologizing for its obscurity. As he explained:

I wrote it last August when I was with Herbert, and it was meant to be very experimental. The idea is that I was thinking how if we had been our age ten years ago, Herbert and I would probably have been shooting each other instead of devoted to each other: and I dare say that in ten years we may be fighting our common friend, a young communist, in a Revolution.

Hamburg in July 1929 was a threshold experience for Spender. The long vacation was, however, not yet over after his return from the Rhine walk with Herbert. He may have seen Auden around the middle of September ('he has become as silent as the tomb again', he complained to Isherwood). Stephen was still, as he records in *World within World*, in the habit of confiding to Winifred Paine things 'which I confided to no one else'. It seems that he told her about what he had experienced, and what he had felt, in Germany. She became so angry with Stephen 'that she made a bonfire on which she burned all the letters I had written her from Nantes and Lausanne'. They were obviously in a juvenile way (on his side) love letters – of some kind. Their relationship eventually settled down to 'friendship'.

There is a blank in the record of what Stephen did over the remainder of the long vac of 1929. There was, it seems, one of the regular family holidays to Switzerland, where he again met Gisa Soloweitschik – a beautiful German of Lithuanian origin. He found her 'exciting and very nice . . . Very funny indeed. Jewish.' As he recalls in *World within World*, 'I was an undergraduate and she was seventeen when I first met her whilst skiing in Switzerland.' Later he would introduce Isherwood to Fräulein Soloweitschik in Berlin (she would figure in Christopher's fiction) and Stephen stayed in her house when he visited the city, after 1929. He confided to Isherwood, in early 1930, that he 'hoped to marry' Gisa, adding, 'Don't for God's sake tell her that, if you see her.' He wrote a poem (never published), celebrating their love on the *piste*:

Taking the easy slope, the breeze fanning my cheek,
The sun on my face, my feet breaking the light
I think of you skiing in a further valley.
Content now under this light, content in this act
My body copies your body, both swing in the great radiance
Without that pain of looking speaking and breaking
We are the same now under the same sun.

The effects of the Wall Street Crash and the subsequent slump did not affect Oxford directly, but the mood changed. Students became more political: 'it was just a beginning', but within three years the students would have their famous Union debate and resolve not to fight for King and Country. After 1929, Stephen observed, with an Audenesque epigram, 'Everything became politics.' Including, of course, his poetry. As a kind of valediction to the 'personal', pre-political, Oxford, he published four of his finest Marston poems in *Oxford Poetry: 1929*, a volume edited by himself and Louis MacNeice.

On his return to Oxford in his final year Stephen moved into new rooms at 63 St. John's Street. There was immediate glory in the recent publication of the 1929 *Oxford Poetry*. Both the *TLS* and the *Cherwell* flatteringly saw Stephen's poems as the anthology's outstanding achievement. And it was in this final year that he formed what was to be the most significant of his Oxford friendships – that with Isaiah Berlin. 'I think I first met him in Oxford late in 1929, or very early in 1930,' Berlin recalled in 1995:

my first impression of Stephen was, as it remained, of a wonderfully handsome, friendly, open, gifted, disarmingly innocent, generous man, irresistibly attractive to meet and to know – indeed, I remember vividly the sheer pride with which I could then claim his acquaintance. I saw him in Oxford from time to time. He read his poetry to me; I think his early verse of those days is among the best he wrote. We used occasionally to go for walks in Christ Church Meadow or the University Parks. I was, as during the rest of our lives, uniquely exhilarated by contact with him, and became devoted to him very soon indeed . . .

As Berlin records, with typical self-deprecation, he himself was not superficially attractive, at least by Auden's tests for young men at Oxford: 'I was everything that at that time he [Auden] was against –

middle-class, fat, conventional (he felt sure), bourgeois, obviously not homosexual, over-talkative.'

Berlin and Stephen seem to have become the best of friends instantaneously. Writing to Carritt in 1931, Stephen records that there are only four people he loves – and it does not matter to him that two of them (Auden and Berlin) are 'ugly'. He and Berlin discovered that they shared a passion for music. In Stephen's last long vacation in 1930 they went to the Salzburg summer festival and heard the operas of Mozart, conducted by Bruno Walter. The summer trips were repeated most years until the Anschluss, in 1938. For each of them it was an annual pilgrimage, a renewal and deepening of their friendship.

Together Berlin and Stephen cultivated their almost religious reverence for Beethoven's late quartets. (Enigmatically, T. S. Eliot told Berlin that in his view these quartets meant 'too much' to Stephen.) It was Berlin who gave Stephen a book of death masks containing a striking reproduction of Beethoven's. It inspired his much reprinted poem:

> I imagine him still with heavy brow.
> Huge, black, with bent head and falling hair,
> He ploughs the landscape. His face
> Is this hanging mask transfigured,
> This mask of death which the white lights make stare.

Berlin confirms that, in his last two years, Stephen was a dazzling and assured presence at Oxford: 'He was extremely popular as an undergraduate: that is to say, he was equally happy in the company of aesthetes, contributors to the *Oxford Outlook* (of which I became editor) and rowing men, footballers and the like: they all fell under the spell of his great charm.' Spender's involvement in college and academic affairs was by now exiguous. He was, however, active as an officer of the English Club, in which capacity he invited Walter de la Mare, Edmund Blunden, J. C. Squire, Humbert Wolfe, E. M. Forster and William Plomer to speak. The last two became friends – Plomer (who looked, as Isherwood thought, 'like a muscular owl') would be particularly close over the subsequent decades.

Stephen shared his duties at the English Club with Elizabeth Harmon. A beautiful and cultivated student, she was less dedicated to work than her fellow undergraduettes ('we all fell in love with her', according to Carritt; Frank Pakenham, later Lord Longford, won her). Rewarding as the English Club was, Stephen by now felt that he primarily belonged to 'a world outside the university'. Among his outer-world friends were Rosamond Lehmann ('one of the most beautiful women of her generation') and her husband, the painter Wogan Philipps.

On their part, these beautiful and gifted people were gratified to know Stephen Spender. His writing was going well, he was being published in any number of little magazines: *Oxford Poetry, Oxford Outlook* (in which Berlin did the music notices) and *Sir Galahad*. More importantly, his poems were being noticed to a degree which was unusual. He had friends who he knew would go far – Isaiah Berlin, of course, and Dick Crossman, who affected to be entirely bamboozled by his friend's latest efforts: 'My dear Stephen,' he would say, 'I don't understand your work nowadays at all' ('Crossman was very arrogant,' Carritt remembers; Berlin recalls him as a bully; Stephen discovered, much later in life and to his amusement, that Crossman was himself furtively writing poetry at college, but was too nervous to show it round).

No longer an acolyte, his opinions were now sought and even paid for. He published his first piece of criticism in the *Spectator* in August 1929, a grand pronouncement on 'Problems of the Poet and the Public'. According to family legend, instead of spending his fee on a new pair of trousers – as Bertha commanded – he blew it on lunch for Auden and Isherwood and a set of Beethoven gramophone records. As undergraduates go, Stephen was now a meteorite blazing across the Oxford sky. The article itself is very much a wild young man's manifesto. It is prefaced by a weak-kneed disclaimer by the magazine's editor:

This is an article giving expression to 'The Younger Point of View', and expressing an opportunity for our readers under thirty to express their views, which are not necessarily those of the *Spectator*.

His poems now made up a substantial corpus. In May he informed his grandmother that:

I am producing a small book of 20 poems from Blackwell's at 5/- a copy, and I am making all my friends buy copies. There will be about 100 for sale [in fact, 175] and 40 of them I am going to sell privately at once. The idea is, that people are always asking me for poems and I simply can't go on typing them out separately, so I am printing a small store for myself, and going to cover my expenses by selling a few for a few days.

Blackwells were the publishers of *Oxford Poetry*. The book was a huge success. Despite the modest remark about its not being an 'official' edition, it was widely noticed. Ernest Rhys (a friend of his grandmother's), Walter de la Mare, William Plomer and others to whom he privately sent the volume 'wrote very nicely'. A new acquaintance and admirer, Professor Ernst Curtius in Bonn, undertook to translate some of the poems into German for the *Neue Schweitzer Rundschau*, laying the ground for what was to be a formative friendship.

As he told his grandmother on 29 May: 'It may please you that Virginia Woolf saw my poems, and Harold Nicholson [sic] says that she was so struck with them that she tried in vain to get a copy. I have written asking for her address, and then I will get Berthella to send one that is left in my drawer.' Nicolson asked Stephen to stay with him and Vita Sackville-West. Through this connection, and through Rosamond Lehmann, Stephen was introduced to the inner sanctum of Bloomsbury. Lytton Strachey, as Frances Partridge records, was very taken with the handsome young undergraduate.

At the same period an unnamed 'friend' sent his poems to Eliot, which led to four of them being published in the *Criterion* in October 1930 ('The Port', 'The Swan', 'Lines Written when Walking down the Rhine', 'Not to You I Sighed'). In his jubilant letter to Carritt, Stephen recalled that Eliot said 'that he liked the poems very much'. In *World within World*, he describes what was to become a famous exchange: 'At our first luncheon he asked me what I wanted to do. I said: "Be a poet." "I can understand you wanting to write poems, but I don't quite know what you mean by 'being a poet'," he objected.' Stephen knew what he meant. Proofs came from the magazine in early August. It was to be the beginning of a fruitful relationship. In October 1931, the *Criterion* would publish another batch of three poems ('Moving through the silent crowd', 'Your body is stars whose million glitter here', 'The Prisoners'), and − following a review of Rilke in July 1931 − he would review regularly for Eliot's journal over the next few years (invariably on poetry, from the young poet's standpoint).

After their initial gratification the Schusters had been much alarmed by *Twenty Poems* − or one of them. In her diary Mrs Schuster recorded that Ernest Rhys had shown her a poem 'which made me very anxious as to how the poetry might be received. I got anxious too and we agreed to consult Edgar' − her son, now head of the Schuster family. A letter would be written to J. A. Spender on the subject. The offending poem, clearly enough, was 'The Port'.

It was the last straw for Stephen's long-suffering Uncle Alfred. When he read, in 'The Port', the inflammatory lines about the pale lily boys flaunting their bright lips for sale, he exploded. He curtly wrote to his nephew (as Stephen reported, jovially, to Gabriel),

saying that he knew it was a pose [among] young men at Oxford to be immoral, but would I please refrain from writing more poems like the Port. I wrote a furious reply and then he let fly in his answer and said I was all Oxford and nothing but Oxford. I then sent both his letters to William [Plomer] in Greece, and he writes 'Thank you for your uncle's letters. I laugh whenever I think of them.'

Stephen was now near enough to twenty-one (just six months away) to take such risks. And the risks, he was assured by critics even more author-itative than Plomer, were justified. On 17 May, T. S. Eliot wrote approv-ingly about the poems which Stephen had sent him. He would, Eliot said, show them to 'one or two friends'. He might even be able to use some of them. Eliot added, prophetically: 'I think the time will come when you will have to choose between writing verse and writing novels; because I do not believe that any human organism can be stored with enough energy to cultivate two such different modes of speech; but meanwhile you are right to try both forms and time will tell you which are yours.' Over the next few months Eliot would repeat his encour-agement that the young man concentrate on poetry, 'deploring' his devoting so much of his creative energy to prose.

Spender's achievement at Oxford – in the aspects that mattered to him – was crowned with glory. There was only one fly in the ointment. His degree. He made one last despairing stab at getting a half decent result by going on a reading party to Crackington, in Cornwall, over the Easter vac. He did not, however, read the right books. Instead of politics, he plunged into Lawrence's *The Plumed Serpent* and Gide's *Les Faux Monnayeurs*. He drafted two fine poems, 'The Swan' and 'Cornet Cornelius'. He watched a beautiful sunset with a fellow student called 'Douglas' (a pseudonym, as was revealed seventy years later, for Richard Crossman). The sun made Stephen sad for Germany. Crossman was evidently some-thing of a lost cause. As Stephen jauntily told Isherwood:

I have spent some weeks trying to seduce someone this term, and at last one evening feeling that the time had come I began a moral discussion. But this one before I had properly got going interrupted me: 'You know, Stephen, since I met you my life's entirely altered. When I first knew you I used to masturbate and I used to read pornographic books. But now, after being with you, all that's stopped. I don't masturbate and I'm absolutely pure!'

Stephen's studies were another lost cause. He was not deluded, nor did he try to delude others, about where it would all end. On 28 May he wrote to his grandmother: 'I can't stay in England after July *whatever happens*, because I must get away after my examination. I am sure to do badly in my examination, so I want to get started on my novel at once, in Germany. My idea is to go away the very day after my viva which will be about July 20th.'

Exile was in order. Stephen came a cropper in his exams, failing even to get a pass degree. He felt no great shame. As he explained to his grandmother:

I dare say it seems intolerably hypocritical that having ploughed in Schools I should be self-righteous about it. But, in a sense, I do feel righteous. It all had no *meaning* for me, and in spite of everyone saying that Oxford is an excellent training and everything I was afraid I didn't want to touch it: I don't want to be efficient and have a trained mind any more than I want to be a motor-car. I want to be a human being, and to have an intense sympathy with the life around me.

His grandmother, as always, was understanding. So was everyone whose opinion meant anything to him. Most importantly his friends ('they mostly got Firsts') were 'very nice about it and accepted my little book of Poems as a consolation'. As Isaiah Berlin observed, Stephen resolved to leave Oxford naked as he had entered, three years before:

before he went down (I don't think he knew that he had not done well in his final examination), he asked his friends to come and see him in his rooms in St John Street [. . .] He told them that they could take with them anything that they found there – desks, chairs, tables, clothes, books, manuscripts, whatever there was – it was a general distribution of all his worldly goods. I remember Richard Crossman walking off with a book of manuscripts of Stephen's poems – as for me, I think he gave me a book, I cannot remember what it was, I think a book of his early poems, inscribed 'To Isaiah, this book made valuable by the author'.

Oxford was not, from Stephen's point of view, 'failure'. As he patiently explained to his grandmother, from Hamburg in August:

It is no use. I am most awfully sorry, but I cannot do examinations; and Schools I never really had any ambition to do properly. I was only a little anxious not to let down my friends and relatives; but if they feel let down, that has to be. I only care really for poetry and writing . . . I dare say that my behaviour all last year was very wilful; only please forgive me, because I have conceived the ambition that I may with my life be able to contribute some quite new tradition to English literature, and I work always for that, and I care really for nothing but that.

His novel, of which he had fifty-five pages written, would be finished, he reckoned, by Christmas. Herbert List, who knew about such things, helped him choose a camera ('he is still very much one of my heroes').

After a holiday with Winifred, Stephen moved on to Auden in Berlin, via Switzerland. The strait-laced country, which had been so liberating in summer 1927, inspired a jolly squib:

> A very pious race are the Swiss:
> They never spit and they never piss.

In early October he wrote to Carritt what was, in effect, his valediction to Oxford – or at least, to academic Oxford:

This is chiefly a letter of condolence, because the autumnal bleakness in the air reminds me that OXFORD and all that period of horror is about to put on its leaves again. I hope that it will not be too awful: I look back on it all now as a series of nightmares, peopled by nightmare characters, mostly Wykhamist. However it is a little comforting to remember that three of the same people will still be there, you, Johnny Freeman, and Isaiah Berlin.

The 1930s

Literary history likes to catalogue Stephen Spender as pre-eminently a 'Poet of the Thirties'. It was a label he was pleased to bear – although he might have preferred 'writer' to 'poet'. Or perhaps even activist. The decade was, as he incarnated its spirit, one of active rejection, rebellion, and radical political ideas. Spender's generation had not, like their 1920s predecessors, been traumatized (or decimated) by the Great War; but they rejected everything that they associated with it. And they were haunted by the premonition that an even greater, more horrible, war than 1914–18 was coming. As Spender later confided to Orwell, he knew from 1929 onward that 'catastrophe' was inevitable. Was flight or engaged resistance the proper response? Spender's departure for Germany in 1930 was part flight. It was part Lawrentian pilgrimage. It was partly a gesture of solidarity with Isherwood and Auden, sexual rebels who were already in Germany. Partly it was a search for intellectual and artistic freedoms. But mainly it was a rejection of England and what the country stood for. Cultural repression, in a phrase. The 1930s were, for Spender, a long, restless itinerary: Hamburg, Berlin, Greece, Yugoslavia, Vienna, Portugal, Spain. It was sometimes exploration, sometimes voyage of discovery, sometimes utopian quest, sometimes merely tourism. Whatever, it was world-wide in its scope and range. His account of this phase of his life in World within World *emphasizes the enlargement of his vision. During these years (English poet that he always was), his country was, essentially, his friends (in the same way that the exiled Joseph Brodsky would later say that Auden and Spender were his 'family'). Now adult and free, Spender was, during the 1930s, as much an adventurer in sex as in ideas. From unsatisfactory and brief liaisons with German boys he moved to a years-long relationship with a male partner into heterosexual marriage. All these experiments in love (and occasionally loveless sex) eventually failed. But they moved him a step further along. The general trajectory of the 1930s was, for Spender, from idealism through struggle to disillusionment and moral realignment. It was a useful, if painful, process. He would discover more realistic bases for his life and career in the 1940s. And, by 1939, he would have returned to the England which he rejected in 1929. Indeed, by remaining in the country (when he could easily have emigrated to America) he showed himself ready to die for England. 'Making one's name' had been the great mission wished on him (in his character of 'ambitious son') by Harold Spender. He satisfied his father's wish with the publication of his volume* Poems, 1933. *There were other literary ventures: into fiction, critical books, verse drama, higher journalism, even a political treatise. All had a measure of success. But it was as a poet of the 1930s that he established the fame which outlived the decade with which he is indelibly associated.*

1. Germany

Stephen left Oxford in June 1930. He had resolved to take up residence in Hamburg. Before leaving he spent a few days at Fieldhead with his friends Wogan Philipps and Rosamond Lehmann. After meeting them the previous winter he had sent them some poems in progress. Rosamond had shown these poems to her brother John, whom Stephen had not yet personally met. Already prominent figures in the London literary world, 'Ros and Wog' had the eccentricity which Stephen, the raconteur, relished. They both of them furnished good stories. 'Ros' was 'the queen adored by queers'. As the author of the novel *Dusty Answer* (1927), she was already famous both as a writer and as a beauty. This was her second marriage. Wogan painted – badly, and 'with a fanaticism which he later brought to politics'. He later became notorious as the only Communist in the House of Lords. He had 'wide staring eyes and [a] way of saying anything that came into his head. He once came down to breakfast and said: "do you know what I dreamed about last night? Fields and fields of shit with white swans wearing crowns flying over them."' Both were sensitive, clever, and affectionate to the impulsive young Oxford poet. Stephen kept up a chatty correspondence with them over the next few years and visited them at their Ipsden mansion in the Chilterns on his returns to England.

Stephen also corresponded, in a more deferential way, with the grander Nicolsons, Harold and Vita (Sackville-West). They, particularly Harold, had been impressed by *Twenty Poems* and were talking Stephen up wherever they could. He stayed at their house, Long Barn, in Kent. Nicolson – a rising political figure – came across any number of clever young Oxford men, but Stephen – whom he first encountered on 22 June 1930 – struck him as something special. He noted his approving (if ineffably condescending) impression in his diary:

He is an intelligent young man with wild blue eyes and a bad complexion. He takes his work and poetry with immense seriousness, and talks for hours about whether he is more fitted to be a poet than a novelist. He is absolutely determined to become a leading writer. A nice and vital young man whom we both liked.

It was useful to be liked by him. Nicolson passed on various of Stephen's new poems to friendly editors ('I know it is no use for me to send the poems myself,' Stephen told him on 21 August).

After a flying visit to Salzburg with Isaiah Berlin in July, Stephen packed his bags and his 'Hugo' German primer for a long trip. He left on the *Bremen* night boat from Harwich, entrusting to a stranger leaving the boat a farewell letter to post to Gabriel Carritt. It never arrived. An ill omen. Wystan had been in Berlin since he left Oxford, under *his* cloud, in October 1928. 'Be thankful you don't live in Berlin,' he once chaffed Stephen: 'your nose would never stop bleeding.' Christopher Isherwood's intentions in life were clinched in autumn 1928 when he visited Auden in Berlin – a city where 'not even the puppies and kittens are virgins', as Stephen mischievously put it. Behind the heavy leather curtains of the 'Cosy Corner' café the 'novelist of the future' found his future. Soon afterwards Isherwood and Auden, in between tumultuous (and for Auden traumatic) relationships with German boys, became occasional lovers.

Auden's residence in Berlin was comparatively short. He returned 'wounded' to England to take up gainful work in July 1929 (the literal wound in question, a rectal fissure, supplied the subject of an ironic poem). In England Wystan immediately felt 'homesick' for Germany. He did not, however, return 'home'. There ensued six years of teaching appointments, poetic growth and spiritual introspection in Britain. And poverty. In later life Stephen recalled that Auden had suggested – with his characteristic seigneurial grandeur – that his friend split the 'Spender bequest' with him. Spender 'did not like the idea'. 'I might want to get married,' he objected.

Christopher, always the most decisive of the trio, uprooted himself from Britain after a shattering series of quarrels with his mother and transplanted himself in Berlin in November 1929. He would remain there until May 1933, with only the occasional (and unwilling) dash back to the UK, after which Germany was no longer safe for leftist homosexuals. In Berlin Christopher (initially at least) made an ostentatious show of living like the German *Volk*. It mainly meant, as Stephen saw, bad plumbing, cold rooms and unspeakable food:

He lived very poorly, scarcely ever spending more than sixty pfennigs (about eightpence) on a meal. During this time, when I had meals almost every day with him, we ate food such as horse flesh and lung soup, which for some years ruined my digestion, and for all time my teeth, as they had long ago ruined his.

It seems more likely that the dental damage was done by the huge amounts of toffee in which the two young men indulged daily. There was stern doctrine behind the depressing regime: 'Auden and Christopher were in full revolt against all forms of hygiene.' Hygienic, fastidious, and a lifelong lover of good food, Stephen dutifully went along with his friends' foibles.

There was an artistic benefit to Christopher's immersion in the destructive element of the Berlin *Lumpenproletariat*. His underworld experiences would eventually flower in the 'I am a Camera' Berlin stories (as they were much later called – rather to the author's irritation; he saw himself as something grander than a Leica with legs). At the time he was pinning his artistic hopes on longer and more ambitious fictions. After *All the Conspirators* (which had been received coolly) he was working on *The Memorial*. Christopher was ever the most absolute of the three in his disdain for England. It was he who adopted most enthusiastically the subversive teachings of Magnus Hirschfeld's Institute of Sexology and 'Lane-Layardism'. He was by temperament an exile.

On his part Stephen set out for Germany (as he had in 1929, primarily to escape the censorship in his homeland – embodied in the tyrannical, and literature-persecuting, figure of the Home Secretary, Joynson-Hicks ('Jix'), darling of the *Daily Express*). It was in Germany that he would find the newest and most radical mutations of the 'liberalism' which he had imbibed with his mother's milk and at his father's knee. In the first instance, this meant the freedom to write books like *The Temple*.

The years 1930–33 stand out as a high point in Spender's poetic career. It was a period when, as he put it, 'I was living a life dangerous to myself and impossible to justify to others [but] was writing my best early poems.' It is a judgement with which the anthologizers have always concurred. His output over the German years is, however, marked by two irreconcilable tendencies. The driving force is a youthful, Shelleyan enthusiasm for the new styles of living emergent in Weimar Germany. He embraced the brash styles of Expressionism, as they were manifested in film and industrial design. German Expressionism inspired his most anthologized poem of the period, 'The Pylons', a homage to the National Grid which has all the graphic starkness of a 'Ufa' film poster:

> Now over these small hills they have built the concrete
> That trails black wire:
> Pylons, those pillars
> Bare like nude, giant girls that have no secret.

With Oxford's antiquities still in his nostrils, Stephen found every-thing in Germany new – intoxicatingly so. He loved Bauhaus:

There were buildings with broad clean vertical lines crossed by strong hori-zontals, which drove into the sky like railroads. There were experiments in the theatre and opera, all in a style which expressed with facility the fusion of naked liberation with a kind of bitter pathos, which was characteristic of this Germany . . . Roofless houses, expressionist painting, atonal music, bars for homosexuals, nudism, sunbathing, camping, all were accepted.

'Nakedness,' he declared in *The Temple* with a melodramatic flourish, 'is the democracy of the new Germany, the Weimar Republic.'

Running against Stephen's enthusiasm for things German, artistic and naked was his anxiety about the increasingly visible manifestations of the world slump. The Depression increasingly depressed him. Alongside his anthems to German Modernism are laments on the conditions of the swelling masses of the unemployed, written in a limpid unorna-mented idiom:

> In railway halls, on pavements near the traffic,
> They beg, their eyes made big by empty staring
> And only measuring Time, like the blank clock.

His work of this period yearns towards what he called (in correspon-dence with William Plomer) 'real values – food, fucking, money, and religion'.

Like Christopher and Wystan, sex at this stage of his career meant principally boys of the lower classes. Although his own educational back-ground was more egalitarian than that of his friends (and of future friends, like the Etonian John Lehmann), Stephen seems at this point to have subscribed to, without ever wholly accepting, the public schoolboy's imperative that there should ideally be a class difference (class in either the social or the public school sense) in sexual relations between men. The 'other' must be proletarian and junior. In a much-quoted remark in later life Stephen claimed that sex 'would have been almost impossible between two Englishmen of our class . . . Men of the same class just didn't; it would have been impossible, or at least very unlikely.' 'I could never face the electric shocks and the pain of having an "affair" with someone who was my "intellectual equal",' he told John Lehmann at this period. On the other hand, he confided to Plomer his dislike of mere 'whores'. Relationships with young men which could hover between the erotic and the Platonic, and in which the emotional investment was relatively shallow (although caring), were – over these years – convenient. Even though, as he was to discover, Christopher was right in his judgement that 'all boys are sharks', for a year or two Stephen would swim with them. In his German years he was never without what Isherwood called his 'little chum'. In his retrospective 1939 *Journal* he would conclude that his interest in young men was, at least in part, born of a fear of women.

Stephen's thinking on the subject of sex, as on many subjects at this period of his life, was extravagantly idealistic. In his September 1939 Journal, he noted:

I was 20 in those days, and I was caught up mostly with the idea of Friendship – *Freundschaft* – which was a very important part of the life of the Weimar Republic . . . It was not cynical, shamefaced, smart, snobbish, or stodgy, as so often in England. It was more like Walt Whitman's idea of camaraderie.

Stephen saw Pabst's film *Kameradschaft* with Christopher, in 1931. It was, he told John Lehmann, 'the best film I have ever seen'.

When he disembarked in Hamburg in late July 1930, Stephen's first reaction was 'a tremendous sense of relief, of having got away from Oxford and home'. He initially took up residence at Innocentia Strasse 11 (an address which would be the occasion of mirth). Gisa stayed with him a day, on her way to Berlin in early August. There was a possibility that Isaiah might come out. His lodgings in Innocentia Strasse were 'adequate' (for himself), he told Gabriel Carritt. In *The Temple* Stephen offers a densely remembered description of the establishment, with its 'chintz-covered sofas and fleshy armchairs', its framed photograph of Bismarck and the huge cast-iron oven that in winter made everything smell 'like the inside of a cardboard packing case'.

Stephen's principal contacts in the city were Erich Alport and Herbert

List and their shifting circle of young friends and lovers. To get him through the impending German winter his grandmother had given him his Uncle Alfred's greatcoat: 'She had bought it for him when he was on leave in London from the Western front,' he recalled. 'Killed in France a month later, Lieutenant Schuster had only twice, when on leave, worn the greatcoat.' The handsome garment is immortalized in one of Humphrey's fine photographic portraits of young Stephen in Germany.

Winter was, however, still some months away when Stephen arrived. This was the season of 'swimming in the Alster and excursions in canoes', living 'from day to day, enjoying to the utmost everything that was free: sun, water, friendship'. Sun, above all, symbolized the mixture of eroticism and essential innocence that Stephen craved (half a century later he and Humphrey would pay for the craving with skin cancer).

Stephen recounted, in late August, a strange anecdote to the Nicolsons which throws some illumination on his creative practices at the time:

I started the poem about 'Upon my solitary peak there is no light' two evenings ago at about 11 p.m. I worked at it till 12.20 and then went to bed. The next morning I worked at it for two hours, and thought I had finished it. Then I had lunch, went to swim, etc. All this interval I felt so ill I thought I really must be having cancer or something, and I took the final plunge that I have never dared to take before – I made an appointment at a hospital for next Wednesday. I went home, I read the poem through and I rewrote it very quickly. I felt instantly as well as ever. It was very funny.

There was a typical epilogue to this illustrative anecdote. Stephen, after admiring it for a month, suppressed 'Upon my solitary peak'. As he told Vita Sackville-West, 'I am always writing poems like that, and thinking they are terribly good, sending them to everyone, and then, lying awake at night, blushing at the very thought of them.'

The procession of August visitors continued with Christopher and his current Berlin lover. 'I remember Stephen's explosive laugh as he greeted [me],' wrote Isherwood with his characteristic impishness in *Christopher and his Kind*: 'it was the laugh of a small boy who has done something forbidden: "I've just written the most marvellous poem!" A pause. Then with sudden anxiety: "At least, I *hope* it is."' In Berlin Christopher had set to work on *The Memorial* – an ambitious Döblin-like saga covering three generations of English post-war society. His first novel, *All the Conspirators*, had not set the literary world on fire and it was not clear that Cape would leap at any successor. Meanwhile – almost without intending to – Christopher was gathering the material (notably zoological specimens such as Gerald Hamilton, 'Mr Norris', Jean Ross, 'Sally Bowles', and the fantastic Francis Turville-Petre, 'Fronny') that would eventually feature in his sequence of shorter Berlin stories.

Stephen hated solitude. To keep him company during his first Hamburg months he had brought with him, *faute de mieux*, Moore Crosthwaite, who was killing time before joining the diplomatic service. Mid-August found Stephen in bubbling high spirits: he wrote to Isaiah pronouncing that Hamburg was 'incredibly amusing'. He had, of course, 'ploughed in schools', he told Berlin (whose academic career was progressing mete-orically). But that did not matter, as he was 'getting on fine with my novel'. As he told the Nicolsons, even more enthusiastically, 'the novel is so terrific I hardly dare touch it now!' He had also acquired 'a most wonderful camera', a Voigtlander reflex, with which he could take what he laughingly called 'masturbatory pictures designed for narcissists'. Herbert List gave him some useful instruction (on photography, that is).

Stephen was, during his Hamburg period, reading voraciously in the German classics. Summer evenings were devoted to hedonism. He was now a habitué of the Port area commemorated in the 1929 poem. Moore was 'funny beyond belief', he told Isaiah:

I took him down to St Pauli, and he went there murmuring that he couldn't stand effeminate or decadent people and that it wouldn't amuse him at all. Then when we had gone a little way I introduced him to a young boy. He said 'How charming and delightful he is.' Then I said 'Yes, that's the boy I live with.' He was silent for a long time, and then he began to say how wonderful the place was. I think though that it was about half an hour later that he suddenly stopped being so enthusiastic to remark dubiously: 'But of course he *isn't* a gentleman.'

Hamburg was congenial, he told Gabriel Carritt. He had two firm and knowledgeable friends in the city, although they were different kinds of friend:

Erich [Alport] I do not like, but I sympathize with him and he interests me absorbedly. Herbert [List] I suppose I love. I love him as I love a few other people, Wystan, Humphrey, Isaiah Berlin and you, Gabriel. I love them out of a generous response to their generosity which seems to spring from me. I love

them physically – even the most ugly of them, but I am content only to be
with them.

But even in the first flush of Hamburg's paradisal freedom, Stephen was
afflicted by dark moments: 'I have a most charming boy when I want
to,' he told Gabriel. 'At the same time I am still liable to fits of depression, and the periods of that kind of physical poisoning which in England
I was subject to. In a word, myself is not changed as I hoped it would
be.'

It is clear that Stephen had a number of transitory experiences with
young lovers in Hamburg. In *World within World* he recalls one as illustrative – 'Walter'. Walter was unemployed and Stephen met him idling
in a *Lokal*. The young man had 'large clumsy hands, an intent expression of his eyes in his pale face, under the cloth cap which he nearly
always wore'. Dull and vacuous, he was addicted to amusement arcade
games. Walter systematically wheedled money from his English protector
on outrageously improbable pretexts. Finally, on List's advice, Stephen
bought the parasitic Walter a railway ticket and packed him off to his
relatives in South Germany. The only alternative, as Stephen told the
Nicolsons, was for the hapless youth to 'go on the streets' as a male prostitute. Typically the Walters of the world were homosexual less by choice
than by economic necessity: it was the last resort of the (physically desirable) unemployed.

Spender reflected on the relationship, twenty years later, in *World within
World*:

Now I look back with amusement at the episode of Walter. Yet at the time I
took his problem seriously, and I tried to believe the stories he told me. If I
had not tried to believe him, or if I had not thought that his stories were ways
of expressing a need for money with which I could sympathize, the relationship would have been more cynical. Because it was not so, I can still think of
it as a friendship in which there was something more significant than a kind
of mutual exploitation.

In late August Stephen made an *Ausflug* from Hamburg. It is not easy
to piece together his itinerary accurately at this point. He evidently holidayed in Venice in September with Winifred, Humphrey and Christine.
The family were taking their annual (and last, as a group) continental
holiday, paid for by Mrs Schuster. Afterwards he and Winifred spent five

days in Verona. The family were bright and cheerful. Stephen, however, was 'in every way worse' and 'listless'. He had a 'poisoned neck' (the result of an infected razor cut) which blackened his mood. He had, anyway, outgrown the simple rituals of Frognal life.

On 10 September he went on to Berlin, again in the company of Moore Crosthwaite. The young Englishmen stayed with Stephen's friends the Soloweitschiks, at their house in Wilmersdorff, Konstanzer-Strasse 10. He introduced Christopher to Gisa, the girl 'whom I hope perhaps to marry', as he had recklessly told his friend. She never became Frau Spender, although she did resurface as Natalia Landauer in Christopher's Berlin stories: 'a young Jewish girl who lived with her wealthy parents . . . She had dark fluffy hair, far too much of it – it made her face, with its sparkling eyes, appear too long and narrow. She reminded me of a young fox.'

Stephen wrote to Isaiah from Berlin telling him that 'I am in the middle of the sixth chapter of my novel':

Moore is a great social success, rather to my annoyance. I alternatively feel infuriated with him and rather like him. I feel at home with him on the whole, because under his veneer of public schoolishness, and his pompous aestheticism, he is a neurotic.

Lane-Layardism had infected him to the degree that 'neurotic' was now a term of high praise. He has, he goes on to tell Shyah (as his close friends called him), 'for the first time for about a year and a half . . . fallen deeply in love. It is just like an illness.' The current object of Stephen's love was a Hamburg boy, called Arnold. He was 'unfortunately the only person I have met in San Pauli who will not go to bed with me. He is lovely beyond words, an engineer, sportsman, and efficient; very happy temperament, rather like Freeman, but easier to get on with.'

On this trip he saw the film *The Blue Angel*, and the sultry tune which Dietrich huskily crooned ('Ich bin vom Kopf bis Fuss' – 'Falling in Love Again') inspired a poem. He also, during this stay, wrote his fine poem about the unemployed, 'In railway halls'. In both works he was, as he told the Nicolsons, 'trying for something new, and I dare say that I have only achieved the ludicrous'. All in all, this Berlin visit was a success. As Stephen recalls in *World within World*, Christopher invited his friend to leave Hamburg and come and live 'near him' (not *with* him) in the capital. Arnold was not included in the invitation.

One of Stephen's main motives for going to Germany had been to find a teacher. Isherwood, as *Christopher and his Kind* makes clear, was only too happy to take on the task of civilizing Stephen Savage. Stephen found a less mischievous mentor in Bonn, in the person of the eminent literary critic, Ernst Robert Curtius. Curtius had made a name for himself among English intellectuals by translating *The Waste Land* into German. He was a personal friend and translator of André Gide. Born in 1886, Curtius had served as an officer in the trenches in the First World War. He had been appointed a professor in Bonn in 1919, at the precocious age of thirty-four. At the period when Stephen met him he had a few weeks earlier married one of his former students, twenty years his junior.

Stephen was known, as a poet, to Curtius – who had already indicated an interest in translating his work. He was introduced personally through the good offices of Erich Alport. From the first Stephen felt immensely attracted to Curtius. It was he who was primarily responsible for the high European flavour of Stephen's reading in his last terms at Oxford and his subsequent fascination with German romanticism. 'With Curtius,' he later wrote, 'I was in contact with the Germany of Goethe, Hölderlin, and Schiller. That is an Apollonian Germany, a Germany of the sun, not the Dionysian Germany of Hitler . . . We read Hölderlin together and later on the poems of the Greek anthology.' Curtius exercised on Stephen what he called a 'mental seduction'. He was not homosexual or bisexual, although intellectually sympathetic with the 'Hellenic cult of beauty'. He thought Stephen ('a child of the sun') had enough imaginative energy 'to run a factory'. And he loved his young English friend's 'shamelessness'. He remained professorially critical, however, of the 'formlessness' of his disciple's prose.

Stephen's initial plan, on arriving in Hamburg in August, had been to go to Bonn in October, but Curtius had put him off. It was his *Urlaubsmonat*. On his eventual arrival in Bonn in late November, Stephen was welcomed into Curtius's home – an honour, in terms of the starchy etiquette of the German university. Stephen found Frau Professor Ilse Curtius 'a very beautiful and intelligent woman'. Jestingly he declined to impart to Isaiah Berlin any 'scandal about Curtius'. But, he mysteriously added, there had been 'one or two shocks about his character' (a covert taste for pornography, according to a suppressed passage in the 1939 *Journal*). None the less, 'I think he is the most affable man I have ever met and one of the ablest critics.'

A thesis remains to be written about the influence of Curtius's thinking on Spender's writing. Relics of these formative tutorials in Bonn can be discerned in all his subsequent prose writing. As articulated in his 'great work' (as he called it), *European Literature and the Late Middle Ages* (1948), Curtius's literary theory was formed on three big ideas. The first was that European literature (and latterly American literature) formed an indivisible supranational entity. What he advocated was a kind of literary study without frontiers. The whole domain of the world's poetry, he argued, was a single enchanted island, like Prospero's. Secondly, Curtius discerned a long and fruitful quarrel through history between the discourses of philosophy (intellectually inert) and literature (intellectually vital). Thirdly, and most significantly for Spender, Curtius conceived medieval European poetry to be the first manifestation of 'modernism' – or, as Spender would later put it, the voice of the young rebel. Dante, Stefan Georg, T. S. Eliot were all, for Curtius, modernists. It was a version of literary history peculiarly congenial to the young English poet, on the brink of his career.

Initially in November Stephen stayed in a Bonn pension, at Koblenzstrasse 108. He was 'studying' (his word) and furnishing written work for Curtius to comment on. They read Goethe and Schiller together. The practice of travelling to a professor and working under the Great Man was an honoured one in German universities and Stephen fell naturally into it. Discipleship always suited him better than discipline.

Stephen's reputation was meanwhile consolidating in England. Influential people were talking about his poetry and he had been marked as a young man to watch. He had, as he told Gabriel Carritt, 'God knows why', been offered 'by a publisher, through a literary agent, £75 down for a book and in addition to this very big royalties'. The publisher's offer pricked him into what he called an 'orgasm of work' at the end of the year. Was it worthwhile work? On 20 October T. S. Eliot wrote 'deploring' Stephen's devoting himself to prose. Poetry, Eliot thought, was his proper occupation.

Stephen had in fact promised Faber a volume of poems 'that will probably not be ready for two years or so', as he estimated. Under Auden's influence, he had moderated the tumultuous speed of his poetic composition and was subjecting his poems to rigorous revision. Auden complained at the wanton 'richness' of Spender's poems – the need for more 'dull lines' and more severity with his work. Of the many hundreds of poems he wrote in these years, only thirty-three would reach print in *Poems, 1933*. Meanwhile with his left hand Stephen was writing occasional short stories and was turning out a fluent stream of commissioned reviews. He had a quick pen and a smart turn of phrase. Editors had marked him down as reliable.

Under Curtius's influence Stephen turned his hand to translations of 'Hellenic' Stefan Georg. In lighter mode he dashed off a charming *vers d'occasion* for a young friend, Wolfgang Clemen. Clemen was another disciple of Curtius's and, like Alport, a dedicated Anglophile and Cambridge man (he had studied at Downing – Alport's college). Like Stephen, he was passionate about music. Clemen would, in later years, become a professor of English at Munich and establish himself as an internationally influential Shakespearian critic.

Stephen's poem, strikingly imagistic in style (he had, one suspects, recently been reading Pound), commemorates the walks on which his friendship with Clemen was forged:

> After the town I am fulfilled in peace
> The coral flowers above us in the trees
> The country girls stare at us through the gate
> Under the boughs how sweetly pouring laughter
> We walk, fanned by pale lights
> I love the small wires running through the orchard.
> At evening with my young friend Wolfgang Clemen
> I reach the hill.
>   I am tired after town
> Our eyes on the horizon are gazelles
> Which drink the liquid and transparent line.

This friendship with Clemen would come under strain when the German, six years later, tried to enlighten Stephen on the virtues of a militarily resurgent Germany.

Crosthwaite had left Bonn and Stephen was now, as 1930 drew to an end, sharing rooms in the Koblenzstrasse pension with Arthur Calder-Marshall. Another Oxford contemporary and stalwart of the Poetry Society, Calder-Marshall was training himself as a novelist. Arthur composed a couple of limericks for the delectation of their Oxford friends. The first reads:

A young German student called Clemen
Once travelled to Bremen to see men.
　And though they agreed
　He was running to seed
He said 'not to seed but to semen'.

Arthur added considerably to the bawdiness of life, Stephen told Gabriel.

Stephen, after six months in Germany, was now himself an intrepid adventurer. He jauntily recounted one alarming escapade to Carritt:

I have lived now in the most perfect virtue for four months, with the exception of one day on which I entered Köln in order to do a little mountaineering. On this occasion I was a little too much filled with Wystan's Holy Ghost, which turned round and bit me. For I was abandoned later in a sinister hotel which had no locks in the doors where I was robbed of all my money and my watch. This was very funny, but it was rather a shock and has finally put an end to my activities in this direction, I think.

The episode was stored away, to be resurrected in a story, 'Der Unschuldige', written in 1954. In this story (which Stephen never published – and which would probably have been unpublishable before 1960) the hero, 'Richard Aveling', confesses all to the Professor Curtius figure who offers him moral absolution: 'My dear Richard, you can do what you choose. You may plunge in filth, or may, as I hope, lead a wise and beautiful life. You are capable of error, but I assure you, you are incapable of sin.'

One thing is very clear. Germany had confirmed in Stephen his sense of literary vocation. 'My whole life', he told Carritt on 8 December:

is resolving itself into the struggle of poetry versus prose: with further minor conflicts as to how much I should work, what I should read, etc. I find myself reading Blunden's book on Leigh Hunt and his friends, E. M. Tillyard's Milton, and especially Beethoven's Letters – all of which I have been studying in lately – in order to find some *rules* by which I may escape the struggles with my conscience and simply follow out someone else's plan of life. It is absurd. My only reward in reading the lives of artists and poets is to find that they had the same difficulties.

'My writing goes on, like a continual wrestling with the devil,' he told Isaiah Berlin. The young philosopher was entertained by his friend's letters and instructed. As Michael Ignatieff records:

Stephen Spender did most to bring home the realities of European politics to Berlin and his circle . . . His letters back made it impossible for Isaiah to ignore what was happening as Hitler edged closer to power.

Stephen's German letters served as bulletins from the real world – something with which Oxford always has a tenuous relationship. He put it well himself, in a letter to Isaiah in 1932:

I didn't mean [as he evidently was mistaken to imply in a previous letter] that rawness and violence were better in themselves than Oxford. What I do mean is that if our world is a world of violence, of rawness, then [when] one leaves Oxford one is bound to have to deal with it, so it is best to accept the real conditions of contemporary life as soon as possible. One has got to put up with them for better or worse, and the only hope of changing them is in facing them, not in living in a dream of the old world. But I am tired of saying what is so obvious to me.

On 8 December Stephen left Bonn for the even more real world of Berlin. As he told Gabriel, 'I came to Berlin chiefly to see Christopher.' Arnold had by now gone his way. His successor was not entirely satisfactory. 'My boy Walter went out with a girl and caught clap,' Stephen reported to Gabriel, 'so that I was rather worried when he last wrote to me when I was at Bonn. However, fortunately the infection is not serious; and things are more cheerful.'

Stephen's first impression in Berlin was how much worse the effects of the slump were. As he told Isaiah, 'One [cannot] buy things in a shop without being troubled by beggars, and signs of poverty are sufficiently evident in the Kurfürstendamm.' Christopher, however, was living in less ostentatiously impoverished style. 'He has been having sunlight treatment and is much better,' Stephen noted. 'Herr Issyvoo' was now installed, famously for posterity, in Fräulein Thurau's Nollendorfstrasse lodging-house. It was in a more desirable area of the city, not far from the Kurfürstendamm. Among his fellow lodgers was the leggy chorus-girl Jean Ross – 'Sally Bowles', as she was to be immortalized. Thanks to Stephen, Christopher was now friendly with the Soloweitschiks ('she is *really* a very sweet girl') and had a new set of Berlin friends, many of whom would be translated into the Berlin stories.

After what was a flying visit to Berlin, Stephen decided to go back to England on 20 December for Christmas, 'because Wogan and Rosamond have asked me to stay with them', as he told Isaiah (whom he was equally keen to see). The trip home also had a business motive. Stephen had two novels to bring to market: his own *The Temple* and Christopher's *The Memorial*. Stephen packed Lewes's life of Goethe in his bags with the manuscripts and set off. At Fieldhead over Christmas Stephen was introduced to Rosamond's brother, John Lehmann. It marked the beginning of a vexed friendship. Much later in life, in the privacy of his journal, Stephen wrote a reminiscence of this first encounter with John. At the time John was a junior partner in the Hogarth Press. His position in the firm had been bought for him with family money, and he was eager to establish himself as a commissioning editor. He was a potential buyer of Stephen's wares.

Rosamond offered a pen picture of their house-guest at Ipsden for the amusement of her Cambridge friend, Dadie Rylands: 'that absolute lunatic Stephen Spender is still with us . . . he has been booming, droning, pouring, bursting out of doors like a northeaster, into rooms like a fiery sunrise, beaming, beaming, beaming'. In introducing Stephen and John, Rosamond may well have seen herself as a Pandarus to the two young men − fire and ice, respectively. She built the meeting up to 'a great event', as Stephen recalled. John Lehmann's sexual tastes were undeviatingly homosexual. He was tall, blond and handsome. Initially the two young men took to each other. Some Lawrentian *Blutbrüderschaft* was in prospect, as Stephen mischievously recalled. Overhearing their initial conversation, as they walked along the Thames bank at Fieldhead, Rosamond recalled it as a chorus of 'I, I, I, I − like a flock of cawing crows'. It seems that, in the excitement of their first meeting, they projected a new and quite revolutionary publishing house, devoted (as Stephen fondly foresaw) to the Gang's writing.

From the first Stephen was uneasy − less about business than personal matters. 'The moment I met him I had that feeling of mixed attraction and repulsion which makes lovemaking impossible,' he later recalled. On their return to London, Lehmann invited Stephen to his apartment in Bloomsbury. Ostensibly, they were to discuss publishing plans. The conversation turned to Oxford and Cambridge and old lovers. 'Then, after lunch, John said, "Don't you think it would be *splendid* if we went to bed?"' The word 'splendid' tickled Stephen's fancy. He saw in his mind a ludicrous 'vision of us both, blue-eyed, blond-haired, giants with pink flesh and large bones, wrestling till dawn on a white sheet'. The invitation was politely declined.

With 'a part of my mind', Stephen was always 'repelled' by Lehmann. His 'steely will' put him off. 'What really made me reject him,' Stephen later recalled, 'was what seemed to me his lack of sensibility and relaxedness . . . I regarded him in some ways as a failed version of myself – but I also regarded myself as a failed version of myself.' Others had similarly mixed feelings about John. Cyril Connolly (for whom Lehmann had no libidinous feeling) said that having lunch with him was like a visit to the dentist: painful and inhibiting to conversation.

Stephen was evidently making up his winter itinerary as he went along. He would, he declared, rejoin Christopher in Germany at the beginning of February – even if he had to emulate Captain Webb to do so:

How nice that will be! But how many years will it take before I can emerge from the waters at the point where you have emerged? It is as though I had to *swim* that rotten Channel. I have always been trying to build tunnels under it. Now I shall give up. I see it has got to be swum.

He was, he confided to Christopher, feeling glum. One of the factors adding to Stephen's melancholy was the fact that, even at this embryonic stage of his career, he provoked intense envy and malice in fellow-writers to whom his own feelings were entirely benign. It was perplexing. 'I rather love Roy Campbell,' he told Gabriel on 30 December. But:

Campbell, Wyndham Lewis and (now) Graves are carrying on a great campaign against homosexuals. They all attack them in writing and by wild and inaccurate gossiping . . . It seems that every *modern* writer who happens to be normally sexed, is so overjoyed to find himself normal in one rather unimportant respect, when he is wildly abnormal in all other ways (as are C., W.L., and G.), that he must needs spend all his energy in attacking buggers.

More pleasantly, in the couple of weeks that remained to him Stephen visited old friends (Gabriel, Isaiah, Freeman, Crossman and 'my sweet cousin John [Schuster]'), at Oxford. He also went to Cambridge 'for a day or two. There I met a wonderful boy,' he told Gabriel Carritt. Stephen invited the wonderful boy (Wynard Browne) to visit him in

Germany. Stephen also spent some time at Frognal and with his grandmother (who had been faithfully sending him copies of the *New Statesman*
on his peregrinations round Europe). Humphrey recalls him enthusing
about Germany in the kitchen at Frognal. The house, less full than it
used to be, was still under the reassuring superintendence of Berthella
and Winifred. He read extensively – most influentially *Lady Chatterley's
Lover*, 'which I did not like at first, but which now I am enthusiastic
about', he informed Vita Sackville-West.

The Christmas trip to England confirmed Stephen's sense that he
could not happily live in England; at least, not yet. As he told Lehmann,
just before returning to Germany, 'you must remember how hard I find
it to live in London, because I so hate the whole Game, the whole Push
that we are in'. He had left London without any final meeting with
Lehmann. The other man was hurt at what he took to be a snub, and
wrote an angry letter to await Stephen in Berlin. Stephen civilly thanked
him for not 'bottling up your annoyance'.

Stephen booked a passage from Harwich back to Germany on 29
January. He stopped off *en route* for a couple of days in Hamburg, 'chiefly
spent in seeing Herbert List'. The port city, once so exciting, no longer
interested him. The hedonistic excesses of the previous summer had been
therapeutic (after Oxford), but it now seemed irresponsible to live for
pleasure. There was so much visible suffering. As he told Isaiah on 30
January (while still in the city):

I have little desire now to indulge in my usual transports at Hamburg, particularly as, owing to the economic distress of this country, where formerly the
bodies of prostitutes could be regarded as merchandise, now I cannot think of
them except as carrion: and it is no pleasure to imagine myself as playing the
part of the foreign vulture.

He moved on to Berlin, where, for a few days, 'I lived in a perfectly
foul room for couple of days which stank.' These quarters were arranged
by Christopher as some kind of induction ordeal. Stephen moved on to
the Pension Gramatke, Motzstrasse. His room here was 'excellent', he
told Gabriel Carritt on 10 March. It was only a few hundred yards from
Isherwood's rooms at Nollendorfstrasse. The aspect of the street depressed
him, dominated as it was by 'grey houses whose façades seemed out of
moulds made for pressing enormous concrete biscuits'.

The city's 132 homosexual cafés and clubs, swollen by the ranks of the prostituted unemployed, were no longer joyous in his eyes. Christopher's taste in friends (notably 'Fronny' and Hamilton) raised the horrible suspicion that, perhaps, one could not live this life and remain entirely *unschuldig*, morally intact. He was also, as he told Vita Sackville-West in a letter of 26 April, not sure that Christopher (whom he saw as selfishly 'cactus-like') was good for him:

Knowing, as I do, that if Xtopher is a hot-house plant he is a cactus, and liking him as I do, ought I not perhaps to leave him? I am always divided between the solitary life of the plains, etc. and the more human life of companionship. On the whole though I've decided that the best thing is to stick through thick and thin to the best one can find in one's fellow creatures, even though one is humiliated by having one's weakness and lack of pride exposed by one's dependence on them.

Whatever else, Berlin was culturally exciting in a metropolitan way that Hamburg could never be. In October 1977, almost fifty years after his first visit to Germany, Stephen visited an exhibition of 1920s Berlin and wrote up his reminiscences of the place for the *New York Times*. His and Christopher's Berlin was not, he admonished, the glossy place made chic by the film *Cabaret*. 'There is not a single meal, or club in that movie,' Stephen noted sardonically, 'that Christopher or I could have afforded.' For them, he recalled, with a grand panoramic sweep:

Berlin was an immensely alive, rather common and vulgar place where there was a very active intellectual life of writers and artists whose much-publicized faces (Berlin was always a place presided over by the camera) were to be seen in the Romanisches Café. It was the Berlin of great theatrical productions by Max Reinhardt and the political theatre of Erwin Piscator. We went to Brecht's *Dreigroschenoper* and *Mahagonny*, Max Reinhardt's production of Offenbach's *Tales of Hoffmann* (in which Jean Ross was a member of the chorus) and to expressionist plays by Ernst Toller and Georg Kaiser. But most of all we went to movies . . . *The Cabinet of Dr Caligari* . . . *Metropolis* . . . *M*. . . . *Der Blaue Engel* . . . *Kameradschaft* . . . *Mädchen in Uniform* . . . We looked at the liveliest magazines: *Simplicissimus* . . . *Der Querschnitt* . . . *Die Weltbühne* . . . in musical life this was the period of performances by conductors such as Furtwangler, Klemperer, and Bruno Walter. There were performances of Alban Berg's *Wozzeck*, Kronek's *Johny spielt auf* and the now-forgotten *Die Burgschaft* by Kurt Weill.

Rich as this cultural feast was, Stephen had not come to Berlin for Berlin's sake. In an interview shortly before his death he admitted that what drew him to the city was the 'hypnotic fascination of Christopher's life there'. In a letter to John Lehmann, in February 1931, Stephen nominated Christopher as 'my hero'. The other writer was not averse to hero-worship. There was not much of it going in Berlin in 1931. He accepted, with serene complacency, the role of Stephen's 'mentor', or 'Rule giver'. Christopher describes the sovereign power this gave him over his 'Pupil' with impish glee in *Christopher and his Kind*. He 'enjoyed preaching Lane-Layard to him and he briskly took charge of Stephen's problems as a writer'.

With disconcerting honesty, Christopher describes the teasing malice with which he literally cut the looming Stephen down to size:

The Pupil, striding along beside the brisk, large-headed little figure of the Mentor, keeps bending his beautiful scarlet face downward, lest he shall miss a word, laughing in anticipation as he does so. There are four and a half years between their ages and at least seven inches between their heights. The Pupil already has a stoop, as all tall people must who are eager to hear what the rest of the world is saying. And maybe the Mentor, that little tormentor, actually lowers his voice at times, to make the Pupil bend even lower.

There were other disciplines. Christopher imposed arbitrary prohibitions on his pupil: 'he disapproved of my going to concerts, was bored when I attempted to discuss ideas, and was cold about friends with whom I shared intellectual interests,' Stephen recalled in *World within World*. In *Christopher and his Kind*, Christopher admits to have been 'violently prejudiced against culture worship'. He hated 'the gushings of concert audiences and the holy atmosphere of concerts'. Stephen thought it was 'in some respects' like 'the Nazi attitude'. It was particularly painful when the brutal sarcasm was turned against figures like the pianist Artur Schnabel and the composer Roger Sessions, both of whom Spender had come to know, and revere, in Berlin. He continued to go to concerts (by Schnabel, Bruno Walter and Furtwangler), defying his friend's philistine edicts.

Absolute intellectual surrender to Christopher was corrosive. Stephen was becoming emotionally dependent, 'living precariously off the excitement of being with Isherwood', as he told Plomer, offering his 'feelings on an altar of Christopher's domination'. He told Gabriel Carritt, bleakly, that: 'Most of my life [here] is spent in allowing Christopher and his boys to live for me. I only see them, and I have practically given up having boys myself.' In this condition small woes became great miseries. Minor aches and pains assumed Job-like proportions. 'Toothache is now a pretty continual thing with me,' he informed Gabriel. He was £26 overdrawn and an irrational fear of poverty nagged at him. His £300 allowance was more than enough to live on. It was quite incredibly cold in Berlin (despite his Uncle Alfred's memorial coat).

Stephen describes the vacuous routines of his daily life in these early Berlin months in *World within World*. Rising relatively early, he would leave his bed-sitting-room and stroll the few hundred yards from Motzstrasse to Nollendorfstrasse. His eye would idly play over the comically imperial architecture of the *Viertel*; its 'display of eagles, helmets, shields and prodigious buttocks of armoured babies', overlaid as it all was by a 1930s 'smell of hopeless decay (rather like the smell of the inside of an old cardboard box)'. It was vaguely ominous. There was, he apprehended, 'a sensation of doom to be felt in the Berlin streets', a barely palpable fore-tremor of the Hitlerian horrors to come.

When he arrived at Nollendorfstrasse 22, Herr Spender would announce himself to the formidable Fräulein Thurau – she of the 'pendulous jaws and hanging breasts, the watchdog of the Herr Issyvoo world'. Eventually Christopher would appear, shaving perhaps, to give some peremptory instruction to the pupil who had come so punctually to his *levée*. In ten minutes Christopher would reappear, 'transformed', his hair slicked down, white cuffs projecting, neatly dressed. Always Stephen would be transfixed by his friend's eyes: 'They were the eyes of someone who, when he is a passenger in an aeroplane, thinks that the machine is kept in the air by an act of his will, and that unless he continues to look steadily in front of him it will fall instantly to the ground.'

The young men would adjourn for an 'execrable' breakfast, while Christopher talked of what he was writing. 'We walked a great deal,' Stephen recalls, enjoying Berlin's lakes and woods, admiring 'the relentlessly handsome German youths with their arms round their doughy girls'. A waste. He and Christopher would amuse themselves inventing reviews for their unpublished novels: 'We are not amused . . . We know that it is the pose of young men to be immoral . . . This is in every way the greatest novel I have read this week.' Despite the young-men gaiety, both Christopher and Stephen were – gradually but irreversibly – becoming convinced that 'this life would be swept away'. Stephen, as he records in *World within World*, first learned the name Hitler from Herbert

List who, 'in between the singing of Bavarian songs had told me of an orator from Austria, who had a power of speech which those who listened to him called hypnotic, whilst realizing that he talked nonsense'. That nonsense was now insidiously beginning to tyrannize the streets of Berlin.

Creatively Stephen was at a low ebb in these early 1931 months and the only thing which seems to have sustained him was his novel. He would, he projected, finish it by May. But even *The Temple*, his great literary hope, was the source of nagging and paralysing doubts. He would, he hoped, place the novel with Cobden-Sanderson, who had paid him £75 for it, sight unseen. After that, as he told John Lehmann, 'I don't think I'll ever do any more novel writing, but shall turn to poetry. I don't think I shall publish any new poems for about three years.' That next collection of poems would, he hoped, be published by Faber. He felt 'pushed' by his agents, Curtis Brown, who were eager to capitalize on their author's youthful fame. Meanwhile the Nicolsons and Eliot were 'pulling' him towards poetry.

It cannot have eased relations between Christopher and Stephen that the older writer's wares were somewhat less marketable. No literary agent was 'pushing' him. On 10 March, Christopher left for England so as to be 'on the spot' when Cape's decision was made. Stephen remained in Germany, 'loyally awaiting' the outcome (out of loyalty he postponed a planned trip to the Bavarian Alps with a 'very nice boy' called Harry). If Christopher thought his presence would induce Cape to be merciful he was wrong. *The Memorial* was 'firmly and politely' turned down. In the event of this disaster, Stephen had advised Christopher to deposit the novel with Curtis Brown. They duly gave Christopher an expensive lunch, so raising his hopes 'irrationally'. He returned to Germany on 21 March. The novel travelled on to Faber. Neither journey can have been very cheerful.

Stephen's relationship with the publisher – at least with its senior editor – was increasingly warm. T. S. Eliot wrote to him on 28 March promising a 'speedy' and as he hoped 'painless' response to his (Stephen's) novel. He went on to say:

I am delighted to hear that you have been at the late Beethoven – I have the A minor quartet on the gramophone, and find it quite inexhaustible to study. There is a sort of heavenly or at least more than human gaity [*sic*] about some of his later things which one imagines might come to oneself as the fruit of reconciliation and relief after immense suffering; I should like to get something of that into verse once before I die.

That Eliot should – at this early stage – have confided plans for what would, over a decade later, be the *Four Quartets* witnesses to the extraordinarily high opinion which he had of his young (still only twenty-two-year-old) friend. And, one suspects, to the hopes which he had of him as a poet.

Stephen, as planned, made his trip with Harry in early May – not to the Alps (which proved too expensive) but to Munich. Harry's 'enthusiasm for cooking' proved rather defective and the relationship fell apart, as such relationships routinely did. In June Christopher, in the company of his lover Otto and Wystan, made a holiday excursion to Sellin on the Baltic island of Ruegen. Stephen had arrived some days before the others, settling himself at the Pension Idyll.

The location was truly idyllic, as he told Vita Sackville-West:

Our house is about three minutes from the sea, and on the other side, about three minutes from an inland lake. There is a little strip of wood between us and the sea, and, when the weather is fine, I am woken up by the noise of birds singing in the branches.

It reminded him, he told her, of Norfolk. Stephen had a 'superb work room' at his disposal where he read 'enormous books', notably Henry James ('*The Ambassadors* was a revelation to me,' he told Vita on 29 June).

The trip (and that of the following year) is immortalized by Stephen's 'masturbatory camera', famously the picture of 'Us three'. Christopher was less pleased with it than his two comrades:

Stephen, in the middle, has his arms around Wystan and Christopher and an expression on his face which suggests an off-duty Jesus relaxing with 'these little ones'. Christopher, compared with the others, is such a little one that he looks as if he is standing in a hole.

Stephen also took some 'animally beautiful' photographs of Otto. He was working, as always, on *The Temple*, 'though he spent much of his time out of doors', he reassured his English friends.

His chief recreations, he mischievously informed John Lehmann, 'are lying in the sun and bathing and looking vainly on the pier for boys'.

Humphrey spent a few days at Ruegen and took some 'magnificent photos' as well. The weather was deliciously sunny. Wystan (who 'preferred rainy weather') worked grumpily in his shuttered room on *The Orators* – in which he created his own photograph album, notably a vignette of Stephen:

> Came summer like a flood, did never greediest gardener
>> Make blossoms flusher:
> Sunday meant lakes for many, a browner body,
>> Beauty from burning:
> Far out in the water two heads discussed the position,
> Out of the reeds like a fowl jumped the undressed German,
> And Stephen signalled from the sand dunes like a wooden madman
>> 'Destroy this temple.'

'Wooden madman' is odd.

Isherwood (who testily complained that he had spent all the time alone in *his* room, masturbating) left a memorial of summer 1931 in the short story 'On Ruegen Island'. It opens with a pen picture of the

> birch trees . . . the rutted sandy earth . . . the zig-zag path which brings you out abruptly to the edge of some sandy cliffs with the beach below you, and the tepid shallow Baltic lying almost at your feet.

Somehow he could never enjoy the resort as much as Stephen, with his vibrant animal energies and inexhaustible intellectual enthusiasms.

On 15 June, Stephen finished his novel (again) and sent it off to Curtis Brown, who promptly passed it on to Cobden-Sanderson. He solemnly promised the Nicolsons (always keener that Stephen should attend to his poetry) that 'whatever happens to this novel, I won't write another – not for a long time, at all events'. It was during this holiday in Sellin that Stephen devised what he described to William Plomer as his 'very direct' mode of poetic composition – which resulted in the anthems 'Oh Young Men', and 'I think continually'. He was, he said, 'so excited about writing poetry that I find it difficult to sleep'.

Christopher decided, rather grumpily, to leave Sellin in early July. Wystan had already gone. Stephen decided (as he told Lehmann) that 'I can't face being in a Nazi north-German village quite alone'. He was toying with the idea of a trip to Athens, to join Willy Plomer. In the

event, he returned to Berlin with Christopher. He commemorated the
holiday with a fine *poème de départ*, 'The Sign *Faehre nach Wilm*':

> At the end of our Ruegen holiday, that night,
> I lay awake. Waves' ceaseless fretful scansion
> By imagination scourged, rose to the height
> Of the town's roar, trafficking apprehension.

Christopher and Stephen were back in Berlin on 13 July, when Bruening
formed an emergency coalition of the Right. The city was *awful*, he told
Plomer. Weimar Germany was manifestly falling apart. 'It was,' Stephen
told Lehmann, 'like a day of public mourning.'

'All in all,' Christopher concluded, 'this Ruegen visit wasn't a success.'
There had been squabbling when faithless Otto took off with girls from
the local casino. Christopher cut his toe badly on a piece of tin 'and
was a semi-cripple for several weeks after his return to Berlin'. His bad
mood was compounded by suspense over the fate of *The Memorial*, which
was turned down by Faber, after an interminable delay, in late June. The
manuscript was passed on, like a bad penny, to Lehmann at the Hogarth
Press – through Stephen's good offices. If they turned it down, Christopher
might have to face the uncomfortable conclusion that he had chosen
the wrong line of work. He should have stuck to medicine. It was an
unhappy period at Nollendorfstrasse.

The American writer and musician Paul Bowles was in Berlin shortly
after the Ruegen holiday and has left a vivid pen-picture of the young
poet, in 'Byronesque' pose, with his shirt unbuttoned to the waist, 'blonde
and sunburnt, standing in the middle of his room at the top of the house
in Motzstrasse' with the setting sun streaming through the window,
looking 'as though he was on fire'. Bowles found the English writers
too closely knit with each other for his taste – they seemed to converse
in a code from which he was excluded. Christopher opportunistically
took the American's surname for his 'Sally'.

In August, Christopher and Stephen went their separate ways for
the remainder of the summer vacation. Christopher went to England,
where, through Stephen, he met Lehmann, Plomer and, most valuably,
E. M. Forster. Stephen went to Salzburg, where he was reunited as in
previous years with Isaiah Berlin and Isaiah's young friend Michael
Corley. Music and Oxford gossip were a wonderful tonic and a welcome
change from the *Lokale* and the seedy *Kino*. The attraction of the

performances at Salzburg for Stephen and Isaiah are described by Michael Ignatieff:

Salzburg, in political terms, was an anti-Bayreuth. When Toscanini refused to play the *Giovinezza*, the fascist hymn, and was assaulted by fascist thugs in Milan in the 1920s, and when he refused to play at Bayreuth, he became a hero to anti-fascists throughout Europe. In Salzburg in 1935 he gave the famous perform-ance of Beethoven's *Fidelio*, where – as both Spender and Berlin remembered – the prisoners' chorus, as the men cast off their chains and rose up into the light, seemed to give voice to that 'humanistic piety' that was everywhere under attack in the Europe of the 1930s.

Otherwise Stephen did not much like the Austrian town. Fascists bullied their way round the streets. It was physically uncomfortable. He was obliged to live in an 'inferior' *Gasthof* without running water. But it was cheap and he planned to remain there for the whole of August, saving money, listening to good music, and writing.

There were other recreations. He had brought with him 'a very nice schoolboy from Hamburg'. The young man had inspired a poem which communicates Stephen's infatuation rather than any clear image:

> Abrupt and charming mover,
> Your pointed eyes under lit leaves
> Your light hair, your smile,
> I watch burn in a land
> Bright in the care of night
> And protected by my hand.

After two weeks, the schoolboy turned less nice and Stephen was obliged to 'behave as harshly as I can' to him; which seems not to have been particularly harsh. He invited John Lehmann to join him, which he did in the first week in August. John was suffering from a 'very nasty . . . unofficial sort of illness'. It was, evidently, a tense encounter. Lehmann did not stay very long.

On 23 July, Stephen had received the bad news that Cobden-Sanderson had turned down *The Temple*, 'on the expert advice of their legal adviser'. The novel was too dangerous for England. They accompanied rejection with 'a most tearful letter'. The manuscript was doing the rounds with Cape – Edward Garnett had made some encouraging noises. If 'Cape do not dare to look into the dragon's mouth of British Law', Stephen promised the novel to Lehmann at the Hogarth Press. 'Would publishers be any braver,' he asked the publisher, 'if they had shown the MS round to a few people and obtained guarantees that, if it were attacked, the Nicolsons and a few people like that would stand by it?' – as Virginia Woolf and the Nicolsons had stood by *The Well of Loneliness* three years earlier? Stephen was 'sick' at the thought of *The Temple* being so unwanted. There were, as he told Lehmann, more material considerations:

Financially, this puts me in a very bad way, and in other ways it is much worse: for I had thought of my novel as a kind of declaration of independence, and I had imagined that its publication would give me some sort of position from which to consider my next work. Besides this, I love the *Temple*: and I often lie awake thinking of what a nice book it is.

In his innocence, Stephen had sent a carbon copy of *The Temple* to Uncle Alfred. 'JAS' had refused to read the profane thing, sending his nephew 'a very threatening letter'. Another rejection. Cape kept the MS barely long enough to read it before returning it as something obnoxious.

By 1 September, *The Temple* was on its rejected way to the Hogarth Press. Among his friends, the jury was out. Wystan liked it; or said he did. Shyah Berlin 'is of the party who think it should be rewritten'. Lehmann and Isherwood were enthusiastic. Despite the rejections, Stephen's ideas were already forming for his next novel, dealing with his childhood experiences, tentatively called 'Letter to a dead self'. It would eventually emerge, ten years later, as *The Backward Son*.

Poetry was going better than prose. While at Salzburg, lifted by music, he wrote the valedictory and thunderous piece with which he thought he might conclude his Faber book, when it came out in January 1933:

> From all these events, from the slump, from the war, from the boom,
> From the Italian holiday, from the skirring
> Of the revolving light for an adventurer,
> From the crowds in the square at dusk, from the shooting,
> From the loving, from the dying, however we prosper in death.

The poem – with its tremendous imagery and paratactic looseness of form – embodied Stephen's current belief, as he told Lehmann, that 'there is no reason why we should not bring mechanics, Communism and all the contemporary world within the range of poetry. To my mind that is the *duty* of the poet.'

At Salzburg Stephen received a flattering invitation from Eliot to review regularly for the *Criterion*. There was now a degree of familiarity between them. Eliot had instructed him to drop the 'Mr' in his letters. Stephen returned to Berlin on 22 August, earlier than projected, but he was relieved to be 'away from that frightful climate' (the Austrian town was not sunny enough for him). He moved in with Christopher at Nollendorfstrasse for what would be a brief stopover. He may have come back a day or two early to meet, for the first time, the Communist schoolteacher Edward Upward (Isherwood's close friend from Cambridge) on his way back from the USSR. The encounter is recalled in *World within World* (where Upward is masked as 'Allen Chalmers'). Stephen was taken with Upward's 'miniature sensitive beauty of features . . . his finely formed fingers of a chiseller's or wood-engraver's hand'. He was less taken with his finely-formed politics. A card-carrying Communist, Upward quizzed Stephen on issues of socialism. When Stephen returned 'stumbling answers' expressing his hatred of all forms of totalitarian oppression, Upward listened intently, smiled to himself, and muttered 'Gandhi.'

Upward's firmness of political conviction evidently made an impression. Immediately after the August meeting Stephen informed John Lehmann, 'I think we have all become communists,' adding, however, 'I have been hesitating for a few months, and I still can't *quite* admire the virtues of the Communist Party.' He would read all the stuff up when he got home, he vowed. About the current state of British politics he had no second thoughts. Ramsay MacDonald's coalition with Baldwin (the politics of the 'jellyfish' as he called it) was disgusting: 'it seems as if English policy is now dictated by American bankers'.

Stephen's own income was, of course, solely derived from (British) bankers. He was a *rentier*, that most despised animal in the Marxist menagerie. It was something that must have uneasily crossed his mind in conversation with *engagés* like Upward. None the less, he became over the next few months a regular attender at the Communist *Lokal*, the Bunte. His friends, he told Vita Sackville-West in December, were now 'almost exclusively . . . young communists'. Christopher was, however, 'less class conscious'. Or less impulsive.

Stephen made a trip back to Britain in the first week of September. There was immediate good news: the Hogarth Press had agreed to take Christopher's much-rejected novel. Stephen – who had worked hard for this result – phoned Christopher's mother to tell her. 'He must have wanted,' Christopher deduced, 'to let her have the pleasure of telegraphing the news to Christopher, which was truly considerate of him.'

Stephen's main reason for coming to London was to consult with Faber (T. S. Eliot, that was) about the contents of the poetry book. His poems were coming out prominently in magazines and – even before his first proper book had been published – he was a lion in the London literary world. Janet Adam-Smith had been appointed assistant literary editor of the new magazine the *Listener*, with responsibility for poetry. On a train journey to Cambridge she asked a friend travelling with her, John Maud, who were the 'young poets' to watch at the university. Maud had been Dean at University College while Stephen was there, in the fraught Marston months, and was one of the privileged recipients of *Twenty Poems*. He enthused about its author. Adam-Smith requested some poems from Stephen and prevailed upon her (somewhat reluctant) editor to print them. They began to come out in the magazine on 25 November 1931, with 'I think continually' (in the *Listener* it has the last line, 'And left the air signed with their vivid honour'. Shortly after, Christopher brilliantly suggested the transposition 'vivid air'). At the same period, J. C. Squire at the *Adelphi* took 'How strangely this sun', and Eliot, at the *Criterion*, continued his promotion of Stephen's career by publishing 'The Prisoners'. The name 'Spender', if not in 'letters inch-tall', was everywhere.

From comments in letters, it seems likely that Stephen was at this period seriously contemplating repatriation and a 'New Life'. He was ready for his 'London phase', as he jestingly told Lehmann. He was not sure he could stand 'the biting, vicious cold' of another Berlin winter. He was confident (with his friend Lehmann in his corner) that the Hogarth Press would surely take *The Temple*.

In the event the Hogarth Press's nerve was not up to taking it on. They were as gutless as every other London publishing house. Lehmann informed Stephen in mid-October that the 'Woolves', Leonard and Virginia (whom the author had not yet met) had decided to reject his novel. It was a bitter disappointment – doubly so since the publisher had evidently raised the author's hopes unreasonably. Stephen was devastated. The rejection, his last serious hope of publication in England, meant the extinction of two years' work. He could not but be angry with the friend who had raised his hopes. 'I think it is better we do not meet,' Stephen told Lehmann, frostily, on 18 October, 'as I'm afraid it would be upsetting to us both to do so.'

The shock of *The Temple*'s being rejected by Hogarth – on the grounds of its being too frank a treatment of forbidden topics – steeled Stephen's resolve to return to Berlin. Better that city's winter cold than England's moral chill. There would be no 'London phase', at least not yet. He decided to go back to Germany at the end of October. When he returned to Berlin, Stephen proposed, might he not move in with Christopher? Christopher blew cool on the proposal. 'I think I could find you something cheaper two doors away,' he wrote: 'I think it is better if we don't all live right on top of each other, don't you? I believe that was partly the trouble at Ruegen.'

In the event, Stephen moved into Kleistrasse 15. Despite the landlord's name ('Weiss') it was a 'very dark . . . sordid and bad . . . room' – so dark that he could not take photos in it ('sad', he told Lehmann, 'as I was wanting to learn portrait photography'). Compared to shabby-imperial Motzstrasse, his new room was in an 'inferior' quarter of the city. There was a good reason for this come-down. Stephen was no longer as well off as he had been. No Englishman abroad was. On 21 September 1931 Britain came off the gold standard. The effect was calamitous for expatriates living on sterling. Stephen's £300 p.a. Schuster inheritance would never again go as far as it had.

The rift with John Lehmann was mended temporarily when the publisher, evidently hoping to soothe his aggrieved author, came up with an interesting proposal. The previous year Michael Roberts, a thirty-one-year-old schoolteacher with a love of poetry, had moved from Newcastle to London to take up a position as senior maths master at the Mercers' school in Holborn. Roberts had published poems and articles in the *Spectator*, the *TLS*, and the *Listener* (whose literary editor, Janet Adam-Smith, he would marry in June 1935). Modestly successful himself, Roberts was excited by the 'new poets' of the time, who, as he generously realized, had greater talents than he did – particularly Auden, Empson, MacNeice, Day-Lewis and Spender. He conceived the idea of an anthology to publicize their work; a collection that would weld the leading spirits of the modern age into a 'school', or 'movement'. This would eventually take its published form as *New Signatures* (everything was 'new' in the 1930s, Stephen wryly observed). Roberts had, as Janet Adam-Smith recalls, simply walked into the offices of the Hogarth Press and 'sold' the venture to John Lehmann. When it came out in February 1932, with a thirteen-page polemical introductory essay by Roberts, *New Signatures*, more than anything, created what was in subsequent years hailed as the 'Auden Generation' and jeered at as 'MacSpaunday'.

As he had with Stephen's poems published in magazines like the *Listener*, Eliot good-naturedly agreed to release eight poems from the forthcoming Faber collection for prior, or simultaneous, issue in *New Signatures* – a volume to be published by his principal rival. The concession was the more generous since Lehmann picked a number of plums from Faber's pie: 'The Express', 'My Parents', 'Who live under the shadow', 'The Prisoners', 'Without that One Clear Aim', 'I think continually', 'After they have tired', and 'How strangely this sun'.

New Signatures appeared in February 1932. The effect, with many of his poems having been published in leading magazines over the previous months, was that Stephen seemed ubiquitous. Like Byron in March 1812, he awoke and found himself famous. If not famous, Christopher was at least on the literary map again. *The Memorial* finally came out in February 1932, as well, and also under the Hogarth imprint. Bound copies arrived in Berlin on 20 February. There were one or two good reviews. As authors Stephen, Auden and Christopher were running neck and neck. Of the three, however, Stephen had temporarily nudged ahead.

'Things in Berlin are very hard,' Stephen told Lehmann on 11 January:

but at the same time there is a feeling of the poverty not being so shut-in and horrifyingly compressed as it is in London. The sufferings of the poor here are the sufferings of Germany: they are a collection of individual cases of extreme misery. I don't see what one can do quite except to get on with one's own job, and if one's job is writing to try and relate that to the world we live in.

He has, he says in the same letter, broken off with all his Communist acquaintances (of whom he knew 'a lot'); 'almost the only person I see is Christopher'.

By 'persons' he meant equals. In that separate compartment of his life where he kept his love affairs he was, he told Lehmann, 'very lucky in having an extraordinarily nice boy, much the nicest I've ever had here'. The son of Russian *émigrés*, Georgi was 'complete Berlin'. As the relationship stretched into months, Georgi – for all his niceness – irritated Stephen, however, by demanding to be 'mothered'. 'I cannot be responsible for waifs and strays,' Stephen observed rather testily, as the glow of their early relationship wore off in January. 'I wish he were more sexy,' he elsewhere complained. 'No, he is not a bit literary, I'm afraid,' he told

Lehmann. On other occasions he realized that he was being unjust to the young fellow, 'however a Berlin street boy can put up with a good deal of injustice, I'm afraid'.

Harold Nicolson came out in late January. 'I suppose that we shall survey all the dens of Berlin,' Stephen wearily told Lehmann. 'It would have been so much nicer if he'd asked Christopher and me to lunch and given us a very delicious meal. But anyhow I am genuinely glad to see him, as I like him.' Nicolson visited Stephen in 'sordid' Kleistrasse. There he sat reading Stephen's latest poems 'amidst the dirt, the stench of condensed milk, and without troubling to listen to the noise of bullets whistling in the streets outside', observing only, 'The grammar of that sentence might be improved.' The demonstration of English sang-froid amused Stephen hugely.

A recurrent note in Stephen's letters over these months in early 1932 is financial hardship. In January he began to give conversation lessons at the Marxist School ('learning very rapidly to speak in broken English', as he jested). He was, he told Lehmann, 'obliged to publish everything I can, as I find I can't pay off my debts from my income'. He spelled out his exact financial affairs on 11 February in the context of apologizing for selling a poem that John had particularly wanted for a forthcoming anthology ('the aerodrome poem') to *Life and Letters*. 'I live on £25 a month.' Of this £4 went to Georgi; £4 went on rent; £8 went on food 'and the necessities of the day'. There were, of course, 'extras'. He simply 'cannot live under my income to pay off a month's overdraft'.

In March he moved under financial duress into a 'cheaper and much nicer room away from the centre of Berlin'. The new accommodation was at Lützowplatz 10, bei Voss, Berlin W 62. Rather forlornly he asked Lehmann on 20 February if there were any possibility of his 'representing' the Hogarth Press in Berlin. If that was a non-starter, would Lehmann ask 'Miss Adam Smith or any other person in authority . . . to try and get reviewing for me?' 'That swine' Desmond MacCarthy at the *New Statesman* had not, for almost a year, replied to the offer of some poems: 'If one were trying to sell coffee no firm would treat one with the same insulting rudeness as a man like that does if one tries to sell him poetry.' There was some relief from financial pressure when *New Signatures* came out in February, bringing a welcome ten guineas and great *éclat*. Commissions flowed in.

Spring was late in Berlin. There was still slush and snow in April – not to mention jackboots and bullets. Stephen attended an Iron Front

meeting in early March, where 100,000 Communists displayed their
metallic solidarity. He got wet through and caught a bad cold which
left him weak and feverish for weeks. The political scene in Germany
was ever more ominous. On 10 March, Spender wrote to Eliot, saying:

The presidential election is in full swing here, and the most terrific propaganda
for Hindenburg is going on. I have an uneasy feeling that perhaps people will
be sensible enough to realize that he is a complete puppet, and that the only
motive for voting for him is one of blue funk at what the other candidates
might do if they came into power. It is quite possibly insanely stupid of the
middle parties not to have put up a young active man instead of someone who
is a puppet whose only qualification is the quite superstitious reverence everyone
has for him. Heaven knows what will happen here if he is not elected. Hitler
is so passionately hated that it is even possible the moderates will put in the
Communist at the second vote rather than him. However, almost as soon as
this letter reaches you the results will be known. Also the idea that Hitler might
be elected at the first vote has only occurred to me very recently as being a
disturbing possibility.

Hindenburg failed to achieve the expected walkover, gaining only 49.6
per cent on the first vote against the Nazis' 30.1 per cent. He was forced
into a second ballot, when he got the necessary absolute majority of 53
per cent; but the Nazis increased their share to 36.6 per cent, which
Hitler (correctly) regarded as a victory.

In April 1932, Christopher went off to Mohrin (a village east of Berlin)
with Erwin Hansen and Heinz Neddermeyer (Heinz was Otto's successor
– his relationship with Christopher would last for almost a decade).
Francis Turville-Petre had a house (more a primitive log cabin) by the
Mohrinsee. 'For some reason,' Stephen told Lehmann, 'they are very
anxious I shouldn't come.'

More plaintively, he wrote to William Plomer that being banned from
the trip was 'a great blow to me'. So much so, that he contemplated
leaving Germany altogether:

I would come home except that whenever I think of returning to Frognal I
have the same nightmare in which I dream that I am home and everything is
black and I realize that I will never be able to get away again. This dream is
so persistent that I really now take it as a warning.

Christopher (very belatedly) explained why they hadn't wanted Stephen at Mohrin in *Christopher and his Kind*: '[Christopher] hated having Stephen and Stephen's camera invade the scene of his love affair with Heinz . . . It was Stephen, not Christopher, who ought to have said "I am a camera" in those days.'

As things now stood, Stephen would stay in Berlin till June 1932. Then he would give up his room in Lützowplatz. The landlord, Voss, was a 'Nazi of the most unpleasant, cowardly, bullying type'. He might perhaps join Humphrey and his friends in the Austrian Tyrol. (Humphrey was currently staying with him in Berlin.) Georgi would be left with a weekly allowance large enough to keep him from starvation and small enough to keep him from temptation ('girls'). Ten marks would do it, he thought. Stephen would work in the mountains on his Faber book of poems. Or perhaps he would go to England. It was all very vague. One thing that was clear was that he and Christopher were not entirely happy in each other's company at the moment – although he assured Lehmann that they had *not* quarrelled. After Mohrin, Christopher travelled on to England where he met J. R. Ackerley, who was editor of the *Listener* at this time (an 'aesthete in a trench-coat', Stephen later described him). E. M. Forster entrusted Christopher, as he had earlier Stephen, with a copy of his homosexual testament, *Maurice*, in return for *The Memorial*. He returned to Berlin at the end of April. The reunion with Stephen was warm, if brief.

In early May, Stephen at last received permission to visit Francis Turville-Petre in his house by the lake in East Prussia. Turville-Petre – a doomed, fantastic, and inspirational figure – survives as Wystan's 'Fronny' and in Christopher's Berlin stories as 'Ambrose'. A talented anthropologist, he was a religious fanatic, alcoholic and terrifically self-destructive. Stephen rather liked Fronny's East Prussian retreat (Christopher hated its 'steppe-like' bleakness). He evidently liked Turville-Petre as well. There was some thought that he might lease Fronny's London flat in Chester Street, from 1 November, for £85 a year. The lease on Frognal was about to expire. Stephen was not sorry, much as the Hampstead family house had meant to him. 'Half my income goes to 10 Frognal,' he told Lehmann. The Chester Street plan fell through, however. In other ways Stephen was uncertain about the future. 'I'm not sure whether it wouldn't be better to sell everything,' he told Lehmann, 'and live nowhere fixed . . . London seems so impossible; more impossible the more I think about it.'

By this stage, Stephen's summer plans had firmed up. He would go to Sellin at Insel Ruegen on 1 June. Humphrey and a friend would join him there in the middle of the month. How long they would stay, he did not know. He (Stephen) would probably stay until the end of August 'in order to save money, as it is very cheap'. One could live there on 7s. 6d. a day at the wonderfully named Pension Idyll. Money was still the pressing consideration. His income was sadly and inexorably deteriorating with the erosion of the value of sterling and falling stock values. Christopher would probably join them in July, or later. He hoped that Lehmann would come – perhaps in the first fortnight in June? (He did come.) Georgi would be dispatched off 'with a club of Russian boy scouts'. This sensible arrangement made Stephen feel 'rather like a mid-Victorian parent'. In the relaxed solitude of the Ruegen holiday Stephen intended to think out his future authorial plans. 'I have no idea whether I shall write any more novels,' he had told Lehmann. 'I have very little idea what I shall do.' T. S. Eliot was encouraging him (for the sake of his writing as much as anything else) to return to England – or, at least, to leave Germany.

Stephen arrived at Ruegen on 1 June, having effectively burned his bridges in Berlin. He had vacated his room. The weather was fine, he was 'quite alone', and was looking forward to his first visitor, John Lehmann, who arrived on 7 June, remaining only a week or so. Stephen met a nice boy, living on the beach. 'Occasionally I have him, in a rather desultory sort of way,' he told Lehmann, but he was careful not to encourage him with extravagant gifts, 'otherwise he would never leave Sellin so long as I am here'. He had become world-wise about such things. Life on the beach for such boys struck Stephen as idyllic: 'The poor really *are* better off here you know,' he mused, 'even when they are poorer.' Or, as Scott Fitzgerald might have put it, the poor were different.

He was, in fact, rather impatient with emotional interruptions, since the desire to write poems had again taken him. It had even momentarily taken his mind off the fate of *The Temple*. His mood this summer was erratic in the extreme. Solitude did not suit him and precipitated attacks of hypochondria and depression. Both he and Lehmann had come down with what he took to be some form of food poisoning ('drains?' Stephen wondered). The summer was 'the worst ever': never-ending cloud and rain.

Christopher arrived at the end of June with Heinz, which lifted

Stephen's spirits. And the weather at last improved. Humphrey arrived in July, which added even more to the general gaiety. Things in Berlin were, by contrast, anything but gay. Martial law had been declared. The Pension Idyll had been invaded by hordes of schoolchildren ('perhaps he could get *us* some boys', quipped Christopher). Stephen and company were obliged to move to an Evangelical establishment, where 'the coffee is made of petroleum'. But, with this company, he could be cheerful even about that.

Among the visitors to Ruegen that summer was Christopher's friend Wilfrid Israel (the 'Bernhard Landauer' of the Berlin stories), 'an elegant, distinguished, dark-eyed young man, whose family owned one of the great department stores in Berlin'. At thirty-two Wilfrid was somewhat older and considerably richer. He was, as Christopher recalled, 'a smiler who seldom laughed'. On a walk with Stephen in the forests at Sellin, Wilfrid outlined a plan of Gandhiesque passive resistance for 'the Jews when Hitler seized Germany – an event which he seemed to anticipate as certain'. Spender had, to this point, observed but not formulated his strategy of resistance to the totalitarian nightmare represented in Hitler (a demagogue of the Bavarian cellars). After his conversations with Israel, which made an indelible impression on him, 'I decided that I must study the Nazi point of view: so I bought the Nazi programme and a good deal of the literature of Goebbels and the other Nazi propagandists . . . after I had read this literature, I knew that I hated the Nazis.' Israel eventually escaped certain death by fleeing to Britain.

They returned to Berlin on 12 July. Five days later Stephen travelled on to Salzburg, where he remained until the middle of August. Despite the presence of Shyah, there were gloomy moments. He now accepted that despite all the revisions he had subjected it to, his novel was wholly unpublishable in England. Any firm that took it on 'would probably be raided by the police'. If not (as Faber had discovered), any publisher foolhardy enough to put their imprint on *The Temple* would be sued for libel by the infuriated Erich Alport (to whom Eliot had prudently sent the manuscript). In Salzburg Stephen lost his camera and his mackintosh – much needed, since it was sopping wet, even in July. What else could he lose, he plaintively asked Plomer, 'perhaps my manhood?' 'There will almost certainly be a revolution in Germany this winter,' he told his English friends. The prospect did not add to his good humour.

Before returning to England on 18 August, Stephen spent a few days in Berlin with Humphrey and Winifred ('my stepmother', as he nowadays liked to describe her). Georgi he found, after his virtuous boy-scouting, to be 'plumper and much more attractive'. Stephen by contrast had become extraordinarily thin. By late August, Stephen was again back in England, as was Christopher.

The main professional business in hand was to see his poems through the press. Faber had announced publication in January 1933. These were also the last days at Frognal. The Spenders, after fifteen years, would leave Hampstead. Ella, who married the local postman, and Winifred, who set up house with her retired sister, would go their separate ways. Bertha, with Captain Devoto, agreed to stay on and look after what fragment of the family survived. She and Christine started looking for somewhere else. When Christine failed to do so to Bertha's satisfaction, the servant complained to Mrs Schuster. There was a painful interview in which Christine was humiliated and reduced to tears. She went her own way for several years (she had converted to Catholicism the year before, and had friends in the church who would put her up). Humphrey was happily installed in his bachelor flat at Upper Montagu Street. Michael, Stephen and Bertha took on rather uncomfortable accommodation at 43 Boundary Road in north-west London.

It was a sad period in the family history, and there were tedious things to be done about accumulated belongings. Stephen wrote a poem on leaving Frognal, 'Hampstead Autumn'. It begins:

> In the fat autumn evening street
> Hands from my childhood stretch out
> And ring muffin bells.

After cataloguing a range of nostalgic childhood memories, the poet defiantly affirms, 'now I reject them all'. It was probably easier said than done. Severance from the 'obstreperous' Georgi was also proving difficult. Stephen was obliged to return to Berlin for a couple of weeks at the end of October to clear up some problems in that department.

By the end of 1932, the relationship between Christopher and Stephen had broken down. Stephen (guardedly) recalls the triggering event as something quite minor – conversational 'indiscretions' on his part, exacerbated by professional jealousy: 'He disliked seeing me transformed from his Berlin disciple into a London literary figure. Our quarrel was, on the surface, as simple as this.' The explosion came at William Plomer's house. Christopher made his irritation with Stephen obvious to the company – evidently directing some cutting remarks at his friend. The next day, Stephen went to the house of Christopher's mother in Kensington, where his friend was staying, to demand an explanation. Christopher (as Stephen later recalled) was contrite and insisted that there was no feeling on his side that they should not continue as before – as inseparable comrades in Berlin. Christopher adds 'a memory of my own. Stephen, annoyed by Christopher's evasiveness, exclaimed, "If we're going to part, at least let's part like men." To which Christopher replied, with a bitchy smile, "But Stephen we *aren't* men."' 'The next day,' Stephen recalls, 'I received a letter from him saying that if I returned to Berlin he would not do so, that my life was poison to him, that I lived on publicity, that I was intolerably indiscreet, etc.' It was clearly the end of the road. Stephen resolved that they must part. Christopher returned to Berlin on the last day of September, 1932.

With Isherwood gone, Stephen found himself adrift in London in the tense interval between returning the last proofs and the imminent publication (on 19 January) of *Poems, 1933*. It was in other ways a period of introspection, stock-taking, and consultation about his literary future with friends and advisers, such as Virginia Woolf, Isaiah and Eliot, as to what his literary future should be. Georgi had not been a success. Like his predecessors, he had turned out to be a 'sneak'. Stephen never quite got over the sight of him laboriously copying out his signature, clearly intending to put the skill to use in forging cheques.

The relationship with Christopher was, as it seemed, dead – at least in its former intimate intensity. This was more serious. There were other boys (too many of them), but only one Christopher. As a mark of their 'estrangement', as Stephen called it, he excised the dedication from his proof copy of *Poems, 1933*. The act evidently hurt him more than it did his friend. Christopher was, as always, the cooler of the two. 'Of course I quite understand about the dedication,' he wrote on 14 November. 'In fact, I'd half thought of writing and suggesting it to you myself.' Stephen then asked Curtius to accept the dedication. The German scholar – aware of political dangers – prudently declined.

The international situation was indeed ever more dangerous. In the elections of 6 November 1932 the Nazis lost ground in the Reichstag. 'Berlin is red,' Christopher triumphantly (and prematurely) crowed to his friends, garlanding his letters to Stephen with the slogan '*Rot Front*' and a hammer and sickle. The power struggle that was developing in Germany led to ugly scenes in the Berlin streets. Christopher wrote to

Stephen on 3 November, describing a band of Nazi thugs beating up and blinding a youth by jabbing him in the eyes with their flag banners: 'Six policemen were standing about twenty yards away, but they carefully didn't see anything.' The Communist triumph proved shortlived. Hitler was appointed Chancellor on 30 January 1933. The closures of the bars, clubs, homosexual haunts and political halls began and the diaspora from Berlin (for those lucky enough to get away) began.

What was Stephen to do? His relationship with Georgi was finished. Nor, if he were honest, did he want other friends of the same street-level kind. His relationship with Christopher was fragile. In such circumstances travel – anywhere – was his favourite remedy. On 27 September he told John Lehmann, 'I am planning to go to Ragusa (Dubrovnik) for the winter where I shall do some work, and, I hope, save money.' 'I am not going to live in London,' he declared with some firmness. Nor, if he ever did, would it be in the old 'bourgeois' way of things: 'Later, I shall live in England if the Workers' Education Association want to make use of me, but not in London.'

Stephen did not in the event go to Dubrovnik, on being told by Gerald Heard – Wystan's sophisticated friend – that the climate there was chilly during the winter. Nor did he make any preliminary application to join the earnest ranks of the Workers' Education Association, bringing culture to the English industrial hinterland. While discouraging him from Yugoslavia, Gerald Heard recommended Spain. A friend of Heard's, Chris Wood, knew a young German ('a marvellous young boy') in Barcelona whom he was sure Stephen would like. Wood was a rich dilettante who entertained generously in his flat in Portman Square. He had first met Stephen and Christopher in Berlin, through his (Wood's) association with the Hirschfeld Institute.

To Humphrey's amazement Stephen 'went hurtling off to Barcelona' on Wood's assurance about the unknown German. 'It was very typical of him,' his brother adds. Stephen was in Barcelona by 20 October. The city was 'fever-hot' with political unrest. Quixotically Stephen told Isaiah Berlin that he intended 'to get through some work whilst I am here'. He was consumed with 'remorse' over his failure to move ahead with his writing. The paralysis in part derived from an uncertainty over literary role and ambiguous feelings about what, in black moods, he called 'the literary racket'. It did not help that the advisers whose opinion he trusted most seemed to give contradictory advice: Eliot advised against the writing of fiction and Virginia Woolf encouraged him to continue with the novel. He had already begun the routine of fast reviewing (five pieces for the *Criterion* alone in autumn and winter 1932). Editors liked him because he was prompt and wrote well. Reviewing kept his name in the reading public's mind, which was also helpful for a poet. But it sapped his creative energy. In *World within World* Stephen outlines his reviewer's credo: 'I do not think I reviewed much better or much worse than most reviewers, and I tried to be fair.'

In Barcelona Stephen promptly met up with the young German who had been recommended to him by Wood. Hellmut Schroeder was 'awfully nice', Stephen told John Lehmann. He is described at some length as Till, in the story 'The Burning Cactus':

The young man wore no jacket over his light grey shirt, nearly matched by the darker grey of his flannel trousers. His open collar revealed a graceful eager neck: he had a fair but not unblemished complexion, long fair hair, good features, large eyes and sensitive nostrils. The refinedness of his features was purely external: small spots on the skin, a rubbed redness of the neck, a loose-ness of the lips, the overarched nostrils, and slightly bloodshot eyes showed places where the surface seemed already tarnished by something altogether coarser and more violent which threatened in time to alter the whole face. His hands were shapely and yet tactile, in contrast to his heavy lips.

Humphrey, who knew Hellmut, confirms this as an accurate sketch, although he struck the other Spender as unpleasantly 'effete' (he had a penchant for transvestism). He was not bright ('Dunkelmut' would be a more appropriate name, Christopher quipped) and spoke virtually no English. Stephen conversed with him in his fluent but 'incredibly ungram-matical' German. As Humphrey recalls, Stephen thought it would be 'too Michael-like' to master correct grammar.

At twenty-two Hellmut was no 'boy'; Stephen himself was only a year older. In the impulsive way that would mark his relationships over the next few years, Stephen immediately proposed setting up house with him. A cocktail waiter in Berlin, Schroeder had been recruited to come to work as house-servant for an expatriate doctor in Barcelona. His employer lived in an ultra-modern apartment built 'in the new German style' with a roof garden for sunbathing. Hellmut's role was, apparently, to be decoratively German around the flat, mix drinks, and be available when required for sex. When Stephen met him, Hellmut had been in Barcelona for six months and was bitterly unhappy in his work.

Almost as soon as they began living together Hellmut was diagnosed as having a stomach ulcer. Stephen was extravagantly solicitous and only too willing to act 'as nurse and hand-holder, tasks for which nature has made me peculiarly well suited', as he archly told Plomer. 'It really is a good thing that I am here,' he told John Lehmann:

because Hellmut knows no one else hardly in Barcelona . . . His job is to look after the flat of a very rich business man who is German and a sadist. This man keeps two boys and the boys of course try to show Hellmut in every possible way that he is only a servant. At night Hellmut hears the man beating one of the boys in the next room. He has been eight months here quite alone in the household, so it is no wonder he has got ill now.

This extraordinary ménage furnished the title story to *Burning Cactus*.

Stephen took Hellmut away from Barcelona on 17 November on a cargo boat to Malaga. It took four days to limp along the coast at eight knots ('whatever that may be', Stephen added in his account of the trip to Lehmann). On the third day the holiday turned sour. There was a storm and suddenly the shipboard food tasted as if it had been cooked in 'lampoil', as Stephen complained. 'I was very sick indeed,' he told Christopher. Hellmut was sicker. His ulcer made 'things cooked in oil absolutely disastrous'. A diet of bread, water and countless cigarettes was all his finicky gastric system could handle.

They arrived at Malaga on the morning of 23 November, and Stephen promptly decided that the city was 'too civilized for us . . . it is run for rich old ladies'. Parking their heavy luggage at the railway station and with knapsacks on their shoulders, they set off on foot – two *Wandervögel* – to walk down the coast to Gibraltar. *En route* they determined to find somewhere to live.

That evening found them footsore in a *fonda* at Marbella. Rural Spain was less picturesque than Stephen would have liked. Malnourished 'syphilitic' children, idiots, beggars, ugly packs of libidinous dogs 'fucking themselves stupid' offended their eyes. The fish they were served up in their *fonda* was fried in olive oil and made Hellmut – who was so hungry from the unaccustomed exercise that he would have eaten a fried horse – very ill. It quite put them off Spanish village life. And walking. They made the next leg of their pilgrimage by bus to a village where they intervened only long enough to 'stop some children stoning a cat'. The children turned their stones on the foreigners, together with volleys of foul-mouthed street Spanish. Finally they surrendered to bourgeois necessity and took a taxi to the Hotel Victoria in Gibraltar.

There ensued what in later life Stephen called the 'Hellmut fiasco'. The two of them made their way back up the coast, stopping off in Malaga, before finding themselves, thoroughly out of spirits and out of love, in Barcelona on 6 December. By 9 December they had located some rooms which might be suitable. But Stephen continued to feel 'dread' at the social types Hellmut was connected with in Barcelona. 'I wish I had protested more strongly against returning there,' he wrote. They moved into an apartment on 14 December. It was, as Humphrey recalls, 'pretty small and dim', although big enough for a spare bedroom ('into which Hellmut came', Humphrey recalls, wryly: the young German was no model of fidelity). Stephen was by now acutely short of cash, and reckoned himself £50 overdrawn on his London account. A distant uncle, Arthur Loveday, helped them out. But the English gentleman 'refused to meet Hellmut on the ground that he hated all Germans'. Stephen too may have been going off them. His uncle advised him to join the polo club 'if I wanted to meet anyone at all decent'.

On 5 January 1933, Stephen wrote to Christopher to confess that the experiment of living 'domestically' with Hellmut had proved a 'failure'. The young man had returned to Berlin. Stephen could not grieve at the end of the affair. His epitaph was delivered in a letter of 29 December to Isaiah Berlin: 'Hellmut is a nice person, very hysterical, beautiful, uninteresting, sensation-mongering, and second-rate who has the incredibly petit bourgeois mentality of most German homosexuals.' He had, as he noted in his journal, learned something from the fiasco: 'I have the stupidity and the intelligence, the openness and the tiresome subtlety of an educated savage. Tiresome to be with.' Hellmut Schroeder evidently concurred. The parting was bad-tempered.

Stephen decided to remain in Spain until the end of January; mainly because Humphrey had come out to Barcelona for three weeks during his vacation from the Architectural Association. Stephen's brother witnessed the last explosive end of the affair (his recollections of Schroeder's behaviour in these last days are, he says, 'wholly unpublishable'). The normality of his brother's company would be a refreshing tonic, Stephen felt. Meanwhile, in Barcelona, he became involved with a drunken American called James Kirk, who rivalled Fronny in his outrages on decency. A photograph survives of Hellmut, Humphrey, Stephen and a clearly collapsed Kirk. He was, ironically, a dancer by vocation; but his legs were no longer what they were.

Kirk had been sent to Barcelona by a Dr Möring, who was a Hamburg friend of Curtius. Cut loose from his custodians, Kirk indulged in 'macabre' feats of drunkenness. Möring had prevailed on Stephen to keep some kind of watch on his young American. It was an impossible task. One morning Stephen and Humphrey set out for a constitutional walk only to see Kirk, who had made an early start on his day's debaucheries, 'in the distance in front of us making water in front of a telegraph post'. Later that same day, he gave Humphrey 'a love letter 8 pages long', which 'extremely alarmed' the young man. (Kirk was, he recalls, 'awful-looking'.) After Humphrey departed for London, at the end of the first week Kirk's outrages became unbearable. Stephen gave him money to telegraph Möring, and he promptly spent it on drink. In a final debauch 'He drank 3/4 of a litre of alcohol for lighting stoves with this morning. That was taken away from him so he started drinking hair oil.' At last, after much imploring, Möring sent money for the wastrel to be sent off to Ibiza, where he could drink himself to death without disturbing honest English poets. Stephen used Kirk and the details of his self-destructive alcoholic orgy for his story 'The Dead Island'.

With Humphrey gone, Kirk shipped out, and revolution abroad in the streets, there was little inducement to stay on in Barcelona. Stephen left for England after the first week of January 1933, cutting short his trip. He seems at this point in his life to have realized that he would have to balance a twin need for the stabilities of England and the stimulus of abroad: 'From now on,' he informed Christopher, 'I am going to try and live at least six months a year in England. If my book pays off my debts I shall go abroad in May.'

By 10 January Stephen was back in Britain and 'my new dwelling, 43 Boundary Road, N.W.8' – a pleasingly Audenesque name. It was designed as a kind of way-station after Frognal had been broken up. Michael and Stephen paid the rent, the faithful Bertha acted as house-keeper. The flat had a workroom outside the flat proper which raised Stephen's share of the rent £13 a year. It was somewhere he could be 'very much alone', if he so wanted. It was very cold in winter; so cold, as he joked to Christopher, that he was positively constipated from reluctance to make the necessary dash from his study to the Arctic bathroom. Stephen would keep the Boundary Road establishment till the end of 1933.

Plunged into the London literary world, Stephen was increasingly excited about his volume of poems, scheduled to appear, at 5s. under the Faber imprint, on Thursday 19 January. Among other 'complimentaries' Stephen sent a copy to Christopher, less the excised dedication, but inscribed: 'For Christopher in admiration and with love from the writer January 10, 1933'. Thanking Stephen, Christopher asked about the blurb: 'portentous tripe – what idiot wrote it?' The idiot was probably T. S. Eliot. The offending remarks were:

If Auden is the satirist of this poetical renascence Spender is its lyric poet. In his work the experimentalism of the last two decades is beginning to find its reward . . . Technically, these poems appear to make a definite step forward in modern English poetry. Their passionate and obvious sincerity ranks them in a tradition which reaches back to the early Greek poets.

Stephen professed himself embarrassed by the blurb, which he anticipated 'will annoy Wystan'.

On its appearance on 19 January Stephen's volume of thirty-three poems for 1933 was an unqualified success. What impressed the reviewers – predictably, perhaps, given the mood of the times – were the political poems. In the *London Mercury* Eiluned Lewis likened their impact to a 'modern poster'. Herbert Read in the *Adelphi* (February 1933) applauded Stephen as the laureate of 'chaos and despair', the authentic voice of the 1930s. 'Another Shelley speaks in these lines,' Read declared. The *Fortnightly Review* found the collection 'an unmistakable declaration of genius'. In *New Verse* (May 1933) Allen Tate thought that the quality of the verse 'is not surpassed by any other English poet since the war'. 'In 1929,' Tate went on to claim, 'is one of the finest English poems of the century.' In America, Archibald MacLeish, in *Hound and Horn*, thought that Faber had scandalously undersold Stephen with their 'cautious little blurb'. 'As a spectator who loves poetry,' MacLeish wrote, 'I listen only for that clean sharp stroke which is heard when the axe goes into living wood. In Mr Spender's poems at their best I hear it.' Tate and MacLeish would become known personally to Spender in the next decade. Another American who responded warmly to *Poems, 1933* was Lincoln Kirstein, the founder of the little magazine *Hound and Horn*, begun while he was still a student. A rich connoisseur, a patron of ballet and famously eccentric (he once made out a cheque for $2 million to the Queen of England, politely returned from Buckingham Palace), Kirstein would be among the first editors to publish Stephen Spender in America and promote his reputation there. The two men would become firm friends.

Among Stephen's family circle there was one stentorian voice of dissent. 'My book has brought me into great disgrace with the J. A. Spender part of the family,' he told Lehmann:

incredibly, as it seems to me, on account of the poem 'My parents quarrel in the neighbour room'. At my eldest brother's wedding my aunt refused altogether to speak to me and my uncle writes that a letter I wrote explaining that it wasn't and couldn't be *my* parents 'weighed on his spirits'.

'Such silly misunderstandings irritate me,' he added tetchily.

Michael had married in February. He had met his wife, a cosmopolitan German with a mass of golden hair, in Osnabrück. The J. A. Spenders may have been upset as much about Michael's wedding as about Stephen's indiscreet poems. Michael, as Humphrey recalls, 'had an eye for beautiful women', and Erica – although not beautiful – was 'terrifically sexy'. According to Humphrey, before the wedding she invited her future brother-in-law into her bed; when he indignantly demurred she murmured, thoughtfully, 'how peculiar you British are'. Stephen found Erica, 'my brother's corn-cob bride', amusing. But they would see little of each other. Michael's work in photographic cartography meant that he was often abroad.

A case can be made for seeing *Poems, 1933* – early as it comes in his career – as one of Spender's most lasting creations in poetry. The collection is constructed more or less chronologically. It begins, loyally, with two Marston lyrics ('He will watch the hawk', 'Marston, dropping it in the grate, broke his pipe'). There follows, *inter alia*, the expatriate meditative poem, 'Different living is not living in different places', and the works directly inspired by his conversations with Isaiah Berlin, 'An "I" can never be a great man' and 'Beethoven's Death Mask'.

There follows a nucleus of retrospective poems of childhood – 'My parents quarrel' (surely Harold and Violet, despite what Stephen told his uncle), 'My parents kept me from children who were rough'. Then come three pieces about Stephen's exploration of his own sexual identity: 'In 1929', 'Your body is stars', and 'The Port'. The collection, at midpoint, moves to the poems which so affected contemporaries, reflections on Europe ravaged by unemployment: 'The Prisoners', 'Who live under the shadow of a war'. The collection is concluded by the 'technological' poems, so much to Christopher's taste ('The Express', 'The Pylons', 'The Landscape near an Aerodrome'), and full-throated exercises such as 'I think continually' and – as finale – 'Not palaces, an era's crown'.

'What shall you do now?' Christopher asked Stephen in mid-January. 'I hardly see you sticking it out in London for long.' What should Stephen do now? Survive, most importantly. In the short term, he threw himself into reviewing and writing for the prints. In 1933, he began to produce higher journalism with extraordinary facility – there are no fewer than seventeen reviews and essays, and almost as many single poems, published in London journals, between January and December 1933.

At between two and five guineas a shot, these pieces kept him financially afloat. 'From now on,' Stephen told Isaiah Berlin, 'I shall publish no poems for a good long time – at least a year I hope.' His immediate intention was to write three short stories, and rewrite his novel. 'The stories will be strange, I think.' Even these might have to wait or be hurried. He needed money quickly, and only reviews and publisher's advances for 'hack books' could supply ready cash.

Not that he was capable of working at anything with his old vigour in February 1933. On his return from Spain Stephen discovered what it was that was making him so thin and so chronically fatigued – a tapeworm. He had picked up the parasite from eating 'uncooked swine in Spain' as he told Isaiah. The curse of Hellmut had struck again. The condition was serious enough to require hospital treatment at the end of February. He wrote to Isaiah on 1 March from a nursing home, describing the starving and purging treatment he was being subjected to. 'Yards of the thing have emerged,' he informed his friend (who may not have enjoyed his dinner at All Souls that evening) 'but apparently not the head.' If he was where it was, E. M. Forster wryly observed, he too would keep his head hidden.

The tapeworm sparked a number of good jokes in Stephen's circle, most hilariously that which Christopher relates in *Christopher and his Kind*:

The problem, in removing a tapeworm, is to get rid of its head, which hooks itself to the lining of the alimentary canal and hangs on, even when the entire chain of segments attached to it has been evacuated. Sometimes the head can't be found in the stool so the doctor doesn't know if it has been lost or is still inside the patient. Christopher bought a particularly repulsive postcard photograph of the head of Goebbels and sent it to Stephen, inscribed: 'Can *this* be it?!!!'

Although there was no clear-cut valediction of the *Farewell to Berlin* kind, Spender's life takes a distinct new turn at this point. He became less an impulsive and reckless 'rescuer' of those he loved or cared for. There would be no more casual 'boy-relationships'. Indeed, casual love relationships of any kind would become a thing of the past. He grew out of them. Warm as the connections were, this inevitably made something of a separation between such friends as William Plomer, Joe Ackerley or John Lehmann – all of whom continued to follow the more adventurous sexual habits of their youth.

2. The Tony Hyndman Years

Late in February Stephen received a letter from Christopher which left him, weak as he was from treatment for the tapeworm, 'trembling with joy'. The 'estrangement' was over. 'You are the one person who *could* always understand me,' Stephen told Christopher, 'whether we are together or not, if you are willing to try. Freeman is another.' The reprint of his poems was dedicated to Christopher, as a mark of reconciliation. 'I am 24!' he exultantly exclaimed at the end of his letter.

He was intending, at this stage, to come out to Berlin in May. The accession of Hitler and the meeting with Tony Hyndman, the man with whom his life would be involved for the next five years, intervened to forestall the trip. It seems that Stephen met Tony in late March or early April 1933. As he puts it in *World within World*, 'by chance I met a young man who was unemployed . . . I asked him to live in my flat and work for me.'

As *World within World* tells it:

Tony Hyndman came from a small town near Cardiff where his father kept an hotel. He had run away from home at the age of eighteen, and been in various jobs, including, for three years, the Army. He was pleasant-looking, friendly, quickly intelligent in certain ways, and capable of learning. He read a good deal and had a response to poetry which often astonished me.

Isherwood expatiates on the 'pleasant-looking' remark in *Christopher and his Kind*: 'His appearance was attractive: curly red-brown hair, sparkling yellow brown eyes, big smiling teeth. He would call Stephen "yer silly thing!" and tell him, "Don't be so daft!" with a Welsh (Cardiff) accent.'

Stephen's recollection was that the accent was 'slight' but 'perhaps because he was Welsh he did not think of himself as "lower class"'. Everyone agreed that Tony was full of fun and loved argument – left-wing political argument or just argument for its own sake. Telling Christopher about his first meeting with Stephen, he said: 'That was when the curtain went up, for me.' Humphrey Spender, less infatuated, thought him 'a bit of a sponger' and incorrigibly lazy. 'He always wanted sex.' Humphrey remembers Tony as 'jolly' company until (as increasingly happened) he tried to converse like an intellectual.

Tony Hyndman was, as Stephen says, a great story-teller. Many of the tallest were about himself. Thomas Arthur Rowett Hyndman, known in his childhood as 'Tommy' but in London usually as 'Tony', was born in Cardiff on 26 June 1911. This made him just two years younger than Stephen ('Jimmy Younger' is his pseudonym in *World within World*). Tony was the third of seven children, and the only son, of Thomas and Sarah Hyndman.

Tommy's 'dad' was the dominant influence in his early life. He had wanted many sons and expected too much of the one he had. Thomas Hyndman the elder had joined the Coldstream Guards aged eighteen and had served in the Boer War. He was a model guardsman: a boxing champion, marksman, and a senior NCO. On his return from South Africa he was stationed in London, where he met his English wife, Sarah.

On his discharge in 1907 Hyndman returned to Cardiff, where he found work as a publican. His family grew with a child every year. As his daughters recalled, Thomas Hyndman was 'a very hard, very strict man'. His daughters could not wear jewellery. He insisted on silence whenever he entered the room. He ate alone, even on Christmas Day. Much of his attention was centred on the boxing ring that his public house contained. Tony did not match up to his father's expectation. The older Thomas Hyndman despised the younger, the younger 'disliked his father intensely'.

Tony went to local schools in Cardiff and left at fourteen. Despite the slump, the Hyndmans were well off materially. It was only emotionally that they were deprived. Realizing that his son could never go down the pits, and suspecting that he was not up to a man's job, his father paid for Tony to go to Bloggs's secretarial college in Cardiff for a course in 1925. Here he learned shorthand and typing. (The term 'secretary', applied to Hyndman in his service with Stephen, was not – as it is routinely taken to be – a euphemism.)

Having got his certificate from Bloggs's in 1926, Tony started work as a clerk with Matabele Davis, a firm of solicitors in Cardiff. His father was now proprietor of the Neville Hotel, Bridgetown, Cardiff, and life at home was physically comfortable. But Tony was unhappy. And he was radicalized by defending working-men prosecuted for disturbances of the peace during the General Strike.

In 1929 Hyndman came to London to join the Guards. He did not, as is usually recorded, 'run away' from home and have a succession of jobs before joining up. It was his father's suggestion that he join the Coldstreams. He still wanted to 'make a man of him'. It was a disastrous move. In later life Hyndman was a pacifist and a conscientious objector in the Second World War. His 'cowardice' in the Spanish Civil War had its origins in his pacifist instincts rather than any constitutionally craven character. His hatred of war and army must have been confirmed, if not inspired, by his experience in the Brigade of Guards. According to his sister, he had a 'dog's life'. He seems not to have got into serious trouble (there was a spell of glasshouse for falling asleep on duty in Hyde Park). But his army career was undistinguished. Luckily he did not have to fight. He served with the regiment in Khartoum, which furnished some old soldier's anecdotes for his London friends.

Knowing that the Brigade (which in peacetime is usually posted in London) was the target of cruising homosexuals, and that casual prostitution around the barracks was rampant, Hyndman's father warned him before he went in: 'you're a pretty boy, keep yourself clean'. It's not clear that he did. Tony left after three years, well before his term of service was up. The persistent rumour (confirmed by Cuthbert Worsley in his docunovel, *Fellow Travellers*) is that Guardsman Hyndman was bought out by a male lover. If so, the relationship did not last. What was Tony Hyndman doing between discharge from the Coldstream Guards in late 1931 and the 'curtain going up' in early 1933, when he met Stephen? According to Richard Felstead, he was 'plying his trade'. Scraping by, that is, as a male prostitute or by doing casual work as a kitchen porter.

Humphrey recalls being invited in April to Boundary Road 'to meet the great new event in Stephen's life'. According to *World within World*, Stephen had invited Tony to live with him and work for him shortly after their first meeting. Such impulsiveness would have been in character. His relationships tended to open with whirlwind speed.

Tony and Stephen left England to tour abroad in the first week of May, travelling by train. Stephen was charmed by Tony's calmly wrapping his greatcoat around himself and 'dossing down on the floor of the compartment'. Old soldier that he was, Tony was used to the tedium of troop-trains. Tony and Stephen were in Paris on 9 May and in Florence by the 20th. Stephen was joyous at being able to show off the cities to Tony. In Florence they stayed at a 'villino' for a week, with Roger Sessions and his wife Barbara. He knew the brilliant young American composer from his Berlin days (they had plans for Stephen to do a libretto and Roger the music). The villino belonged, as Stephen casually noted in a letter to Isaiah, 'to some people called the Berensons, who are the sort of people Moore [Crosthwaite] would swim in'. This was Bernard Berenson, the connoisseur (the Berensons took to Stephen but not to Tony Hyndman, who they specifically instructed was not to be brought to their table).

From Florence, Stephen wrote a comic postcard to Isaiah to report, 'My worm has turned again, so I am going to Rome on Monday to have it out at the British American hospital.' It was not, in point of fact, all that comic. He sadly informed Isaiah on 25 May that despite the starving procedure, to which he was now wearily habituated, 'as before everything but the head has appeared'. There would have to be another treatment in twelve days. He was keeping himself entertained by reading Henry James. The second treatment was as unsuccessful as the first. 'I get thinner than ever,' he told Rosamond Lehmann. 'It really is a bloody nuisance.' If he survived the worm, he might still go hungry. 'As the result of this illness I have got so hard up,' he told John Lehmann, 'that I will have to go home and place things in papers to earn money.' He had sold the last bit of 'sellable stock' he owned at his bank's insistence. Otherwise they would not honour his cheques.

Stephen and Tony went to Levanto on the Italian Riviera to convalesce in the first week in June. Stephen was 'trying to learn Italian, but I find languages more difficult than most people seem to do', he told John Lehmann. He was, he told Plomer, reading *Don Quixote* and the *Odyssey* because 'I want to read all the epic works I can.' They were staying at the Hotel Stella d'Italia, Levanto, Golfo di Spezia. Despite the grand name, the establishment was a pension. Stephen, as was his habit, compiled a merry account of the guests for William Plomer, including 'the German who is disguised as Bernard Shaw'. For the first day or two it rained. Stephen instructed William to tell Joe Ackerley to change the BBC weather forecasts so that they could have some sun.

There were olive groves at Levanto to stroll through and hills to walk up. The hotel was comfortable, clean and only cost twenty-four lire a day, inclusive. They planned to stay until the end of July, when Humphrey could join them. Stephen was, despite his lowered physical condition, in a honeymoon state of mind. 'Tony is marvellous,' he bubbled to Rosamond Lehmann in mid-June:

It's impossible to write about him. It's so terrific being with him that I almost feel as if I'm physically changing. He's such a real person that it's a mixture of pleasure and pain; because I am so used to having been with tarts whom I had either to ignore because they were so bloody or who were just reflections of me, that it causes me suffering even to realize the *differences* in a person who is so different from me as he is.

'I am dazed by Tony,' he told her a week later.

In more sober mood in *World within World*, writing almost twenty years later, Stephen recalls that 'Levanto passed off almost without incident. [Tony] liked the life of swimming, bathing, and conversation of pensions.' (He was an 'adequate swimmer and a first-class sunbather', Humphrey recalls.) This beach-lounging was, if pleasant to Stephen, less than he wanted from life. There was, too, the occasional and ominous cloud, as Stephen looked back on the episode:

Quite early in our relationship, when we were at Levanto on the Italian coast, he said: 'I want to go away. You are very nice to me, but I feel that I am becoming completely your property. I have never felt like that before with anyone and I can't bear it.'

The idyll on the Italian Riviera could not last. Stephen's plans were vague and uneasy. 'When we come home,' he told Rosamond Lehmann, 'I think that Tony is going to do work in the East End, assisting Winifred's sister Clémence Paine who is a probation officer. If this comes off it ought to be the ideal for him.' It didn't come off (Miss Paine confided to Humphrey that she 'would never dream of giving Tony a job'). On 3 July, Stephen wrote to John Lehmann with a wilder plan:

In the autumn or winter Tony and I are going to start a hotel fairly near the Vale of the White Horse. It will have five double bedrooms for guests, and a bar and a library, and two radio gramophones, and a small car fetching people from the station. All our friends will come, and undergraduates will come over for the day from Oxford, I hope. Tony, whose father is a hotel keeper, will manage it entirely and I will provide the clientele, and, apart from that, will get on with my work. I think I'm going to raise a capital of £1000 at 3½% and become a company, very shortly. Would you care to invest?

Idyllic as Levanto was, and incredibly cheap (more so since all that the young men wanted was sun and each other), money problems gnawed away at Stephen. He wrote to Isaiah in reply to a suggestion that he might consider living permanently abroad, since he was so happy:

I would love to stay on, but I'll explain what the position is: at the end of this quarter I'll be £45 overdrawn: on July 1st I have £50 coming into the bank [his Schuster money, evidently]: £26 has to go to Bertha [who is housekeeping for him and Michael, in their London flat]: I may have a cheque for £25 (at the very least, I suppose) from Faber: so I have in actuality, precisely nothing till October. My idea was to go by boat from Genoa on the 15th and have a free week on the sea (it is as cheap as the second class fare home), and then when I got home simply to sell things and slave until Oct. 1st (when I get £150) to keep going. You see, my position really is impossible: besides that I have this expensive illness, for which I haven't paid the doctor's bills, and which may or may not be cured.

Levanto suddenly went sour. They had intended to stay through the summer months, but as July broke, the resort was overrun by holiday-making Italians. Stephen and Tony left for London on 3 July, cutting short their stay by three weeks. When they returned to London, Tony took up work as Stephen's secretary. It was not what either of them wanted. As Stephen recalls in *World within World*, 'I really did not need a secretary.' The result was never-ending squabbles.

Virginia Woolf, later an affectionate friend, was initially sharp in her diary, after meeting Stephen and Tony Hyndman, as a couple, for the first time (it was shortly after they had moved into their new flat at Randolph Crescent, in October 1933):

he's a nice poetic youth; big nosed, bright eyed, like a giant thrush . . . He is . . . married to a Sergeant in the Guards. They have set up a new quarter in Maida Vale; I propose to call them the Lilies of the Valley.

On her part Rosamond Lehmann, presuming on their by now very warm friendship, chided Stephen for treating his friend like a plaything. He wrote back, passionate and hurt, on 14 August:

Please believe me, I don't think of Tony as a toy. I wanted you to like him simply because he is such a central part of my life now, and I wanted you to see how worth while he was; but it was stupid and fussy of me to have rushed you . . . Every move in our relationship comes so from my guts and is so full of pain that I lose all sense of proportion in it and feel sometimes as if I were going dotty . . . How can I ever expect anyone like him to like me? It is really asking far too much . . . Tony is an extremely nice person and I'm an extremely dotty and neurotic one . . . I hope still to love Tony without ruining him and tying him up in my muddles.

Stephen saw clearly enough that the solution was to get 'an independent life, and some kind of work' for Tony. But there was nothing suitable. His efforts would become increasingly desperate, and his friend's complaints at being 'kept' increasingly bitter, as the months rolled by. Even Humphrey was asked to find something for Tony. But what could he do? 'All he was fit for was coffee boy, and he wouldn't do that.'

There was no shortage of work for Stephen. That autumn, he threw himself into a hectic round of reviewing 'in order to try and earn £3 a week'. Never had he written so much, so fast, for money. In addition to their day-to-day living expenses, he and Tony were about to move into 25 Randolph Crescent in the first week in October. Stephen loved Maida Vale, 'a part of London which almost rivals Berlin in its atmosphere of decay', he recalls in *World within World*:

Along the banks of the canal were rows of stucco houses, whose doors and windows, flanked with yellowing, peeling, Corinthian or Ionic columns, 'tactfully struck a soft Egyptian note, varied by a Greek one,' as Plomer pointed out to me. Steam rose from the canal, covering the lower parts of the houses and washing everything in sweat, as though this part of London were a Turkish bath.

Tony and Stephen decorated the flat themselves. They were comfortably installed by mid-December. Mrs Schuster gave the couple new curtains for Christmas (she approved of the arrangement with Tony, on the grounds that he would discourage her grandson from returning to

Germany). Tony was now formally Stephen's 'secretary' and primarily responsible for cooking and looking after the flat. Stephen did not give him a regular wage but reckoned, for income tax purposes, that Tony cost him £200 a year, or £4 a week. In the new flat Stephen could entertain again as he had at Frognal. There was now a close-knit circle of friends in London: Humphrey and his circle of architecture friends; Plomer, Heard, Ackerley. They all took to Tony, with the exception of Stephen's brother, who was never impressed.

As a poet Spender was, as he told his new friend Herbert Read, looking for a 'subject'. The London literary world was uninspiring and fretful for him: 'I do so hate the clique that one seems doomed to write poetry for,' he told Read. 'I *hate* their tittle-tattle criticism.' In later life he put it more precisely. London critics of the 1930s, particularly those like Geoffrey Grigson, who prided themselves on their severity, made it as

difficult for a writer to see beyond them as for a batsman to see beyond the fielders who are in a ring round the wicket to the crowds on the edge of the field far away.

They crowded an author – Spender would not be crowded; or type-cast. In December 1933 he proposed a volume of short stories to Eliot at Faber, sending him 'By the Lake' as a sample. The poet-publisher observed, sagaciously, 'It seems to us that you have a special gift for a form which we may call the "diary".' Faber accepted the proposed volume of short stories 'of the diary kind' in January. It would eventually be published as *The Burning Cactus*.

Meanwhile, as 1933 drew on, the political situation got blacker. 'The ship continues to sink,' Stephen bleakly told Christopher, now in Greece with Heinz and rather out of it. 'I've stopped publishing poems,' he added, so as to concentrate on the Henry James book and 'earn money'. Stephen's worm had been suppressed by the skilful Italian doctors (it would not, however, be entirely destroyed until 1934). But Tony had now developed excruciating stomach pains. He saw a series of doctors, the third of whom diagnosed it to be 'pyschological'. Despite this disability, 'he helps me more and more', Stephen assured Isaiah, who probably disapproved of Stephen's partner. When Spender reprinted 'By the Lake', his most personal story, in *New Stories* in February 1934, it was prominently subtitled 'For Tony'.

New year of 1934 found Stephen, for the first time in his life, in a stable domestic situation at Randolph Crescent. Following the critical and sales triumph of *Poems, 1933*, he was recognized, at twenty-four, as one of the country's leading poets. His work was now the nucleus around which a major poetic movement was forming. On the publication of *Poems, 1933*, he recalls, 'immediately the names of Auden, Day-Lewis and Spender were linked by the critics'. Around this nucleus was a constellation of other associated names: MacNeice, Lehmann, Warner, Plomer, Bell, Prokosch (in later life Spender recalled that the eccentric Frederic Prokosch, owner of one of the flashiest cars in London, carried a naked photograph of himself for purposes of introduction). What linked this poetic company was energy, youth, modernism and – above all – political commitment.

'We *were* the 1930s,' as Stephen puts it:

The writing of the 1920s had been characterized variously by despair, cynicism, self-conscious aestheticism, and by the prevalence of French influences . . . the qualities which distinguished us from the writers of the previous decade lay not in ourselves, but in the events to which we reacted. These were unemployment, economic crisis, nascent fascism, approaching war.

Their predecessors had reacted to a past war. The writers of the 1930s anticipated the war to come.

Poems, 1933 had been, for a slim volume, extraordinarily successful. There were two impressions in 1933 (the second was 'inscribed' to Christopher Isherwood – who gracefully acknowledged, from Greece, that we 'have buried that little hatchet'). In September 1934, Faber brought out a new 'revised and enlarged' edition. In London, Stephen's social life also enlarged on a number of fronts. His fame, social aplomb, attractive appearance and that curious inability – which he laments in *World within World* – to turn down any invitation plunged him into the 'literary social life'. 'At home' cards summoned him to the drawing-rooms of the now venerable Bloomsbury set, literary grandees for whom 'I never lost my awe'. Awed as he might have been, Spender was now himself an influential player in the London literary scene. It was he, for example, who introduced the work of George Barker to T. S. Eliot in January 1934, starting the other poet on his career with Faber.

Over this period he consolidated his friendship with the Nicolsons, with 'Ros and Wog', and became a regular guest of the fantastic Ottoline

Morrell – 'Lady Acetyline' and 'Ottles' as she was irreverently nicknamed by the mischievous Plomer. Tea in Gower Street with 'Ottles' was not without its excitement. 'In the last years of her life (when I knew her),' Stephen recalls:

she always had the air of falling apart, with hair like a curtain suddenly drop-ping over one eye, or a bodice dropping open. On one occasion, when she was in the middle of a sentence, a large ear-ring fell off the lobe of one ear and dropped into her tea-cup. Without interrupting what she was saying, she fished it out and attached it to her ear again.

It was at a Morrell 'Thursday' in February 1934 that Stephen met W. B. Yeats, now seventy, with 'the appearance of an overgrown art student, with shaggy, hanging head and a dazed, grey, blind gaze' (and a 'curious pot-belly', as he irreverently reported to his American friend, Lincoln Kirstein, with whom he was enjoying a lively correspondence at this period). When the Great Irish Poet asked the young poet his views on 'the Sayers' (a troupe of choric reciters of poetry), Stephen blunderingly thought he meant Dorothy L., the detective novelist. Lady Ottoline phoned for Virginia to come by taxi and rescue him.

Separate from this upper tier, Stephen and his Maida Vale neighbour William Plomer had a circle of lively literary intimates of their own generation who were on regular visiting terms. They included the influ-ential journalist J. R. ('Joe') Ackerley, eventually to be one of the most powerful editors in London; René Janin, an old friend from Frognal days; the publishers John Lehmann and Rupert Hart Davis; the South African Laurens Van der Post (currently a farmer); and the man of letters Peter Quennell. In 1934, Stephen began a lifelong friendship with an older man, Herbert Read. Read had offered what Stephen considered the most judicious review of *Poems, 1933*. Read liked to write long, chatty, intellectually probing letters. Stephen, as was habitual with his close friends, offered in return impulsive confidences about his private affairs and drafts of his poems in progress. 'I seem to have reached a stage,' he told Read in an early letter, 'where all my work is back in the melting pot.' Read (a First World War poet, anarchist and publisher) constantly endeavoured to move his young acolyte away from 'descrip-tive' verse. He himself was moving from imagism to the new school of surrealism.

Above all, Stephen and Plomer had become close friends. Stephen was one of a privileged few to know William 'behind his mask', an inscrutable exterior which Stephen likened to a carapace of 'hard, light coloured wood'. Plomer's comments on Stephen's poems were invariably sensible (in 1937, he would become a professional 'literary adviser' to Cape). Unlike Read he preferred the old, lucid, lyrical mode of Stephen's writing.

On another, less literary, front, there was the Bohemian set of Architectural Association friends to which Stephen was introduced by Humphrey – notably 'Lolly' (Margaret Low – nicknamed because, short in stature, she was 'low Low'), Helen Gibb (with whom Stephen would, in 1935, have a brief affair; she married Lolly's shiftless brother Oliver), Humphrey's particular friend, Bill Edmiston (with whom Stephen would also have a fling in 1935), and the gifted artist Bobby Buhler, who would leave to posterity fine portraits of Stephen Spender in his early twenties.

There remained friends from his earlier life: Isaiah Berlin and the brilliant set of young philosophers he was gathering round himself (notably in 1936 Stuart Hampshire, who would become one of Stephen's closest intimates), Winifred and Clémence Paine (it was through Clémence's work in the East End that both Stephen and Humphrey had first-hand accounts of social suffering in the slump). Stephen moved easily through these sets of interlocking friends.

For liberals like Stephen and his friends, the situation in Europe was worse with every newscast. 'We seem,' wrote Christopher from Berlin in August 1934, 'to be in the final circle of the whirlpool.' Fascism had triumphed in Germany and Italy. It was resurgent in France and latent in Spain. Even in Britain the 'Sedition Bill' which would punish anyone (particularly any writer) undermining the allegiance of the armed forces presaged authoritarianism – even dictatorship. Sedate liberals, like E. M. Forster, were driven to agitate publicly against it. And, of course, there was Mosley.

Tony and Stephen left it all for the Adriatic sun, in the first week of April 1934. They had let the Randolph Crescent flat. The two young men travelled by third-class train through Europe. For part of the way, to Milan, they were accompanied by Isaiah Berlin. 'Shyah and I each had a whole side to ourself and Tony slept on the floor, which he says is very comfortable,' Stephen told his grandmother. Mrs Schuster had tipped her favourite grandson 10s. to see him through the trip. He had also borrowed £50 from her, to cover his current overdraft. The hope was he could repay it with the advance on his forthcoming short-story collection. Income from reviewing, while he was away from the telephone, would dwindle.

By 8 April Tony and Stephen, having dropped off Isaiah, were in Venice. Tony was 'mentally unprepared' for the impact of the city on his provincial sensibility:

This overwhelming flesh of marble with arteries of water, which he had been told was the most beautiful place in the world, simply dismayed and depressed him. All he noticed was the dirt and the smells.

After this unsatisfactory interlude, they travelled on to a pension at Mlini, six miles along the coast from Dubrovnik (a 'perfectly preserved' town, Stephen told Plomer). The small resort had been recommended to them by Geoffrey Grigson as somewhere idyllic, secluded and unbelievably cheap. 'Cheap' was the principal consideration. As Stephen told Lincoln Kirstein, 'since Tony's illness we have been rather short'.

When they arrived by boat from Trieste, in the second week in April, the weather was already warm enough for bathing. Mlini was, as Stephen pictures it:

a little village on a stretch of the Adriatic coast, south of Dubrovnik, where there was a stony beach. The pension was a building not unlike a stone farm-house. In front of it was a terrace with chairs and tables under trees, where the guests ate outdoors . . . Above the beach, to the north of the pension, there was an orchard on the hillside where I used often to write at a table under the trees.

The air was 'crystal', he told Herbert Read, 'the atmosphere timeless'.

Stephen had brought with him working materials for 'my book for Cape' (*The Destructive Element*, as it was to be when written; a study of Henry James). This he thought he might finish by July. It was overdue by a year. This 'James book' was proving fiendishly difficult to bring to fruition. '70,000 words of criticism is a hell of a lot to write,' he wearily told Plomer in mid-May. There were also reviewing odds and ends to tidy up. Within days of arrival Stephen had posted back to Russell Square a long essay for the *Criterion*. He also intended to have a 'play for Faber to publish at Christmas'. The theme of the proposed verse drama was 'German justice, the thing I feel most strongly about', as he told Kirstein.

This obsession crystallized into a poem, which created much stir. In February 1933 the Reichstag had burned down. It was, as everyone outside Germany suspected, perpetrated by the Nazis as part of their methodical destruction of the apparatus of German democracy. There was a cinematically staged show trial, in which a Dutch cretin, Marinus Van der Lubbe, was indicted and humiliated by Goering as prosecutor, for the benefit of the world's cameras. The luckless defendant was found guilty, as the script determined, and executed by beheading in January 1934. The spectacle triggered a blisteringly angry poem from Stephen:

> Yes. No. Yes. No. Shall I tell you what I know?
> Not to Goering, but, dear microphone, to you.
> I laugh because my laughter
> Is like German justice, twisted by a howitzer.

Daily routine at Mlini was simple. Spender painted an idyllic picture for William Plomer. The young men got up early, bathed and break-fasted frugally on rolls, honey and coffee. The village was still, apart from the never-ending sound of the waterfall which splashed through it to the sea. Stephen wrote and Tony typed till eleven. Then they bathed in the sea, after which came a long leisurely lunch. For the rest of the day they read, smoked, took a siesta, wrote letters and lounged. In the evening, Stephen and Tony would stroll through meadows sprinkled with 'lovely spring flowers' or play chess ('which Tony is good at'). Once a week they went into Dubrovnik to see a movie and 'keep in touch with civilization'.

Although Edenic, their mode of life in Mlini was, as Stephen reas-sured his grandmother, 'very cheap'. Full pension cost only 5s. 5d each a day. Apart from the occasional storm and a strange hot wind (a 'sirocco', as he later learned to call it) that gave Stephen headaches, the only fly in the ointment was the omnipresent swastika. The hotel was full of vacationing Nazis.

Despite the Nazis, Mlini was otherwise so pleasant that Stephen thought, in May, that he and Tony might well stay until January next, if his grandmother could land them a long-term tenant for Randolph Crescent. It was so economical to live in the Adriatic village, he reas-sured her, that 'I really may be able to pay off my overdraft', repay the money he owed her, and settle his and Tony's doctors' and dentists' bills. He had himself had two false teeth inserted before leaving London. He was paying (in 14-carat gold, as he jested) for all that jaw-breaking toffee he and Christopher had chewed in Berlin.

At the end of April, there was a visitor to Mlini who would change Stephen's life utterly. Muriel Gardiner, née Morris, was a rich American, eight years older than Stephen. Muriel's family wealth was old money. It originated in the Chicago stockyards. Like Stephen, she was Jewish on one side of her family and highly cultivated on both sides. Muriel had been educated at Wellesley and Oxford. She had been married twice – the second time to an Englishman, Julian Gardiner. That marriage, like her first, was breaking up. She had initially come to Vienna intending to enter analysis with Dr Freud (Muriel was never one to be fobbed off with second best). His casebook was full and she was taken on by one of his disciples, Dr Ruth Mack Brunswick. Her sessions with Dr Brunswick led her to determine that she too must be a psychoanalyst. At the time when Stephen first encountered her in April 1934, Muriel had enrolled for a two-year course at medical school in Vienna (she needed an MD to practise as a Freudian analyst in America). By 1934, her marriage with Gardiner was effectively behind her. They had separated 'amicably'. She had assumed custody of their daughter, Connie, now three years old and in the care of an Austrian nanny, Gerda.

Freudians apart, Muriel's social milieu was among the artists and musicians who thronged Vienna in the early 1930s. In the spring of 1934, she had a spacious apartment in the city and a small wooden cottage – the 'Blockhaus', as it was called – at Sulz, in the Vienna woods. Up to this point in her life, Muriel had taken no great interest in politics. She dated her political awakening to 12 February 1934, one of the blackest days in Austrian history. Earlier in 1934 all political parties had been dissolved, except for Chancellor Engelbert Dollfüss's fascistic Fatherland Front. A General Strike was mobilized in protest at these drastic measures. Brutal repression ensued.

Over the next few years (bloodily punctuated by Dollfüss's assassination and, in 1938, Nazi Anschluss), Muriel would be recruited into the socialist underground. As an agent ('codename Mary') she was directly involved in smuggling out refugees from Vienna with faked passports to Czechoslovakia and safety. It was an activity which could have led to her being executed, well-connected American national though she was.

Stephen coincided with the crucial political moment in Muriel's life. It was, however, not politics but the accidents of tourism which brought them together. Muriel, little Connie, the nanny, Gerda, and Muriel's current lover (an elegant but taciturn young Austrian) had taken a boat-trip passing through Mlini during her spring vacation. 'I had selected this spot from various circulars,' she recalls, 'because it was the only one that advertised a sand beach.' (Stephen recalls it having a stony beach; brochures fib.) The proprietor of the hotel, where they stayed, told Muriel, as she checked in, that 'two distinguished English journalists' were also in residence.

In her mind Muriel 'pictured two elderly men in tweed jackets'. The 'journalists' were the spectacularly un-tweedy Spender and Hyndman. Muriel found Stephen to be

strikingly handsome, very tall and well built with a slight tendency to stoop, probably because of his height. He had curly fair hair and round, intensely blue eyes. His expression was youthfully idealistic but at the same time a little sad.

Tony she found 'less striking but very personable . . . his neat, well-proportioned body with its natural ease of movement suggested a graceful animal'. On his part, Stephen recorded his first visual impression of Muriel Gardiner, when he saw her on the beach:

her profile, as she looked out at the sea, reminded me of my mother in certain photographs taken at an age before I can remember her: black hair and eyes, a clear complexion slightly tanned but not expressionless with sunburn. In her appearance there was a look of having suffered at some time.

It was Tony who effected the introduction: 'He's *Stephen Spender*, the poet . . . I'm his secretary.' Stephen and Muriel hit it off. With only Tony and Nazis for company, he was starved of the kind of cosmopolitan stimulus she brought to the little seaside pension. Steeped as he was in the writings of the Master, he saw Muriel as 'certainly a James character', as he told Plomer (who may have been baffled by the allusion). Stimulus apart, Muriel had much in common with him culturally: Oxford, music, psychoanalysis. Above all he was, as she discovered, 'passionately concerned with the political situation in Germany and Austria' – on which she communicated expert and up-to-date intelligence.

After a day or two, Muriel continued her journey by boat on to Greece. Stephen had said at Mlini that he hoped they might meet again. An unforeseen emergency supplied the occasion for the reunion. Tony had, for months, been racked again by stomach pains. A series of doctors over the last year had offered diagnoses ranging from psychosomatic illness, ulcers, to grumbling appendix. In May, medical opinion hardened around the appendix diagnosis. The Dubrovnik doctors recommended an operation – in Vienna, preferably.

Stephen wrote to Muriel. She arranged things (as she well could, being herself a surgeon in training). Within two days of their arriving in the city, on 24 May, Tony was in hospital. There was an operation two days later. (The cost, as Stephen told his grandmother, was 300 schillings, 'just £11', for 'one of the best surgeons in Vienna'). The appendectomy was uncomplicated but – as was normal medical practice – Tony was kept in the hospital for a week or so after.

In the ward there were an English boy and a dying man. Out of this experience – and Tony's irrepressible jauntiness – Stephen wrote one of the *Burning Cactus* stories, 'A Strange Death'. He also rashly introduced a representation of John Lehmann (grossly defamatory as Lehmann thought) as 'Landin', which would cause ructions. At the moment, however, relations with 'Bonny Johnny' were very friendly. Stephen rented his Vienna apartment when Lehmann was away from the city, cruising Europe in his dazzling 'passion waggon', a vehicle whose silvery ostentation, in Stephen's eyes, rivalled Goering's.

Muriel and Stephen visited Tony daily. 'Vienna,' he told his grandmother, 'is all on edge, and bombs keep going off, even when one is in the street.' He himself had heard two. His letters must have caused some alarm at Albert Court. Every evening, Muriel and Stephen would talk far into the night. 'We quickly grew to know each other well and were soon in love,' Muriel recalled. Her former lover was no longer in the picture. She evidently took the next step:

Stephen was perfectly open about the fact that his previous relationships had been only with men. I remember his saying, before making love to me the first time, 'I'm a little embarrassed. You see, I've never been in love with a woman before, never even been attracted to a woman.' We were both concerned about hurting Tony. The fact that we could all speak openly and sincerely about this and that we all felt true friendship for one another made the situation less difficult than one might expect.

To William Plomer, Stephen sent a poem allegorizing his love affair with Muriel in the Vienna woods (it was later published in *The Still Centre* as 'Experience'):

> There was a wood
> Habitat of foxes and fleshy burrows
> Where I learnt to uncast my childhood, and not alone,
> I learnt, not alone. There were four hands, four eyes,
> A third mouth of the dark to kiss. Two people
> And a third not either; and both double, yet different.
> I entered with myself. I left with a woman.

Stephen wrote enthusiastically to Christopher, recording the momentous 'change' which had taken place in his life, insisting, however, that 'it has not made any difference to my relationship with Tony'. Heterosexuality was amazing to him. 'I find sleeping with a woman more satisfying,' he wonderingly concluded.

When Tony came out of hospital on 6 June, Muriel offered Stephen the use of her house in the woods in which to convalesce. John Lehmann had also offered the use of his flat. Everyone was being very kind. But Vienna was too hectic. Stephen took Tony into the mountain air for a couple of days at Mariazell. It turned out to be a 'horrible place', Stephen told William on 19 June. They left as soon as Tony felt well enough. It was, however, less places than the ambivalence of his personal life that was troubling Stephen and making him restless. Part of him felt obliged to care for his friend, another part drew him to his new lover: 'All these days, I was feeling that Tony's illness, which had brought us to Vienna, was now keeping me from Muriel.'

On his return to Vienna and Muriel, around 20 June, Stephen and Tony camped in Lehmann's atelier flat in Vienna, Invalidengasse 5. Stephen was amused by the grandeur of John's baroque writing desk. The address of the flat, given Tony's convalescent condition, was almost too good to be true. Unfortunately, their arrival coincided with an infestation of bed-bugs of biblical proportions, which it cost 18 schillings a room to remove.

The two of them would remain at Invalidengasse till the end of July with occasional visits to the Blockhaus in the woods, where there were happily neither bugs, fascists nor John Lehmann's grandiose furniture to overawe them. Now that Tony was fit they enjoyed a serene interval. Stephen told William, exultantly, that all the 'dangers seem to be averted, and I have returned to the status quo'. It was Tony, he confided to his London friend, 'that is most holding me together'.

There was, in June, the first stirring in Stephen's mind of an ambitious long poem about Vienna. 'I read a lot of documents about the February Revolution, which gave me the idea,' he told his grandmother. 'I have never had so many *ideas* as just now,' he told Plomer. The sexual experiences of the summer had unlocked something in him: 'In some strange way, I am leading for the first time now a life I have really wanted to lead,' he declared. As the summer progressed, and with Tony recovered, the poet scrawled and the secretary tapped at his keyboard daylong in Muriel's cottage and John's flat, with Austrian history being made with the machine-gun and jackboot in the streets outside.

Muriel gave a party for Tony's birthday on 27 June. The young man was by now fully recovered and in Stephen's judgement fitter (physically) than he had been for years. Emotionally, things were strained by the love triangle that had developed. Stephen contrived to write through it all. In the last week of June he wrote 300 lines of his new poem, before putting it aside to finish *The Destructive Element*.

Lehmann's flat was still 'absolutely over-run by bugs'. Stephen and Tony were, however, obliged to stay at verminous Invalidengasse until the end of July. They were utterly broke. Muriel was currently between apartments (they were hard to come by in Vienna, even for the rich), and could for once not help her English friends out. They sought refuge in her cottage for periods of up to ten days, when bugs and politics made Vienna utterly impossible to work in. Meanwhile in Vienna itself events were coming to crisis. History was boiling over. On 25 July, Dollfüss was murdered in a Nazi putsch. Stephen happened to be in the city that day with Muriel. There were machine-guns set up in the street and wild rumours that 3,000 socialists had been arrested. Roehm had been exterminated three weeks earlier in Germany. This internecine slaughter was ominous. Was it reassuring or frightening when fascist murdered fascist? 'Everyone is very roused by this murder,' Stephen told his grandmother, adding, 'I can't help wishing that Hitler and Mussolini would be disposed of in the same way.' Except that 'murder seems to breed murder'.

By the end of July, *The Destructive Element* was finally dispatched to Rupert Hart Davis, who promptly returned it with demands for revision, 'which will mean a lot of typing', Stephen wearily noted (in later life he would judge Hart Davis to be the best editor he ever worked with). At this point, he was still thinking of staying out of England until January 1935, and letting Randolph Crescent. In the first week in August he rejoined Humphrey and Winifred at Mieders, for a fortnight (a wet fortnight, as it turned out) in the Tyrol. Muriel meanwhile had gone off to escape the wet at Juan-les-Pins. She would stay for a month in the Riviera. Stephen returned to Vienna, for a few days, on 20 August. At the end of the month he intended to go to Salzburg, where, as was now an annual ritual, he would meet Isaiah and other Oxford friends for the music festival.

On 16 August, it was decided that Tony would go back to London in September and stay with Joe Ackerley (Randolph Crescent was still occupied by tenants). Stephen's debt to his grandmother still troubled him, although she had generously written off the £30 for Tony's operation. He owed her £50 or so, and had no immediate way of clearing the debt until Cape were satisfied with his book – which they obdurately declined to be. Tony would travel home third class and his being in London would be cheaper than keeping the young man in Vienna, Stephen reassured his grandmother. Tedious redrafting of *The Destructive Element* kept Tony in Vienna until 10 September.

By this point, Stephen was reunited with Muriel, now tanned and back from France. His plan was to return to London in October via Bonn, where he could see Curtius. It might also be possible to catch up with Christopher, whose peregrinations were taking him from Greece to the Low Countries – anywhere that he might find some 'papers' for his companion, Heinz, who was threatened with the horrors of conscription if he returned to Germany.

By the end of August Stephen could congratulate himself that he had 'done my two books for the winter' (*The Destructive Element* and *Vienna*). Cape's revisions were satisfactorily completed, which would release a £50 advance he desperately needed, and the poem was finished. Stephen had a few blissful days in the first week of September, living with his lover in her new apartment at Rummelhardtgasse 2. It was a happy ending to what had been an exciting summer. By now, after her return from France, their love was at its most intense and physical. On 14 September, he wrote to Christopher, with an unconvincing show of casualness:

By the way, almost I hate to tell you, but I have been having quite a lot of normal sex lately. The effect is funny, because I find boys much more attractive, in fact I am rather more than usually susceptible, but actually, I find the actual sex act with women more satisfactory, more terrible, more disgusting, and, in fact more everything. To me it is much more of an experience, I think, and that is all there is to it. Also I am just as happy when I don't have much sex with Tony, and I want him to have a more independent life. The idea of sex with any other male (than T.) however attractive, just makes me sick.

He is, he adds, glad to be out of the 'lost whirlpool' of the *Lokale*, and their sexual promiscuities.

What he should have done was to part amicably from Tony, as Muriel had parted from Julian Gardiner. But Stephen felt responsible for Tony. He was not like Muriel, who, as he told Lehmann, lived 'entirely for love'. He could not bring himself to break off the relationship with a partner who so obviously depended on him. Under the pressure of all this emotion Stephen – aged twenty-five – made his last will and testament. Dated 29 July 1934, it is a symptomatic document. In it, Stephen Spender declares that he wishes to leave T. A. R. Hyndman £300, the sum to be deducted from his 'Schuster capital'. The rest of his estate is to be divided among his brothers and sister, with two small bequests for the executors. A codicil adds that he wishes the executors to act as trustees for Tony's £300, and 'to undertake, as far as they find it possible, to see that this money is spent in teaching him languages, or secretarial work, or whatever they believe will help him most to find independent work'.

The good news in early September was that Faber were agreeable to publishing *Vienna* as a book in November. Eliot must have assented by return of post. It would mean a mad rush to get the proofs done. The whole poem had been dashed off too quickly – but so fast were political events moving that there was no choice. Stephen got back to England in the last days of September after what had been the most epoch-making six months of his life.

Money was a pressing problem. Christopher and Heinz in Copenhagen, which Stephen and Tony visited in October, had set their sights on distant and lawless Mexico. As Stephen patiently explained to Tony (who was aching to go to South America and start a new life, preferably with Christopher and Heinz and no Muriel):

I shall be very glad to talk with all of you about our plans. The chief difficulty about leaving Europe – if that is what C. wants to do – is that it would cost us £100 to get out of this flat, and a further £100 travelling expenses. If we wait till the end of summer [1935], we won't have to pay to get out of the flat, and in fact we can let it till we go. Apart from this I still have 8 months of

work that I wd. rather, on the whole, do in Europe. Of course, I feel that this
life in London is unsatisfactory for us all. It all comes down to finance really,
because if we had the money, we could go, and then if we found nothing satisfactory, then S. America, and treat the whole thing as a journey.

Over the next three months (October–December) in London Stephen
began a sporadic friendship with Helen Gibb. She was a colleague of
Humphrey's and Margaret Low's (Humphrey's future wife) best friend
at the Architectural Association. Helen fell heavily for Stephen. He made
it clear that he was not interested in a long or serious relationship and
may have found her unsophisticated compared with Muriel. Helen was
not pretty ('rather beaky' is Humphrey's description). Lolly, fond as she
was of Stephen, was 'rather cross' with him about his treatment of her
friend.

Stephen was more and more concerned about what best to do with
Tony. The hope that he might find social work in the East End had
fallen through. In some desperation Stephen toyed with the idea of total
rustication. Things were always easier, he told William Plomer, 'when we
are quite alone together'. 'Next year,' he told Lincoln Kirstein, 'we are
going to settle in a cottage in the English country, so that means, I think,
that we won't get abroad till 1936.' This relocation into the backwoods
of England would have been disastrous.

In other moods, he toyed with escape to far-off places. In November
he inquired of William whether there was any chance of 'my getting
the Japan job'. It would be 'better than reviewing', he explained. (Plomer
had spent some time in Japan, teaching, in the late 1920s; it left an
indelible impression on him.) To Kirstein, Stephen confided a hope that
he might come to America. The American – who as editor of *Hound
and Horn* had been among the first to publish Spender's poetry in his
country – strongly encouraged this plan.

Vienna was published by Faber, in a rush, in November 1934, 'among
the Christmas books', as T. S. Eliot joked. There was little seasonal goodwill for Spender's latest effort. Few commentators, in 1934 or later, have
had a good word to say about *Vienna*. None the less, the long poem
(Stephen's first) represented a major advance – or could have done, given
a more clement reception. In *The Destructive Element*, the manifesto-book
which he was writing *pari passu* with *Vienna*, Stephen identifies three
elements as necessary for the modern writer. He must, as Conrad puts
it in *Lord Jim*, 'in the destructive element immerse'. Take risks, that is. It

was in this spirit that Stephen had immersed himself in the anarchic underground life of Berlin. And now, in 1934, he was in the front line in Vienna. The second necessary thing for the modernist writer was to forge a style both politically subversive and artistically subtle. Stephen's masters were James in prose and Eliot in verse. The third necessity, to which the final section of *The Destructive Element* is devoted, is 'proper subject'. Increasingly for Stephen this could be glossed as 'political subject'.

The historical significance of Austria in 1934 is overshadowed by the Spanish struggle a couple of years later and the late 1930s triumph of German Nazism. For Stephen, as tutored by Muriel and her socialist comrades, Vienna was a test case of overwhelming urgency. Could democracy mobilize and assert itself sufficiently to resist the onslaught of totalitarianism?

The SDP had been elected by two-thirds of the Austrian electorate in the mid-1920s. A ruthlessly anti-socialist policy was introduced by Ignaz Seipel when he came to power in 1926. To this end Seipel mobilized the Heimwehr fascistic party. It was, as the name ('return to our roots') implies, essentially Austrian, not German. The leaders of Heimwehr in 1934 were Dr Engelbert Dollfüss, Prince Stahremberg and Major Emil Fey (the 'wet dream dictators', as Stephen calls them in his poem).

Heimwehr's policies were articulated in 1933 with a compact between Dollfüss and Mussolini. These swaggering potentates agreed on a policy for the ridding of their states from the plague of socialism. In Austria this entailed low-level civil war against the Social Democrats, who armed themselves for the struggle to come. In Vienna a Socialist Republican Defence Corps was formed to resist the Heimwehr assault.

In February 1934 there was a failed coup d'état by the socialists. A general strike led to violence, and ruthless suppression. The working-class areas of the city, Social Democrat strongholds, were shelled. An estimated 2,000 or more socialists were killed or executed. The socialist mayor of Vienna was dragged from his office and thrown into prison. Martial law was declared. Machine-guns were set up at street corners. In the countryside the first concentration camps were established. Against this cataclysmic background Tony Hyndman was having his appendix removed and Stephen Spender was enjoying his first sexual experience with a member of the opposite sex.

By August 1934 the Heimwehr Fascist Movement had effectively destroyed the Socialist Democratic Party as a viable political entity. Its members were forced into underground resistance as its only mode of

survival. Its leader, Dr Otto Bauer, fled to sanctuary abroad. The situation was complicated by German subversion and Italian meddling. This
was the period of Roehm's assassination. Fascist was killing fascist, and
Germany had always seen Austria as its Reich in Osten. Nazi bomb-
throwers spread panic in the Vienna streets in the months after February,
with the aim of destabilizing the country to ready it for a putsch.

In May 1934, when Stephen and Tony arrived, Vienna was a powder
keg. The keg blew in late July, with the assassination of Dollfüss. The
leading assassin was not a socialist, but a Nazi, an ex-army sergeant, Otto
Planetta. The rebels' aim was to wipe out the whole cabinet. The pro-
German faction had, it transpired, moved too soon and too nakedly.
Major Fey took over on a wave of revanchist anti-German anger. Hitler
promptly disowned the failed putsch and Planetta was hanged, together
with his accomplices.

Events had moved with blinding speed in Vienna, and with great
uncertainty as to the outcome. So volatile was the situation that any one
of the three forces in contention might have triumphed: Austrian
Nationalism, International Socialism, Pan-German Fascism. Like Madrid
two years later, Vienna was, in summer 1934, where European history
was being made. 'The Place meets the Time', as Stephen portentously
puts it in his poem.

Although in 1934 Stephen was seen as leader of the 'New School',
Vienna is, in form at least, a filial homage to *The Waste Land*. Like Eliot's
poem it is in distinct 'parts'. The first section of the poem, 'Arrival at
the City', records Stephen and Tony arriving in May. Thematically, the
section revolves around 'the man living' and 'the man dying'. Literally
(as in 'Two Deaths') Tony surviving while the victim of the February
uprising dies alongside him in the hospital ward. Stephen's 'new life' (his
sexual resurrection) is seen as coinciding with all the death in the city.
The second section of the poem, 'Parade of the Executive', sweeps like
a panning camera over the Heimwehr leadership ('Dollfüss, Fey,
Stahremberg, the whole bloody lot'). The tone is one of blistering
contempt. The puppet-leaders' Ruritanian regalia are contrasted with
'the unemployed at the pavement's edge'. The third section, 'The Death
of Heroes', is a lament for the fallen of February and a scathing satire
on 'Fey's swine'. The last section, 'Analysis and Statement', is a medley
of five voices, depicting the poet's internal turbulence. Its highpoint is
a lyrical anthem to Muriel:

I think often of a woman
With dark eyes neglected, a demanding turn of the head
And hair of black silky beasts.

Vienna, when it arrived at Faber's office in Russell Square, must have caused some alarm. In the *New Statesman*, on 27 October (a week before the poem was published), G. W. Stonier roundly branded Stephen a 'Red' and a 'Communist poet'. In addition to its extremist politics, *Vienna* was liberally sprinkled with what were, in the literary culture of the time, near-obscenities. The poet referred freely to 'oil-tarred pissoirs', 'wet dreams', 'arses' and 'nipples'. There were other references, far from veiled (and not ostensibly critical), to 'those who hang about at [the] jaws of lavatories, advertising their want of love'.

This was not the tone which Faber had carefully created for their verse over the years of Eliot's management of the poetry list. Eliot's own position was difficult. Stephen was a protégé, a friend, and a long-term investment of the firm. He did not want to lose the young man as an author. He admired his poetry. On the other hand, *Vienna* was clearly *not* a Faber book. T. S. Eliot had blazoned Stephen as 'the lyrical poet of our generation', and this latest effort was by no stretch of the term 'lyrical'.

The firm's dislike of the poem was expressed by a virtual boycott on advertisement. In the *Spectator*, which gave the poem its first important review on 9 November, I. M. Parsons's columns face a full-page advertisement for Faber's autumn books which does not even list *Vienna*. Parsons's review offered no balm for this snub. 'Mr Spender, we cannot help feeling,' he noted with insufferable condescension, 'is in a sense too involved in his material.'

The reviews were generally hostile, shockingly so for Stephen, given the chorus of approval for *Poems, 1933* and its revised successor. The *TLS*, echoing the *Spectator*, found the poem 'hardly lucid'. The *Mercury* found 'lumps of quite crude stuff in it; and parts are written in too great heat, and too dubious a heat'. *New Verse* found the work vitiated by 'gang-belief' and 'anti-poetical'. Mr Spender 'has forgotten the true function of poetry . . . *Vienna* is a bad poem'. Montagu Slater in *Left Review* agreed that '*Vienna* is a bad poem' but for the opposite reason. Its politics were 'disfigured' by Spender's ineradicable 'poeticism'. Even Isherwood, the most reassuringly sympathetic of critics, felt that *Vienna* was 'unnecessarily obscure'.

Stephen was overwhelmed by the critical response to this 'bad poem' and was demoralized by his publisher's apparent lack of faith. He wrote to Eliot, suggesting that *Vienna* be withdrawn. Eliot talked him out of such a suicidal step. He was alarmed at the young man's depression. 'Don't worry about your work,' he reassured Stephen on 10 December. *Vienna* had actually earned 'over £11 . . . I don't think in the least that it will damage your reputation'. But the blow to Stephen's confidence was palpable. *Trial of a Judge*, his next ambitious project in verse (and another 'political' production), went into limbo. It would not appear until 1938. Nor would he produce another collection of verse until *The Still Centre*, five years later.

Over the winter of 1934–5 Stephen threw himself into an orgy of reviewing. He was doing 'two or three a week', he told Christopher. Money was tight. His Oxford bank stopped payments on his cheques in early January until the next quarter's Schuster money came in. Poverty was 'rather fun', he bravely told Plomer – although it did put a cramp on one's travel plans. So did international politics. Every year in Europe there were fewer places where a socialist poet with a bohemian lifestyle was welcome. The era of interwar tourism was drawing to an end.

'Please write often,' Muriel had implored when Stephen left Vienna. He did. On the evening of 3 October 1934, only days after his departure from the city, she wrote from a café replying to his first letter: 'Darling, I was so happy to have your letter today – and I'm glad you miss me because I am missing you very much. Vienna is very different without you.' They had agreed he would return (without Tony) to Vienna for the month of January. 'We'll have some lovely days and nights, darling,' Muriel promised. The January 1935 visit to Vienna is described with nostalgic vividness in Stephen's memoirs. The couple spent some idyl-lically wintry days in the cottage in the Vienna woods:

we ski-ed in the sloping fields and down the steep snowy paths through the woods. When, after some hours outside, we returned to the Blockhaus and, throwing off our outdoor clothes, cooked a meal on the oil-stove, there was something sparkling and joyous about our life, which seemed an inheritance from the past Vienna of horse drawn sleighs with tinkling bells.

These stolen weeks with Muriel were what Stephen calls 'a kind of lived poetry'. 'In poetry,' he wrote to Herbert Read, on 14 January, 'love can be a creative experience.' Muriel had explained to him 'the amazing vindication of love contained in modern psychoanalytic theories'.

Stephen had deliberately gone without Tony. 'My money affairs still don't quite permit it,' he explained to William Plomer. That he was acutely short of cash was true enough. But it is also clear that at this juncture Stephen did not want the added point of his personal triangle protruding into his affair with Muriel. If he *did* propose marriage to her, now was the time.

Vienna, in its mantle of new-fallen snow, was 'very beautiful'. In Muriel's new flat in Rummelhardtgasse he would sit writing, reading or correcting proofs of *The Destructive Element* (scheduled for publication in March) while she attended to her studies at the hospital:

Then she would come in from the snowy streets, her face like cold marble under her fur cap, and when I kissed her it was as though my lips, warm from sitting indoors, were like fire against her cheeks.

And, of course, they would make love with the passion and tenderness of honeymooners. Not that it was all romance. It was on this trip that Stephen was wholly inducted into Muriel's (Mary's) underground activities and the 'haunted lives' of her comrades. Above ground, he met the writer Hermann Broch, who told him 'Ihre Gedichte sind *wundervoll*' ('Your poems are brilliant').

During this January 1935 stay in Vienna – which was extraordinarily productive in terms of writing – Stephen worked Muriel into what would be the lead story in *Burning Cactus*, 'The Dead Island', which contains an etherealized Jamesian portrait of her. The reader is also given an un-Jamesian 'Muriel desnuda', a snapshot description which contrasts her rounded femininity with the boyish figures which had hitherto represented sexual beauty to Stephen:

her black hair, her wide too-ponderous hips, her thick thighs tapering with relief of the knees to the small feet, her small hands which were her only really ugly feature . . . her delicate ears, the fine nape of her neck, her firm breasts.

The question arises – why *didn't* Stephen marry Muriel? Manifestly he was tempted. She might well have consented had he seriously proposed. She certainly loved him. Her theory, as he knew, was that although she had two broken marriages behind her, 'there was no reason why one shouldn't just go on trying with marriages until one succeeded'. Stephen might have been the partner she was seeking. What seems to have prevented marriage was what they called his 'ambivalence', for ever 'keeping watch between us like a sword'. And, of course, there was his other lover. 'I cannot abandon Tony,' Stephen bluntly declared. The January opportunity was lost. 'Although we did not dream of it at the time,' Muriel writes, 'this was to be our last month as lovers.' On his part Stephen hoped he might be able to keep the affair alive until, three months later in April, he next returned to Vienna. By then some arrangement might be worked out.

Things did work out, but not as Stephen planned. In February Muriel became connected, through her 'Codename Mary' activities, with another socialist, Joe Buttinger (codenamed 'Wieser'), who was forced to go underground 'shortly after Stephen left'. He took refuge in Muriel's cottage – a risky move on her part. Again there were long, intimate, candle-lit conversations far into the night. In March, a couple of months after Stephen had gone, Muriel experienced what she calls an 'erotic spark'. She and Joe became lovers.

'I was immensely happy except for one thing – parting with Stephen,' Muriel later wrote. 'Nothing had happened to make me care less for him, but someone had entered my life whom I loved more.' She wrote a long letter to her English (and less-loved) lover, 'explaining as best I could what had happened and hoping that he and I could remain friends'. Stephen took the news philosophically, although it must have shaken him horribly. 'The letter was not entirely a surprise,' he records, stoically, in *World within World*.

It would have been possible to change their travelling plans, and perhaps advisable to do so. None the less, he and Tony went out again to Vienna ('our second hometown', as Tony called it), as arranged. His ostensible purpose, as he told Eliot, was to do some research for a new verse translation of Hölderlin. Stephen and Tony left London on 29 March. The two of them had canvassed round Maida Vale, up to the last minute, for the Labour Party in the forthcoming General Election. They would be out of the country in June when, to Stephen's chagrin (and Tony's increasingly Communist fury), the conservative Stanley Baldwin succeeded Ramsay MacDonald in another 'National Government'. Stephen regarded these ramshackle coalitions as impotent against the mounting tide of European fascism.

Stephen and Tony travelled to Austria via Germany. They called on Curtius in Bonn for a couple of days. The professor, as his friend Gide noted, was 'distressed' by Hitler's regime, but had resolved to be passive under its oppressions. What Stephen saw in Germany in April convinced him 'that a war is inevitable', as he told Christopher. He visited an exhibition of *Deutsche Kunst* in Munich. It had huge gaps where Goebbels, in a towering Nazi rage, had peremptorily ordered that 'foreign' pictures (i.e. by Jews and modernists) be removed. 'The strings were left dangling,' Stephen told Plomer, 'as a sort of gallows, I suppose, to warn artists.'

There was no excursion, as in previous years, to Paris or Venice. 'My money affairs still aren't going too well,' Stephen explained to Plomer. Nor was Stephen's heart in sight-seeing this year. He and Tony arrived in Vienna on 4 April. The meeting with Muriel was tense. 'We hardly ever see her,' Stephen told William, forlornly. Soon after his arrival she took herself off on political business to Paris and London during the spring vacation from her hospital, having (at last) passed her examinations. As always, she generously allowed her English friends to use her properties in the city.

In Vienna he wrote a poignant poem of love, now never to be fulfilled.

> If it were not too late!
> If I could mould my thoughts
> To the curved form of that woman
> With gleaming eyes, raven hair,
> Lips drawn too tight, like a scar,
> Eye sockets dusted with migraines
> Memories of earlier loves and wars
> And her smile learned in being human!

If only.

In a letter of 18 April he confided to Rosamond Lehmann his verdict on the end of the affair with Muriel:

She and I had a talk, and although I felt rather upset at first for a few days, I don't any longer now, though at moments I feel slightly embarrassed with her . . . Primarily it was our circumstances that made the whole affair transitional. Also there was my friendship with Tony which made difficulties to begin with, but not more recently . . . I'm very grateful to her for our affair, and I'm even grateful that it has dissolved so easily and with so slight a break in our friendship. Above all, I've had the experiences I wanted, in the way I wanted, with as little emotional tangle as possible, and that's enabled me to get over a very difficult and bad period without much fuss. Because now I am a different person. And I feel it all the more freely and strongly just because I'm not bound any more to her. When I first had this change of feeling about sex, I could hardly believe in it, because it seemed to make so little difference. But now I can accept it, because I can see it has made no difference. There has been no violent switch-over. All that's happened is that a whole part of my life which I had ignored suddenly became significant.

On 31 April Stephen and Tony returned to Mlini. As it had been the year before, the seaside resort was restful, and was as yet undisturbed by the summer flood of Nazi visitors. At this period Stephen wrote up what he called his 'Elementary Classroom Poem'. It would be an anthology favourite over the years, and witnesses to an increasingly angry flavour in his verse. 'An Elementary School Classroom in a Slum' (its printed title) was presumably inspired by a visit to Clémence Paine in the East End. Stephen had been immersing himself in Yeats, who also wrote a famous poem about visiting a school. Spender admired the patriarchal poet, but was contemptuous of his mystical 'Parnassianism'. There was also the inexpungable feeling that Yeats, like Wyndham Lewis (another fallen god), was soft on fascism. The anti-Yeatsian campaign would climax with a blazing condemnation by Spender of Yeats's *Oxford Book of Modern Verse* in the *Daily Worker* under the sarcastic title: 'Modern Verse – Minus the Best of It'.

'Elementary School Classroom' is written to controvert 'Among School Children', and Yeats's auto-iconic 'smiling public man'. Stephen is not smiling. The poem rises to a Blakean climax:

> Unless, governor, inspector, visitor,
> This map becomes their window and these windows
> That shut upon their lives like catacombs,
> Break O break open till they break the town
> And show the children to green fields, and make their world
> Run azure on gold sands, and let their tongues
> Run naked into books the white and green leaves open
> History theirs whose language is the sun.

Stephen's anti-Yeats animus in this poem and elsewhere in his writing of the period raises the question of where he stood vis-à-vis Eliot. Did he agree with his friend and mentor Herbert Read that the Christianized

Eliot of *The Rock* was 'shameful . . . merely parochial, in the proper meaning of the word'? 'Read *Tropic of Cancer,*' Herbert advised Stephen in May 1935. 'It is unbelievably scatological, but the man is so fucked out, physically and spiritually, that he has become something bodily pure,' adding, gratuitously, 'It makes a very illuminating contrast with Eliot.'

Spender was still at Mlini in early May when the reviews of *The Destructive Element* came in. Most were 'really quite favourable', he told his grandmother, with cautious relief. He was, however, annoyed by Desmond MacCarthy's suggesting that he (Stephen) thought Henry James was a Communist. The book had faults, he protested, 'but I am still only learning to write'. In *New Verse*, Geoffrey Grigson opened his review of the book with a wisecrack which was to pursue the poet for the next half-century: 'Stephen Spender is the Rupert Brooke of the Depression.' Writing privately, Herbert Read congratulated him on the 'extraordinary *wisdom*' of the book. Cecil Day-Lewis applauded 'your remarkable faculty for accurate generalization'. Eliot wrote with his usual sagacious approval, noting, however, that there were 'a few spots where the actual writing might be improved'. Stephen must, he chided, let Faber have 'first option' on any future book – prose or poetry.

The most judicious review of *The Destructive Element* came from Cyril Connolly, writing in the *New Statesman* on 4 May. Connolly was almost persuaded by the opening section of the book, which argued that Henry James – in his late phase – was both a modernist and a subversive. It was of the book's later sections, where Stephen argued for political commitment in the contemporary artist, that the review was most critical. And, woundingly, Connolly – writing as always with lapidary elegance – found *The Destructive Element* 'awkwardly written, arid, inconsequent, and hard to follow'. None the less it was, he conceded, 'an important book'. The hurried and ragged quality of his prose worried Stephen. 'I must really write much better,' he told Plomer. He put himself out to meet and cultivate Connolly on his next visit to London. The connection would lead, five years later, to the two writers' collaboration on *Horizon* and lifelong friendship.

By June 1935, there were added strains evident in the relationship with Tony. With *The Destructive Element* out of the way and Stephen's new political book, *Forward from Liberalism*, not yet begun, there was no typing to keep him out of mischief. But Stephen's sexual ambivalence was the most pressing and uncomfortable factor. 'Lately I have discovered,' he wrote to Geoffrey Grigson, on 6 July, 'that I am not even consistently homosexual.'

It was decided at this time that Tony would go to Vienna for two months
in September: 'to learn German really well'. Tony, whose politics were
becoming daily more radical, was excited by what he had picked up
about Muriel's underground work. He would be recruited three years
later, in 1938, to take on various missions for her.

In the event September was too distant and Tony, the impossible
companion, was dispatched to Vienna in late July. The German lessons
seem not to have worked out and he returned, early, to England in
August. 'He is a very different person lately,' Stephen reassured Plomer
(whose patience with the Welshman was limited):

He is going back to London . . . to try and find a job. I hope he will get one.
If he doesn't he'll do free-lance secretarial work for me and others, I expect,
but in any case he'll have a little flat of his own. The effect of living with me
is that our life together becomes a barrier which prevents or protects him from
having any life of his own. We've lived through the logic of all this: but we
might have realized it with a little forethought. In any case, I want to be alone.

'Personally,' Stephen told Lincoln Kirstein on 5 August, 'I don't feel now
that I want any "marital" relationship with anyone.' On his part, Tony
made the first of what would be a series of melodramatic 'running away
from Stephen' motions. He proposed to volunteer for the Red Cross in
Abyssinia, where Italy was embarking on an ugly-looking war.
'Homosexuals of his type,' Stephen told Kirstein, 'are obviously the best
nurses.' It came to nothing. Tony was capable of nursing nothing but his
grievances.

Stephen spent the whole of July at Mieders in the Tyrol, as he had
done the year before. He was by now reading Hölderlin furiously. 'I have
hopes that my German is improving a great deal,' he told his grandmother. On 12 July, he wrote an odd letter to Christopher, apologizing
for Humphrey's having injudiciously said that he (Stephen) felt 'superior
. . . re: buggers'. He was only normal, he reassured Christopher with a
breezy allusion to mad Hamlet, 'when the wind blows nor nor east'.
Christopher was, however, uneasy about his Berlin comrade's steadfast-
ness where sex was concerned. William Plomer, who had received the
full blast of Stephen's enthusiastically heterosexual bulletins in January,
was similarly uneasy.

Winifred Paine arrived at Mieders on 4 July. Still a redoubtably energetic woman, she dragged Tony off on long mountain hikes. Humphrey,

as he usually did, had made up the family party for a week or so before going on his way (he was travelling very widely at this period). Later in the month Lolly (i.e. Margaret) Low dropped by with Giles Romilly, Gavin Ewart and various of Humphrey's Architectural Association pals. It was all very convivial. Stephen, with his confirmed dislike of solitude, was glad to have the company, hard-worked as he was this summer. Like others at the time, he was particularly taken with Romilly, Winston Churchill's graceful and talented nephew. A dissident runaway from Wellington and the author of a successful book while still an under-graduate at Oxford, Giles was, Stephen told William, 'amazingly quiet and unspoilt, and . . . amusing. He reminds me of Wystan a lot.' Tony got on well with Giles as well.

Muriel passed through Mieders for a day, on her way to Jugoslavia where she was doing who knows what. King Alexander – a Serbian monarch – had fallen to a Croat assassin in October 1934, and the country was seething. Doubtless she had some underground mission in hand. The brief encounter between the two former lovers caused an inevitable pang. 'I probably won't see her again now for a year or so,' Stephen glumly told Plomer:

I ought never to have left Vienna [in summer 1934, he meant], but, as it is, I wasted almost a year making up my mind about her, and when I had done so it was too late. However, I dare say it is all for the best.

Stephen's work on Hölderlin was interrupted when John Lehmann had passed on to him, by Christopher, the proofs of the story 'Two Deaths'. Lehmann went through the roof when he recognized himself in the depiction of the English *flâneur* Landin, 'a man with certain tastes'. Stephen wrote a carefully apologetic letter: 'Of course I absolutely under-stand why you are hurt, and I am very sorry about it . . . The point is that the narrator of the story is no more I myself than you are Landin, or Tony, for that matter is Tony.' Lawyers were threatened. Stephen went on to explain at length the interior ironies of his narrative. But he changed Landin into the wholly unobjectionable Dr Mur: 'a middle-aged ex-schoolmaster, grey-haired, and wearing khaki shorts, who is leader of a communist *Zell*'.

Stephen was – in between his devotions to Hölderlin – writing poems of his own in what he saw as his 'new' mode: 'people like Edwin Muir and Herbert Read, whom I most trust like them very much, but editors

don't like them, because I have changed my style', he told his grandmother, insisting none the less, 'It's a better style.' By 10 August Stephen
was, as usual, in Salzburg with Isaiah and an assortment of Oxford friends.
Toscanini was conducting this year (Stephen was contracted to write an
article on the event for the *Yorkshire Post*). Stephen left the festival on
26 August. On the way back to London he spent another five days with
Curtius in Bonn before meeting up briefly with Christopher in
Amsterdam. His German mentor went over the Hölderlin translations
with him.

Stephen returned to London in early September to find, inevitably,
that Tony had found neither job nor flat. They renewed the lease on
Randolph Crescent for a year. Back in London, Stephen picked up the
familiar threads: visits to the Woolves, Lady Ottoline Morrell and
Fieldhead. A proposed volume of Hölderlin translations with Edwin
Muir came, alas, to nothing. A summer's labour was largely wasted. All
that survived were a few poems published in various journals over 1935–6
(notably a bunch in the first issue of Lehmann's *New Writing*, spring
1936).

A striking vignette of Stephen at this period of his life is given by
the American Emily Hale (T. S. Eliot's friend). Miss Hale took tea at
Tavistock Square (the heart of Bloomsbury) with Virginia and Leonard
Woolf in late November 1935, 'in the company of Tom Eliot, who is
one of a closer circle of friends, admitted to their life'. Also present was
'young Stephen Spender'. For the most part, she observed, 'the conversation was upon topics and personalities, known to the other four,
Stephen Spender being very much at home with his hosts also, and by
his very boyish open eyed, gentle manner, affording an interesting contrast
to the profundity of his remarks'.

Stephen's time was at this point (autumn 1935) almost completely
taken up with finishing the five stories which made up *Burning Cactus*.
The task took until well into November. Rewriting these pieces for the
umpteenth time left him in 'one of those awful moods of depression
about my work', he told Christopher, 'which completely undermine my
confidence and make it impossible for me to do anything'. He was, he
told Read at the same period (October 1935), 'going through a crisis of
extreme self-dissatisfaction'.

A symptom of Spender's extreme self-dissatisfaction was his miscon-
ceived resolution to expatriate himself (and an even more self-dissatisfied
Tony) to Portugal. The Cintra interlude finds no direct mention in *World*

within World. None the less it represented a resolution of kinds to the 'crisis' he complained about to Read. From one aspect, the six months taken up by the Portuguese experiment (late November 1935 to late March 1936) were the last throw of the communitarian ideal which had taken root in Auden's rooms at Christ Church and which was enthusiastically proclaimed in Stephen's 1931 letter to John Lehmann:

There are four or so friends who work together . . . Whatever one of us does in writing or travelling or taking jobs, it is a kind of exploration which may be followed up by the other two or three.

Isherwood, the main mover in the Cintra adventure, was primarily moved by a less than Utopian need to save his friend, Heinz Neddermeyer, from conscription. His plan was to renationalize the twenty-year-old Heinz in some South American country, where the necessary papers could be bought. To this end, they had been skipping ahead of the dreaded summons through various European countries.

The idea of founding a Utopian community in Portugal arose from conversation among a congenial band of visitors who descended on Christopher and Heinz in Amsterdam in late August 1935. On the 26th of the month Stephen and Tony arrived. They were joined on the following day by Forster with his policeman friend Bob Buckingham, and Brian Howard with his Bavarian friend Anton ('Toni') Altmann. Together with Klaus Mann and the ubiquitous Gerald Hamilton, the party celebrated Christopher's birthday at lunch in The Hague.

The notoriously degenerate Howard (immortalized by Evelyn Waugh as Anthony Blanche) was experiencing problems in domiciling Toni similar to Christopher's with Heinz. Altmann had been refused entry to England. On 1 September Christopher's diary recorded:

Brian wants to go to Portugal, buy a ruined palace, and keep hens and goats and grow oranges. Toni keeps making objections and warns Brian in advance that he won't clean the shit off the goats. Brian got angry with him and alarmed that his lack of enthusiasm would put us off. Actually, I don't want to go unless we can get Gerald or Stephen to come with us.

Christopher prevailed on Stephen and Tony (currently residing in a pension in Belgium) to join them in Portugal. But it would be a month before they could leave. Howard and Altmann had reconnoitred Portugal in October, after outlining the project to the others. The German remained living with (and sponging off) the expatriate painter John Strachey and his wife. The stipend of £3 a week which Howard remitted barely covered his friend's addictions. At an early stage Stephen and Christopher evidently decided that Brian and Toni were not suitable housemates.

On 10 December the quartet, Stephen and Tony, Christopher and Heinz, embarked on a steamer bound for Rio via Lisbon. They had fourteen pieces of luggage (immense steamer trunks, suitcases, rucksacks), two typewriters and a gramophone. Despite some heart-stopping moments, Heinz escaped official notice and as they left port, Christopher was 'light-headed with relief'.

The trip and segments of the subsequent sojourn in Cintra are recorded in a joint travel diary, assembled intermittently by the three Britons. The journals were evidently undertaken for recreational purposes 'in a tone of shipboard humour and were meant to be read aloud at once, before they could go stale'. The early entries by Stephen catch the excitement of departure and the boredom of the voyage, written in his packed, sub-Jamesian descriptive style with glints of mischievous comedy:

Thursday, Dec 12th. 1935
On Tuesday, when we left Brussels for Antwerp, Gerald came to say goodbye to us, wearing a huge fur-lined coat with a skunk collar in which his chinless, thick-lipped, flat-nosed face nestled. He was wearing no jewelry, but there was such a smell of scent in the room after he had come in that I said, 'What lady has been here with scent?' 'I'm still here,' he answered, bridling a little. We all kissed him goodbye.

This boat is very old and goes very slowly. The cabins are quite nice but stuffy as there is no draught through them. There are two lounges, one a drawing-room, very decorative, with a yellow-keyed grand piano, the other an Olde Tudor lounge, clawed over by five enormous electric fans, hanging from the ceiling like vampires. Here we read or write. In the other room, Tony strums on the piano and Heinz sings.

One of the songs Tony strummed and hummed was 'Cheek to Cheek' (from the Astaire–Rogers film), with its refrain:

> And the cares that hang around me through the week
> Seem to vanish like a gambler's lucky streak.

Christopher asked Stephen what he was thinking as he listened to the words. The ruminative poet replied:

'I was thinking about the lucky streak. If I'd written that, I thought, I should have made it somehow terrible and terrific. And how boring, I thought to myself, that I can only write about things terrifically.'

The voyage, as Christopher put it, was coloured by 'constipated oyster-grey boredom'. The communal diary is largely composed of malicious sketches of their travelling companions. The most spiteful observations were reserved for a family of 'colonial Nazis'. The wife patriotically jangled *Deutschland über Alles* on the ship piano for the benefit of her husband after dinner, displacing Tony and terrifying Heinz. The ship touched at Oporto on 16 December and the four young men went ashore to inspect the town (it rather reminded Tony of Torquay). They posted letters, bought newspapers, took photographs, sipped coffee, and drank too much port. Stephen 'got very tipsy' and giggly. Everything was incredibly cheap. 'We were going to like Portugal,' Tony concluded.

They landed at Lisbon the following day in sleet, fog and intermittently dazzling sunshine. Inevitably Anton ('Brian's Bavarian friend'), who was meant to meet them at the dock, was not there. They made their own way through customs ('remarkably efficient') and took a taxi (remarkably cheap, at 30s.) to Cintra, some fourteen miles away, where they were met by an effusively apologetic Anton at the farmhouse which Brian Howard had rented.

Anton took his steward's duties seriously. As Stephen pictured him:

He was followed by two farming mongrels, and carried a switch, and was either wearing breeches, or the kind of tweeds that a country gentleman who paints or translates or plays the pianola wears when he is doing nothing in particular.

His striking good looks were 'rather spoilt by alcoholism', Stephen thought. John Strachey, the English painter who was living in the house, was revealed to have a similar weakness for the bottle. His face was a 'darker shade of red' than even Anton's. His boozy cheerfulness made him good company. His wispy 'stork-legged' wife, as Stephen reported, 'greeted us in a voice that we could hardly hear, that hovered about the room like the noise of a mosquito'.

They were all taken with the beauty of the village, overhung as it was by cliffs, 'sprouting with fern-shaped trees and sub-tropical plants, like an enormous rock garden'. They stayed a couple of nights at the Hotel Nunes ('comfortable but bare') while finding their bearings and moving into a large cottage called Alecrim do Norte (the name of a kind of evergreen bush). Alecrim was surrounded by moors speckled with gorse and stone. When the sun shone – which it rarely did in the early weeks – it reminded Stephen, in his cheerier moods, of a Van Gogh drawing. In less cheery moods, it was like being imprisoned on Dartmoor.

Alecrim, they concluded, would 'do for three months, until we have looked round, learnt some Portuguese and acquired the necessary experience of prices and servants'. Then they would move into '*the* house', as Christopher called it. Meanwhile the two senior partners would settle down to read and write. Stephen had buckled down to 'a play about Germany and his book on Communism'. He was also teaching himself Greek, 'in order that I may read Greek tragedy in the original', he told Lincoln Kirstein, 'and write about Hitler'. He had been advised on the topic by Isaiah Berlin, who was keen to share his enthusiasm for the classics. On 7 December, shortly before the hopeful colonists embarked on their Portuguese adventure, Stephen wrote to T. S. Eliot ('Dear Tom') promising that 'I will do the play this summer. I am longing to get settled down.' The 'play' was what would two years later emerge as *Trial of a Judge* (at this stage provisionally entitled 'Death of a Judge'). A verse drama of martyrdom embraced, in the face of Nazi totalitarianism, it grew – in large part – out of what was by now a three-year-old discussion with Eliot on the subject of conscience and authority. The older poet had recently expressed his thinking in his verse drama *Murder in the Cathedral*. The themes were similar but the analyses were different.

For Spender the issues were essentially political, and focused in his complex ideas about 'liberalism'. *Death of a Judge* was the 'undoctrinaire' partner to his 'Gollancz book' (*Forward from Liberalism*, as it would be). For Eliot, Becket's martyrdom was essentially spiritual. Stephen's play was assured of publication by Faber and had already been promised performance by Rupert Doone's Group Theatre – when, that is, he was able to get the work on paper. It might not be easy. During January the proofs of *Burning Cactus* arrived from Faber. Eliot accompanied them with a letter hoping that Portugal would be 'favourable to work' but fearing that the diet might be 'constipating'.

Tony was appointed major-domo. He had for the purpose 'a huge account book'. It was his responsibility to keep the two housemaids in order (he found the 'southern races' incurably 'lazy'). It was also Tony's vexatious responsibility to work out which of the two couples owed the other what. There were the inevitable squabbles. Heinz had nothing to do but odd jobs about the garden. He was set to read P. G. Wodehouse in German. Tony, knowing little German, could not speak to Heinz, even about Jeeves. Neither of them knew Portuguese and they could not speak to the servants.

The cottage was rented from a 'businesslike' and tweedy Englishwoman, Miss Mitchell, a watercolourist and a spiritualist, who lived opposite. A disciple of J. W. Dunne (the evangelist of mystical time-travel), Miss Mitchell's former lives were more colourful than her current drab existence, or even her daubs. She had written up her various autobiographies, Strachey told them. One previous incarnation took Christopher's fancy. 'She started as a Syrian lad and had the bad luck to fall in with some Roman legionaries (the number is uncertain) who took advantage of her – I mean him – in a manner which makes her manuscript unpublishable.'

Within five days of landing at Lisbon, the fractures that would eventually break up the ménage were already showing. It rained incessantly. They ran up a massive 461 escudo coal bill (the bulk of which was charged to Stephen). Walks across the moors were an ordeal. The atmosphere inside the house was 'curiously directionless'. They felt, as Stephen put it, 'like fish and weeds in a tank of stagnant water in which the air was rapidly evaporating'.

There was a community of English expatriates in Cintra: but too old, gin-sodden, too respectable (*Daily Telegraph* readers all), and too boring – even the exotics and eccentrics – to amuse let alone sustain Stephen's cultural needs. Nor did the young Britons endear themselves to their new acquaintances (Tony's pro-Abyssinian outbursts went down particularly badly). It was in the company of some of these stuffed shirts that they heard the BBC bulletins about the deaths of King George V and Rudyard Kipling, on 18 January (the Britons evidently did not have their own radio). As Tony listened, he privately recalled 'how disappointed everyone was when old George got better last time'.

Portugal was cheap and safely out of harm's way. But its artistic, cultural and architectural heritage could not satisfy Stephen's appetite. None of them had any interest in Portuguese language and literature (Tony picked up enough to haggle over butter). Salazar's regime had effectively exterminated any intellectual or even bohemian life in the nearby capital. Unlike Germany, or Belgium, it was too far afield for frequent visitors.

Gerald Hamilton and Humphrey loyally came out (separately) in early January and furnished some welcome distraction. Stephen's brother was recovering from a minor operation. On 15 January, Heinz shaved all Humphrey's hair off. As Christopher noted sardonically: 'He has been meaning to have this done ever since I have known him – so the event was historic. Humphrey retired into Stephen's beret immediately the operation was over and now only uncovers himself in the privacy of the family circle.' Hamilton had a more painful mishap at the Hotel Nunes when he tried to use a hand washbasin as a bidet and 'the entire fixture was torn out of the wall and the bowl shattered, wounding him embarrassingly in the buttocks'.

In the absence of any other society, Stephen was thrown into close contact with Christopher, who he thought was manipulating him. Heinz was 'maddeningly' sulky as the weeks passed. He was furious at Tony, who 'bossed him about'. Tony cocked up the household bills, and stormed off to Lisbon shouting 'I don't want to stay' (he was a great bolter). They were not sorry to see the back of him; he talked 'endlessly'. But he returned that evening, still defiant and still talking nineteen-to-the-dozen.

Unluckily Anton introduced them to the Casino at Estoril in early February. Ennui led them to plunge headlong into play, with the inevitable damage to their collective (and modest) exchequer. Anton's growing debts to the Stracheys and bad behaviour were making social relations difficult. The weather remained appalling. Portugal was experiencing, Spender complained to Elizabeth Bowen, 'the longest spell of rain since the year of the great Lisbon earthquake'. The wet had given Stephen rheumatism. Heinz's chickens ailed and died despite his neurotic mothering of them. The news from England about the reception of the performance of the Auden–Isherwood play, *The Dog beneath the Skin*, was not uplifting. Nor could Stephen enthuse about it convincingly. As he told Herbert Read, he thought his friends' play 'suitable for 8-year-olds'. Humphrey left on 15 February for Malaga, 'infuriated by being in this damp, cold, raining climate – no better than England'. Christopher's novel was going badly, Tony had made no progress with his army memoirs (which Stephen had proposed, on his behalf, to Faber), and Stephen was half considering abandoning his 'book on communism'. On 8 March Hitler marched into the Rhineland.

For a while Stephen went along with the resolution that they would all move into a larger, permanent house on 1 April. As the weeks passed, the project became increasingly unattractive and finally out of the question. On 2 March Christopher confided to his diary: 'our attempt at living here together has been a complete flop. The schemes of taking another and larger house have been tacitly dropped.' Stephen and Tony departed on the Ides of March for Spain. The Portuguese months had not been entirely wasted. Stephen had on paper, as he told Eliot on 29 February, 'more than a third of my play about liberalism . . . I've put a corpse in the first scene and a parrot in the next.' Both body and bird disappear from *Trial of a Judge* when finally delivered, two years on. Stephen sent his copy of the two written scenes to Isaiah, for safe-keeping. His Oxford friend read the fragment carefully, objecting, perhaps, that there might be too much *larmes* – 'tearfulness'. Stephen replied (on 6 May) that 'when I think of the future of civilization one either has to be a satirist like Evelyn Waugh or Auden, or else, in one's work, one breaks one's heart.' In 1936 tears were in order, with Fascism insurgent.

Stephen and Tony were hugely relieved to put Cintra behind them. Domestic difficulties apart, Portugal was, as Spender told Kirstein, 'a bloody Germano-Italo-Hispano-Fascist Colony'. The rain continued to aggravate Stephen's rheumatism and sheltering indoors had led to friction with Christopher. Their relationship was always closer when they were apart. There was a comic farewell from the spiritualist lady when Stephen said that they were off to Athens. She hadn't been there herself, she solemnly informed him, 'for two thousand years'. Stephen and Tony spent four weeks in Spain. In Barcelona he wrote a poem, 'On the North Shore', which Herbert Read complained was too 'deliberately descriptive'. Stephen and Tony visited Madrid in mid-March. They made an excursion to admire the El Grecos at Toledo ('rather a poky little town'), visited the Prado and the Escorial. Stephen found Madrid 'even more characterless than Berlin'. It was in Madrid that they finally caught up with Chaplin's film *Modern Times*.

It was a good place to see Chaplin's 'Red comedy'. The Spanish capital was now a socialist paradise. In February 1936 the Popular Front (an alliance of Communists, Socialists and Liberals) had defeated the Conservative government of Alejandro Lerroux. As he had witnessed the twilight of Weimar Germany and democratic Vienna's dying moments, so Spender would be present at the birth (shortlived, alas) of Spanish Republicanism. Stephen was meanwhile learning Spanish in order to read Lorca, a 'modern poet . . . whose poems are extremely beautiful', he told Plomer. He continued studying the language and reading Lorca's

'beautiful poems' throughout the summer and recommended them unsuccessfully to Eliot. Barcelona – somewhere Stephen had positively disliked
during the 'fiasco' with Hellmut in 1933 – was now 'a town I am very
fond of'. The fact that he and Tony could live in some style for half-a-
crown a day helped. In a letter to Herbert Read, Stephen proclaimed
himself 'a communist'.

On 6 April the two young men took a cargo boat from Marseilles
to Piraeus. Fired by his study of the Greek dramatists, Stephen was eager
to see the country. In Athens, he visited his old family friends the
Stavridis. Spender was still an honoured name in the country. In early
May, they voyaged on to visit Fronny on his island at St Nicholas, where
he had built himself a villa. Turville-Petre was not, Stephen discovered,
an honoured name in Greece. Fronny, ravaged by syphilis, was in the
process of destroying himself, as scandalously as ever. In one of his infrequent moments of sobriety (and even more infrequent moments of self-
pity), he complained to Stephen 'that none of his servants had ever heard
of Homer'. Stephen picked up a touch of paratyphoid and his stomach
would be troublesome for a year or so after.

They stayed in Greece for six weeks before pushing on to Vienna –
by the Orient Express – where they arrived on 17 May. Muriel met
them at the railway station and whisked them off by taxi to the Blockhaus.
On the 22nd they took up residence again in John Lehmann's plush
atelier flat. Lehmann, who was buzzing round Europe like a self-important
bluebottle, had meanwhile gone back to Fieldhead. Stephen could have
the Vienna apartment for six weeks.

It was in John's Invalidengasse flat that Stephen drafted his 'communist book' (*Forward from Liberalism*, as it would be). Muriel was able to
get him much of the reading matter he needed from local libraries.
Victor Gollancz wanted 'An Approach to Communism' (the provisional
title) by 1 August, and was 'rushing' him, Stephen complained. He and
Tony charged through draft after draft, doing 2,000 words a day, leaving
enough waste paper behind them to keep Lehmann's flat in firelighters
all winter.

The Left Book Club was first advertised to the British public in
February 1936. Gollancz solicited postcards from those who wished
reading matter which would enable them to 'play an intelligent part in
the struggle *for* World Peace and . . . *against* Fascism'. This mailing list
constituted the so-called 'club'. Newly commissioned books, costing a
budget-price half-a-crown, and in uniform soft covers, were delivered

to members through bookshops or direct from the publisher (the books cost 7s. 6d. for non-members). The scheme was boosted by various news-letters and political rallies – often overtly Communist in spirit. Gollancz's was, Spender told Cecil Day-Lewis, 'the best of the publishing rackets'; the least capitalistic, that was. Cecil had joined the Party in 1935.

Stephen's book was advertised as forthcoming in the first advertise-ments of February 1936 as '*Approach to Communism* by STEPHEN SPENDER – in which a famous poet explains how he is approaching the communist point of view'. As Stephen wryly informed his grand-mother, 'a lot of people will buy it, under the impression that it is by uncle Alfred'.

The first two LBC titles were published in mid-May 1936. At this point membership stood at 9,000. By the time that Orwell's *The Road to Wigan Pier* was published a year later in March 1937, membership had soared to 47,000. Stephen's volume, aggressively retitled *Forward from Liberalism*, was offered as the 'book choice' of January 1937. This would mean, Stephen calculated, sales as high as 35,000 and a scale of payment far beyond anything he had hitherto received.

In *World within World* he recalls taking the completed manuscript of *Forward from Liberalism* to the Blockhaus, where he, Muriel and Joe spent a weekend discussing it. Few LBC titles can have been field-tested by discussion with practising revolutionaries. Writing *Forward from Liberalism*, Stephen told John Lehmann, 'has changed and strengthened my attitude both to politics and to work'. Jubilantly Stephen wrote on 27 July to tell Christopher that he finished the 'Gollancz book today'. He was off to Salzburg for two weeks 'to recover'. Recovery meant an orgy of music, good conversation, and gossip with Isaiah Berlin. Moore Crosthwaite – now a junior diplomat – would also be at the festival this year. Tony would leave Salzburg early (Stephen's Oxford friends did not have much time for the obstreperously talkative Welshman).

In mid-August Stephen undertook what was another summer ritual in the 1930s – a few weeks in the Tyrol at Mieders with friends and family. Why did his friend travel so much, William Plomer once asked. He was baffled by the bombardment of letters which he received in Maida Vale with exotic stamps and at erratic intervals. Plomer, after his two *Lehrjahre* in Japan, found everything he needed in W9. Indirectly, of course, William was inquiring why Stephen, now twenty-seven, did not 'settle down'. How could he consolidate his career (let alone his private life), gadding about as he did?

It was a good question. 'I am very unsettled,' Stephen explained, 'and I dare say I shall be always.' If he stayed in London, like William, 'I would acquire a mask. I would become a "figure", and I would gradually freeze into my little group.' But all this rushing around was not, as Stephen realized, good for his writing – any more than it had been for his father's.

In mid-July 1936 Spain exploded with the Generals' Uprising in Morocco. Franco crossed from North Africa with his Moorish troops, and the Civil War began. 'I think the Spanish business is the most terrible European disaster to date,' Stephen told Lincoln Kirstein. Even more terrible to him was the complacent reaction of his countrymen: 'The English bourgeois don't care enough: they are on the upsurge of a Boom which makes them think they are unaffected by the rest of Europe. The boom is due to armaments.' (In March 1936, the British defence budget allocation had jumped from £122 million to £158 million. This was also the year of the Jarrow Hunger March.) Spender's affiliations would shift over the next turbulent years but his opposition to Franco and Britain's spineless (or worse) 'non intervention' policy was a constant element.

On 16 April 1936 Faber had published *The Burning Cactus*, at 7s. 6d. The stories dated, in their different versions, from as far back as 1927. The volume had a bipolar dedication 'To W.H.A and T.A.R.H.' Unlike Christopher's Berlin stories, with their series hero Mr Norris, *The Burning Cactus* items lacked a central focus or location, moving as they did (and their author had) between Barcelona, Vienna, Mlini, Lausanne and the home counties. They registered different strata of their author's development. 'By the Lake' was a 1920s story, 'Two Deaths' firmly anchored in July 1934. The most substantial piece in the collection, 'The Dead Island', was impenetrably personal. It was, the author told Read, 'an attempt to recapture the second movement of Beethoven's Opus 111, Sonata, as performed by Schnabel'. Herbert cannot have been much enlightened.

John Lehmann, who had been so annoyed about the representation of himself in 'Two Deaths', generously praised the collection as 'a remarkable bit of work'. It gave him 'a powerful sense of one's bowels being eaten into' (not, when one thought about it, entirely gratifying to the author). It was another friend, Herbert Read, who put his finger on the main weakness in *The Burning Cactus* (Stephen had sent him the proofs, as he now did with all his important books): 'You don't, I feel, *invent* enough. You don't *lie* freely enough.' As Christopher said in another context, it was really Stephen who should have taken the slogan, 'I am a camera'. The stories are too literally autobiographical. And he seems to have written and rewritten them too often, over-cooking his literary effects.

The reviews were mixed. Since the awful shock of *Vienna* Stephen had inured himself to the critics' vagaries. He was steeled for bad notices. It was, as he explained to his grandmother, the tax he must pay for the extravagant praise lavished on his earlier volumes: 'I am treated to a certain amount of spite, just to make up for this equally ridiculous praise.'

Reviews of *The Burning Cactus* arrived on 23 April. Its author was still in Greece at the time, and not feeling at all well. Fleet Street provided no tonic. The *Evening Standard* summed the book up as 'unreal people in unreal situations'. (The lackeys of the Beaverbrook press had always had it in for him.) The *Observer* was only slightly less sniffy. The *TLS* thought that 'Mr Spender has by no means mastered the art of prose.' The paper was also offended by the homosexual tone of the stories: 'These young men burst into tears on the slightest provocation, dislike games, shudder at a woman's touch.' There were some good reviews by Geoffrey Grigson, Cyril Connolly and Graham Greene. L. P. Hartley, in the *Observer*, commended the stories' 'subtlety' and 'originality'. The *London Mercury* wrote that 'he has crystallized in poignant terms a civilization that must break through to a new life or perish'. But the consensus was against the collection. Some of Spender's friends professed to be embarrassed for him. 'Stephen's book has had *pulverizing* notices,' Rosamond Lehmann wrote to her brother John, who probably wanted to hear bad news: to Stephen, however, Rosamond wrote much more favourably about *The Burning Cactus*. Christopher did his best to reassure his friend: 'Cactus,' he wrote, 'is by far the most interesting book of stories since Lawrence. People are scared of it.' Which was probably true. In the way of some of Spender's other work, *The Burning Cactus* eventually found its own, minority, constituency. Ned Rorem, the extraordinarily gifted, gay and self-destructive American musician, recalls, as a young man, coming on a copy of the title story, 'The Burning Cactus', in an old copy of Lincoln Kirstein's *Hound and Horn*, and 'devouring and redevouring' it – identifying, all the while, with the mysterious hero, Till.

There were, however, not enough Kirsteins, Isherwoods or Rorems to make the book a sales success. Just as the reception of *Vienna* killed any inclination to write another long poem, so the reviewers' slighting regard for *The Burning Cactus* inhibited further experiments in that direction.

There were other forms to master. As Stephen told Geoffrey Grigson, he had 'an almost mystical feeling that I must go through the stage of disappointing all my backers'.

Spender's political positions consolidated over the summer of 1936. They were given shape by the intellectual effort of writing *Forward from Liberalism* and sharpened by polemical exchanges with ideologues like Dmitri Mirsky about 'where he stood'. From his time in Berlin and Austria, Spender had a first-hand knowledge of what street-Nazis were like. They were not literary coves. But he could see the pointlessness of socialist schismatism, which merely split anti-Fascism into factions. In an open letter in August 1936 in *Left Review* he argued, as he did consistently at this period, for a Popular Front in which divisive opinions, along the spectrum from liberalism to Communism, should be submerged for the greater good of democracy. In some sense he was pulled along by C. Day-Lewis, the most radically Communist of the new poets, and by John Lehmann, whose politically committed *New Writing* was launched in spring 1936, with the proscription that it would not 'open its pages to writers of reactionary or Fascist sentiments'.

The inevitable break-up with Tony came in September. It was sparked off by an ugly row about keeping on the flat at Randolph Crescent. In the heat of the moment Stephen told his friend he could no longer support him now that unpaid political activities were eating into his reviewing income. Their quarrels had anyway become intolerable for both men. Tony's increasingly rabid political views were the cause of a new kind of bitterness between them. In October 1936, Hyndman took the plunge and formally joined the Communist Party. He was evidently a lot further forward from liberalism than Stephen.

In *World within World*, Stephen asserts that the decision was his: 'I decided that I must separate from Tony.' With whatever heartbreak and recrimination, the thing was done. After the break-up, Spender took over Clissold and Diana Tuely's fourth-floor flat at 11 Queen's Mansions, Brook Green, Hammersmith. The Tuelys were moving to Kent, where they intended to grow apples and otherwise cultivate their garden. Diana was Margaret Low's younger sister (later Stephen's sister-in-law). He had come to know them through Humphrey and his Architectural Association set. The new apartment was furnished in the contemporary 'Finnish' style that Stephen admired. Louis MacNeice, in *The Strings are False*, recorded, without much admiration, that Queen's Mansions had a 'colour scheme out of *Vogue*, a huge vulcanite writing-desk and over the fireplace an abstract picture by Wyndham Lewis'. It was 'not quite big enough for Stephen', the other poet drily observed.

In Queen's Mansions Stephen could spread his wings with the advance that Victor Gollancz gave him for *Forward from Liberalism*. As he recalls in *World within World*:

I received a cheque for £300, most of which I spent on modernizing my high-up studio flat, looking towards the river across a view of many roofs . . . I bought three-plywood chairs and tables like those I had seen in Herbert List's flat in Hamburg. I had copper-bowl lamps which threw indirect light up at the ceiling, and lamps of tubular ground glass which also resembled Herbert's.

List actually came to stay at Queen's Mansions, a couple of weeks after Stephen moved in. It was not a happy experience. The carefree Hamburg of '1929' was long gone. The German, an alien refugee with nothing to do in London, mooned around the small apartment all day. Stephen eventually billeted him with Tony in his new place across the river. The two of them could moon together.

True to its Communist principles (and Gollancz's legendary tightness with money), the *Left Review* did not yet pay its contributors. Tony had taken 'a small flat [in Battersea] in which Cuthbert Worsley has the use of a room when he comes up to town', Stephen informed Lincoln Kirstein. Worsley – a former public school teacher, now a journalist – was one of the so-called 'bookshop crowd': Popular Front supporters, Communists, bohemians who hung around David Archer's bookshop in Parton Street. Worsley describes its political, freewheeling, sexually liberated ambience in his 1971 *roman-à-clef*, *Fellow Travellers*:

I had sought out Harry [i.e. Tony] at the Pleiades [Archer's] bookshop, where one could usually find him of a morning. The Pleiades Bookshop – or just the bookshop as we called it – was on the edge of Bloomsbury. It was run by a kindly dedicated male spinster, Edmund Gladstone [David Archer], who had stocked it with the powder and shot of every revolutionary movement and splinter group of the period, and it had become a kind of haven, or club, for young intellectuals, poets, artists, left-wing layabouts.

Hyndman fell plump into the last category. On his free days Tony still did some odd-job typing for his friend. This was the pretext for

Stephen continuing to dole out money. None the less, as he told Christopher, Tony was now 'semi independent'. In politics he had gone entirely his own way: he had 'joined the CP, who make him work for them from eight till midnight most evenings'. Tony's formally joining the party was worrying. But, as Stephen consoled himself, 'they also take the trouble to educate their followers: Tony is taught Marxism and also to speak in public.' Speaking had never been the gabby Welshman's problem.

As the political scene darkened, Spender's politics sharpened. Sides had to be taken. On 1 September 1936 he wrote for the *News Chronicle* a particularly angry piece recalling (with calculatedly bad-mannered indiscretion) his conversations, over dinner, with the Consul General in Barcelona, Norman King, during his visit there (on the rebound from Cintra) the year before. He had been appalled by the overt fascism of the diplomat's unbuttoned opinions. The newspaper published the article as by 'Stephen Spender, the well-known, 27-year-old, left-wing poet'. In his furious correspondence with London, King called him 'a communist poet who is known to be quite irresponsible'. The Consul had realized 'young Spender' was a 'nasty piece of work' when, showing 'extreme rudeness' he 'did not send even a card to my wife for our kindness and hospitality to him'.

The truth was, young Spender had been too appalled to be courteous. In his *News Chronicle* article he catalogued King's casual, postprandial insults against 'in particular the Catalans: their food, women, behaviour as husbands, ways of bringing up their children ("never send an English child amongst those corrupt little beasts"), their literature, their language ("insipid, bastard, Latin"), their painting – all were discussed and nothing was too bad to say about them'. Moreover, these ostensibly 'neutral' diplomats were wholly sympathetic to the Fascists. Spender's article provoked an extraordinary quantity of infuriated internal Foreign Office correspondence and intervention, at the highest level, with the editor of the offending newspaper. In the official mind, he was marked down as a 'declared communist', which, at this stage, he wasn't. Undeniably, however, he was sympathetic with Popular Front republicanism. And in his writing Spender was a main exponent of the idealism which, elsewhere in October 1936, was leading to the formation of the International Brigades and the British Battalion and, in progressive literary circles, to the cult of Lorca.

In early October Stephen met Inez Pearn, a postgraduate student at

Somerville College. They came together at a lunch after a Spanish Aid Committee meeting in Oxford where Stephen was speaking. The lunch was given by Isaiah Berlin – whom Stephen had, over the years, kept informed with eye-witness bulletins from the European front. As Philip Toynbee recalls, Stephen had 'semi-deified' status in Oxford at this period. If Spain was the poets' war, he was the iconic poet. Whenever he appeared, 'the hall would be packed'. His political chic was aided by a glamorous and dashing appearance. Sally Graves, one of Inez's contemporaries at Somerville, who saw him for the first time at this period at Oxford, recalls that her initial impression was undergraduate wonder at his 'extreme beauty'.

In a city of young men, Inez was a very rare bird: a pretty, clever, politically conscious girl. She was twenty-two, and had 'an oval, childlike face, under fair hair cut almost to an Eton crop'. Her habitually solemn expression ('horseheaded', as Virginia Woolf put it) is well caught in the William Coldstream portrait of *Mrs Spender*. Her dominant mood was, as her Somerville classmate Sally Graves recalls, 'deep seriousness' ('humourless' was the unfriendly epithet). Inez was committed to the Republican cause. In witness of her dedication, she had changed her Christian name from 'Marie Agnes' and renounced Christianity. She was in other ways a self-made woman. Her father played no part in her life. Anglo-Irish, she had been brought up by her mother and aunt in a series of seedy boarding-houses. Educated as a 'charity pupil' in convent schools in Portugal, France and England, Inez had conceived a bitter hatred of Catholicism, which fuelled her animosity against Franco to the pitch of fanaticism.

She had got a scholarship to Oxford in 1933, and studied modern languages under the formidable communist Enid Starkie. She got a First. At that period it was unusual for women students to enrol for second degrees. Inez had, however, won a scholarship to pursue postgraduate studies. When she met Stephen she was working on an edition of the metaphysical poetry of Luis de Góngora (this meant research trips to Brussels, from time to time). It was expected that she would follow the bluestocking (and Communist) example of Dr Starkie.

In the summer vacation of her final year, 1936 (as Franco launched his assault on the mainland), she had been in San Sebastian doing a vacation job as a 'governess to the children of rich Spanish reactionaries'. She had managed, as Stephen discovered (on their first meeting apparently), to slip away from her chaperone for love affairs with a diplomat and a

Spanish painter (the latter a Francoist, regrettably). Under the pseudonym 'Elizabeth Lake', she described this episode in a later *roman-à-clef*, *Spanish Portrait* (1945).

Isaiah's lunch party of 11 October was, apparently, very lively. Rosamond Lehmann, writing to her brother John the day after, noted that 'Stephen has just left [Ipsden, where he evidently spent the night]. We went to a colossal lunch-party with Shayah Berlin yesterday, and met numbers of young men, and John Sparrow, and two girls from Somerville who have been fighting in Spain – one of them quite ravishing, called Inez Perne [sic].' Although he did not at the time know it, Stephen was about to play a part (the leading male part, as it would flatteringly emerge) in a version of *Zuleika Dobson* – 1930s style. On 10 October, the day before the lunch-party, Philip Toynbee (then an undergraduate and severely Communist) had met, for the first time, 'the famous Inez', reputed to be 'the most lovely woman in Oxford' – a judgement with which Toynbee, having seen her with his own eyes, enthusiastically concurred. On discovering she was 'half Spanish' (she wasn't, of course) and a socialist, he recruited her for his Spanish Defence Committee. Walking home with his friend Bernard (surname unknown), Toynbee ('I find virginity repulsive') was excited to hear that Miss Pearn was 'a woman of wide experience': experience which he intended to enlarge even further. 'She loves desperately, chaotically,' he was told, 'and is thought not to be engaged at the moment.' Bernard sagely advised him not to woo her 'on the sex basis'. Politics was the royal road to Inez's heart.

Others had followed that road into her affections. Before meeting Toynbee, or Spender, Inez had conducted an affair for some time in England with Dennis Campkin (the son of Stephen's dentist, and a journalist). Over the next few weeks she would 'comfort' Dennis from time to time. She was, according to Humphrey Spender, 'enormously promiscuous' at this period of her life. As, indeed, were other young *doctrinaires* who extended Leninist anti-bourgeois liberations into their personal lives as 'free love'.

Inez called on Toynbee on 15 October – ostensibly on Spanish Defence Committee work. She was, he wrote in his diary, 'very lovely but somehow aggressive'. He invited her to dinner at the Union, where she ate and drank 'expensively'. Afterwards she sat in his room 'smoking like a chimney and talking about communism'. The next day he called on her, bringing with him the scarf which she had 'accidentally' left. 'She pretended she hadn't noticed she'd forgotten it.' He pursued her the next day, with the 'uneasy feeling she's not the least interested in me'. None the less, in his rooms they spent the day 'kissing on the sofa'.

The relationship progressed rapidly. On 19 October, he invited her into bed with him. She had, he recorded in his diary, 'no contraceptive [a diaphragm, presumably] so [we used a] French letter which I regretted'. She had, he noted admiringly, a 'perfect brown body like a Gauguin'. She was 'insatiable' as a sex partner, he found. Inez sportingly warned her new admirer that she had been engaged five times, and was currently involved with the 'mysterious Dennis'. She had also had at least one lover of her own sex (also in the background, although she was discreet on the matter, was the young philosopher A. J. (Freddy) Ayer. Philip must, she said, meet Dennis and 'convert him to communism'. On 21 October, Inez's landlady discovered the young couple in bed. They would, Philip feared, both be sent down. Inez, however, talked her way out of it. She was evidently skilled in such matters. They adjourned to the Cotswolds for a weekend, where the landladies were more complaisant. The following weekend, Philip was informed, she would spend with Dennis: not, apparently, with the aim of converting him to communism. She was also, she told him, seeing her new admirer, Stephen Spender, at lunch with Isaiah Berlin and other Oxford functions. This was the famous lunch-party.

By this point Philip was 'UTTERLY' in love with the irresistible Somerville scholar. He planned to be engaged to her by the end of the term. On 26 October, they too had lunch together and did some perfunctory committee work. There was, regrettably, 'no bed as she feels frigid'. They listened to Bach on the gramophone. Four days later, on 30 October, Philip made a promising conquest: he persuaded Inez to join the CP.

Inez evidently was beginning to reciprocate Philip's passion. On 12 November he recorded in his diary that she had, she told him, informed Dennis that she was now in love with him (Philip). Perplexingly, however, she went the same day to Stephen's housewarming party at Queen's Mansions. Inez was spectacular. 'Her looks,' Stephen records, 'made her the success of my party.' Young men jostled to be next to her at table. Stephen and Inez found themselves alone in his bedroom, where he kissed her and made a declaration of love. 'I asked her to luncheon next day at the Café Royal,' he later recalled, 'and later in the afternoon I proposed to her.'

It is not clear that Inez immediately accepted; although she certainly did not refuse. Philip (rather in the dark about what was going on) was informed by a well-meaning mutual friend, a couple of days later, that 'Spender means business'. There followed another evening of Bach on the hearthrug in her digs. It was clear that she was inclined to be 'Mrs Spender'. Philip wept, and she stroked his head. He was told that Dennis, to whom she had written confidentially after the party, had replied saying he approved of the relationship with Stephen; he, Dennis, was off to the USA – whether to nurse a broken heart is not known. On 16 November, Stephen was in Oxford. He and Inez went to dinner with Philip. 'I didn't in the least like him,' the bested rival wrote in his diary that night: 'they smiled joyfully at each other and after dinner, in the rain, she announced, "I'm going to marry Stephen."'

Things looked bad, but Philip was not a man to give up. He called on Inez on 17 November. Perverse as ever, she now thought she 'would not marry Stephen' (currently staying with Isaiah in Oxford). It was all, she felt, 'too dreadfully practical'. She was not, for the moment, inclined to be practical. She admired the other man, but 'loved Philip'. She was tearful about Dennis, whom she had once loved. Over the next few days, Philip pressed her to come to a decision. Marrying Spender, he thought, would be 'utterly idiotic'. On 19 November, Philip called on Inez in her lodgings in Walton Street and learned that she had determined to marry Stephen. Philip resolved not to be bitter and stoically decided that they would not, that day, make love. A week later, after seeing her with Freddy Ayer (with whom she had clearly just made love), Toynbee decided that he now 'detested' the woman he had loved a few days before.

Undergraduate adulation doubtless played a part in Inez's deciding in Stephen's favour. The imminent publication of *Forward from Liberalism* and his 'approach to communism' also supplied common ground. They also had Lorca in common. She agreed to help him with his translations of the poet. Did he, one wonders, know about her lovers, or the five previous engagements? One doubts it – at least, in their full and amazing intricacy. He wrote a rather awkward letter to Christopher, on 22 November. He was going to be married, he explained to his friend: 'I am in love with her and I think she with me.' Isherwood replied three days later, saying that he had heard rumours about Inez. 'I am very fond of all my friends' wives,' he said – enigmatically. 'Poor Tony,' he sighed. 'As you say, I expect he'll get used to it sooner than he thinks.' Privately he expressed his opinion that Stephen's marriage was 'absurd'. Stephen had also impulsively confessed his intention of marrying Inez to his new Oxford friend, Stuart Hampshire. He thought the woman a crashing bore – especially when she held forth about the iniquities of Franco against the background of thunderous flamenco music in the 'political' restaurants she favoured. And she was always holding forth.

Stephen's other bosom friend at Oxford, Isaiah Berlin, regretted to his dying day that he may unwittingly have played Cupid ('he was a terrible old matchmaker', Sally Graves recalls). Shortly after the first meeting in Oxford, he met Stephen bounding up the stairs at All Souls. Stephen's ingenuous admiration for Inez had been a matter of mirth to his friends. 'Are you going to marry that girl?' Isaiah jestingly asked. It might, he later realized, have popped the mad idea into Stephen's head.

Rosamond Lehmann found Inez:

attractive, with the look of a neat clever little boy, really a lovely shaped head and remarkable eyes. She is as cool as a cucumber, the most detached girl I've ever known. She's 22 and has had a brilliant academic career at Somerville . . . she gives one an antiseptic feeling, is highly egotistical, rather pleased with herself – and seems almost entirely devoid of emotional content.

Inez was, Stephen's Oxford friends thought, too fond of laying down the law and emotionally unstable. Even Stephen's dentist (Dennis Campkin's father) warned him against the match, as he drilled Stephen's teeth, a week before the wedding. Writing in *World within World*, Spender confesses that he finds it difficult to understand why he proposed to Inez. Clearly there was a political affinity – but no more so than with many progressive young women at the university. 'I hated living alone' seems to be the best answer he can come up with. To his confidant, Christopher, he was slightly more analytic as to why he felt impelled to this 'final step':

I'm just not capable any more of having 'affairs' with people; they are simply a part of a general addiction to sexual adventures. She also wants to marry me, and I think that we shall be able to build up a satisfactory life together.

If Tony 'will accept himself as my best friend rather than lover' all would be well, Stephen thought. It was a big if.

To Christopher a couple of days earlier he had reported that 'Tony is very upset indeed.' But he now had 'a flat of his own, and a job, and lover'. He had made a 'terrific scene' when Stephen told him about the marriage. But paradoxically the row seemed 'to cheer him up a bit'. As he admits in *Christopher and his Kind*, Isherwood was 'implacably' displeased with the marriage. He put himself out to be especially nice to Tony. To Stephen he wrote, on 25 November, 'I won't make any comment – except that I hope you'll be happy . . . Poor Tony.'

Stephen and Inez married in an 'abrupt little ceremony' on 15 December at the local Hammersmith Registry Office. It would, Stephen told Elizabeth Bowen, 'be very curious indeed', and so it was. Mrs Schuster was a witness and hosted the reception at 33 Albert Court. She also loaned her grandson the money to buy a wedding ring. On the way in the wedding car, Inez turned to Stephen, 'laughed and exclaimed "Oh, I am so happy!"'. Stephen kissed her 'and this moment was like an enormous load suddenly lifted from my mind'. But, he sadly noted, 'I did not completely share this exquisite moment with her . . . Part of my mind stood aside.'

Present at the reception at 33 Albert Court were William Plomer, Lady Ottoline Morrell, Auden, and J. A. Spender. A few anecdotes survive. 'JAS' scrutinized Wystan and sagely murmured, 'A remarkably self-possessed young man.' Isaiah Berlin could not bring himself to attend. Stephen, in a spasm of socialist benevolence, distributed the wedding presents to the 'paupers' among his guests. Inez's disapprovingly Catholic relatives kept to themselves, 'like the masked avenging figures in Don Giovanni, all in black', Stephen told Elizabeth Bowen, who could not be there. During the reception a courier arrived with a set of proofs which the groom absented himself for a few minutes to correct for immediate return. First things first. Inez told Philip, also forlornly present, that she hoped he wouldn't be killed in Spain. He went home, glumly, and read up on dialectical materialism.

Some of Stephen's militantly gay friends (most aggressively, John Lehmann) wondered how married life would suit him. He explained the nature of his contract with Inez, and his feelings about a wife, to Rayner Heppenstall, who had observed that he found female physiology 'disgusting':

we don't intend to have children for at least three years and at the moment I feel that Europe is so awful that I won't ever want to have children . . . The Spanish Civil War, hatred and various other things do disgust me. Phenomena such as menstruation, shit and morning sickness don't.

The one thing which does seem to have disgusted him was disloyalty. Shortly after their wedding Stephen discovered that, in November, while he and Inez were newly engaged, she had had a fling with Freddy Ayer. Spender was shocked enough to back out of an arrangement to co-write an LBC volume with the other man. Stephen's friends were shocked for him. Inez's conduct was 'squalid', Isaiah told Elizabeth Bowen, adding, 'Freddy is an absolute Italian, but I am surprised that Inez is thought suitable for even a temporary flutter.'

As he prepared for the publication of *Forward from Liberalism*, Stephen saw himself as an author transformed. The marriage with Inez had confirmed his new political commitment. Politics meant meetings and rallies. Stephen was, he discovered, an effective public speaker. By autumn 1936 he was lecturing in places like Birmingham, Manchester and Sheffield for the Popular Front. His oratory went down particularly well with earnest undergraduates in the provincial universities. So confident was he in his new platform abilities that in November he was toying with the idea of a lecture tour to America the following year, if Lincoln Kirstein could help arrange it.

The year ended with a personal crisis. Without Stephen to restrain him, Tony hurtled off the rails. The ex-Guardsman had threatened to run away and fight in Spain in the immediate aftermath of the marriage to Inez – probably during the 'terrific scene' that Stephen described to Christopher. The International Brigade had been formed that same month, November 1936, and was calling for British volunteers (there would in time be 2,762 of them; 500 would be killed in action). As Stephen told Christopher, he had on that occasion contrived to dissuade Tony from any such craziness – probably with the guarantee of continued 'financial assistance'.

A month later, in late December, Tony again declared that he was leaving to join the International Brigade. This time Stephen 'didn't try' to stop him. In his Christmas letter to William Plomer, Stephen reported that Tony had just left for Brussels, *en route* to Spain with Giles Romilly and another ex-guardsman, Bert Overton. Romilly – nephew of Winston Churchill and brother of the more famous rebel, Esmond (an even earlier volunteer) – had dropped out of Oxford, amazing contemporaries like Philip Toynbee with his determination to fight or die for socialism. As Tony Hyndman recalled (to Philip Toynbee) forty years later, Giles phoned him from Oxford and they met the following day in wintry Hyde Park: 'We walked slowly along the main footpath. I

told him I would go with him as soon as possible; that once decided
it was fatal to hang around.'

'Tony is really confident about it,' Stephen gloomily told Plomer, 'and
convinced that it is his duty as a party member with military experience.' He told Rayner Heppenstall on 20 December that 'I do most
bitterly weep about this; for selfish reasons his going away and staying
away are almost unbearable to me.' He wrote at greater length to
Christopher, with whom Tony, Bert and Romilly would stay in Brussels
before making their way to the Spanish border:

Tony will tell you that he is on his way, via Brussels, to Madrid, to join the
International Brigade, where several other of his friends are going. My own
first reaction to this has been a selfish feeling of utter misery. Apart from Inez,
Tony is my only intimate friend in London.

Christopher was sympathetic. 'I am as miserable as you are about this
business.' It came on top of the news that Wystan and Wogan (Philipps)
were also going to Spain (with 'Medical Aid'). 'Let's see if we can't both
arrange to get reporter jobs and go out together in the Spring,' he
suggested. 'I suppose Inez would come too?'

Tony's volunteering for the International Brigade was an act of madness.
He was a semi-invalid, by nature a pacifist, emotionally unstable and
incurably insubordinate. He should have gone to Spain as a medical
orderly, if at all. It is unlikely that Stephen *was* the decisive influence on
Tony's enlisting. His work at *Left Review* and his hanging around David
Archer's Communist bookshop in Parton Street had thrown him together
with a group whose motto was 'action'. As James K. Hopkins notes, in
the early months of the war there was a rush to join up by young British
engagé homosexuals (like Tony) and at this stage – before the ritual degra-
dation of Gide a year later – the Party was only too pleased to use them.
After the defeats of mid-1937 (especially the decisive loss at Brunete),
the International Brigade would be thoroughly militarized. Romantics
like Romilly and misfits like Hyndman (and, as it would turn out,
Overton) would thereafter be unwelcome. But in December 1936 it was
still what Stephen famously called it, 'the poets' war'. Romantic gestures
were in order and misfits welcome.

Stephen saw the trio off from Victoria Station. He pressed £30 into
Tony's hand 'in case, he said, I changed my mind and wanted to get
back home'. It was a prescient parting gift. Tony, Giles and Bert spent

Christmas (as planned) with Christopher and Heinz in Brussels. 'It was a success,' Christopher reported. And, he told Stephen on 27 December:

You can set your mind absolutely at rest about one thing: Tony is not going to Spain on account of your marriage. And he's not feeling badly about it any more. I am absolutely certain of this, because we had a conversation when we were very drunk and the way he said it was really convincing.

He, Heinz and Gerald had seen the volunteers off on the train (with a UF Salute) on 27 December. *Le Soir* had sent a reporter: 'Giles and Tony were pleased,' Christopher thought, 'to have this opportunity of striking a blow for intervention.'

Stephen wrote back to say that he was very grateful for Christopher's letter and the confirmation that 'you have the same impression as I did about Tony's motives for going away'. He had been in touch with one of Tony's sisters, however, who thought 'it is the fault of my ideas that he has gone to Spain'. It was horribly ironic. For almost two years he had been trying to launch Tony into 'independent' life, without success. Now he had made his move for independence in a way that must, as Stephen foresaw, end in tears. This 'awful business' about Tony, he told Christopher, 'undermines everything'. So it would.

The relationship between Stephen Spender and Tony Hyndman has been more exhaustively depicted and mulled over in print than any since Bosie and Oscar. It forms the nucleus of Cuthbert Worsley's *Fellow Travellers* ('not a novel – a memoir', he insists in his 'Author's Note' – not always a reliable memoir, one should add). It features centrally (and courageously, given the date of publication) in *World within World*. It is gone over in Isherwood's *Christopher and his Kind*. And it is distorted in David Leavitt's *While England Sleeps* (in both the suppressed and unsuppressed versions). The relationship is discussed by any number of critics, biographers and annalists of the 1930s. Hyndman himself intended, at one point, to write a full-length account but only managed a summary in his chapter for Philip Toynbee's *The Distant Drum: Reflections on the Spanish Civil War* (1976).

Various accounts are given as to why the relationship broke up. Most authoritative is Spender's own, in his autobiography. Most sympathetic is Worsley's. He was close to both men in 1936–7. The break-up was necessary, Worsley records, because of Spender's 'experiments in heterosexuality'; successful experiments, as it would turn out. By 1936, Hyndman 'had virtually ceased to perform any function in [Spender's] life. If he had begun as a sort of secretary-wife he had by now ceased to be either.' Quixotically, Spender had tried to 'improve' Hyndman but by so doing he merely exacerbated the other man's incompatibilities and resentments. As Worsley (a friend of Hyndman's) puts it, bluntly, 'Perhaps [Tony] ought to have stayed a tart really. He had all the qualities of a really high class tart.' Spender now needed much more from his partners. But it would require more 'experiments' – some very painful – before he would get what he needed.

Spain and After

On 11 January 1937 Victor Gollancz published 42,000 copies of *Forward from Liberalism*. Spender's political book opens with a proverb from the poet Blake: 'Religion is politics, and politics is Brotherhood.' The subsequent text is in three sections, which form the image of a pilgrimage: 'Journey through Time', 'The Inner Journey', 'The Ends and Means'. Journey's end in *Forward from Liberalism* is, necessarily, Moscow. The book concludes with a eulogy on the Soviet Union's new constitution, which rings hollow and must have tasted sour in Spender's mouth, even as he wrote it. 'In the new constitution,' he intoned, 'the Soviet has removed the main barrier to real liberty of thought and discussion: terror' (with the appointment of Nikolai Ezhov as head of the NKVD in September 1936 Stalinist terror would, in fact, reach unprecedented peaks). Spender was, in later life, remarkably candid about his short-sightedness in this politicized phase of his career. But, as Natasha Spender points out:

Stephen had experienced Fascism during the years before he went to Spain. He had seen Nazis beating up and killing not only Jews but Communists in the streets of Berlin, and in Vienna he knew through Muriel Gardiner's Socialist group the Nazi horrors of pre-Anschluss times. In England he'd seen the ugliness of Mosley's blackshirts beating up people in the East End and the iniquitous 'non intervention' pact.

What he had not seen were the iniquities in the Soviet Union. 'Russia was known indirectly', by hearsay and propaganda.

What strikes one reading *Forward from Liberalism* is how undutiful Spender is. Quoting his admired Otto Bauer (the exiled Viennese socialist leader), he condemns the persecution of the kulaks, and the callous removal of whole populations in the service of Stalin's grandiose schemes. Spender as defiantly opposes the party line on the Moscow show trial of Zinoviev and his henchmen in August 1936. In the last section of the book, 'Ends', Spender dramatically interrupts his disquisition (he finished the book in late July 1936):

Since I wrote these [immediately preceding] pages, the execution of Zinoviev and his fellow-Trotskyists has taken place. This trial emphasizes the fact that unless the democratic constitution is quickly introduced, there must be many more such trials. For at present opposition to the Soviet government can only take the form of conspiracy against the leaders of the state. If criticism in Russia is not to become a pernicious disease, it must be legalized.

What Spender demands is that the USSR should go backward to Liberalism. As likely (in January 1937) as water flowing uphill.

Spender had wilfully defected from the shabby Left Book Club line on the Moscow trial. As early as 3 February, Victor Gollancz had written trying (vainly) to argue his author out of 'your misconception of the undemocratic nature of the Soviet regime'. Spender must have inserted his interruption about the Zinoviev trials into the final proofs of *Forward from Liberalism* – which meant that it escaped the notice of the LBC's doctrinaire general editors, Harold Laski, John Strachey and Gollancz himself. The hardliner, John Strachey, was publicly critical of Spender's 'deviance'. In *Left Review*, the more dutifully Communist poet Randall Swingler noted severely that Spender would not admit the 'irrefutable' truth of Zinoviev's guilt because he was still trapped in 'Liberal solipsism'.

The *Daily Worker* was likewise displeased by *Forward from Liberalism*. So, doubtless, was the Party hierarchy. But they were not so displeased as to risk losing such a valuable fellow traveller. Stephen Spender – with his 'semi-deified' status among the undergraduates of Oxford – was worth battalions, Liberal Solipsist though he might be. In his study of British intellectuals in Spain, *Into the Heart of the Fire*, James K. Hopkins tracks down several young idealists who volunteered to serve in Spain under the direct influence of *Forward from Liberalism*. The book spoke to the undergraduates of Britain. Stephen Spender incarnated the values they would fight for. Almost sixty years later, Tony Benn fondly recalled it as 'one of the books that converted a generation'.

One afternoon shortly after the publication of *Forward from Liberalism*, in the first days of January 1937, its author was summoned to the Party's dingy headquarters in King Street to meet Moscow's man in London, Harry Pollitt, Secretary of the British Communist Party. Pollitt was, at this time, methodically recruiting charismatic intellectuals from the ranks of the LBC – probably with the connivance of Gollancz and the club's board. Spender was disarmed by 'Comrade Harry's' avuncular warmth, his 'friendly twinkling manner', and his proletarian bona fides (he had seen his mother die of starvation, as a Manchester millhand). Stephen, he felt, did not have the virtue of *hatred* for the capitalists. Hating Fascists was insufficient. He goodnaturedly took Stephen to task on the matter of the August 1936 Moscow trials. Of course young Spender had been wrong to suspect anything fishy. Moving on to more congenial matters, Pollitt suggested they were, at least, of one mind on Spain. It would help the Republican and Popular Front cause greatly if Spender joined the party. In return, 'Pollitt was willing for me to write an article, in which I put my point of view, to appear in the *Daily Worker* at the time when I joined.' Spender agreed to this bargain 'and Pollitt at once gave me a membership card [and] a few days later my article was published in the *Daily Worker*'. So, at least, Spender recalls in *World within World*.

It is clear, however, that Spender (writing eleven years later) mis-remembered some details. The first meeting with Pollitt took place in early January. He did not receive his party card until 16 February, and his article 'I join the Communist Party' appeared in the *Daily Worker* on 19 February, six weeks after his interview in King Street. Between the first meeting with Pollitt, and the public declaration of his party membership, Stephen made a trip to Spain, on behalf of the Party but not as a declared member. In his heart, as he told Herbert Read on his first visit to Republican Madrid 1935, he had been a communist (of his own idiosyncratic kind) for a year. Indeed, together with Christopher, he had proclaimed as early as 1932 that 'we are all communists now'. He had been reviewing poetry in the *Daily Worker* since October 1936. Cards were not entirely rele-vant to his convictions.

At this first meeting Pollitt evidently intimated that, as a strapping young man, Stephen might join the newly formed International Brigade. He, Harry, was alas too old to bear arms. Stephen objected, reasonably enough, that he had 'no qualifications as a soldier'; and, as he knew, the Brigade did not at this stage want amateurs whom it had no time to train. Nor, since he could not drive, could he join the ambulance brigade (as dangerous as front-line soldiering). According to legend, Pollitt jovially retorted that he could at least 'get himself killed, to give the Party its Byron'. Spender demurred. But if there was some other capacity than shooting or being shot, he would be glad to do his bit.

According to *World within World*, 'Shortly after Tony's departure for Spain and a few days after my joining the Communist Party, the *Daily Worker* telephoned me and asked me to report on the case of a Russian ship which had been sunk by the Italians in the Mediterranean.' Moscow was worried about the fate of the crew of the *Comsomol*, which had been lost transporting military supplies to the Republicans. This assignment from the *Worker* was in fact delivered some six weeks *before*, not after, Stephen publicly joined the Party.

Before accepting the *Comsomol* mission, Stephen weighed up the issues. He could see that the *Daily Worker* was asking him to spy for Moscow. But 'it did not involve betraying my country, nor obtaining military secrets, nor indeed anything outside the run of ordinary journalism'. He agreed on two conditions. He would accept no payment other than out-of-pocket expenses. Secondly, he requested that he might be accompanied by Cuthbert Worsley. Worsley was a close friend and resolutely anti-Fascist. He was also a close friend of Tony's. Both men were concerned about him. Mail from Spain was erratic and censored.

Stephen wrote to Christopher, on 5 January, to tell him that 'Cuthbert and I are going for 14 days on rather an important job to the rebel part of Spain . . . I shall tell you all about it when Inez and I reach Brussels' (in the event, she would go by herself at the appointed date, in mid-January). Stephen went on to disclose his other motive for the Spanish trip: 'Since Tony went, I have felt frightfully unhappy and this feeling has grown worse, on account of all the news in the papers.' He was not, as he revealed, at all fit for a trip to Spain. His stomach was still giving him trouble: 'I get colitis and shit blood.' But, as he told his grandmother, 'It is really the least I can do, considering how much other friends of mine are doing.'

The two 'fellow travellers' (as Worsley wryly called them, in his 1970s novel) flew from London to Alicante via Marseilles and – through a storm – to Barcelona, where they arrived on 6 January. The poet's eye devoured the 'outspread map of a country torn by war . . . like a mutilated corpse' which, under perverse sunlight, 'had an appearance of incorruptible morning peace'.

One of Spender's less poetic qualifications for undertaking the

Comsomol mission was that he knew this part of Spain well, having tramped over it extensively with Hellmut in 1933. And, since the trip in April 1936, when he had decided to translate Lorca, he had learned passable Spanish. It is also clear, from a letter he wrote to his grandmother on 5 January, that the party wanted him to report on 'the influence of the Germans and Italians' in southern Spain. Although he later played it down, it was no jaunt, nor mere tourism, that he and Worsley were embarked on.

After landing, Stephen and Worsley made their way south to Gibraltar. The Spanish consul they found to be 'courageous and sympathetic'. They were, however, turned back at Cádiz on 14 January by Franco's guards, who were suspicious of the two Englishmen. Resourcefully, Stephen recruited Lord Marley – *persona grata* with the Fascists – to make inquiries on their behalf at the Italian consulate in Cádiz. He and Worsley meanwhile made day trips to Tangiers, Oran and Algiers. Here it was that Franco's insurgency had begun, and where the Nationalist headquarters were still located. Again, although Spender never stressed the fact, it was a risky business.

They returned to Gibraltar on the 21st. Marley had discovered that the surviving crew of the *Comsomol* was indeed interned in the city – 'an obvious step which could easily have been taken without our leaving London', as Spender later claimed. Perhaps not. Spender is typically self-deprecating about this episode in *World within World*. Later commentators follow his lead and scoff at the idea of Stephen Spender, secret agent. Isherwood is nearer the truth when he points out that Stephen and Worsley could easily have got themselves shot had they got into Cádiz.

Worsley got to know his companion well on this trip. Thirty-five years later he would publish a sympathetic and acute account of Spender's complex personality, based on these weeks together:

He was in constant conflict with himself. I often think of him as having combined in his remarkable person about as many of the current neuroses as could easily be filled into one man. But whereas these, in a less extraordinary person, would surely have produced a breakdown, if not madness, he was somehow able to contain them. He had a remarkable capacity for enduring contradictions and never minded being caught out in them.

As Spender records, during these weeks in Spain and North Africa a less official part of his and Cuthbert's minds was 'preoccupied with Tony'.

His friend was, as Stephen later learned, undergoing his month's basic training near Albacete. It was an unremitting shambles. Tony had already disobeyed an order he 'didn't agree with', and was given an unpleasant few days in the glasshouse with the warning that he was in 'a real army where orders had to be obeyed'. In his later recollections of this period, Tony claimed that Giles Romilly (whose brother, Esmond, and other influential friends were serving in Spain) had assured him that the International Brigade was different from 'real armies'. If you didn't agree with an order, you could 'democratically' disobey. He now knew different.

In the relaxed regime of Randolph Crescent the former Guardsman had quite fallen out of the habit of taking orders. It was, as he later told Stephen, 'Profound disillusionment No. 1'. It may have been another profound disillusionment that his comrade, Giles Romilly (younger and less experienced in military matters than Hyndman, but a 'toff' and well connected), was promptly inducted into the Brigade's (unofficial) officer corps while he, Tony, sweated with the gutter riff-raff of Glasgow in the other ranks, even though he was a trained ex-Guardsman. Communism had its limits. Comrades they may have been on their way to Spain. But during their month's basic training in Albacete Giles and Tony went their separate ways.

On 22 January Spender and Worsley returned to the UK as they had come, by air via Barcelona. According to *World within World*, they stayed two days in the city. In order to leave, as Stephen recalls, he had to get clearance from a British Communist official. This jack-in-office refused to issue the necessary document until Spender could prove that he was indeed Spender. He did so by showing 'the article I had written in the *Daily Worker*, where it had appeared with my photograph', upon which clinching evidence 'even he could not prove I was someone else'. The episode rings true, but it must clearly be misplaced. The *Daily Worker* article did not appear until a couple of weeks *after* Stephen returned to England. The episode with the officious apparatchik must have happened at the end of his second trip to Spain, in April. Spender and Worsley arrived in London on 5 February, mission accomplished. Intending to stay two weeks, they had in fact been away four. Worsley promptly went back, to serve with 'Medical Aid' in the ambulance corps (he seems to have caught up with Tony in February). It was a courageous act. Front-line medics were as likely to be killed as combatants.

After his return from Spain there was the obligatory debriefing with Harry Pollitt on 7 February. Britain's top Communist was pleased. Again he worked his bluff charm on his glamorous new recruit. Again Stephen succumbed. It was the day of the first great LBC rally at the Albert Hall and 'Comrade Spender' was applauded by the 7,000-strong audience. 'The transformation of Great Britain into a Socialist State is *imminent*,' Gollancz announced, to thunderous applause. Spender would be part of that utopian event.

They had further plans for him, Pollitt told him:

In future the C. P. are going to make use of me, sending me as a journalist with Hunger Marches, to the Distressed Areas, etc. I am very glad. It will make me cross a barrier I have wanted to cross for a long time.

He was no longer, he felt, trapped in the *vie littéraire*, as he told Plomer. He wrote in the same enthused spirit to E. M. Forster, who wryly sent him a gift copy of *Das Kapital*. It was at this point, evidently, that Spender resolved to make public his joining the party.

Two days later, on 9 February, he left to join Inez in Brussels, where she was grinding away at her seventeenth-century Spanish manuscripts. It was a flying visit. He reported himself to William Plomer a happily married man:

I don't feel the kind of reticence I felt about our being married up till now . . . I used to be a clockwork machine with a regulator which was my life with Tony, ambition, money, etc. Now the regulator's gone, and I feel like one of those fireworks children put on pavements which zip about the road and crack.

He would stay only a week with Inez before zipping off again. He had an engagement to speak about Medical Aid to the Quakers at Friends' House, and was back in London on 12 February. Inez remained un-zippingly in Brussels. The visit had not, apparently, gone as well as Stephen suggested to William. Philip Toynbee noted in his diary, on 16 February, having received a

Strangely illiterate letter from Inez − Stephen isn't living with her − is going to spend a day with her on his way to Valencia. Exceedingly odd. She sounded genuinely depressed about Spain and I liked her for the letter and wrote back at once, very inquisitive and frank, saying I'd sleep with her if ever I came to Brussels . . . Freddy [Ayer] reading Inez's letter said 'the dog it was that died.'

On his return to London Stephen made speeches and on one occasion marched down Regent Street carrying a sandwich board with Republican slogans on it. He attended meetings and learned that the Party, in its wisdom, had a new assignment for him. They wanted him to return to Spain – again as a journalist – but now to broadcast radio propaganda from the UGT (workers' union) station in Valencia, currently the seat of Republican government while Madrid was under siege (Auden had also been assigned to broadcasting propaganda from Valencia in January 1937). There was also the possibility that Spender might be assigned as a 'political officer' to Albacete. Pollitt was 'rather keen' about this.

Spender was, as it happened, rather keen himself to get back to Spain. He was becoming increasingly worried about Tony. The Welshman was having a hard time (as were the Republicans generally). His unit – unblooded in combat, poorly armed, and with only four weeks' training – was thrown into the savage Battle of the Jarama River on 12 February. It sustained fearful casualties. Tony had lain for four days in an olive grove, while three-quarters of his battalion was killed around him. Many died, slowly and agonizingly, in the dirt where they lay. They were machine-gunned from the air by German planes. One of his close friends went raving mad under the strain. Another died. Tony recalled it in his fine poem, 'Jarama Front':

> . . . No slogan
> No clenched fist
> Except in pain.

It was scarcely less painful for those who survived. Cuthbert (now serving with the Canadian Medical Unit) saw Tony and Giles on the fourth day of the battle. Both were shattered.

Two weeks later, at Sierra de Pingarrón, in the front line, Tony flatly refused an order to advance. He was sent back under guard to Albacete. It was, as far as Tony was concerned, the end of the war. It was agreed that he would remain in service with the Battalion, but only in rear echelon duties – away from the bullets. It was an unusually sympathetic privilege, probably awarded in view of Hyndman's clearly being unwell, shell-shocked and possessed of friends in high places.

Stephen was unaware of the hell that Tony was going through. He did, of course, like other thoughtful observers, suspect that the war was

going badly. Other things were going badly. At tea with the Woolves on
16 February he complained about Inez's not being with him in England
and gave Virginia to understand that he was coming to regret his marriage
to her. There was a lot of pressure on him. On the same day that he
took tea with Virginia, he had received his Party card and had written
his lead article for the *Daily Worker*, which would appear on 19 February
under the headline 'I join the Communist Party'. In the article, Spender
grits his teeth and publicly retracts his earlier criticisms of the show
trials, accepting Pollitt's solemn assurance that there had, indeed, 'been
a gigantic plot against the Soviet Government and . . . the evidence was
true'. His friends were dismayed by the article. Isaiah wrote to Elizabeth
Bowen on 3 March, 'I am frightfully upset about Stephen's public renun-
ciation of his book & joining of the Com. Party. Partly out of pique,
because of my wasted eloquence (you remember, at lunch). I think it is
all due to Tony & sentimental & therefore is bound to lead to embarrassing silliness.'

'The Communist Party warmly welcomes Comrade Spender to its
ranks,' the *Daily Worker* declared, with its usual reptilian salutation. But
the welcome never reached West London. The local Hammersmith cell
never got in touch with Comrade Spender, and apart from his original
half-a-crown subscription he was never asked for, nor paid, any dues. It
is unlikely that he was ever, in any formal sense, a member of the Party.
Spender informed readers of the *Daily Worker* that he was about to leave
for Valencia, 'in order to broadcast anti-fascist propaganda from the UGT
station'. In *World within World* he says that the invitation was to be head
of the outfit – which would have meant being in Spain (and away from
Inez) for a long time. In fact, his second Spanish expedition of 1937
would last just six weeks. He left around 20 February, by train. The Party
was, evidently, paying his expenses. He must have seen Inez again in
Brussels but did not stay for his birthday on the 28th.

In Barcelona, where he stayed a few days (under the shadow of huge
pictures of Stalin and Lenin), he met up again with Cuthbert who now
told him about the carnage at Jarama, Tony's subsequent insubordination,
and his having been confined, in semi-imprisonment, at Albacete. Tony,
Stephen further learned, was in a state of nervous collapse, and his stomach
ulcers had flared up again. His battalion Medical Officer at Albacete recommended honourable discharge from the Brigade. His commandant Captain
George Nathan (an ex-British Army NCO and gay) had been very kind.
The British Commissars (political officers) were, however, proving tricky.

Shell-shock and peptic ulcers were popular ailments with cowards and malingerers. Tony had disobeyed an order. And he had made few friends in the Brigade – however many he had in England.

Also in Barcelona was Wogan Philipps who (like Worsley) was serving in a front-line ambulance unit. He offered to give Stephen a lift on his way south. Wog's personal life was in ruins – it was over between him and Ros. He went into painful detail as their truck lumbered on its way to Valencia round road blocks manned by 'dark grizzly ruffians'. Their guides, as much English strangers in Spain as Stephen, misguided them and they were in some danger of blundering into the rebel lines. Since Wog's vehicle carried the patriotic sign 'Fuck Franco' it would have been a prompt and ignominious death.

In Valencia, Stephen's path almost crossed with that of Auden, who had also come out intending to be an ambulance driver (a project which came to nothing). Wystan left a fond note pinned on Stephen's door at the Hotel Victoria. When he turned up next day at the Broadcasting Station in Valencia, Spender discovered that his job no longer existed. The UGT station 'had been abolished with the unification of parties'. This must have been in the first week of March. It was the usual wartime shambles. Stephen and Wogan could not even get a bath in Valencia, let alone a job.

With nothing else to detain him, Spender now determined to make contact with Tony. He went on with Wogan to Albacete, garrison town of the International Brigade. Here, at last, he met Tony, still shell-shocked and practically gibbering from his experiences at Jarama. As soon as they were alone, Tony demanded, vehemently, 'You must get me out of here!' He hated war.

Stephen introduced himself to the local Commissars, Peter Kerrigan and David Springhall – high-ranking figures in the Brigade and uncompromisingly hardline. They told him that despite Tony's disability, 'no one, or almost no one can now be released from the Brigade'. Kerrigan was Glaswegian, Springhall 'thick-necked, tough and friendly'. Unyielding as they were on honourable discharge, Stephen was reassured by them that 'on no account' would Tony ever be sent back to the front. Noncombatant duties could be found for him. He was, of course, a clerk by training. This was not, of course, what Tony wanted. But evidently Stephen persuaded him that it was the best deal that he could get. Tony could not be bought out of the International Brigade as he had earlier been bought out of the Brigade of Guards by his previous friend.

As a quid pro quo, the Commissars asked Spender, in his capacity as a liaison officer and journalist, to make a trip to the front near Madrid. He was given travel and accommodation warrants. Any copy he filed would pay his other expenses (Stephen got a piece for the *New Statesman* out of it, and the clutch of fine war poems that make up the third section of *The Still Centre*). Tony's friendly commandant, Captain George Nathan (for whom the Welshman had served as a runner at Jarama), went along as Spender's minder.

It may have been a ruse to get this obstreperous civilian out of the way. As Edgell Rickword confirmed, forty years later, Spender was irritating the Party by the 'fearful fuss' he was kicking up about 'his young friend' (there was some anxiety he might start writing about it in unsympathetic newspapers). The hard men in the Brigade simply could not understand why there should be so much fuss about one dubiously courageous private soldier. Shortly after Stephen's departure Tony was informed that despite the Medical Officer's report 'ulcer of the stomach . . . was no reason against his going back to the Front, where he would be sent next day'. In *World within World*, Stephen says it was the emergency of the forthcoming battle of Guadalajara, which blew up in the first week of March, which overrode Tony's compassionate arrangement. There could well have been a more sinister reason. As everyone in Spain knew, sending 'difficult' soldiers to the front was a convenient way of getting rid of them – for good, if necessary.

On hearing that they were going to be thrown into another bloodbath, Tony and a fellow soldier, John Lepper, ran away on 8 March to nearby Valencia. Lepper was something of a poet – author of the poignant lyric 'Death stalked the Olive Trees' (Spender would give it a prominent place in his 1939 collection, *Poems for Spain*). Like Tony, Lepper had been at Jarama and had been traumatized by the slaughter in the groves. He had bad eyes and should never have been put in the front line.

'Unfortunately I was in Madrid so knew nothing of all this,' Stephen told William Plomer. It seemed that Tony and Lepper had gone to the British authorities and applied, as British citizens, for repatriation. The British consular officials kept them waiting (probably deliberately), and on the third day of waiting they were arrested by the Spanish police, who handed them over to the International Brigade.

At this period, Stephen had his closest and most nerve-racking experiences of war. He visited the front near Madrid, where the 'bullets spat round us like shrieking starlings'. His party had been joined by a congenial

Indian journalist, Mulk Raj Anand (there were Indian volunteers fighting for the Republican cause). Captain Nathan (a veteran of the Great War) was a model of amiable gallantry: 'an elegant, cane-swaggering, likeable type of adventurous Jew'. He obviously enjoyed war.

Nathan, old soldier that he was, advised Stephen to stoop when walking through the trenches. Stephen bowed his head an inch or two beneath its habitual inclination (stooping came easily to him). Anand, who was five-foot nothing, bent himself double. At a machine-gun emplacement Stephen was invited to fire a ritual few shots into the Moorish lines. He did so 'positively praying that I might not by any chance hit an Arab'. At the HQ, after lunch, someone asked whether he had once had 'a secretary who was a member of the Brigade – a chap called Tony Hyndman'. From their eyes, Stephen deduced that Tony did not stand high in their estimation.

Nathan suggested he might stay a week. Stephen refused on the pretext that he was expected in Madrid. 'The fact is,' he candidly confessed in *World within World*, 'I was frightened and wanted to get away as soon as possible.' Madrid was under siege and bombardment, and also held its terrors. Spender and Anand were put up at the palatial Casa de la Cultura. Nathan went his way, but Stephen now had the company of Dennis Campkin, the former lover of Inez, now a sympathetically socialist journalist. Philip Toynbee, another lover of Inez's, was also in and out of Spain. They could practically have formed a brigade.

March was a cold month in Madrid:

At the Casa de la Cultura we spent most mornings in our beds, crouched down under our purple velvet bed covers. Then we got up and went to a café, where the crowds of people wearing their greatcoats, seated at tables and sipping a little atrocious cognac (coffee was unobtainable), slightly raised the temperature. Then we went to the hotel where the journalists lunched.

Spender was in Madrid in the middle of the month as the ferocious Guadalajara Offensive (9–18 March) reached its bloody climax. The Republicans finally succeeded in throwing back Mussolini's attacking forces, relieving the pressure on the city. It was a great moment for the cause. Immediately after the victory at Guadalajara, Spender was on his way back to Albacete to find out what he could about Tony 'as I felt so worried about his state of mind'. At this point he fondly thought that Kerrigan had kept his word. He was shocked to discover that Tony was now in prison. There had been the charge of desertion, the repeated insubordination and, more seriously, some suspicion of espionage. The sentence passed on the men was two months in a camp of correction.

Lepper had been tried together with Tony. He had at first argued that cataracts of the eye disabled him from combat. Finally he 'confessed' to cowardice. Like Tony, he received two months. The sentences were minimal for the most serious of military crimes – desertion (and in Tony's case earlier cowardice) in the face of the enemy. Tony and Lepper were lucky that their trial coincided with the afterglow of the Republican victory at Guadalajara, when the apparatchiks felt they could afford to be generous. Later, when the war turned decisively against them, the verdict might have been harsher.

On learning the facts, Spender returned to Valencia and wrote a plea to the Judicial Commission of the International Brigade, imploring that Tony be allowed to return home at once, on medical grounds. He found their response 'extraordinary'. The head of the Commission agreed that 'the case of Hyndman is utterly pitiful'. But none the less the two-month sentence must stand. Stephen was informed, 'you ought, as a communist, to be *pleased* that he is going to be disciplined by us'. Stephen was not pleased nor was he, it might be thought, any longer a Communist.

Spender describes at some length the gloomy journey to Valencia. He had to wait seven hours on the railway platform. It was a scene out of Hieronymous Bosch, crowded with wounded soldiers, 'calling, whistling, urinating, expectorating'. On the train, a hard-faced young Scotsman abused deserters and cowards unmercifully. 'I could not answer,' Stephen recalls. At this point he evidently conceived his poem for Tony, 'The Coward'. It was 'a turning point in my affairs', he records in *World within World*.

'The Coward' represents his answer to the hard-faced young Scotsman, his sympathy for what Tony had undergone at Jarama, and his disgust with the propagandists' cult of heroism:

> Under the olive trees, from the ground
> Grows this flower, which is a wound.
> It is easier to ignore
> Than the heroes' sunset fire
> Of death plunged in their self-willed desire
> Raging with flags on the world's shore.

In Valencia Stephen cooled his heels and waited. Almost the first person he bumped into at the Hotel Victoria (famous as the resort of 'spies and harlots') was a friend, the First Secretary of the British Embassy, Barry Thomas, who offered to refer Tony's case to the Republican Foreign Minister, Del Vayo, for compassionate consideration. Stephen was realistic enough not to plead at this stage for the Brigade's sentence to be commuted. He merely wanted an assurance that, having served his two months, Tony would be invalided home. 'I am going to do everything I can,' Stephen told Plomer, 'to prevent Tony's being killed for a cause in which it is quite impossible for him to believe, owing to the bullying of the commissars.'

In Valencia, Stephen had made new friends. The most glamorous was Ernest Hemingway, who was in the city from the night of 16 March to the morning of the 20th. As Stephen much later recalled, 'We would go on walks together, and then he'd talk about literature.' Stephen was fascinated by his schizoid switches from sensitive artist to tough 'public Hemingway' when they got back in company. Hemingway liked to upbraid Stephen – as he did most men – with being 'yeller'.

Another, warmer, friendship formed at this time was with Manuel Altolaguirre, 'a lean, tall, handsome quixotic figure, dressed in blue dungarees'. With Latin impulsiveness, 'Manolo' gave his *querido camarado Spender* an eleven-volume edition of Johnson's 'Shakespeare' (Stephen would not travel light, on his way home). Stephen loved the 'child-like' quality of this gentle friend whom he had met in a 'violent time'. He translated his poetry and wrote a dedicatory poem for him, 'To a Spanish Poet':

> You stared out of the window on the emptiness
> Of a world exploding:
> Stones and rubble thrown upwards in a fountain
> Blasted sideways by the wind.

It was Altolaguirre who suggested they simply forge some papers, drive across in an official-looking car and abduct Tony from the labour camp. 'This happens all the time in Spain,' he blithely explained.

Tony's letters to Stephen from the labour camp were harrowing:

My Dear Stephen . . . I think of you all the time and wonder how you are and what you are doing. I look forward to being with you again more than anything, but I am almost consumed with a feeling of despair, absolute helplessness, and with no idea of what the future will bring. I dream the whole time of our days together, our freedom, our happiness . . . I want to stop thinking of these things, and yet I cannot. Oh my darling, it all seems so terribly unfair . . . But do come if you can.

Stephen had been told he could see Tony when the sentence was promulgated (the Communists were addicted to this kind of protocol). He duly returned to Albacete, only to find that the Commissars were now spitting mad at *him*, Comrade Spender. Kerrigan, in his Glaswegian whine, arraigned him for communicating with the 'Kluss Ennimey'. The British Embassy that was to say. They evidently had spies in Valencia. Out of spite, they refused to allow Stephen access to Tony. It was maddening.

The only remedy, Stephen now realized, was to get help through the internal power structure of the Party; to persuade, that is, some high official to intercede with the judges over the heads of the inflexible Commissars. Stephen wrote directly to Edgell Rickword (a poet as well as a Communist high-up) with the request that an impartial report on Tony be forwarded to Harry Pollitt. Rickword was impatient with Stephen, and thought his anxiety about one private soldier, when regiments were being slaughtered for the cause, extravagant. But he evidently did as requested.

On 2 April, Stephen crossed the border and gathered his shattered nerves in a hotel in the French Pyrenees. He was 'completely dazed', but obsessed to the point of mania with 'the one very important matter of Tony's future'. Over the next few months he would organize a writing campaign to everyone he could think of who could help. This single issue had become the whole Spanish Civil War, as far as he was concerned.

He rejoined Inez in Paris on 5 April. Would she understand his going off to Spain to help Tony? It would be nice to think that it was on this occasion Stephen wrote the poem called 'The Indifferent One', later collected in *The Still Centre*:

> I take the lift to the eighth floor
> Walk through the steam of corridors
> And knock at the numbered door.
> Entering the porch, I pass
> My face reflected palely in a glass,
> Lean, with hollows under the eyes,

A heightened expression of surprise,
Skin porous, like cells in a hive,
And I think: 'Can you forgive?'

Did she forgive him? The poem only states that she 'accepts'. They returned to London on 7 April.

Three days later, on the morning of the 10th, Spender had a 'long and remarkable' interview with Pollitt. Pollitt was, as before, nice to Stephen 'personally'. But the party had 'now elaborated Tony into a sort of monster which they used to label an "intellectual"'. Pollitt initially refused to intervene,

until right at the end of the interview when he said 'Tell me, is there any sex in this'. I said yes. He said 'I know'. Then he went off the deep end and said people like that were no use at the Front, no use in the Revolution, no use anywhere, so Tony would be brought home and then he would be 'in the mud'.

As far as Stephen was concerned, 'the great thing' was that Tony was going to be brought home. Mud was irrelevant. He (Stephen) would not be 'sane till I see him'. Pollitt threatened that the party would 'publish everything' if Stephen used his forthcoming article in the *New Statesman* to publicize Tony's plight or blacken his Communist superiors.

At lunch with Stephen, Inez and Cuthbert a couple of hours later, Philip Toynbee recorded the conversation as being entirely about 'this business about getting Tony back – Christ how they talked!' Pollitt, Toynbee was told, had threatened to 'blackmail' Stephen as 'a bloody homosexual intellectual worrying about his boyfriend' if Stephen publicly attacked the party. Toynbee (still staunchly loyal to the cause) 'implored' Stephen to criticize from 'within'. Inez, Toynbee thought, was 'very cold'.

In *Life and the Poet* (1942), Spender recalls being summoned on his return from Spain to a meeting of Communist writers. He was instructed to 'explain my attitude to the Party'. On his complaining about brutalities committed by the Republican side on their own 'deviants', Comrade Spender was declared to be a hapless victim of 'bourgeois propaganda spread by fascist agents' (this by colleagues who had never been to Spain). After this, Spender records, 'I gave up.' He was Comrade Spender no longer. His position, in late spring 1937, is summed up in a letter to Virginia Woolf, recommending that she advise her favourite nephew,

Julian Bell, not to join the International Brigade. He was supported in his efforts by Kingsley Martin (both men may have spoken to Bell before he left for Spain): 'What I am convinced of,' Stephen told Virginia,

is that politicians are detestable anywhere . . . I have not seen Julian Bell at Albacete, so I suppose he has not joined the Brigade. In any case I hope he will not do so. The qualities required apart from courage, are terrific narrowness and a religious dogmatism about the Communist Party line, or else toughness, cynicism and insensibility. The sensitive, the weak, the romantic, the enthusiastic, the truthful live in Hell there and cannot get away.

Despite all the advice, Bell eventually joined the ambulance corps and was killed. Spender would, of course, keep up his own kind of fight: principally for Spanish aid, Spanish art (at constant risk from vandalism) and, above all, the Spanish people, for whom the terms 'Popular Front' or 'International Fraternity' no longer meant anything.

On 6 May (the day after a large dinner party at the Woolfs' house, for the newly knighted Hugh Walpole), Stephen returned to Brussels and Inez. The two of them had the shortest of breaks in Corsica, before returning to Paris where Sylvia Beach had arranged a reading at her bookshop for 12 May. Hemingway also read from his fiction in progress, *For Whom the Bell Tolls*. Stephen read an assortment of his Spanish War poems. James Joyce was in the audience, but slipped away before Stephen could be introduced. The Spenders stayed on in Paris until July, seeing something of Gisa and her new relative by marriage, André Gide (whose problems with the Communist Party were similar to Stephen's). In early July, Humphrey married Lolly ('at last', as Stephen observed to Tony, in a letter of 11 June).

Despite Pollitt's assurance to Stephen, Tony's troubles were far from over after he had served his two months in labour camp 10R. At the end of April he was confined to barracks in Albacete with his now inseparable comrade, John Lepper. He later learned that a prison informer had told the authorities that he (Tony) was planning a Trotskyist uprising, on the symbolic first of May. It may have been routine Stalinist paranoia or a garbled version of what Tony, talker that he was, had injudiciously fantasized about. His mouth was always getting him into hot water.

As he waited in the camp without any charges being laid against him, Tony was increasingly terrified that he was going to be murdered. He was being employed, in a desultory way, as a mess orderly, washing dishes. Gradually, the camp at Albacete emptied as all able-bodied men were sucked into battle. Battle that was increasingly going the wrong way. By 5 May, Tony told Dennis Campkin (who was keeping an eye on things for Stephen) that 'There are very few people left, and I believe the [camp] is being closed down.' He was told that he would be released, on condition that he returned to the front. 'My first fear,' he later told Stephen, 'was that being sent to the front was the easiest way of killing me off.' Someone would be assigned to shoot him from behind during a fire fight. 'This, according to other prisoners, was the favourite way of getting rid of undesirables.' Tony was by now extremely undesirable.

Stephen launched another letter-writing and telegram-sending campaign, asking friends like Leonard Woolf and Morgan Forster to intercede and protest on Tony's behalf. One of his requests was to Giles Romilly's mother, who got on to her brother-in-law, Winston Churchill. The old warlord was inclined to send a battleship out, to bring his nephew (not Tony, alas) home. This failing, he intervened with the International Brigade to keep Giles from the front. On hearing of his uncle's meddling (from Stephen, 'inadvertently'), Giles was furious and also deserted, running off to Valencia. But his intention, unlike Tony's, was to force the Brigade, on his surrendering himself, to send him to the front by way of punishment. After serving his time in the same camp as Tony (which he found 'rather amusing'), Giles was duly dispatched to the terrible battle of Brunete in early July 1937, where he distinguished himself. It was a strange war.

Three of them had left Victoria Station in December. Bert Overton had been the unluckiest of the trio. As James K. Hopkins records, the International Brigade court-martialled him after

he failed abysmally as a company commander at the Jarama, losing the lives of many because of his fear and incompetence. He was then sent to a labour battalion. At Brunete [in July 1937] he was killed while carrying ammunition 'to a forward position'. Some wondered if putting Overton in harm's way wasn't simply a means of getting rid of a soldier who had become a dangerous embarrassment.

Tony and Lepper feared, constantly, that 'they would shoot us and then tell our friends we had been killed fighting at the front like heroes'. Luckily, Tony eventually came into the care of a sympathetic medical officer who X-rayed his insides and testified that he was, indeed, organically sick. This, together with Stephen's unrelenting pressure on the authorities and the fact that his mother (who died a few months later) had fallen ill, eventually led to Tony's repatriation, as an invalid, in late July 1937. His file was marked 'Recalled for Political Reasons. Undesirable.' At least he was alive. Harry Pollitt sardonically noted that 'Tony Hyndman has been more trouble to me than the whole British battalion put together.' It would, presumably, have been much less trouble to shoot him (discreetly), Overton-style. It was at this point that Stephen wrote the poem which is called 'Sonnet' in *The Still Centre* and 'To T. A. R. H.' on the dedication page of *Trial of a Judge*. In it, he apostrophizes Tony as 'The other self for which my self would have died':

> We being afraid, I made my hand a path
> Into this separate peace which is no victory
> Nor general peace, but our escape from fate.

The poem is written in a spirit of relief and love. But the episode with Tony and Spain was, as he says in *World within World*, 'the greatest distress of my life'. It may well have provoked another great distress – Inez's desertion, eighteen months later. According to Christine, who was seeing something of her over these months, Stephen's wife was lonely and resentful. And resolutely Communist. Her health seems, at times, to have been poor.

During June Stephen made a number of appearances as a leftist intellectual, recently returned from 'active service' in Spain. His speeches were studiously non-political. His contribution to the June 1937 pamphlet *Authors Take Sides on Spain* studiously omits any reference to the Popular Front, the Communist Party, or even the War. It begins 'I am opposed to Franco.' This, at least, had not changed. And he might have added 'and opposed to the CPGB'. His subsequent meetings in 1937 with Harry Pollitt are not recorded. But it would seem that, as part of the deal for Tony's return, and out of respect for comrades still fighting, Stephen agreed not to make any public declaration of his defection from the party. There would be no waves. Tony too had had to agree to a gag order (Stephen undertook to Pollitt in April to 'guarantee that when Hyndman returns he will say nothing against the Brigade'). It also seems likely that Stephen agreed, for appearance's sake (and out of solidarity with the Spanish people), to go as a delegate to the Second International

Congress of Writers in Defence of Culture, in Madrid, in early July 1937. This was in the cat-and-mouse phase when Tony's return was promised, but not yet ensured. The Commissars could still change their minds. The conference was held at the invitation of the (desperate) Republican government, with the aim of demonstrating the solidarity of the intellectual élite of the world behind socialist democracy.

The second conference was a very different affair from the first. That glittering event had been held in Paris in June 1935, under the chairmanship of Gide and Malraux. Among the 230 delegates were Aldous Huxley, Forster, Brecht, Pasternak, Babel, Musil and Barbusse. The second conference took place during a grim juncture of the war. Madrid was under daily bombardment. The Fascists were clearly winning, and many in England (including most of the government) were relieved to see the Bolshies lose. As Edgell Rickword (whom Stephen respected) recalls:

I went to Madrid with Sylvia Townsend Warner, Valentine Ackland, and of course Spender. We were about the only people the Writers Delegation could rustle up. All the others were either fighting, or clearing out, or were on the other side.

It would be a bleak event.

Stephen wrote two accounts of the visit: one in *New Writing* (Autumn 1937) and another – more savage – in *World within World*. In both recollections he expresses qualified admiration for the European writers and intellectuals who attended: André Chamson, Rafael Alberti, José Bergamin, Miguel Hernandez, Octavio Paz, Ilya Ehrenberg, Ludwig Renn, Julien Benda, Tristan Tzara, Alexei Tolstoy (the Congress chairman) and Michael Koltzov. Above all, he admired Pablo Neruda, Altolaguirre and André Malraux.

Stephen's sense of comradeship with the charismatic Frenchman was forged (literally) when Malraux procured a fake passport for him. The Foreign Office had refused him a visa. 'Cultural reasons' were judged inadequate justification for visiting a war zone. 'Non intervention' had a harder edge nowadays. Among others whom the FO had refused a visa was Wystan, who may at one time have considered keeping Stephen company. The name that Malraux came up with for this pseudo-Spaniard was Ramos Ramos – 'a name which seemed to involve a minimum of invention', Stephen wryly noted. At the frontier on 3 July, Malraux:

amused himself by explaining that I was a very special kind of Spaniard, tall and with fair hair and blue eyes, speaking a dialect undistinguishable from English, and coming from a remote northern mountain district.

(Malraux in fact arranged false passports for the whole English delegation; the Spanish officials were, of course, complaisant.)

Across the border, there was no amusement. Stephen was embarrassed by the Rolls-Royces in which the English delegation were driven along the coastal road from Port Bou to Barcelona and Valencia. The limousines, like the champagne, rich food and luxurious accommodation, were, he thought, 'a thick hedge dividing us from reality'. The reality was what Hemingway (who wasn't at the Congress) called 'the Spanish Earth'.

The English delegation arrived at the provisional capital on 5 July, to be met (with a speech in Castilian and much hammering of the fist) by their countryman, Comrade Ralph Bates – 'an English Communist novelist', as Stephen disguises him in *World within World*. The 'fat and fussy' Bates exuded a 'hysterical conceitedness'. He decked himself in uniform and paraded his Commissar's power. Spender was obliged to deal with him over the final arrangements for Tony's repatriation. He could, Bates sadistically declared, have had the man shot. He had done such things before – for the Party, of course.

Valencia, like Madrid, was now under constant aerial bombardment. They were woken up at four o'clock by the bombs. The delegates moved on to Madrid on 6 July, where the real business of the Congress ensued. The English delegation was put up in the still sumptuous Hotel Victoria. The 'great, tall, ugly town' was still 'sublime'. By day and night in the Congress Hall the Russian delegates spewed party-line spleen against their former darling, André Gide, for his mild criticisms of Stalinism in his *Retour de l'U.R.S.S.*, which had been published in November. For the first time, Spender discovered – from a source he trusted – the appalling things which had been going on in the Soviet Union.

On a personal level Spender was particularly irritated by Sylvia Townsend Warner and her (female and habitually drunken) lover, Valentine Ackland, with whom he shared a limousine back to Valencia. In *World within World*, Stephen disguises them as 'a Communist lady writer and her friend'. Warner looked and behaved 'like a vicar's wife presiding over a tea party given on a vicarage lawn':

Her extensory smiling mouth and her secretly superior eyes under her shovel hat made her graciously forbidding. She insisted – rather cruelly I thought – on calling everyone 'comrade', and to me her sentences usually began, 'Wouldn't it be less selfish comrade', which she followed by recommending some course of action highly convenient from her point of view.

Townsend Warner, on her part, thought Stephen 'an irritating idealist, always hatching a wounded feeling'. She made no secret of her desire to have him publicly drummed out of the Party (too late, as it happened; he had already left).

The delegates made their way back to Port Bou on 13 July. Before leaving the country Spender reassured himself that Spain's artistic treasures were not – as the right-wing press in Britain insisted – being looted. A luxury train took them from Port Bou to Paris, where there was a final session of the conference. Stephen was disgusted by the petulance of some of these 'distinguished intellectuals' on discovering that they could not have berths in the wagons-lits. He got back to London on 26 July.

Spender returned from Spain physically prostrated and politically disillusioned. *Il faut s'agir!* – Malraux's call to arms – had proved the emptiest of slogans. There was no meaningful action to be taken. Gestures were all that remained. As such a gesture he signed (with 148 other writers on the left) Nancy Cunard's petition, 'The Question' ('Are you for, or against, the legal Government and the People of Republican Spain'?). The pen was anything but mighty at this period of history. George Orwell's response was typically savage:

Will you please stop sending me this bloody rubbish. This is the second or third time I have had it. I am not one of your fashionable pansies like Auden and Spender. I was six months in Spain, most of the time fighting, I have a bullet-hole in me at present, and I am not going to write blah about defending democracy or gallant little anybody . . . By the way, tell your pansy friend Spender that I am preserving specimens of his war-heroics and that when the time comes when he squirms for shame at having written it, as the people who wrote the war-propaganda in the Great War are squirming now, I shall rub it in good and hard.

'War heroics' were, as it happened, the least appropriate description for what Spender was currently thinking and doing. On 1 May he published a bitter piece for the *New Statesman* entitled 'Heroes in Spain'. 'I like the Spanish *people*,' he declared,

because it seems to me that they are emotionally honester than any other people. There are few heroics, no White Feathers, and genuine hatred for the necessity of the war in Spain.

As Orwell would later realize (after they became friends a couple of years later), he and Spender were, in fact, of one mind.

For a while after his return from Madrid, Spender withdrew from speaking engagements, limiting himself to some letters to *The Times* denying the *Daily Mail*'s allegations that Spanish art treasures were being looted by the Republicans. Over August 1937 he recuperated from Spain, with Inez, at Church Farm, Wareham, near Ashford. Auden came to stay. In summer 1937 the other poet was moving towards a more religious view of life and politics. There were necessarily differences between him and Stephen (and Inez) on Spain. Wystan was repelled by Republican anti-Catholic atrocities. None the less, he and Stephen optimistically projected a lecture tour of America followed by a book on the country. Contracts were signed but, in the event, Wystan would have to go with Isherwood.

Stephen was working methodically to repair his relationship with Inez. He was worried about the deleterious effect of 'breaks in our married life'. He and Inez had resolved – as he told Humphrey – not to have children. They were reluctant to bring innocents into a world of Francos, Hitlers, Mussolinis and Mosleys. Stephen was still harassed by the Hyndman business, which – since he had shouted his friend's plight from the rooftops – was the tittle-tattle of literary London. His friends suspected that the relationship with Tony Hyndman was still romantic. On 27 April 1938 Christopher Isherwood wrote, mischievously, 'how is your dear little wife? And that delightful fellow your . . . secretary?' Elsewhere there were moves to publicly expel him (if only he could be clearly demonstrated to belong to it) from the Communist Party. Despite his disillusion with party politics, he had committed himself to a wearing schedule of public speeches on Spain later in the year.

For some months, Stephen went into a therapeutic retreat – from the 'Uncreative Chaos' of politics into the 'Still Centre' of himself. Withdrawal from politics also meant that he could, for the first time in years, explore new developments in English art – specifically the return to pictorial realism represented by the 'Euston Road Group'. The leader of the group was William Coldstream. Auden had been associated with the artist in his work for the GPO film unit in 1936. Coldstream, together with Victor Pasmore, Claude Rogers, Graham Bell, Bobby Buhler, Rodrigo Moynihan and Lawrence Gowing, established the loose-knit group in 1937 (Coldstream's studio was in Fitzroy Square, a few hundred yards from the railway station and UCL's Slade School of Art).

There was much mingling among the young writers, artists and critics who were defining the 'New' British culture. Some of the personnel of the Euston Road Group (notably Coldstream) had links with the Group Theatre and the Mass Observation Project – both of which would figure in Stephen's life over the next three years. Although graphic realism was not entirely to his taste (he was fonder of the work of Graham Sutherland and Henry Moore), Spender admired Coldstream's work and commissioned an expensive portrait of Inez from the artist, in August 1937. He was also interested in developing what skills as an artist he himself might possess. 'Since he was a boy he always wanted to be an artist,' according to Humphrey. Stephen jokingly called this artistic alter ego 'Redneps' – the reverse Spender. At twenty-nine, he hoped 'I might still become a poet and painter, as others had done' (Blake, notably). To this end he enrolled himself as a student with the group.

Coldstream and the others liked Spender enormously but did not think much of Redneps, nor – in the rough and tumble of their studio life – did they trouble to hide their low opinion. Nancy Coldstream recalls a legendary anecdote among her friends: Stephen looking thoughtfully at a blank canvas, then going across to it and solemnly signing his name 'very large' in the bottom right-hand corner. He was, almost certainly, making a joke at his own expense.

As an apprentice artist Stephen laboured at landscapes from his window in Hammersmith and on weekend painting-parties in Suffolk. He submitted to many portraits of himself. He got some paid modelling for the always impecunious Tony Hyndman. But by the end of 1937 he had discovered, ruefully, that although he had 'creative feeling' he lacked the technique fully to express it. He could paint in his 'mind's eye', but not on canvas. He continued throughout life, as a skilled amateur, to sketch and paint for his own satisfaction.

The months of study with the group heightened his awareness of line and colour – something which can be felt in his poetry. And it is from this period that Stephen's close and intellectually fruitful association with Francis Bacon dates (Henry Moore had been a personal friend for some years). He developed practical skills as a discriminating collector and writer on art history. He cultivated a discerning 'eye' and a shrewd sense of who the really good, but as yet unrecognized, artists were. He was an early collector of rising British artists. Humphrey recalls how appalled he and other members of the family were at Stephen's 'recklessness' when he would 'blow' as much as £20 on a Moore or a Sutherland (Humphrey – an avid hunter round junk shops – made it a rule never to spend more than a shilling). Unfortunately Spender had all the skills of the collector bar one – he did not always hold on to what he acquired.

Spender paid the physical price of his exertions in Spain. His stomach had been giving him chronic pain – colitis, it was first thought. In late August appendicitis was diagnosed. He had an operation on 1 September. Afterwards he spent some time in a convalescent nursing home and was visited by Giles Romilly, who was 'very interesting about the war and very nice'. The war was, in fact, going very badly for the Republicans. Giles bore no hard feelings about Tony's conduct nor about Stephen's 'inadvertence' in the business with Winston Churchill and the unwanted warship.

Tony Hyndman was, predictably, proving difficult. His experiences in Spain had not made him more employable. The *Left Review*, where he had worked before the war, did not want the deserter back. He was – without question – a sick man; and the International Brigade did not pay medical pensions; least of all for 'undesirables'. It was increasingly clear that he had deep-rooted psychological problems (Muriel Gardiner suggested that he go into analysis, which he did in 1939–40).

Stephen felt that any drift by Tony back into 'dependence' would be disastrous for both of them. 'I agree with you,' Stephen told his friend, in his sternest tone,

that it would be a good thing for you to find a job *as soon as possible*, because otherwise it means you are leading a kind of life which is really quite un-related to what you may do in the future and for which I am automatically responsible, whether I like it or not, because it is entirely dependent on my resources.

Even at this stage, Stephen could not do what was crying out to be done: cut Tony loose and let him sink or swim.

At the end of 1937, having failed to find a job himself, Tony was sent off (by Stephen's good offices) to Vienna. Muriel needed help with her refugees and, as an old friend to the two of them, she was prepared to shoulder the burden of supporting Tony for a while. Tony's (fond) hope was that, with her powerful contacts, she could arrange for him to get on the quota for America, where he could start a new life and shoulder his own burdens. Muriel was arranging emigration for any number of deserving cases from Nazi Austria at this period. Why not slip in a deserving Welshman among them?

On 17 September, Stephen having been discharged from his nursing home, he and Inez went off to Salcombe for a fortnight's convalescence. It was the Devon resort where he had spent his happiest childhood holidays. But the blight of the war penetrated even this West Country haven. Stephen's recovery – or at least his determination to get back to London – was accelerated by a blimpish holiday-maker with a 'walrus moustache' and 'loud check tweeds' who proudly revealed himself to be an arms supplier to the Francoists. His guns, he gleefully told Stephen and Inez, would 'smash your friends in Madrid to pieces'.

On his return to London Stephen gave a lecture at Kingsway Hall where the seventeen-year-old music student Natasha Litvin first heard him, wondering at his willowy form, 'Etruscan profile' and passionate but soft-voiced oratory. His address was prefaced by thunderous and belligerent chanting: 'Arms for Spain means Arms for Peace!' Stephen's theme was, by contrast, the pathos of war – the suffering of the people; the horror of being dive-bombed, or 'smashed to pieces in Madrid' by shells supplied by English men in loud tweeds. There was no Marxism. He was speaking, at this period, exclusively to raise funds for medical and civilian aid. He still enjoyed his prestige with the students of Britain. Laurie Bates, in 1938 an undergraduate at Cambridge, recalls Spender speaking 'passionately about Republican Spain and the evils of Fascism. Brilliant stuff.' But politically Spender had undergone great changes between January and October 1937. History, as Samuel Hynes puts it, 'had brought him briefly into the Communist Party . . . And history took him out again.'

Spender articulated his feelings about the Spanish imbroglio in the poems which make up the third section of *The Still Centre*. Hynes singles out 'Ultima Ratio Regum' as the representative poem of this dark period. It was written after Stephen's experience in Madrid. The arrogant Latin motto – 'Force is the final argument of Kings' – was embossed on the

cannon of Louis XIV. The poem contrives to be both anti-capitalist
('money') and anti-war ('guns') but reserves its Owen-like 'pity' for the
boy – an anonymous victim of the Jarama bloodbath – lying dead in
the olive grove:

> The guns spell money's ultimate reason
> In letters of lead on the Spring hillside.
> But the boy lying dead under the olive trees
> Was too young and too silly
> To have been notable to their important eye.
> He was a better target for a kiss.

In addition to experimenting with painting, Stephen explored the
recesses of his sensibility by psychoanalysis. He had read Freud as a
schoolboy. Through Muriel he was familiar with the subtler theses of
Freudianism and through Auden the crazier theories of Lane-Layardism.
His London analyst was Karin Stephen – Virginia Woolf's sister-in-law.
Stephen arrived at Freudian therapy by the side-road of Bloomsbury. Dr
Stephen was, as Frances Partridge recalls, 'tremendously deaf'. In later
life Stephen recalled the problems of roaring out one's innermost sexual
secrets to a superannuated analyst who needed an ear-trumpet to hear
what her patients were saying.

As 1937 drew to an end, two major literary projects occupied Stephen:
a volume-length translation of Rilke's 'Duino Elegies' (commissioned by
the Hogarth Press) and the verse play for the Group Theatre on which
he had been working on and off for six years. Inez, who had suspended
scholarly work for her dissertation, was writing the first of her series of
autobiographical novels under the pseudonym 'Elizabeth Lake' (*Spanish
Portrait*, as it would eventually be titled).

For the Rilke project, the Hogarth Press teamed Spender with J. B.
Leishman, a crusty professor of English at unfashionably redbrick
Southampton. Leishman, it was fondly hoped, would bring stringency
and Spender creativity to the venture. The partnership was not harmo-
nious. Stephen – much as he revered scholarly mentors like Curtius –
did not take well to this English don. Decades later (in his 1981 journal)
he candidly acknowledged that he reverted to his old undergraduate
tricks: 'I kept putting off meetings with Leishman.' He was exactly the
kind of academic Stephen least liked: 'although (I think) a Yorkshireman
he had a grim Germanic character of total seriousness – the kind of

man who can exhaust a subject like a Hoover taking dust out of a carpet'. When Stephen eventually met Leishman in the flesh he discovered him to be a 'grey mountaineer attired in pepper-and-salt tweed . . . solitary rock-climbing seemed to be his substitute for sex'.

Stephen set to and drafted his translation of the first elegy by mid-August 1937. Illness and the business of his crammed life then intervened. In October, he was obliged to write, reassuring Leishman (who had been complaining bitterly to Leonard Woolf) that he was still on board. He was 'overwhelmed with work', Stephen explained to their publisher. There was his play and his obligations as a literary director of the Group Theatre, which would stage it in 1938. There was journalism (to earn his bread) and, as he told Leishman, 'I have to speak often several times a week in different parts of the country about Spain.' But he would do his best to keep up with the professor. He did not inform his collaborator that he was distracting himself, when he should have been working on Rilke, with more congenial translations of Lorca.

If 1937 had begun with *Forward from Liberalism*, in 1938 it was backwards from communism all the way. The Marxist God had failed. Liberal doubt, not socialist dogma, was worked into the later strata of Spender's major literary effort of 1937–8, *Trial of a Judge*. He had a complete draft of the play done by 22 October, and sent it to Lehmann. If Faber turned it down (on political grounds), the more left-leaning Hogarth Press would be the obvious second choice. Lehmann liked the play greatly. Eliot liked it as well, and Faber undertook to publish it.

Stephen's involvement with Rupert Doone's Group Theatre absorbed much of his energy between January and April. Doone, a former ballet dancer and acquainted with Auden through his (Doone's) lover Robert Medley, had founded the 'London Group Theatre' in 1932. It was not a club, as such, and – on principle – had no fixed premises. As its manifesto declared: 'it is a community not a building'. The group's programme was as grandly socialist and cooperative as its slogans. By personal magnetism Doone attracted a coterie of talents from many more fields than traditional theatre. There were play-writing poets such as Yeats, Eliot, Auden (with prosaic Isherwood), Louis MacNeice and (late in the day) Stephen Spender. Artists such as Henry Moore, John Piper and Duncan Grant designed sets and the plays' expressionist décor. Musicians such as Benjamin Britten and Michael Tippett provided incidental music.

Humphrey Spender did the photographic stills ('for nothing,' as he even now complains). The Group organized lecture series at their Great

Newport Street headquarters, with speakers as eminent as T. S. Eliot (some of whose work they staged). Auden and Isherwood were the Group's star playwrights, although, like Spender, they were thought by Doone to be rather lacking in high seriousness on occasion. They called the director 'Boopy-Doop' behind his back.

Spender had been a paid-up Group member since 1933 and had occasionally taken the chair at Great Newport Street meetings. Doone had, for years, given him an open commission to write a poetic drama for the Group, and *Trial of a Judge*, during its long gestation, was devised with this end in mind. The germ of the play was the sadistic murder of a Polish-Jewish Communist, Konrad Pietzuch, by a team of drunken SA stormtroopers in Silesia in 1932. After Hitler intervened personally, the murderers – having been sentenced to death – had their sentences commuted and were, when soon after Hitler assumed absolute power, released and fêted as heroes of the Party. The murder of Pietzuch was a significant moment in the perversion of the German judicial system.

Auden had evidently pricked Spender's interest in writing drama during the August 1937 vacation in Kent, when – following his travails in Spain – he was at a loose end. In October 1937, Doone had cunningly appointed Stephen a 'literary director' (unpaid, like Humphrey). He took the post seriously. He told Lehmann, on 22 October 1937, that 'we are trying to double the membership'. He even solicited the sour don, Leishman, to put up programmes in the corridors of Southampton University.

Spender's main contribution to the Group was *Trial of a Judge*, which was finished, revised, and discussed collectively into its final stageworthy form by early 1938. Stephen sent a copy of the printed text to Kirstein in America on 13 March with the gnomic comment that its pages 'will tell you everything there is to know about me during the past four years'. As surviving drafts indicate, the play was much changed from what Isaiah Berlin had seen (when it was called 'Death of a Judge') in 1936. *Trial of a Judge* was published by Faber and performed by the Group in March 1938. The *Anschluss* in Austria that month gave it welcome topicality.

As finally revised, the play is set in an unnamed middle European country, ambiguously Germany or Austria. The principal theme is, as Stephen earlier put it, 'German Justice' – the Fascist dismantling of democratic 'separation of powers' and an independent judiciary. As the action opens a judge has just sentenced a gang of Fascist thugs to death for murdering a Polish Communist Jew. He similarly sentences three Communists, for less brutal crimes of armed self-defence and dissemination of propaganda. The Judge (unnamed, patriarchal, but childless) decides, however, that he cannot be impartial, and reprieves the Communists. There is a putsch, and he is shot. The judge in his court, like Beckett in his cathedral, dies for conscience. He leaves for the firing squad with the Eliotesque observation:

> I have become
> The centre of that clamorous drum
> To which I listened all my life.

The last words in the play are given to the Chorus of Red Prisoners. They echo the majestic refrain in *Fidelio*, which had so moved Stephen and Isaiah at Salzburg in 1935:

> We shall be free.
> We shall find peace.

The action ends with 'three loud drum taps' (an effect added, as the manuscript suggests, during stage rehearsal).

The play was put on for a week at the end of March, at the Unity Theatre Club (a proudly anti-Fascist establishment), in the slums behind King's Cross. There was some ideological friction, since the Unity practised a harder-line socialism than did the Group and its members were suspicious of the poet (and lapsed comrade) Spender. The premises were a converted nonconformist chapel which sadly cramped John Piper's set – the first he had done for the Group. The audience capacity was under 100, the seats as hard as pews, and on some nights of *Trial of a Judge*'s run the auditorium was half empty. Entrance was one shilling.

E. M. Forster and his policeman friend Bob Buckingham came up to London to see Stephen's play. As Morgan guardedly put it, they 'particularly enjoyed the second act'. Virginia Woolf and Eliot also came as honoured invitees. Woolf found it 'a moving play: genuine; simple; sincere . . . I like [Stephen] always: his large sensitive sincerity better than the contorted nerve-drawn brilliancy of the others'. The 'others' were Auden and Isherwood, whose *Dog beneath the Skin* had been put on in 1936 and *The Ascent of F6* in February 1937. Eliot was polite about *Trial of a Judge* in conversation with Stephen. In a letter he declared himself 'impressed and moved', although he ventured to object that the play might, perhaps, be *too* poetical. None the less he was proud to have published it.

Friends who received complimentary copies of the printed text were more than polite. Christopher wrote from America on 5 July 1938 to pronounce that he and Wystan (in the same letter) regarded it as Stephen's masterpiece: 'the Trial of a Judge (just received) is, in both our considered opinions, really *great*. I mean that literally . . . It's in the same class, as poetry, as Shakespeare or Goethe. One day, people will see this.' The phrase 'one day' indicates that he knew of London's coolness. Wystan wrote confirming their superlative verdict: 'Stephen, with all seriousness, I say that I'm certain it is the greatest poem of our time.' Wystan concurred that it was essentially a poem: 'I don't feel it is a play at all, but then I haven't seen it, even with Boopy Doop's spittle on it.'

The most sensitive response was from Isaiah Berlin, with whom Spender had conversed and corresponded on the play for several years. He gave his verdict on the performance on 18 March:

I wished to make remarks about the play, which I was enormously moved by, not more, but as much as by reading it: I have now read it twice and the cumulative effect is very great . . . the whole thing is so musical & stands to an ordinary prose play so much like an oratorio to an opera, that I almost wd like the actors to have better singing voices, & speak your poetry with less conscious underemphasis . . . I shall now read it for a third time & so acquire a certain amount by heart: the whole Fidelio–Destructive Element theme is more sympathetic than I can say.

Spender had not enjoyed the rough and tumble of rehearsal and performance. Having a play on, he told Plomer, 'is really a very upsetting experience'. Nor did the upset end with the final curtain. Louis MacNeice recorded a hilarious account of the post-performance discussion of the play on the night of 27 March by a group of Unity 'Comrades', who set themselves to correct Spender's 'wavering' ideology. John Strachey took it on himself to 'put across the Party point of view'. Cyril Connolly was recruited to offer a literary appreciation. A pretty but 'ice cold' blonde declared that *Trial of a Judge* 'had been a great disappointment to herself and others in the Party'. Then, 'one after one the Comrades rose and shot their bolts. Marx, Marx and Marx.' Stephen protested. Finally, an old Comrade got up and criticized Spender for his incorrigibly 'mystical' faith in 'Justice'. Beethoven and Fidelio went down badly. Stephen stuck to his guns but it would be thirty years before he wrote another original verse play, even though Eliot strongly encouraged him to do so.

In early May Spender took a short holiday in Corsica, by himself, apparently. In his recoil from the stage and from politics he was writing a lot of poetry. Inez joined him in Paris on 15 May. He had by this date formed what was to be a close friendship with Peter Watson. Stephen had first met him in Paris, in 1935, through their mutual friend, Herbert Read. An Etonian, Watson had been, briefly, a contemporary of Stephen's at Oxford, although they never met. He was Maecenas-rich on his family's margarine business, which had prospered during the First World War. He was highly cultivated, cosmopolitan, debonair, handsome, homosexual and generous. Watson had, Spender observed, 'more sensibility than cleverness'. But that sensibility was refined, and in advance of its age. He was a patron as well as a connoisseur. As a patron, he was non-intrusive but unfailingly supportive. Reminiscing about Watson with Henry Moore years later at his country studio, Spender observed that being helped by Peter was 'different from the way that people like the [Kenneth] Clarks patronized artists (Clark being Moore's most generous patron). Henry said "Yes, being helped by the Clarks was rather like being helped by the Ford Foundation."' Being helped by Peter was like being helped by a friend.

In pre-war Paris, Watson was the centre of a coterie which included the surrealist-anarchist poet David Gascoyne and the sexual anarchist Denham Fouts. Fouts − a drug fiend (he put Hyndman on the road to addiction) − was handsome and dangerous to know. An American, he was Watson's lover. When Stephen and Inez were in Paris, over the years 1938–9, they habitually stayed at the apartment which Watson and Fouts shared. They were, at this period, also seeing a lot of Cyril Connolly. The Connolly–Watson–Spender triumvirate would, a year later, form the foundation of *Horizon*.

In late summer 1938, Stephen toured with Watson through Switzerland in his friend's great dark-green chauffeur-driven Bentley. Peter insisted that Stephen buy a new suit at his (Peter's) expense and was so vexed when the poet turned up in pin-stripes that he peremptorily forbade him ever to wear the new outfit. On this visit they visited the dying Paul Klee. Watson was a legendary bon viveur and knew, for example, that 'the best food in Switzerland is often to be found at the buffets of railway stations'. His personality, Stephen thought, was entirely that of 'a self-made person . . . He detested politics, officialdom, priggishness, pomposity and almost everything to do with public and bureaucratic life'. It was a philosophy which chimed well with Spender's own.

Tony Hyndman remained a heavy cross for Stephen to bear. On arrival in Vienna, in the early months of 1938, he had proved surprisingly serviceable to Muriel and her underground comrades. He had undertaken missions of some danger. In the anxious days after the *Anschluss* on 11 March, Tony was invaluable as an intermediary able to move freely – as a foreign national – through the heavily policed city streets. Muriel was frantically busy at this period, trying to get as many endangered comrades out of the country as she could. She was also arranging for the evacuation of her daughter Connie, her lover Joe Buttinger, and close members of the household (particularly Fini, Connie's Austrian nanny). Tony was dispatched, as courier and travelling companion, to Switzerland, Holland and France.

In late March, Tony wrote a long letter to Stephen from Paris. He had volunteered himself for a fake marriage, to get Fini the passport that would allow her into England. Auden had done the same for Erika Mann, in July 1935. Tony's wedding took place in Paris. Muriel Gardiner married Joe Buttinger at the same period – also primarily with the aim of making him legal and getting him to the safety of America. Stephen admired Tony's conduct over these early months of 1938. For once, his friend was acting decisively, unselfishly and heroically. This explains Stephen's choosing to dedicate the *Trial of a Judge* to 'T. A. R. H.', with the sonnet, 'The world wears your image on the surface' when the play was published by Faber in March 1938. The gesture may not, however, have pleased Inez.

Stephen was himself in Paris in the middle of May, where he met the newly-wed Mr and Mrs Buttinger. His admiration for Tony's heroism earlier had by now evaporated. Having done his bit for Austrian socialism, Tony was again jobless and again drifting back into parasitic dependence on Stephen. His complaints about his 'suffering', as Stephen complained to Christopher, were maddening:

I have inflicted an injury and I have tried to atone for it by getting Tony back from Spain, supporting him, etc. But every time we meet, he hammers into me all the facts about my 'unforgiveableness' . . . Even if one accepts the fact that one's in the wrong, one can't go on liking people indefinitely who keep on drawing one's attention to the fact.

A job which he had helped set up for Tony in Paris had fallen through. America was still a hopeful prospect, but there would inevitably be difficulty with the immigration quota. Although in one breath Tony reassured Stephen that 'you have no obligations whatsoever', in the next breath he blithely claimed that he couldn't possibly emigrate unless Stephen came across with £200 for his passage and guaranteed (by affidavit, for the immigration people) an income until he found his feet. America was in the grip of an unemployment crisis worse even than England's. The prospect of Tony making good was remote.

In August, on his return from Europe, Stephen and Inez moved into the Great House at Lavenham, in West Suffolk. The house, one of the finest in the village (enriched by the medieval wool trade), dominates the central square. Stephen purchased the building (for £1,200) together with Humphrey on a mortgage provided by their grandmother. Their capital in the Spender–Schuster settlement could not be touched, but would provide the repayments. Stephen was, at this period, close to Humphrey and adored Lolly, whom he had married in June 1937; they were intending eventually to start a family (as, Stephen may have fondly thought, he and Inez might when the political situation improved). Humphrey was cramped in his bachelor flat in Upper Montagu Street, as was Stephen in Queen's Mansions – although both couples would keep London *pieds-à-terre*.

Humphrey's career was going well. He had moved from architecture to journalism and – most effectively – photo-journalism. The *Daily Mirror* was paying him £11 a week; big money in 1936. Never comfortable in salaried work, he went freelance for *Picture Post* when it was launched in 1938. This gave him more money and more spare time. Out of interest he enrolled as photographer-in-chief (unpaid) on 'Mass-Observation'. The enterprise had been formed by the social scientist and poet Charles Madge, in collaboration with Tom Harrisson, in January 1937. Madge's brother, John, had been a fellow student of Humphrey's at the Architectural Association.

M-O's aim was to subject urban Britain to the scrutiny which Harrisson (an Oxford-trained anthropologist) had earlier applied to the natives of the New Hebrides. The English savages they had chosen for their fieldwork were the industrial under-class of Bolton ('Worktown'). The photo-records which Humphrey produced for the survey are regarded as classics of their kind. Through the connection with Humphrey, Stephen and Inez saw quite a lot of the M-O crew. They included (in addition to Madge, Harrisson and Humphrey) the artists Humphrey Jennings, Graham Bell and William Coldstream (whose 'Euston Road' realism was powerfully influenced by M-O). The operation was run on a shoestring budget. Harrisson contrived to raise money from the Bolton self-made millionaire William Lever (later Lord Leverhulme). But the team was paid very little or nothing by way of salary. In Bolton they pigged it in a wretched artisans' dwelling in Davenport Street. The project was none the less immensely successful. By 1939 it had 2,000 voluntary observers working for it. During the war it was absorbed, usefully, into the Ministry of Information.

From the first, Stephen took against Charles Madge. Born in South Africa in 1912, Madge came to university in England. At Cambridge he was already a hardline Marxist. While still an undergraduate he had an affair with the poet Kathleen Raine, then married to the don Hugh Sykes Davies. There had been an ugly divorce. Sykes Davies was provoked to 'homicidal madness'. Madge left Cambridge without a degree. By 1937 he and Raine were living in her fine Vanbrugh House at Blackheath. Inez saw a lot of the 'Blackheath set' (through Mary Elliott, her best friend at school, now a friend of the Madges). Stephen did not much like them – particularly Madge, who had the reputation of a 'marriage breaker'.

It was Madge's responsibility on M-O to keep the observation diaries and reports in good literary order. His health was not good, which may explain his absence from the Republican ranks in Spain – a cause which he supported with undeviating Stalinist orthodoxy. Madge was also regarded as a coming poet, whose work, like Stephen's, had been featured in W. B. Yeats's *Oxford Book of Modern English Verse* (1938). It did not help relations between the poets that Madge had written a venomous review of *Vienna*. He found Spender's poem lacking in Marxist rigour. Spender was infuriated beyond measure in 1937 when Madge used the columns of *New Verse* (with the connivance of Lehmann, as Stephen thought) to attack him for lack of Marxist correctness in an article he wrote for *New Country*. It added to the soreness that Wystan (whom Madge had quoted approvingly against Stephen) was, as he told Michael Roberts, 'a great admirer of and believer in Madge'. Auden's admiration was, as none knew better than Stephen, not easily won.

Over the period 1938–9 Stephen would suspect that Madge was setting his cap at Inez. When Spender asked Madge outright, he was assured there was nothing 'serious' between them. He was, as he concedes in *World within World*, 'extremely jealous'; so much so that he may have frightened Inez into dishonesty. His temper, as Humphrey recalls, could flame up alarmingly at this period. The 1930s was, however, a period in which progressive couples allowed each other considerable freedom within the ideal of the 'open marriage'. Stephen evidently bore with patience Inez's going to parties with Madge, and even going on holiday with him. Stephen's understanding was that he and Inez had a 'fundamental loyalty'. He did not, as he later said, mind his wife having affairs, 'because I was told that whatever happened she would never leave me'.

It was against this emotionally complicated background that Stephen set up their second home at Lavenham. Stephen knew Suffolk well, from the cottage which he, Tony and Worsley had once rented at Bures (some ten miles away). It was served by the same main-line LNER station, at Mark's Tey (there was a branch line to Lavenham). The village was idyllic, particularly in high summer, when the four Spenders moved in. The Great House had been previously owned by twin brothers, John ('J. G.') and 'Pum' Gayer-Anderson. Both were outrageously gay. Pum was a doctor, J. G. an art dealer who acted on behalf of the royal family of Egypt, among other clients. They were both of them distinguished Egyptologists. (The 'Gayer-Anderson cat', immortalized on innumerable BM posters, is their best-known monument; they also founded the Gayer-Anderson museum in Cairo). Their conduct in Lavenham testified either to the villagers' worldly tolerance or to yokel innocence about cosmopolitan vice. J. G. – an amateur artist – drew portraits of local lads. When he died in the 1940s Humphrey, as his appointed executor, donated these alarming sketches to the Ashmolean, who prudently filed them under 'psycho-sexual-pathology'.

Humphrey and Lolly, with their Architectural Association background, remodelled the house into two separate halves (Stephen and Inez had the section which now comprises the dining-room of the present Great House Restaurant). Humphrey was already an indefatigable collector of china and bric-à-brac. He furnished the house (Stephen's side as well) with furniture chosen well and acquired, at bargain price, from local antique dealers. He also made himself a north-facing studio in the attic. Humphrey – always 'mad about cars' – had a Standard Flying Twelve coupé which he parked facing down the hill outside the house, because it was tricky to start in the wet. They could get to London in under two hours – if the Standard got them to Mark's Tey. Stephen did not drive at this date.

Lavenham was idyllic. But it put strains on Stephen's finances. Inez, now at work on her novel and making frequent trips by herself to London, brought nothing into their bank account. Her scholarship had long since expired (she had not, however, finished her B.Litt.). They were still paying rent on the Queen's Mansions flat. There were payments for the conversion, remodelling and furnishing of the Great House. There were payments for pictures (including £100 for the Coldstream portrait of Inez). There were medical bills and the fees for Stephen's psychoanalysis.

And, of course, Tony needed to be supported (at the rate of about £2 a week, Stephen calculated). In August 1938, Stephen wrote a despairing account of his finances to Christopher:

entirely on account of my own stupidity and extravagance . . . I am at least £292 in debt. £100 of this I pay interest on to Humphrey for the furnishing of this house – so it does not matter (incidentally, the rent of this house is only £30 a year from each pair of us to Granny, so that does not count as one of my follies).

He needed to pay off debts 'within a very few months'. Tony had thrown up his latest job. On learning this: 'I immediately assumed that I would have to give up being analysed and go and live in the country so that all the money I have beyond my immediate needs could go to him.'

By pulling all the strings at their disposal, he and Christopher got Tony yet another job, this time with Lehmann, just back from America. It was nothing very grand. The Hogarth Press had a bit of a rush and needed the services of a part-time typist. Tony got on well with Lehmann, and the hope was that it would keep him occupied, and partly solvent, until he was shunted off to America, where Christopher might be able to find something for him.

The Leishman arrangement was not progressing at all well. By 12 August, Stephen had furnished provisional versions of the first three Rilke elegies. He was working 'six hours a day' at Lavenham, where he was undisturbed, he reassured his co-translator. He would keep his nose to the grindstone for a month, at least. He had five elegies finished by 31 August. But by this stage the relationship was fraying badly. On 31 August 1938 Stephen was constrained to tell Leishman that 'you write to me not so much as a collaborator, but with the sort of patronizing and discouraging air which you might adopt to one of your students at Southampton University'.

Hogarth Press wanted the completed manuscript by the end of October. Stephen continued to prevaricate and do other things (a visit to Paris, to see Peter Watson at the end of November, for example). On 10 December he wrote, contritely, apologizing to his collaborator for his delays in sending drafts, adding (hopefully), 'I think you will understand when I explain that during the past three months I have had lectures to give every weekend, all over the country; in addition to this I have done a translation of *Danton's Death* with Goronwy Rees; a translation of a new play by Ernst Toller; about half a volume of new poems; and all the usual reviewing by which I largely exist.'

In addition to the works he cites to Leishman, Stephen was working on three other volumes to be published in 1939–40. Most pressing (in view of events in the Civil War) was the anthology *Poems for Spain*, co-edited with John Lehmann. The sixpenny pamphlet he was writing alongside it, *The New Realism*, redefined his aesthetic, post-Spain and post-Communism. He was meanwhile making notes for a novel, *The Backward Son*, as it was to be. All these projects had been commissioned by Lehmann, who was, after April 1938 and the retirement of Virginia Woolf, a full partner at the Hogarth Press. He had expansionist plans – many of them built around Stephen. Once again, the utopian idea of a Lehmann–Spender publishing combine, or possibly a joint editorship of *New Writing*, was aired. Pressed as he was for money, the author took on more than he should.

The year 1938 came to an end with Inez finishing her novel, Stephen within sight of completing both the Rilke *Elegies* and his forthcoming collection of forty poems for Faber, and Catalonia falling to the Fascists. Stephen performed an unobtrusive but immensely valuable service for English literature by converting Cecil Day-Lewis from his doctrinaire, card-carrying Communism in early December. He joined Stephen in the growing ranks of the politically disillusioned. There was a huge Christmas party thrown by Cyril Connolly, which Christopher nostalgically recalled a year later as 'the last great blaze of European culture'.

On 2 January 1939 Stephen went to Paris for a short trip with Inez, to celebrate, at last, the completion of her novel and his *Duino Elegies*. They returned for a round of farewell parties for Wystan and Christopher, who were leaving for America. Stephen commemorated Wystan's departure with a valedictory essay, 'The Importance of W. H. Auden', for the *Mercury* in April. No valediction for Hyndman. The plan for Tony's going to America fell through in January, just as Stephen's other friends were leaving. Muriel wrote at the end of the month from Paris to say that he had been turned down by the immigration authorities. She was 'not altogether surprised'. Moreover she was disinclined to pull strings for him because influence ought to be reserved for 'urgent cases from Germany'. Tony's case was not urgent. He only wanted to go for 'some experience and fun' – while Western civilization was going up in flames. His plan to become a 'political secretary' for someone important was ludicrous. He had asked her for £200 (he was shamelessly cadging at this period) to take a typing course – as he said.

There were other reasons for Muriel's being unhelpful. She had entrusted to Tony a large sum to settle his 'wife' in London. Fini got a housekeeping job with Anna Freud and separated, as was expected, from her husband of convenience. But Tony kept Muriel's money (it was legally his) and frittered it away on himself. Tony's continued presence on the scene added stress to Stephen's marriage. It was a further source of stress that Inez finished her novel in December 1938, but by February had found no publisher. Her B.Litt. was dragging on interminably. Stephen was sick of the name of Góngora. In December 1938, the tattered remnants of the British Battalion, leaving 500 dead behind them, came home from Spain. The cause which had originally united Inez and Stephen was lost. Fascism had won; and would, it seemed, keep on winning.

In early March the Spenders took a spring holiday at Mousehole, near Penzance. Stephen was going over the proofs of *The Still Centre* and was well ahead with the novel that would follow, *The Backward Son*. It was, as regards his literary output, a hopeful time. He had solved his position *vis-à-vis* socialism and could again write from a secure ideological standpoint. The couple were in the process of moving to a larger, rather grander, flat at 6 Selwyn House, Lansdowne Terrace, WC1, opposite Coram's Fields. His money problems were not, for once, pressing, with all the advances Lehmann had thrown at him.

Spender and Lehmann's militant volume, *Poems for Spain*, had been slow in appearing, and when it eventually came out in late March it coincided exactly with the fall of Madrid and the *de facto* defeat of the Republic. It was the more ironic since many of the poems (including one by Tony Hyndman and another by John Lepper) had been composed with the expectation of inevitable victory. Spender's introduction was pointedly apolitical. 'To these writers,' he wrote, 'the Spanish War is, in the words which Keats used of Peterloo: "No contest between Whig and Tory – but between Right and Wrong".' But, as in 1819, the forces of Wrong had triumphed. Sales were, inevitably, poor for the collection which the *New Statesman* called 'Alas, a valedictory work.'

It was a cause of some anger to Stephen that Faber, in March, published Roy Campbell's anti-semitic, homophobic and triumphantly pro-Fascist verse epic, *Flowering Rifle*. It reiterated sneers which the Fascist poet had been making for years about 'Spauden', the 'sodomites, cranks and cowards' who supported the Republic. Stephen (who had always had a good word for Campbell's lyric verse) reviewed the volume, under the biting headline 'Talking Bronco', in the *New Statesman* of 11 March. It was, he said: 'an incoherent, biased, unobjective, highly coloured, and distorted account of one man's experiences of the Spanish Civil War, seen through the eyes of a passionate partisan of Franco'. Parts of Campbell's poem, he declared, 'make me physically sick' – nausea heightened by the fact that the volume had come out (like his own poetry) with Tom Eliot's firm.

Faber had, however, done well by Spender in 1939. In March they published the text of *Trial of a Judge* and in May his volume of poetry *The Still Centre*. It marked Stephen's return to romantic lyricism and re-established him at the age of thirty (with Auden now in exile) as England's leading young poet; a pre-eminence contested only by Louis MacNeice, whose impressive *Autumn Journal* came out this same year. Eliot had suggested the strikingly effective title for Stephen's collection (the poet had originally intended 'The Silent Centre'.) As Christopher told him, on reading his inscribed copy, 'you have kept your integrity in a world of publicity. You outsplash headlines . . . I wish you could go on writing for ever, and always about your immense eyeballs, genitals, entrails.'

The volume, which is dedicated 'To Inez', has only one poem which is unequivocally inspired by her, 'The Little Coat' (an embroidered jacket). The love lyric is written with the simplicity of a parent talking tenderly to a child:

> The little coat embroidered with birds
> Is irretrievably ruined.
> We bought it in the Spring
> And she stood upon a chair,
> A blazing tree of birds;
> I leaned my head against her breast
> And all the birds seemed to sing
> While I listened to that one heavy bird
> Thudding at the centre of our happiness.

Why is it 'ruined'? The poem does not tell us (according to Natasha Spender, Stephen's second wife, it was damaged by bad laundering).

As Stephen explains in his foreword, the poems are arranged 'in the order of development' – that is, the poet's development between 1934 and 1939. He also indicates the trend of that development: 'I have deliberately turned back to a kind of writing which is more personal.' The first part contains poems written mainly in the period of impersonal socialism, such as 'Experience' and 'An Elementary School Class Room'. The second section dates mainly from the the 1935–6 period, and is headed by the meditation on *furor poeticus*, 'Hoelderlin's Old Age'. The third section contains poems from Spain. It opens and closes with experiences of marginality, 'no-man's-land' poems – 'View from a Train' and 'Port Bou'. The collection ends with poems which constitute a personal statement, in recoil from the war. The valedictory piece is 'To a Spanish Poet' – Altolaguirre. What will survive of the horror is poetry and friendship. Or so the collection affirms.

The reviews were strong. Some, like the *TLS*, felt that there was perhaps too much 'self absorption', and in the *New Statesman* G. W. Stonier ordained that rhyme would discipline the 'shapeless charm and undeveloped beauty' of Mr Spender's lyrics. But the general tone was one of warm approval for a poet now in his artistic maturity. Only his former Party comrades were critical. For them he would always be a renegade. Alick West in the *Daily Worker* pronounced what was, in Party terms, a verdict of death: 'Spender is not interested in solving his conflict, but in having one. For he can then feel that his special task is to stand aside and watch it.'

There was to be no still centre in his personal life. Things were going badly between him and Inez. Her behaviour was increasingly irrational. Stephen had been translating Ernst Toller's play *Pastor Hall* with Hugh Hunt (it was Spender's final commitment to Doone; Auden also did some translation for the production). Toller was a German-Jewish refugee and a disillusioned communist. In May 1939, there occurred the strange episode which Stephen records in *World within World*. Toller wanted Stephen to collaborate in 'an appeal through high functionaries to the conscience of the world on behalf of the Spanish Republicans'. Stephen was weary of such initiatives (more so as the war was clearly lost). But he was polite enough to discuss the scheme over dinner, with Toller and Inez, at the Gargoyle Club. At the end of the dinner, 'Toller, rather surprisingly, fished a silver brooch out of his pocket and presented it to Inez.'

'A few days later', as *World within World* records, on 22 May (as *The Times* records), the German hanged himself in a New York hotel. Stephen read about the suicide in the newspaper, and was 'deeply shocked'. Inez's reaction was ominous:

her face became distorted with anger as I had never seen it before, for she did not as a rule dramatize things. She turned on me furiously: 'You understand why he committed suicide. You *would* know someone capable of doing such a thing. That's what I can't bear about you,' and she threw the brooch which Toller had given her, across the room.

The anecdote is interesting not just as a sign of marital tension but as an example of Spender's habitual trick of retaining the essential truth of events, while actual details bent in his mind. The discussions with Toller about Spain took place in October 1938 – not 'a few days' before his death but eight months. Toller indeed gave Inez a present, but it was a bracelet, not a brooch. He sent it by registered mail, to Lavenham. He left for New York – to continue his hopeless Spanish campaign – in January 1939. Here it was that, five months later, distressed by the Francoist victory, he hanged himself.

It is extremely likely, however, that on the morning of 23 May Inez threw the tantrum Stephen describes. Humphrey (who saw a number of such tantrums) surmises that over the months Charles Madge had been blackguarding Stephen to Inez. In early July, Madge and Inez went on holiday together to Wales. Their respective spouses acquiesced in the arrangement. Stephen was meanwhile working on his writing in Suffolk. Kathleen Raine was in her second home, a cottage in Devon. Allegedly, Charles's last remark to her was, 'I've got to go away with Inez for a fortnight. My God, how *bored* I'm going to be!' Neither Raine nor Stephen anticipated the storm that was about to break over their marriages. But both, apparently, knew that Charles and Inez were sexually involved.

Throughout the spring Stephen had been drafting *The Backward Son*. He was confident he would finish it by the end of the summer. There was, however, an interruption in June when he and Peter Watson motored through Switzerland to examine Spanish pictures, in safe storage from Franco. Spender wrote up the trip for the *New Statesman* (24 June). He was putting some final touches to the manuscript of his novel in Lavenham on 16 July. Inez had just returned from her holiday with Madge. That morning she woke up, turned to Stephen, and said: 'Could Charles be a cat? Because I dreamt that a cat (Charles) was killing a rat (you).' Stephen did not, evidently, decipher this sybilline message.

It became clearer during the course of the day what Inez meant about cats and rats. As Humphrey recalls, he, Lolly and Stephen went for a walk through the summer lanes after lunch, leaving Inez in the house. When they returned Stephen found a letter on the bed. She had gone, and would not return, as the note coldly informed him. She had left most of her clothes, most woundingly the 'little coat'. Her belongings were scattered untidily all over the bedroom. She must have intended to tell Stephen to his face that she and Charles were going to live together, but lost her nerve. On the spur of the moment she packed an overnight bag and rushed off to catch a train at Lavenham Station. Stephen 'took one look at the letter and simply ran out of the room'.

Over the next two days he fired off a series of telegrams to their flat (and their friends) in London, demanding to see her for some explanation. He wrote, in his despair, to Mary Elliott on 24 July, protesting, 'I love Inez. I cannot imagine loving anyone else.' He intended, in his grief (and if she did not come back to him), to sell his flat, his pictures and travel for six months. Anywhere. On 24 July Stephen at last received an explanatory letter from Inez informing him that he must regard the marriage as over. There was no question of face-to-face discussion:

Dear Stephen, If I saw you now it would make both of us very unhappy and protract the uncertainty and anxiety. Please believe me when I say that I've thought about this carefully and I'm sure that we should not meet for some time . . . So as not to leave the slightest vagueness, because that too prolongs the anxiety, I must say what the position is again; I cannot live with both you and Charles, that has been proved to be unworkable and destructive to all, and at the same time I cannot live entirely with you because of my feelings for Charles and because, even if there were no Charles, although our affection is very solid, we could not get any further with our relationship and should both be profoundly dissatisfied.

She gave him no return address. But she and Charles were camping in his cramped lodgings in Bolton. They had decided, as Madge told Mary Elliott, that they must live together during their 'lovely time in Wales'. They had furnished his Spartan quarters in Davenport Street, Bolton, with 'a new mattress and a chest of drawers'. Raine was as devastated as

Stephen. Madge had deserted her (regarded as one of the most beautiful women in London) after only a year's marriage. She had two children by her earlier marriage. Scandal was inevitable.

For Stephen the world seemed more apocalyptically symbolic than even a poet could have devised. Inez's departure happened on the eve of war between Britain and Germany. The old fig tree in the walled courtyard behind the Great House, recalling the lightning-blasted chestnut in *Jane Eyre*, chose this moment to fall to the ground with a mighty crash. What next? Would the sun go out? He hurried back to London, to lay down (as he told Mary) a 'background of love' for Inez to return to. If she did come back, he would undertake to love her 'my whole life':

At the moment I feel rather shattered. Everything – the wireless, the papers, food, my relations – gives me a sense of nausea, and I haven't recovered from the stupid fact that some guests whom I hadn't invited played a record from Don Giovanni yesterday at Lansdowne Terrace . . . It makes me unhappy to think that it is precisely because I care and feel so much that Inez cannot live with me.

He wrote 'a bitter poem called "The Separation" which was about one weekend only'. The poem evidently recalls an earlier flight by Inez. 'This is by far the most important and terrifying thing that has happened to me,' he told Mary Elliott. On her part, Raine told Elliott (with whom all parties were communicating over this hectic period), 'I loathe this so much that I feel ready to step into the grave to escape it.'

At this early stage, Stephen hoped that a trial six-month separation would lay the way for reconciliation. 'I'll go to Paris for some time, and stay at a cheap hotel and write my books,' he told Christopher, unaware at this point that the Wehrmacht might get to Paris before he did. If (as he hoped) Inez came back, 'it will be on my terms'. At the same period, he told Mary Elliott that 'there can be no question of Inez staying with Charles . . . if she ever in the dim future asks herself why Charles, in spite of all his cleverness, is a total and vacuous failure as a poet, the answer will be that his work lacks all moral feeling . . . I love Inez a hundred times more than anyone else does . . . I don't cheat and lie.'

He remained emotionally paralysed for most of August. He repeated to Lehmann his plan to go to Paris till the new year, 1940. London with its wagging tongues would be unbearable. It was at this point, evidently, that he decided to publish the violently Oedipal poem he had been working on, 'The Ambitious Son'. The poem was much changed in its various appearances in print over the next fifty years. In its first form, in *New Writing* (December 1939), it blazes on the page with Stephen's accumulated rage against his father, Harold:

> Old man, with hair made of newspaper cutting
> And the megaphone voice,
> Dahlia in the public mind and strutting
> Like a canary before the clapping noise,
> My childhood went for rides on your wishes
> As a beggar's eye strides a tinsel horse.

It was the last straw for J. A. Spender, who cut this parricidal nephew out of his will. He died, two years later, unreconciled.

Meanwhile, Europe was moving inexorably towards cataclysm. On 22 August, Stephen wrote to Mary asking if she knew what Inez's plans were 'in case of war? Does she intend to come to Lavenham?' If so, Stephen would welcome her – so long as the serpentine 'Madgiarelli' were not in the picture. He had heard rumours that 'Charles is not serious about Inez.' Other malicious gossips informed him that the couple were publicly 'crowing over me'. He was being driven frantic by Inez's silence. As he told Mary ('the only human person in the affair'), 'We have been married two and a half years and during the last eighteen months I have strained myself to give her whatever she wants, however now she cannot even answer a letter . . . if Inez is such a callous little bitch, the best thing is to try and forget her.' But he could not forget the callous little bitch. He was firing off two or three letters a day. His health was suffering. Two of his teeth, he told Mary, 'have died as the result of shock. I think you might tell Inez that as a person who doesn't believe in violence she might be more gentle in her methods in future.'

Virginia Woolf, when she had tea with Stephen on 19 August, discovered him 'full of regret and bitterness' – so violently so that the encounter gave her bad dreams. He was, she noted, writing 'reams about himself'. This was evidently preliminary notes for what later became *September Journal*. The form, which Gide had successfully turned to artistic purposes, had attracted the autobiographer in him for some time.

He chose, for the purpose of synchrony, to begin the journal on 3 September 1939, the day that war was declared. Personal and historical cataclysm converged to form his starting point. As for the war, he realized that it was 'madness' but must be fought. He would not, he resolved on 3 September, 'run away . . . to save my skin or get on with my work'. According to Humphrey, he and Stephen were actually in Lavenham when Chamberlain's declaration of war came out over the radio at 11.15. Stephen, his brother recalls, walked across the square and bought a seven-pound tin of bully beef, in the solemn expectation that there would be a blockade; it was, of course, a joke – even in this dreadful time.

On 12 September Spender applied for a job as translator in the War Office. It would, he thought, fill in the few weeks before his age group was called up. No one knew how fast the War Department would react: it could be hours, days or months before the King's summons came. He was not sure, even so, that translation was an adequate way of doing his bit: 'I feel that I ought to be doing stretcher work or filling sandbags.'

On 26 September he bought a printing press, which he set up in Bobby Bühler's flat, intending – as he claimed – to produce volumes by 'unknown poets'. It is likely that he was nervous about a possible Fascist coup or invasion. As he knew from Muriel, a clandestine press was invaluable for underground resistance. Buhler (as he originally was), a refugee and a left-wing painter, could expect to be on the Gestapo's lists when they marched into London. As could Stephen. He was under no illusions about what his decision to stay in Britain might mean. He and Leonard Woolf, a couple of months later, planned a suicide pact in the event of the invasion which looked probable. Stephen favoured cyanide: Woolf carbon-monoxide poisoning, for which he prudently put aside a store of rationed petrol. (They may have made the resolution on the weekend of 26–28 September, which Stephen spent at Rodmell.)

September Journal in fact runs from 3 September to 16 November. There are three main literary sources: Christopher Isherwood's 'Berlin Diary' (which was currently being serialized in *New Writing*), Gide's journals, and Wilde's *De Profundis*, which is alluded to twice in the first entry. Wilde wrote his journal in Reading Gaol, after disgrace and the break-up of his marriage. Spender was working on the diary in the last week of September, when he made another weekend visit to the Woolves. 'A loose jointed mind,' Virginia wrote in her diary, 'misty, clouded, suffusive. Nothing has outline . . . we plunged and skimmed and hopped – from sodomy and women and writing and anonymity and – I forget.'

During the period of emotional crisis described in the journal, Stephen was sustained by friends – notably Lolly and Humphrey, to whom he wrote his 'Dearest and nearest brother' tribute (published some years later in *Ruins and Visions*). Eliot (who had his own domestic crisis over the preceding years with his crazed first wife, Vivienne) was extraordinarily kind and attentive. He discussed Faber's plans for the wartime publishing (as had happened in 1914–18, there was a boom in poetry books). Stephen visited Isaiah Berlin at monastic Oxford and read Shyah's recent book on Marx with all the eagerness of a committed ex-Marxist.

Stephen published his 1939 journal, or substantial parts of it, at least five times (most dramatically in *Horizon*, 1939–40, while it was still white hot). But in every version which he allowed into print during his lifetime he suppressed a main strand in the manuscript text, his tortured (and infinitely humiliating) relations with Inez and Madge, immediately after her bolt to Bolton.

On 3 September, in his initial entry, he noted that the outbreak of world war was only comprehensible to him through the breakdown of his marriage: 'Everything I read in the papers about broken faith, broken pledges, disloyalty, etc seems about her.' Madge was, he told Herbert Read, 'a crook', who seduced women like Kathleen and Inez with 'Wykehamist flattery'. Were Inez and Madge 'happy'? he tormentedly asked himself.

On 4 September there was an air-raid warning. 'Inez seems so far away,' he wrote. 'I imagine her in her red dressing gown and she looks pale and dazed.' He was 'humiliated' by his 'need of loving'. A few days earlier he had dreamed of Madge: 'He looked unctuous, like he does look, and I threw stones at him' (he was, after all, the man taken in adultery). But, as happens in anxiety dreams, Stephen could not throw the stones hard enough to break his enemy's bones. 'They were very light pebbles, but all the same they hurt him.'

Stephen meanwhile was still bombarding Inez with letters. She was working now, picking up a few shillings clerking for M-O. Spender had lunch with Cyril Connolly on 3 September. In addition to the obvious topic of conversation (war), Cyril – a world-class womanizer – told Stephen that if he wanted Inez back he must make her jealous. Tell her that he 'had another girl', Connolly advised. The trick worked. On 8 September, Inez told Mary Elliott that Stephen reported having met 'what he called a beautiful and charming girl'. Her curiosity was piqued (was she more 'beautiful' than Inez?). On 14 September Inez finally replied to his barrage of letters with a phone call from Bolton. She was coming down to London for a few days to accompany Charles, who was helping negotiate M–O's absorption into the Ministry of Information. Stephen and Inez arranged to meet at 'the Chinese restaurant in Piccadilly Circus' for lunch on 15 September.

Stephen was so excited at seeing her again that he arrived far too early. But, to his surprise, he found that she had arrived even earlier than he. It was another surprise that Inez – so charming in his fantasies – looked worn in the flesh:

she had dark rings under her eyes, she looked older, and her hair was rather greasy and untidily fastened by two hair pins. She seemed to me more *ordinary* than before.

Her lost beauty was 'a load off my mind'.

They soon got down to business. Did she want a divorce? She replied, 'No, but if you do, of course we must have one.' What about the other girl? she asked – clearly curious (Connolly knew the female mind). He confessed that it was a ruse (not something that Cyril, having gained the advantage, would have done). Was she liking her new life? he asked. She replied, dully,

It's all right, but we have to work so hard, and there's practically nothing to eat but bread and marmalade, and we only have 10/– a week pocket money each [from M–O]. When I used to go away with him for weekends it was very different.

She 'hated Bolton', she said. Davenport Street was 'absolutely disgusting' (it was, Humphrey confirms). They were having 'very violent rows'. Although she was still 'fascinated and physically attracted' by Madge, Stephen guessed that 'the whole thing will last another month or two'. They discussed 'with a completely open mind the prospect of her coming back'.

He realized, however, that Madge had given her something which he never had – a job, and with it a sense of self-worth. Inez needed, he now saw, 'independent work of some kind to do, which is regular and scholarly, and which is not like novel-writing, setting her up in a rather hopeless rivalry to me'. They spent the day together. It ended with Stephen confident that she would come back – probably quite soon.

On 26 September, Stephen resolved that when she returned he would be magnanimous. Over the next forty years of married life, 'I can accept there being periods of three months or so every few years when you run off.' Poets could be complaisant (like Robert Graves and Laura Riding, or Yeats and Maud Gonne). Insidiously, however, his mood was hardening from quivering pain into cynical resentment. Three days later, on 29 September, he had lunch with another of her discarded lovers, Dennis Campkin. Man to man they discussed Inez in the terms of a tart. They had both suffered, they agreed, from

her habit of keeping us both on a string, and he said that she was like a species of female spider which almost destroys the male but keeps him partially alive in order to have him again. Bitching. Keeping one on a string. Playing one person off against another. Cockteasing.

Gradually, Stephen pulled himself out of the trough. By 23 October he was having symbolic dreams about Charles Madge in which his cuck-older was dead and cremated into harmless ash. What most worried him, as he noted at this point of his journal, was the vindictiveness which the episode had evoked in him. He was ashamed of his own emotional violence. In the creative sector of his life he was picking up threads again. He had founded *Horizon* with Connolly and Watson; he was back at work on his 'childhood novel' for Lehmann (he would, in fact, finish *The Backward Son* by December); poems were being written. As Eliot told him, over a club lunch on 30 September, the important thing was to 'keep the engine running'. To write, that is.

He was, meanwhile, spending a lot of time with Humphrey (also anxiously awaiting call-up) and Lolly. Suffolk was beautiful in autumn, its beauty 'rich as though laid on with a trowel'. They went mushroom picking in the early morning, like Russian poets. Sonia Brownell and Cuthbert Worsley came for a weekend to Lavenham, and Sonia recorded in a letter a comic row which began with Cuthbert trying, vainly, to open a tin (in the absence of a proper opener) with a dinner fork. 'Stephen is very funny,' she wrote affectionately. Everyone was very kind and hospitable, the Woolves (now at Rodmell), Isaiah, Bobby and Eve Buhler. Stephen was reassured that his friends still loved him. There were, he concluded on 26 October, 'advantages of living alone'. He had more energy and 'can indulge without qualms of conscience in the self-ishness of being a writer'.

There was a final flare-up of hostility. In mid-November Inez wrote to say that her relationship with Madge would, after all, be 'permanent'.

Stephen felt as unhappy again as 'in those awful first days at Lavenham'. Divorce was the only option. And he would divorce her. The usual 'gentlemanly' code was that the husband, right or wrong, would go to Brighton and make an arrangement with some complaisant lady of the night and a private detective. Stephen resolved to be 'puritanical'. Inez had deserted him. *Her* misconduct would be the grounds for divorce. He instructed his solicitor to institute proceedings.

Stephen's intransigence provoked alarm in Bolton. Inez had just submitted her B. Litt. thesis on Góngora. She had hopes that it would lead to a fellowship at Oxford. Public scandal might damage her prospects. She and Charles had 'no money and overwhelming debts'. Madge was in negotiation for a job with the Ministry of Information. Scandal would not help him (nor did the fact that, even after the Russo-German pact, he remained resolutely Stalinist). Inez wrote angrily to Stephen in late November. 'Remember that you have money and position,' she pointed out, 'and stand to lose nothing by being divorced.' She accompanied her remarks with a clear threat: 'You forget, perhaps, that on the level which you decide thus to act I have as much or more grounds than you to complain.' She would, that is, drag Tony Hyndman into the picture.

Stephen dismissed the threat as 'blackmail, and nothing else'. He was surprised Inez would stoop so low. It was, he told Mary, 'the end of my relationship with her forever'. As he explained:

I did not suggest her divorcing me, partly because this is expensive, sordid and will upset my family, partly because I have now been a victim of her and Charles for 15 months and do not see why I should fall into this particular trap, and partly because I do not see why she, of all people, should object to being divorced.

Inez and Madge agreed, reluctantly, to be the guilty parties. Inez got her B.Litt. but failed to get her fellowship at Oxford. She taught in school for a year or two and continued writing fiction, with middling success. Madge broke with Mass-Observation in 1940, objecting to Harrisson's merging operations with the Ministry of Information. After September 1940, he worked with J. M. Keynes at the National Institute for Social and Economic Research. In this capacity, he did useful research on wartime saving measures. He was, for a while, a director of Pilot Press before, in 1950, finding his true vocation as a professor of sociology at Birmingham. He published little poetry in the years after his running away with Inez. He died in 1996; an eminent academic. He and Inez married in 1941 (when their respective divorces came through) and had two children. Inez changed her name, yet again, to 'Enes Madge'. She wrote three novels, in all, under the pseudonym 'Elizabeth Lake'. Her path did not cross Spender's after October 1939. She died, relatively young, in 1977. In later years, Spender could even be philosophical about his first marriage. It was, he says in *World within World*, the fracture of something that had never properly joined.

The hardest blow of this awful year was, however, still to come. Humphrey's wife Lolly had been visibly thin and fatigued for months. Her father – a Harley Street doctor – obdurately refused to admit she was ailing. His suggestion was that she had picked up 'rat bite' fever at Lavenham (Dr Low did not think much of the accommodation Humphrey had provided for his daughter). Humphrey finally took his wife to a specialist who diagnosed Hodgkin's disease. She had two years to live. Five if she underwent deep X-ray treatment, whose side-effects were crucifying. Humphrey elected for it as offering the only hope.

Following the medical practice of the day, Lolly was never informed how ill she was. Friends were told merely that she had a 'serious illness'. Humphrey was obliged to move her to London, under the care of a nurse, during her treatments. It put a horrible strain on his finances. When the Great House was requisitioned by the Army as an officers' mess, in early 1940, she was moved to the School House at Sutton Veny.

It was, as Humphrey recalled, 'a cruel illness' (his eyes still visibly moisten, sixty years later, as he describes it). On occasion her weight plummeted to four-and-a-half stones. She suffered a miscarriage in 1940, probably as a result of the radiotherapy. She would, in fact, survive until Christmas Day, 1945. Through it all her good humour and patience were saintly. In the period of his marital breakdown, Lolly was Stephen's principal confidante and an example to him. She showed him 'courage and hope which seemed the final development of a line throughout her fearless and happy life which even illness could not break'.

Stephen's main literary venture in the period following Inez's desertion was the establishment of *Horizon*. He saw a lot of Connolly during that awful September. Connolly had earlier in the year been making overtures to Peter Watson, inviting him to put money into a new magazine. Watson was not interested in backing a London magazine from Paris. All this changed with the outbreak of war. Watson fled Paris in a troop-train on 7 September (it was feared the Germans would sweep across France in days). In his precipitate haste he left much of his art collection behind. Like Stephen he had resolved to remain in Britain (although his wealth could easily have assured him safe passage abroad). On 28 September Stephen records in the *Journal* having lunch with Watson. A day or so before, at a party of Elizabeth Bowen's, Connolly had renewed his proposition about the new magazine and Watson had made a tentatively affirmative response.

Watson, who was generous but no fool where his money was concerned, wanted Stephen on board to provide stability. Connolly, for all his literary talents and famous charm, was a self-confessed idler, *bon viveur*, cadger and philanderer. As Stephen recalled forty-five years later: 'Peter asked me specifically to help edit *Horizon* because he wasn't absolutely sure about Cyril. He wanted to have three editors, and then if Cyril didn't work out, I would be there to help Peter carry on.' Connolly was, prudently, not informed of his colleagues' low estimate of his reliability. On his part, he was only too glad to share the editorial chair with Spender – on the usual principle that, when two men ride a horse, one must ride behind.

The next day, 29 September, Stephen spent the evening discussing with Connolly 'his project for a magazine'. Cyril was 'rather vague about what it would cost', but they were already thinking about names. Stephen 'said I would give him any amount of help but *did not want my name used* as it has been used too much in this sort of way'. 'Spender' would appear neither on the masthead nor on the notepaper. The most practical way he could help was by leasing to the magazine the flat at Lansdowne Terrace – the larger residence which he had hoped, when he took it on in April, to share with Inez. With the expansion of Whitehall, office space and office staff were at a premium. Stephen threw in the clerical services of Tony Hyndman, for good measure. He reserved a small bedroom for himself at the back of the apartment.

Lehmann (who had fondly thought that he and Stephen were going to start a new magazine – *New Writing*, as it would be) was apoplectic when he found out about Watson's project from a coat-trailing article ('The Ivory Shelter') by Connolly in the *New Statesman* on 7 October. He blamed Spender. 'I know he is my enemy in the deepest sense,' he wrote in his journal. It seemed to Lehmann a betrayal of the partnership offers he had been making (without any reciprocation) since 1931. Stephen's scrupulous anxieties about affiliation to Watson's magazine he saw as the 'egotism' of a writer 'utterly corrupted by years of extravagant self-deception'. Virginia Woolf, the receptacle of Lehmann's bile (and a former co-manager of the Hogarth Press), was also annoyed at Stephen's defection. The rifts were eventually healed. Relations were resumed with the completion and publication, to some acclaim, of *The Backward Son* under Hogarth's imprint. *New Writing*'s thunder was not stolen and, as *Penguin New Writing*, it made its own wartime mark.

If Stephen was at all to blame it was merely in being slow to tell Lehmann. Or anyone. It was not until two weeks after Connolly's *New Statesman* article that he broke the news of his association to Plomer. 'I'm not officially connected with it,' he told his friend, 'as I don't want to start any rivalry with the Vesuvius of 45 Mecklenburgh Square (who casts a red glow across Bloomsbury in the blackout).' The eruptive Lehmann's premises were in the square, some 200 yards from Lansdowne Terrace.

Horizon's wartime success is one of the legends of the British book trade. The first issue, of December 1939, had a print run of 1,000. At its height, the magazine would sell 100,000 an issue. This despite Geoffrey Grigson's sourpuss prediction that 'magazines called *Horizon* never last for more than two numbers'. In fact, it would last a decade. As an active, but only partly visible, element of the editorial team, Spender's working relationship with Connolly was a crucial factor in establishing the magazine. The relationship, unlike that with Watson, was complex. Spender was a generation younger than Connolly in Oxford reckoning. His first encounter with the older man had arisen out of a not entirely favourable review. When Connolly had delivered his judicious verdict on *The Destructive Element*, in 1935, the author had written to his critic (whom he had never personally met): 'You are quite right about the bad writing. I am very sorry. It disturbs me very much.'

Unlike Auden, however, Connolly could not maintain this ascendancy over Spender, who respected the other man but who, by the end of the 1930s, felt (as clearly Watson felt) that they were now equals. Equals but temperamentally different (something that Watson clearly appreciated when he put together his editorial mix). The difference is summed up in one of Connolly's witticisms: 'You are entirely without integrity,' he once told Stephen: 'you not only sign contracts for books, you actually *deliver* them.' Connolly was notorious for pocketing publishers' advances and never delivering. It was, in the long term, self-destructive. To be the finest stylist of your literary era was pointless if no (or in Connolly's case no substantial) literature was produced. Connolly made a virtuosic cult out of his wilful failure as a writer with the one book of his which has lasted, *Enemies of Promise*. He was, as friends observed, his own enemy; the extinguisher of his own promise.

Spender enjoyed an intimate relationship with Connolly over the following three decades. They brought the best out in each other's conversation. 'Oh God, how I miss you, Cyril,' he wrote on one of his American stints in the 1950s. But it is clear that Connolly came to resent his younger colleague's outstripping him in public reputation. He took refuge in petty acts of revenge, insisting, for example, when in the early 1950s his time came to an end at *Horizon*, that the magazine be wound up – not continued, as Watson wanted, under Spender's editorial control. The later phase of their relationship is marked by even more petty acts of misappropriation (theft would be the blunter term) of Spender's books: notably such collector's items as the hand-printed 1928 Auden volume, and an inscribed *Poems, 1933*. A bibliophile, Connolly took extreme care of his library (he would, at the end of his life, sell it at great profit at Sotheby's). Famously, he took less care of the women with whom he had relationships. One of the women whom he had treated badly concluded that 'he was ruthless'. If you got involved with Cyril, 'you just had to take it on the chin'.

Spender's carefully positioning himself on the editorial edge of *Horizon* was strategically astute. It enabled him to participate, bringing stability into the journal, without coming too dangerously into Cyril's orbit. This involved, but slightly marginal, positioning of himself would be a consistent feature of Spender's professional life over the next fifty years.

The 1940s: An Englishman Again

Most importantly for Stephen Spender, the 1940s were the end of the 1930s. The first major phase of his creative life also terminated in 1939 – with a combination of shattering personal and historical break-ups: divorce, world war, the departure of friends, and ideological disillusionment with all forms of radicalism. These breakdowns inspired two major literary achievements: his September Journal *and* Ruins and Visions *– a volume which represented a distinct advance in his progress as a poet. His style and manner would develop further with the essentially private* Poems of Dedication *in 1947 and the more publicly voiced poems in* The Edge of Being *in 1949. With his first published novel,* The Backward Son, *his first 'journal book' (*European Witness), *and a string of thoughtful literary critical essays, the 1940s mark a creative highpoint. New, post-1930s, stabilities helped. Over the decade Spender assembled a new self, a new career, a new life. Ideologically he returned to the 'Liberalism' of his youth. He remarried: more wisely the second time. His marriage to Natasha Litvin would be lifelong and would supply the durable foundation to his later career (and hers). After 1941 Spender was, among his many parts, a family man: husband, father, provider. He was also, for much of the war, a fireman. Disqualified by chronically bad health from military service, he contrived to enlist in the NFS. Based in London, he was able to play a leading part in the literary and cultural life of the capital. He was a co-founder (with Cyril Connolly) of* Horizon *and a leading contributor to Lehmann's rival* Penguin New Writing. *He was a founder of the Apollo Society, which offered programmes of music and readings by leading performers and writers. It was in line with other changes of direction in his life. The early 1940s saw a turn from personal preoccupations to more public concerns. As a fireman Spender pioneered outreach educational activities for his comrades. In the immediate post-war period he served in the Allied Control Commission and the newly formed UNESCO. Spender would be for the rest of his life as much a public intellectual as a man of letters or lyric poet. In 1947 he made his first visit to America. The year he spent, as a visiting professor, was formative. Until his death there would be few years without visits, or longer residential stays, in North America. Unlike his expatriated comrades, Auden, Isherwood and Aldous Huxley, Spender would labour to create Forsterian connections between the two great English-speaking cultures, traditionally separated by their* *'love-hate relationship'. The decade ended with a decision to retire from publishing poetry: a resolution which, for many years, he stuck to. In the 1930s, Eliot had hailed him as the lyric poet of his generation. What was he in the 1940s? Still a poet (now one of his country's best known), but also, in embryo, and with his habitual reticences, what Noël Annan later called him: 'a cultural statesman'.*

As 1939 ended Stephen was alternately *never* seeing Inez or – as he ingenuously told Herbert Read – seeing her regularly 'without our being reconciled'. At this point the aim was less to mend things than to achieve a tidy ending to the marriage. As tidy, that was, as the times and British law permitted. The charade of provable 'infidelity' would have to be stage-managed for the divorce court.

'The thirties,' as Spender later put it, 'was being wound up like a company going into bankruptcy.' Over the new year he went off for a month to Beddgelert, in north Wales, to complete *The Backward Son*. How best to bring up 'difficult' or 'backward' children (such as young Stephen had been) preoccupied him. He had for some time been toying with the idea of school-teaching. With this change of career in mind he had been giving the odd class at Bryanston school, in Dorset, and had become friendly with the senior boys there. Over his month's writing in the Welsh wilds in January he was accompanied by two Bryanston pupils and would-be artists – Lucian Freud, and Freud's friend David Kentish. 'It's a very good arrangement,' he told Mary Elliott:

He paints all day and I write. Lucian is the most intelligent person I have met since I first knew Auden at Oxford, I think. He looks like Harpo Marx and is amazingly talented, and also wise, I think.

Freud did a dozen studies of Spender, 'reading, typing, or just looking like a well-meaning head of house', which, in a sense, he was.

The seventeen-year-old Freud was already displaying artistic genius. He, like the poet, had been spectacularly 'backward' as a child. Legend had it that he could neither read nor write until he was eleven. But he could paint. His precocious brilliance had impressed Stephen and, through him, Peter Watson, who subsequently became another of Freud's early patrons. Spender took Lucian, in April, to the Cedric Morris School at Dedham, in Suffolk. Tony Hyndman (currently Michael Redgrave's lover) was modelling there and Stephen was still a keen weekend painter. Redgrave's diary recalls 'wild and amusing conversation' and some malicious observations on Stephen's 'solicitude' for his young protégés.

Friendship with Lucian brought Stephen into contact with the young artist's architect father, Ernst, and his aunt, Anna Freud. Their father, Sigmund, had been driven from Vienna and Berlin by Nazi persecution in 1938 (Ernst had left with his family on Hitler's accession to power, in 1933). With the outbreak of war Stephen could not but be conscious of his own part-Jewishness. It pleased him and Lucian to play-act being 'two old Hebrews, Freud and Schuster'. In more serious vein, for the *New Statesman* Spender wrote powerful denunciations of the 'barbarous' persecutions Jews were suffering in occupied Europe and Germany. With the expectation of imminent invasion, he had no illusions as to what his (or Lucian's) fate would be when the Gestapo knocked on his door at 3 a.m.

The period 1939–40 represented the most influential phase of Spender's connection with *Horizon*. He commissioned such heavyweight contributors as Auden, MacNeice, Herbert Read and Geoffrey Grigson. Connolly was troubled by the political flavour these Spender recruits brought to his magazine. More to Cyril's taste was Stephen's introduction, in February 1940, of a dazzling young friend of Bill Coldstream's – Sonia Brownell (later Orwell) – 'the Venus of the Euston Road Group'. Only twenty-one, Miss Brownell was subsequently poached from the government department where she was working and taken on as one of *Horizon*'s Girl Fridays. In addition to being ornamental she turned out to be usefully efficient.

At this period, Spender drafted the first version of his poem 'The Double Shame'. He sent a copy to Mary Elliott (who, poor woman, was also getting a stream of confessional verse from Charles Madge). The poem represents an attempt to untangle the complicated skein of emotions between him and Inez ('you' is Stephen):

> At first you did not love enough
> And afterwards you loved too much
> And you lacked the confidence to choose
> And you have only yourself to blame.

Although he might shoulder the blame, and the double shame, Stephen was resolved to go ahead with the divorce. In early February, as he told Mary Elliott: 'Inez turned up. As soon as she looked at me she started crying. However, as far as I could make out from asking her, she is (a) happy (b) she wants to go on living with Charles indefinitely (c) she is hard up (d) her only objection to the divorce is to do with her career.' She feared, that is, the scandal might damage her prospects of a fellowship at Oxford. Stephen resolved: 'it will be better not to see her again. These have been the worst six months of my life.'

Spender's major literary achievement in early 1940 was the completion of his 'childhood novel'. *The Backward Son* would be his first published long work of fiction – a trail littered with innumerable false starts and hopeful projects. 'It is,' he told Lehmann in a note accompanying the typescript, 'very naked, for the simple reason that something has happened to me which makes it only possible for me to write from my heart.' The 'something' was Inez's treachery.

The complete manuscript of *The Backward Son* was delivered to Mecklenburgh Square on 30 January 1940. The work was oven-ready. But the lawyers required some changing of names to protect the guilty (those Charlcote schoolteachers who had made young Stephen's and Humphrey's lives hell). With the general mobilization of civilian Britain the Great House at Lavenham was by now taken over by the War Department. Neither Stephen nor Humphrey regretted surrendering their Suffolk home to the nation. Lolly was now in nursing care at the Old School House at Sutton Veny, in Wiltshire (formerly the country studio of a family friend, the painter Sir William Nicholson). Stephen grimly expected her to die there. He told Mary Elliott in mid-February, 'Lolly can live only a few weeks now . . . Humphrey is nearly crazy.'

Stephen continued to work at improving his artistic gifts. Painting remained therapeutic. As he notes in *World within World*, the 'apparently disconnected activities, of being psychoanalysed and painting, did in fact have a secret connection, a kind of complicity even. Strangely enough they were both attendants on the breaking up of my first marriage. They did not cause it, but they made it more bearable.' Christopher Isherwood recalled, from his haven in Hollywood, that one of the things he most missed about Britain was Stephen telling him funny stories about his shrink. When might his friends expect to see a Spender hanging at the RA? Christopher archly inquired.

For a year or two, laughs between the men would be few and far between. In early 1940 there was a row with Christopher and – less directly – with Wystan. The cause was an editorial in *Horizon*. Christopher had been notably friendly during the magazine's start-up period. He ordered ten copies of the first issues to sow among his West Coast acquaintance and submitted strong pieces for publication. All friendliness towards *Horizon* evaporated, however, when he read Connolly's 'Comment', in the February 1940 issue.

Connolly declared portentously that 'the departure of Auden and Isherwood to America a year ago is the most important literary event of the decade'. Its importance lay in the fact that Auden 'is our best poet, Isherwood our most promising novelist'. The 'Comment' continued with a remark clearly intended to wound: 'They [Isherwood and Auden] did not suffer from lack of recognition in England where they received a publicity which they did everything to encourage.' These suavely barbed words reminded a reading public, steeling themselves for aerial destruction, that some of their compatriots had retreated to safer climes where the only risk from the skies was sunburn. The 'emigrant authors' story was picked up by the press and provoked ugly questions in the House of Commons.

Christopher fired off a response to Stephen on 17 February, accusing him of complicity: 'I know it must have been written by you, or by Cyril with your approval,' he wrote. Quoting the 'which they did everything to encourage' crack, Christopher turned on his friend:

Stephen, what the hell do you mean by that? In what way have either Wystan or I 'encouraged' publicity? . . . All that really concerns me is that *you* have written or, at any rate, approved this article. Because it can only mean that consciously or unconsciously, you are turning against us both. And I want to know why.

Stephen replied on 6 March. He had better say, 'straight away that I am not really very upset by your letter, because a year or so ago I certainly would have been'. As for the offending 'Comment', it was entirely written by Cyril, although he (Stephen) had had the power to censor it. He *didn't* censor it, however, because he felt the editorial was 'fair comment'. Moreover, in the context of Lolly's imminent death, 'the whole thing seems to me frightfully unimportant'.

The issue was further stoked up when on 19 April Harold Nicolson, in his 'People and Things' column in the *Spectator*, attacked those 'eminent Georgians', like Auden, Gerald Heard, Isherwood and Aldous Huxley, who had 'retired within the ivory tower'. Auden's 'friend, Mr Spender, remains', Nicolson went on (urbanely retailing what was evidently club gossip), 'yet I fear that the siren calls which reach him from America may induce even that great bird to wing silently away'. Spender wrote to the magazine the following week, indignantly contradicting Nicolson's imputation. 'This great bird,' he wrote, 'has every intention of staying where he is put, and of helping to the best of his ability, and until he is called up, Mr Cyril Connolly with the editing of *Horizon*.' There would be no white feathers. He went on to defend Isherwood and Auden. Artists could not, he asserted, be judged by the same rules as others. He likened his absent friends to Gauguin, renouncing Western civilization for the South Seas.

Wartime provoked florid reactions in British writers. The latest cry in poetry was the school of 'New Apocalyptics' – end-of-the-worlders. Spender, now mid-career, was amused by their juvenile 'tremendousness' and their incorrigible descent into 'gibberish'. Reviewing the manifesto volume *The New Apocalypse* in the *New Statesman*, 11 May 1940, he observed that most of the disciples of the movement had nothing in common other than a sense of artistic equality with 'Da Vinci, Goya and Van Gogh . . . and a desire to imitate Mr Dylan Thomas'. Among the apocalyptics, he was most sympathetic with their senior colleague, David Gascoyne, with George Barker and – of course – Mr Dylan Thomas; the boy genius. He was in two minds, however, whether even the best of them had 'the intellectual strength to grow' – or were their poems nothing more than 'a firework display?'

Nowadays Spender's personal preference was for the 'sensitive, delicate and genuine gift' of Roy Fuller, whose talent he recognized and encouraged very early. He had also over the years grown into an admiration for the 'always remarkable, often beautiful, often arid, cantankerous, difficult and forbidding poems' of Robert Graves, on whose *Selected Poems* he lavished a rave review – something he very rarely did, even for Wystan.

As regards his own poetic theory, he still had a Yeats problem, and had been judiciously sniping at the Irish Nobel laureate since his death in 1939. He wrote an unusually bitter piece for the *New Statesman*, 'Wise Man and Fool', in response to a vexingly adulatory tribute volume in August 1940. Yeats, he said, was like a majestic old building, all grandiose façade in front and decayed ruin behind. The writers in this book, Stephen observed, 'skirt round the fact that a great deal of Yeats was humbug'.

As a poet, Spender's strongest allegiance at this period was to Rilke,

Hölderlin and Lorca. His adherence to German models, in 1940, was foolhardy as his friends may have thought; outrageous as his critics proclaimed. But for Spender, the current conflict was less a war of power politics or ideology than of values – European values. His dissident thoughts on the subject were expressed in a thoughtful article in the *New Statesman* in July 1940 ('Rilke's Letters to this War'). Under a German bombardment more ferocious than any European capital had ever received, Spender insists that after the war, with democracy victorious, the mistakes of 1918 and Versailles must not be repeated:

Whatever else happens, the Europe of 1918–40 is at an end. There cannot be a 'victory' of the sort that the British and the French seemed to envisage at the beginning of the war. There cannot be a super-Versailles or a super-Munich. Whether we like it or not, we are fighting for the entirely new situation which will arise if we are able to 'hang on' until Germany collapses. That situation will demand remedies and plans and cures rather than crushing terms.

Remarkably, Spender in 1940 thinks ahead to 1945. More importantly, he is thinking of the preservation of the European values incarnated in pre-Hitlerian Germans like Rilke. True Germans.

When it came out in April 1940, *The Backward Son* received mixed but generally enthusiastic reviews. It was not entirely what his admirers expected. Virginia Woolf liked it, saying it gave her 'three good hours'. In the *Spectator* Kate O'Brien applauded the author's 'brave' depiction of schoolboy life. Spender had not failed, she declared, 'in any essential of this delicate task'. Cuthbert Worsley, in the *New Statesman*, agreed. *The Backward Son* was 'a fascinating document of our time . . . its great merit is its candour'. The *TLS* chose, however, to attack the novel as 'trivial'. Their motive, Stephen suspected, was low. He had declined to write a belligerent poem for their columns, feeling himself still sufficiently Owenite (if not pacifist) and a lover of *his* Germany not to supply jingoism on demand.

There was a particularly warm piece on *The Backward Son* by Orwell in *Tribune*. After an inauspicious start, with Orwell's vituperations against 'pansy poets', Spender and he had formed a friendship, following on some joint BBC work together, in April 1938. Both men were by now profoundly disillusioned by their experiences in Spain. 'I was very upset when Cyril told me you were ill [with TB],' Stephen wrote, 'if you are bored in hospital, I would like very much to come down and see you.'

By 1940 they were on intimate terms. Orwell was (at Stephen's invitation) a regular contributor to *Horizon*. Both men were frustrated by the slowness of the authorities to call them up – either into the colours, or the intelligence services. They were unsure whether it was age (Orwell was six years older), ill-health, or their 1930s 'premature anti-Fascism' which was responsible. Both were profoundly gloomy. As Orwell noted in his diary, 8 June 1940: 'I have known since about 1931 (Spender says he has known since 1929) that the future must be catastrophic.' Spender was under no illusions as to what 'catastrophe' would entail.

On 16 May, Winston Churchill took over as Prime Minister. Stephen approved – 'we all despised Chamberlain', Natasha Spender recalls. On 4 June, there was the military disaster of Dunkirk and the evacuation of 300,000 soldiers of the AEF. On 16 June the Germans occupied Paris. Invasion was imminent and bombardment inevitable. During this fraught period, June to August 1940, *Horizon* evacuated to Thurlestone Sands in Devon. It was conveniently close to Salcombe, the resort that Stephen had loved since the family holidays there twenty years earlier. The magazine took up residence at 'Thatched Cottage' on the coast. 'Peter Watson paid for this, as he did for everything that concerned *Horizon*.'

It was an idyllic summer. Stephen would go off 'by himself on a bicycle to Salcombe harbour, where he would rent a boat and spend an afternoon rowing'. He was entertained by the gangs of Breton sailors, promenading round the harbour in 'wooden shoes'. He gave the occasional lecture or lesson at Bryanston. He was friendly there with a sixth-former, James Iliffe ('such an entirely good and honest person,' he told Mary Elliott, 'that I love being with him'). Iliffe would later make a name for himself as a composer. It was for him that Spender wrote (in London, in April) the poem 'At the Window':

> As I sit staring out of my window
> Wasting time the traffic does not waste
> I think of you James, at another window
> With your stubby hands relaxed and your blue gaze
> Invaded by a sense of emptiness
> Startled as if a gust of air
> Had blown through the interstices
> Of your mind and hair
> Ruffling your forehead with despair.

In the last week of June, Spender's decree nisi came through. He could not go up to London for the event, because, as he explained to Mary Elliott, 'I have ruptured a varicose vein in my leg.' This timely disability 'solved a lot of problems'. He added enigmatically, 'there is a half-Siamese cat here which reminds me of Inez and upsets me a lot'. There was further vexation when Madge refused to pay the costs of the divorce, telling his solicitors, 'Spender can pay as he has a private income of £500 a year' (an over-estimate; the true figure was £300). Spender thought it 'one of the meanest things I have heard of'. Divorce, he concluded, 'is a sad business. I still haven't been persuaded that mine need ever have happened if we'd all behaved in a more grown-up way.'

Despite this personal distress it was a good time for Spender's poetry. From the summer 1940 interlude in Devon came his poem 'The Air Raid across the Bay', published in *Horizon*, September 1940:

> Above the dead flat plane of sea
> And watching rocks of coast,
> Across the bay the high
> Searchlights push to the centre of sky
> Rubbing white rules through dull lead,
> Projecting enormous phantom
> Masts with swaying derricks,
> Sliding triangles and parallels
> Upon the abased wasted distances.

Spender was fascinated by the paradoxical beauty of the destruction of England (an England which, in his wild days of youth, he had *wanted* destroyed). It was a poem much admired by Spender's late-life friend, Joseph Brodsky, who pointed out the influence of Futurism and Vorticism in the poem's striking pictorial design.

The three-month lease on Thurlestone was not renewed. *Horizon* returned from the rural safety of the West Country to London a couple of weeks before the Blitz began, on 28 August. Watson had found Connolly a difficult house-guest. Nor did the gourmet editor of the magazine much like country life. He sulked. Apart from anything else, Watson had not brought a car with him because of petrol rationing. The nearest bus stop was two miles distant and the nearest restaurant five. Cyril was not one to cycle for his lunch and the thrill of catching and cooking his own lobsters soon palled.

At what seemed like the period of its extinction London was experiencing a strange renaissance of artistic vitality. As Spender later put it,

Thinking of the war as viewed from London, I remember not only streets full of shattered glass the night after an air raid; flames and the smoke of gigantic fires from the docks seen against the silhouetted foreground of Bloomsbury eighteenth-century squares; and a dinner party at Elizabeth Bowen's house in Regent's Park and walking out into the street afterwards to find it lit whiter than daylight by dropped flares: but also of concerts at the National Gallery with programmes by Myra Hess, Clifford Curzon, or some famous quartet; magical Shakespearean performances with John Gielgud and Peggy Ashcroft; the series of 'Shelter' drawings by Henry Moore; paintings of burning buildings by Graham Sutherland and John Piper; poetry readings and lectures at the famous Churchill Club at Westminster; T. S. Eliot's poignant *Four Quartets*; the grim and realistic poems of Roy Fuller; the apocalyptic ones of Dylan Thomas and the unaccountable, weirdly inspired ones of Edith Sitwell. A little island of civilization surrounded by burning churches – that was how the arts seemed in England during the war.

Cool indifference was the approved response to vulgar German bombardment among their circle. Natasha Spender also recalls dinner at Elizabeth Bowen's house on a warm autumn 1941 evening. After supper the guests went for coffee on the terrace. The sky was incandescent with magnesium flare and searchlight. 'I do ap-ap-apologize for the *noise*,' said the imperturbable hostess, with her characteristic stutter.

After its return to London, in early autumn, Stephen detached himself from the month-to-month business of *Horizon*. He remained a regular contributor, a consultant editor and a luminary in its pages. But increasingly he fed his pieces to other outlets such as Lehmann's *New Writing* and its phoenix resurrection as *Penguin New Writing*. It was a boom period for literary magazines.

The momentous event of summer 1940 was Stephen's falling in love with Natasha Litvin, the woman whom he would marry eight months later and with whom he would share the rest of his life. Natasha was the daughter of the actress Ray (Rachel Rebecca) Litvin. The Litvins, like other Jews, had fled the Tsarist pogroms in 1900 (when Rachel was ten), coming to Scotland from the Baltic States. Rachel grew up to be an accomplished actress, taking the stage name 'Ray'. She established herself under Lilian Baylis's management at the Old Vic, where she struck up a close friendship with the daughters of the banker Daniel Meinertzhagen, one of whom had also gone on the stage and was in the company.

During the Great War (a period of relaxed morality in London), Ray Litvin began a love affair with the music critic Edwin Evans. Evans – the offspring of a famously musical family – was at this time an influential figure in the London concert world. He had been instrumental in introducing Debussy, Stravinsky and Ravel to English audiences. When told that his young lover was pregnant, Evans, aged forty-three, informed her that he was not free to marry. He already had a wife. He was, however, quite willing to free himself, if Ray so desired. She did not require him to leave his wife and the affair ended.

Born on 18 April 1919, Natasha was kept uninformed during her childhood of the fact that she had a living father. She did not discover his existence and identity until she was eleven years old. Ray Litvin was, by the 1920s, a well-known figure on the London stage. The actress's career was, however, blighted when, after an attack of typhoid fever, she was afflicted with near-total deafness in 1926. For a while she managed to do monologues, but her future as a company actress was finished. Always temperamental, she was for the remainder of her long life prey to depression. She was also chronically hard up and partly dependent on others for her survival.

Natasha Litvin was fostered by a small family in Maidenhead for nine years. Later, through the intervention of the Meinertzhagens, she was taken into the family of George and Margaret Booth. A son of Charles Booth, author of *Life and Labour of the People in London*, and related to the Sidney Webbs, George was wealthy from the family's interest in shipping. Natasha came to regard 'Uncle George and Aunt Margy' as her 'other family' and their Funtington house as her 'other home'.

The Booths observed and helped cultivate the little girl's musical talents. The piano was her instrument. She won a scholarship to the Royal College of Music in 1935, aged sixteen. Here she studied for five prizewinning years. At the college Natasha Litvin belonged, with Livia Gollancz (whose instrument was the French horn and whose father the redoubtable socialist publisher, Victor), to the 'Progressive Student Musicians' society. In 1937, as a 'progressive student', Miss Litvin heard the Left Book Club author Stephen Spender give an 'electrifying' talk at the Kingsway Hall on what it felt like to be under the bombs of Fascist divebombers in Spain. She was struck by the speaker's lack of jargon and the gentleness of his address.

During the early months of the war, before the Blitz, Natasha had access during the day to the grand piano in the small ground-floor apartment of Ian and Lys Lubbock in Great Ormond Street. The Lubbocks were friendly with the *Horizon* crowd, a few hundred yards away. Ian was 'a struggling actor and schoolteacher'. Lys would, in the very near future, become Connolly's mistress and a secretary to the magazine.

One Friday evening in late August, after the twenty-one-year-old Natasha had done her day's practice and the Lubbocks had returned for drinks and conversation, Tony Hyndman dropped by to invite them, and anyone else, to lunch next day at *Horizon* (which Natasha, in her student innocence, thought must be the name of a pub). In 1940 Tony was still subsidized by Stephen and was doing odd jobs around the *Horizon* office. When Natasha demurred, Tony – 'bubbling constantly' – simply talked her into it: 'Oh come on ducky, you'll love it.'

At the Saturday lunch at Lansdowne Terrace, Natasha Litvin's eye lingered wonderingly on Stephen's personal properties still decorating the office: the small Picasso on the wall, the huge horn of his gramophone with its electric turntable, and the glistening expanse of the famous ebony desk. Of particular interest to the young music student was his record collection. He had the Glyndebourne twelve-inch discs, 'a lot of Schubert, a lot of Mozart, a lot of Beethoven – exactly my own musical preferences'.

It was a crowded party. Joe Ackerley was there among the ruck, and Rose Macaulay. It was Ian Lubbock who introduced Miss Litvin to Stephen. After the party, Natasha and Stephen went for a walk around the gardens in Mecklenburgh Square and adjourned for dinner in a nearby Italian restaurant (not unpatriotic at this stage of the war). They 'talked politics and music', among much else. They would meet every day over the next fortnight, dining together most evenings – mainly at the Café Royal ('very, very French' at this date) and a staunchly Republican Spanish restaurant, the Barcelona, in Beak Street or the nearby Quo Vadis? in Wardour Street. They fell in love 'rather soon'.

'I'd never met people like these before,' Natasha Spender recalls. She had been admitted into a 'totally new life ... I was amazed'. Stephen was also amazing. He had something of the paradox about him. Possessed of a 'radiant beauty', he was wholly indifferent to his appearance. 'He never looked in the mirror which is why he cut himself shaving so much.' His trousers were usually unpressed. He got his suits 'from any old place', and would wear them until they fell to pieces. His 'dark-mouse' hair was usually tousled. And yet, 'he was marvellous to look at'.

Spender fretted as he waited for his (relatively antique) age group to be called to the colours. There were, however, no land battles imminent and no hurry to conscript thirty-two-year-olds. Stephen meanwhile decided he needed a break from *Horizon*. He had been thinking about some temporary school-teaching. In June, he offered his services to Blundell's in Devon. The headmaster, Neville Gorton, was keen to have Spender on his staff. Stephen wrote a letter to Mary Elliott, in America, on 23 July, on getting the position:

Dearest Mary . . . I have got a very good job, it seems. I am afraid that something may still prevent my getting it, such as the army, or my not having a degree. Blundell's is a very good progressive public school. I have to teach all the sixth forms English, which is delightful. The headmaster is a charming person and the boys seemed very nice. The county is beautiful. The head offered me £400 a year with keep, which gave me such a shock that I said £300 would do . . . My finances should soon be in order. We have big air raids here now, which is bloody depressing really.

Stephen and Gorton had a mutual friend, Mervyn Stockwood – a socialist parish priest at Bristol and Blundell's School Missioner. Gorton (known universally as 'Gorty') was an extraordinary and charismatic headmaster. He had taken Blundell's over in 1934 and would run the school until becoming Bishop of Coventry in 1942. 'Half eccentric, half saint', Gorty flouted traditional notions of how a British public school should be administered.

Stephen's feelings about his new vocation were mixed. He had a visceral dislike of school architecture. It reminded him of Gresham's. He was oppressed by timetables and syllabuses. He hated being a 'master' and 'sir'. On the other hand he admired Gorty. He loved helping with the plays and magazines which the boys produced. He loved Devon, and Blundell's was a continuation into autumn of the summer Thurlestone idyll. Above all he enjoyed the company of intelligent, sensitive and unusual boys – such as he himself had been. He was particularly kind and useful to Oliver Russell, a budding artist, the son of the designer and furniture tycoon Sir Gordon Russell, who did not entirely approve of his son's artistic ambitions. Spender published a poem ('A Childhood') in *Ruins and Visions* addressed to Oliver Russell:

> I am glad I met you on the edge
> Of your barbarous childhood.

Their friendship was formed, he recalls, in 'the black frozen landscape / Of those grey-clothed schoolboys'. Russell died, tragically young, of TB.

The German bombing campaign had shifted from military targets like Plymouth to the capital. Blundell's 'might as well have been on the moon', Natasha Spender recalls. Spender decided he would see the term out – but resolved to leave when it was over. Two main motives dominated. 'I am not a good teacher,' he discovered, 'as I don't ever really want to teach anyone anything.' And, as he told Lehmann, he was convinced that '*Horizon* cannot really carry on without more active aid from me.' He now 'detested' the routine of school life – a life with 'no poetry in it'. He delivered his letter of resignation to Gorton in November (he, like his colleagues and the pupils, had in fact found Spender to be a good teacher).

Natasha Litvin meanwhile had followed her Bechstein piano to Oxford, where she had a small room in St Clements. The piano was housed in the library at St Mary's church. In this austere setting she could play 'to my heart's content, except when there was choir practice'. The Bechstein had been given to her by her father. Stephen had given her one of Robert Buhler's portraits of him for her room (she has it still). She came up to London to study and perform. She was also giving recitals in Oxford. Stephen made it down to Oxford on some weekends.

That Christmas they were reunited, and spent the holiday with Clissold and Diana Tuely (née Low, Lolly's sister) at their remote house, Underhill Farm, at Wittersham, overlooking the Romney Marshes in Kent. Clissold and Diana, on transferring Queen's Mansions to Stephen in 1937, had become thoroughly rusticated. Clissold was now an apple-farmer and a lieutenant in the Home Guard.

It was an idyllic vacation. Stephen locked himself in his study in the morning writing poetry. He was, Natasha recalled, 'just like a boy let out of school for the holidays' – which, in a sense, he was. She played the piano for as many hours as he wrote (sixty years later, Clissold greeted her after a long separation by humming the Schubert piece she had been practising in December 1940). There was lots of good country fare; Clissold had hens and a much-loved, but none the less eaten, pig. Ham and bacon were plentiful. The landscape was lovely, even in midwinter.

After the holiday break Stephen and Natasha returned to a Blitz-blasted London where they helped Rose Macaulay, whose flat had been destroyed by a direct hit, salvage what she could from the wreckage. Contemplating the ruin of all her library and papers, the author declared that she wished she had died with them.

On 20 January 1941, Spender got his divorce from Inez. By now he and Natasha were engaged in all but name. Although moral codes were relaxed in wartime, they had resolved not to live together. It was not merely apprehension of that guardian of public decencies, the King's Proctor. As Spender explained to Mary Elliott: 'I think it is better not to do things in too much of a hurry, so that people get used to the idea of our marrying.' In early January his fiancée was invited to Sutton Veny, where Lolly's first impression was that she was 'stunningly beautiful'. Humphrey, whom she first met in the bar of the Ritz, concurred. He was now a lieutenant in the army; Michael, on a faster track, was in the RAF doing 'hush hush' work of national importance. Christine, now working in the censorship office, agreed with her sister-in-law in finding Natasha 'the most beautiful woman I had ever seen'.

Natasha made the ritual call on Berthella at Cricklewood. These honorary Spenders were equally impressed by Stephen's new attachment ('she's illegitimate, and don't care *who* knows it,' Bertha wonderingly observed). More daunting for the young woman was her first audience with Mrs Hilda Schuster at 33 Albert Court. On arrival Miss Litvin was ushered into the Kensington flat by Mrs Schuster's fearsomely taciturn factotum, Clara. All the furniture was under white shrouds. There were pale patches where the pictures once hung. The apartment was freezing cold and barely lit. In the drawing-room a single coal glowed feebly in the fireplace. Mrs Schuster's frugal lunch of cabbage and pudding (nestling on the same plate) was on a tray, as were the small sachets of ersatz coffee and sugar which she had prudently saved from the First World War. Also visible was the hefty pile of banknotes under the glass paper-weight which she distributed to worthy refugees.

Famously, Mrs Schuster had 'no time for *girls*'. And she rather put Miss Litvin down by intimating her disappointment that 'Stephen is going to marry a *Jewess*'. Natasha was just twenty-one, but not without spirit. She pointed out that she was only *part* Jewish – 'just like Stephen himself'. And she trumped her elderly inquisitor with the added infor-mation, 'but on the other hand, I *am* illegitimate'. The display of spirit went down well. The two women became friends, especially over the years of Mrs Schuster's lonely wartime evacuation from Albert Court to Boar's Hill Hotel (where she would, in fact, live the remainder of her long life). Natasha would make the bus journey from Oxford, to be taken back to the hotel for tea. The old lady, puritan that she was, fretted that the management would not let her scrub the floors of her room. She would meet Natasha at the bus-stop in her heavy velour hat and mittens 'looking *so* pinched and cold'.

In London both Natasha and Stephen were leading peripatetic lives. Stephen would normally stay with his old friend from Spanish days, Cuthbert Worsley, in his house at 44 Bourne Street before it, like so many others, was bombed out. The 'school-masterly' Worsley (he had once taught at Wellington) was now on the staff of the *New Statesman*. His connection with Hyndman had ended amicably – as had Stephen's. The mercurial Welshman was no longer with *Horizon*. The magazine's business manager, Bill Makins, 'did not have much time for him'. Tony, sexually adventurous as ever, was still involved in an affair with Michael Redgrave and working in the London and provincial theatre. Sometimes Stephen would stay overnight with Christine, in Hampstead, or at Humphrey's flat, in Kensington Park Road. For postal (and divorce) purposes, his address was still Lansdowne Terrace. He kept his small room there, although the racket of *Horizon*'s business made it an uncomfortable berth. Peter Watson had a spare room in Athenaeum Court, Piccadilly, which was available to him when he needed it.

Natasha – who was still coming up from Oxford midweek for music instruction at the Royal College – would go back to sleep at Primrose Hill if her mother were in town. If her mother were out of town, she had various 'ports of call'. She and Stephen dined together whenever they could. They made social calls on Stephen's friends including, for an awestruck Natasha, lunch with the 'slightly explosive' H. G. Wells. But the nucleus of their society was 'the *Horizon* crowd', particularly Connolly, Watson and their associates.

After her day's practice Natasha would join Stephen at the Lansdowne Terrace office around five. Typically the editorial discussion would still be in full flow. She became familiar with the way in which the editorial trio played off each other. Watson, she noted, was more dominating than his self-deprecating and affable manner might suggest. Stephen would speak his mind. Connolly – by nature a 'soloist' (and temperamental with it) – would typically dig his heels in and sulk. The crisis would be defused by Watson and would end, good-naturedly, 'with Cyril doing some wonderfully funny parody of the piece they were going to publish'. The evening would dissolve into drinks and a jolly dinner-party.

Spender's affairs were gradually sorting themselves out. Over the eight months' period of his and Natasha's courtship, he was waiting for the decree separating him from Inez to be finalized. Freedom, in a word. He was also waiting for 'his number to come up' – and the end of freedom. The army medical for his age-group was interminably delayed. In the meantime he had applied for various things at Whitehall without any official response. London was, meanwhile, beginning to feel the savagery of the German bombing campaign, which had shifted from military to indiscriminate civilian targets.

In January 1941, Stephen wrote his stark poem 'Air Raid', for February's *Horizon*. It ends with a snapshot of one of the thousands of ruined civilian dwellings in the capital:

> But the home has been cracked by metallic claws,
> Years of loving care ground to rubble in jaws,
> And the delicate squirming life thrown away
> By the high-flying purpose of a foreign day.

The poem, in its austere, rhymed newsreel objectivity, expresses Spender's sense that this was, above all, a war of machines. Bombing, he observed in an essay of the period, reduced one to a condition of 'peasant-like' simplicity. Stimulating and terrifying.

Theirs was, as Natasha Spender recalls, 'an odd courtship'. Normally they could expect to meet in the middle of the week. Sometimes Stephen would go down to Oxford. The engagement became formalized in March. Although it had been clear to Stephen for some time that he was going to marry Natasha Litvin, he had absent-mindedly forgotten to pass the news on to his intended. She learned that she was to wed when someone came up to congratulate her after a performance at Oxford. She at first thought the compliment was for her playing.

When Stephen and Natasha discussed their impending marriage, 'I was very very conscious,' she recalls, 'that a writer's interior monologue has to be entirely free . . . I never said a word about anything he was writing, except that occasionally when I was invited to I would say something about rhythm.' Her career would continue separate but parallel with his. It was a strange time to enter into 'until death do us part' contracts. As Stephen recalls in *World within World*, 'in the summer of

1940, when invasion seemed imminent, a friend could say to me: "Within six weeks from now, if I blow out my brains and they spatter all over the carpet, in my own home and with my family in the room, no one will think it worth noticing."' The author of this startling speculation was probably Herbert Read. The thought of the earlier suicide plans with Leonard Woolf must still have been in Stephen's mind. There were, Natasha Spender recalls, 'so many ifs and buts about the war'. The pact with Leonard was given awful poignancy when, on 28 March, Virginia Woolf drowned herself.

Stephen viewed this calamity, he recalled, as if through a thick pane of glass. He wrote a 'Tribute' in the *Listener*. In a period of national blackout, 'the death of Virginia Woolf cannot strike her circle of friends and admirers except as a light which has gone out'. There was, as always, a human dimension. Writing to Julian Huxley, on 2 April, he said that – on reflection – he felt that Virginia Woolf's suicide was 'reasonable' (although 'appalling for Leonard') since 'she just couldn't face going mad a third time . . . she had done her life's work, she had enjoyed so much happiness'.

There were other services than funerals to think of. Stephen Spender and Natasha Litvin were married on 9 April 1941, ten days before her twenty-second birthday. He was just ten years older. The ceremony took place at St Pancras Register Office. The Booths were Natasha's witnesses. Stephen's were Peter Watson and Tony Hyndman. Stephen put his profession down as 'editor'. It was, Natasha recalls, 'a pretty odd affair'. The Registrar (very busy in these wartime days, with soldiers queuing up to marry on leave) was 'officious and perfunctory'. On his part Tony was 'very funny and airborne' and 'plonked a bottle of whisky on the table of the Registrar who was not amused'. Natasha's mother, locked in deafness, could not hear or understand a word of what was going on. Uncle George and Aunt Margy looked on benignly. As Stephen walked with his bride across Russell Square he turned to her and joked: 'You look *too* radiant.'

There was a lunch party at the Etoile in Charlotte Street for the principals (hosted by Cyril Connolly – who was famously good on lunches), followed, as Stephen recalled,

by a drinks party in the studio of Mamaine Paget (who later married Arthur Koestler). Cecil Beaton took a photograph of this party. Among the guests were Cyril Connolly and Lys Lubbock . . . Sonia Brownell (later Sonia

Orwell), A. J. Ayer (in Guards Officer uniform), Guy Burgess, Erno Goldfinger, the architect, and his wife Ursula, Louis MacNeice and Nancy Coldstream (then married to William Coldstream but later to marry my brother Michael).

Also present were Tambimuttu, Julian and Juliette Huxley, John Lehmann and William Plomer. Stephen gave his bride a Steinway piano – for wherever it would be in London that they might live. That question was very uncertain. She gave her husband a Nonesuch Dante, with illustrations by Botticelli.

Stephen confided his feelings about his bride to Julian Huxley:

I am very thrilled about starting this new life of my marriage, etc. Much more than I was about my first marriage, strangely enough. I think this is because being married to Natasha will be quite different from just living with her, as she is really a very remarkable person, with, in perhaps your sense of the word, a deeply religious nature. This has a revolutionary effect on me.

The couple spent the first night of their honeymoon at the Savoy Hotel. They were telephoned a number of times during the night by an intoxicated Louis MacNeice and Nancy Coldstream, engaged in less legitimate lovemaking.

The next morning, on 10 April, Mr and Mrs Spender took the train from Paddington to Cornwall. There they spent a fortnight at a little hotel at Carbis Bay, on the coast near St Ives (the artist Adrian Stokes, a friend of Stephen's, was spending his Conscientious Objector's war in the neighbourhood). 'We wanted to get as far away as possible because we couldn't go abroad,' Natasha recalls. In Cornwall they took long walks in the afternoon or sat on the beach or were taken sailing by a charming young man, Michael Ventris, later famous as the classical Greek scholar and decoder of 'Linear B' (Natasha was, she remembers, 'desperately sea-sick').

On the way back, in late April, they stayed a few days with Dorothy and Leonard Elmhirst, proprietors of Dartington Hall, near Totnes. The Elmhirsts had set up what was, in effect, a commune on their huge Devon estate. The utopian aim was to create an 'organic' community that needed nothing from the town. Dartington had its school, its farms, its cider factory, its library and even a resident ballet and theatre company. When the Spenders were there, it had its poet and concert pianist. Artists and intellectuals were frequent visitors. It was at Dartington that Natasha first met Arthur Waley, and Francis and Frances Cornford (the most confusingly named couple in literary England). After dinner in late April, as they looked over the Tilt Yard, Leonard read aloud from Froissart. Natasha then played for the company on the concert grand in the Great Hall. While in the West Country they also called on Robert and Beryl Graves, in their house on the Dart Estuary. It was at this meeting that the older poet told the younger he must, at all costs, procure a copy of the thirteen-volume OED. Spender duly sold off a Picasso and his Rolleiflex to do so.

In early June the newly-wed couple were at Bristol, where their marriage was blessed in a private ceremony by Mervyn Stockwood, in the chapel at St Matthew Moorfields Church. Stockwood was 'an unconventional minister' and notorious at this period for his proclaimed socialist views. 'It was the first time I had married a divorced person,' Stockwood recalled in his autobiography. There were prayers, and at evensong that day Stephen gave a sermon to the congregation. His text was 'The Sabbath is made for Man, not Man for the Sabbath.'

After the extended honeymoon the Spenders returned to Oxford, where one of Stephen's first acts was to draw up a deed of covenant to support his mother-in-law, Mrs Litvin. Natasha's little room at 107 St Clements was too small for a married couple, one of whom was a concert pianist, the other a poet. The historian A. J. P. Taylor and his wife Margaret invited them to stay with them, as paying guests. Stephen could use the St Clements room for his study. Natasha could continue to practise at St Mary's. The next house guest of the Taylors was Dylan Thomas, who would, notoriously, have a hugely disruptive affair with Margaret Taylor. Natasha remembers her running down the drive instructing her and Stephen to bring back 'someone, *anyone*' for the weekend. They brought back (unwittingly) the silver-tongued Welsh serpent.

Stephen and Natasha were still living with the Taylors at the time of the Russian invasion, on 22 June. At the end of the month, on 1 July, they again rented the Tuelys' farmhouse on the Romney Marshes. In this seclusion, Spender told Huxley, 'if God so wishes, I will finish two books before being called up'. They had resolved, despite the hazards of war, to start a family. Natasha would, later in the year, have the first of what was to be a series of miscarriages – an anxiety for the couple over the next three years before the birth of their son, Matthew.

The Spenders remained at Underhill during August and September. Various people came to stay. Ray Litvin's visit was memorable, since this part of coastal Kent was a 'reserved area' and she did not bring her Identity Card with her. As a (putative) foreigner she was suspected of being a spy. Less vexatious was a visit from Arthur Bliss, who wanted Stephen to write a libretto for a proposed new opera – 'some grandiose Greek theme'. It was too heroic for Stephen. His main creative efforts were directed towards gathering, redrafting and composing poems for his forthcoming Faber collection, *Ruins and Visions* as it was to be.

Natasha's career was moving forward. She had, by now, left the Royal College of Music. That summer (1941) she played for Clifford Curzon at his house in Highgate. He took her on as a pupil. She did not at this period get much work from agents ('because I was married', she suspects). Nor was there much work to be had, other than ENSA work for the forces; the musical world was disrupted by war. Her career would take off two years later, when she started playing regularly for the BBC.

Early in the summer Stephen had the bad news about his first medical. Colitis, poor eyesight, varicose veins, lingering organic weakness from his childhood illnesses and the 1934 tapeworm rendered him totally unfit – grade 'C'. He had always been hopeless at exams. He requested another medical, and was again declared unfit for heavy duties by the doctors.

After his second rejection he could decently have accepted the judgement of fate and the advice of his physicians and devoted himself wholeheartedly to the literary life like Connolly, Orwell and Louis MacNeice (who had come back from America, only to be turned down at *his* medical). Instead he contrived, by arguing the toss with his doctors and 'pulling strings', to get himself reclassified as 'B', which would allow him to serve in the Auxiliary Fire Service.

They were stirring times for firefighters in the capital. In August 1941, the 1,400 brigades across the country (assisted by the Auxiliary Fire Service) were reorganized into thirty-three units of the National Fire Service. This force was directly under the command of the Home Secretary, and £6 million of public money was pumped into equipping and setting up the hugely enlarged service trained to deal with aerial bombardment. A recruiting drive was launched.

From September 1941 until June 1944 Stephen was a uniformed fireman in the AFS/NFS. He was not promoted, leaving the service as he joined it – a lowly fireman, first class. He never made Leading Fireman, nor commissioned rank. One of the things he most liked about the service was its matey indifference to protocol; one did *not* salute officers (who were merely promoted ordinary firemen). Nor did one kill people.

Frustratingly, with the opening of the Russian Front in June 1941 and until the V-1 raids in mid-June 1944, there were no serious fires to fight; just the odd hit-and-run. It was a happy outcome for Londoners, but deadly boring for the NFS. For Spender to have sat in a fireman's barracks for three years seems a spectacular waste of national resources, even for Britain in wartime. He was neither over-age nor in a reserved occupation. He was not a Conscientious Objector. Spender spoke German fluently. He had intimate knowledge of enemy country (including areas of military importance on the Baltic coast). He was one of the country's leading writers and enjoyed international recognition, particularly in neutral America where his voice would have been worth battalions to his country's war effort.

In late summer, while a still unwell Natasha remained at Wittersham, recovering from the first of her three miscarriages, Stephen went off to do his three weeks' basic training at Parson's Green, in south London. His fellow recruits were, like himself, either dubiously fit, misfits, or too old for military service. It was 'back to school' – if not quite as traumatic as Holt had been. There was no kipper hole (but neither was there a Greatorex). 'I very much like my fellow firemen,' he told Plomer:

but my life seems completely wasted at present. We do drill from 9–10 in the morning. Then we clean up the station as slowly as we possibly can manage till 1. Then I sit in a room full of shouting and swearing people, playing snooker, darts, and telling dirty stories till midnight. I try to read and write but it is pretty well impossible. However, it gives some sort of satisfaction to the British Lion, I suppose.

With the rest of his intake, Trainee Fireman Spender wore un-leonine blue dungarees 'like rompers' which 'smoothed out the excrescences of middle-age' and was given 'humiliating and often ridiculous orders' by absurd officers. There were graphic lectures on high explosives, incendiary devices, unexploded bombs and poison gas (this last topic affected Stephen so painfully that 'I hid for half an hour in a telephone box, overwhelmed by the vision of human beings asphyxiating one another in poisonous over-sweet scents'). There was what his cockney comrades called the 'eavy work – lifting and aiming full hoses, sledgehammer and axe wielding. Worst of all, he had to undergo training on fragile, wobbling, high ladders fifty or sixty feet up in the air.

Despite these pains, it is astonishing how well recovered Stephen was, after the troughs of late 1939. As he mused, during the course of a review of Edith Sitwell's latest volume in the *New Statesman*, 'Perhaps the war acts like that treatment of certain types of insanity which, by giving the patient a violent shock, integrates his scattered personality and brings him to his senses.' Shock therapy and marriage to Natasha had put him back together again.

In September 1941 he was posted to the Cricklewood sub-station, Willesden area, at Dyne Road. His fireman's pay was £2 a week, plus uniform and supplementary rations while on duty. By happy chance, Berthella had retired to 31 Chiltern Gardens, within a mile-and-a-half's walking distance of the substation. It was convenient for Stephen and Natasha to move into Berthella's house as paying guests. The best of servants, they were now the best of landlords. There was a spare double room for them upstairs, a back room with French windows on to the garden, and space in the front room (normally only used on special occasions) for the Steinway. Ella (a shadow of her former sweet self) had married her postman of Frognal days, Frank. Bertha was still ruling the roost. After the war, she would marry another old friend of Sheringham days, Captain Devoto.

Bertha had a soft spot for Stephen's new wife. She it was who took charge of her paying guests' ration books. The redoubtable woman had her own allotment, and produced 'the most wonderful vegetables' for her guests. There was fresh broth every day (in the absence of meat or bones, Bertha improvised with bacon rind). As in the old days, Sunday lunches were a big event. Humphrey, Michael and Christine would turn up – if duties permitted. The family had not been so together since Frognal.

At Dyne Road, Sub-station 2A, Stephen was normally on duty for forty-eight hours and 'off' for the following twenty-four. At the station there were four crews – three of whom were ready for action at any time. Action, however, rarely came. Bells were polished, but rarely rung. During their 'on' days, the men lived in four Nissen huts. At the centre of their day's duty was 'the rec.' or recreation room. It boasted a round bakelite radio 'shaped like an empty face' which was always set, at maximum volume, to the Light Programme. There was also a snooker table, which was constantly in use (never, however, by Fireman Spender). There was a bunkhouse where the men slept. The third hut was the kitchen and communal mess room. The fourth supplied bathroom and lavatory facilities.

It was early winter when Stephen joined his unit at Sub-station 2A. The station had been thrown up in haste, and without any idea of amenity. Daily drills and turning fire-engines churned the unpaved grounds into a morass. Everything in the huts was filthy: 'Mud from the paths and duck-boards got into the Rec-room and kitchen and bunkhouse.' Stephen found himself

cleaning up lavatories, spittle off duckboards. Often I used to feel humiliated at having to spend my time like this. As I saw it, my humiliation was not personal, it was more a feeling that this was the only use they could put poetry to.

It was not just the harshness, but the crushing banality of life at the sub-station which, as he discovered, destroyed the creative spark. Stephen was maddened by the omnipresent Light Programme. 'We listen to *jazz* all day,' he peevishly noted in his notebook. 'If any good music at all comes on the wireless, someone turns it off at once.'

Much as he hated the blare of the Light Programme and the inter-minable click of snooker balls, Stephen took to his comrades. The close-ness of Dyne Road 'brought out the warmth, good-nature, humour of all the men'. It also brought out a natural courtesy in them. His fellow firemen were all 'exceedingly considerate to me, in many unexpected and uncalled-for ways'. He was addressed as 'Mr Spender – half seri-ously, half facetiously' but always affectionately. It was a 'bad moment' when somebody discovered one of his poems in a magazine. He was constrained to read it aloud ('someone even went so far as to switch off the Light Programme'). To Stephen's surprise, 'no one sneered'. One comrade said, 'When you read we can understand it.' His months at Cricklewood, Stephen realized, 'fulfilled one of the aspirations which had been a part cause of my joining the Communists. This was to get to know the workers.'

He would later articulate this sense of comradeship in his post-war book: *Citizens in War – and After* (1945). It was something which would profoundly shape his future views on politics, progress, and social reform:

Vulnerability, closeness to unkind realities, and physical proximity to each other are the foundations of working-class tolerance. On these foundations a way of life requiring the exercise of good-humour, wit, forbearance and active kind-ness, is played. It is a comedy of Every man in His Humour. Every one accepts a part, and creates a part, for his fellows. Human qualities are treated, not as though they were moral attitudes towards life, but masks assumed for the purpose of adjusting one's temperament to that of one's fellows. In this way, even anti-social qualities can be made part of the drama of the station.

The mild bawdy of the bunkhouse neither shocked nor much interested him. Just married himself, he was, however, curious about his married comrades' views on matrimony. They did not, he discovered, 'think much to Dr Marie Stopes's thesis about periodic intercourse, though, of course, they agreed with birth control'. The men had a pragmatic code about looting. If a house was clearly ruined, anything was fair game – 'except a kid's cash box'.

There was a fund of shrewd good sense and humanity in working men. They did not at all, Stephen was surprised to find, hate Germans. In their view, the enemy were 'just like us'. 'Blokes doing a job', that is. They distrusted trade unions. It was during these weeks at Cricklewood that Stephen began to meditate an article on 'Civil Defence Education', which he would later expand into an educational course for his firemen comrades.

In the New Year of 1942, Spender was transferred, at his own request, from Cricklewood to another sub-station – a converted girls' school in Maresfield Gardens, Hampstead. It was a stone's throw from Frognal, near Stephen's beloved heath. Lucian Freud had made the necessary connections. The boy's architect father, Ernst, had leased the ground floor of a large house at 2 Maresfield Gardens, a few hundred yards from the sub-station. The Spenders could rent the four-roomed attic suite – 'Flat 4' – (Stephen called it a 'poet's garret'). Lucian (who had 'rather complicated feelings about his parents') was allowed to use the largest room of the Spenders' flat as his studio (later it would become Stephen's study). The room was, as Stephen later recalled, 'full of dead birds' – *nature morte*.

Stephen's double bed was brought from Lansdowne Terrace. Natasha's Steinway was transported from Chiltern Gardens and some old curtains from Lavenham were taken out of store. Granny Schuster (who threw *nothing* away) helped out with some tattered turkey carpets from Albert Court. With Fireman Spender's £2 a week, the Schuster bequest, the two or three hundred pounds a year he was making from reviewing, and Natasha's performance fees, they 'scraped through'.

It was a bonus that Ernst Freud, in his capacity as architect, had stoutly fortified the ground floor of 2 Maresfield Gardens, making it in effect a bomb-proof shelter of pillbox durability. The Spenders were welcome to take refuge downstairs when the air-raid sirens sounded. This was a weight off Stephen's mind, should there be a warning while he was on duty.

At the Maresfield Gardens sub-station Stephen found more leisure in which to write. There was a higher level of culture and more congenial comrades, notably the painter Leonard Rosomon and the writer William Sansom, with whom Stephen would later collaborate on a collection of 'Fire Station Stories'. There were also musicians from London orchestras among the crews. No 'jazz'. Despite the 'agreeable' company, he missed the 'sense of unity' he had found at Cricklewood and there was less camaraderie. He *could*, however, work at Maresfield. The atmosphere at the new station had, as he later put it, 'parallels with the ideal uncelibate monastic life Rabelais dreamed of in his account of the Abbey of Thélème'. In the character of Rabelaisian monk, Spender wrote the sonnet sequence *Spiritual Exercises*. He showed it to John Hayward, who recommended the less liturgical title 'Explorations' – 'only saints go in for "spiritual exercises"', he warned. And Stephen Spender was a fireman, not a saint.

The *Exercises/Explorations* were privately printed in 1943 and dedicated to C. Day-Lewis (currently in the throes of a complicatedly extramarital affair with Rosamond Lehmann). It was a graceful gesture, acknowledging the dedicatory verse 'To Stephen Spender' which Day-Lewis had, in October 1940, prefaced to his translation of the *Georgics*. Spender was at this thoughtful stage of his career exploring the disciplines of rhyme, half-rhyme and prosodic patterning. In September 1941, he noted to himself in his commonplace book that rhyme 'organizes sense' while free verse 'leads naturally to the development of assonance'. He further investigated the technicalities of 'form', using a consciously Eliotesque idiom. Typical of the tone of the sequence is the third exercise, which has the mortuary sonorousness of Donne's 'Holy Sonnets':

> Since we are what we are, what shall we be
> But what we are? We are, we have
> Six feet and seventy years, to see
> The light, and then release it for the grave.
> We are not worlds, no, nor infinity,
> We have no claims on stone, except to prove
> In the invention of the city
> Our hearts, our intellect, our love.

Although he still wrote for *Horizon*, Spender was no longer integral to the magazine's management. Nor, in many ways, to its thinking. He was, if anything, more sympathetic with *Penguin New Writing*'s progressive agenda. As Michael Shelden notes, 'Connolly did not really regret losing Spender as an active editorial associate . . . he complained that Spender's influence had pushed the magazine too far into politics.' Relations were not helped when, broadcasting for the World Service in March 1942, Cyril chose to describe Spender as 'an indifferent poet'. His explanation that his airborne words 'were intended "only for India"' was amusing but not an entirely satisfactory *amende*.

As at Cricklewood, the duty roster at Maresfield Gardens was two days on, one off. Stephen was now close enough to pop home when he had a free hour or two. It was at this station that he began to think of ways in which he could employ the tedium of watch and ward with useful instruction – useful, that is, for those proletarian comrades whom he had so much liked at Cricklewood. He propagandized for something to be done for workers' education in a number of articles published in 1942.

Official minds were turning in the same direction. In August 1942, the Select Committee on National Expenditure reported that the NFS was largely idle, 'standing by' for a bombardment that (happily) never came. Herbert Morrison made a statement in the House. There would be a new policy. A large section of the NFS was released for work in the factories, where even unskilled workers could earn twice the fireman's £2 weekly wage.

As Spender recalls, other practical steps were taken at grass-root level:

A group of ordinary firemen started an education scheme among the London firemen, and they invited me to be a discussion group leader. A great virtue of the scheme was the modest and simple way in which it functioned. A few scores of firemen, without being given any rank or relieved from fire-fighting duties, were given facilities to spread the gospel of progressive education, planning and war aims among their fellow firemen. We simply went from station to station, opening discussions on Russia, China, the Law, History, Art, and many other subjects.

As a moving spirit in this initiative, Spender was officially appointed 'director' of the 'Discussion Group Scheme', responsible for No. 34 London Regional Fire Force. Every Monday morning, he and fellow leaders would meet as a committee to work out a weekly programme. Spender was particularly ingenious in assembling 'brains trusts', calling on the services of distinguished friends such as Julian Huxley or the art critic Kenneth Clark, who lived with his wife Jane just up the hill from the fire station. On one memorable occasion, Spender recruited the exiled Prime Minister of Hungary, Count Karolyí, who – perceiving the NFS uniforms in his audience – declared, thunderingly, 'I don't say to you, firemen, put out fires, *light them up, all over Europe!*' Spender was duly marked down by the top brass as a 'dangerous man'; a veritable firebrand.

Towards the end of Spender's service, in 1943, the 'educationists' were all assigned to one fire station, at Holland Park Avenue. Natasha Litvin was meanwhile doing her bit for the nation's morale with concert performances for ENSA, travelling with a troupe of singers (including MacNeice's latest love, Hedli Anderson). She was paid 'minute sums' – two guineas a performance. Performing for ENSA entailed uncomfortable travelling and performances in large, windy aircraft hangars, works canteens, north country town halls and other strange venues. Given the fact that some of the audience were just returned, or about to embark, on dangerously active service, it was 'immensely rewarding'. She was still studying with Clifford Curzon.

In July 1942, Spender formed what was to become a close friendship with Robert Graves. The two poets had met the year before (in April 1941) and were by now on first-name terms. Graves reassured his young colleague that the quarrels with Auden and Isherwood were all for the good – 'as a result of all this recent shake-up you will soon be doing your best work. I would say more, but it would be an impertinence.' It was a source of strength 'that you no longer belong to a school' (of poetry, he meant). Graves was worried about Stephen's young wife, as were other friends. 'How is Natasha?' he solicitously asked in January 1943. 'It is no war for anyone with delicate insides and so much hard work to do at the piano.' She was, as it happened, in blooming health.

The Elmhirsts supplied an escape from London for the Spenders at Dartington Hall, in Devon. When in town, despite Fire Service duties, health problems, rationing, and blackout, the couple contrived to entertain a circle of friends with shared literary and cultural interests. They regularly dined with, or had to dinner, Jane and 'K' Clark (whose house, Capo di Monte, was only minutes from them; Clark was currently engaged with the war-artists project); Rosamond Lehmann and Cecil Day-Lewis (now at the Ministry of Information); William Plomer (now at the Admiralty); and Graham Sutherland. They went on overnight excursions to Whipsnade, with the Huxleys (Stephen had been since childhood an enthusiastic zoologist), and had weekends, when Stephen's off-duty time permitted, with the flamboyant Stephen Tennant at Wilsford Manor. 'In a sense,' Natasha recalls, 'it was a marvellous time, the war.'

Guests, she was grateful to find, were 'very indulgent' and a kind of picnic atmosphere ruled. E. M. Forster, for example, replied to an invitation to Maresfield with the query whether he should bring some sardines and Algerian wine. In the absence – particularly – of prime meat (even if coupons were saved up), Natasha became adept at improvising meals around unrationed offal (as it would be thought in peacetime), such as 'stuffed ox-heart' or ingenious variations on tripe. Having done her work in the kitchen she would later play for the company.

Spender had a social life outside the home – when duty allowed. He became friendly, at this period, with a young American serviceman, Harry Brown (editor of the army magazine, *Yank*). Their friendship is commemorated in a high-spirited piece of laddish doggerel: 'To Sergt. Harry Brown from Fireman S. Spender':

> The problem which confronts us, Harry
> When we enlist, slave, drink and marry
> Is to write poetry, though we're harried
> Enlisted, enslaved, drunk and married.

In his fireman's notebook, in July 1942, Stephen recorded that he was interested in writing '*about* poetry as well as in writing verse, because I am interested in the truth'. His major discourse on his craft was *Life and the Poet*, which came out in March 1942 as one of Secker and Warburg's 'Searchlight Books'. The series was put out under the joint editorship of George Orwell and Tosco Fyvel (then working at the BBC but connected, as later emerged, to the country's intelligence agencies). 'Searchlights' cost 2s. The editorial rubric instructed that they be written with Orwellian limpidity and 'without the rubber-stamp of political jargon of the past'. The volumes were aimed principally at soldiers and workers in factories. They sold some 10,000 a title.

Spender's argument in *Life and the Poet* rests on simple theses. The book opens with a straightforward *j'accuse*. Over the last twelve years poets had applied themselves so exclusively to politics as to lose their essential role as poets. This role, which Spender conceives in Arnoldian terms, was to articulate – in all its multifariousness – the civilization for which the nation was currently fighting and its airmen dying. Since 1930 poets had descended to impotent Utopian dreaming – only to be jolted awake by world war. What, then, is the 'function of poetry' at the present time?

Spender offers by way of explanation a metaphor. A man is 'shot up to the moon' in a rocket, with all the resources of modern technology. The astronaut is 'in constant communication with the earth, to which he is every day sending back messages'. This allegory, Spender suggests, supplies the 'simplest possible account of the poet's creative activity in life. He retains throughout all the situations in life in which he is an artist the sense of being the man who lands on the moon, steps out of his rocket, and stares at the unexperienced landscape for the first time.'

Spender's poetic output follows two main streams in 1942. There were the *vers d'occasion*: poems written in hot response to the war – such as the outraged lyric 'On the Executions in Poland' (published in the *New Statesman*, 19 December 1942):

> Such is the waking Polish night:
> Behind the bars, the visionary scream
> Of the murdered moment, blinds our sight
> With the drama of a naked dream.

Alongside these topical poems were the works which he wanted to last – the poetry which represented the best he could do. In the second category he produced, in April 1942, what was his most impressive collection to date, *Ruins and Visions*.

The principal aesthetic problem which Spender had to solve in this volume was one which he had discussed at length with T. S. Eliot in the dark days of late summer 1939. 'Coherence', in a word. In a draft poem of the period, Spender asked himself

> How can I piece together
> These many imperfections
> Of my life, full of headaches,
> Weakness and darkness
> Interrupted by distraction
> And fading in putrefaction?

The problem lay in the paradoxical phrase, 'piece together'. Spender wanted both fragmentariness and wholeness.

The solution which he worked towards in *Ruins and Visions* was (for him) unusual. The collection is organized as a four-part narrative ('Separation', 'Ironies of War', 'Deaths', 'Visions'). The sequence moves from personal breakdown, through public cataclysm, to personal re-integration. 'Separation' opens with nine poems probing the break-up with Inez. The first ('Song') commemorates the awful day at Lavenham when she went 'over the hills' with 'another':

> Lightly, lightly from my sleep
> She stole, our vows of dew to break.

The poem opens with a savage imprecation against Madge, the 'stranger' who had stolen Inez, satisfying 'the hunger of beasts', leaving Stephen

> . . . beneath a bitter
> Blasted tree, with the green life
> Of summer joy cut from my side.

'Song' broods on the idea of homicide — murdering the guilty couple — or punishing them with his own suicide.

'Separation' is a wholly subjective set of poems. In the second section of *Ruins and Visions*, 'Ironies of War', he is again the Public Poet. In 'The War God', the first poem in the sub-sequence, he warns sagely that after victory the allies must beware the 'semen of new hatred' (good advice, if the war cabinet happened to be listening). Most affecting (and least ironic) among 'Ironies of War' are the poems in which Spender contemplates the young men he has known — and in some cases taught — dying as airmen in defence of their country. In his notebook he composed innumerable variant drafts of the elegy 'To Poets and Airmen'. The printed version of the poem is dedicated 'To Michael Jones in his life, and now in his memory'.

Spender explains the dedication in *World within World*:

Michael Jones [was] killed in an accident while training. [He] stayed with me during one of the worst nights of the Blitz. He went out into the East End of London during the heavy bombing, and returning with shining eyes described the streets full of glass like heaped-up ice, the fires making a great sunset beyond the silhouette of St Paul's, the East End houses collapsed like playing cards. If I tried to commemorate some of these men in poems, it was because poetry was exactly what I had in common with them and it was this that they came to me for. It is right to say that the service they required of my generation was that we should create.

Jones was one of the 'few' – young warriors with Hermes' 'Iron wings tied' to their 'Greek heads' (one of many lines lost in the poem's re-writings).

The third section of *Ruins and Visions*, 'Deaths', opens with the Oedipal denunciation of his dead father, 'The Ambitious Son'. The poem was rewritten many times over its many subsequent printed appearances. In the context of 1942, it portrays Harold – brutally – as a hollow man.

> Old man, with hair made of newspaper cutting
> And the megaphone voice,
> Dahlia in the public mind, strutting
> Like a canary before a clapping noise.

None the less (with biting irony), *Harold Spender c'est moi*:

> O Father, to a grave of fame I faithfully follow!

The fourth section, 'Visions', opens with the hope that 'I . . . might glide into another I'. The poems now linger on Arcadian spring and summer settings drawn from Suffolk, Wiltshire and Devon. On the flyleaf of the notebook for *Ruins and Visions* which he began to put together in early 1940, Tony Hyndman (who evidently gave the book to the poet as a present) had scrawled: 'Dear Stephen – Write some poems in this, Tony.' Underneath 'N.L.' scrawled a postscript: 'and one for me'.

Spender indeed wrote several poems for Natasha Litvin (although she discouraged him from publishing many of them). The sequence, and the whole volume, ends with two deeply felt love poems to Natasha Spender (as she now is): 'Daybreak' and 'To Natasha'. They celebrate union, as the first poems in the collection lamented separation. In the first, the couple awake together, to richer dreams:

> Our dreams
> Flowed into each other's arms, like streams.

'To Natasha' rejoins the circle of two broken in 'A Separation'. There is, of course, no security: the war goes on – they can only have a 'terrible peace' in the haven of their love. But the poet is no longer, as he was, alone.

Ruins and Visions was well received. In the *New Statesman* G.W. Stonier, mixing censure and praise, observed that 'Mr Spender is, perhaps, a poet of muddle; but even slipshod sentences and hazy feelings are justified so far as they enable him to produce experience and thought further.' The *TLS* discerned 'a deepening and widening of experience . . . a purer imaginative art . . . Mr Spender's poetry has unquestionably ripened.' The *Listener* was unequivocal in its praise. *Ruins and Visions* confirmed Spender's position 'among the most individual and gifted of living poets'. It was a good note on which to end the year.

Nineteen forty-three would be a year of holding on. With America now in the war, and after Stalingrad, it was clear that the Axis powers would be defeated – but not in the immediate future. Stephen and Natasha Spender consolidated their careers, their vision for post-war life, and dedicated themselves to schemes of public service. She was now getting commissions from the BBC in addition to as much ENSA work as she could manage. 'Fireman Spender' was by now a familiar public sight, giving readings or attending them. In his reviewing and essay-writing, he was still revolving large aesthetic questions. What was the 'creative spirit'? The place of 'sensuousness' in modern poetry? How should modern poets address themselves to the 'symbolist heritage'? To what degree should they embrace or reject 'personalism'? He wrestled with these questions – particularly in the pages of Connolly's *Horizon* and Lehmann's *Penguin New Writing*, where he now had a virtual free-hold for leading articles. And as he pondered these poetic cruxes he was not, for the moment, himself writing poetry. 'The fact is,' Spender told Edith Sitwell (whom they had come to know a year or so earlier), 'I am becoming a kind of war casualty: a Pavlov dog who goes mad through having to react to so many stimuli coming from so many directions.'

In April 1943, the Spenders were together with Sitwell at a reading from *The Waste Land*, by T. S. Eliot, at the Churchill Club (a cultural society, with an Anglo-American membership). The event took place during a week of 'dream-like fairy-tale weather' and was for Sitwell, as she told Stephen later, her first happy experience 'since the War and hideousness began'. She impulsively appointed the younger poet, whom she associated with this happiness, as a soulmate. On 26 April 1943 she informed him that: 'you and I *do* feel about poetry as people feel about salvation. We haven't the *cold* outlook.'

Natasha and Stephen, in 1943, had helped found the Apollo Society, one of the most successful cultural innovations to come out of the war effort. Since 1941, Peggy Ashcroft and Edith Evans had been giving dramatic readings in the Globe Theatre to audiences composed, in large part, of soldiers and war-workers. Natasha had meanwhile been giving recitals to the mixed audiences that wartime threw up. Both activities had been well received. As Sean Day-Lewis records:

The idea of expanding this work into the Apollo Society occurred when Peggy Ashcroft found herself in a Cambridge to London train in 1943 with Stephen Spender and his wife, and Cecil [Day-Lewis].

The society had actually been tentatively launched, earlier that day, 30 May, at the Arts Theatre, Cambridge. The core troupe comprised the actors Peggy Ashcroft, Robert Harris and John Laurie. Natasha Litvin was the featured instrumentalist. Poets such as Dylan Thomas and C. Day-Lewis figured in the programmes, as, occasionally, did Spender. It was a cause to unite the great and good. Maynard Keynes (later an architect of the Arts Council), the Cambridge don Dadie Rylands and the Poet Laureate, John Masefield, all participated in the launch event. Members contributed a voluntary £10 to get the society going. Organizational meetings were, initially, held at the Troika restaurant in London – Stephen or someone else taking notes and drawing up provisional programmes (the society had no formal secretary until 1951). Concerts and recitations were given all over the country – the performers wearing evening dress, Stephen Spender his uniform. The Apollo would run successfully for the next three decades. Natasha remained actively involved, as an organizer and a performer, until well into the 1960s.

Over the period 17 to 21 February 1944 the Luftwaffe launched its heaviest raids on London since summer 1941. Ernst Freud's fortifications to 2 Maresfield Gardens were again put to the test when the house opposite sustained a direct hit. The noise, Stephen recalled, 'was like that of a train emerging from a tunnel, and one felt oneself to be tied to the rails'. Supposing himself about to die, he recalled thinking, 'This is something I have all my life been waiting for.' ('What a solipsist you are,' Wystan jested, on being told of the experience.) Stephen would (happily) have to wait half a century more. The attic ceiling came down, but nothing much was broken. Natasha, who as Stephen noted, 'is without fear, seemed scarcely affected'.

I looked out of the window and saw London lying below me, black and calm, with a few isolated fires rising from scattered areas, like tongues of flame fallen from the heavens upon a darkening view of Florence, in some late morbid visioning of Botticelli.

Surveying the apocalyptic landscape he felt impelled to go out and walk the streets, towards a pillar of flame in working-class Kilburn (in fact it was a flaring gas main). Natasha remembers his coming back, semi-dazed, at daybreak. There were holes in the roof where, by now, the morning light was glinting through. Amid all the fallen plaster, disorder and stench, 'he dusted a small portion off the kitchen table, and started writing'. What he wrote was the first draft of his poem 'Abyss':

> When the foundations quaked and the pillars shook,
> I trembled, and in the dark I felt the fear
> Of the photograph my skull might take
> Through the eye sockets, in one flashlit instant.

As his 'Yank' friend Harry Brown put it, the Blitz was 'almost worth it, to have produced such a poem'.

The February 1944 raids also meant active service for Stephen as a fireman. It was, he told Sitwell, 'a relief' after the years of waiting. From Holland Park Avenue the fires he was called to fight were in Kensington. 'The flames themselves,' he told Sitwell (sending her his 'fire poem'), 'have a wonderfully *calming* effect.' He regarded it as symbolic that they had occurred 'nel mezzo del cammin di sua vita' – on his thirty-fifth birthday.

Stephen was, for some time after, deeply disturbed and excited by these near-death experiences (he rewrote his will at this time). He mused on the subject of mortality to Edwin Muir (the British symbolist poet he most admired), now working with the British Council in Edinburgh. Muir wrote back on 21 March:

I was much struck by what you say about death and the fortuitous snuffing out of life. I can't find or think so closely about it, for though I've lived much longer, I have never come in contact with it. It is the most horrible thing in the world, probably: I don't know. I still stick to my belief in immortality.

The February raids were the Germans' last throw – at least by manned bombers. Spender applied, at last, to leave the NFS. He had cast-iron health grounds. The varicose veins were now disablingly painful. 'They took one look at them and simply shot him out,' his wife recalls. Spender was discharged on 13 June 1944. Ironically, it was the same day that the first of the V-1 buzz bombs fell on London.

Amid all the wreckage, they carried on with their lives and work. On 18 April 1944, Natasha Litvin made her début at the Wigmore Hall. Her recital (featuring Beethoven's 'Tempest Sonata', Ravel's 'Gaspard de la Nuit' and Schumann's 'Etudes Symphoniques') elicited a warm review in *The Times*. She was described as a 'promising pianist . . . only the mellowness of riper years is needed to make her a distinguished player of Beethoven'. Stephen had been there, 'very anxious. Not much of a help really – always more anxious than I was.'

On leaving the Fire Service Stephen was recruited into the Foreign Office's Political Intelligence Department, housed in Bush House, the peacetime premises of the BBC World Service. Kenneth Clark, influential in the Ministry of Information, had been helpful (another friend, Lys Lubbock, from *Horizon*, had also been working at the PID for some months). Stephen's main assignment in the agency would be to compile information about the history of Italian Fascism, as 'background material for the British force occupying Italy'. The Allies had entered Rome on 4 June 1944.

Spender managed to squeeze in three months' leave before taking up his duties at Bush House on 31 July. As high summer came on he retired to Oxford, to work up his autobiographical Oxford novel, 'Instead of Death', which he intended submitting to the Hogarth Press. He was also writing up a critical book for Cape. He had some £250 from publishers' advances to see him through the year (his new agent, A. D. Peters, had proved more energetic than Curtis Brown). His new post located him in the centre of London, and made it possible, once again, to lunch in town. On 23 October he lunched with Cyril Connolly and E. M. Forster. His impression of himself was typically self-deprecating:

Morgan Forster always gives me the impression that, in his extremely diffident way, he is making moral judgements on everyone. The very reticence of his personality shows up everyone else like a patch of colour, which placed beside other colours, makes them seem tawdry and vulgar. The effect of his presence was that I talked a great deal about myself. All the time I was thinking, while he looked at me with his head a little to one side, 'how abominably vulgar I am'.

Cyril took a more materialistic line on Forster's moral censoriousness: 'When I served the steak I wondered whether Morgan would notice that I had taken the largest piece?' While Stephen talked too much Cyril munched – without any uncomfortable remorse. Connolly's way.

At PID whatever *folie de grandeur* Spender may earlier have had was promptly extinguished. It was boring work, when it wasn't 'appallingly sad. Everything I read is about the endless suffering of people in Europe.' His main task consisted in 'rewriting and putting into shape large amounts of factual material which other people have amassed'. He asked his friends to help him to something more fulfilling. Goronwy Rees and Noël Annan (both, like him, German speakers) had been recruited for the Political Division of what, after the war, would be the Allied Control Commission (that is, the Civil Service administration, for occupied Germany). Through Julian Huxley's good offices, Spender was inter-viewed by the Joint Selection Board of the Commission, on 29 November.

The interview was a disaster. He described it at length to Huxley, four days later:

When I went into the Board Room there were three people there seated at a table. They asked me to sit down. The officer on my right looked through my papers and said: 'Mr Spender, your qualifications don't seem very concise. You describe yourself as a writer and a Fireman. What do you mean by that?' I explained I had written several books. My interlocutor asked me what sort of books, and I attempted to explain. I added that I had experience in the NFS of organizing Discussion Groups as I had been Organizer for No 34 Fire Service. I added that I had considerable journalistic experience. I was next asked how long I was willing to commit myself for in this work. I said that I did not want to bind myself for more than two years after the war was over. Asked why, I said that the reason was that I also had an obligation to do my literary work, which I thought was very important . . . 'In other words,' my interlocutor said, 'you put your – er – journalistic work before this work?' I answered that I did not consider myself a journalist. I considered myself a writer with definite obli-gations to literature, and a task to fulfil. This was precisely why I might be useful to them. After the war I thought there would certainly be some kind of literary and cultural movement in Germany, as there was after the last war. The interviewer at the end of the table said: 'Do you think that after the Nazis there can really be such a development? Among what class of people?' I said I thought there might be amongst the students, and I pointed to the case of Professor Curtius at Bonn University, who had steadily retained the interest of a group of students all through the Hitler period, at any rate until the war. Before these remarks about Curtius had been made, one of the interviewers suggested that I was the sort of person who did not stick at anything and that therefore I was not suitable for this work.

On 1 December, Spender received a note 'stating that the Board had found there was no suitable vacancy for me'. He protested bitterly. Eventually, a short-term assignment (of six months' duration) would be offered to him.

There were some better things to report to his friends. On 30 November, he wrote to Julian Huxley to say that Natasha was pregnant and that both of them were 'very happy'. He had done 100 pages of his Oxford novel and was 'very excited about it'. He had also finished his other book for Cape, 'The Creative Element': 'but I refuse to send it to the printers until I can get 14 days completely free in which to revise it. God knows when that will be' (1953, as it turned out). The Spenders spent a happy Christmas 1944 at Sutton Veny — the happier since Lolly had, miraculously, survived another year.

By the new year 1945, it was clear that the Spenders were at last going to have the child they desired. Among the gloom of bomb-damage, blackout and winter, his wife's pregnancy was, for Stephen, 'one candle burning on an altar in a dark cathedral'. The child was due in March. With luck, it might be born in peace. It was not for Natasha Spender an entirely peaceful nine months — although with continuing rocket-raids candles were prominent enough. Given her history of miscarriages, she was, in the critical months, subjected to 'gargantuan injections', which effectively paralysed her (particularly nerve-racking during buzz-bomb raids).

Rosamond Lehmann — veteran mother of two — offered the advice 'just scream' (during the birth, she meant). Natasha received more constructive help from Anna Freud, who invited her to her Netherhall Gardens nursery to 'learn how to look after babies'. The Spenders had been active in the previous couple of years in raising funds for Freud's childcare centre. Stephen had advised on fire safety. Fini, Tony Hyndman's ex-wife and Muriel Gardiner's ex-nanny, was now a full-time helper of Miss Freud's, in charge of the 'baby room'.

On the night that Matthew Spender was born the nunnery next door to 2 Maresfield Gardens took a direct hit from a V-2. Ernst Freud's fortifications again proved their worth – but the exposed top flat was, as before, temporarily uninhabitable. Natasha had anticipated that her child might be born on the ominous 'Ides' of March – the 15th. He in fact arrived two days earlier, on the unlucky 13th. The baby was 'slightly jaundiced, and looked like a red Indian'. Six weeks later, when W. H. Auden first saw him, he was inspired to his much-repeated wisecrack, 'all babies look like Winston Churchill'. In fact, as he grew up, Matthew would bear a facial similarity to his father. Nor did misfortune attend him.

Thirty years later, Stephen recalled his first paternal visit to Cheniston Gardens:

Riding on top of a bus which went from Swiss Cottage all the way to Kensington, where Natasha and Matthew – our son – were in hospital, again I had the feeling of mystery as though the dreary, almost trafficless, partly-wrecked streets were the base of a Jacob's ladder which stretched into the sky, upon which the born and the unborn children climbed from heaven to earth and earth to heaven.

Early choices of names included 'Benjamin'. But Clifford Curzon, one of the boy's godfathers, objected that 'Ben Spen' offended his musician's ear. They settled on Matthew Francis. 'Michael' was added as a third Christian name, in commemoration of Stephen's brother. Squadron Leader Michael A. Spender was killed, on 5 May, in a plane crash in Germany a couple of days before the christening and just before VE day. It was a dreadful death. The RAF Anson plane, in which he was a passenger, had crashed into a wood. The pilot, a friend of Michael's, was horribly injured but survived. Michael lingered for two days in an oxygen tent, his second wife Nancy (whom he had married in 1943) by his side. He was buried in the British services cemetery at Eindhoven.

The obituaries made impressive reading. Michael had made his mark with a brilliant First in science at Oxford. His university friends were convinced that he could – had he wished – have been a great musician. In 1928, he had served as surveyor to the Barrier Reef expedition.

Thereafter, he had been on a major Everest expedition and had done ground-breaking work in commercial optics, and important research for his country in photo-reconnaissance analysis during the war. His relationship with his brother, although intense, had never been easy. As Stephen explained to Edith Sitwell:

No one will ever realize now what he *might* have done. He died because of the blind, destructive stupidity of war . . . I was never very intimate with him, as we had been rivals since childhood, and we never got over a certain embarrassment with each other . . . he got firsts and scholarships. I have never passed a single exam in all my life and yet I have had more public success than he had . . . He probably felt there was a mystery about my being well known, despite my failures.

Stephen composed an elegiac poem, 'Seascape: *In Memoriam M.A.S.*', which plays with the idea of human fragility in the image of butterfly flight:

>Then from the shore, two zig-zag butterflies,
>Like errant dog-roses, cross the bright strand
>Spiralling over sea in foolish gyres
>Until they fall into reflected skies.
>They drown. Fishermen understand
>Such wings sunk in such ritual sacrifice.

Matthew Spender was christened at St Mark's church, North Audley Street, in early June. The godparents were William Plomer, Clifford Curzon, Edward Selwyn and Edith Sitwell. Miss Sitwell informed Christine Spender, as they returned from the service, that the 'babe leapt in my arms' as she held it ready for its ritual anointment. Less ecstatically, Natasha noticed the sibylline poetess give the baby a 'sharp little tap' with one of her massive rings when he ventured a cry during the service. He was instantly silenced.

The Spenders had been househunting for several months. In September 1944 Natasha had found exactly what they wanted (and could currently afford) at 15 Loudoun Road, NW8. The property was being offered for rent by the Eyre Estate. A detached early Victorian structure a few hundred yards from St John's Wood underground station (useful – they would have no car till the 1950s) and Lord's cricket ground ('of no interest whatsoever'), it was a fine house gone to rack and ruin with wartime neglect and bomb damage. The Eyre Estate charged a pepper-corn rent for the first year (thereafter £125), on condition that the tenants put the property in habitable order.

The move to Loudoun Road in March was undertaken while Natasha was in the nursing-home. There was not much to move from Maresfield Gardens. When mother and child returned, the furnishings in the spacious new house comprised the couple's much-travelled double bed, Natasha's Steinway, Stephen's books, typewriter, gramophone, favourite pictures and some other bits and pieces. Natasha got hold of some red linoleum, which cheered up the basement kitchen and top-floor nursery. Ernst Freud gave them a huge glass acid jar, enclosing a cherry bough, to decorate the living room.

On the evening of VE Day, 8 May, Stephen and Natasha took a walk down to Regent's Park to observe the lights of London, blazing, 'divinely', for the first time since the blackout of 1939. And what should the Spenders do in the new era of divine sweetness and light? Natasha Spender knew where she was going professionally. Stephen Spender did not, any more than he ever had. 'He never talked about his career at all. Things just cropped up.'

One of the things that cropped up was work in Germany – a country so changed from what he had known in the early 1930s that it might now have been another planet. With the end of war, PID ceased to have any reason for being. Spender was transferred on the six-month assign-ment which the Allied Control Commission had grudgingly awarded him. One of the commission's first tasks was to guide post-war Germany back to democracy. A first step was building the ravaged country's cultural, educational and intellectual infrastructure – *Deutsche Geist und Kunst*.

This was a cause dear to Spender. He was particularly interested in working in German universities, prostituted by the Nazis since 1933. His 'private reason', as he later admitted in the *Journals*, 'was to go to Bonn and concern myself with the fate of my friend from pre-war days . . . Ernst Robert Curtius' – the teacher who had taught him how to read Rilke, Goethe and Hölderlin.

Over the course of his service in the ACC, Spender held a brevet commission (as an army lieutenant) and was obliged to wear khaki uniform. From his training in the NFS, he knew how to bear himself as a soldier – although returning salutes must have been awkward. He would need special permission to interview ('fraternize with') members of a German population which was being punished by being sent collectively to Coventry by its conquerors – a prohibition Spender thought crazy.

Spender's German mission was a few months away, after the military occupiers were bedded down. In the meantime, with victory, W. H. Auden came to London in late April ('the rats return to the unsunk ship', was Robert Graves's acerbic comment). Auden was himself on an official mission as a brevet-Major in the US army, assigned to assess the impact of the air-raids for the Morale Division of the US Strategic Bombing Survey in Germany – 'Uzzbuzz' as it was nicknamed.

As soon as he arrived, Wystan was invited to supper at Loudoun Road with Louis MacNeice. Stephen committed the *faux pas* of giggling at Auden in his uniform – his friend did not have a military carriage. Major Auden was not amused at Stephen's amusement. 'You have a son,' he brusquely announced, with an inspecting glance at Natasha's bundle. It was Natasha Spender's first sight of Stephen's friend, about whom she had heard so much. When Wystan spoke, she was astonished by his American accent ('where's my gaas maask', he said, as he put his things down by the umbrella rack). When he arrived, a minute or two later, an amused MacNeice looked on, a languid elbow on the mantelpiece, 'his rather lofty self'.

With drinks, the atmosphere relaxed and the poets sat over dinner 'for ages' talking about the war, about literature, about Oxford. Auden did not, however, remove his overcoat during the evening. As the guests left, they gathered on the steps of the house and enjoyed the lights blazing in the road, even though their unfamiliar brilliance revealed seven years' decay and aerial destruction. Earlier, Auden had made his sublimely tactless remark to the effect that London had suffered much less bombing damage than German towns. Perhaps so. But it had suffered rather more than Manhattan.

As war ended and the post-war era began, Spender – like other young(ish) intellectuals of his time – was obliged to work out where he stood in this new world. Final positions were premature, since 1945 would be a year of thinking and horizon-broadening. The most restless of writers, Spender had been confined for six years in one country. Never, since adolescence, had he been so tied down. The first few months of peace were an orgy of travel, the fruit of which was the travel-book-cum-testament, *European Witness*. Before undertaking his cultural reconnaissance of Germany for the Control Commission, Spender visited Paris for three weeks in late

May–early June 1945. He had been invited by the British Council (thanks to Edwin Muir). Natasha remained at home with newborn Matthew at Loudoun Road.

As he passed the frontier Spender was amused that his passport, on which he had inscribed as occupation 'Poet and Journalist', was over-stamped with the words 'Government Official'. It seemed, as he later told his French hosts, to symbolize something. Stephen had never liked France, ever since the adolescent wretchedness of Nantes. In May 1945, he fell head-over-heels in love with Paris. The three weeks that he spent in France were, he recorded in his journal, 'amongst the happiest in my life'. His first two days in the capital were spent wandering around the streets. Paris, an 'open city', had been spared destruction. Coming as he did from bomb-torn London, with the 'corpse cities' of Germany in prospect, he was entranced by the unruined beauty. The French people were something else. They were consumed with a sense of national 'disgrace'. Collaboration had corroded French civic virtue. The country was, Spender felt, starting at 'year zero'. This spiritual blankness was exac-erbated in Spender's mind by the novel he was currently reading, Camus's *L'Étranger*, and the hollow doctrines of existentialism. The whole French population seemed convulsed with a 'sob of fury and despair'.

In Paris Spender gave a lecture in the British Council Centre in 'bad French' on the 'Crisis of Symbols in Poetry'. It was a subject he had been worrying at for some time, in his pieces for *Penguin New Writing*, and in his own verse. In Paris he met everyone. The literary editor Henri Hell became a close friend. Hell (known to his companions as 'José') was the amanuensis of Francis Poulenc, a music critic and would, a year later, join the music division of UNESCO. In Paris Spender was reunited with his pre-war friend and Joyce's publisher, Sylvia Beach. She told him the shocking story of a Jewish assistant, 'a beautiful girl aged eighteen' whom she was instructed by the Germans to dismiss if she herself wished to stay out of trouble. Beach, who refused, was interned. 'The girl was put on a train for Poland. She was never heard of again.'

Spender learned the equally horrifying experiences of his pre-war love, Gisa Soloweitschik (now Drouin) over a five-course meal in her Paris apartment. He had not seen Gisa (now a niece by marriage of André Gide) for six years. They talked about old days in Berlin – when her solicitous mother had stuffed the pockets of the impecunious and clearly malnourished *Engländer* with fruit – and her recent immortal-ization by Isherwood as 'Natalia Landauer'.

The Soloweitschiks had lost everything. The parents had been deported by the Nazis to Poland. During the war in Paris Gisa had been obliged to wear the yellow Star of David on her coat. She was excluded from shops and areas of the city and Métro. She had lived in constant fear of deportation (only the connection with Gide protected her). Through the Drouins Stephen was put in touch again with their eminent relative Gide, now returned to Paris from North Africa. He would meet the Grand Old Man of French literature several times over the course of the year. ('Y-a-t'il beaucoup d'immoralité parmi les ruines de Berlin?' Gide delicately inquired, after Stephen's 1945 German visit.)

From Paris Spender travelled south by train on to 'the hot vermilion courtyards of Toulouse'. The British Council's arrangements were less than perfect. Their distinguished guest was obliged to spend a night sleeping on the corridor floor of his railway carriage, to be 'woken from my half slumber by a lady being sick over me'. He none the less felt 'exaggeratedly happy' and imagined himself as one of Camus's Arabs – an *étranger*, a vomited-on 'outsider'.

After Toulouse Stephen travelled on to the 'intensely serious sun of Montpellier' (intoxicating after five years of cool English summers and northern light). The British Council had improved its service and he was now travelling first class. With the seething masses in the corridors it was, if anything, more uncomfortable than the trip to Toulouse had been. Stephen was now, he realized, 'on the wrong side of the barricade'. A first-class passenger in life. An insider. It was at Montpellier that he received his first (honorary) degree. Spender made two other brief stopovers in Paris in 1945, on his journeys back from the Rhineland in August, and from Berlin in October. The Parisian experiences of 1945 were formative. It was not just the relaxation of being in an unbombed and enduringly beautiful city. In Paris, Spender moved easily among an intellectual stratum which was still vital. He visited and revisited Picasso in his studio; called on Louis Aragon in his 'book-lined flat'; conversed at length in *rive gauche* cafés with the minimalist Francis Ponge and Paul Éluard (whose poems he would later translate). He promenaded through the gardens of Palais-Royal with a wry Jean Cocteau; debated politics with intellectual communists like Loys Masson; learned about *résistant* poetic strategy from Raymond Queneau. This, Spender felt, was the world to which he now belonged.

Spender was back in London in July 1945 for the Labour landslide victory and the 'nationalizing' government of Clement Attlee. Some of his contemporaries – such as Dick Crossman – were now in Parliament. Herbert Morrison (who had been Home Secretary when Fireman Spender had pioneered his civil education schemes) wanted to put him forward as a candidate. But the feelers came when Spender was abroad. He was, anyway, disinclined to accept any such invitation.

Since autumn 1944, Spender had been revising his undergraduate novel, 'Instead of Death', with a view to its being published by Lehmann at the Hogarth Press, as a sequel to *The Backward Son*. By summer 1945, he had a (professionally) typed version of his manuscript. The narrative centres on 'We three'. The setting is Oxford 1928. The ingenuous hero is 'Benjamin Saschen' – Stephen Spender. Wystan dominates, as 'Vernon Hunter' – a character who instructs Benjamin, in true Auden style, 'do not run away from your balls'. The Isherwood character breaks up Vernon's romance with a nurse; saving his friend's balls for homosexuality. 'Instead of Death' was an eminently publishable work. But it would not see print (after much further revision) until 1988, as a section of *The Temple*.

At noon on 6 July 1945 Spender took off from Croydon airport for Germany. The RAF transport plane had been due to depart five tedious hours earlier. There would be a lot of waiting around over the next four weeks. His mission was to go to the Rhineland, investigate, and report back on the intellectual climate of German universities to the British authorities. His main source, as he expected, would be his teacher of fifteen years earlier, Ernst Robert Curtius.

On arrival in Germany, Spender was driven through 'Niebelung landscape' to the headquarters of the occupying 21st Army Group, at Bad Oeynhausen. He then kicked his heels, waiting for transport from the motor pool to take him on to Bonn and Cologne, his official destinations. He wandered around picking up vignettes of German life under British occupation for his forthcoming book, *European Witness*.

Spender did not arrive at his destinations until the 11th, after 'incredible adventures'. They revolved mainly around an obstinately deflationary tyre. It took three days to cover the short distance across the British Zone. As they picked their way through Cologne's war-torn thoroughfares, for the first time Stephen 'realized what total destruction meant'. The population trudged wearily through the streets and rubble pushing handcarts and prams, or carrying cans to fill from the few operating standpipes. Cologne was a 'putrescent corpse city'.

Having at last arrived at Bonn (similarly ravaged), he made a beeline for the house of Curtius. His old mentor was astonished to see 'der Unschuldige' on his doorstep in military uniform. He and his wife Ilse (a former student, whom he had married in 1931) insisted he stay for dinner, sharing their 'Tolstoyan diet' of potatoes and cabbage. The once magnificent library was bereft of books (the few treasures Ernst Robert had left, Spender learned, he would sell on the black market to stave off starvation in the coming winter). Ernst Robert and Ilse seemed to be living in utter emptiness, their lives ticking away, 'like a clock in a cellar'.

Spender explained to Curtius his official purpose in coming to Bonn. His mission was to 'inquire into the intellectual life there'. Curtius retorted, gloomily, that 'there was no intellectual life'. He then launched into the first of a series of depressive 'tirades'. The German nation, he concluded, were by nature 'servile and stupid'. Unlike other Europeans, the Germans had 'never governed themselves'. He was frank about guilt: anyone who denied that Hitler started the war 'is either ignorant or a liar . . . the German people *are* guilty of these frightful crimes'.

It was tormenting for Stephen to confront the possibility, but had Ernst Robert himself been too acquiescent over the last decade-and-a-half? It was a question that Spender posed obliquely in his December 'Rhineland Journal' for *Horizon*. Since 1933, he recorded, 'I have often wondered why Curtius didn't leave Germany . . . After Hitler's seizure of power it would have been easy for him to leave Germany and go to Paris, Madrid, Rome, Oxford or Cambridge.' He was childless, honoured abroad, and cosmopolitan by temperament. Why work for Hitler and his academic goons?

Curtius's position in the late 1930s was, in fact, complicated. In 1933 he had published *Deutscher Geist in Gefahr (German Spirit in Peril)*, a passionate attack on the totalitarian threat to universities. The book was anti-Nazi but 'nevertheless a defence of the German tradition, written in a nationalist spirit. Besides attacking the Nazis, it attacked the prole-tarianization of literature and it criticized the influence of Jewish ideas.' Curtius had evidently displayed a dignified silence during ceremonial book-burnings at universities in May 1933 (Cologne's was particularly fiery), through the wholesale purge of Jews, Communists and legal scholars from his university. He must, like other academics, have made a formal declaration of allegiance to the Führer, whatever his private reser-vations. He must have witnessed Jewish colleagues dismissed (and worse).

Spender assumed that Curtius had remained in Germany, and silent, out of 'rootedness' and a sense that, like Goethe during the Napoleonic

Wars, it was his duty to be 'like a mighty cliff towering above and indifferent to the waters hundreds of feet beneath him'. It was a pose easier to adopt in a Weimar principality than a modern totalitarian tyranny. He got no clear answers from Curtius on these painful questions – not that they could be asked directly without giving mortal offence. Nor could Ernst Robert give any satisfactory response to Stephen's objection that 'it was difficult to understand how the *whole* of the German educational system should have become so subservient to Nazi doctrine'.

Curtius's gloom, silences and intellectual despair cast a shadow over Spender's subsequent interviews with Bonn and Cologne professors and educational administrators. All in all, it was a bad four weeks. On 20 July Spender suffered a moral-nervous relapse. He felt 'terribly depressed and homesick'. Whenever he heard a baby cry he thought of Matthew. Whenever he saw flowers, he thought of Natasha. His physical surroundings were something out of Dante – 'vast sandy wastes of blowing dust, derelict walls and maimed monuments', all the more horrible for memories of idyllic 1930s days walking down the Rhine. Bonn in summer 1945 was afflicted by a biblical plague of green midges, engendered by the city's filth. The tales of revenge atrocities perpetrated by DPs (displaced persons – mainly Poles brought to the Reich as slave labour) were an added torment. 'In every corner of Germany,' Spender recorded, 'one stumbles on some new horror, a mass grave or a prison camp.' He had come out as a missionary of sweetness and light. He had found himself Marlow in the Heart of Darkness.

The redeeming event in the first German trip, typically, was Spender's being able to save one single victim of war (as ten years earlier he had saved Hyndman in Spain). In a hospital in Bonn was a young German boy, Rudi, who was dying. The only thing that could save him was penicillin – impossible to procure through normal channels or even (like Harry Lime) on the black market. Spender none the less got hold of some of the antibiotic, and visited the boy, lying in bed 'with large leaden blue eyes through his dead white face'. The next day, he brought the lad a Wilhelm Busch comic book, and elicited a faint 'prima!' from the bedclothes.

Spender returned to Britain, via Paris, in early August. Over summer 1945 – a blissful few months of good weather – he wrote poetry, drafted his report for the Control Commission, and made notes for *European Witness*. They spent much time in Sutton Veny, with Lolly (very ill) and Humphrey (now demobilized). In the autumn both Stephen and

Natasha were contracted to visit Germany. She had been commissioned by the 'Malcolm Clubs' – an RAF officers' association – to do a three-week concert tour in October.

Spender had been sent out a month earlier than his wife, in September, on a wide-ranging mission through the British Zone. He was charged by the Control Commission to inspect German libraries, all of which had been closed down with the Occupation in May. Where appropriate he was empowered to authorize their reopening. The non-fraternization law had at last been lifted, to Spender's relief and the gratification of his soldier-drivers, who could now consort with 'Fräuleins'.

He left Croydon military airport on 7 September, amid the usual confusion. His flight was hours late taking off, diverted mid-flight by fog, and Spender contrived, meanwhile, to lose the haversack containing his toothbrush and razor. When he did eventually manage to scrounge a new toothbrush, he promptly lost it through a hole in his trouser pocket. Once he reported for duty, his mission was handicapped by comically inadequate transport arrangements. Everyone in Germany wanted a car and a driver. Temporary lieutenants working for the Commission carried little clout with the car-pool spivs. Spender always ended up with the clapped-out vehicle, in this case a 'rachitic Humber', whose unreliable entrails he and his drivers came to know well over the next few weeks. 'I have acquired a whole philosophy of life from this Humber,' Spender later wrote – a cosmic indifference to arriving on time that even Christopher's Krishnamurti could not have taught him.

Spender was unconvinced of the worthwhileness of his mission. His liberal conscience rebelled at the thought of having to act as a *censor librorum* – inspecting books for political correctness. 'I could never make up my mind whether I approved of the policy of "purging" libraries of Nazi books,' he later wrote. As before, the nucleus of the trip for Spender was less his official duties than his personal contacts. Little Rudi, he was gratified and amazed to discover, was – thanks to the penicillin – transformed from a living skeleton into 'the Fat Boy in *Pickwick Papers*', with 'bulging cheeks, bulging thighs, and complexion like a suet pudding'. The change was so marked that it was difficult – on aesthetic grounds – not to regret it.

As before, it was the encounters with Curtius that were most perturbing. On 13 September, Spender met his teacher in the streets of Bonn 'by chance'. The two of them wandered past the university (still not reopened) and walked along the bank of the Rhine together. 'No

one worked in Germany unless they were given cigarettes', Curtius
sardonically observed – as Stephen gave him a cigarette. They smoked
away in gloomy silence. A couple of days later, at supper (more Tolstoyan
cabbage), the Curtiuses told him in graphic detail about the dreadful
phosphorus raids on Wuppertal, where Stephen had just been to open
a library. German civilians had been burned alive, in their thousands.
What did books matter?

The Spenders made their way separately to Berlin, on 13 October.
It was not an easy trip, requiring as it did a 100-mile journey across
the new Russian Zone. The city itself was under a four-power *Kom-
mandatur*. As Natasha was driven down the Hannover–Berlin Autobahn,
the driver of her car stopped to help a fellow-Briton who had evidently
broken down. Driver and passenger were peering glumly into their
engine. It was, by the happiest of flukes, Stephen's Humber, up to its
usual tricks.

Stephen was taken aboard Natasha's car. In Berlin the Spenders
checked into the Hotel Bristol, by the Kurfürstendamm. Stephen was
so excited that, leaving Natasha to rest, he rushed out after dinner to
explore the city. He wanted to 'recapture something of the mood of the
Berlin I knew'. Were the *Lokale*, cafés and dubious nightclubs still there?
Was any *life* surviving? To his astonishment, he could not even find the
'Kudamm'. It was obliterated. All that remained were 'skeletons', under
'an enormous shroud of sameness'. His Berlin, Christopher's Berlin, Mr
Norris's Berlin, no longer existed.

Later in the week, he and Natasha crossed into the Russian sector of
the city and inspected the ruins of the Chancellery and its underground
bunker. Stephen picked up as a souvenir a polished stone fragment of
Hitler's desk. In the remains of his bedside table in the bunker they
found some marked-up architecture books (the Führer had consoled his
latter days with fantasies of rebuilding Linz as his shrine-city). These
relics were subsequently placed, as trophies of war, on the mantelpiece
at Loudoun Road. Lolly, on her last visit to London, picked the Hitlerian
fragment up – without knowing its provenance. 'I've never touched
anything so evil,' she said, dropping it as if it were red-hot. 'Get rid of
it!' she instructed Stephen and Natasha. They did as she instructed. For
good measure Stephen threw away the books.

Lolly, now emaciated to five stone, was dying. She had guessed what
the doctors would not tell her. During her last months the Spenders did
week-on, week-off spells at Sutton Veny. Humphrey was by his wife's

1. Granny Schuster, 1940s

2. Harold and Violet Spender's wedding day, 1904

3. Spender
children, 1915

4. Stephen, *c.* 1914

5. Bertha and Ella,
'Berthella', Frognal,
late 1920s

6. Harold Spender and children, *c.* 1922

7. Stephen at Oxford, taken by his brother Humphrey

8. Stephen,
Ruegen, 1931

9. Stephen and Tony Hyndman, Malcesine, 1934

10. Stephen, Tony Hyndman and Winifred Paine, 1934

11. Stephen in Cintra, Portugal, with Christopher Isherwood,
Tony Hyndman, et al., 1935

12. Inez,
Roegate,
1937

13. Muriel Gardiner,
Vienna, 1936

14. Helen Low, Margaret (Lolly) Spender
and Inez, 1938

15. *Trial of a Judge*, Group Theatre, 1938

16. Michael Spender, 1943

17. Christine
Spender, early
1940s

18. Leonard Woolf, Stephen and Natasha at Monk's House, 1941

19. Stephen in Fire
Service uniform with
Arthur Bliss,
Wittersham, 1941

20. Stephen and
Natasha at Sutton
Veny, 1941

21. Lucian Freud, Tony Hyndman and John Craxton on the balcony of 2 Maresfield Gardens, 1942

22. Natasha Litvin, 1946

23. Natasha Spender and Isaiah Berlin, Geneva, 1946

24. W. H. Auden, Stephen and Christopher Isherwood, Fire Island, 1947

25. Matthew Spender and friend outside Loudoun Road, 1951

26. Stephen with Lizzie and Matthew Spender, 1952

27. W. H. Auden and Lizzie Spender, Loudoun Road, 1954

28. Stephen and Francis Bacon, Montmajour, 1967

29. Christopher Isherwood, Stephen and Don Bachardy, 1970

30. Joseph Brodsky and Stephen, Venice, 1977

31. Iris Murdoch, Mas de Saint Jerome, 1977

32. Reynolds Price, North Carolina, late 1970s

33. David
Hockney and
Greg Evans in
China, 1981

34. Lizzie Spender
marries Barry
Humphries,
Spoleto, 1990

35. Stephen and Humphrey Spender, Maldon, Essex, 1991

36. Golden Wedding lunch, Mas de Saint Jerome, 1991

bedside day and night. Stephen was two days into his week with her when she died, with awful coincidence, on Christmas Day (a festival which, ever since childhood and his mother's death, he had disliked). They brought a distraught Humphrey back to Loudoun Road. During her death throes over the previous months Stephen had written the lament which heads *Poems of Dedication* (1947), 'Elegy for Margaret':

> Darling of our hearts, drowning
> In the thick night of ultimate sea
> Which (indeed) surrounds us all, but where we
> Are crammed islands of flesh, wide
> With a few harvesting years, disowning
> The bitter black severing tide.

There was trouble at the very end of the year from an unexpected quarter. Connolly wanted Spender's article 'Rhineland Journal', in a hurry. It was not an easy piece to write. Stephen had to clear what he had written with the War Office. He had also assured Curtius, who was punctilious about such things, that he would show him the proofs of anything he wrote arising out of their conversations in July and September.

The 'Rhineland Journal' piece draws heavily on these conversations. In the rush of late 1945, with Lolly's condition distracting him and with *Horizon* breathing down his neck, Spender neglected to get Curtius's imprimatur. As he later said: 'Cyril was very anxious to publish it immediately, so thinking that there was nothing in it unfavourable to Curtius I published "Rhineland Journal".' Carelessly but innocently, he had not done what he had assured Curtius he would do.

Curtius was enraged to the pitch of madness by the references to himself in 'Rhineland Journal'. As Spender notes:

He could not, of course, in any circumstances have taken action against a journalist publishing reports which were entirely favourable to him, but he took the line that it was only because he was a member of a defeated people, living under an occupying power, that he had no legal recourse against me. Believing this, he wrote protesting his helplessness to the Archbishop of Canterbury, T. S. Eliot and others.

How the primate replied is unknown. T. S. Eliot wrote back an emollient letter, designed to calm. It was an error of youth. 'I saw Stephen's article,' Eliot wrote. He had been 'disturbed by . . . the element of pure bad taste and stupidity':

He [Stephen] really is a good and affectionate young man – though very callow for his years; but he has sometimes offended me – and I think, others – by the tone he adopts. He is a Liberal, and therefore tends to intolerance and judging others; and he tends to take an unconsciously superior tone on the basis of very imperfect understanding. But I see that you are very deeply hurt indeed. I have written to him (as he showed me his letter to you) to say that he has put himself in the wrong.

In another letter he declared himself 'appalled' by Spender's suggestion that no 'good German' could have remained in the Reich.

Eliot – clearly acting as something of a broker – wrote to Stephen on 12 February:

While I think that Curtius may be in a peculiarly nervous state at the moment (his letter to me rather confirms this impression) I do feel that you have put yourself in the wrong toward him by publishing this account of your visit without getting his approval first. It seemed to me that it would have been better either to have printed his name in full or to have disguised his identity to a greater degree. And I don't feel that you give a particularly favourable impression of Curtius himself. You discuss the reasons for his not leaving Germany after 1933 but I don't think that you attempt to justify his remaining there, you merely go a certain distance toward condoning it.

Eliot's criticisms were evidently overstated to soothe Curtius. They are less than fair. Ten years later Spender attempted a reconciliation with Curtius by offering to dedicate to him the 'Early Poems', in *Collected Poems, 1928–1953* (1955). He refused, and the dedication went to Auden.

The ice was, however, broken. In October of that year, Ilse phoned Stephen when he was in Berlin, asking him to call on them on his way back to England. Curtius had suffered a stroke (he would in fact die in 1956). Conversation was difficult, but finally Curtius made his gesture of peace with an inscribed copy of his essays on European Literature, his 'great book', as he called it, with touching vanity. 'It was not exactly that I felt I was forgiven,' Stephen wrote, 'but I felt that what was unforgiven could not be forgiven and that a great deal else had always been forgiven and could not be unforgiven.' Their friendship had been one of the casualties of war. Ilse, much younger than her husband, outlived him by many years. Stephen met her in April 1985, in Munich. She was 'charming, bearing no grudges . . . she hoped I understood that when she had quarrelled with me about my Rhineland Journal, her remarks had not been meant personally. All was forgiven.'

The 1945–6 holidays were overshadowed by Lolly's death. Edith Sitwell, the most confidential of their friends, wrote to the Spenders on 4 January to condole about 'this terrible time, this most dreadful Christmas'. She had not herself known Lolly. But 'Natasha loved her, and the way in which she loved her tells me *everything*.' Spender had poured out his grief to Sitwell as he watched Lolly slowly die, racked by 'the devouring love of humanity'.

As the year turned, Spender worked on the manuscript of *European Witness* and the final draft of *Poems of Dedication*. John Hayward, T. S. Eliot's closest literary adviser and for some years the poet's flatmate, read and commented on the poems. Grievously handicapped, Hayward had been confined for years to a wheelchair. He was a formidably meticulous reader, with a fine ear for poetry. Headed as the collection was with his 'Elegy for Margaret', the new collection included the most deeply felt poems Spender had hitherto put into print. After this, he assured Hayward in February, 'I'm going to write the most impersonal things imaginable.'

Approaching forty, it was necessary to redefine himself as a poet. In the *Partisan Review* (March 1946) he published his much reprinted 'The Making of a Poem', a mirror-study of himself at work. The *mise en scène* stresses his muse's need for physical triggers:

Schiller liked to have a smell of rotten apples, concealed beneath the lid of his desk, under his nose when he was composing poetry. Walter de la Mare has told me that he must smoke when writing. Auden drinks endless cups of tea. Coffee is my own addiction, besides smoking a great deal, which I hardly ever do except when I am writing.

Making poetry was, in 1946, a less intuitive activity for Spender than it had been fifteen years earlier. In the wake of his encounters with French writers he was wrestling with the doctrines of *poésie pure*. In a thoughtful article for *Horizon*, 'Poetry for Poetry's Sake' (April 1946), he concluded that: 'Poems are hypothetical and theorematic' (not terminology one encounters in the pre-war Spender). In practice he was gradually coming round to the conviction that the essence of a poem was the *ligne donnée*. 'Stephen was always looking for the "golden line",' Stuart Hampshire recalls. These elusive filaments were hunted for through innumerable drafts and trial copies of his poems, often with only the tiniest variations or renuancing (his working notebooks reminded his wife of her own practising the same phrase or passage of music over and over again).

No more than in the pre-war world could Spender live by poetry's golden lines (more so as there were now three mouths to feed at Loudoun Road – not counting the many who came to dinner or to visit). His agent, A. D. Peters, reported that between April 1945 and April 1946 he had earned £567 6s. 3d. (less agent's commission) from his pen. Add to this the £300 p.a. Schuster bequest and the Spenders were not, by the standards of 1946, poor. But it was only just enough for their needs. And, of course, literary earnings were precarious.

He had tentatively accepted the offer of a post in the newly formed United Nations Education, Science and Cultural Organization in late 1945. The invitation came from Julian Huxley. In July 1945, the principles of the fledgeling organization had been thrashed out in a Preparatory Commission, based in London. Huxley (executive secretary to the Preparatory Commission) was appointed the first Director General-elect. He would be the only Briton ever to hold the post and he owed his election in 1946 to the UN's desire to get the 'S' (or science) into the acronym. There was, cynics noted, no 'L' in UNESCO.

On 16 September 1945, seventy-seven members of the embryonic UNESCO left London to take up residence in the Majestic Hotel, in Paris. Two months later the organization's constitution was formally ratified. Its founding principle echoed Spender's own sentiments at the period – and may well have originated with him: 'Since wars begin in the minds of men, it is in the minds of men that the defences of peace must be constructed.' UNESCO, as conceived by Julian Huxley (an incorrigible *improvisateur*, as his starchier colleagues complained), would oppose 'official thought'. This, and Julian's explosive temper, would inevitably bring him and Spender into conflict with the officials of the UN.

Julian and Stephen had been intimately friendly throughout the war and frequent guests at each other's houses. Natasha Spender remembers meetings long into the night at Loudoun Road, or at the Huxleys' place in Pond Street, discussing what the new body should stand for, and what it might usefully achieve in the post-war world. Spender's title at UNESCO was 'Literary Councillor to the Section of Letters'. He would serve under the Communist Pole Anton Slonimsky (a 'slyly entertaining poet'). Among other colleagues at UNESCO were Spender's countrymen Max Nicholson and Jacob Bronowski. The organization moved its *apparat* to Paris in early 1946. The first session of its cultural activities ran from 19 November to 10 December of that year. Spender had considerable latitude as 'literary councillor'. His initial brief was to arrange a series of lectures on general cultural topics. He recruited, among others, Anna Freud to give a lecture in November 1946 on 'The Child in Wartime'. Another visiting lecturer in the inaugural session was J. B. Priestley. 'Still writin' poetry, Spender?' the Yorkshire man of letters asked, in his broad accent. Yes, Spender was writing poetry. 'Not a bad idea,' the Sage of the Ridings replied, 'if yer wants ter do summat serious later. Did it meself, once.'

In March 1946, Natasha and Stephen toured Belgium and Italy. He lectured on the way, on Anglo-European modernist topics and European romanticism (a topic on which he and Isaiah Berlin had jointly developed a long-standing interest). The trip was an opportunity for Natasha to recuperate from the strains of wartime winter. For the last two years she had been under great pressure, what with a new house, a baby and the demands of her concert career. For her the European trip was both a tonic and an education – she had never been to Italy. While the couple were abroad Matthew was looked after by Berthella in Cricklewood.

In Milan, the Spenders met the handsome and charismatic Sicilian Elio Vittorini, and in Florence, where they remained a couple of weeks over Easter, Montale, Ungaretti and 'all the Italian poets'. Neither of the Spenders spoke Italian fluently and they conversed with these literary grandees in somewhat formal French. In Florence Natasha also met her husband's Uncle Arthur for the first time. A Catholic convert, founder of the British Institute in Florence, and the blackest sheep of the Spender family (nicknamed 'the Queen of Florence'), he had built up a notable art collection over many years, only to have it plundered by the Nazis, and what was left bombed into rubble by the RAF during the invasion of Italy. He took the disaster with Spenderian stoicism.

In Rome, the Spenders met among other notables Carlo Levi and Ignazio Silone – a novelist and former communist with whom Spender would have close dealings over the years. Stephen's pre-war acquaintance, the venerable Bernard Berenson, had come with them from

Florence to take them round the capital. Still the grandest of art connois-
seurs, Berenson took the Spenders in his chauffeur-driven limousine to
the British Embassy, surrounded by barbed wire and guarded by British
soldiers. None the less, Berenson solemnly presented his visiting cards
to a bemused tommy, the corners turned down, *comme il faut.* Some
things not even the RAF's bombers could destroy. Berenson was intran-
sigently conservative in his aesthetics. 'Everything they build today is
filthy,' he confided to Spender. Fortunately there remained many old
things in the Eternal City. Out of the experiences of this trip Spender
wrote a slim volume on Botticelli (a painter whom he had long admired),
brought out by Faber in May.

After the trip, in April 1946 Spender went on to Paris to prepare for
UNESCO's first session at the end of the year. Natasha returned to
England to pursue her musical career, to look after Matthew, and keep
things in order in Loudoun Road. The family was reunited in England
in June, to enjoy a last summer in Lavenham. The Great House was now,
at last, de-requisitioned from War Department ownership. Spender,
Natasha and – when he could get away – Humphrey spent part of
summer 1946 there. Returning to Lavenham after five years was a poignant
experience. Humphrey recalls neat piles of woodworm sawdust heaped
under his treasured antique furniture. A wondering Natasha went through
the drawers and wardrobes, where she discovered, among other moth-
balled relics, Inez's 'little coat', about which Spender had written his
poem six years earlier.

The brothers decided to sell their country house. The Stephen Spenders
had no car. The train and taxi journeys were tedious with a child and
nanny in tow. The place had unforgettably painful associations for both
Stephen and Humphrey. But deciding how best to divide the property
led to one of their rare rows. Humphrey was by temperament propri-
etorial ('I have inherited the Jewish aspect of the Schuster character,' he
blandly explains). Stephen always disbelieved in possessions. They ended
up owning you. For this reason he did not, as he might perhaps have
done, buy 15 Loudoun Road – preferring to remain a tenant on long
lease ('I have a horror of "real estate",' he once told his American friend
Reynolds Price). It took a little while to sort things out and for the
brothers to get back on friendly terms. The Spenders would not have a
second house again until they took over Red Brick Cottage at Bruern,
in 1956. Humphrey remarried in 1947, and would live thereafter in rural
Essex, at Maldon.

The Spenders made the most of their last summer at the Great House. It was unusually hot. Matthew was now toddling. There were the usual interesting visitors. Among them was Michel St-Denis, a leading Gaullist and Free French spokesman during the war. He and Stephen talked post-war European politics – a topic in which Spender was becoming increasingly interested. The London literary scene was meanwhile going through one of its uglier spasms. Roy Campbell had launched his MacSpaunday (i.e. MacNeice, Spender, Auden, Day-Lewis) attack with his volume-length verse satire *Talking Bronco*, which came out in May 1946. It contained virulent slanders – particularly against Spender, who was closest to hand and who had – disparagingly – invented the insulting equine title which Campbell now chose to wear as a badge of pride. It added to the insult that the volume carried the imprint of Spender's own publisher, Faber, and – presumably – the imprimatur of Tom Eliot.

Campbell's scurrility was tiresomely predictable: the Auden Gang were self-promoting, sexually degenerate, yellow-bellied cowards who had let *real* men, notably a certain South African, do their fighting for them. Campbell, whose war service (for General Franco and King George) was a matter of record, was furious that MacSpaunday had never been properly denounced for the scrimshankers that (in his drunkenly chauvinistic view of things) they manifestly were. To Spender's rage, he further alleged (libellously) that MacSpaunday had written Communist propaganda during the Spanish Civil War for financial gain.

The quarrel with Campbell flared into warfare in early June. Spender took particular exception to the allegation in *Talking Bronco* that he had gone to Spain in 1936–7, financed by 'red gold' – or, as Campbell ludicrously put it, 'stolen pelf'. Spender wrote a private letter to Campbell, on 2 June. There was, he scathingly said, 'no point in attempting to use the ordinary language of civilized beings with you'. Released from such restraint, he went on to label the South African 'a liar, a gross slanderer, an empty-headed boaster, a coward, a bully, and a Fascist'. He defied Campbell to produce 'any evidence whatever that any of the four writers concerned [MacSpaunday] received a penny in payment from the Spanish Republic'.

Campbell replied, on 11 June. His letter reiterated the insults about MacSpaunday's cowardice and 'stolen pelf'. He offered the interesting information that 'Eliot and Faber had my entire co-operation in eliminating a third of the poems in case they might excite your well known hysterical paranoia.' He denounced Spender as a 'chairborne shock trooper of the knife and fork brigade . . . a guzzling poltroon and a banqueteer'.

Spender then wrote to C. Day-Lewis, who advised consulting 'Louis'. Campbell, like MacNeice, held a position at the BBC. Perhaps, Cecil suggested, 'we should raise such a stink that Campbell [will] be chucked out of the BBC as a Fascist and a calumniator'. He was, however, strongly against going to court, or airing the matter in the press by jointly-signed letters of protest. 'I cannot help feeling,' he added, 'that Tom Eliot is not blameless here.'

Over the first half of 1946 Spender was frantically preparing *European Witness* for press. It was essential that its reportage should come out while it was still news. The book was published, to acclaim, on 21 October. *Vogue* gave $500 for the Berlin and Picasso extracts. Viking gave $500 for the American rights. With subsidiary and foreign earnings, and Hamilton's remittances, the book would net Spender the highest payment of his career (around £2,000, from all sources). It deserved to succeed. In the *New York Times*, Alistair Cooke described it as 'the journal of a mature and compassionate man looking without pride or prejudice on a country that has become one vast monument or tomb of lost freedom'. Hamish Hamilton, reviewing the typescript, said he hoped 'it will be the first of several equally fine "witness" volumes'.

The other great work of 1946 was the collection of verse *Poems of Dedication*, for Faber. It proved somewhat problematic. After *Ruins and Visions*, Faber had advanced £100 for the next volume of verse. But this new collection, impressive as the poems were, was only half the length of its predecessor. The publishers saw it as short measure. Spender, of course, had poems with which he could have bulked out the book. But, as always, he composed the architecture of his collections with great care. He wanted *Poems of Dedication* to be terse. After some grumbling, Faber agreed to accept it as an 'interim book', outside the contract. They advanced a secondary £75 for it. This tiny sum, Eliot said, 'seems to us right'. Poetry was not well paid in 1946.

The late summer would be professionally hectic. Stephen took up work, formally, with UNESCO, in June. Natasha was playing a concerto in Bournemouth on 10 August. For three weeks, from 28 August to 20 September, the couple were in Switzerland, attending the first of the *rencontres internationales de Genève*. The conference was the brainchild of Ernst Ansermet (orchestral conductor and mathematician) and of the philosopher Karl Jaspers. As Spender recalls, the *rencontre* was not without its comic aspect. Sartre's *L'Être et le néant* hung over the conference like a thunderstorm. The event

provided the occasion for the first post-war meeting between the French and German existentialists. Merleau-Ponty, who was an atheist, was leader of the French; Karl Jaspers, a Christian, led the Germans. Jaspers infuriated the French by asking them whether the most prominent French existentialist, Jean-Paul Sartre, would accept the Ten Commandments.

Sartre wasn't there and wouldn't have. But the attendance at Geneva was otherwise star-studded, international and politically ecumenical. Among the *conférenciers* (there were no delegates, as such) were Georg Lukacs, Hannah Arendt, Georges Bernanos (who brought his confessor, Père Bruckberger, with him) and Julien Benda ('a pompous little man'). The amassed intellectual force of the age was directed to cogitation on 'the spirit of Europe'. *Life* magazine sent two photographers and a reporter. No British paper thought the spirit of Europe worthy of coverage.

There were, oddly, no other poets in attendance at Geneva. Some years later Spender composed a lyric tribute to the intellectually and physically elegant Merleau-Ponty, with whom he had been immensely impressed, entitled, 'One More New Botched Beginning':

> I walked with Merleau-Ponty by the lake.
> Upon his face, I saw his intellect
> Energy of the sun-interweaving
> Waves, electric, danced on him. His eyes
> Smiled with their gay logic through
> Black coins flung down from leaves.

The poem was inspired by Sonia Orwell seeing in the Spenders' family album a photograph of Merleau-Ponty (formerly her lover, now dead) taken at the *rencontre*. She asked if she might have it as a memento. Her evident emotion stirred Spender's own memories.

As it happened, Isaiah Berlin was in Geneva in September 1946, not conferencing but visiting a friend at the League of Nations. 'We hadn't seen a lot of him during the war,' Natasha Spender recalls. It was on this trip to Geneva that Natasha heard her first complete performance of *Fidelio*, an opera which (like Beethoven's late quartets) had a religious potency for Stephen and Isaiah. Also present at Geneva, enjoying the music, was the composer Samuel Barber with his current lover, the beautiful and gifted poet Robert Horan (nicknamed 'Kinch'). Spender had not seen the American composer since before the war, although they had kept in touch by letter (Barber had done a musical setting for Spender's poem 'A Stopwatch and an Ordnance Map' in 1942). 'Sam always liked Stephen,' Gian Carlo Menotti (Sam's partner, earlier and later in life) recalled, fifty years later.

Old friendships were revived at Geneva and new friendships formed. After the two weeks of the conference the Spenders resolved to see something of the Alps. They were invited by the Benedictine monk Dominique de Grunne, whom they had met in Geneva, to stay a week in the Bernese Oberland with Baroness Lambert, a close friend of his mother, the Comtesse de Grunne. Dominique was currently tutor to the Belgian royal children, exiled during and immediately after the war with their family in Switzerland. De Grunne (who came across to England at Christmas 1946) and Hansi Lambert would be the Spenders' warm friends over the next fifteen years. Hansi Lambert had been born in 1900, into a devout and aristocratic Austrian Catholic family. She had made a second marriage with Henri Lambert, a senior member of the Belgian branch of the Rothschild banking family. Now widowed, she had three children and had spent the war exiled in America. Rich, cultivated, and again head of the Banque Lambert, she was hostess in the post-war period to a distinguished salon at her house in the Avenue Marnix, in Brussels. Here it was that the ideals of European unity were being forged. Through Lambert the Spenders would meet Paul-Henri Spaak and other leading pro-Europeans; a cause for which Spender would be an early proponent.

On returning from Switzerland, at the end of September Spender was called away to duties in Paris until 24 November. UNESCO had by now moved to its new headquarters in the Avenue Kléber, and was in 'General Conference' (i.e. up and running). Now that he had a salary, Spender was better off financially than he had been for years. But what with house, family and travel his outgoings were considerable. He never mastered the art of putting aside money from his windfall literary earnings for tax.

The level of physical comfort was grindingly low for the British population at this period. Isherwood, visiting in 1947 from sun-drenched Southern California, was astonished, on going to the theatre, to observe that the audience wore their overcoats through the performance. His American eye was appalled by London's grimy streets, unrepaired bomb-sites, and the general dullness, with continuing restrictions on public lighting and advertisement display. There was still clothes rationing, and even the British overcoats were drab or pre-war threadbare.

Money, or the lack of it, was on everyone's mind. In September 1946, Spender (with other writers) was sent a *Horizon* questionnaire, 'The Cost of Letters'. His answers were mischievous and self-revealing. Connolly's blunt first question was: 'How much do you think a writer needs to live on?' Spender replied with equal bluntness:

I should say an unmarried writer needs £500 or £600 a year (free of tax), if he lives in London. A married writer, if he makes his wife cook, needs £700. However, if he has children, if he does not wish his wife to be a domestic slave and if he has any social life, he needs £1000 a year or more.

One should multiply these figures by fifty to get current levels.

Spender's most controversial answer was to Connolly's third question, on *deuxième métier* – what second job should an artist have? He offered in reply the Spenderian version of Joyce's silence, exile and cunning:

For God's sake never be in a position of responsibility and have no ambitions. Do not seek honours and do not refuse them. One should aim at being a rather superior and privileged office clown who attracts no one's envy, and on whom one's colleagues project a few fantasies. One encourages all this by arriving always a little late (but not too late). Prepare for the worst, when the boss shows you his (or his wife's or his son's) poems. Pretend to like them, ask for a testimonial and resign immediately when this happens.

No freelance writer of the twentieth century kept more irons in the fire than Spender. At almost no point in his career, from 1945 until the late 1980s, does one find him with fewer than three or four ongoing professional activities: poet, journalist, reviewer, lecturer, editor – all this with a full domestic life and a bewildering itinerary of overseas travelling. How he contrived, among all the bustle of his life, to write creatively – with the concentration that act requires – was something of a mystery even to him. He reflected on the topic in his journal (9 July 1979):

How can one write with passion, intensity and yet in a dilatory way, with many interruptions, going downstairs then coming up again, taking up the newspaper and reading an editorial, taking a book from the shelf reading someone's poem and passing judgement on it, answering the telephone, turning on the radio, making a cup of tea, getting – how unjustly annoyed – because one's wife or child came in just now and interrupted one, deciding after all one must answer someone's letter before one goes on to anything else, and so on? The only kind of answer I can give is because at the back of one's mind one is aware of a pattern with a blur or blank in it, which is a space that has to be filled in. One is aware also that there are pressures of rhythm, imagery, intensity of feeling around this space, and it is out of the combination or resolution of them that there will be the words.

In mid-October Spender received a letter from Christopher Isherwood. What with the war and separation they had drifted apart. 'This is a shot in the dark,' the American (as he now was) began his letter, 'as the international grapevine whispers that you are in South America.' 'Did you know Heinz is (a) a P. O. W.? (b) married, and the father of a six year old child?' Christopher asked in this letter, harking back to happy pre-war days. He signed off with the salutation: 'My love to Tony Hyndman.'

On receiving Spender's enthusiastically newsy reply (containing much about Natasha and Matthew), and an inscribed copy of *European Witness*, Isherwood wrote to say he found the book 'the best thing you have ever done in prose. It really amounts to an autobiography – all the old Stephen I knew is in it and also a new Stephen who impresses me without in the least scaring or repelling me (is this the effect of being a father??).' It being a bitter December in Britain, Christopher sent a Christmas food parcel to 15 Loudoun Road, largely made up of a huge packet of sugar with the arch motto: 'sweets from the sweet to the sweet'. It arrived, belatedly, in February (nothing worked properly in these years) and was very welcome. These were not times for false pride. Sugar was gold dust in 1946.

Nineteen forty-seven opened hectically for both Spenders. Stephen's UNESCO duties obliged frequent trips to Paris. There he would stay at the Majestic Hotel (now majestically renamed UNESCO House), with the Huxleys at their apartment, or with friends. At some point, when the UNESCO post firmed up, he planned to get something permanent for himself in France. Other than the occasional weekend,

Natasha could seldom make time to come to Paris. As the year opened she was rehearsing for a recital in Manchester in early February. Matthew was at kindergarten. With the war over, there was a round of visitors from abroad. Isherwood announced that he was coming to the UK in the New Year and he would be in London for Spender's birthday on 28 February. It would be his first meeting with Spender's second wife. 'I feel sure I'm going to like her, provided she'll like me!' he wrote nervously. Christopher spent a couple of nights at Loudoun Road in between visiting his family and other friends. In London he had some wild sex with, of all people, Tony Hyndman.

On 15 January, Spender left for Prague and Austria. Out of this trip came a wealth of journalism and, more ruminatively, his deeply felt poem 'Return to Vienna'. Spender wrote and rewrote this work – his most ambitious since 'Elegy for Margaret' – over most of 1947. A meditation, written in nine parts, 'Return to Vienna' is a startlingly eroticized performance, opening with the image of the city (where he lost one of his virginities) as a vagina:

> Feminine Vienna, where the Ring
> – Girdle embossed with Palaces –
> Guarded the City's virginal imperial Cathedral –

(The city's virginal imperial cathedral is named after St Stephen.) Vienna was the city both 'of my loving my first woman' and of the 'Red martyrs', massacred in 1934. Now, thirteen years later, his imagination would exhume the 'Vienna raped within Vienna'. The poem ends with the image of the almond tree which was, for Spender, allegorical of his hope for the post-war world. Elsewhere this almond tree – inspired by that which had serenely defied German bombs in the garden of the Freuds' house at 2 Maresfield Gardens by blooming in spring 1944 – inspired one of his war lyrics:

> In the burned city, I see
> The almond flower, as though
> With great cathedral-fall
> Barbarian rage set free
> The angel of a fresco
> From a cloister wall.

Spender returned from Austria on 6 February. His major poetic effort in 1947 was *Poems of Dedication*, which had just been published by Faber. It was eagerly awaited and despite its exiguity (60 per cent of his usual 'slim volume' length) it received respectful reviews. The *TLS* applauded the poet's 'honest hesitation' and 'spiritual sincerity'. The *Listener's* reviewer observed, astutely, that 'the three poems that make up the section "Seascape and Landscape" rank among the best work of their author . . . this is Mr Spender at his least ambitious, and there is nothing else so perfect in the whole collection'. In the *New Statesman* G. W. Stonier declared Spender 'the most lyrical and most uncertain poet of his generation'. His best poems achieve 'a curious intimacy, as if feeling one's way, produced by no other writer'.

The first section of *Poems of Dedication* is headed by 'Elegy for Margaret' – to Lolly, that is, who had died on Christmas Day, 1945. Spender evidently completed the poem in the full flow of his grief. The first section also includes two pieces from *Ruins and Visions* alluding (bitterly) to Inez's flight. One of the poems ('Dearest and nearest brother', addressed to the loyal Humphrey) had been written as long ago as 1939, during the turmoil of the break-up of his marriage with Inez. As Spender notes, the poems in this section of the volume are influenced by Rilke's *Duino Elegies*, which he had been translating (in unhappy collaboration with Leishman) in 1939.

The second section is dedicated 'To Natasha' and is constructed around the themes 'Love, Birth, and Absence'. It comprises a narrative of the poet's relationship with his second wife. The third section, dedicated to C. Day-Lewis, reprints the 1943 (even slimmer) volume, *Spiritual Explorations*. The fourth section is dedicated to his wartime friend and ally, Edith Sitwell. It contains the elegy, dedicated to Michael, 'Seascape', with its imagery of the dying butterfly.

Spring butterflies were late arrivals in 1947. In February Britain experienced a cold snap of Siberian severity which lasted until well into April. There were power cuts, frozen pipes, fuel shortages, massive industrial shut-downs, and universal misery across the land. Eliot fell ill with bronchitis. His years of chain-smoking would eventually kill him. None the less at this period he and Spender exchanged matching anacreontics, spontaneously spun off, on the joys of nicotine.

Spender's verse, 'With a Transparent Cigarette Case', accompanied a gift and was addressed with mock humility 'To the Master of Russell Square' (where the Faber office then was):

> When those eagle eyes, which look
> Through human flesh as through a book,
> Swivel an instant from the page
> To ignite the luminous image
> With the match that lights his smoke –
> Then let the case be transparent
> And let the cigarettes, apparent
> To his X-ray vision, lie
> As clear as rhyme and image to his eye.
> (To T.S.E. from S.S.)

By return of post the Master of Russell Square sent a similarly complimentary verse '*à l'Organisateur Des Nations Unies Pour l'Education, la Science, et la Culture*' (as John Hayward mischievously divulged, he stayed up 'all night' composing it):

> The sudden unexpected gift
> Is more precious in the eyes
> Than the ordinary prize
> Of slow approach or movement swift.
> While the cigarette is whiffed
> And the tapping finger plies
> Here upon the table lies
> The fair transparency. I lift
> The eyelids of the aging owl
> At twenty minutes to eleven
> Wednesday evening (summer time)
> To salute the younger fowl
> With this feeble halting rhyme
> The kind, the Admirable Stephen
> (To S.S. from T.S.E.)
> August 20th and 21st, 1946

Eliot's verse was framed, and stood for the next thirty years on the chimneypiece at Loudoun Road. Many of the country's most distinguished smokers regarded it with puffing complacency over the decades until, in the 1990s, tobacco became a proscribed substance even in the Spenders' house.

Eliot would be ill, on and off, for the whole of the year. The Spenders paid several visits to his bedside. Natasha too fell ill in this most inclement of winters. Spender informed Julian Huxley, on 28 February, that his wife 'has had a haemorrhage of her duodenal ulcer . . . I am anxious about her.' Her condition meant that he must put off his planned move to Paris, on 10 March, to take up full-time UNESCO duties, 'as I want to look after Natasha'. Her illness was perhaps stress-related. Was *he*, Spender asked Auden, somehow the cause? It worried him.

On 12 March Spender wrote again to Julian Huxley to report that

Natasha is much better. We are off to Belgium on March 24th and the Baronne Lambert (if you will forgive me!) has very kindly lent us her chalet in Gstaad where I hope Natasha will get completely well. I shall come to Paris from April 1st, go on to Brussels, and join Natasha, Matthew and the nurse a week later on April 8th.

For the newly Francophile Spender, the arrangement with UNESCO was a happy one in that it allowed him to travel at a period of stringent exchange control for Europeans. He had always craved movement across borders to sustain his intellectual and literary life. As he put it, 'foreign travel was poetry, England prose'. The British intelligentsia were currently forced to stay prosaically at home by the £10 annual limit. Sterling, the Labour government determined, must be defended: if necessary by quarantining the whole British nation in their island. You could blow your tenner on a single meal in Paris.

In other ways the UNESCO experience was fraught, unhappy and (as it turned out) short: both for Spender and for his patron Huxley. Institutional life had never been congenial to either of them. Spender describes his brief career as a Parisian *fonctionnaire* in the *Journals*:

When UNESCO moved to Paris I went to live there, but resigned when the General Assembly failed to re-elect Julian Huxley as a result of his lack of support by the American delegation, already influenced by McCarthyism. Julian was suspected of being 'soft on commies' employed in the secretariat of UNESCO.

Even if the UNESCO berth had been more comfortable, it would not have suited him. Spender was appalled by the apparatchiks and bigwigs he met in Paris and on his official trips round post-war Europe. 'When I met M. Rákosi, the Communist Deputy Prime Minister of Hungary,' he recalls, 'almost the first remark he made to me was that the British Labour Government was "Fascist". When I asked him what he meant by this, he said: "For two reasons. Firstly, they have not filled the British Army with Socialist generals. Secondly, they have not taken over Scotland Yard."'

Spender drifted away from the organization in early 1947. A project he proposed for an anthology of literary writing was, evidently, denied funding. Huxley also suggested (somewhat hurtfully) in early 1947 that he 'thought the Section on Letters could be dispensed with'. There survive two letters from Spender to Huxley, dated 28 February and 12 March [1947] in which he says that the news from the organization is 'very depressing' and protests strongly. Julian Huxley strenuously denied any intention to 'wipe out' literature. But at this point, around March 1947, Spender cut his links with the organization, although he and Julian would remain personal friends for another twenty-five years. His interests were, at this stage, turning towards American rather than European employment.

Over Easter, the Spenders took another trip through Italy. It helped that Hamish Hamilton had just come through with £300 (in addition to the £200 advance) for *European Witness*. His author, the publisher recalled, 'was in a state of ecstatic gratitude and said he had never received such a large cheque on any of his books before'. Hamilton's big cheque would not pay for everything. Stephen was again singing for their supper, lecturing as they went (mainly, as usual, on British modernism). In late April their paths crossed with those of Dylan and Caitlin Thomas in Florence. The two poets had known each other professionally for a decade. As early as February 1934 Spender had offered appreciative comment in print about the young and then entirely obscure Welsh poet. Thomas – a world-class cadger – promptly wrote imploringly from Swansea. He was buried, he unpatriotically complained, 'in this worst of provincial towns . . . so utterly removed from any intellectual life at all'. Spender, good-natured as ever to fellow-poets in distress, did indeed help with discerning reviews, by talking Dylan Thomas up, and in June 1940 by raising a subscription with Herbert Read and Henry Moore. 'Spender raised more lovely, important money than I'd dared to hope,' Thomas gleefully told Hugh Walpole. Eliot declined to contribute on the sensible grounds that the Welshman would blow anything he got on drink, as he did any cash that came his way.

Dylan Thomas was extravagantly polite to Spender to his face, and

Puckishly mischievous behind his patron's back (among his party tricks was a hilarious burlesque of the 'Pylon' poem). In March 1947 Thomas was awarded a Society of Authors Travelling Scholarship of £150. Edith Sitwell was insistent her protégé must go to Italy, rather than America. 'We don't want what happened to Swinburne to happen to him,' she argued. Bibulous America, Dame Edith thought, was not a wise choice for a poet with 'a certain habit'.

Dylan's certain habit was not to be denied. When the Spenders came across him in late April he and Caitlin were in the process of drinking Tuscany dry on the Society of Authors' largesse. When sober, Thomas had significant differences of poetic opinion with Spender. On 29 May 1947 he wrote to John Davenport:

I met Spender [in Florence] a few weeks ago. It was very sad. He is on a lecture tour. It is very sad. He is bringing the European intellectuals together. It is impossible. He said, in a lecture I saw reported: 'All poets speak the same language.' It is a bloody lie: who talks Spender?

In midsummer, the family was back in England. Spender's ties with UNESCO were by now effectively severed. In front of him was a newer world than Paris or Geneva. Harold Taylor, the president of Sarah Lawrence College, invited Spender to come as a visiting professor for a year, 1947–8. Thirty-two years old, Anglophile and alarmingly boyish, Taylor had visited the UK over summer 1946. He had been President of SLC since 1945. Both Stephen and Natasha took to him at first sight. She remembers him as 'a very bright, very clever, curly-haired, clarinet-playing former philosophy student. He was the youngest university president in America.'

Taylor was Canadian by origin and had an English wife, Muriel. The poet Randall Jarrell (a part-time teacher at Sarah Lawrence at the same period as Spender) had little time for 'the boy president', as he scathingly called him. In his letters and in the campus satire, *Pictures from an Institution*, which began appearing serially in 1952, Jarrell offers a merciless depiction of 'Benton College' and of 'Dwight Bennington' – 'an assistant professor metamorphosed into a president'.

Sarah Lawrence was itself a vigorously young institution, if not quite as juvenile as its boy-president. It had been founded in 1928, when businessman William Van Duzer Lawrence converted his Bronxville estate in Westchester County into a Liberal Arts College for genteel

young New York ladies, to commemorate his recently dead (and femi-
nist-inclined) wife. Taylor was the college's third president. SLC was
still largely segregated. In 1946, however, the college patriotically
admitted forty-four veterans, under the GI Bill. These lucky ex-soldiers
were surrounded by 352 of America's most nubile and affluent young
women.

Satirized as he might be, under Harold Taylor's dynamic leadership
Sarah Lawrence had gathered a 'starry faculty', as Spender recalls,

> including Mary McCarthy, novelist, Robert Fitzgerald, poet and translator, Horace
> Gregory, poet, Joseph Campbell, anthropologist and author of books on
> mythology, Rudolf Arnheim, psychologist of art, Robert and Helen Lynd, soci-
> ologists and co-authors of the famous study *Middletown*, Mark Slonim, Russian
> historian, and Randall Jarrell, poet and critic.

If Spender agreed to join Sarah Lawrence's constellation he would
need to leave England in August, as the American academic year
commenced in early September. It was inconvenient for Natasha to
accompany him. She had, by now, done three recitals and had bookings
with the BBC through August. Most importantly, she was engaged as
soloist for a promenade concert, on 13 September, Malcolm Sargent
conducting. It would be the first concert in the world ever to be tele-
vised. It was, as Spender told Harold Taylor, 'a tremendous thing for her'.

Spender accepted Taylor's offer in November. It was approved by the
SLC faculty later in the month. Terms were agreed in early December
– 'Seventy Five Hundred Dollars for Ten Months beginning September
23, 1947'. It was agreed that Stephen would go ahead, travelling light.
Natasha would follow later in the autumn with child, nanny and the
bulk of the family luggage.

Some of Spender's oldest friends were living and working in America:
Auden and Sam Barber in New York, Muriel (Gardiner) Buttinger in
New Jersey, working at the state hospital for the insane, Aldous Huxley
and Isherwood in Hollywood. Spender liked American academics, and
thrived in their company. UNESCO and its commitments were now
behind him. Matthew was two and a half, and his education was not a
factor. There were, however, problems. The sale of Lavenham had not
yet been settled. House-sitters would have to be found for Loudoun
Road. Most vexingly, from the point of view of Natasha's career, a year
away from London was 'unfortunate' (her word). She would necessarily

miss any follow-up engagements from her solo appearance on the final night of the Proms.

There might, to cap it all, be difficulties with American immigration authorities. Spender had been, albeit momentarily, a 'premature anti-fascist', with a top billing on the front page of the *Daily Worker* prominent, presumably, in his FBI file. That file, which has innumerable blacked-out pages, records that as early as 1944 a 'reliable anonymous source' in London had (mis)identified him as a practising communist. For the next fifteen years whenever he entered America (as he frequently did) he would be 'looked over' by the INS and, after the paranoia of the late 1940s, the FBI would be informed of his arrival. Spender entered America in 1947 'on the quota', as it was called (that is, the UK entitlement for immigration and permanent residence), because he was employed for the whole year. It is likely that he was conscious that he might stay in the US for longer than a year – at Harold Taylor's instigation.

Edith Sitwell reacted with her usual warmth and operatic exaggeration to the news of her dearest friends' departure from British shores. It was 'very wretched'. None the less, 'I try to comfort myself by thinking and saying to myself what wonderful work you will be doing for poetry out there.' She evidently saw New York as scarcely less distant than the moon. But she was encouraged by Spender's example (and by the lecturing fees which a famous but impecunious British poet might earn) to follow him 'out there' herself, in December 1948 and again in December 1949.

'Come early,' Harold Taylor demanded, 'so I can take you round America a bit.' Going a bit early would also enable Spender to touch base with Frank Taylor (no relative of Harold's), a publisher who was acting as his unofficial agent and could set up lecturing engagements. After a flying visit to Paris, to wind up his business there, Spender left England, first class, on the *Queen Mary*, on 20 August. On the boat were Lillian Hellman and John Dos Passos – currently moving away from Socialism as fast as he could (Hellman was still as faithful to Joseph Stalin as to her partner Dashiell Hammett). Harold Taylor met his newly appointed poet-professor as he disembarked at the quayside and saw him through customs. Harold then 'spent the morning showing me New York, which is absolutely staggering', Stephen told Natasha, 'quite as wonderful in its way as London, Florence and Paris'. High on this metropolitan thrill, he had lunch with Harold, 'then Frank [Taylor] took me to the house he has on the Atlantic with his family and we bathed in the sea. It was really a marvellous first day.' Spender was 'very tickled' at having bought himself 'a cotton suit with salmon pink stripes'. He smoked a pipe at this period and quite looked the part of the American academic. *Vogue* welcomed him to America as the most voguish of poets: 'He is 38 years old and is a charmer with deep set, very blue eyes. Probably he will wear his shirt open at the neck, just the way Shelley and Byron did.'

The boy president kept up the hospitable pressure by taking Spender off on a five-day tour from 25 August until 2 September. 'Taylor his dog and I are motoring all over New England,' Spender told Natasha, with the wide-eyed enthusiasm of the new visitor to God's Own Country:

It is exactly the introduction to Sarah Lawrence that I had dreamed of as the nicest possible. I am amazed by the beauty of the architecture. Every town and village here for hundreds of miles is in the lovely simplest colonial style, set in streets which have lawns on either side. It really is a great surprise.

The president and his new recruit spent two idyllic days on the side of a lake by the Green Mountains, fishing for bass, and living the pioneer life. Ever since his childhood holidays at Salcombe, Spender had enjoyed the ruminative pleasures of angling. 'Yesterday,' he told Natasha Spender on 30 September, 'we caught four fish and made a bonfire and cooked them and ate them with our fingers.'

Spender and Taylor arrived from their motor tour in time for the new semester at Sarah Lawrence on 1 September. Spender had not yet contrived to meet up with Auden, who was away in his summer home in Ischia, near Naples. Later in the month there was, at last, a grand reunion of 'We three' – Wystan, Christopher and Stephen – in New York. It had been ten years since they were all together. As a snapshot of mid-September records, they spent some time in Auden's shack on Fire Island, replaying their Ruegen roles of fifteen years before.

Christopher was 'just as nice as he was in London', Stephen informed Natasha. And Wystan was just as endearingly grumpy. An overnight stay with Auden at his Cornelia Street apartment was the occasion of an anecdote, ruefully recollected in *World within World*. Stephen woke early and clumsily yanked down the curtains trying to open them, eliciting Auden's furious and wholly typical reproof, 'idiot! . . . there is no daylight in New York.' Wystan was long past *his* wide-eyed enthusiasm for the place. And his theory about curtains was you never drew them 'because you only have to close them again at night'. Stephen, writing to Connolly, declared himself amazed at the 'appalling squalor' of Wystan's domestic arrangements. Even more amazed that 'he can live like that and not *notice*'. Wystan, preoccupied with theology, ignored the horrible smells and lived, apparently, on a diet of Lifesaver mints (at least his breath should not smell).

World within World was forming in Spender's mind as his next major work. He had made a tentative agreement with Hamish Hamilton for an autobiography of 120,000 words on 6 August 1947; to be delivered by 31 December 1948. This work, he told Hamilton, would explore 'the dark and ambiguous experiences which are the night side of my day'. He also projected an 'American Witness' volume to Hamilton, who advanced £400 for the two books. Taylor was, he told Natasha on 29 August, 'sympathetic about everything . . . I've told him about "Autobiography and Truth"' (this was the working title for what became *World within World*; another provisional title was 'My Life and Truth' – which sounded rather too Thurberesque). In fact, Harold was 'really keen'. His own ambition, he had confided to Spender, 'is not to be a college president but a writer and therefore he understands our situation very well . . . I now think of him as one of our friends and not a college president.' 'Generally America means money,' Spender candidly told his new friend. But money meant time off from weekly deadlines for creative writing.

His urge to write poetry was somewhat dampened by his September 1947 annual royalty cheque from Faber (for four in-print volumes of verse). Seven shillings and three pence. One dollar, precisely. More cheerfully, A. D. Peters secured £250 for the film rights of his short story, 'The Fool and the Princess' (Merton Park Studios eventually produced a rather inferior movie; Spender's fireman comrade William Sansom did the script). This £250 was urgently needed by Natasha, as she made arrangements to travel with the family.

On 1 September Spender wrote to his wife:

I've now been in America for six days. I've spent four of them going all over New England and my whole physical condition is altered by an open air life with quantities of sunbathing and so on (not to mention clams and ice cream). I feel very sad you are not here to see me.

The couple were longing for another baby at this time, and hoped one might be conceived in America. By the early weeks of the semester,

Spender's impressions had settled down from his initial excitement into something more indulgently amused and occasionally even critical. 'I don't think America will surprise you tremendously,' he told Natasha:

the life is extremely pleasant and easy but everything we hate is very much in evidence . . . So far the one or two parties I have been to have been very forbidding with silent young men who chew pipes and look superior and negative and young women with long straight hair who look rather chic and forbidding. They talk mainly about their own literary gossip but you are expected to interrupt and indulge in a long monologue to which they all listen respectfully. It is all terribly unlike France and also I feel more embarrassingly foreign in America than anywhere I have been. I am frightfully conscious of my accent much more conscious that is of my English English than I ever am of my English French.

In a few days, he wistfully added, 'we shall be *en famille* which will be nice'.

Spender had never taught at a university before. The beginning of the academic year at Sarah Lawrence, on 29 September, he found 'quite a strain . . . the girls are amazingly ignorant, most of them, and everyone is embarrassingly eager to please'. Himself included. He gave what he called his 'coming out lecture' (i.e. inaugural) on 'Europe'. It was an ordeal. None the less, he was 'in the midst of writing as I haven't been for twenty years'. He had, by the end of September, four sections of the twelve-section *Return to Vienna* worked into final shape. Frank Taylor arranged a publisher's party for him in New York, on 6 October.

Natasha arrived in America in early October by the *New Amsterdam*. It was a rough crossing, and the voyage was made difficult by the nanny's prostrating sea-sickness. Natasha was obliged to look after her as well as Matthew. She was met at the quay in New York by Stephen and Frank Taylor. They had found it difficult to rent a house in Bronxville. Stephen may have added to the difficulty. He was not sure that he wanted to get sucked too deeply into college life. He disapproved of Bronxville's being 'restricted' (closed to Jewish residents). Something off campus might suit them better.

The house which Harold Taylor eventually found them was on the edge of the golf course in Scarsdale, two stops up the railway line, and the snobbiest town in the Westchester County area: 8 Stratford Road was early colonial, spacious (three bedrooms) and 'comfortably but not elaborately furnished'. It was not, at $225 a month, cheap. It was a mile away from the railway, which made connection with New York easy.

Connection with Bronxville was slightly less easy. The college arranged a chauffeur-driven car three days a week for Spender, who could not drive at this point. Scarsdale was a pleasantly rural environment for little Matthew (after the first snow falls, in November, Spender took his son tobogganning, something both of them loved). There was a piano, no close neighbours to disturb. A cleaning woman came once a week.

For Spender Sarah Lawrence was less an opportunity to teach in America than to be in America. Particularly its cultural centre, New York. Scarsdale was close enough to Manhattan (three-quarters of an hour by train) to meet up with Auden and pre-war American friends like Lincoln Kirstein and *their* friends. In his day-to-day teaching activities, Spender discovered himself to be more than competent. In a confidential report to the Rockefeller Foundation, on 13 February, Taylor confirmed that students reported 'great enthusiasm for Spender's philosophy and his poetry'. Formally unqualified though he was (the only letters after his name were the honorary degree from Montpellier), Spender could confidently accept offers from other top-ranked American institutions, in the knowledge that he could now hold his own in the classroom.

During the academic breaks the Spenders journeyed as far afield as Washington DC, where in Easter 1948 they stayed at the British Embassy with their friend the Ambassador, Lord Inverchapel. They also knew Nicko Henderson, then second secretary, a close friend of their London friend Hugh Gaitskell (Henderson would later himself become Ambassador to America). Names well known to Stephen for their poetry and criticism – Cleanth Brooks, Robert Penn Warren ('charming southerners'), Archibald MacLeish ('rather pompous') – became acquaintances over these months. There were also other English visitors, notably Edith Sitwell, who crossed the Atlantic in grand state in November 1948. She chose to lecture on 'Modern English Poetry'. Spender's stand-by lecture was 'Modernism in English Writing'. Auden figured high in both their accounts of current British verse.

There were other and newer poets than Miss Sitwell and Wystan for Spender to meet. Robert Lowell, for example, came to read at Sarah Lawrence while Spender was in residence. Lowell was currently the Consultant at the Library of Congress (a post Spender himself would occupy, fifteen years later). Randall Jarrell performed the introduction.

Spender liked both men's poetry, and wrote appreciatively of them for English readers. Spender also saw a lot of the '*Partisan Review* crowd' in New York. He had been writing for the journal, from England, since their serialization of *September Journal*, in 1940.

His links with this congenial set of New York intellectuals were strengthened when Mary McCarthy joined him on the faculty at Sarah Lawrence. McCarthy was a regular contributor to *Partisan Review* and a former lover of its editor, Philip Rahv. She came to teach at Sarah Lawrence (desperately needing the stipend) for the spring semester of 1948. Being a woman, and American, she was paid significantly less than Spender – $200 a month, as against his $750. She didn't like the work much, 'because the students were so poor'. It was a characteristically sharp judgement. Mary McCarthy got her money's worth by skewering the college, its dumb students, and the luckless Harold Taylor in her 1954 campus novel, *The Groves of Academe*.

Sarah Lawrence was also close enough for the Spenders to stay weekends with the Buttingers at Pennington (near Princeton) or in their New York apartment. The post-war friendship with Muriel was to be important both for Spender and for Natasha. More immediately important for her, as a musician, was the couple's friendship with the pianist Artur Schnabel in New York. The maestro (who had known Stephen since his Berlin days) 'adopted' Natasha as his 'first (musical) granddaughter', as it pleased him to fancy – she having been taught by his pupil Curzon.

There were less formal musical occasions with the composer Samuel Barber, only a few stations up the line at his sprawling house, Capricorn, in Mount Kisco, where the English couple spent Christmas 1947. Through Barber, the Spenders met the composers Gian Carlo Menotti (co-owner of Capricorn) and Leonard Bernstein, all three of whom were rising in the American musical world. Through Bernstein they were introduced to Tanglewood, the music academy in Massachusetts frequented by composers such as Aaron Copland and Serge Koussevitsky (the originator of the Tanglewood Festival), and home of the Boston Symphony Orchestra during the hot months of summer. It was, Natasha Spender discovered, an 'amazingly energetic musical ambience'.

Spender got on amicably with his faculty colleagues – notably Mary McCarthy. The friendship led to the famous Christmas party which in turn led to one of the more bitter feuds in modern American literary history. In December 1947 Spender asked his Sarah Lawrence class who they would like to have come and talk to them, as an end of term treat. Hellman and McCarthy, the young women replied. These were the two literary heroines of the day. Presuming on their shipboard friendship last August, Spender duly arranged for the author of *The Little Foxes* to come – as guest of honour.

It was easier to arrange for McCarthy to be present at the same party, since she was coming to teach in the New Year. 'We did not know there had been a tremendous *froideur* between the two ladies,' Natasha Spender recalls. As the party got under way, both women sat in the centre of a circle of student admirers on separate sides of the room. At first Hellman mistook her rival (whom she could not see clearly) to be 'a younger faculty person of no importance'. On her part, McCarthy could both see and hear Hellman and caught her 'red-handed in a brainwashing job' – blackguarding her erstwhile shipmate, Dos Passos. The inevitable chill fell on the company, rather blighting the Spender party (it was not, as sometimes reported, a blazing row – but bitter none the less). Hellman was convinced for the whole of her life that the whole thing had been elaborately set up by Spender and McCarthy to humiliate and 'red-bait me'.

On 25 April, Spender published an influential article in the *New York Times*, 'We *Can* Win the Battle for the Mind of Europe'. In it he argued that Communism did not have all the best intellectual and ideological tunes. It was the first shot in what was to be a long campaign to establish new (and distinctively European) liberal values as a middle way between the opposed ideologies of America and the USSR. There was, he believed, a *via media*, but 'what Europe needs today, almost as much as economic aid, is a reaffirmation of the idea of the West, not as politics and strategy, but as civilization'.

As the academic year drew to a close, Spender found himself increasingly weary with classroom duties. 'Outside teaching spoiled rich progressive girls and lecturing and writing,' he told Connolly in March, 'I have scarcely no existence.' America too (at least the American campus) had lost some of its charm. It was, he told Cyril, 'just a large commercial hotel full of commercial companies, with lavatories down behind where one can sit occasionally and write poetry'. Even Wystan, he thought, was incapable of filling a whole, vacuous, continent. It was, however, overflowing with the good things his friend lusted after. He sent Cyril regular parcels of butter and other luxuries (necessaries, as Connolly would have seen them) denied a rationed Britain.

Classes ended at Sarah Lawrence in June 1948. Despite his moans to Connolly, it had been a stimulating and rewarding experience. Spender wrote a parental sonnet on leaving Scarsdale, 'Empty House':

> Then, when the child was gone,
> I was alone
> In the house, suddenly grown huge.

There remained one formal piece of business to complete his first year as a professor. In early June Harvard awarded him an honorary Phi Beta Kappa. The university asked for a poem, and Spender wrote to Eliot, on 8 June, saying that he had written one 'which is also in honour of your birthday'. The poem was 'Speaking to the Dead in the Language of the Dead' – not, as his friends later pointed out, an entirely happy choice of title.

'We are just off for three weeks to the West Coast,' he jauntily informed Eliot, adding dutifully, 'I shall have a new volume of poems for Faber's in September' (in fact, *The Edge of Being* would be a year delayed beyond then). Now free agents, the Spenders made their planned trip west. Matthew was meanwhile looked after by Muriel Buttinger and his nanny – in the 1940s cross-continental travel still had something of pioneer hardness about it and was not for very young children (or encumbered adults).

The trip would be exhausting and exhilarating. In three weeks they (sometimes Stephen by himself) covered Illinois, Indiana, Montana, Minnesota, Oregon and California – all this long before the rise of mass tourism had made such itineraries common and convenient. 'Stephen worked our passage like a troubadour,' Natasha recalls, giving readings and lecturing all the way (principally on 'Modern Poetry in Modern America'). Harold Taylor had arranged for them to stay, *en route*, with congenial Sarah Lawrence alumni. They managed to visit the National Glacier Park, the Grand Canyon ('a little bit of a honeymoon'), and Big Sur, where they met Henry Miller (the two writers, Spender noted, sniffed around each other like wary dogs). In Los Angeles, Christopher Isherwood gave them a tour of Hollywood Babylon.

Their grand American tour terminated in New Mexico. Here they were the guests of Frieda Lawrence, to whom they had an introduction from Auden, at Taos. Frieda had invited them to lunch at her house on the outskirts of Taos, at El Prado. She met her English visitors at the gate with the welcome, 'Isn't it *vonderful*! Lady Chatterley has just been translated into Hindustani.' As she cooked their food (omelettes) they were overwhelmed by her 'gusto' and good nature. She later showed them some of the novelist's manuscripts and his paintings which, friendly as he was disposed to be, Stephen could never honestly admire.

While they were at Taos, Stephen took the two-hour trip up the mountain road to the Kiowa (now the 'Lawrence') ranch at San Cristobal, 7,000 feet above sea level. Also in residence at Taos were the Hon. Dorothy Brett – another living connection with D. H. Lawrence – and Mabel Dodge Luhan, heiress to the Dodge fortune; she it was who had given the ranch to the Lawrences. The three women were still competing among themselves as to which was the great author's favourite. Spender was amused that when she had made a particularly effective case for herself Brett promptly removed her hearing aid, so as not to hear her rivals' claims. On his return to England Spender would consult Lawrence's disciple, Samuel Koteliansky, now a neighbour in St John's Wood. 'Kot' confirmed that:

Lawrence took Brett with him to New Mexico in order to protect himself from Frieda: and that his relations with women were an elaborate defence system in which one was being used to neutralize the other. Until finally at Taos, he left a kind of self-perpetuating system of women loving him and hating one another, and revolving round his memory, in a mind hell of their making, like Sartre's *Huis Clos*.

Hell as it might have been for Lawrence's harem, the Spenders' stay at Taos was a huge success. Frieda's warmth was overwhelming. Lawrence's shrine was a holy place for Stephen. It was also, he thought, a place in which he could find peace to write. If nothing else, it was one of the few places in North America where he would not be required to lecture on Modernism and Modern Poetry. At a party, on their second day, Natasha confided to their new friend that she was worried about Stephen getting on with 'Autobiography and Truth' without her there. Frieda, who found Stephen engagingly like Lawrence, promptly invited him back later in the summer to work on his grand project. It was arranged that he would stay on for three sabbatical months, at one of the three rugged cabins at the ranch.

Natasha, eager to get back to her career in London, left Taos before Stephen. On 29 July she flew back to England from New York, having put Matthew, Nanny and the heavy luggage on a homeward-bound liner. Stephen, who had seen his family off on their way to England, had kept a room in Bronxville but used his vacation time to see something of rural New England in summer. He went to Vermont, where he stayed with the publisher Claude Fredericks. Then he moved on to the Tanglewood Music Centre, in the Berkshires, where New York's musicians and composers had gathered to escape the city's blistering heat. Spender was, by now, very friendly with Leonard Bernstein. The composer and conductor had decided he also wanted somewhere utterly quiet to work on a great project, the ballet adaptation of Auden's *Age of Anxiety*. Bernstein, who would, ten years later, achieve superstar celebrity with *West Side Story*, liked Spender, whom he nicknamed 'LP' (Lyric Poet), immensely.

It had been a costly few weeks and Spender was short of ready money. Bernstein had a new Buick saloon. He suggested to Spender that they club together and drive to Taos, with Lenny's seventeen-year-old brother, Burtie. The three of them could then get their heads down and do their respective creative work in the New Mexico wilderness. Spender was not at all keen. 'I don't want you to come Lenny,' he protested, 'if you're there working *I* won't do any work.' On the other hand, the prospect of an overland trip was an overwhelming inducement – apart from anything else, it would be a great adventure.

The unlikely trio duly hit the pioneer trail in mid-August. Years later, Burtie wrote up the episode in a hilarious article for the *New Yorker*. The pilgrimage was immortalized by his snapshot of Spender, serenely sitting by the roadside thinking about his poems while the handier Bernsteins, in their American can-do way, wrestled with the inevitable flat tyres. There were four blowouts, Spender later recalled. Doubtless they inspired four poems.

For the Bernsteins, it was better to travel to New Mexico than to arrive. They left after a week at the ranch, finding the solitude, at the end of its long dirt road, intolerable. 'Which Stephen knew would happen,' as Natasha recalls. For Spender, once the Bernsteins had motored back to civilization, the interlude at the Rancho San Cristobal would be blissful, writing under the shade of the 'Lawrence pine' (immortalized by a later resident, Georgia O'Keefe), fifty yards from where Lawrence's ashes were destined to rest. Crusoe solitude was exactly what he needed. Every so often a basket of food or can of soup would be delivered (there were by the time he left 'billions' of old cans in his shack). Ten years later, on Roy Plomley's *Desert Island Discs* (appropriately enough), he recalled these six weeks at the shack as the only time in his life that he had truly experienced loneliness (a condition he normally abhorred). During these lonely weeks he produced a first draft of what would become *World within World*.

On his eventual return down the hill to Taos, Spender took over the 'boys' house' as Frieda Lawrence called it. These 'two boys' were William Goyen and Walter Berns (both of them in their unboyish mid-thirties). Goyen, who was gay, and Berns, who was straight, had formed their friendship in the US Navy. On being demobilized in 1945 they had worked for a while as waiters or whatever casual work they could pick up. Goyen, who had writing ambitions, was following the classic American author's hobo route. Berns — more studious by temperament — would become an academic social scientist. They had hit it off with Frieda Lawrence, who gave them free run of her house and land.

Over the years 1945–7, the boys had built for themselves an adobe shack next to Brett's house. In between building their place the young men ranged as far afield as Dallas picking up casual work — teaching or labouring. When Stephen moved into their house in September 1948, they were working at Reed College in Portland. Stephen took to the boys immensely. 'We are a perfect mutual admiration society,' he told Dorothy Brett, 'like I assume the three Graces to have been.' He saw in Goyen the makings of a good writer. The young Texan was, with infinite pains, composing his first novel, *The House of Breath*. He showed the work-in-progress to Spender, who gave advice and practical help. By early June, Spender was describing Goyen to Frieda as 'my best friend in America, one of the most wonderful and extraordinary people I know'. Spender arranged for his friends at Random House to look at the work-in-progress manuscript of *The House of Breath*, securing the young author a $250 advance in the process.

To introduce his protégé to the benefits of a literary community, Spender invited him to come and stay in London with him at some future point. 'It was a wonderful thing that he did,' Goyen later recalled: 'the stipulation was that I would bring a girl who had come into my life with me.' This was Dorothy Robinson, to whom Goyen was briefly, and pointlessly, engaged. An art student, she was keen to come to Europe and study in Paris. Spender put himself out to get Goyen's patrons (Mabel Dodge, notably) to come through with the cash that would enable Bill to travel.

Over autumn weeks of 1948, from September to October, Spender, living almost in a state of nature, had delivered the first draft of *World within World*. He wrote and rewrote, searching for what he called 'the translucent style'. He published five sections of it under the title 'Life in Literature' in *Partisan Review*, from November 1948 to September 1949. They deal principally with his Oxford encounter with Auden (who demanded some changes), his Berlin apprenticeship, and pre-war Bloomsbury. He dropped a planned section on his recent American experiences. A few other sections were tried out in other American journals.

Alongside his memoir he was also composing another autobiographical piece, his chapter for the volume which would eventually be called *The God that Failed* – provisionally entitled, in 1948, 'Lost Illusions'. It, too, centred on his brief encounter with Communism, in the 1930s ('my commie essay', Spender liked to call it). Here the translucent style proved more elusive. He wrote despairingly to Hamish Hamilton in early September to report, 'I have written this essay five times.'

In early October Spender took his farewells from Taos. With a virginal first draft of 'Autobiography and Truth' stowed in his briefcase, Stephen first flew north to see Goyen and Berns, in Portland, Oregon. 'Stephen has arrived,' Goyen wrote, 'and we are terribly happy with him. It is a sort of divine gift.' After his solitary confinement, Spender was evidently as happy on his part to see his American friends. He sat on their verandah, composing poetry.

It was a short remission. His next port of call was further down the coast at Redlands, in Southern California. Here he would teach a week for an urgently needed $250. It was hard earned. Redlands, he told Brett, is 'oh, so *dull*!' The university was even duller. And puritanical. At Redlands, Spender told Harold Taylor, 'no one is allowed to smoke on the campus and if a Faculty member drinks a glass of anything, he then spends half a day eating peppermints'. It was not really a joking matter. 'My time is systematically being wasted and I lie awake at night thinking about it,' he forlornly told Brett.

Spender travelled back by train to the East Coast at the end of October. He wrote a high-spirited letter to Dorothy Brett, in his private compartment (purchased at an extra cost of $15), as western America flashed by his window:

Here I am on the this train steaming away from you all, and feeling in a rather divided and torn state of mind, much as I wish to be home. I have taken a 'roomette' in the train in order that I may work and be quite alone, as I feel I want time to think things over, and as I have work to do, as always . . . This has certainly been a bad summer financially and I still will only scrape through, it seems . . . I am so fond of the boys that I find it quite hard to leave them. They lead a life which I admire and respect which makes me feel that I would like always to be with them.

Spender returned to England on the *Queen Elizabeth* at the beginning of December. He wrote a farewell letter to Dorothy Brett: 'It will be very nice to be home and with Natasha and Matthew. Otherwise, if I didn't have my family in England, I think I might have stayed in America.'

The initial literary task for Spender in 1949 was to polish up, yet again, his confessional chapter for the anti-Communist 'symposium', *The God that Failed* (it would eventually be published in January 1950). Spender had been selected by the book's originators, R. H. Crossman and Arthur Koestler, as the representative British intellectual to line up with other Europeans and Americans who, like him, had fallen out of love with Communism. The invitation to contribute had come from Crossman, whose name would stand on the title page as 'editor'.

Now a rising Labour MP, 'Dick' had served in the psychological warfare division during the war. He was still suspected of having connections with MI6. The book's other co-originator, Arthur Koestler (also connected with British intelligence operations), had been a friend and dining partner of Spender's since the Hungarian first arrived in England as a refugee in the early 1940s. He was notoriously difficult to deal with. If you had a Hungarian friend, the jest went, you needed no enemy. The other contributors recruited for the project were the black American novelist Richard Wright (anti-Communism's Paul Robeson); the American political commentator Louis Fischer; the Italian political philosopher and novelist Ignazio Silone; and a piece on behalf of André Gide, awkwardly ghosted by Enid Starkie. Koestler unsuccessfully tried to get Malraux and Camus.

The publisher of *The God that Failed* was the Anglo-American Hamish Hamilton, who, like Crossman, had connections with Second World War psychological warfare operations. According to Crossman's introduction the book 'was conceived in the heat of argument' when he was staying with Koestler in the wastes of north Wales, in 1947–8. Koestler had expostulated, 'we ex-Communists are the only people on your side who know what it's all about'. Koestler's biographer, David Cesarani, contradicts this 'heat of argument' scenario. The book was coolly and 'explicitly conceived as anti-Communist propaganda' by the British and American intelligence agencies.

Spender was unaware of the political machinations behind the book. But it suited him to make a proclamation of his beliefs, and his lost beliefs. His essay concludes with what was to be, effectively, his manifesto for the 1950s: 'My duty is to state what I support without taking sides. Neither side, in the present alignment of the world, represents what I believe to be the only solution of the world's problems.'

Spender's non-combatant neutrality was put to the test in the famous encounter with Roy Campbell, at the Ethical Church, Bayswater, on the night of 14 April. There are many versions of the event. The most concise and amusing is Spender's own, to John Hayward, the day after:

Last night I had to read some poems at a thing called the Ethical Church in Queensway. In the afternoon I was rung up by someone who pretended he was a woman I had met in Spain then revealed that he was Roy Campbell and trailed off with 'you fucking cunt. You bloody cunt, you fucking cunt, etc.' until I put down the receiver. At the meeting, when I got up to read my poems, someone said, 'I'm just a sergeant in the British Army. I want to complain about this fucking Stephen Spender. He said I was a coward. Where is he? Where is he? He's a coward. He hasn't dared to come here. I'd like to have a fucking talk with him, etc.' He came up to me and hit me in the face with an honest sergeant's fist, before he was dragged away by Mrs Campbell, Miss Campbell, and John Gawsworth. He went away shouting, 'What's more, he's a fucking lesbian.' After this I read my poems which were so well received that a section of the audience concluded that the whole thing was a put up job by collusion between Roy C. and me to arouse interest and sympathy. Another section thought that Roy Campbell was some poor boy out of one of my previous incarnations, to whom I had given 10/- when he thought he had earned an honest £1.

Bernard Bergonzi, who was in the audience, recalls that Spender 'was applauded for his Christ-like passivity'. He refused to have the police called, quietly saying of his assailant: 'he is a great poet, he is a great poet. We must try to understand.' He insisted on going on with the reading.

Later in April, Spender embarked on a six-week lecture tour to the

US. The political temperature there was rising uncomfortably. As he observed in Syracuse, 'Everywhere this week when I have met members of faculties at universities, there has been talk of Communism.' China was 'being lost' to the Reds. Berlin was still (until May) under blockade. NATO had been set up in April – as a clear preparation for World War Three. There was a palpable 'increase of fear' among the American academic profession, a premonition of the McCarthyite purge to come. He managed, amid his speaking engagements in late April, to stay with the Buttingers in Princeton and with Barber and Menotti at Mount Kisco. He found he liked the deep south, which he had never seriously visited before. Tennessee had 'a mysteriousness that I find lacking in the North', he discovered. He made forays in late May to Kansas City and Chicago, lecturing all the way. In Chicago he stayed with the poet Allen Tate and his novelist wife, Caroline. The half-drunk Tate (he was always, apparently, half-drunk), whom Spender liked (although he had his doubts about the Southern Agrarians), took it on himself to tell his English guest ('smiling most amiably'): 'you have no idea how we *hate* you. We hate all the British, but most of all we hate Auden, MacNeice and Spender. You are much cleverer than us and we can't forgive you for it. You come over here and everything is much easier for you than it is for us.'

In mid-May, Stephen was in Los Angeles, with Isherwood, who did not hate him. They managed a trip together to Santa Fe. In Washington State, in Seattle, Spender hit it off with the boisterous poet Theodore Roethke, about whom he wrote enthusiastically for English readers and with whom he corresponded over the subsequent years. Roethke (as his principal American advocate, J. M. Brinnin, pointed out) had much in common with Dylan Thomas – the poet whose death, Stephen thought, had been catastrophic for post-war British poetry. Like Thomas, Roethke, prey to shattering mood swings, was not always easy to be friendly with. Introducing the English poet to the audience, on Spender's first reading in Seattle, he took the opportunity to make a blistering critical attack; followed by fulsome praise. At the end of May, Spender finally made it to Portland, where he met up, at last, with his particular friends, Goyen and Berns, at their apartment. It was at this point that – recklessly – he returned Goyen's adobe-shack hospitality at Taos by renewing the invitation that the young novelist come and stay at Loudoun Road, while he was finishing his novel.

By early July, Spender was homesick and yearning for his family. He had arranged for Natasha to be sent a $300 money order from his American earnings to tide her over and to enable her to come with Matthew and the au pair to Portofino in late July. They had planned a long holiday in the Italian sun. 'I'm simply existing for the sake of getting to Italy,' he told his wife, in his last week in the US.

The house in Portofino had been found for them by Stephen's American friend, the artist Hugh Chisholm. He was rich, and rather over-estimated the Spenders' means. There was a cook ('a sweet old Italian lady with a turban') in residence. A vast piano was hired from Genoa, and its tones 'boomed across the port'. It was, Spender told Dorothy Brett, 'rather excessively pretty'. The house was big enough to entertain visitors. Mervyn Stockwood (still vicar of St Matthew Moorfields in Bristol) came, as did the psychologist Yves Gallifret (whom Stephen had met in 1945), the choirmaster Robert Shaw and Michael Duff (a Welsh landowner, and close friend of Chisholm). There was lively conversation; especially when the strenuously anti-Catholic Stockwood got on to the subject of the Whore of Babylon.

On this long Italian vacation, Spender was able to observe how startlingly precocious his son Matthew, now four, was becoming. On one occasion, he found the child on the balcony of the house at night, looking into the sky and saying: 'Look at all the stars, shivering with their eyes.' On another occasion he slipped into his parents' bed at night and when asked what he was doing replied, sedately: 'I needed the companionship.' His son's sayings over the subsequent years would be a source of delight.

In September, they wrapped up their Italian summer with a visit to a PEN conference in Venice (here it was that their daughter, Lizzie, born on 30 May 1950, was conceived). Auden and Cecil Day-Lewis were also delegates to the conference, which made for good conversation. As Day-Lewis recalled in his autobiography, *The Buried Day*:

Though Auden, Spender, MacNeice and I have known each other personally since the mid-thirties, each of us had not even met all three others till after the publication of *New Signatures* in 1932, while it was only in 1947 that Auden, Spender and I found ourselves together in one room.

As Ed Mendelson notes, the four of them had in fact assembled on 18 October 1938, for a BBC broadcast from Manchester. Also in Venice in September were Silone and their old friend the Scottish poet Edwin

Muir, currently director of the British Council in Rome (he and his wife Willa were, in their spare time, translating Kafka).

The two months in Italy had been a wonderful tonic; one could clearly live a literary life there; why not, then, stay for ever? Spender told his friend Edwin that he was tempted by the idea of taking over the British Institute in Florence, when the incumbent left in 1951 and it was absorbed into the British Council (this merging of Institute and Council was happening all over Italy). In the event the idea came to nothing. It was perhaps for the best. Spender would have been too big a fish for the small Florentine pond.

Bronzed and relaxed, the Spender family returned to Loudoun Road and the rigours of an English winter. Those rigours were not eased when, in mid-October, William Goyen turned up, with his fiancée, Dorothy Robinson, in tow. Dorothy left almost immediately for Paris, and the 'engagement' ceased abruptly at that point. They were important months for Goyen as an author. *The House of Breath* was finally completed while he was a guest at Loudoun Road. In other ways, Goyen's stay at Loudoun Road was not a success. It was difficult having two creative writers in the house. Not that it much helped when one of the writers – Spender – was called away in mid-November to America to lecture in Harvard, on Goethe. Goyen proved to be neurotic, a poseur 'obsessed with his image of himself'. Natasha Spender also found him – for a man who had served in the US Navy – extraordinarily peculiar about lavatories. He insisted on buying a new lock, and screwdriver to fit it with, for the first-floor bathroom on the grounds that the one in place was too flimsy. On one occasion Stephen found him 'so outrageous that he went off to Paris, and I [Natasha] had to cope with him'. It got worse. Goyen went off for three weeks to Italy in January where he 'busted the hell out of my right knee'. He fell, he rather proudly told Dorothy Brett, 'down about 60 magnificent marble stairs designed by Michelangelo'. It took three weeks in hospital to fix him up. Natasha Spender, now pregnant, had other things on her mind than nursing Bill Goyen. He was politely told it was impossible for him to return to Loudoun Road and he returned to America. He remained eternally grateful to the Spenders – to Stephen, particularly, for launching his career.

The trip to lecture at Harvard turned into a minefield. When he applied for his visa to the American embassy, in late October, Spender was turned down. He had been formally asked, like other applicants, if he had ever been a member of the Communist Party. He responded, honestly, that he had: for 'about a fortnight', before breaking with them, over the *Daily Worker* article. New regulations meant that it was impossible for the Embassy to grant a visa to an ex-Communist – even if they had only had a card for ten minutes. He would have to apply personally to the Attorney General of the United States for a 'waiver'.

It could have been handled tactfully and quietly. Spender was, by now, a VIP. Less for himself than for other European intellectuals, he told Harold Taylor that he intended to 'make as much of a row as I can'. He wrote an article-length letter for the *New York Times* which inspired a sympathetic editorial ('this country seems to be putting itself in a ridiculous position'). The Attorney General's office grudgingly granted Spender a three-month visitor's visa. There is a quantity of material obliterated in his FBI file, relevant presumably to the visa problem.

December 1949 was overshadowed by the urgent need to get *World within World* into shape. He had, Spender assured Hamish Hamilton, rented a room where he could work, undisturbed, from nine in the morning until six at night. Frances Cornford meanwhile was going through the text. At the end of the year Faber published Spender's volume, *The Edge of Being*. Dedicated to Natasha, it contains some of his best poems, such as the tribute to Eliot, 'Speaking to the Dead in the Language of the Dead', the love-in-recollection lyric (for Muriel) 'Ice', and an abbreviated version of 'Return to Vienna'. Spender also chose to reprint his grim piece 'Responsibility: The Pilots who destroyed Germany, Spring 1945' with its devastating line: 'Oh, that April morning, they carried my will.' But the collection generally is somewhat overwhelmed by the prevalence of exclamation. The first poem, 'O Omega', opens:

O, thou O, opening O

and the second:

O Night O trembling night O night of sighs
O night when my body was a rod O night
When my mouth was a vague animal cry
Pasturing on her flesh O night.

In the *TLS* the anonymous reviewer (Philip Tomlinson) fixed – almost exclusively, and most unfairly – on the two opening pieces. Alluding to

Spender's historical role as the voice of the 1930s, the reviewer observed that:

While most are emerging from the twilight of the coteries to make use of an idiom more generally comprehensible Mr Spender becomes less readily understandable as his feeling for humanity increases . . . A symbolic 'O' runs through much of the verse. It is not always so clear to the reader that he can see through the hoop. It has a vague meaning for him, and a full one for the poet.

The collection had been well reviewed elsewhere. The *Listener* compared Spender, favourably, with Yeats. In the *Spectator* Barbara Cooper pronounced him 'the most consistent of the distinguished group of poets to which he belongs'. In the *New Statesman* G. S. Fraser applauded the 'touching directness' of the poems. But the *TLS*'s sarcasms were deeply wounding. Spender resolved 'not to run the gauntlet of another volume of new poetry ever again'. It would be twenty years before his next original collection would appear. Whatever poems he wrote (and he would write many) he would keep to himself and a few friends.

The 1950s: Middle Years, Mid–Atlantic

As the war and its upsets receded, the 1950s were years in which Spender laid down the work pattern that would dominate the rest of his life. It entailed a home-and-away relationship with America, where he would take up a number of prestigious chairs and lectureships over the decade. Relationships with his expatriated comrades (Isherwood and Auden, primarily) resumed – if less intensely than in the 1930s. Over the same period he assumed a dominating position in the literary world of London. This ability to work in two literary cultures led, logically, to his being appointed the 'English' editor of the new Anglo-American magazine, Encounter. *It would mean the longest salaried association in what was, in other ways, a freelancing professional life. The decade began with the publication of his autobiography – a book which proved to be his most popular and best received to date. It ended with the writing of what would be one of his major critical works, and a different kind of personal testament,* The Struggle of the Modern. *Although no significant volume of new poetry was published during these years, Stephen Spender could legitimately be seen as his country's most eminent international man of letters (his stature as a poet was strengthened by the first of his 'Collected Poetry' volumes). New friendships were formed over this period: with the young writer and protégé Reynolds Price, the composer Igor Stravinsky, the English novelist Angus Wilson (with whom he enjoyed an eventful writers' conference in Japan), the American novelist Raymond Chandler. Spender's family now included a daughter. His life was never fuller than in the 1950s – if more settled than ever before. These were years of promise achieved.*

Early 1950 was dominated for Spender by the final touches to the composition of *World within World*. He had, more or less, three-quarters of the text as he wanted it. But he passed the first months of the year 'in a daze of correcting typescripts'. With Bill Goyen gone, domestic arrangements at Loudoun Road returned more or less to normal. Their household staff was now added to with the 'adorable' Italian au pair, Franca, and a cook, Maria, immortalized in family annals when she stopped Spender going out of the house because he was wearing two ties. With all these bodies, Loudoun Road was bursting at the seams. At the end of January, the Spenders bought another house round the corner, in Blenheim Road. Stephen set up a study there in the basement. Here, as he told Dorothy Brett, 'I can work all day.' They rented the top storey out, which furnished some useful income.

Preparing *World within World* for press took forever. The revisiting of his past in the book had a strangely disturbing effect. On 8 January he woke having 'slept little as I was remembering during the night how confused I am about the events of 1936–7'. On 9 January, as he recorded in his journal, he was 'entirely absorbed in thinking and writing about Spain, so that I can hardly sleep'.

On 11 January he went to see George Orwell, in his private room at UCH. The other writer – never plump – had lost two stone, and was 'very thin and weak'. On the subject of *The God that Failed* (a copy of which Stephen had given him) he advised that his friend 'was wrong to attempt to *reply* to the communists. "There are certain people like vegetarians and communists whom one cannot answer."' Stephen and Natasha made a number of visits to Orwell who was, in fact, dying of TB.

Spender's grand project in early 1950 was for the *New York Times*, which, following the publicity stirred up by *The God that Failed*, commissioned him to do a gallery-portrait of the leading European intellectuals – particularly those, like Ignazio Silone, who had renounced Communism. It was a well-paid assignment and one which – as himself a leading renouncer – he could do well. On 13 March, having celebrated Matthew's fifth birthday at breakfast, Spender flew to Brussels to stay for a few days with Hansi Lambert. As a house-guest of his friend, Spender planned to gather his thoughts for the intellectuals-of-Europe project. Much of the research would be done 'over the dinner table'. He was met at Brussels airport by a chauffeur and whisked off in a 'great American car' to the Lambert residence in Avenue Marnix, opposite the royal palace.

While in Brussels Spender read – for the first time seriously – Dostoyevsky. The Russian novelist, he recorded in his journal,

suddenly seemed to me a key how I should write and I regretted the twenty years during which, influenced by a remark by Ernst Robert Curtius, I have read no Dostoyevsky. The central vision of an utterly simple contractual relationship between people which is betrayed on all sides, but which remains constantly through certain situations with the force of revelation is exactly my own.

The comparison of Stephen Spender with Dostoyevsky's 'Holy Fool' would, over the years, become a critical commonplace. He seems to have first discovered it himself.

Spender left Brussels for Italy on 17 March. His first interview was with Silone. The philosopher lived in industrial Rome – the bleak terrain of 'Rossellini's films, not the guide books'. The two men knew each other quite well by now and were co-contributors on *The God that Failed*. Spender was ushered into Silone's presence by his deferential wife, Darina. He explained the *New York Times* project. What did Silone foresee? He replied 'slowly and carefully in his French with its vibrancy of an Italian accent'. In his view, 'The uniting of Europe must not be a *fétiche*.' Silone had doubts about Spender's compatriots. 'In the present European situation,' he said, 'the worst lacuna is the passivity of the English socialists.'

On 28 March Spender journeyed to Milan to meet Elio Vittorini. The writer asserted that he 'belonged to no party'. Physically, the Sicilian was 'wonderfully attractive', with black cropped hair and glinting eyes. He had 'never had a party card', Vittorini told Spender, 'because he associated party cards with Fascism'. He talked 'in illuminated moments of real passion' interspersed with epigram. Perhaps capitalism, he archly suggested, 'should abdicate and become constitutional capitalism'.

Next on Spender's list was Eugenio Montale, now literary editor of the *Corriere della Sera*. 'I was struck by his extreme irony,' the Englishman recorded. 'Being the most famous poet in Italy,' Montale told him, 'was a grave disadvantage which he had long to struggle against.' He had evidently read an Italian translation of *Enemies of Promise*.

At the end of March Spender flew to London via Paris. Here he would spend a few days and revise the last 100 pages of *World within World* for press. On 13 April he returned to Paris to interview Arthur Koestler and André Malraux. Malraux bluntly told Spender that 'England had interests which put her quite outside the project of a United Europe'. His view of things was by this stage staunchly, if unfashionably, Gaullist. Spender ventured his own pro-American sentiments to little avail.

Koestler roundly told him that 'left and right have lost their meaning'. Like Silone, he felt that 'Labour England is the main obstacle to European Union . . . Every British government is bound to be isolationist.' He called down plagues on every house. Post-war France was completely 'pourri' (rotten). But the British Labour government was worse than rotten: 'it is *provincial*'.

Koestler celebrated his marriage to Mamaine Paget, at the British Consulate in Paris, on 15 April. The woman he would marry next, Cynthia Jeffries (then his secretary and mistress), joined the celebrations. Spender, who was meanwhile staying in the spacious Paris flat of a friend, Henri Louis de la Grange, was swept up – unwillingly – in Koestler's gruesome wedding breakfast. It all began as Spender was having lunch with Peggy Bernier at the Café de Flore. Koestler's wedding party breezed in. He was 'very drunk' and even by Koestler standards very offensive. He quarrelled abusively with Spender, who said he hated ideology because 'it prevented ideas of the past having validity in the present'. Spender was 'arrogant', Koestler shouted. Stephen formed 'the curious feeling that Arthur would like to be back in the Communist fold'. The company lurched from one 'expensive place' to another, in a seething condition of 'altercation'. As David Cesarani drily records:

Finally, Koestler screeched away into the night, leaving his newly minted wife, secretary and wedding guests standing in the middle of St Germain des Prés. Mamaine took refuge on a sofa in Spender's flat, with Cynthia Jeffries as chaperone. The next day Spender joked, 'I've always wanted to spend a night with you, it's too bad it was your wedding night.'

The Spenders' next child, Elizabeth ('Lizzie'), was born on 30 May (the date that Spender notes as completing the proofs of *World within World*, whose narrative ends with the death of his mother). Stephen, as

Natasha recalls, turned up at the hospital with Dominique de Grunne to see his new child but, oddly, 'didn't seem to take much notice'. The indifference, if that is what it was, did not last long. He would dote on his daughter and made a private vow that she would have a better life than other Spender women. Six weeks after her birth, he wrote the paternal lyric, 'Nocturne':

> Their six-weeks-old daughter lies
> In her cot, crying out the night. Their hearts
> Are sprung like armies, waiting
> To cross the gap to where her loneliness
> Lies infinite between them.

'It's *terrific* having a daughter,' he told Harold Taylor, archly inquiring: 'May I put her down for Sarah Lawrence?' Lizzie's godparents were Elizabeth Bowen, Laurens Van der Post, Muriel Buttinger, Lucille Curzon and Dorothy Elmhirst. Stephen hadn't thought of a girl's name. 'Elizabeth' was chosen because, as a newborn, 'she looked incredibly imperious'.

On 15 June, Hamilton remitted £250 on account for *World within World* 'to help out with hospital and other expenses'. It was both good and bad news to learn, in early August, that it had been selected as a Book Society choice. It would mean big sales. Hamilton told Spender he might expect 'at least £3,000' – the largest payment he had ever received. But publication would now have to be held back (to synchronize with the club's printing) until April 1951. It was frustrating. 'We were all so thoroughly worked up about this book,' he told Harold Taylor, 'that there is a feeling of coitus interruptus.'

There were other interruptions to his writing career. On 4 September, Spender told his agent, A. D. Peters, that 'I do not want to collect my poems for another ten years, or indeed to publish *any* poems until 1960.' He might, he conceded, allow a 'selected poems' volume. But, as regards original work, he would be silent for a decade. Partly his self-denying ordinance was provoked by the sour reception of *The Edge of Being*. But mainly it was because he planned to work on a large autobiographical poem, of *Prelude* scale, to partner his prose memoir. T. S. Eliot – famously parsimonious about the publication of his own verse – approved the idea of a 'ten year break'. He also approved the idea of a Faber 'Selected Poems' (which they would none the less call 'Collected') to keep the poet's name fresh in the public mind.

On 25 November Spender wrote a letter to the *New Statesman*. Noting the abysmal sales of English poetry (he was himself just getting six-monthly returns on *The Edge of Being*), he had a novel suggestion as to how poetry might be supported in future:

My proposal is that there should be a Poetry Book Club run on lines different from those of other book clubs. A committee of poets and critics representing several trends should recommend a list of approximately twelve volumes a year to subscribers who, on payment of, say, 30s annually, will be entitled to buy four of the volumes.

This was the blueprint of what would later become the Poetry Book Society. Spender's shrewd suggestion was taken up by Eric White, at the Arts Council.

The end of 1950 found Spender in cheerful mood. 'Our life,' he told Dorothy Brett, 'gets nicer on the whole – despite debts, etc.' The baby, he told Harold Taylor, 'weighs about two tons and increases by geometrical instead of arithmetical progression'. An end-of-year visit to Italy (now his favourite European country) raised his spirits further. 'I have never known Rome to be so beautiful as it is in December,' he told Taylor. London, if not beautiful, was merry. There was a big party at Loudoun Road, with a recital by Natasha (in fact 'a slight dress rehearsal' for her forthcoming concert). Spender's brain was fizzing with ideas. He was, he told John Hayward as the year ended:

indulging myself by putting other things aside and writing a play about Coleridge, Wordsworth, Mr, Mrs and Miss Hutchinson. I think that it is a good thing to give way to one's most crazy ideas for writing, work through them, and then throw them away if they do not succeed. Who knows I might turn out to be a Terence Rattigan, if not a Shaw.

He was, of course, joking. The year 1951 marks the beginning of Spender's involvement with *Encounter* – although the launch of the magazine itself was still two years away. *Encounter*'s parent organization, the Congress for Cultural Freedom, was founded in 1950 as a first move in the American 'roll back' of Soviet cultural aggression. A bid, that is, for the minds and sensibilities of western Europe. Up to this point the Communists had made remarkably successful inroads into western intellectual and artistic élites, building substantially on 1930s recruits whose God had not yet failed. It was Moscow's Cold War Fifth Column.

The CCF was, in its secret depths, the creature (as is now known) of Allen Dulles's CIA. It was run by demobilized veterans of the wartime OSS. Spooks. The prime movers in the Congress – Michael Josselson, Melvin Lasky, Nicolas Nabokov – had all served with distinction in US Army intelligence during the Second World War. In the CCF they would fight on. The Congress's secretariat was set up in Paris, with Josselson as executive director (he would later be based in Geneva) and Nabokov its front-line director at the Boulevard Haussman. Josselson's 'favourite son' was Lasky (currently, in the early 1950s, editor of the Berlin-based magazine *Der Monat*, a CIA client publication in which *The God that Failed* had been serialized). As Stephen Dorrill records:

Secret CIA funding for the CCF came via nearly forty different American trusts and charitable foundations – 'notional donors' as they were technically known by MI6 – with the principal conduit for covert funds being the Farfield Foundation. Its philanthropic president, Cincinnati multimillionaire Julius Fleischmann, was a director of the Metropolitan Opera in New York and fellow of the Royal Society of the Arts in London.

Allen Tate, whose brother Ben was Fleischmann's brother-in-law, also seems to have been involved in the formation of the Congress. Link figures in the UK were the journalist Malcolm Muggeridge (at this period probably an MI6 operative), the BBC man Tosca Fyvel (ditto), and the London publishers Fred Warburg and George Weidenfeld.

From first to last Spender knew nothing of the CCF's covert political connections with the CIA. He was not invited to the Berlin conference (organized by Melvin Lasky) which brought the Congress into being. Unlike many of his friends (A. J. Ayer, Richard Crossman, Muggeridge, Stuart Hampshire), he had been entirely outside the intelligence community during the war. He was a fireman, not a spook. None the less, he was idealistically aligned with the proclaimed aims of the CCF. During 1951, he wrote powerful articles in the *New York Times* arguing the case for intellectual freedom and 'combative' liberal values with which to resist 'the totalitarian enemy'. A main aim, he declared, 'is to *humanize* the concept of America in the rest of the world'.

World within World was published in late April. Over 50,000 copies would be sold in the year. The memoir has many sides to it. It evokes, with Wordsworthian sensitivity, a wartime childhood. It chronicles the genesis of an interwar literary generation (the 'Auden Generation', as it would be called), pre-war political agitations, wartime service, and post-war hopes. *World within World* is, in one of its aspects, a strenuous declaration of Spender's passionate liberalism. But, in passages dealing with 'Jimmy Younger' (Tony Hyndman), the autobiography broke dangerous ground. The book came out four years before the Montagu witch-hunt, six years before the Wolfenden Report, and sixteen years before the liberating Sexual Offences Act. In 1951, Britain was decades away from being entirely ready for honesty about 'love relationships' between men. Reviewers, such as the *TLS*, carefully omitted to refer to this aspect of the book.

World within World cost 15s., was handsomely embellished with a portrait photograph of the author and was dedicated to Isaiah Berlin, who was 'immensely proud' and returned the compliment by dedicating *Four Studies in Liberty* to Stephen. To those friends, like Berlin, who had known him longest, a new Stephen was visible in the book. Isherwood thought it 'wonderful . . . the best book you have written . . . one of the first-class autobiographies of this highly autobiographical time'. Auden discerned, for the first time, the artist's necessary 'calculation and coldness of heart'. An Audenesque, if entirely wrongheaded, compliment. In his review of the book, Cyril Connolly made his much repeated distinction between Spender I ('an inspired simpleton, a great big silly goose, a holy Russian idiot') and Spender II ('shrewd, ambitious, aggressive and ruthless'). A malicious and typically Connollyan compliment.

Stephen and Natasha were busy in the Festival of Britain year. The festival itself was a summer event, running from June to September. It meant concert work for Natasha and her Apollo Society colleagues. And, to crown what looked like being a wonderful year for Stephen, his verse play *To the Island* (a modernized Oedipus, on the theme of sons striking the father dead) was accepted for production by the Oxford Playhouse, as part of that city's Festival programme. Spender spent a large part of May 1951 working with Frank Shelley, who was producing and starring in the piece. Given the vogue for T. S. Eliot's and Christopher Fry's verse drama in the early 1950s, there was every hope of success for *To the Island*. The first night was scheduled for 9 July.

With the prospect of a hardworking autumn ahead of both of them, and with money in the family purse, Stephen and Natasha could take a working vacation of three months. Lizzie was now one, Matthew six

and a half. They went to Torri del Benaco, by Lake Garda. Torri, a fishing
village unspoiled by post-war tourism, had its ruined castle, its harbour,
and its bustling quayside. To the eye, it was unchanged from medieval
times. Spender described their lodging to John Hayward:

We have an entire wing of a hotel, given us at a very low rate by the hotelier
because André Gide once had these rooms. I could write an interesting illustrated monograph on the local fisher boys' simple memories of *le maître*. The
children of the village run after me screaming 'Poeta!' I suppose that Catullus
set them doing that with visiting poets.

From the balcony of their bedroom, the Spenders could look across the
centre of the lake to the mountains. Full pension was 2,000 lire – something under £2. The many friends who visited them that summer 'were
astonished at the moderateness of their bills'. Visitors included Cecil and
Jill Day-Lewis, on their honeymoon; the Robert Lowells (his personal life
was almost as complicated as Cecil's); Frances Cornford, who saw Venice
for the first time with the Spenders; the poet Henry Reed, who, rather
embarrassingly, fell for a local actor; Marion and George Harewood; Peggy
Ashcroft, who gave advice on the play; and Jeremy Hutchinson. There
were expeditions on the lake and to Sirmione peninsula – a trip which
inspired a love poem for Natasha, subsequently printed as an 'Ariel' pamphlet
by Faber. The cook was found to be drunk while in charge of Lizzie and
was discharged. This led to the hiring of two house-servants, Francesca
and Idelma, who were brought back with the family to London to live-
in at Loudoun Road, where they would become lifelong friends.

Matthew 'entered very fully into the drama' of boyhood life in the
village, accoutred in his toy sword and buckler. Within a few days he
was fluent in Gardanese phrases and expletives and had an army of loyal
followers. On one occasion, walking with his father, he observed with
his strange precocity: 'I think these people must be very poor.' Why?
'Because they are so kind,' he replied. In later life Matthew would elect
to live in this country of kind people.

Things turned momentarily sour at Torri with the 'missing spies'
imbroglio. The diplomats Guy Burgess and Donald MacLean had been
fingered as two of the 'Cambridge spies'. Burgess was a homosexual and
MacLean a reckless womanizer. Both were covert Communists (their
superiors were, apparently, too polite to inquire on these matters). Both
diplomats were drunken – MacLean spectacularly so. He had suffered

what was euphemistically called a 'breakdown' and was on open-ended 'gardening leave' in early 1951. Both men had been inserted by the KGB, years before, as moles in the British Foreign Office.

Burgess was warned around 23 May that the net was closing on them. In his alcoholic condition MacLean might spill everything. The flight plan was triggered. MacLean would decamp to Moscow as a spent asset. Burgess would accompany him as far as Prague. MacLean was too far gone to find his own way. If, as was hoped, things blew over and the coast was clear, Burgess might return to the FO and soldier on for the Kremlin. They needed their spies. It was a period of great international tension. The Korean conflict had swung to and fro until, provoked by MacArthur's adventurism, China had invaded the Peninsula. Many in Europe expected a third world war by the end of the year. They also expected nuclear annihilation – for which they, and the American public, blamed British espionage, which had 'given' the bomb to the Soviets. There was, at this period, a hysterical fear of 'the enemy within'.

On the evening of 24 May 1951, Natasha had received an urgent phone call from Guy Burgess for Auden. The poet was staying at Loudoun Road on his way to Ischia, in the Bay of Naples, where, since 1950, he had rented a house annually. Auden was out when Burgess phoned. There was, Natasha told him, a possibility that he was at their other house, 5 Blenheim Road, chatting with Stephen in his study there. Her actual words were: 'Wystan *might* be at the other number and anyway I know Stephen is there.' She gave Burgess the other number. Auden was not there. But Burgess went on to have a longish conversation with Spender in which he said: 'I want to congratulate you on *World within World*.' The book summed up, Burgess said (meaningfully) 'the predicament of a generation'. Spender, who vaguely suspected that Burgess had long-standing communist sympathies, found the compliment 'strange'. It was, Spender later recorded, the first conversation he could recall having had with Burgess in five years. His social relationships with the Cambridge spies (as they later turned out to be) had always been strained. As he wrote in his journal, in March 1982:

Blunt, Burgess and MacLean all treated me with near contempt when I met them. I don't know whether this was because I was an ex-communist, or as a Liberal, or an innocent – what they all had was the arrogance of manipulators who thought they could manage other people.

When Auden returned that evening he had evidently dined well. Spender told him about the calls. Would he call back? 'Do I have to?' Auden drawled: 'he's always drunk.' He did not call back. Later he would muddy the water by telling the press that Spender had *not* told him about Burgess's call.

As it happened, the time was past for phone calls. The spies fled England that night, travelling to France from Southampton. On 7 June, the Foreign Office announced the diplomats' defection. The fact that they were by now in Moscow was not publicly divulged until February 1952. There was, in the meanwhile, a hue and cry in the press, led by the *Daily Express*, which had set itself up as Fleet Street's spycatcher in chief. It was plausibly suspected that the two traitors might have taken 'secrets' with them. Newspapers alluded darkly to 'widespread sexual perversion in the Foreign Office'.

The British press soon found out about Burgess's phone calls to Loudoun Road. On 10 June, in an interview with the *Observer*, Spender said that, given the remarks about his book, he found it 'very difficult' to believe that Guy Burgess was a Communist spy. The *Express* published an interview with Auden, on 13 June. The next day, Auden wrote to Stephen complaining, 'The combination of that phone call and some lady who thought she saw "La B." in the train on his way to Ischia, has turned this place into a mad-house. The house is watched night and day by plain-clothes men.' He told Stephen, 'I still believe Guy to be a victim, but the horrible thing about our age is that one cannot be certain.'

By now the Spenders themselves were besieged by reporters at Torri del Benaco. Spender staunchly continued to believe Burgess innocent until, on 15 June, he received an alarming letter from John Lehmann, written five days earlier:

Just a word, after reading what you said in this morning's *Observer* about Guy's disappearance. I was in touch yesterday with someone whom you know very well, who told me that she worried for *years* about Guy, owing to a piece of information that came her way during the war, and that now all the pieces fitted together. She was absolutely sure.

Lehmann also wrote to warn Wystan. The 'someone', as Spender realized, was John's sister, Rosamond. She had been a lover of Goronwy Rees who, as later emerged, was also murkily involved in all this spy business.

Spender was placed in an awkward position. There were reporters hounding him and his family. He was on record as defending Burgess. And now, it seemed, Guy was probably a traitor. On 15 June Spender innocently showed Lehmann's letter to Owen Seaman, the young *Express* reporter who had interviewed Auden on 13 June. His intention was to demonstrate his complete ignorance, until very recently, of Burgess's activities. Spender imprudently let Seaman keep the letter, having received the journalist's solemn word that he would only use it as unattributed background information. Natasha, who was in the room at the time, heard Seaman say: 'My night editor won't believe me if I don't show him hard evidence.' As he left, Seaman pledged: 'I have been on the job a long time, and I can assure you, you can have complete confidence in me, Mr Spender.'

It was too much of a scoop for any hack to hold back on mere 'ethical' grounds. A photocopy of Lehmann's letter, with its writer's name, appeared in the London edition the next day under the headline, 'DIPLOMATS – THE SECRET: Mystery Woman Phones MI5.' Lehmann himself was doorstepped on the evening of Friday 15 June. 'My bewilderment and anger were boundless,' Lehmann later recorded. In his boundless anger he wrote a 'stinker' to Spender on 16 June. It began:

Dear Stephen I don't think I can find words to describe to you what I feel about your conduct – or what anyone else feels who's in any way connected with it or us. It would never have occurred to me that a friend could calmly, without asking permission, give a private letter to the press [it is] without parallel in the dealings of gentlemen . . . You can't expect me to want to have anything more to do with someone who has been guilty of so gross a breach of trust.

Spender wrote back saying he was 'appalled and frightfully sorry'.

He wrote to Edith Sitwell, on 21 June, saying, 'Natasha and I have been so worried we have not been able to sleep . . . I feel that through my own idiocy I have set a kind of gulf between John and our mutual friends and myself.' Lehmann turned the screw by instructing his lawyer to write to Spender 'informing him that I still held him firmly responsible for what had happened'. Rosamond took a more sensible line on the matter. Isaiah Berlin put the affair firmly into context. John Lehmann, he said, 'definitely considers himself some kind of instrument in the orchestra of history' – adding, mischievously, 'a triangle, perhaps'. It was a storm in a teacup.

The Burgess scandal cast something of a blight over the late summer. It was compounded by the failure of *To the Island*. The production was a 'horror'. After ten days of working with the cast, Spender and Natasha, who returned to England for the opening, had the mortification of a first night in which – as *The Times* recorded – the audience fidgeted. The play is a good one, but the production was hopelessly botched. Spender stoically gave up his ambition to be a 'Rattigan or a Shaw'.

Spender returned to Torri in early August. He had experienced months of up and down – from the triumph of *World within World*'s launch, through the turmoil of the Burgess affair to the disappointment of *To the Island*. There was, however, another high point in 1951 – his first meeting with Igor Stravinsky. The introduction came through their mutual friend Hansi Lambert on the occasion of the first performance of *The Rake's Progress*, for which Auden did the libretto, at La Fenice, Venice, on 11 September. They stayed overnight with Hansi and walked back through the town with the composer and his wife after the performance. Italians in restaurants stood up as the maestro passed, and applauded. Over the years the Spenders would see the Stravinskys, Igor and Vera, frequently. Their encounters, Spender later recalled, were always enlivened by merriment and hilarity. For Natasha, whose father had been instrumental in introducing Stravinsky's music to an English public (for which the composer was profoundly grateful), the friendship was something wonderful.

The family returned to London in autumn. For so long a young writer, Spender felt, in 1951, a premonition of advancing age. His hair had silvered early. It made him look distinguished but, to young eyes, also ancient. Matthew, now almost seven, was still at the Hall, in Hampstead. In early November 1951 Spender went early to the school, and watched the gym class. As he recalls in his journal:

on the way home in the bus where I sat with Matthew, one of his little friends who was seated directly in front of us suddenly turned round, pointed at me with butting finger, and said, 'Spender, is that old, white-haired man with spectacles your daddy?' 'No,' said Matthew with perfect self-possession. When we got off the bus and were at a safe distance from his little friend I asked Matthew why he had said I was not his father.

The boy at first replied: 'Don't talk about it.' When his father persisted, Matthew burst out: 'Because you aren't . . . You aren't like what he said you were.' In his journal the next day Spender jotted down some 'notes on being middle aged'. At this time of life, Spender discerned a pervading 'disgust with oneself, as with a partner with whom one has lived too long. Desire to spare other people one's company. Loss of physical mystery.'

In this section of his journal, Spender also records being 'increasingly disturbed' by world events. The income tax people were again hounding him – their nostrils quickened by the scent of all the money he had earned in this *annus mirabilis*. Incredibly, he was £500 overdrawn at the bank. He could, of course, manage; his energy was adequate. But he would have to do more, faster, more efficiently. On 30 November he noted '"a brutal hurry" occurred to me yesterday as a phrase which adequately described a good deal of my life'. That same day he attended at Covent Garden the dress rehearsal of Britten's *Billy Budd*, for which his friend E. M. Forster had done the libretto. He was there, with his cloth cap and satchel, looking, as Stephen thought, 'like a piano tuner' (William Plomer thought that Morgan was more like 'the man who came to wind the clocks'). Britten's music was never quite to Spender's taste. He judged *Billy Budd* good, but inferior to *The Rake's Progress*, which he had seen a few months earlier. Britten's score lacked Stravinsky's 'wonderful purity and profound heartbeat'. None the less, Spender left the opera house 'elated and purified by the gloomy yet exhilarating *Billy Budd*, which has the quality of a great white snowy night shining through a mist'. The nebulous image was appropriate. This was the last great season of British smogs – when the whole of London was suffocating under pea-soupers of toxic density. He telegrammed his congratulations to the composer.

As the new year, 1952, broke Spender found himself unsettled and restless for new challenges. Should he leave England? It was important too that he and his family should have a source of income more secure than journalism, lecturing and visiting academic posts could supply. He wrote on the subject to William Plomer, his 'most reliable' friend and Matthew's godfather, on 4 January:

Dearest William, Could you dine with me after Wednesday the 9th . . . I want to ask your advice. I'm applying for a job as Byron Professor in Athens University. I don't suppose for one moment I'll get it, but would rather like to talk things over all the same. Gradually I'm finding it unbearable to support a whole family by free-lance writing, and yet much as I'd love to go to Greece I am worried on our boy's account.

The possibility of the Byron Chair had been mooted the year before during a visit to Greece – one of the many officially sponsored trips Spender had undertaken in the last twelve months. The salary was £1,381 p.a. with generous living allowances. He had influential backers in Athens: Louis MacNeice (teaching), Wilfred Tatham (Director of the British Institute), the Hellenophile Patrick Leigh Fermor, the artist Niko Ghika (on whose work Spender would write a monograph with Leigh Fermor), and Moore Crosthwaite, at the Embassy. The committee in the event chose an un-Byronic university man to be their professor. There were other reasons than his being a poet for Spender's being passed over. He had put down Harold Nicolson as a referee, together with Harold Taylor, who was typically encomiastic. Years later, Spender discovered that Nicolson had supplied an unhelpful reference; he never found out why. It was, he thought, 'really rather ratlike'. Spender was, his friends thought, 'dashed' by this failure. He told Ronald Bottrall, head of the British Council in Italy: 'The idea of going to Greece had immense meaning for me, and I had thought of it as a turning point in my work and my life.'

On 5 January the politician Woodrow Wyatt, publisher George Weidenfeld and Spender went to Paris to confer with Nicolas Nabokov about a possible new magazine – *Horizon* was the model they had in mind. George Weidenfeld, now, like Nabokov, a CCF officer, was not a publisher with whom Spender had previously dealt. A fervent Zionist, Weidenfeld suggested that he might write a 'Report on Israel', sponsored by the Jewish Committee of Refugee Children. It was an attractive invitation. Spender was, however, warned by friends that 'George never pays for anything.' George's prudence in money matters was evident when, as they were clinching their deal on 13 February, the publisher looked up and said to his new author: 'Why should I sign a contract with you? Your friends never deliver their books' (he was thinking of the dilatory Cyril Connolly). Weidenfeld duly wrote in a clause stipulating that the £500 advance must be repaid, if a manuscript were not forthcoming by 31 July. The publisher did not want a political treatise. 'As a political writer' Weidenfeld thought Spender 'naïve. But he was a gifted *creative* writer.'

Spender left in early March for two months. His journey began by train to Marseilles. Here he met a boat's cargo of Jewish children, in transit from Morocco to Haifa. Youth Aliyah, which was sponsoring their emigration, was an organization dedicated to bringing 'home' young refugees from North Africa. Spender would accompany them through all the steps of their 'return'. *Learning Laughter* is written as journal-reportage: a style of writing which, with the success of *European Witness*, had become one of the author's most effective forms.

Before embarking on the *Artza* Spender blew 3,000 of his meagre 5,000 francs French currency allowance on writing materials and a copy of Baudelaire's *Fleurs du Mal*. The single cabin assigned to him on the vessel was, it emerged, to be shared with an immigrant from Poland, with no English but many sacks of onions whose un-Baudelairean fragrance permeated the voyage.

The *Artza* was not Cunard and bounced sickeningly around the Mediterranean like a cork. Once arrived at Haifa Spender's work began. 'In Israel,' he recorded, 'I worked for fourteen hours a day, taking notes on everything I did.' *Learning Laughter* is made up of vivid first impressions of the integration of African-Jewish children into Israel, which was efficiently done, he thought; of kibbutzim, which he approved of; of the Middle Eastern desert, which moved him; of Jerusalem, whose partitions made him uneasy; and Tel Aviv, which he hated – the capital's buildings were 'architectural whores'.

Learning Laughter is also remarkable for what it omits to mention. The 1948 War of Independence is never referred to. Nor, more contemporary readers will note, is the Holocaust (not that this horrific crime was much mentioned by any commentators until the 1960s). This absence was not coyness on Spender's part. He constructed his book around the vision of a newborn state as lacking in history as a new-born baby. The children whom he accompanied on his pilgrimage from Marseilles *are* Israel. As with *World within World*, which begins and ends with the author's earliest childhood memories, the child is father to the man – and in Israel's case, to the state.

On his return from Israel in late April, Spender was plunged into arrangements for the 'Festival of Twentieth-Century Masterpieces of Modern Arts' in Paris. Sponsored by the CCF and directed by Nicolas Nabokov, the festival aimed to demonstrate that Western culture – specifically American modernist culture – could be mobilized as ideological resistance to the Soviet Union's *Kultura*. The CIA's International Organizations Division, which had an annual budget of $250 million, clandestinely helped underwrite the operation. Nabokov serenely took the credit for raising the money from a (supposedly) private source. The programme was scheduled to last a whole month. A huge cast of speakers and performers was recruited. The main expense (costing a massive $166,000) involved transporting the entire Boston Symphony Orchestra to Paris, for an overture performance of Stravinsky's *Rite of Spring*. Literature and Philosophy were represented by Auden, Faulkner ('only sign of life the empty whisky bottles he threw out of the window'), Katherine Anne Porter, Malraux, Silone, Denis de Rougemont and Allen Tate. Camus and Sartre disobliged.

Learning Laughter was published on time (under Weidenfeld's whip) in late November and received good reviews. The *TLS* thought the four-year-old country a 'good field for the observation of so sensitive a writer as Mr Spender, who combines an acute awareness of the problems of the day with something of the humane aloofness of an intellectual exile from the 1930s'. Youth Aliyah was less pleased. They took exception to the book's mild poking fun at aspects of Israel.

Nineteen fifty-two was a year in which Spender covered thousands of miles in cultural diplomacy for the CCF (including lecturing tours as far afield as South America) and wrote – in consequence – very little. Other than *Learning Laughter*, there was no major book or collection of verse. There would, in fact, be no major new collection until *The Generous Days*, in 1971. A large hole had developed in his career, where his published poetry used to be. His tally for the year is barely a dozen reviews – the lowest figure of his mature writing career. There was, however, a new development in this casual line of work. In 1952, Joe Ackerley began using him in the *Listener*, as a reviewer of fiction. Spender read and reviewed no fewer than twenty-seven novels for the paper between October 1952 and January 1953.

Nineteen fifty-three was the Coronation Year. Entering a new Elizabethan age gave all Britons a bit of a lift. There were other causes for rejoicing at Loudoun Road. Spender was invited to take up the Elliston Professorship at the University of Cincinnati. The chair had been specifically endowed for distinguished poets. John Berryman preceded Spender, Robert Lowell and Robert Frost succeeded him (the last with the disdainful proviso that he would come from New England for only one weekend during his tenure). Spender's appointment was for two academic quarters; February to June. His principal duty, as Elliston Professor, was to deliver the six public lectures on modernism which would by the end of the year be published as *The Creative Element* (a monograph on which he had been labouring since 1944). His theme, as he told the university, was that the modern writer 'is a kind of superegotist, a hero, and a martyr, carrying the whole burden of civilization in his work'. The stipend was a little under $10,000.

At the turn of the year, Spender wrote in his new diary a résumé of 1952 and his resolutions for 1953:

The year – 1952 – has had a great disappointment – not getting the Byron professorship – a blessing hardly disguised as far as all the others are concerned, which hardly consoles me. There was my visit to Israel . . . *Learning Laughter* is a book of a kind I will never do again – pure reportage – but quite useful, and not in any way a disgrace . . . During the summer I wrote some poems – a beginning for something better – a new style and new subject matter – a turning point I have been waiting for.

'In general,' he concluded, 'I am in favour of planlessness.' Two of his good resolutions for the new year were 'to clear up the huge waste paper basket in my mind' and 'never to run the gauntlet of publishing a volume of poems ever again'.

There was the usual rush to get things ready for his trip. Spender would go by himself, even though it was a five-month stint. It was too much disturbance to remove Matthew from the Hall. Lizzie was still a toddler and household help was needed if her mother was to function professionally. Natasha had engagements in the UK for 1953 which could not be put off. Spender would, perforce, be a grass widower for a month or two. He was contracted to go to Cincinnati on 5 February – assuming his visa came through. It might not. There had been McCarthyite furore in Washington and much paranoia about 'Reds'. The resulting McCarran act made it difficult for anyone who had ever had, however tenuous, a relationship with the Communist Party to enter America. In the *New York Times*, 7 December 1952, Raymond Walters, President of the University of Cincinnati, publicly announced that 'the record of Stephen Spender, British poet, indicates that he is now hostile to the Communist doctrine'. None the less Dr Walters conceded that the fact Spender had *ever* been a member of the Communist Party 'came as a complete surprise to the university officials'. It was not, as Spender's voluminous FBI file witnesses, a surprise to the authorities. Whenever the poet entered America over the next ten years, the Bureau was alerted.

As Spender worked on his first lecture in mid-January he had heard nothing from the Embassy about his visa, applied for three months since (he had been amused, at the time, by having to take a Wasserman test, to prove he was not syphilitic). By the end of the month, with only days to go, he was 'crazy' with anxiety. At the last minute another 'waiver' was arranged. Spender was never entirely sure who to thank. As he told friends later that year, he discovered it was Robert Taft who 'got him through the McCarran barrier'. Taft was a Republican politician 'so far to the right that he regarded Senator McCarthy as a vulgar upstart'. Taft was also a powerful man in the smaller world of Cincinnati: the local art gallery, among other city monuments, was named after his family. He died later that year, but not before Stephen had a chance to thank him and talk about pictures with him.

Spender left England's fogs on 5 February. 'Natasha and I rather silent and sad' and Matthew 'really unhappy', he noted, as he left the house. Lizzie was, at two, too young to take in Daddy's going away. But her father felt the separation keenly. With his uncanny precocity, Matthew had announced three weeks earlier, 'We oughtn't to have christened her Elizabeth. We should have christened her just Beauty, that's all.'

Spender arrived in Cincinnati on 8 February. He took up residence in a small apartment 'just opposite the campus'. He was particularly struck by the room's 'wall paper of broad pink and cream stripes'. The ugly furnishings inspired a poem, 'Missing my Daughter', built round the conceit of Lizzie trapped in the wallpaper's 'bars'. It is written in what he called, in his journal, 'my new style and subject matter':

> This wall-paper has lines that rise
> Upright like bars, and overhead
> The ceiling's patterned with red roses.
> On the wall opposite the bed
> The staring looking-glass encloses
> Six roses in its white of eyes.

His principal task was to give a weekly public lecture, the first two of which were on Rimbaud and Yeats. He was also contracted for a creative writing class and the occasional follow-up tutorial. He could look forward to a three-week break at Easter between the winter and spring quarters. His timetable at Cincinnati was relaxed enough for lecture trips across the country. There was the inevitable ordeal by publicity. Local newshounds had got wind of 'Mr Spender's communism'. Red heresy was abroad. The campus paper, the *Recorder*, published an article about 'the ex-communist on the campus'. Its journalistic style, thought the English ex-communist in question, 'would have disgraced a boy of 10'. Even more shaming was the way in which the head of the English department, Dr William Clark, a scholar of some eminence, truckled to the ignoramus student reporter. 'I had the strong impression we were throwing ourselves on the young man's mercy,' Spender tartly noted.

Having been 'processed', Spender settled down to a quiet scholarly routine, interspersed with the familiar academic hospitalities. He saw a lot of the poet Allen Tate – now a warm friend. He also made what would be long-term friendships with Professor George Ford, a congenial Lawrentian, and Gil Bettman, a lawyer and future judge. His Elliston lectures – with their strong biographical emphasis – were well received and the creative writing course, with its fifteen enrolled students, went 'very well'. He met some of the great people of Cincinnati society. He also met the multi-millionaire Julius Fleischmann. 'Junkie', as his friends called him, lived with his wife Dorette in a nobs' compound, Indian Hill, outside the city. The head of the Farfield Foundation had been enriched by Fleischmann's table products – notably margarine.

When she came out in April, Natasha was impressed by the city's musical ambience:

I was immediately lent a piano, sent for my use to a university room. Apart from the many symphony concerts we enjoyed Sunday morning chamber music at the house of Mrs Wurlitzer [heiress of the electric organ firm]. The very German atmosphere of Hausmusik, leisured yet devout, solemnly vital yet nostalgic, transported us happily back, Stephen to his years in Germany and I to my Funtington childhood.

The plans for what would be *Encounter* were meanwhile forging ahead. On 14 March, Spender noted in his journal that 'Irving Kristol came here yesterday and spoke of the new magazine.' He had discussed the possible appointment of himself as co-editor with Natasha, before leaving England. He wrote to Paris on 14 March accepting the position, 'in principle'. On 30 April, Frederick Warburg wrote from the BSCF (the British offshoot of the CCF) to say that:

The Magazine, still nameless, appears to be firmly on the map. Nabokov and Josselson came to London yesterday and I had a long session with them at the Garrick Club and a restaurant. A firm decision was made to offer you the joint editorship with Irving Kristol, at a salary of £2,000 per annum, of which possibly £500 per annum can be paid as an expense allowance and thus be tax free. It was the feeling of all present that your salary should be the same as Kristol's. Your engagement would be from the first of July next, on the assumption that you will be back in London by that date, and it will run for a minimum period of eighteen months . . . Your salary will in fact be paid by the British Society, and we have taken on this obligation together with responsibility for a secretary.

The blueprint for the new journal was laid down at a CCF meeting in Paris on 13 July. Arising out of this meeting, Josselson formally submitted to the Farfield Foundation in New York a request for £40,000 to indemnify the first twelve months' publication. It was now settled that the American Kristol and the Briton Spender would share editorial responsibility. It had been decided, while Spender was still in America, not to have an advisory board. Instead, there would be regular dinners in London with Muggeridge, Warburg, Tosco Fyvel, Kristol and Spender in attendance. Less regularly, the officers and trustees of the magazine would dine with Josselson in Paris. This lack of formal structure would, over time, become intensely frustrating to Spender.

The magazine was to be London-based, answerable to Paris, Anglo-American flavoured, and international in its circulation. It was a complex mix. Kristol's constant refrain was that *Encounter* must not become a 'house journal'. On the issue of 'independence', he and Spender were of one mind. The crux was money. If the support was predominantly from the CCF, and its American patrons, how could they *not* call the tune? 'Muggeridge,' as Goronwy Rees recorded (in a memorandum dated 12 May 67), 'thought it wrong it should be *all* American money.' He duly raised some British money, ostensibly from private donors including Alexander Korda and the *Daily Telegraph* (where Muggeridge currently worked), to finance the English editor (Spender) and a typist-administrator, Margot Walmsley. The English Foreign Office also, as it much later emerged, clandestinely made unacknowledged subventions, details of which have never been clearly made public.

Kristol was paid directly and entirely by the CCF, in dollars, in America. This enabled him to evade the 'fantastically complicated British tax situation'. Kristol also had a 'local overseas allowance' which financed him to live in some style in London with his wife Gertrude Himmelfarb and their son William. London, Kristol airily informed a friend in May, is 'a charming city and needs only some good chefs and attractive women to be inhabitable'. In addition to his reporter's typewriter, the hard-boiled New Yorker bought himself a bowler hat and furled umbrella to look his new part. He was, apparently, amazed at how many homo-sexuals there were in the city.

Editorial responsibilities were nominally equal. But from the start Kristol was observably better connected with Josselson and Paris. Both editors had impressive credentials. Kristol had been managing editor on *Commentary*, Spender had been instrumental in *Horizon's* success. Both had made the ideological passage from youthful Communism to Liberalism (Kristol would eventually go all the way to neo-Conservatism). The CCF sent £750 petty cash in mid-June, which Kristol used to set up his office (including a state-of-the-art typewriter for himself). For a one-off fee of £250, Secker and Warburg gave technical assistance and the goodwill of the firm's name to get the first issue launched. The magazine established itself at Panton House, off the Haymarket. It was central – but, as visitors invariably noted, 'pokey'. The name of the maga-zine provoked much head-scratching. They finally settled on *Encounter* (Natasha Spender's inspired suggestion).

The editors established the payment schedule as '£10 for a thousand words' and 'four shillings a line for poetry'. When Spender left in 1967, *Encounter* was paying ten guineas a thousand words, and the same four shillings a line for verse. From the first Spender thought *Encounter* a regret-tably miserly paymaster. It was important to him that they broaden the magazine, as he had helped broaden *Horizon*, beyond the merely literary and political. He recruited, inter alia, David Sylvester and Peter Watson as commentators on art; Humphrey Searle on music; and philosophers such as Richard Wollheim and A. J. Ayer. It was a matter of regret that Eliot eluded him. The great man of Anglo-American letters was wary. He was chronically suspicious of the 'American auspices' of the magazine.

From the start there was evident a difference not just in areas of responsibility between Spender and Kristol, but in editorial style. The American tended to commission contributions concerned with big ideas, politics or current affairs. Spender cultivated a certain kind of contrib-utor – typically using his circle of literary and personal acquaintance (the 'Piccadilly commandoes', as Kristol and his friends sarcastically called them). For most British readers the 'literary' section, or 'back half', of the magazine was its main attraction.

Since Spender was away until July, Kristol necessarily did much of the spadework for the inaugural October issue. He and Fyvel decided on yellowish paper, quarto format, double columns, and prominent capitals speckling every page. Spender never quite liked the physical look of the magazine (particularly the spindly columns) – although he managed, over the years, to get some cover illustrations that pleased his eye. On his return, Spender took a full part in the commissioning of articles for the first issue. He secured two plums: an extract from Virginia Woolf's diaries and a short story from Isherwood.

For the first issue Kristol's lead piece was by Leslie Fiedler, whom he commissioned in May to write on the Julius and Ethel Rosenberg executions. Fiedler's thesis was that the spies had indubitably been guilty of passing atomic secrets to the Soviets. Feelings ran high about the grisly electrocution, particularly of Ethel Rosenberg, only eighteen months earlier. It was an article designed to provoke. Kristol nurtured and painstakingly 'edited' (i.e. rewrote) the piece. He was sure, he told Harold Kaplan, that it was 'the best article' in the issue. Spender thought it betrayed 'rather obvious anti-communism'. Kristol's friends affected to find a 'musty odor' in 'Spender's part of the magazine'.

As early as 22 January 1954, after the fifth issue, Spender wrote to Josselson to say that although they had made a 'good start' he was very unhappy about the 'political side' of the magazine:

> It is very unfortunate that the side of the magazine which is owing to America is inferior in quality to the English side. It is this inferiority – inferiority in style and content – which gives the impression that we are dictated to by a committee of tough Americans . . . It is very generally thought here that I am in some way obliged to publish certain tendentious material.

Whatever suspicions there were about American influence the first issue promptly sold 10,000 copies: twice what the editors had expected. Sales of 20,000 were confidently projected within the year. The magazine out-*Horizoned Horizon*. Ian Hamilton, on his deathbed in 2002, recalled it as the only magazine of his time whose new issues he had awaited with impatience. There were many like him. In America, Robert Silvers (later the co-editor of the *New York Review of Books*) thought *Encounter* 'was for a while the best journal of its kind – anywhere'. But, Silvers adds, it had one 'obvious defect. It was inherently uncritical of the American situation' (unlike the *NYRB*). Such subjects as race and Vietnam got little attention.

From the first Spender was also anxious about the polemical anti-Communism of *Encounter*. William Empson bombarded the magazine with 'rather mad' letters. The opinions of old liberals like E. M. Forster, who had hated the Rosenberg article, weighed strongly with Spender, as did Eliot's polite refusal to have anything to do with it. 'The political atmosphere emitted by *Encounter*,' E. M. Forster declared, 'has been regrettable, and I don't see how it is to be dispersed while your present co-editor remains.' Spender felt, as he told Josselson on 22 October, that he was being viewed as an American stooge by his British friends. This was 'naturally very painful to me'. From surviving correspondence in the CCF archive it is clear that politically sensitive articles – from the first – were cleared with Josselson. He was, on the whole, light-handed. But the hand was always there.

In late 1953, having worked with his co-editor for six months, Spender wrote in his journal his impressions of Irving Kristol.

Irving Kristol fascinates me. He looks rather like a caterpillar which has pale bright blue eyes placed rather flatly in his head. He sits at his desk all day long, usually arriving at the office early, but it is very difficult to see what he does. All his friends are called by names like Pfeffersuss or Opalblut. I think he probably writes them long letters about the goddam English. His occupation, of course, is editing – which indeed, he is meant to do. But he means something quite different from what we mean by it. He means rewriting, chopping about, and tailoring all the articles that come in. He regards a contribution as a chassis to which he then adds the coachwork. He loves doing this. He will arrive at the office saying that he has been up all night 'editing' Nathan Glazer's or Leslie Fiedler's piece. 'Hope he won't mind', he says. Then adds, reassured, 'Nah. He won't. He does the same to mine'. One day he told me that his real ambition was to be on the editorial staff of *Time* . . . his contempt for writers is absolute. 'You have too much respect for writers' he's always telling me: 'It's *our* magazine isn't it?' . . . He thinks the magazine should consist exclusively of editors, plus one over-worked secretary.

Despite the sarcasm, Spender would – over the years – see Kristol as the best American editor he worked with on the magazine. But incorrigibly American.

There was more to 1953 than magazines. On his return to England, in July, Spender had a family to bond with again. On 8 August, he took Lizzie and Matthew on a weekend outing to Swanage. Lizzie was up at six, chanting, 'Seaside, Matthew, seaside!' The station was so appallingly crowded that they had to travel first class. They chattered away to each other in Anglo-Italian – 'exhibitionistically', as Spender indulgently thought. In Swanage they stayed three days in a hotel, took excursions in a motor boat, and bathed. Spender took a wry pleasure in the spectacle of his compatriots on vacation:

The English occupy their own landscape. They arrive with deckchairs, Sunday newspapers, tea-kettles, and their own native ugliness, relieved occasionally by extraordinary beauty. They sit down in front of a mountain or the ocean, stick their legs up in front of them, and sit out their holidays . . . Here at Swanage the beach is a close-packed mass of deck-chairs. These are as it were the front-line trenches beyond which lies the enemy itself, the sea. Reading their papers and making cups of tea, the front-line heroes feel that they are going over the top for the sake of the kiddies, who are supposed to be enjoying it.

At the end of each day, as he put his own kiddies to bed, Spender felt 'strangely sad as though something immensely important might have happened in the last half hour'.

Later in August, he and Natasha took a holiday in Corfu with Hansi Lambert and her daughter, Lucie. As they cruised round the coast in the yacht chartered by Lucie Lambert, sitting on the deck in canvas chairs, Spender recalled the *Odyssey*; a literary afflatus rather diminished by the hordes of 'delinquent children' (less regimentally disciplined than their Swanage counterparts) who swarmed round them wherever they touched shore. He loved the new sensory impressions, particularly the late afternoons. The conversation was good. Spender was particularly struck by Lucie's glamorous companion, Michel. 'People like Michel,' he wrote in his journal, 'always disturb me very much. They live their dreams and they make me dream of a life I might have lived.'

The Creative Element, the fruit of Spender's Elliston lectures, was brought out by Hamish Hamilton at the end of the year. It was dedicated to his comrade of his stint in Cincinnati, Allen Tate. The *TLS* was sour. It was affronted by the author's 'lack of academic caution'. Spender was always vulnerable, in his critical writing, to this kind of lordly sneer. But viewed sympathetically, his meditations on Yeats, Lawrence, Rimbaud, Rilke and other 'moderns' mark a significant shift from the moderate Marxism of the book's predecessor (*The Destructive Element*) to something more avowedly spiritual. Other reviewers (in the *Listener, New Statesman* and

Spectator) picked up this aspect of the book more sympathetically. The balance of reviews was distinctly favourable. And the sales were healthier than more 'academically cautious' monographs might expect.

The death in November 1953 of Dylan Thomas, aged thirty-nine, cast a pall over the 'summer of the Elizabethan age'. Spender had hoped he might get Eliot to write an obituary in *Encounter*. In the event, he wrote it himself (it boosted the circulation of the December issue palpably). A month later he had a disturbing dream about Dylan, in which the Welsh poet was standing, 'transparently alive', at his own funeral, in King's College (an unlikely resting place for the unlettered roaring boy).

Matthew was sleeping in his father's bedroom, Natasha being away from home at the time. One morning, Stephen saw his son looking out of the window at Household Cavalry horses, cantering down Loudoun Road. The boy shouted, excitedly: 'Look, look! Their heels are on fire', as he saw sparks being struck from the road by the horses' hooves. This, Spender thought, was 'how Dylan saw'. He wrote a poem on the pyrotechnic theme, consciously imitating the Dylan mode, playing with his favourite pub (the *Catherine*), and his dying around Guy Fawkes Day:

> In November of Catherine Wheels and rockets,
> This roaring ranter, man and boy,
> Proved Guy Fawkes true, and burned on a real fire.

Unlike the roaring, ranting Welsh boy, he thought, 'I myself see things clearly from the outside, at a distance, through the instrument of what I am.'

Early in 1954 Spender was again in America, lecturing at Ivy League colleges on the East coast. As a critic of literature he was becoming increasingly impatient of the narrowness of contemporary British literary culture. It was the theme of a string of influential articles for the *New York Times* in 1954. The first, on 10 January, 'A Literary Letter from London', expounded the main ground of his quarrel. 'The only new writers,' he declared, 'are the old ones.' Spender pressed his paradox home with a satirical 'Letter to a Young Writer' ('Henry James Joyce Jr.') in *Encounter*. Literary youth, he suggested (*pace* Virginia Woolf) had been a diminishing commodity since 'about 1910'. The theme was again picked up in other 'Letters from London' for New York readers in May and August. The writers of the 1930s had many weaknesses but at least they were not, like today's crop, 'complacent'.

There were important changes taking place at the *Encounter* office.
Since April 1954 there had been negotiations with Dwight MacDonald
to take over as the 'non-literary editor' to replace Kristol. Initially the
arrangement was presented as the American taking a year's sabbatical
from the *New Yorker*, with the unstated rider that, if things worked out,
the sabbatical would become a tenured editorial post with *Encounter*.
Allegedly, 'this was done quietly, and Kristol later claimed that he knew
nothing about it until Michael Josselson informed him he was being
replaced'. In the light of later revelations, MacDonald, although a brilliant journalist, was not an obvious choice, and why the cold warriors
of the CCF should have wanted him is perplexing. He was radical, energetic and still very much a man of the left. The negotiations went on
throughout 1954. Spender pushed energetically for the appointment, as
did Muggeridge. Much as he had come to respect Kristol, Spender, as
he explained to Josselson, found it

impossible to work with him because there is no basis and no machinery for
cooperating. He is, and always has been averse to having any editorial consul-
tations. If one insists on having them, he accepts but in such a way as to make
them not worthwhile . . . I therefore think it would be quite dishonest to go
on working with Irving because there simply is no basis for collaboration. In
our personal relationships I find him very agreeable, and I cannot understand
why he is like this about our work. Finally, I think it must be because he is so
intensely competitive that he regards every decision as a kind of conflict in
which he has to score a victory, either by keeping the decision to himself or
by sabotaging it if it is made by his colleague.

Stephen could, however, leave the office and its worries behind for
a while. The second half of 1954 would be a long intercontinental
pilgrimage – the longest journey of his life. He was now serving as a
free-ranging cultural ambassador for the CCF. He left England at the
end of August. His first stop was in Paris, and the headquarters of the
Congress at the Boulevard Haussman. He, Natasha and Matthew then
travelled on to Rome for an International Congress on Contemporary
Music. He also lectured on 'Freedom in Art' (it was later worked up
into his *Encounter* article 'Inside the Cage'). Matthew, already a budding
historian, solemnly lectured his father on the Holy Roman Empire. In
Rome there was a reunion with Aaron Copland and Sam Barber and
with the Stravinskys. From Italy Stephen flew on to Athens for more

lectures. His life was increasingly that of the international man of letters. It was pleasant to be able to combine it (as he often could not) with the role of family man.

On 5 September, now travelling alone, he arrived in Northern Australia. His first impression of the country was stark: 'The countries of prose and the countries of poetry: this contrast struck me the moment I arrived in Darwin.' Australia he would find to be very prosaic. A crowded schedule of meetings, interviews, and lectures had been set up for him. He had also been charged by the CCF with investigating the possibility of founding a journal. As it happened Natasha was also in the country, on a six-week concert tour with the Sydney Symphony Orchestra, 'playing five concertos and two concert programmes from morn till midnight', as Stephen told Edith Sitwell. For this she would get, he esti-mated, some £500, which they needed. The Spenders bent their Australian schedules to meet 'once or twice'.

Spender stayed six weeks in Australia before being 'pumped full with injections against every imaginable disease' and flying north. On 17 October he stopped over in Kandy and he was in Madras by the 29th of the month. He was met by a delegation, which he describes (as he describes the whole of the Indian trip in his notebook) in high comic terms:

The men looked terribly scruffy, with dirty clothes, dishevelled grey hair, and stomachs protruding under their costume. There was a writer who looked like an Indian dressed up as E. M. Forster dressed up as an Indian in the days when Forster wore a walrus moustache.

He was promptly 'whizzed off' to give lecture after lecture to 'audiences utterly stupefied by the combination of heat and me. As I was, also.' He was stuffed with meals, comprising innumerable courses, all vying with each other in 'inedibility', and lodged in hotels with 'insects the size of bats' clustered on the bedroom ceilings and 'Kafka-sized' beetles in the lounges. He wrote in comic despair to Nicolas Nabokov, on 3 November, from Trivandrum:

Dear Nicky, at last I have 3 solid hours alone! Indians are worse than Americans, worse than Australians, worse than anyone. Hearing of our approach they take up a sheet of paper, decide that you rise at 7 and go to bed at 11, and then fill every minute of the day with lectures, interviews, etc. When there is a blank, they fill it in with a visit to some minister. If you do get a moment alone people call on you (to demonstrate this, five have called since I began this sentence: one, with a questionnaire 'Pound, poet or pedagogue?' 'Would it be right to call this the age of T. S. Eliot?' 'What are the three or four Lehmanns, brothers or sisters, now writing?' 'If that God failed, Mr Spender, did you find another God, who succeeded?' Two – for one had to write down all my answers – to interview me. One with an autograph letter from Julian Huxley, dated March 1925, to say he could not give him a job. (This one asked for 5 rupees).

Spender returned to London in mid-November, via Paris. Towards the end of the year he was troubled by a resurgence of the Tony Hyndman problem. His friend's life had not gone well since they had drifted apart, fifteen years before. His career as a stage manager, which Spender had helped fix up, went wrong. Tony fell out badly with his erstwhile lover, Michael Redgrave (following a particularly fierce quarrel, Hyndman sprinkled tin tacks on a couch on which the actor was obliged to throw himself during the performance of a Strindberg play. Redgrave was quite seriously hurt and very seriously angry). In September 1950, William Plomer had written to Spender saying:

the other day the tail of my coat was twitched as I was peering in a window in Kensington Church Street. I turned round and there was Tony (Hyndman). I hadn't seen him for a long time, and I got a curious and really rather disturbing impression of him – he was so like and yet so unlike my memory's impression of him . . . he said he was going to Australia.

He did not go.

Spender had been careful to send Tony a complimentary copy of *World within World*. The description of himself as Jimmy Younger infuriated him. Stephen suggested, unmaliciously, that he publish his own autobiographical account. In January 1952, a few days before Spender left for Paris, Isherwood, who was in London, phoned up to say that Hyndman had rung him from Bristol, to report that he was in a very bad way. Tony had been passing bad cheques – most seriously one for £10 with Peggy Ashcroft's signature forged on it. 'I've committed a felony,' he had bleakly told Christopher. Over 1953–4 another friend, E. M. Forster, wrote more than once to say that Hyndman (now based in Norwich) had appeared in Cambridge to cadge money from him. 'Is pilfering among Tony's troubles?' he delicately inquired. Things had a habit of disappearing when the Welshman was around. It was embarrassing – and occasionally frightening. Hyndman had also turned up at Loudoun Road when Natasha Spender was alone with the children. On one occasion, Matthew recalls, he cadged the little boy's half-crown pocket money off him. More seriously, there had been thefts in the house while the Spenders were away and Hyndman (who had been asked to keep an eye on the property) was suspected by them of having been involved.

Something had to be done about Tony. At root were drink and drugs. He had picked up a heroin habit, pre-war, from Peter Watson's lover, Denny Fouts. Spender helped Hyndman get treatment for his addictions. He underwent various courses of detoxification and rehabilitation over 1954–6. Natasha visited him regularly in hospital. Over the subsequent years, Spender would get letters from well-meaning clergymen, when Tony suffered a relapse.

It ended peacefully. There survives a series of letters from the early 1970s, in which Hyndman makes contact again with Spender. Hyndman had gone back to Cardiff. On 16 June 1974, he tells Spender that pressure of work at British Steel, where he had found a job as a clerk, had proved too much for him. At the age of sixty-three he had taken early retirement. In his spare time, he works with recovering alcoholics, like himself. He has bought himself a typewriter and is writing his memoirs. But he is afflicted with spells of giddiness and cannot concentrate. According to Richard Felstead, Spender sent Tony a radio in his last years and helped his old friend out with money. He died in 1982, of emphysema, aged seventy-one.

The big literary event of 1955 for Spender was Faber's publication in April of *Collected Poems: 1928–53*. The poet's method of collecting his work was idiosyncratic. He copied out candidate poems in an exercise book, feeling the work of twenty-five years through his pen again. The result was a combined sieving and fine-tooth combing. Rewriting enabled him, while selecting the final 111, to revise and rewrite as he went – sometimes drastically. The dimensions of the book were marked by the first poem: 'He will watch the hawk with an indifferent eye'. This anthem to Marston recorded the discovery of his mature voice. *Collected Poems* was issued in the shadow of Dylan Thomas's death, in November 1953. The elegy with which Spender chose to end the volume was a pastiche of the brilliant, doomed Welsh poet's New Apocalyptic, firecracker style.

The premature death of Thomas represented a terminus in British poetry. Now that Auden was American, and Eliot (if English) aged and quiescent, the force had gone. In totality, the poems were arranged in what Spender called 'autobiographical', rather than 'chronological' order. Bravely, he included – as witness to his growth – poems which he knew might embarrass himself or his friends (he cites, as examples, 'The Pylons' and 'The Funeral'). The result, he trusted, was 'a weeded, though not a tidied up or altered garden'.

The *Listener* pursued the horticultural theme. Spender had 'done well to put his garden in order by ruthlessly sacrificing the failures of early phases'. As re-ordered, the collection 'imports a vivid sense of freshness and colour, like the work of some minor Impressionist painter'. 'Minor' was somewhat barbed, but the tone was generally favourable, as was Anthony Hartley in the *Spectator*, who thought the collection 'presents a meditative, introspective type of poetry, owing something, no doubt, to Rilke and something to symbolism'. Spender's poetry was like 'a faulty electric light but when it comes off it has as little to do with the "Thirties" movement as the best poems of Mr Day-Lewis'. In the *New Statesman* G. S. Fraser admitted to liking the poet's 'deliberate flatness'; his work had 'an awkward grace' and 'clumsy adroitness'. The volume was 'impossible to read without feeling respect for the slow patience of the craftsman and an affection for the gentle heart and honestly groping mind of the artist'.

The *TLS* review was anything but affectionate. Leavis's protégés were graduating into posts of cultural power. Their blackest beasts were Spender and the British Council (whose favourite lecturer was Spender). There emerged a standard Leavisite method for anathematizing Spender. As he later told Reynolds Price: 'they review *me*, not my poems'. Spender's friends felt that as a poet he was, nowadays, comprehensively under-estimated by his contemporaries – and routinely vilified. Edith Sitwell wrote to him, on receiving her presentation copy of the *Collected Poems*, on 4 May to say: 'When I look round at the silly *little people* priding themselves on their non-existent "cleverness" and then at your poetry, I wonder why they should trouble to write anything down.' Spender was stoical. But he felt he was being forced out of English poetry. He renewed his resolve to preserve a ten-year sabbatical.

In the higher echelons of the CCF, things were stirring. The magazine's discreet negotiations with Dwight MacDonald were still progressing. There was, however, some uneasiness at the prospective new editor perhaps being too leftist and notoriously headstrong – although it was accepted that he would, in this respect, be closer to Spender than some of the harder men in the Congress. On his part, MacDonald gave assurances that he had no 'unfriendly' feelings towards his new employers. He was given a kind of roving correspondent role over 1955, to write for *Encounter*, preparatory to something firm being offered. He and Spender were getting on well, but it was clear that MacDonald was not in line for quite the powerful position Kristol had enjoyed.

Domestically 1955 was, for the Spenders, somewhat complicated by the Raymond Chandler problem. With the invention of the 'private eye' Philip Marlowe, Chandler had established himself as the living master of the hard-boiled detective story. Marlowe's creator was, alas, sadly soft-boiled. Writing was never easy for him and his main support during his career had been his wife Cissy. Twenty years older than Raymond, Cissy dressed and acted twenty years younger. When she died in the early 1950s, he fell apart.

Chandler had always garnered more respect from literary Britain than literary America. His English publisher, Hamish Hamilton, treated the American writer with flattering deference. Chandler himself was extravagantly proud of having spent part of his boyhood at a British public school. In April 1955, a man of means (thanks mainly to film rights on the Marlowe novels and his own film work), he moved to the UK for an extended trip, taking up residence at the Connaught Hotel. Chandler was at this period drinking heavily. He frequently threatened suicide and made a few fuddled attempts at self-destruction.

Hamilton and his wife, Yvonne, gave a luncheon party to introduce Chandler to the British literary élite. The Spenders were present, and Natasha 'saw he was having a miserable time and, in hopes of cheering him up, invited him to dinner the following week'. As it happened, Chandler already knew their name. He had admired extravagantly Stephen's contribution to *The God that Failed*. Natasha Spender and her friends put themselves out to rescue the obsessively self-destructive Chandler. He, on his part, found the attention of these Englishwomen intoxicating. Over the summer Chandler threw himself into London society and its literary parties. To get him through the bad spells, Natasha Spender and her friends formed what they called a 'shuttle service'. One of the shuttlers, Alison Hooper, wryly recalled: 'There was a lunch-hour patrol, a drinks-and-dinner shift – even on occasions a dawn watch.' Natasha found that taking Chandler sight-seeing in a car was useful. 'It gave him something to do and kept him away from the bar.'

As Spender noted in his journal, 'things I do other than writing seem to take up a larger and larger place in my life'. His time was divided between editorial work for *Encounter*, lecturing, and travel. On 22 May he left for Vienna, after the family had spent a weekend at Funtington (the Booths' house, where Natasha had spent much of her childhood). The trip was accompanied by an ill omen. As they were leaving the Booths' house, Matthew caught his hand in the car door. As they drove him to the nearest hospital the ten-year-old boy 'sat in the back of the car, blood streaming from his finger, and tears in his eyes'. All he said was: 'Oh God, how it hurts. Oh damn, oh damn, oh damn.' The event recalled other tragedies in the boy's little life; the running-over, for example, of his dog Bobby – a 'rather lugubrious looking spaniel' and a present from his godmother, Edith Sitwell. Six-year-old Matthew had been disappointed by the hound's demise not being reported in the obituary columns of next day's *Times*. Most traumatic had been the massacre of his pet canary, Hector, by the family Siamese cat, three years earlier. It inspired the tenderly paternal poem, 'Boy, Cat, Canary':

> Once, hearing a shout, I entered his room, saw what carnage:
> The Siamese cat had worked his tigerish scene;
> Hector lay on the floor of his door-open cage
> Wings still fluttering, flattened against the sand.
> Parallel, horizontal, on the rug, the boy lay
> Mouth biting against it, fists hammering boards.
> 'Tomorrow let him forget.' I prayed, 'Let him not see
> What I see in this room of miniature Iliad –
> The golden whistling howled down by the dark.'

In Vienna – 'the great centre of hallucinations', as he called it – Spender consulted with the Austrian editor of *Forum*, 'a kind of sister magazine of *Encounter*'. He went (as he usually did in that city) to the opera, wondering, in a world-weary way, whether he could still, as a listener, 'rise to the height' of Wagner's *Tristan*. The production, to his dismay, was 'banal'. Not worth rising to; nothing here was. Vienna – a city which was immensely important to him – had become, of all things, *bürgerlich*, under a crust of 'phoney boom'.

In August Stephen and Matthew took a trip with the Lamberts on their yacht in the south of France. For the boy it was a terrific adventure, seeing himself, as his father perceived, in the heroic role 'of the young sailor in the crow's nest who sighted land for Christopher Columbus'. For Stephen it was an opportunity to read Wordsworth, and to ponder the egotistical sublime; more particularly how it connected with his own poetic practice. 'I', he wrote in his journal:

is Wordsworth's whole sentient being, the instrument of self that through the senses responds to, and is part of, nature. This sentient 'I' has direct communication with nature and therefore is not bookish – regards books as dangerous lore and intellect as only a part of being.

It was as much himself that he was thinking of and his own lifelong search for immediacy in his verse.

Nineteen fifty-five was a bumper year for *Encounter*. The magazine garnered a huge increase in sales and readerships with Nancy Mitford's skit on 'U and non-U' usage. Spender had initially commissioned a piece from his friend in early March on the 'British Aristocracy'. What he had in mind was something satirical illustrated by Osbert Lancaster and appropriate for the Christmas 1955 issue. Mitford's article was published in *Encounter* on 22 September. It was sensationally popular. A thousand offprints were run off for separate sale. The whole population of the country seemed to be asking themselves whether 'loo', 'lav' or 'toilet'; 'serviette' or 'napkin'; 'lunch' or 'luncheon' were the approved 'U', or the dreaded 'non-U' alternative.

In early October Spender went on a lecture tour (one of many at this period) to Germany for the Deutsch-Englische Gesellschaft, lecturing on Lawrence and Orwell. *En route* to Berlin he called on Curtius in Bonn, now, amazingly, the German capital. His old teacher had declined the dedication of the early segment of *Collected Poems*. Spender was in some doubt as to whether he would even be allowed entry in Joachim Strasse. Ernst Robert had suffered a stroke, and had difficulty speaking. Stephen was admitted by his wife, Ilse, and went down to Curtius's study. There was some conversation, in halting German. Despite the impediment of his stroke Ernst Robert mustered his old magisterial instincts into a rebuke: 'You were a communist and now you go on yachts in the Mediterranean . . . ja . . . ja . . .' Spender patiently explained (1) that he could no longer live in a bedsitter (morally worthy as that might be) and (2) 'I have never been in any real sense a communist.' The encounter ended amicably, if awkwardly.

Berlin was, inevitably, a disappointment – haunted as it was by the same memories of 1931–2 that had hovered over the meeting with Curtius. The Western sectors of the city had been rebuilt, but without any indigenous style. The East sector of the city was oppressed by the ideological uniformity symbolized by Stalin Allee – which, in its tiled grandeur, reminded Spender of a gigantic public lavatory (not, *pace* Mitford, 'toilet'). The 'glittering promenades' of West Germany reminded him of 'false teeth'. Like Germany of the 1920s, Germany of the 1950s was a 'laboratory demonstration of the effects of history'. He preferred the 1920s experiment.

History had moved on. Nineteen fifty-five was the era of the H-bomb, the four-minute warning, CND, and the fear of global annihilation. Peggy Ashcroft gave a prize to the Hall School, for the best poem written by one of its young pupils. 'With the best will in the world she couldn't help giving it to Matthew,' recalls his mother, 'who wrote a grimly apoc-alyptic poem called "Doomsday", all about the atom bomb.' The young pessimist was already a talented painter.

For Spender the crucially influential event of 1956 was a meeting in March of the European Cultural Association, in Venice. This 'very select gathering' was historically momentous: 'the first of its kind, I think, since de-Stalinization – between Soviet and Western European intellectuals'. On 25 February at a closed session of the 20th Conference of the Communist Party, Nikita Kruschev had denounced Stalin as a tyrant. It threw off-balance the whole complicated business of 'peaceful co-existence'. No one was sure what the 'thaw', as it was called, would mean. Was it even a ruse? The CCF view was suspicious. For them the war was still as cold as it had ever been. Josselson strongly discouraged Spender from attending. Spender insisted that he must go: 'If we refuse to meet the Russians, then in the *dégel* we risk being left behind by events, for the *dégel* is likely to become a *déluge*.'

Spender recalled precisely what his first reaction was, on 17 March, when he read Kruschev's speech. He felt 'the kind of horrified satisfac-tion one gets with the end of *King Lear*, when Edmund exclaims: "the wheel has come full circle. I am here."' His other, less lofty, reaction was surprise that *anyone* had ever believed *anything* the old crook in the Kremlin ever said. The Soviet premier's speech was made public just six days before the Venice meeting. The conferees were distinguished, inter-national, and intellectually high-powered. The existentialist Jean-Paul Sartre and Merleau-Ponty represented France – currently world leader in philosophy. The Communist scientist J. D. Bernal and the men of letters Alan Pryce Jones and Stephen Spender came in under the English flag. The Russians – wholly disoriented by events at home – were a bunch of party hacks, headed by the 'old buffer' (as Spender called him), Fedin. Among the Italians were friends such as Ignazio Silone and Carlo Levi. Signor Compagnolo, the head of the Italian delegation, presided impotently over the events.

The Conference kicked off, on 26 March, with a keynote debate on 'the Idea of Literature *Engagée*'. That is, what could the printed word *do*? The Frenchmen, Sartre and Merleau-Ponty, argued for the necessity of 'engagement' – but from radically different positions. In the chair, Compagnolo was useless. He had organized the discussion on a round table so vast in its circumference that – symbolically – dialogue was impossible. The debate 'was quickly reduced to absurdity by Sartre putting forward the view that discussion between the Russians and ourselves was meaningless because we were inhabitants of incommunicable ideological worlds'. The Russians, however, were so unsure of what fate awaited them in the USSR that they did not want to communicate about anything, even assuming, *contre Sartre*, that such a thing were epistemologically possible. Bernal, inflexible until death, cleaved to the old Stalinist line. Pryce Jones was ironic. Before the débâcle stage of the conference Spender got in his point, 'that the only writer who *had* to be *engagé* was the one whose social conscience could be realized in the results of his imagination'. Poetry, that is, mattered.

The March 1956 conference, as it descended into farce, would – two years later – inspire a comic novella, *Engaged in Writing: A Collage*. In it Spender himself is the uneasy Olim Asphalt, a LITUNO (i.e. UNESCO) representative who, in the climax of the story, publicly resigns. Asphalt's *non serviam* was, in a sense, his creator's. Spender lost faith, in March 1956, in the power of international meetings of mind. The vision which had so enthused him at the Geneva *rencontre* in 1947 was dead. The Venice conference was as formative an event as that meeting of writers in 1937 in Madrid, when he had lost for ever what was left of his Communist ideals.

Nineteen fifty-six saw one of the great shifts in British poetic taste. 'The Movement' came into being as a school with Robert Conquest's *New Lines* (a title that inevitably evoked Michael Roberts's *New Signatures* – new no more). Conquest's anthology contained work by Philip Larkin, Kingsley Amis, Thom Gunn, Ted Hughes, Donald Davie. Spender's review of *New Lines* in the *New Statesman* began sharply: 'Introductions which attempt, while not quite daring, to be manifestos, are always tiresome.' Nor did he much like the ironic complacency of Donald Davie's 'Remembering the Thirties', written by someone who was a schoolboy safe in his playground when he, Spender, was under Fascist bombs in Spain:

> The Anschluss, Guernica – all the names
> At which those poets thrilled, or were afraid,
> For me mean schools and schoolmasters and games.

Spender was one of 'those poets'. It was hard to hand the baton over to this grown-up, irreverent schoolboy and his pals. He penned a retaliatory 'Remembering the Thirties' poem for the 5 December issue of *Encounter*:

> When we put pen
> To paper, in those times,
> We knew our written
> Ten lines and five rhymes
> Before you could turn
> The page, might well burn.

Spender had a more amused distaste for the 'Angry Young Men' and their academic cheerleaders, 'young instructors in provincial "red brick" universities . . . intellectuals divided between cabbage beds, teacups, and text books . . . registering complaints about their boredom'. The 'New Provincialism' and its aggressive proletarian philistinism were not to his refined, metropolitan taste. If there was a hope for the modernism he admired, it must be sought in America.

Anglo-American relations (that fascinating 'love-hate' match, as Spender would call it) came under severe strain in 1956. On 2 April the wife of the premier, Clarissa Eden, was invited to Loudoun Road for dinner. Stephen had known her since the early 1940s, through their mutual friend Isaiah Berlin. It was an impressive company. Charlie Chaplin and his wife Oona were also present, Harold Nicolson, Elizabeth Jane Howard and James Pope Hennessy. The Spenders bought a new dining-room table for the event and arranged, unusually, to be waited on at table (an ancient retainer, 'Squires', was borrowed for the occasion from their friends the Hutchinsons). Chaplin was 'rather courteous and deferential' and talked about his deprived childhood in South London and about the Russian leaders, Bulganin and Kruschev ('Bulge and Crush', as Fleet Street called them): 'he said that he did not like Bulganin but he found Kruschev very sympathetic. Obviously Chaplin sympathizes with people like himself,' Spender observed, 'whom he feels to be little men who have become enormously powerful big men.' His friendly feelings for Communism were apparent.

Lady Eden, wife of the Tory Prime Minister, might well have been preoccupied by events at Downing Street. The Suez crisis was brewing up. It would mean an upheaval as consequential for Britain as Kruschev's speech had been for the USSR. The last British soldiers left the Canal Zone in June 1956. A month later, Colonel Nasser nationalized the Suez Canal, expropriating French and British property without compensation. Eden decided to send the gunboats. British and French forces invaded Egypt in late October, with the collusion of Israel. Taking advantage of the distraction, the USSR overran Hungary in November, savagely putting down that country's insurgents. It was a dramatic year, and brought the world close to the 'unthinkable' – nuclear war. Spender tried, vainly, to get a contingent of British writers to go to Budapest, as human shields against the Soviet invasion and the purge which would follow. Some were willing – although Auden refused. The human shield project came to nothing. But Anthony Sampson remembers a great protest march on the Soviet Embassy, organized by Philip Toynbee and other veterans of the Spanish Civil War. 'It got no further than a pub in Knightsbridge.'

Nearer home, Spender had to deal with a crop of deaths. Hilda Schuster died in 1951 and Winifred Paine three years later. Both women had loved and looked after him, in his youth. Peter Watson died on 3 May 1956. It was a terrible shock. On 4 May, a comparative stranger, John Hall, the business manager of the magazine, walked into the *Encounter* office and said, 'Do you know this fellow Peter Watson? He's just been found dead in his bath.' Spender wrote a short, deeply felt, obituary for the *New Statesman*. 'Peter Watson's death,' he wrote:

seems like the extinction of the last of a rare, disinterested, pure and questing human species. No other patron was so individual, so non-institutional: even the word 'patron' seems wrong for him – perhaps a better word would be 'friend'.

Privately, in his journal for 5 May, Spender recorded that his friend and patron 'had more sensibility than cleverness'. It was not a criticism.

It was the more disturbing since the circumstances of Watson's death were mysterious. He had drowned in his bath (with the door locked from the inside) in the flat he shared with his lover, the sculptor Norman Fowler, at Rutland Gate. There was widespread suspicion that, somehow, Fowler, who was dissipated and emotionally deranged, was responsible. He was the main beneficiary in Watson's will, inheriting his partner's art collection. All those who, like the Spenders, knew Watson well (and knew about his weak heart) disbelieved the gossip about Fowler. Watson was cremated, with an 'inhuman service', at Golders Green on 9 May. For Spender, an era had passed with this dismal ceremony.

In February 1956 Auden was elected Professor of Poetry at Oxford, in succession to C. Day-Lewis. He would hold the post for six years. It meant his English friends would see more of him. Auden stayed at Loudoun Road in late May to mid-June, in preparation for his inaugural lecture in June. It would be his pattern to reside in Oxford for three weeks, each summer term. As always, he took over Spender's study at the front of the house as his own and was treated less as a guest than as a member of the family. He loved, and was loved by, the Spender children. On one visit, he made a list of his closest friends in England. 'I'm glad to say that we were near the top,' recalls Natasha Spender; 'but heading the list was Bill Coldstream. So we invited him for dinner. "No, for God's sake *don't!*" said Wystan.' It was perhaps for the best. Dinner parties with Auden as the guest of honour, Natasha quipped, 'were like being in a car with a driver who resolutely charged through every red light'. Why, Lizzie once asked, did Uncle Wystan tell every story twice the same evening? In private conversation, feeling 'incredibly brave', Natasha asked him how he reconciled his religion (strict Anglo-Catholicism) with his sexual practices. 'OK. I sin. OK,' Auden declared, patiently. He trusted the 'Good Lord' would forgive him. Stephen always treated Wystan royally at Loudoun Road, giving him ample room to be Wystan. It was, Joseph Brodsky observed, less out of any sense of inferiority than as a gesture of 'spiritual generosity'.

Spender was in Rome in mid-June for a 'meeting of editors'. He disliked committees and had difficulty concentrating. On one memorable occasion, after doodling away a long discussion, he absent-mindedly voted for his own dismissal. He felt it keenly when bohemians like Lucian Freud, still, in middle age, looking like Struwwelpeter kitted out by Oxfam, twitted him for having become a dark-suited bureaucrat. From 3 July he was in Bologna, on CCF business. It was on this trip to the city that he formed what would be a long friendship with Giorgio Morandi, whose painting he particularly admired. He wrote a long, painstakingly inventorial memorandum of his visit to the artist's studio:

In the centre of the studio is an easel. The rack is thickly covered with a heap of what looks like petrified dust – really, I suppose, paint mixed with dust or sand. Round the room various still lives are arranged – one on a flat table, another on what looks like a revolving table; a stage set or a miniature cyclorama. These exhibits have the air of having been there, in exactly the same position, for years. The tops of bottles and objects like cans are covered with that dust which was perhaps deliberate, 'part of the picture'.

On 7 July he and Natasha went to stay with Nicolas Nabokov at Verderonne, the château outside Paris which he occupied with his third wife, Marie Claire. 'It was very pleasant to be alone with him and not in the usual tangle of committees and dinners,' Spender recorded. The two men got on well together and had agreed to collaborate on an opera, *Rasputin's End*. Spender would do the libretto, Nabokov the music.

The Spenders returned to London on 9 July. That week, as happened quite often this year, he found himself drawn into a row over *Encounter* and its 'ugly American' connections. Michael Ayrton, a Tribune Labourite, made the familiar cracks. Spender was particularly incensed by Ayrton's saying 'that political issues today were as simple as they had been in 1930'. To say this, Spender thought, 'one would either have to be exceptionally perceptive or exceptionally stupid'. Everything was more complicated nowadays. Intellectuals could not be lined up like soldiers on a battlefield.

The regime was changing at the magazine. In January 1956, Dwight MacDonald had been taken on as a roving contributing editor (his role was never clearly defined), and was still evidently being groomed as a potential 'American editor' of *Encounter*. He and his wife Gloria, who joined him in June, with their children, were now installed in London. His initial impressions were favourable and his relations with Spender good. But MacDonald would, during his two-year tenure at *Encounter*, prove to be a difficult colleague. Not least because of his inveterate and growing suspicion of what was going on between the CCF and the US government, and its agencies.

How much *was* known, by those in the know? George Weidenfeld says that he knew from the first that there was government agency money in *Encounter*. At a meeting in 1951, when any new magazine was still a distant project, given the government rationing of paper, he had heard Muggeridge say that funding would be no problem: 'we can always get money from the war office.' Koestler also claimed to have some early inklings. Robert Silvers recalls coming back to New York in 1958 from France, where he had been editing the *Paris Review*. He had been hired as an editor at *Harper's Magazine* and was told that he was in luck: the first in line, Cord Meyer Jr, had turned it down 'because he was having such a good time running magazines for the Congress for Cultural Freedom'. Meyer was known to have connections with the CIA. There were, in fact, always rumours swirling around New York. But, as Silvers puts it: 'everyone *sort of* knew that the Congress had this sort of govern-ment backing – but no one could prove it'. Spender had never met Meyer nor heard rumours that seemed anything other than rumours. And, as such, they were always convincingly denied by the Paris office.

Spender and Natasha spent their summer 'as usual' with the Lamberts. Cyril Connolly, who comically fantasized marrying la baronne Lambert as a solution to his chronic financial problems, had furiously angled for an invitation for himself. His marriage with Barbara Skelton was over (she was now involved with George Weidenfeld – whom she would marry, before returning again to Connolly). Cyril promised Spender faithfully, 'he was not going to bore any of us about it'. The second part of the summer vacation took Stephen to Gstaad. Should Cyril come? They tried to put him off, assuring him that he would be terribly bored in Switzerland. But Cyril's telegrams were 'persistent'. He declined to be put off. He arrived, and 'for the first three or four days was an absolute model of good behaviour'. There was an enlivening excursion to see a Klee exhibition in Berne. But, inevitably, the old Cyril reasserted himself and with him came the familiar chaos. Everyone was plunged into 'the awful maelstrom of Barbara's and Cyril's marriages, divorces, and remar-riages'. There were phone calls at all hours, telegrams, and an air of crisis. At one point, it seemed Barbara Skelton might be coming herself to Gstaad. The upheaval dwarfed the Suez crisis.

Natasha and the children spent the midsummer months at Westwell, in Oxfordshire. The house was leased from Rex Warner and his wife, Barbara (the couple were in the process of separating). On his return from Switzerland, Stephen joined them. For him it was a brief respite during one of the busier years of his life. In mid-September, now back in London, he went into Hendon District Hospital, 'having at last gone through a long overdue operation for varicose veins in my right leg'. He traced the ailment back to cadet service at University College School, and the khaki knee breeches ('puttees') he had to wear tightly wrapped round his calves. The disability had got him out of military drill as a schoolboy, as he recalled. His first pacifist gesture.

Much of the last part of 1956 was spent in the US: Stephen lecturing, Natasha playing and making arrangements for an imminent American tour. In December Stephen was back in London, where, one evening at the Savoy, he arranged a first meeting between Stravinsky and Eliot, two giants of twentieth-century modernism. The conversation was in English and French – 'which Eliot talks slowly and meticulously'. Spender kept a full record for posterity of what was said. The subject moved to health (neither man was well) and the condition of their respective blood. Stravinsky recalled a doctor telling him that his was 'too thick'. His blood was so thick, he went on, 'so rich, so very rich, it might turn into crystals, like rubies'. Eliot said meditatively: 'I remember that in Heidelberg when I was young I went to a doctor and was examined, and the doctor said: "Mr Eliot, you have the thinnest blood I've ever tested."' And Spender's blood? Probably a happy medium.

Not only were the Spenders moving with bewildering speed across the globe at this period of their lives, they were, after 1956, a two-house family in the UK and clocking up many miles on British roads. For some time they had been friendly with Michael Astor and his wife Barbara, who had a large country establishment at Bruern, in Oxfordshire, close to Westwell. In the grounds was a red-brick Queen Anne dower house. In late 1956 Astor goodnaturedly suggested: 'You might like to live in my garden.' When Spender said they would indeed like to take over the cottage (as it was called) and what would the rent be, Astor insisted they should remain his guests, not tenants. They would in fact use Bruern on this friendly basis as their second home for ten years, until buying their 'ruin' in Provence. It was a delightfully convenient getaway from London – more so since both Spenders now drove (Stephen passed his test in January 1956; Natasha in December). Natasha had a grey, red-topped Hillman Minx called 'Paddy' (after Patrick Leigh Fermor's red beret, a relic of his commando days). Spender drove a grey Austin (nicknamed 'Teddy'), before acquiring – with something of a flourish – a Jaguar. Not everyone admired his prowess at the wheel. As Anthony Sampson recalls, 'Stephen drove a large car, slowly, and *very dangerously*.'

Bruern was of less interest to Matthew, now growing up, than to Lizzie, who loved horses, as did the Astors' daughter, Jane. For the adult Spenders, it would become a second centre of their social life. With the Astors they created an intellectual and cultural ambience distinctly different from that at Loudoun Road. It was, as Anthony Sampson recalls,

a wonderfully old-fashioned atmosphere – what I rather imagine life was like before the War. What I remember most is the impression of a world of serious intellectuals. Not very English, really. It was flattering to think one belonged to this world [Sampson was, at the time, a journalist on David Astor's *Observer*]. A couple of dons would come down from Oxford. Selwyn Lloyd, Willy Douglas-Home, Jo Grimond, the Duke of Devonshire would be brought on. Stephen was the resident poet, of course. It was rather like living with Jane Austen. Michael [Astor] of course was very 'Establishment'. He had always wanted to be a journalist. Stephen was a wonderful listener; he gave a wonderful impression of disarming curiosity.

Nineteen fifty-seven marks the beginning of Spender's friendship with a young American writer, Reynolds Price. A graduate of Duke University, Price had been since 1955 a Rhodes scholar, working in Oxford on a B.Litt. thesis on Milton. He was gifted and possessed of huge charm. He intended to be a writer, as well as a scholar. He was fortunate to coincide with Auden – an immense stimulus to ambitious young writers at the university in the late 1950s. He admired his supervisor, Lord David Cecil. Price's literary god, at this stage of his career, was Eudora Welty, who had taken an interest in his writing – although he was as yet unpublished in any significant way.

Price's introduction to Spender came through a letter, written on 25 September 1956 and posted, evidently with delay and trepidation, on 6 October:

Dear Mr Spender, I saw you once in Venice. We passed twice in the streets and then there was the mass on Easter morning in San Marco when I fancied that we saw one another, almost with recognition, through all that space. I thought then that you were the kindest looking man I'd ever seen, and in the memory of those encounters I have been bold to write this. I am an American – 23 and a Southerner – reading English at Merton. I have written three short stories set in my own state – North Carolina. Unpublished. They caught the eye of Eudora Welty, who introduced me to her agent, Diarmid Russell. He has not succeeded yet in placing them. I thought perhaps you might find time, somehow, to read them and to say if you think they would be at all understood in England. I mean: are they too alien lives and tradition to have meaning here? I suppose that only postpones the vital question: do they succeed or fail? This is too bold, of course. You need only say no, if you like. Still, I hope. Yours sincerely, Reynolds Price

Late 1956 had been an unusually hectic period, even for the Spenders. Stephen was off to America for a month, from mid-October to mid-November. Natasha was gearing up for an extended concert tour in America. She would be away from December until late January, throwing the sole parental responsibility for a couple of months on to her husband. Spender, although he was impressed by Price's letter, could not immediately respond. He suggested a meeting much later in the year. It might, in fact, be most convenient to see the young man the next time he addressed the Oxford Poetry Society. Price promptly offered to put him up in his Headington digs – an invitation which Spender drily said he was 'disappointed' not to be able to accept. He usually stayed at All Souls.

In the meantime, Spender suggested that Price send the stories by post; which the young man duly did. Spender did not expect any great literary accomplishment from a student. But Price turned out to be that rare thing, a writer of Keatsian precocity. Spender wrote back in some excitement, six days later, to say he 'liked the stories very much'. He was particularly impressed with 'Chain of Being'. It was 'quite beautiful, a poem or perhaps very poetic cinema'. He determined immediately to 'bash it through' his co-editors and get it published in *Encounter*.

An informal lunch at Loudoun Road was arranged on 15 December. It was a huge success with Stephen Spender and with the children: 'Smashy' (as Matthew was sometimes nicknamed), Lizzie and Dmitri (the live-in servant, Francesca's, child). It was arranged that Reynolds would come to stay during the Christmas break, in the New Year. The January visit was another huge success: 'the house is golden when you are here', Spender told Reynolds (it was also a relief to have someone to help him keep the children occupied). The American visitor camped in the study, as had Auden, his eminent compatriot.

Over this period the warmest of friendships was formed. It was not sexual. Had their relationship been romantic, Spender later observed, it

would never have lasted – as it did – forty years. As he told Reynolds
Price, 'every relationship with a man in which I felt intense love has
broken down'. None the less, for a year, at least, the word 'love' was used
freely if platonically between the men. It amused Stephen to address
Reynolds in his letters as 'honey' (as had Reynolds's father – the affectionate term, Stephen was charmed to know, was routinely used between
men of different generations in the American South; and now in north-
west London). In the enthusiasm of their new friendship the two men
exchanged confidences and their thoughts about life and literature. It
helped that they shared a sense of humour. As Spender said on 22 January,
'What I really most share with you is that we find the same things funny.'
In writing to Reynolds, Stephen could be entirely unbuttoned. He
confided, with startling candour, his frustrations at *Encounter*. Kristol was
nicknamed in their letters 'Oiving' and Dwight MacDonald 'Cracklepot'.
Reynolds was regaled with hilarious descriptions of dinner *chez*
Cracklepot: 'soup with lumps of porridge in it and Lyons' cakes'. Reynolds
and Stephen had a running joke about the 'Midwestern editor' – that
dull academic dog, who would one day edit their letters for posterity.
Spender, who was notoriously bad at dating letters, took to appending
elaborate dates and addresses, with the parenthesis 'this is for you, you
old Mid-West sod'.

One of the things that most amused Reynolds, who like all Americans
of his background had been driving since kindergarten, was Stephen
and the motor car; specifically the Jaguar. Spender was not, Price recalls,
a bad driver. But he drove with British amateurism. When Humphrey,
who had been a fanatic about cars all his life, asked Stephen how he
kept the Jag running, Stephen coolly replied: 'I simply go to the garage,
ask what their best petrol is, and tell them to put it in until there is no
more room' (a quarterly petrol bill for £83 none the less caused some
alarm at Loudoun Road). The austere Edward Upward was frankly
disgusted that an ex-Communist should own such a vehicle; he rather
rejoiced on hearing, later, that Spender had pranged his Jag (he overturned it, driving in rain, back from Bruern).

During a lonely few weeks of Spender's life, with Natasha away until
the end of January, Reynolds was a tonic. He offered 'amazed thanks'
for the gift of the young man's friendship. In a role reversal, Spender
submitted his novella in progress, *Engaged in Writing*, for Reynolds Price
to read and comment on. Reynolds effectively became his consultant.
His judgements, comments and praise renewed the older man's confidence

in himself, releasing him 'to re-read and I hope rewrite'. Spender had received £1,100 for *Engaged in Writing* (together with a 'travel book', which would never be written) in March 1956. The story was also scheduled for serialization in *Encounter*. Delivery was overdue and he was under some strain.

Momentously, Price was in April getting to work on what he called 'the Rosacoke story', which would become *A Long and Happy Life*, his first novel. He was in full flow. Everything was going right. On his part, Spender simply could not get *Engaged in Writing* to come right. He stayed up tinkering with the story until two in the morning, his right hand shaky with fatigue. It ballooned to over 50,000 words (might it be published as a novel, he wondered? His agent thought not). Reynolds offered suggestions. Some of them made his English story, Stephen joked, sound as if it had been 'written down in Tennessee'.

Finding the appropriate narrative tone for *Engaged in Writing* proved difficult. What Spender had in mind was a mix of 'parody reportage with wild invention'. The story opens with Olim Asphalt (the name was symptomatic of a certain rigidity of conception) arriving in Venice for an international conference. He is a fifty-year-old employee of LITUNO (i.e. UNESCO). It is March 1956, the world is reeling from Kruschev's 20th Congress speech. The plot revolves around a quarrel between two French existentialists, Sarret and Marteau, transparently based on Sartre and Merleau-Ponty. The story ends with Olim's climactic resignation from LITUNO. Spender felt the novel was a tract for the time. But on the page it did not work. He was seriously considering dropping it altogether in February. Reynolds would have none of it. He manfully read up to six radically corrected drafts and sets of proofs. His main criticism was that the story lacked 'focus'.

Spender was somewhat unwell at this period. His body was no longer young. In the second week of February he was back in hospital for two days to have 'a general anaesthetic and a lump on a toe cut off'. He wrote about the experience with his rueful wit to Price, from his bed: 'all my red corpuscles, all my white corpuscles, billions of good microbes, fifty bad microbes, and all my spermatozoa have been slaughtered, and I feel like an empty old trash can.'

Largely through Reynolds, Spender began to take a more sympathetic interest in the Angry Young Man phenomenon, which was attracting great excitement in 1957 Britain. Colin Wilson was a main object of attention. 'The Outsider' as he was called, after his bestselling book, was currently on the front page of every English newspaper. It was partly philosophical *réclame* and largely his chaotic love life that attracted the headlines. His wild hair, his Aran roll-neck sweaters, and his having made his residence on Hampstead Heath made for good photo calls. On 12 February the Spenders invited Wilson to supper at Loudoun Road, where he amused his hosts with 'his really insane conceit'. As Natasha Spender recalls, 'success had completely gone to his head'. Liquor had gone there in some quantity as well. He sat on the stairs, murmuring: 'I can't help it . . . I'm like that . . . Jesus Christ was like that too.'

Over Easter Spender made a visit with Hansi Lambert to the Mediterranean. Cyril Connolly, finally separated from Barbara Skelton, was with him. The two men arrived in Madrid, having made contact with Hansi Lambert in Paris. She would join them later, with their mutual friend, Dominique de Grunne. Lambert had rather recklessly given Connolly 10,000 pesetas 'for our meals, etc'. Incorrigibly naughty about such things, Cyril fantasized blowing the money on some tart, getting clap, and successfully talking his way out of the pickle, as he always did. As he lay in the bath in their shared apartment in Madrid, Stephen reflexively glanced at his friend's genitalia. 'Hot stuff, eh?' Cyril chortled.

On another occasion, Stephen came down to breakfast where Cyril put on a self-mocking exhibition of his famous weakness for the pleasures of the table:

He said: 'Cyril you seem to be eating an awful lot today. Surely you shouldn't be having bread and marmalade. That way, you'll never get thin. Never mind, Cyril, you might have a few grapes. They won't make any difference. Maybe Cyril, you ought to have some cheese, because you might have to go for a swim this afternoon. All right, Cyril, you'd better have a little cheese. Goodness, your plate's covered with banana skins, grape skins, bacon rind and cheese rind. What will the Lamberts say, if they come down and see all this on your plate? Better put it on *Stephen's* plate.'

(He duly placed on Stephen's plate the debris of what he had methodically consumed.)

No sooner was he back from holiday on 30 April than Spender dashed off to Stratford, where Natasha was giving an Apollo Concert with Peggy Ashcroft and John Gielgud. As he ruefully told Reynolds, 'Poor Natasha had a frightful time while I was away.' Johnny Craxton had been redecorating the study in his absence, and the builders he contracted (nicknamed the 'Aggrevations' [sic] – that being their favourite word) left 'a frightful mess'. Aggravating indeed. Both children had to be brought back early with measles from the farm in Sussex where they were to spend the whole Easter holidays. Once the crisis was over, they were sent off to Bognor. 'So Natasha, while practising, had to manage all this, and of course, the usual household problems.'

Life otherwise went on much as normal at Loudoun Road; manageably hectic, that was. They saw a lot of Craxton during the repainting of the house. The warmest of friends and a fine artist (whose work Stephen admired), Johnny's good nature towards unfortunates could be something of a trial. He employed a number of ex-jailbirds, some of whom seemed not entirely rehabilitated. One of these friends left a sack full of 'Chippendale clocks' at Loudoun Road, then phoned up the next day urgently instructing Spender to 'break them up and get rid of the pieces'.

The respectable Robert Graves was a frequent visitor at Loudoun Road. 'He looks very strange,' Stephen told Reynolds; 'his whole body tubular, his face rather puffy . . . a botched inspired look'. Graves invited the Spenders to Majorca, where he and Beryl had made their home. Stephen (like Cyril) was, at this period, a little worried about his own 'tubularity' and, as he told Reynolds, was taking a course of Alpine Spa Slimming Pills. Perhaps Reynolds would not be able to see him, he mused, if he stood sideways. Spender was both jocose and melancholy during the year. He came on a remark of Joyce's, which struck him as apposite to his mood: 'I lie awake and listen to my hair going white.'

Later in June, the Spenders accepted Graves's invitation to Majorca. The MacDonalds were invited to join them on the trip. It turned out unhappily. 'I hated every moment of it,' Stephen told Reynolds. His fellow editor's 'Cracklepottiness makes me want to run a mile', he complained. Natasha had an appalling time with Gloria MacDonald, whom she had earlier brought out by herself. A former southern belle, Mrs MacDonald arrived with no money, no toiletries, 'saying she had to lie down all the time . . . She proceeded to use Natasha as though she were some kind of negress before slavery was abolished.' On her part Natasha summed up Gloria as 'a bulldozer disguised as a powder puff'. Dwight 'bored the pants off Robert'. The MacDonalds left early and, for a few relieved days, the Spenders had Graves's house, and its owners, to themselves.

Engaged in Writing came out in two issues of *Encounter* in June. The *TLS* reviewer admired Stephen Spender's anatomy of the conversation of the deaf between East and West: 'Instead of communication there is only a gigantic squealing and rattling as massive platitudes are shifted from one language to another.' But the reviewer found the 'serious bits of this short novel are far too serious'. In the *New Statesman* Walter Allen, astutely, perceived the personal element. Spender, 'one of our leading soldiers in culture', had lost his faith: 'his disillusion finally crystallizes, and the result is an invigorating display of controlled exasperation, a splendid exposure of the pomposity and futility of men of letters . . . the satire of this particular kind of solemn and farcical unreality is brilliant, and done with a pungency and panache reminiscent of Wyndham Lewis' – the Wyndham Lewis, ironically, who had once satirized young Stephen Spender in *The Apes of God*. The reviews were good, the sales less so. As he had with *The Burning Cactus*, Spender concluded that the short story was not his proper line of work.

The event which most affected Spender, and influenced his poetry, in 1957, was his trip to Japan. He left on 30 August for the 29th International PEN Conference, to be held in Tokyo (the first such event to be held in Asia). It was an expensive affair. Angus Wilson and Stephen Spender were the stars of the British contingent. During the event, the two writers formed what would be a close and lasting friendship. As Margaret Drabble records, 'both had a keen sense of the absurd. Each found the other amiably dotty.'

The Conference opened on 2 September. Wilson relayed a jaunty account of the proceedings back to his partner, Tony Garrett, in Suffolk. It was Wilson's first 'Grand Tour of the East'. Spender was the more travelled man. But he had never spent long in Japan. The two writers – innocents abroad – tried on kimonos, slept on futons, drank sake and made excursions to naughty nightspots. At one striptease joint, Wilson told Garrett, 'when word went round that we were Spender and Wilson – every single person in the place asked for our autograph'. They were interviewed 'at least 12 hours a day'.

After the business of the conference, Angus and Stephen toured the country. They made friends, in particular, with two Japanese: Osamu Tokanagu (a waif-like, eighteen-year-old student who looked, as Wilson said, like 'a small boy') and the translator Shozo Tokunaga. Shozo would, in fact, be Spender's Japanese translator for years to come and a close friend. Osamu became desperately attached to Stephen. When Spender and Wilson left Japan for Bangkok, Osamu was, as Wilson recorded, 'in great distress – I even feared he would throw himself over the [airport] rails'. On his part, Spender was strongly affected by Osamu's plight (he is called 'Masao' in the published journals). Summing up the trip for Reynolds after he returned, on 9 October, Stephen wrote that:

Apart from anything else, it gave me an appalling insight into the utter hope-lessness of the lives of most students in Japan. What really distresses me now is all I know of Osamu's situation and how difficult it is to help him.

None the less, the Japanese experience had been inspirational:

I seemed to have in Japan something I had always been looking for and never found before with the consequence that I know now what it is I am looking for . . . On the other hand, there is no possible future in Japan for me, and if I go back there it will be on a different basis.

Nineteen fifty-eight began for Stephen with a two-week visit to Paris and Switzerland. The libretto for *Rasputin's End* was pressing. A first perform-ance of the opera had been scheduled for mid-April. There were other pressures – mainly financial. Spender's frequent spells of unpaid leave from *Encounter* depleted his main salary. Domestic expenses were high. The Spenders had two homes, two cars, two children, and two careers, each of which entailed separate travel. In London, Stephen could not do his many jobs of work without taxis and restaurant lunches for contributors. The Spenders entertained generously at Loudoun Road and Bruern.

The children were growing up and at private schools (Matthew was preparing for Common Entrance; public school fees were imminent). There was some welcome relief when an offer came, in spring 1958, to take up a visiting position in Berkeley, the following year. It would mean a six-month sabbatical from *Encounter*, but would allow the family to straighten out their finances. His principal duty at Berkeley would be to give the Beckman Lectures (the series would subsequently form the nucleus of his 'California Book', *The Struggle of the Modern*). There was further relief for the family when Matthew sailed through Common Entrance. Always precocious and wise beyond his years, he could, at the age of thirteen, hold his own with any adult. He was now in his last year at the Hall. The witty youngster was interviewed for Westminster School in early summer and, after the ordeal, sent a postcard to his parents (at

Bruern) reporting, with his customary urbanity, that he had 'passed entirely on charm'. Spender, recalling his own grisly experience, felt that his son shouldn't board, unless he really wanted to. He did want to, it transpired.

The first performance of *Rasputin's End* was scheduled for Louisville, Kentucky, in mid-April. It was an out-of-town trial run. If the opera were judged a success, it would be picked up by a metropolitan company. Could Spender deliver his words in time? He 'worked like fury' to do so. He left for Louisville via New York on 16 April, amid a hectic whirl of activity, including the redecoration of Loudoun Road. At Louisville, Nabokov found his collaborator, as always, 'charming and detached'. Spender, he cautioned, must expect 'nothing' from the performance by the Louisville Opera Company. The opera opens with the conspirators preparing to murder Rasputin, 'the Holy Devil', by means of poisoned wine and cake – a mock sacrament. Subsequent scenes feature the little Czarevich sick in bed and Rasputin's drunken revels with gypsies. The narrative ends in 'cold, white moonlight' and assassination. The auditorium in Louisville was only two-thirds full and those opera-lovers who attended were clearly baffled, Nabokov observed. *Rasputin's End* was too advanced for Kentucky. It did not help that Rasputin looked like 'a head-waiter'. Spender thought the performance 'better than we anticipated, despite the innumerable blunders'. Some rewriting and more rehearsal might help. He sent off suggestions for revision from St Louis airport, 'waiting between flights'.

From St Louis, Spender flew to Los Angeles, where he stayed a couple of days with Christopher and his young partner, Don Bachardy, in Santa Monica. They exposed him to a bit of Hollywood before he travelled on to San Francisco on 19 April. Spender spent a hectic day at Berkeley, looking over the campus, fixing his lecturing schedule, and arranging a house for the family's half-year visit (the deal included 'two Siamese cats, three lizards and two cars'). He also investigated the possibility of some recitals for Natasha, a school for Lizzie and art tuition for Matthew. In the evening, all duty done, he 'pub-crawled a bit and . . . was more or less greeted by some angry young San Francisco poets': Lawrence Ferlinghetti's City Lights crew of raffish 'beatniks', that was.

Two days later, on 21 April, Spender was in Tokyo to undertake a lecture tour, under the auspices of the CCF. Donald Richie, an American scholar with whom he had been friendly in 1957, greeted him with ghastly news. Osamu had attempted suicide. He had been found on the floor of the apartment of another American, who had rushed him to hospital. A terrible scandal was only narrowly averted. Osamu later confided his woes to Spender. His present job was 'wretched'. His life was hopeless. Spender visited Osamu's home. The young man's room was 'about fourteen square feet. He shares it with his sister and his four cats'. Osamu, Spender told Price, is 'an illegitimate son . . . which in Japan means you had better go throw yourself over a cliff'.

In Tokyo Spender had a dinner-party with the eminent novelist Yukio Mishima. At the age of thirty-two, Mishima had written thirty-six novels (a fanatic nationalist, he would commit suicide, in front of the world's cameras, in 1968). Mishima was, Spender found, 'extremely frank about being homosexual'. He was attended by cultish followers and was a prac-titioner of martial arts. He liked to pose, narcissistically naked, as the martyred and bleeding Saint Sebastian. The world Mishima inhabited 'had very much the atmosphere of Berlin of the 1930s', Spender thought. No longer his world.

Spender's main efforts were directed to lifting Osamu out of his 'rut of humiliation'. It was difficult, given the busy and far-flung programme of lecturing set up for him in Japan. The routine was the 'same every-where':

Met at station by a team of two or three professors with their grey, solemn faces. Such gleam of life as they usually have seems to have sunk deep inside them, like a shell into mud flats. In Japan sake is the best way of retrieving it.

On his trip around Japanese universities, he heard muted gossip about his sake-soaked predecessors ('Mr William Empson – strange behaviour'). 'Boring professors' persecuted Mr Stephen Spender. He was obliged to have 'multitudinous baths' with them (a ritual which he liked to get over 'as quickly as possible' – it brought back the horrors of English public school). One boring professor told his distinguished guest that anxiety about his arrival produced 'a cold and two boils'.

Spender was back in England on 3 June, 'dead tired'. He was met by good news. 'Out of the blue', he learned that the Old Vic was keen to commission from him an English verse translation of Schiller's *Maria Stuart*. The theatre's director, Peter Wood, wanted to open the November 1958 season with Spender. It was a compliment. Traditionally the play-house opened with Shakespeare. It was already decided that Irene Worth, a box office star, would take the lead. The theatre advanced a welcome £200, with another £500 to come.

Spender was impressed by Wood ('marvellously discouraging'). The plan was to run the play for a fortnight at the Edinburgh Festival in September, and open with a fully rehearsed production at the Old Vic in early November. This timetable meant a flurry of writing, revision and shuttling of the manuscript to Price ('I must have read seventeen versions of *Maria Stuart*,' he recalls). The principal problem was to reduce Schiller's massive text by up to two-thirds. By the end of August they had, Spender thought, 'quite an actable play, after we have shoved in a few sword fights, murders, and other scenes of violence'.

What made the piece most stageworthy was Spender's sinewy verse. He had been translating German for twenty years, and his skills were bearing their finest fruit. The play opens with Maria, imprisoned, humiliated, awaiting sentence. Elizabeth, with her 'ambiguous mind' and devious advisers, is held off stage until the second Act. The drama builds up to the *scène à faire*, the meeting of the queens in Act 3. Maria 'humbles' her adversary, in front of the Queen's favourite, Leicester ('England is ruled by a bastard'). The play ends with Maria on 'the frontier of eternity', and the treacherous Elizabeth deserted.

Spender and Matthew drove up to Edinburgh in the family Jag at the beginning of September. They went through the Lake District, staying overnight with the Devonshires at Chatsworth, and looked at Skelgill, where eight-year-old Stephen had spent a summer holiday. Forty years on, his nerves were raw with apprehension about how his latest play would be received. Would it be another fiasco, like *To the Island*? Matthew, observing his father's nervousness, said reassuringly (as he thought): 'I know nothing about theatre . . . But remember this. It can't possibly be as boring as *Hamlet*.' As Spender reported to Price, the play was put on 'at that appalling place the Assembly Hall where the audience sits all round you and there is no scenery and the seats are benches and its stifling and the performance is unseeable and inaudible'. Despite the hard seats, poor acoustics, and the deterring atmosphere of Scottish presbyterianism, the performance was a 'great success'.

The play had its London opening on 17 September, opening the Old Vic's forty-fifth season with the same cast that had won applause at Edinburgh, three weeks before. Irene Worth was Maria, Catherine Lacey was Elizabeth. Spender felt that perhaps Wood had played it rather too safe in his production. Some Group Theatre experimentalism would have been welcome. But, as in Scotland, the critical response was overwhelmingly favourable. Spender's translation was highly approved of, for its 'modern ring', as *The Times* put it. The play ran for four weeks, and would have gone on longer 'if only Irene Worth hadn't left to go into TV'. During its run, it made Spender £30 a night ('helps pay for the Jag', he told Price) and was picked up by repertory theatres across the country.

There were the usual difficulties on the *Encounter* front. Both Dwight MacDonald and Irving Kristol were now gone, to be replaced by Mike Josselson's protégé, Melvin Lasky. Not an improvement, as it would turn out. In 1958, Spender, in his capacity as co-editor, did a favour for an old friend that, in time, he would have cause to regret. Since leaving the army, the career of his Oxford friend Goronwy Rees had been very up and down. After serving in MI6, there were a number of academic positions, culminating in the principalship of the University College of Wales, at Aberystwyth. Spender prophesied disaster: 'There was a sort of anarchism about Goronwy. It was ridiculous really for him to have been the head of a university.'

Goronwy's closest friend, since the early 1930s, had been the delinquent diplomat Guy Burgess. He was terrified, evidently, that Burgess – now a blown spy in Moscow – had something on *him*. In his fit of mad panic, Rees wrote a series of anonymous articles, for the *People* Sunday tabloid, in February 1956. The scoop was headlined: 'Guy Burgess Stripped Bare, His Closest Friend Speaks'. The articles were patently intended to blacken Burgess and to point a finger at the 'fourth man', Anthony Blunt, who would be unmasked much later, in 1979. Spender evidently had early warning of what Rees was intending and warned Rosamond Lehmann, who vainly attempted to dissuade her former lover from his suicidal course of action. He looked 'very sheepish' but 'would not change his mind' about the *People* articles.

In late March, the *Telegraph* blew Rees's cover. He was, after huge scandal, forced to resign from Aberystwyth. He was regarded as a pariah for the Forsterian offence of having betrayed his friends. Stuart Hampshire, among others, never spoke to him again. Oxford, his alma mater, shunned him as something leprous. Spender took pity on his broken friend and put writing commissions his way. And he introduced Rees to his new editorial colleague, Mel Lasky, who sympathized with him as an anti-Red who was being ostracized. As a token of his sympathy, Lasky – the new American co-editor – agreed to Rees working for *Encounter*. Goronwy credited Spender with having saved him from destitution and wrote a letter, saying he would be 'grateful to me for ever and ever'. A hollow promise, as it turned out.

For the first half of 1959 Spender was on sabbatical from *Encounter* in order to take up his two-term tenure of the Beckman Chair, at Berkeley. The whole family and their au pair made the trip by air, in late January. Matthew would stay only three months, before the summer term at Westminster. They found a school for Lizzie in California. They had arranged a house, car and dog swap with the English critic Ian Watt, who was in the process of swapping Berkeley for the University of East Anglia. Spender's duties would comprise small-group seminars and a series of big-occasion lectures (*The Struggle of the Modern*, in embryo). The first was imminent on 26 February. Spender was still writing as Henry Nash Smith, the chair of the English department, paced up and down the dining-room, waiting to whisk him off to the auditorium. Two days later the Spenders celebrated Stephen's fiftieth birthday.

Berkeley, on the eve of the 1960s, was academic elysium. 'We loved Berkeley,' Natasha Spender recalls. Stephen's academic colleagues were congenial (they made particular friends with the Lawrentian Mark Schorer, a Bogart look-alike, currently involved in the American court battles on behalf of *Lady Chatterley's Lover*). 'We hardly dined in once,' Natasha Spender recalls, so overwhelmed were they with invitations. In the city of San Francisco there was the City Lights Bookshop. Haight Ashbury was bohemian but still civilized. The Bay Area had the liveliest poetry readings in the country. The more sedate area round the university had a large, cultivated population. Natasha Spender could do radio work on the classical music station, KPFA. Now that both Spenders drove, they could motor down in the Watts' small, blue and cranky automobile to friends such as Stravinsky, Aldous Huxley and Isherwood in Los Angeles. Natasha was within a few hours' range of the Ojai music festival, where she herself gave a recital and Stephen gave readings. He was also writing. He told Price on 7 February: 'I am terribly glad to be in this place where the sun shines and one feels very far away. For the first time in years I feel time and space in which to read and write.' He resolved to embark on a long autobiographical poem – some 5,000 lines in length, as he initially intended. This project (never quite finished) would preoccupy him for a number of years.

Natasha offers a picture of their daily routine in Berkeley:

Stephen was very occupied with his lectures which engrossed him for a long time each morning. He used to work in Ian's study which was shut off from the rest of the house. He would emerge for lunch in the garden with Lizzie's amusing carry-on about Grizzly Peak School. Every evening we went out, usually to colleagues, amongst whom Stephen particularly liked the poet Josephine Miles, and the laid-back evenings with Mark Schorer. There was a lot of enjoyable musical life. It was the only American stint at which we had real continuous family life with both children, with whom we shared the excitement of a rather exotic country.

Spender had resolved to work his lectures into a book. They had gone down well. His first, over-optimistic, assessment was that he would have it done by mid-September. The University of California Press advanced $500. There only remained to grade his students with a 'universal A' and he was, by the middle of May, a free man again. Their time at Berkeley ended with a round of barbecues and beatnik-flavoured parties. At the end of May Sydney and Cynthia Nolan came to stay for three weeks in their Recreational Vehicle (which, nomads that they were, they parked in the Watts' garden). Spender arranged for Nolan's pictures to be exhibited in the house. He was, at the time, reviewing Robert Lowell's *Life Studies*, for the *New Republic*. Nolan was very taken with the collection (which records Lowell's nervous breakdowns) and 'dived off into a bedroom' to illustrate Spender's review copy (taking it with him, alas, when he left Berkeley, in June). As his subsequent review records, Spender admired Lowell's workmanship. But it was not quite, he felt, the 'new modernism' he had been waiting for. He was more enthusiastic about Theodore Roethke's *Words for the Wind*, which he was reviewing at the same time.

Spender was, as he told Price on 3 June, working on his long poem:

whenever I can . . . I keep getting new ideas for it . . . a mélange of analysed situations, and memories, and portraits and perhaps one or two subjects (one subject would certainly be queer life). I don't think I shall try and write something continuous like *The Prelude*, all in one metre, but a number of set pieces following on one another.

What he had in mind was *World within World* in verse. He had 100 lines on paper by July.

As he wound things up at Berkeley he had a series of lectures lined up and a writers' conference in Salt Lake City 'which will be an absolute penitentiary', he forecast to Price, 'afflicted by one of those plagues of old ladies which seem to get worse and worse in America'. In fact, Salt

Lake City turned out to be interesting. A friendly English student, Robert Pack Browning (propitious name for a poet's guide), took him off on a long hike in the hills – involving picnics, parkas and sleeping bags above the snowline. Natasha meanwhile had stayed on at Berkeley, teaching a master class on Beethoven. She had a great desire to drive across America and found a companion, Margot Dennis, willing to accompany her. Lizzie would meanwhile be looked after by friends in Washington. Spender finished his side of the American trip with a visit to the Buttingers at Brookdale Farm, having flown to the East coast on 3 July. By the end of the month he was back in the UK, having stopped off at a 'boring' PEN conference in Frankfurt. On his return he took Matthew, now a precocious fourteen-year-old, to the Savile Club. 'How can you bear it?' his son disgustedly asked, having seen the membership close-up: 'you're unique.'

That summer Spender had received a letter from Boris Pasternak. He was amazed and gratified to find that the Russian Nobel Prize winner had for decades treasured lines from the poem 'In 1929':

> This poor clerk
> Builds with his red hands . . . peace

As he told Price, 'The idea that Pasternak knew these lines and had perhaps carried them round in his head for 25 years really thrilled me, more than any review I've ever read.' What Pasternak admired in these lines (in which the poet foresees calamity decades hence for the three comrades happily walking along the Rhine) is clearer if one quotes the second stanza of the poem in full:

> Yet to unwind the travelled sphere twelve years
> Then two take arms, spring to a soldier's posture:
> Or else roll on the thing a further ten,
> The third – this clerk with world-offended eyes –
> Builds with red hands his heaven: makes our bones
> The necessary scaffolding to peace.

The 'clerk' (in Julien Benda's sense of 'intellectual') is, presumably, Spender – foreseen here not as a soldier, but a visionary revolutionary.

The letter accompanying the lines he found 'very disturbing'. As he understood the letter (which had been pored over by the censor), the

Russian poet was sending him a 'coded message', conceiving himself as, in some sense, the 'poor clerk'. The example of Pasternak – the writer sustaining principle under oppression – would feed into Spender's later idea for *Index on Censorship* and would supply a main theme for the book he was currently writing, *The Struggle of the Modern*. For Spender, Pasternak was the exemplary modern writer. He wrote back to the Russian on 12 October, sending a copy of his *Collected Poems* and a typically apologetic description of his poetic credo:

I am at that stage of my life when I am most preoccupied with a great deal of work and business – things not poetry . . . In our minds, I think we do not only feel that we should be writing poetry, but that there is also a mysterious aim, which is to live the life of poetry. Unless one lives the life of poetry, one feels unworthy to write. For writing poetry is not simply a matter of using one's abilities and working regularly. It has a connection with being someone who is particularly open to experiences towards which he responds with his whole personality and without being interfered with in that response even by habits of work and the manner and style he has developed in his writing – or by his public personality, or even by the image of him which is present in other people's minds.

By mid-October, the family were reunited at Loudoun Road and at Bruern. Briefly reunited. At the end of the month, Spender flew off again to New York. He would stay a month in the US, lecturing, reading and speaking. On this odyssey he would, typically, be staying in motels which (like that in Austin) 'smelled like cushions stuffed with stale cigar fumes' and talking to 'old ladies like corpses resurrected and covered in talcum powder'. But, as he often admitted, these purgatorial episodes gave him what London did not: an opportunity to write, uninterruptedly. After a brief rest at the Buttingers' New York house, Spender flew on 21 November to Cologne for the opening night of *Rasputin's End*. The performance went well. There were twenty curtain calls and the reviews were good. It seemed that Washington might pick the opera up. But, as Spender told Price, 'the trouble about it really is that there is so little music'.

By 7 December the family were all together at Loudoun Road, where Matthew alarmed his father by announcing that John Wain had given a talk at the Westminster School Literary Society 'and explained that you were a no-good poet'. Was Matthew upset, Stephen asked. 'Well, no,' his son replied. He was pleased to report that all the boys took against Wain. None the less, the episode upset Spender. 'This is really a turning point,' he told Price: 'the first time that Matthew has heard me attacked, publicly as it were.' It was crass of Wain not to ascertain that a fellow poet had a son at the school. Spender felt that for his son's sake if for no other reason he would like to do something 'which lifted me out of the world of the John Wains'.

The 1960s: Young Rebels and Old Rebel

The 1960s would be the most eventful and disturbed decade of Spender's life since the 1930s. He received the highest honour, hitherto, of his literary career with the appointment to the Consultant's position at the Library of Congress (it was the American equivalent of the English Poet Laureate). He was, necessarily, resident in America during the increasingly contentious Vietnam imbroglio and the crisis of Civil Rights insurgency. His own relations with the Anglo-American magazine Encounter *were more and more fraught – culminating in public scandal for the magazine and huge mortification for its founding English editor, who had been systematically deceived for fourteen years. Much of what Spender had worked for since the Second World War was, he felt, betrayed. Towards the end of the decade, Spender's attention and sympathies turned towards the 'young rebels' who were transforming the course of European and American politics. This was a period, after his resignation from* Encounter, *when his personal authority and prestige were at their most considerable. He used them to found, with like-minded colleagues,* Index on Censorship *– a journal and associated pressure group devoted to intellectual and literary freedoms, world-wide. Meanwhile, his children grew up and his wife embarked on a new career. During the decade Spender produced a number of important critical books – but published little new poetry. The end of the decade found him, unusually, without a clear sense of his future but with undiminished energy.*

The 1960s opened with Spender still struggling with *The Struggle of the Modern*. Jamie Hamilton (not by nature a patient publisher) nagged his author remorselessly. This new book, he promised, would be the dawn of a 'Spender renaissance'. As the topic grew under his hand, Spender found this project becoming 'quite strange and original'. And, as always, increasingly autobiographical. He and Hamilton agreed, on 21 January, to cancel the agreement for a travel book, 'The Quality of Places'. Spender would never now find time to write it (apart from anything else, he was travelling too much). He also put aside a projected verse-drama about Sir Walter Raleigh – a follow-up to *Maria Stuart*'s success.

Spender spent two weeks in Moscow in early February 1960. He travelled as the guest of Muriel Buttinger, who was visiting the sculptor Konienkov whom she had known since the 1930s in Vienna, when he was an exile and they were all Communists. While Konienkov was in exile, in New York in the 1950s, she had supported him financially. Part of her motive in going to Moscow was to ascertain that he was safe. She invited Stephen along to give her moral support. For Spender the trip would be an opportunity do some goodwill CCF business (his journal of the trip evidently doubled as a report for Geneva, where Josselson, for health reasons, had now set up his headquarters). He had wanted, for some time, to project *Encounter* behind the Iron Curtain.

In Moscow Spender was warned by the British Embassy not to call on Boris Pasternak, the Russian writer he most admired. It would cause 'difficulty' for the (unwilling) Nobel Laureate. Spender made a duty call on the Writers' Union, whose hacks he did not much admire, and was rudely told that no writer was available to speak with him (when he heard of this calculated snub, Alexander Tvardovsky, the editor of *Novy Mir*, was furious). The most memorable event of the trip was a long conversation with the former 'missing diplomat', now exposed as the 'traitor', Guy Burgess. The meeting was set up by a surprise phone call from Burgess, at the KGB's favoured hour of 1.15 a.m. When he arrived at Spender's hotel the next morning Guy launched into a spontaneous rhapsody of praise for the Soviet Union, somewhat vitiated when he waved, meaningfully, 'in the direction of a corner of the ceiling' where the microphone was placed. Utopia was bugged.

The formerly dandy ex-diplomat cut a sorry figure. 'He had a seedy, slightly shame-faced air and a shambling walk like some ex-consular official you meet in a bar in Singapore and who puzzles you by his references to the days when he knew the great and helped determine policy.' Yesterday's spy. Rather amazingly, Burgess accused Spender of being 'an American agent'.

Shortly after his return from the Soviet Union, at a dinner-party of Hamish Hamilton's, the Home Secretary, R. A. Butler, told Spender that 'there was absolutely nothing' to prevent Burgess coming back to England. 'Of course,' Rab coolly added, 'the fellows at MI5' might take a different view. A deal was, perhaps, being set up, with Spender as a 'back-channel'. In return for a full debriefing (such as Anthony Blunt gave), the spy would be allowed in from the cold. Butler, 'too clever by half', as his colleagues thought him, might himself have been fishing in troubled waters.

There were, Spender soon discovered, those in England who were keen that Guy Burgess should remain in Moscow. The next morning, after Butler's remarks (which evidently flew round London like wildfire), Tom Driberg – the most rascally politician in Westminster and a rampant homosexual – phoned up urgently to dissuade Spender from any initiatives. 'It would be an *absolute disaster* for many people if Guy came back,' Driberg darkly warned. Goronwy Rees was frankly 'terror-stricken' when he learned that his 'closest friend' might return. Spender was never informed what was going on. Nor has it become any clearer since.

He was back working at Panton House in early March. The hundredth issue of *Encounter* was in prospect and Spender persuaded Henry Moore to do the anniversary cover. Office rows with Lasky over the treatment of 'literary' pieces were, meanwhile, becoming ever fiercer. 'My *Encounter* life is not too happy,' Spender informed Price on 30 March. 'If I were offered a decent alternative job I would leave.' Why not then take one of the lucrative 'decent alternative jobs' offered by American universities, his American friend (teaching now at Duke) asked. Because, Spender explained, none of them were in places (even Duke) where he could bear to spend more than a semester. Nor could he commit himself, with his family growing up, to 'a life of vagrancy' in American academia. He was, now, in his fifties: pensionless, with three family dependants, and laying out, as he reckoned, £5,000 a year in household expenses. As he told Price, if he gave up his salaried job with the magazine,

I'd probably end up in some old barge on the East River. None of which I'd care a fuck about if it wasn't for the children having to turn round in the street and walk in the opposite direction because something they'd seen coming up a ladder from the other side was Dad.

On 4 May 1960 the Spenders went to dinner at Tom and Valerie Eliot's flat (they had been married since 1957). The other guests were Ted Hughes and Sylvia Plath. It is a literary encounter recorded from two angles. Spender, himself by now a grizzled lion, benignly thought the young poets a good-looking couple. Ted was possessed of 'craggy Yorkshire hand-someness'. Sylvia, who 'talked more', was 'a very pretty, intelligent girl from Boston'. Eliot was subdued; Spender felt 'I talked too much to keep the conversation going'. He wrote to 'Mrs Hughes', apologizing for 'maybe ruining the evening'. From his angle, it was an unexceptional, slightly tense occasion – no different from thousands of others.

The reverse shot was quite different. Plath was intoxicated by being among the truly great and bubbled with bobbysoxer glee in her account of the evening to her mother in America. The Eliots, she wrote:

live in a surprisingly drab brick building on the first floor – yet a comfortable lavish apartment. His Yorkshire wife, Valerie, is handsome, blond and rosy . . . Then the Spenders arrived; he handsome and white-haired, and she . . . lean, vibrant, talkative . . .

Had he read her raptures, Spender might perhaps have thought the pretty young Boston girl even more intelligent. She sent him some poems, which he published in *Encounter*. He had already, as a Somerset Maugham competition judge, given Ted a prize for *The Hawk in the Rain*, in 1957.

Spender had arranged to give a set of lectures on modern literature at a Brandeis summer school, from 27 June to 4 August. He would fly to Massachusetts after Wystan Auden's regular visit in June – the occasion this year of a big Faber party. He was obliged to go to Brandeis alone: 'Natasha was not offered anything and there really isn't enough dough for us both to go,' he bluntly told Price. Also it would be as well for one of the parents to stay with the children. They were worried, that spring, about Matthew's O levels.

Brandeis in mid-summer was, Spender sourly thought, 'like a modern prison'. The student body and faculty were '200% Jewish . . . which is a bit monotonous and overemphatic'. The classes were 'inhumanly awful, and I am only praying for the six weeks to be over as quickly as possible', he told Reynolds. None the less, there were interesting colleagues (Irving Howe and Philip Rahv). And he was struck with the poems of one of his students – Anne Sexton – whom he invited to contribute to *Encounter*. He was, as always, a shrewd talent scout.

By 16 August Spender was back in London. He threw himself into work, staying up till two in the morning working on the intransigent *Struggle of the Modern*, his nerves frayed with jetlag and anxiety. He was 'in a financial mess again', he told Price. His children's education cost £1,000 a year. To pay the fees he had to earn twice that (income tax was punitively high in pre-Thatcherite 1960). The whole of his *Encounter* salary was needed just to get the children out of the door every schoolday. He could manage: but only by firing on all cylinders – as editor, reviewer, lecturer and teacher.

Stephen, for all his personal vigour and *joie de vivre*, was entering that dark zone of life (the 'posthumous area', as he called it) in which his friends, even his contemporaries, were dying of 'natural' causes. Age, that is. Frances Cornford died in June and a little later Hansi Lambert died under what should have been a routine operation (fatally, she waited for her own surgeon to come from Belgium to the German spa where she had fallen ill). For the Spenders it was a tragic personal loss.

During November Britain was electrified by the 'Lady Chatterley' trial. Penguin had published Lawrence's 'obscene' novel, challenging the DPP to prosecute. He obliged. Spender was recruited as a witness but was not, in the event, called to testify (Jeremy Hutchinson, one of the defence team, was not sure that the author of *World within World* was 'sound on Lawrence'; even less sound was Auden, who announced himself prepared to testify for the prosecution). It was just as well that Spender was not called. He had his doubts about the thirty or so eminences who did go to the stand (the Bishop of Woolwich, for example, who pronounced the adultery of Connie and Mellors to be 'an act of holy communion'). As Spender told Price, 'It was slightly absurd hearing them all have to get up and say Lady C. was the purest book ever written.' Spender put the record straight by publishing, in December's *Encounter*, a jaundiced article by John Sparrow, the Warden of All Souls, pointing out that the seventh 'bout' between the lovers in the novel was clearly an act of forcible buggery – something that had escaped the prosecution's notice.

Spender wrapped up 1960 with another Far Eastern lecture tour, from late November to late December. He was back in England for Christmas. In his absence, Josselson had been in touch with Lasky. As always (and for reasons which Spender never understood until years later), the CCF top brass in Paris, Geneva and Washington was desperate not to lose Spender as editor. Lasky had been instructed to be more 'tender-minded' with his co-editor. Josselson had also informed Lasky that Spender was likely to be away for four months in 1961, in Virginia. When he learned this, Lasky wrote back a letter of breathtaking vituperation:

The Spender matter. I must confess that I look forward with *real* trepidation to my next meetings with him. I will *try*, really *try*. But then, as *good* as these last two years have been, full of work and not a few successes, the *worst* part of them has been Stephen-in-the-next-office. How elated I have been at every prospect of his absence . . . I sometimes indulge in horrified speculation at what my life will be like with him around in the next years (2? 4? 6?) . . . to have to live with that kind of nagging, based on his own troubled guilty conscience, getting a maximum of glory for a minimum of work, doing really his own books, plays, anthologies, articles, reviews, broadcasts . . . sinks me into despair! . . . Must we always live under the cloud of his insincerity and characterlessness?

If any of this slander had been true, Spender would have been let go years before. What is significant is that Lasky could put this kind of thing on paper and still himself be safe in his job. On his return, Spender told Josselson that he had had a 'long and very frank talk' with Mel and that 'I think we are going to make a new start on a better basis.' It was a vain hope. But the inevitable crisis was averted for a while, at least. Lasky, however, continued to dominate the editorial decision-making.

The family spent Christmas at Bruern. Lizzie (now 'ravishing') had been given earlier in the year a black poodle puppy called Topsy (political correctness was decades away). The little girl was desperately worried that if she were obliged to house-train the animal 'she'll stop loving me'. Matthew was 'very highbrow'; he requested as presents nothing but classical LP records. Spender thought him 'very changed – quite grown up'. His O levels had, in the event, gone well. It was a happy Christmas. When, in later life, Spender was asked what he was proudest of in life, he replied: 'bringing up *both* my children in the same house'.

Early in 1961 it was arranged that Spender would take time off from *Encounter* for a long lecture tour in the Middle East, sponsored by the British Council. The itinerary would take in Egypt, the Lebanon, Turkey, Cyprus and Greece. It was a tall order and these trips quite often left him out of pocket. But, as he told Reynolds, 'I accepted because there was a chance to take Natasha. She is wildly excited about it – in fact I haven't seen her so pleased and excited for years.' It would be a *deux-ième voyage des noces* for their twentieth wedding anniversary. It would also, if they returned *en route* through Italy, allow them to look at Renaissance art with Matthew.

Politically, Spender's tour was cleared at high level. It was a mission of some delicacy. Full diplomatic relations between Britain and the United Arab Republic were only resumed – after the total breakdown of Suez – on 26 January 1961. Stephen and Natasha left England on 15 February. The following four weeks had many highpoints: they motored through France and Italy before flying to Cairo. In between Stephen's platform chores the couple undertook an orgy of sight-seeing: pyramids, museums and holy places. They spent 28 February, Stephen's birthday, looking at a mosque and at the Gayer Anderson museum in Cairo, which had, amazingly, a portrait of Lolly (done in her youth) prominently on display. From Egypt they travelled on to the Lebanon. Here they stayed with their friend Moore Crosthwaite, now 'Sir Moore' and British ambassador in Beirut. Moore was set in his ways, 'like a man encased in a carapace', 'absolutely gay', and a passionate lover of music – something that supplied a bond between him and Natasha. Already, to Spender's surprise, Moore was talking of retirement, obligatory at sixty in the Foreign Office. Throughout the trip Spender was lecturing – 'like a trouba-dour': no retirement for the poet. He made an excursion to Cyprus (a hotspot with the EOKA uprising) for the British Council. Natasha remained in Beirut. From the Lebanon they travelled on to Ankara, Istanbul and more lecturing and sight-seeing (on 19 March they visited six mosques in a single day). These excursions were made the more pleasant by the company of friends. They had by chance met up at Broussa with their old friends Baron Philippe and Baroness Pauline de Rothschild (cultivated Anglophiles both of them; he had translated Elizabethan poetry into French; she, née Potter, was American by origin). They had become acquainted in the 1950s through Hansi Lambert. Over the next few years the Spenders would make regular trips to stay with the Rothschilds at Château Mouton.

By the end of March they were in Greece, where they stayed at Lucie Lambert's house at Sounion. The coastal ruins were staggeringly beautiful in the Greek spring. There followed a week of lecturing in Athens. On 2 April the Spenders flew back to Rome, where they picked up their car and motored up to Florence. Here they were reunited with Matthew, whose school year was now over (Lizzie, meanwhile, was with the family of film director John Huston, and her friend Anjelica, in Ireland). There were more museums, enlivened by the young, but increasingly sophisticated, artistic eye of their son.

Florence was so pleasant that they decided to stay on for a few days. Another reason was that their friend Henry Moore was there with his young daughter Mary. He told the Spender family, with immense authority, that there was only one time of day to see the Masaccios at Santa Maria del Carmine – seven o'clock in the morning, when the rays of the rising sun struck the murals at the same angle as in the paintings. The three Spenders duly set their alarm clocks for crack of dawn and motored down to the church. Moore was already there. The sculptor went on to give the children a 'socratic tutorial' on Masaccio. The next day the Spenders passed their twentieth wedding anniversary, 9 April, quietly by themselves. The family was back in England by the middle of the month.

It had been a glorious second honeymoon. But back in London, as Spender told Price, trouble awaited at *Encounter*. Editing the magazine 'bothers me a great deal . . . I am getting to the stage of really *detesting* Lasky, who is the kind of person whom I find it almost impossible to deal with.' Impossible because of his intransigence and high-handedness, as Spender thought, over alterations worked out with contributors to accepted articles, layout and delays in publication. Spender was forever having to apologize to frustrated authors, impatient to see their work in print. The CCF would not hear Spender's increasingly intolerable difficulties because Lasky was, 'in fact, their man'. On 7 June Spender again wrote to Josselson, asking to be 'released from co-editing *Encounter* with the hundredth number' in January 1962. Josselson invited him to Geneva and again talked him out of it, appealing to his loyalty to the magazine he had helped found and make successful.

Spender's unease had been sharpened by a row with an old friend, William Empson. At a party at Louis MacNeice's at the end of May,

Stephen had become so infuriated by the other poet's aspersions against *Encounter's* American backers that he threw a glass of wine at him. Empson wrote, suavely, on 6 June to say that his garments were so 'used' that another wine stain would hardly show. But he renewed, on paper, his allegation that Spender's magazine was 'taking American money, perfunctorily disguised as international money, to confront the British public with innocent seeming American propaganda'. He threw in some scathing sarcasms about Spender's 'American playmates'. Spender replied angrily. Empson declared that their friendship was at an end.

After her BBC Prokofiev concerto and some performances for the Apollo Society with Peggy Ashcroft, Natasha moved to Bruern for the summer with Lizzie. Stephen would drive down from London and, during term, Matthew could get the train down at weekends. In early August, Stephen took a two-week holiday by himself in Denmark with the Rothschilds, during which he 'vowed to write nothing but poetry'. Here he worked on his poem 'The Generous Years', later retitled 'The Generous Days'. The work would, nine years later, form the title piece in his next volume of poetry. It opens:

> His are the generous days that balance
> Spirit and body.
> Should he hear the trumpet
> Echoing through skies of idea –
> And lightning through his marrow –
> At once one with that cause, he'd throw
> Himself across some far, sad parapet,
> Spirit fly upwards from the sacrifice,
> Body immolated in the summons.

The poem was originally dedicated to Matthew – the 'he' celebrated in it. The dedication was dropped at the young man's request.

The Spender children were growing up. Lizzie was now eleven and Matthew well into adolescence at sixteen. The 1960s was a good time to be teenagers. Less good to be middle-aged parents – even parents as liberal as the Spenders. Matthew had already decided on his future vocation. As he wrote in his autobiographical statement, prepared for university entrance: 'My first occupation is drawing and painting. I suppose I began painting because I did not need to think while doing it.' He had, in fact, won both the school's poetry and painting prizes. He had, at exactly the same age as his father, lost his faith (would he, William Plomer asked, now have to describe himself as Matthew's 'Science-father'?). It had been agreed with Westminster that he would spend two afternoons weekly at the Slade School at UCL, taking drawing classes. Here he would study under William Coldstream (as his father had done, a quarter of a century earlier). Matthew was becoming, as young men do, increasingly private. As his sister indignantly put it (to her father's amusement), 'All Matthew does is shut himself in his room, lie on his bed, and think about the facts of life.' He was, Stephen told Ruth Witt Diamant, 'slightly adolescent and takes it out a bit on Natasha'.

On holiday in Crete, in August 1961, Matthew had formed a strong relationship with Maro Gorky (two years older than him and the daughter of the artist Arshile Gorky). 'They might as well be married,' was Spender's description to Price, adding, wryly, that he soon expected to be a grandfather. The Spenders felt it was too early for either of the young people to tie themselves down. There were the inevitable child–parent difficulties. They did not want to interfere in their son's private affairs, Stephen assured Matthew, but they felt responsible for him. 'Everyone's responsible,' Matthew serenely replied. 'Children,' he explained to his father, 'feel very responsible for their parents.' He went on: 'Poor old dad. I'd better work very hard and get a scholarship at Oxford, so *you* don't have to work so hard.' But he was adamant that he and Maro must be allowed to go their own way. Confronted with this cool reasonableness, Spender was driven to say, quite unreasonably: 'I wish *I* could run away and live in Crete.' Matthew replied, 'Honestly, why don't you, dad? You'd be so much happier.' Spender had the feeling his son was 'extremely wise' and that he, Stephen Spender, was very innocent.

Spender was, as the year drew to a close, working frantically on the hundredth number of *Encounter* and his 'California Book'. From January through February 1962 he arranged to lecture in South America and the West Indies. The British Council would cover his expenses. It was agreed that the CCF would, somewhat reluctantly, pay his salary and a per diem – in return for which Spender engaged to talk up the Congress and its works whenever appropriate and keep a lookout for likely new contributors. From March to April, Stephen Spender would be a poet in residence at the University of Virginia (CCF undertook to pay half-salary during this period). He would give three lectures at the Library of Congress, at the beginning of March (they were subsequently published as *The Imagination in the Modern World*).

Charlottesville was something of a trial. There was little to do other than read undergraduate poems and make the appropriate pedagogic noises. Spender had no close friends on campus. He was lodged in one of the Jefferson-designed residences round the central green. His apartment comprised 'three dark smelly stuffy rooms on the top floor of a small wooden house: the most hideously furnished rooms I have had anywhere'. Fortunately, he would be moved in a month to something comfortably un-Jeffersonian. Why, one may wonder, did he inflict these ordeals on himself? Partly because they gave him, despite the discomforts attendant on being away from home, a chance to work uninterruptedly. And, of course, they were remunerative. They enabled him both to write and to support his family. The lecturing that Spender did in America was such easy work, and so remunerative, that it inspired a thoughtful letter to his agent, A. D. Peters – currently pressuring him to finish *The Struggle of the Modern*:

I can earn $2,000 in a week or ten days lecturing without doing a critical book. So is it not wiser to do this? I earned $1,400 last week in five days with no effort. What I would like to discuss with you is a kind of five year plan for me to earn the money I need with the least possible amount of hack work, so that I can devote more time to the writing that matters.

Spender was back in the UK by 11 May. Natasha was due to perform Stravinsky's *Capriccio* with the BBC Symphony Orchestra (Malcolm Sargent conducting) the next day, on 12 May. Lizzie was staying with the Astors at Bruern and was not there to meet her father. Matthew was nowadays spending all of his time with Maro Gorky's family. His study at the Slade had been rewarding ('all the models look like elephants', the blasé youth told his father). But he was nervous about his impending A levels. It was not just for himself that he worried. On 13 May he inquired: 'Dad, if I get a scholarship to Oxford, will you promise to leave *Encounter*, and do nothing but write poetry?' Both his children had become 'very grown up' in his absence, the father thought.

As soon as he arrived back, Spender was recruited to accompany the Soviet poet Yevtushenko, who was in Britain to give a reading for the ICA at the Royal Court theatre. Spender did not take to the Russian. Neither did Isaiah Berlin, who confided to Stephen that he thought the author of 'Babi Yar' 'an operator'. Spender was particularly offended when, in reply to a planted question about Pasternak and his mistress

Olga Ivanskaya (the original of 'Lara'), Yevtushenko disdainfully retorted that he 'did not discuss the work of currency smugglers'.

Spender picked up the threads of his *Encounter* duties. There was some resentment in the office at what Lasky insultingly called his 'jaunts'. In fact, as Spender pointed out, he was careful – wherever he went – to publicize their (international) journal and to recruit new contributors. There were other irritations. Spender was affronted by Al Alvarez's popular Penguin anthology, *The New Poetry*. Alvarez had prefaced his collection with a polemical introduction, attacking 'the gentility principle' (embodied, implicitly, in Spender). It was the old story: *New Signatures* (1932) was superseded by *New Lines* (1957) to be superseded by *New Poetry* (1962). Spender wrote 'a rather violent attack' on Alvarez for *Encounter*. He was careful, as he said (ironically), 'not to advance a single step beyond what is perfectly genteel'. Spender's point, a strong one, was that there could have been nothing *less* genteel than the great achievements of modernism, which Alvarez apparently wanted to consign to the dustbin of literary history.

On 12 July, at their friend Annie Fleming's, Spender had a first (rather chilly) meeting with a couple destined later to be warm friends, Iris Murdoch and her husband John Bayley. The politicians Tom Driberg, Edward Boyle and Hugh Gaitskell were also at Fleming's table. Murdoch (politically *engagée* at this period) informed Spender that 'she knew a lot about politics. I said I realized I knew nothing. She talked a lot to Hugh [Gaitskell]. I suppose trying to convert him to CND' (the Campaign for Nuclear Disarmament – Gaitskell, famously, had fought, fought, fought to save the party he loved from the dead-end of unilateralism). A little later, Spender would publish in *Encounter* Murdoch's famous essay, 'Against Dryness'. Bayley would also become a regular contributor.

That summer, as Spender told Price, '*Everyone* I have ever met is now in London, and most of them staying with us.' Everyone included the Tates, Mary McCarthy and her husband, Moore Crosthwaite and Auden. One morning, during Wystan's stay (in mid-July), Stephen came down to breakfast at Loudoun Road. His friend had been there for some time since, had drunk his many cups of coffee and had finished the *Times* crossword. He was, Spender observed, making notes for his, Stephen's, obituary for the country's journal of record. 'Would you like having anything said?' Wystan asked. Spender, meanwhile, had been charged with doing Wystan's obituary for *The Times*. The poets eyed each other like two humorous undertakers, wondering which would lay out the other.

The coincidence (together with the CBE which he had been awarded in the 1962 Queen's birthday list) inspired in Spender a résumé of his life – an autobituary, so to call it:

I felt I was like a hole in the map of history . . . There's always been a fringe of friendship with people who were outside the set patterns and the routine of life – above all not to do with literature. Looking at our generation – Wystan, Christopher, Cyril – it seems to me that this generation had in our minds when we were young the image of a man or woman of 40 who had become completely stuck in a job, a family, and ideas: we were very determined *not* to be like this: to remain fluid, changing, on the move, and the people whom we *admired* – mostly artists and writers – were those who had not got stuck.

At the age of fifty-three, was Stephen Spender, Commander of the British Empire, 'stuck in a job, a family, and ideas'? Perhaps he wanted to be stuck. He declared in his journal: 'I write poetry for some time each day, getting nowhere. The trouble is I'm not sure I *want* to get anywhere, to finish anything.'

On 19 August, the Spenders left by car for Edinburgh for the sixteenth summer festival. They would stay with the Glenconners at Glen, in Peeblesshire, for the duration of the Festival. The literature programme had been organized by Sonia Orwell and John Calder, the London-based publisher who (with Marion Boyars) was pushing out the barriers of permissiveness and modernism faster than even the 1960s could keep up with. A committee had been set up, presided over by Malcolm Muggeridge: infuriatingly bland, as always. The public events were dominated by furious disputes between the 'internationalists' (Norman Mailer, Henry Miller, Alexander Trocchi) and the Scottish nationalists (led by the veteran Leninist, Hugh MacDiarmid). Sex, drugs, rock and roll, and revolution (it being the swinging decade) were much discussed. Sedately English writers, like Kingsley Amis, Angus Wilson and Stephen Spender felt rather out of it. Muriel Spark spoke for these traditionalists when she said 'she knew nothing about novels because she wrote them'. On her part, Rebecca West grimly declared that 'it would have been no loss to the world if most of the writers now writing had been strangled at birth'. Henry Miller told his (paying) audience that he had nothing to say to them other than that he 'just wrote' (and picked up his expenses, doubtless). Wilson's carefully assembled defence of English 'social' fiction – a line descending from Jane

Austen – was contemptuously contradicted by Mary McCarthy's sarcasms about the 'pretty smallness' of the English commodity, compared to the American. Spender, Wilson and Muggeridge somehow managed to hold everything together. In its chaotic way, the 1962 Literature Festival was that beloved sixties thing, a 'happening'. Spender's account of it, in *Encounter*, is one of the funniest things he wrote.

Spender was back in London in early September, to spend a month on the proofs and last revisions of *The Struggle of the Modern* (due to be published in early 1963, on Stephen's birthday). He had, in his haste, forgotten to seek permissions, which provoked something of a crisis. He was nervous, as he told Hamish Hamilton, 'that it will be reviewed by my arch-enemy, Alvarez'. He left for South America, for yet another six-week tour, from 28 September to mid-November. On his return, Wystan was again back in the country, for his lectures at Oxford. He stayed, as usual, at Loudoun Road and 'made a speech to the effect that we had wonderful children, which touched me very much', Spender told Price. At this point, Spender 'suddenly realized that I want very much that Matthew should go up to Oxford'. If he did not go, 'he will be left behind by the best members of his generation.' On the other hand (there always was an other hand) he was worried about what he called the 'anti-creativeness' of the place:

I thought how little Oxford had done for a good many of my friends, and how it made people in some ways unreal, how as a community it isolated us for the rest of our lives, how the most energetic, tough and creative people will probably now not come from Oxford and Cambridge. But I still wanted him to go. The alternatives of the Slade, travel, London, etc., all seemed scruffy.

Matthew duly won an Exhibition and went up to New College to read history in autumn 1963. It was, he once told his father, 'the greatest sacrifice I made for you'. He remained indissolubly attached to Maro, to whom he was now informally and happily engaged. Matthew had spent the earlier months of 1963 at the Château Noir, in Provence, studying art. Nearby was the ruined farmhouse at Maussane which had caught the family's eye a couple of years before. They would eventually buy it and make it a second home.

Nineteen sixty-three saw what would be the biggest crisis to date in Spender's relationship with *Encounter*. For some years he had received dark hints – notably from Barbara and Jason Epstein, and Mary McCarthy in New York – as to murky 'government involvement'. Friends, as he thought them, like Josselson and Fleischmann always reassured him that these rumours were absolutely false. Spender believed what he was told – implicitly and sometimes to the detriment of his other friendships.

The rumours surfaced into print in 1963. Reviewing *Encounter*'s decennial anthology in the *New Statesman*, Conor Cruise O'Brien noted that the journal had been 'consistently designed to support the policy of the United States government'. There were, O'Brien pointed out, symptomatic silences: on Cuba, Vietnam and 'the Negro problem'. As O'Brien later admitted, 'At the time I wrote this review, I knew nothing of any connection between the CIA and *Encounter*.' But his suspicion that the magazine was a covert tool of American policy was aggressively stated. There were other animadversions on *Encounter*'s backers. In 1963 the *Sunday Telegraph* noted in a leader that the magazine had received a secret and regular subvention from the British Foreign Office. The leak may have originated with Malcolm Muggeridge (a regular contributor to the *Telegraph*), who, as George Weidenfeld recalls, had been dropping hints (although not to Stephen) about *Encounter*'s funding for years.

In the face of these persistent allegations, Spender in 1963 made formal inquiries on the funding issue from the CCF and from his fellow-editor. He received denials ('angry denials', as he later recalled) from Josselson and from Lasky (four years later Lasky claimed he *had* vouchsafed 'suspicions' about CIA involvement in 1963 – a claim Spender indignantly refuted). Much later, Josselson admitted that it had been CCF policy to keep Spender wholly in the dark: by barefaced lies when required. Such lies were evidently required in 1963. Honest himself about such things, it was unthinkable to Spender that trusted colleagues would thus lie to his face. He accepted their denials.

None the less, the published and unpublished aspersions about *Encounter*'s independence had made Spender uneasy. In order to immunize the magazine from any future allegations (particularly about its American connections), he insisted on a new, and wholly domestic, source of funding. The journal was by 1963 established and successful – thanks, largely, to Spender's editorial flair. It could now surely float on British water.

The change in the magazine's patron in 1963 was Spender's initiative (although later Lasky was to claim it had been his). The English backer Spender found, through Basil Burton, was the International Publishing Corporation's chairman, Cecil King. King was, in 1963, the *éminence grise* of British politics. A newspaper tycoon, immensely tall and forbiddingly silent, inveterately hostile to Harold Wilson, King loved dabbling in high politics. On one notorious occasion (shortly after the *Encounter* débâcle) he tried to put together a pro-Royalist *coup d'état*; the idea was that Lord Mountbatten should lead a benign dictatorship to prevent the UK from sliding into neo-Soviet tyranny under Moscow's stooge, Wilson. King liked to see himself a king-maker.

King may not have been what he seemed. In *Not Entitled*, Frank Kermode (following revelations twenty years later by Peter Wright in *Spycatcher*) notes that King had active contacts with MI5 and may not have been averse to playing the CIA game. The important thing for Spender at the time was that King was British and, where *Encounter* was concerned, a Maecenas. He could afford to be. His *Daily Mirror* had a circulation of 7 million. A new directorship was duly set up and *Encounter* appeared under King's IPC regime in 1964. The trustees comprised Victor Rothschild, Michael Josselson, Andrew Shonfield and Arthur Schlesinger. Rothschild (it is now known) had links to British intelligence and so, quite possibly, had Shonfield. The two Americans were well inside the American intelligence community. Over the ten years of its public support (1953–63) it is estimated that the CCF put a million dollars into *Encounter*. This was far in excess of the magazine's annual £15,000 deficit. Later, as a 'farewell gesture', the CCF supplied the money for the editors' salaries for the following three years.

From January to March 1963, Spender spent the first of what would be a series of annual terms teaching, as Concord Fellow, at Northwestern University, on the outskirts of Chicago. This first year he made the error of going in the bitter Illinois winter. In later years, he would visit during the more clement spring term. There were congenial friends among the Northwestern faculty: notably Richard Ellmann (who shared his reverence for modernism, and had been instrumental in recruiting him) and Erich Heller (with whom he had previously collaborated on translating Hölderlin).

Spender was lodged at the Library Plaza Hotel, not far from the college precinct. He was as ever (and unnecessarily) apprehensive about his classroom work. As he confessed, 'I feel profoundly ignorant about the poets I am supposed to be talking about.' In the event he was a successful teacher at Evanston. As he explained to Ellmann, he would be alone for most of his stint there. Nor could he stay after term finished. He and Natasha had decided they must 'not be away too long from our

12-year-old daughter'. His roots were, however, deepening in America. In 1963 the *New York Review of Books* was founded, during a protracted *New York Times* strike. The magazine's founders – Robert Lowell, Robert Silvers, Jason and Barbara Epstein – were all friends. Spender was taken on as one of the magazine's contributing writers. It specialized in long, thoughtful, high-powered dissertation – often with a strong political flavour. In June Spender reviewed Hannah Arendt's study of the Adolf Eichmann trial. It was, Silvers recalls, 'perhaps the most controversial book of the twentieth century'. Spender, he adds (with a laugh), 'reviewed it uncontroversially'. He would, over the next thirty years, do some sixty pieces for the *NYRB*: not all were uncontroversial.

While Spender was at Northwestern, *The Struggle of the Modern* was at last published by Hamish Hamilton (at the steep price of 25s). It had been a tough job. In general the book was well received and sold well. In the *Listener* Bernard Bergonzi praised it as 'personal, alert, and frequently illuminating – as, for instance, in the brilliant chapter on nostalgia'. As a university student at the time I recall its being adopted as the successor (welcome successor) to Leavisite sterilities about 'New Bearings in English Poetry'. Like Spender's other critical works, *The Struggle of the Modern* occupied the open ground between academic and journalistic discourse. This did not guarantee a friendly reception from either establishment, Grub Street or the Ivory Tower. And Spender's apprehensions about its 'being torn to bits by the reviewers' were (at least partly) borne out. The *TLS* found the book 'sensitive and intelligent' but 'soft at the core'. None the less the reviewer conceded the book's central dichotomy (between the transcendently 'modern' and the time-bound 'contemporary') was 'stimulating'.

Northwestern liked Spender. On 1 May, he wrote to Mike Josselson to report that 'I have been offered and have accepted a teaching job for twelve weeks of each year for the next three years.' His next stint would be in March 1964. It would mean, with his ten weeks' paid vacation, at least four months a year absence from *Encounter*. He had no alternative but to accept, he explained. He could not keep body and soul together on his *Encounter* salary. He needed American teaching and lecturing stipends.

He wrote to Josselson again, a couple of weeks later, to say that Wesleyan University, at Middletown in Connecticut, had invited him for a semester as Fellow in Letters at their Center of Advanced Studies. He planned to go in autumn 1964, when Robert Lowell would be in residence. Wesleyan offered $7,500 for three months, travel expenses, accommodation, a secretary, and a piano for Natasha. How would this affect his relationship with *Encounter*, he inquired, implicitly inviting the CCF to let him go, or allow him some semi-detached position.

Lasky went through the roof when he heard that 'Spender will be in the USA for almost the whole of 1964!' And, all that time, the truant's name would still be on the magazine's masthead, alongside his own. But, as before, the senior CCF management were reluctant to let their English editor go. They *wanted* Stephen Spender's name on the masthead, whatever the bruise to Melvin Lasky's *amour propre*. A charm offensive was launched. The Spenders were made much of, in Geneva and Paris. They were 'suddenly' invited, in early July, to join Junkie Fleischmann on his yacht ('it seems to be called Speedo', Spender wryly observed) to sail the Aegean.

The cruise was for Spender 'the first real holiday I've had for ages'. He spent it 'absorbing the light', something that had always fascinated him in Greece. His ship companions – the Hollywood actor Zachary Scott and his wife Ruth Ford (the former Mrs John Steinbeck) – were congenial. They discussed the possibility of a Broadway production of *Maria Stuart*, which, alas, came to nothing. Natasha had resolved to go to university in October 1963, as an 'occasional' student, and was studying elementary Latin on board. Her plan was to enrol at UCL (where Noël Annan was provost) in the autumn, to read philosophy (Richard Wollheim's department) and psychology.

After Fleischmann's marine hospitality the Spenders went off, in the second week in August, to inspect the ruin in Provence which they were now in the process of buying. Matthew was working during his gap year, before going up to Oxford, at a studio in nearby Aix. The family was enthusiastic about 'mother's ruin' (as Matthew nicknamed it). Spender described it for Price: 'It is a marvellous part of the country, near Arles. It's the remains of a farmhouse. You must rebuild it with a do-it-yourself kit, bore a well and get water. It cost $1500 and will cost another $2000 to get in order. So you'll be seeing me before long, in fact you'd better help me get some lectures.' Mas de St Jerome, as they named it, 'will need all my 1964 dollars', Spender told Michael Josselson. Some 18,000 of them, as he calculated. It was a delightful prospect. There was, none the less, Spender confessed (to Reynolds) 'something about having "real estate" that always horrifies me'. Natasha remained in France, over September, arranging the renovation.

On his return Spender found himself caught up again by the 'terrific *involvement* of my life in England'. *Encounter*, inevitably, involved him most. At office level, Spender's relationship with Lasky continued to deteriorate. On his return Spender learned, 'quite by chance that we have apparently left Secker and Warburg and are now going to be "published" by Weidenfeld'. His American co-editor had offered no word of thanks to the ousted Fred Warburg for ten years' service to *Encounter*. There had been no discussion with the English editor. What most vexed him, Spender told Josselson, 'is the uneasy feeling that we have entered into some arrangement with Weidenfeld that I do not know about'. The dispute dragged on. 'We are in the worst mess at *Encounter*,' he despairingly told Nabokov on 18 November. Lasky's conduct was 'deplorable'. Spender had consulted a solicitor (Hilary Rubinstein) to discover whether his co-editor was in breach of contract, by making decisions without consultation.

It was a melancholy autumn for poetry. Sylvia Plath committed suicide. In Washington, Ted Roethke died. On 3 September, Louis MacNeice died. Spender was inspired to write the necessary post mortem poem for his old Oxford comrade. It began:

> Like skyscrapers with high windows staring down from the sun,
> Some faces suggest
> Elevation.

Given his orderly life (unlike the bibulous or gormandizing Dylan Thomas, Roy Campbell, Louis, Connolly and Auden), his strong constitution and the luck of good health (unlike C. Day-Lewis, who contracted cancer in his sixties, or Joe Ackerley and William Plomer with their weak hearts), Spender's sad role would be that of sweeper-up to the thirties group. He would, in course of time, live to write obituaries for everyone in MacSpaunday. It is, probably, no accident that he was, almost uniquely among his contemporaries, happily married. Or that he was happy, *tout court*; something that gave him a reason for living. Ackerley, for example, he pictured as

an aesthete in a trench coat – who would have liked two-thirds of the human race exterminated by some form of Spanish flu and the remainder to aspire to the moral nobility of his alsatian dog, Queenie.

If that was your view of life, why live?

He and Natasha had decided to postpone the Wesleyan arrangement until 1965 (in the event, Spender would not take it up until 1967). There were changes under way in Loudoun Road. Matthew would be settling in at Oxford. Natasha would be (at the same time, October 1963) a first-year student at UCL, having galloped successfully through her A levels. With Lizzie at North London Collegiate School, Spender now had two undergraduates and a schoolgirl to support.

Encounter was in turmoil. Spender remained unhappy about the Weidenfeld arrangement. It boiled over when he discovered, to his amazement, that the publisher had asked Auden if he would be interested in the 'English' editorship of *Encounter*, 'supposing that Spender was no longer editor?' Spender wrote angrily to Mike Josselson from New York (where Wystan had told him about Weidenfeld's overture) on 18 February. He was assured that there were no underhand plans to evict him.

In New York, Spender was forever picking up worrying gossip at parties – particularly from the 'radicalized' *NYRB* people. Jason Epstein (one of the magazine's founders) told him, frankly, 'Stephen, I think this whole [CCF] outfit is being run by the CIA, and you haven't been told and you should find out right now what's going on.' On 25 May, John Thompson (the executive director of the Farfield Foundation) wrote in response to a direct inquiry from Spender denying categorically that there was anything dubious about the funding arrangements. He ascribed such 'rumours' to malice – most of them emanating from the disaffected ex-editor, Dwight MacDonald. 'The idea that the American government is behind Farfield is both ludicrous and false, I can assure you,' Thompson told Spender. Spender found the tone of Thompson's letter 'abusive'. But the import clear enough. *Encounter* was 'clean'. Epstein was wrong.

It was squalid to have constantly to deny these rumours. Spender's strategy was two-pronged. *Encounter* should publicly distance itself, over 1964, from the CCF (using King's money, the Board of Trustees, and a new editorial regime). And, over the same period, Spender would distance himself from *Encounter*. He wrote to Josselson on 15 March saying that he had decided to accept offers to work in the US for at least six months in 1965 and 1966. He was prepared to go on a retainer from *Encounter* of £500 a year. But he was adamant that he must accept the American work because 'lecturing in America I can earn in a month the salary *Encounter* pays me in a year'. This year, it had been arranged that Spender would teach the spring quarter (April to June) at Northwestern. During this period (when he continued to do *Encounter* work by correspondence and phone) it was allowed that he would continue to receive two-thirds of his editorial salary.

Spender's drift to America was not, as he explained to Josselson, 'just a matter of money. America is immensely more interesting than England, which, from here, looks like Cuba with Sir Alec Douglas Home or Harold Wilson instead of Castro.' It added to his disillusion that Hugh Gaitskell, the hope of British socialists, died prematurely in 1963. The first Labour Government since 1951 would come in 1964. But without the leader who had made victory possible. Like many lifelong socialists, Spender distrusted the Wilson administration. It seemed weak-kneed and opportunistic compared to the Attlee 'nationalizing' Labour Government of 1945 and to what he had hoped Gaitskell might have achieved, had he lived.

Spender thought the literary cultural energies of America were more vital than those of Britain – dominated as it now was by 'boom and Beatles' and the sterile hand of F. R. Leavis and his fanatically purist disciples. The other side of the Atlantic was where a poet should now be. Britain could keep Paul McCartney. He increasingly admired Lowell. He also approved of the anarchically Whitmanesque 'Beats', whom he had come to know well in San Francisco (Allen Ginsberg was a particular friend). Spender (with two university students as his next of kin) was sympathetic with the youth movement which was shaking things up in America. *Encounter* was, increasingly, on the side of what young radicals called 'the gerontocracy'. Spender warned Josselson about the journal's cultural obsolescence: 'We have not changed our attitude sufficiently in recent years. We are still thought of as Cold War.'

Josselson and Muggeridge at one of their 'informal' meetings discussed the 'Spender problem' at the end of February. They decided to yield to his demand for an advisory editorial board. Muggeridge thought that 'the relationship between Lasky and Spender would be improved if Spender were not absent from London so much'. And, of course, the only way to keep him on this side of the Atlantic was to pay the going rate. Muggeridge suggested a raise from £2,500 to £4,000. Josselson, ensconced in his Geneva luxury, thought this was 'too steep'. They split the difference at £3,300. But, to sweeten the package, they would not, after all, dock Spender's salary while he was in Northwestern this year. An uneasy concord was again achieved.

Spender managed a couple of flying trips back to the UK in March and April 1964. Over Easter he and Natasha motored to Provence to inspect their 'ruin', which they now owned. Spender stopped over with Josselson in Geneva before flying back to continue his semester's teaching at Northwestern. This year he had taken a 'residential' suite in Chicago's North West Hotel. It was, as he told Price, quite as monastic as last year's lodging:

I lead a terribly austere and model life here, eating a grapefruit for breakfast and a liquid food out of a can for lunch and only meat at dinner. It really has greatly cleared up my mind and my legs both of which were in a pretty bad way. The work is rather overwhelming because I masochistically made myself lecture on things I thought I ought to learn myself.

Two months of this kind of life seemed a long time to him. 'I think Jesus Christ was very lucky,' he told Price, 'to spend just 40 days in the Wilderness.'

He was, during these weeks in the wilderness, revolving ideas for the critical work which would eventually become *Love-Hate Relations*. And, at this period, he published the self-revealing poem, 'One More New Botched Beginning'. He wrote the first draft in Geneva, in April. As published, it climaxes with a vivid recollection of his first great 'beginning':

> Today, I see
> Three undergraduates standing talking in
> A college quad. They show each other poems –
> Louis MacNeice, Bernard Spencer, and I.
> Louis caught cold in the rain, Bernard fell
> From a train door.

Their lives had ended: as would T. S. Eliot's in less than a year. Spender – the survivor – was privileged to make another beginning.

Spender left for England as soon as the Northwestern term ended on 2 June. He expected to be based in London (apart from a short lecture tour to the US in November) until March 1965. Now property owners, albeit of a pile of French stones, the family spent much of the summer vacation in France. In July he and Natasha went to Gian Carlo Menotti's *due mondi* festival at Spoleto, in Italy. Stephen had been invited by Menotti to organize the poetry session. He recruited, among other luminaries, Ezra Pound, who gave a totally incomprehensible reading from the *Cantos*, composed entirely of inarticulate snarls. He later informed Spender, in more articulate vein, that 'only the young should read aloud their poetry'. The event was, none the less, judged a success.

In September, while Spender was away lecturing, Natasha had remained in Provence to oversee the renovations of Mas de St Jerome. While reaching to do something to the floor, she felt a 'sharp cracking pain' in her chest. Cancer was diagnosed and immediate surgery scheduled. Natasha had two operations at UCH in October. 'The next months,' Spender told Price, 'may be a bit anxious for us.' Natasha's operation went well. The most painful recollection of her time in hospital was the exquisite agony of a well-meaning Lizzie putting her hair in curlers. The family was gratefully reunited at Bruern for Christmas after a difficult year.

Stephen and Natasha Spender left England on 28 December 1964 for three weeks in the sun, at Marrakesh. It was recuperation for her (exhausted by two months' radiotherapy) and a rest for him. North Africa was enlivened by the presence of Angus Wilson and Tony Garrett, with whom the Spenders got on well. The novelist was, like Spender, a professor – at the University of East Anglia. It was jolly. The Britons were, however, cast down by T. S. Eliot's death, news of which was telegrammed to them on 4 January 1965. Stephen, who was becoming sadly skilled at writing memorials for his friends, took time away from the others to write an obituary. He would commemorate Eliot further with a monograph published in 1975. He would also be commemorated at Mas de St Jerome by an outlying tract of land the Spenders called 'Eliot's Field' (they bought it with the sale-price given by Northwestern for Tom's letters to Stephen).

Michael Josselson gave a birthday party in Geneva for Stephen at the beginning of March, before he left, as was now his annual pattern, for a quarter's teaching at Northwestern. Ellmann was exploring the possibility of 'some permanent arrangement here' for him. As usual, Spender interspersed his classroom work at Evanston with lectures across the country and social trips to New York. Natasha (who was repeating her first year at UCL) was able to come out to Chicago during the spring term, Christmas to Easter.

Lecturing, teaching and writing in America had made Spender as famous a public figure there as in his home country. In May, he was offered the post of Poetry Consultant at the Library of Congress the following year. The stipend would be $15,000 (twice his *Encounter* salary). Before accepting he consulted with Isaiah Berlin, who wrote back, 'if you really want to do this, do it. Washington does not seem to me ideal for writing, but you may not find it too bad . . . Anyway your step is not irrevocable.' Matthew was opposed to his father accepting – what with Vietnam and civil rights disturbances brewing up he foresaw difficulties. Spender resolved to accept the offer. On balance, he felt he could do good. His tenure would run for an academic year from late September 1965 through to June 1966.

It was a high honour. The Poetry Consultant was, in effect, the American Poet Laureate – and is nowadays so called. Spender was the first (and is still the only) foreigner to have held the post – an acknowledgement not merely of his eminence but of 1965's being 'The Year of International Relations'. Spender wrote to Josselson to say that he realized that his accepting the Consultancy would put *Encounter* in 'a difficult position'. More so with Wesleyan coming up in 1966. But, he added, 'I hope you will feel that my appointment is an honour to the Congress. It is also very important for the future relations of American organizations with English writers.' Josselson was vexed. He asked why Spender had not talked to Muggeridge before accepting. The poet, he thought, had shown himself 'unable to resist the call of a first siren'.

The issue was more complex. Spender was not, as Josselson alleged, deserting his post. Natasha, with whom he discussed these matters, recalls a number of hard-to-reconcile factors. Over there 'he was *appreciated*, not subjected to incessant Leavisite sniping and denigration'. Apart from his £2-a-week in the NFS and a pittance from *Horizon*, he had never (before *Encounter*) been offered anything in the UK amounting to a continuous and dependable salary (and that from *Encounter* was not extravagant). On the other hand, 'Stephen was profoundly English and did not want to disrupt his family and long-established relationships'. He felt a powerful loyalty to the corps of *Encounter* contributors whom he had cultivated (in some cases discovered) over the years, and he was devoted to what he felt was an 'English' style of editorship – less coercive and tendentious than the American. He was obliged, he felt, to keep a foot in both countries and both cultures. It was hard to explain. Nor, perhaps, would Josselson or Lasky understand if he tried to explain it. None the less it was, as he and Natasha decided, both the sensible and the honourable course.

Spender flew back to England from Northwestern at the beginning of June. Natasha had left slightly earlier, to take her sessional exams. Matthew had meanwhile taken his first-year exams, and Maro was wrapping up her year's study at the Slade. Like her, Matthew was resolved, on graduation as a historian, to be an artist. On his return, Spender was in Oxford in July, as Isaiah Berlin's guest, when the Russian poet Anna Akhmatova received an honorary degree. Spender also met the Russian poet in London, where he gave her two long-playing records (one of Purcell's music, another of Richard Burton, reading poetry) and some 'warm woolies' to pass on to Joseph Brodsky, a young poet whom he understood to be imprisoned in the Soviet Union. It was the prelude to one of his most rewarding late-life friendships.

Spender went to Geneva in the first week of September to make arrangements about *Encounter* before flying off to take up his Consultancy at Washington. It would have been very easy for them to have parted with their English editor at this point but, as ever, the CCF was stubbornly reluctant. And he, on his side, retained loyalties to the magazine he had helped create. It was decided that he would continue to be on the masthead as 'American Corresponding Editor'. To fill his place in London, they would appoint a 'locum'. Spender suggested Angus Wilson or – more practically – John Gross. Muggeridge came up with Kingsley Amis. Whoever was appointed, Spender warned, would have to be 'tough' in order to 'deal with Mel' and protect 'Books' from the sociologists and politicos that he favoured. Lasky, like Kristol, had no time for all the 'Elizabeth Bowen crap' which he believed only cluttered up a serious magazine.

In the event, they appointed, at Spender's suggestion, the critic Frank Kermode, currently professor of literature at Bristol University. It was understood that he would be a 'writing editor' rather than an 'editing editor'. Serious editing would be left to Melvyn Lasky. 'I have real hopes of Kermode,' Spender told Josselson. As a sop to the British faction it was agreed in December that Goronwy Rees should have his own gossip column in the magazine, as 'R'. The mercurial Welshman was 'excited' by the prospect.

Spender was now fifty-six years old. It was a period of his life when honours were coming. He was invited in September to do the series of six Clark Lectures at Cambridge, in March 1966. It would involve a month's residence at the university. He would be in the unusual position of taking leave from his post in Washington for which he had taken leave from his post in London. By the second week of September Spender was in office at the Library of Congress. He wrote, on his first day, to Price from his 'gilded cage' above the reading room, 'feeling rather scared'. There were 'at least three secretaries to guard me'. He felt, he told Reynolds, 'like one of those girls in a department store in a glass walled office'. The Library had supplied him with an apartment at 321 Second Street, where Natasha stayed with him until the start of term at UCL in October called her back to England.

Spender at last had leisure to write poetry. Among other pieces that he wrote and sent to Price, who was acting as his literary confidant, was a powerful meditation called 'A Glimpse of Hell', which opens with a dream of Lizzie sleepwalking, Plath-like, into her parents' bedroom:

> with flaying arms
> And hair pointed in flames, as like a pony
> Whinnying.

The poet (and father) wakes up,

> Alone, in bed, abroad. I thought
>   'She's grown
> Gone, is no more a child' – and that my dream
> Betrayed some cycle where I walk in Hell
> Endlessly damned for what I am
> Under the pavement every day.

His day-to-day duties, as Consultant, were miscellaneous. There was some formal lecturing (his first address was on 'Chaos and Control in Poetry'). He was expected to give readings of his own work and occasionally compose verse for public occasions. And, most perplexingly, America being a democracy, he was required to be available for consultation with any citizen who had a query about poetry. Strangers would ring up to ask him over the phone for an image. Other strangers would walk in off the street to show their poetry or ask him what use *his* poetry was. He was forever being interviewed. He was ceremonially present at innumerable functions. At the signing of the Arts and Humanities Bill on 29 September he shook President Lyndon Johnson's hand. It was 'like the hoof of an elephant'.

Meanwhile, on the streets outside the Library, Washington was exploding with Civil Rights, anti-War agitation and the reverberations of the Kennedy assassination. Spender was careful to avoid controversial issues, even with such close friends as the political columnist Joseph Alsop. He was conscious always of being a foreigner in Washington, with the guest's obligations. He none the less picked up some good insider LBJ stories. One of his favourites was from Abba Eban. The urbane Israeli ambassador recalled 'that when he visited the President on a mission for his country, Johnson greeted him with the words, "Ah was just scratchin' mah ass this mornin' when ah started thinkin' of your little country."' Spender kept a diary which, he claimed, 'consists largely of what people say about Johnson and is unpublishable'.

In an offhand remark to Josselson at the period, Spender complained that 'I don't really care for Washington. It is too political for me.' One hundred and ten pages of (unpublished) diary, however, record a vital engagement with the capital's cultural life and people. He loved the art galleries (particularly the Phillips) and befriended their directors. He was a regular attender, and honoured performer, at the Institute of Contemporary Art (whose director, Robert Richman, became another friend). If Beltway politics did not directly concern him, the commentators (particularly those connected with Kay Graham's *Post*) who were forming America's opinions did. He became intimately friendly with Walter Lippmann, Arthur Schlesinger, James Reston and Joe Kraft. Although he forbore (as a guest) from commenting directly on American affairs (particularly Vietnam), Spender's time in Washington laid the foundation for one of his finest late-period books, *Love-Hate Relations* (1974). It was, with 1931, the most educational year in his life.

The Library of Congress post added to Spender's already considerable stature in America. Over the next twelve months he would be elected an honorary member of the American Academy of Arts and Letters. Northwestern wanted him to accept a tenured post, year round. USC wanted him as a visitor for 1967. The Wesleyan offer, which he intended to take up in 1966, was still firm. And, as he told Josselson on 8 December, 'I am going to be offered (I think this is *frightfully confidential*) the Mellon lectures here in 1968.' It must, he thought, 'throw some light on the brain drain that in England all my life, apart from occasional journalism, I have never been offered any job at all'. Better late than never. None the less, he was nearer sixty than fifty, and would have to start 'saving up for our old age'. The family was reunited in

London for Christmas. Stephen and Natasha spent New Year 1966 with their friends the Rothschilds at Mouton.

His year in America enabled Spender to sink roots into the country, as in 1948 and 1959. He was a regular writer for the *New York Review of Books*, for the *Saturday Review* (where he wrote a savage piece on the decline of American education, 'The Age of Overwrite and Underthink') and the *New York Times*. His American agent, Harry Walker, was able to set up series of lectures. He was, as always, in demand with American audiences. Spender liked the bustle of travelling and the stimulus of meeting the academics and intellectuals of America. Walker was a 'scoundrel', 'like everyone else I put you in touch with', as Stephen ruefully warned Kermode. But even after the agent seized his predatory 33 per cent plus expenses, Spender was left 'with a little money'. He could at last see the prospect of less bread-winning drudgery in his life and more poetry. And, as he hoped, no *Encounter*.

By permission of the Library of Congress, Spender returned to England on 4 March 1966 to deliver the Clark Lectures at Cambridge. He stayed on the nights after the lectures at Trinity College, as the guest of its Master, R. A. Butler. The accommodation was more luxurious than the stipend. E. M. Forster was amused to discover that his young friend (as he still thought of Stephen) was getting precisely what he, Morgan, had received for his lectures (*Aspects of the Novel*, as they became) in the 1930s. A measly £150, a couple of glasses of vintage claret, and some high table conversation was all the lecturer walked into the Cambridge night with. Spender's series would, like Forster's, result in a book – *Love-Hate Relations*. The lectures themselves were instrumental in getting American Literature established as a respectable academic subject at the university (which led to the appointment of Tony Tanner, one of Spender's *Encounter* protégés). They were the natural outgrowth of his thirty-year fascination with Henry James and T. S. Eliot.

Spring 1966 was the season in which the Spenders celebrated their silver wedding anniversary and Matthew his twenty-first birthday. While Stephen was over for his lectures in March, the family had a large party at the ICA, in Dover Street. David Hockney supervised the room decorations with his friend Mo McDermott, improvising a 'Douanier Rousseau effect', with a forest of brown paper leaves climbing the walls, crowned with nodding flowers of brightly coloured tissue. Allegedly, the event inspired two *romans-à-clef*. One guest (Nicky Hutchinson) got a tooth knocked out doing a 'wild dervish dance with Bimba MacNeice'. Douglas Cooper 'behaved very badly'. He always did.

Frank Kermode was by now (January 1966) installed at *Encounter*. He had been doing pieces for the magazine 'for some years . . . and knew its editors well'. He was already, at forty-five, the most powerful and innovative literary critic of his post-Eliot generation – a pioneer in liberating academic thought from the deadening hand of Leavis. Currently he was employed as a professor of English in Bristol (in 1967 he would move to UCL). Kermode was a leader among the new generation of British critics who were open not just to American ideas but to the new 'theorists' in Europe. Intellectually he was ideally placed to take *Encounter* forward into its third decade. None the less, he found it 'in some ways a barely credible invitation, and my decision to accept it was delayed and uneasy'. It was agreed that Spender should remain on *Encounter*'s masthead as 'contributing editor' and still on (diminished) salary. Spender acceded, but like Kermode he was uneasy. It struck Kermode as strange that Lasky seemed not to mind that his new colleague was

living in Gloucestershire, had a job in Bristol, and most weeks couldn't spend more than a day, or at most two, in the [London] office. No matter how hard I might try, I couldn't have much influence on the principal content of the magazine.

This 'handicap', Kermode later realized, 'was in fact my chief qualification'.

Spender was at Evanston, preparing his forthcoming lectures on modern American poetry, when an explosive series of 'revelations' ('allegations'?) about the CIA and *Encounter* appeared in the American press. On 27 April 1966 the *New York Times*, in the course of a series of articles on American intelligence operations, reported (without any mincing of words) that the CIA 'has supported anti-communist but liberal organizations, such as the Congress for Cultural Freedom and some of their newspapers and magazines. *Encounter* magazine was for a long time, though it is not now, one of the indirect beneficiaries of C.I.A. funds.'

The *New York Times* was the least likely of American newspapers to publish anything unchecked and double-sourced. The indictment could not have been clearer. *Encounter* had been a tool of the American espionage machine since its inception. Four officials of the CCF wrote immediately to the paper, not to offer an outright denial of any CIA funding, but to assert (rather irrelevantly) the unassailable 'independence' of the Congress's decision-making. 'We took the money, but did what we wanted' was a possible gloss. The following day, in a TV debate with Conor Cruise O'Brien, one of the signatories to that four-handed letter, Arthur Schlesinger, an *Encounter* trustee, admitted knowledge that the CIA had indeed subsidized the congress. But had that stream of CIA money, as distinct from Farfield Foundation money, been discreetly channelled to *Encounter?*

After some hasty consultation with each other, Kristol, Spender (who had been specifically reassured on the point) and Lasky (not Kermode) also wrote to the *New York Times*, on 9 May, asserting that 'we know of no "indirect" benefactions'. Their money was Farfield Foundation money, and clean as driven snow. The letter (which had been drawn up by Lasky) protested: 'we are our own masters and are part of nobody's propaganda . . . *Encounter*'s editors, beholden to no one, are publishing what and whom they please.'

Lasky meanwhile flew to New York, and personally intervened with the *Times*. He hoped to force a retraction – or at least, perhaps, to muddy the water. His intervention was unsuccessful. Lasky much later admitted to Kermode that he had in fact known since 1963 of 'indirect benefactions' (i.e. CIA subsidies) to the CCF and thence to *Encounter*. Lapsing into the favoured euphemism of the period, he confessed to having been 'insufficiently frank' on the matter with his fellow editors.

'It follows,' as O'Brien also later observed, 'that in signing this letter Lasky, like Mr Schlesinger, was seeking to mislead the public.' Lasky's 'insufficient frankness' about the 'indirect benefactions' put Kristol (who probably did not know) and Spender (who certainly did not know) in an impossibly compromised position over the next few months of summer 1966. 'I signed [the letter], believing it to be true,' Spender told Tosco Fyvel (one of the founders of *Encounter*) in May 1967. But who would believe him if the co-editor, with whom he had worked shoulder-to-shoulder for eight years, co-signed the letter knowing it to be untrue?

In the weeks after the *New York Times* articles Spender tried, unavailingly, to pin down the senior officers of the CCF. Was 'the Farfield Foundation a "front" for the CIA?' he asked Josselson on 3 May. In a letter of the same day he posed the same direct question to Fleischmann. There was no reply from Junkie, on the surreal grounds that the millionaire was on an ocean cruise, and not answering his mail. (In fact Spender's letter was making the rounds at the CIA headquarters at Langley; Fleischmann would be briefed on what answer to give.) Josselson meanwhile replied, blandly blaming everything on the mischief-making of 'old Stalinists'. Spender was not to worry.

Both Spender and Kermode were shaken by the *New York Times*'s allegations but still sceptical about their truth. They would rather believe their colleagues than some reporter and his unnamed sources on a foreign newspaper. And, of course, Lasky, Josselson, Fleischmann and any number of Congress and Farfield underlings had given their word, time and again, that *Encounter*'s funding was clean. Spender, as he told Mary McCarthy, was reassured by Josselson that the Congress had recruited lawyers, specifically instructed 'to go through all the CCF accounts to see whether possibly a wild dollar from the CIA slipped through all their nets designed just to keep such funds out'. Cleaner than clean was the message from Geneva.

What was essential at this stage was for an unequivocal and unanimous denial to be proclaimed in the newspapers. All Spender could get were 'private' assurances and the advice to hunker down until the fuss blew over. This left him and Kermode in the front line, harried day and night by reporters. By midsummer 1966 the *New York Times* had obstinately not withdrawn its original allegation, nor had the CCF made any threat of libel action. It was now open season on *Encounter* in America. O'Brien was currently based at New York University, where he could take full advantage of America's lax libel and slander laws. The Irishman set himself up as the scourage of the magazine and its corrupt American patrons.

This vanguard British magazine was, O'Brien asserted, deeply implicated in murky CIA cloak-and-dagger games. He was quite prepared to go public with his allegations. Shout them from the rooftops, if asked. On 19 May 1966, O'Brien delivered the Homer Watt lecture at NYU, in which, with specially invited journalists in attendance, he accused *Encounter* of being an instrument of 'the power structure in Washington'. This phrase was particularly barbed for Spender, whose current position in Washington might be seen, by hostile observers, as some kind of payoff for services rendered to the American 'power structure' (it certainly was not, the senior librarian informed Stephen). The whole atmosphere was becoming poisonous and the poison was spreading uncontrollably. The *Encounter* passage from O'Brien's lecture was published in *Book Week* and distributed to the PEN congress in America in July 1966. International representatives went home to the four corners of the earth (most importantly, to London) with some choice Washington gossip.

In August 1966 *Encounter* retaliated, using its own gossip column – written by Goronwy Rees under the penetrable pseudonym 'R'. Rees composed a scurrilous set of paragraphs for his column, which blackguarded O'Brien outrageously. It alluded sneeringly to O'Brien's conduct as a UN official in the Congo–Katanga episode ('Macchiavelli of peace') and described him as a 'politico-cultural Joe McCarthy'. Dark hints were made as to his financial probity.

Spender had nothing to do with this malevolent effusion and knew nothing about it until it was in print. Nor did Kermode, who wrote twenty-five years later, 'I still don't quite understand Rees's response to O'Brien, nor how it got into print.' It may have been pure mischief on Rees's part, or a tactical intervention by Lasky – using 'R' as his catspaw. Rees confided as much to Kermode in March 1967 – but nothing he said could be believed. It is quite as likely that the article was a calculated move and cleared between Lasky and Josselson. It remains one of the obscurer areas in this story.

O'Brien was enraged beyond measure and convinced that the piece had been carefully composed by the magazine's editorial troika, including Spender, and 'other senior people . . . sitting round a table'. He also perceived, in the comments about his role in the Congo and financial dealings, manifest blackmail. If he sued, *Encounter* would use the privilege of the courts to drag supposed skeletons out of his closet and ventilate them. This was standard defence procedure in British libel suits.

Spender had finally left the 'sultry badlands' of Chicago at the end of June. Meanwhile Natasha, at UCL, was taking philosophy exams. Spender spent most of July in London, before travelling on with the family for a summer vacation at Mas de St Jerome. All through the summer months Spender continued to bombard directors of CCF with demands for unequivocal and publishable clarification. Josselson and his associates wrote back increasingly 'angry' and 'hostile' affirmations marked 'confidential'. On 10 September, while still in Mas de St Jerome, Spender was summoned to Geneva to receive, finally, a 'clear statement' about the *New York Times*'s 'allegations'. The statement clarified nothing. Belatedly, at the same period (on 16 September), he received (finally) a reply from Fleischmann to his letter of 3 May asserting that 'certainly as far as Farfield is concerned, we have never accepted any funds from any government agency'. Josselson sent a letter with the same foggy assurance: 'the only outside donor to *Encounter* has always been the Congress' (but where, one might ask, did the CCF's money come from?).

Spender went off to India, as a guest of UNESCO, for ten days in mid-September. The *Encounter* difficulty pursued him, however, even to the subcontinent. He wrote to Josselson from New Delhi on 22 September about a scurrilous piece which had just appeared in *Private Eye*. It was an *ad hominem* attack, alleging that Spender had knowingly allowed himself to be used as 'cover' for American interests. 'I may have to take an action of my own against it,' Spender told Josselson.

Had the CCF had any ulterior motives, Spender wondered, in keeping him 'on board', even when he clearly wanted to leave, all those years? On 2 October, Josselson wrote confessing that the CCF had used him, and his family, to 'woo' Fleischmann:

yes, I admit we did want you to play up to Junkie in the hope that he might make an endowment to the Congress and, since he had taken an immediate liking to you, and also to Natasha, it was only natural that we should try to make him feel as if he were the real angel of *Encounter*.

'Natural'?

Another question which Spender wanted answering was whether, over the last thirteen years, he had been on the same footing as his co-editors. Were they 'in on it'? In the same letter of 2 October, Josselson insisted that 'neither Mel nor Irving were ever on the *staff* of the Congress'. Like Spender, they were entirely free agents. 'We always wanted you to be a more *active* editor of *Encounter*,' he wrote. But it was Spender, Josselson alleged, who had made difficulties, always straining at the leash. The truth, of course, was that Spender had been consistently overruled without consultation by his fellow editors and CCF managers.

It was damage limitation on every front. On 17 September 1966 Josselson sent a letter to Kermode, pointing out that although funds received by the journal were 'fungible' (that is, no single donor to CCF could be nominated, money ran fluidly from account to account), 'Junkie's Farfield Foundation is clear of the suggestion that it was a funnel for governmental funds.' This was not crystal clear, but was an unequivocal assertion, on paper, from men of (ostensible) honour, that *Encounter's* principal benefactor had clean hands. Whatever the CCF might have done with its other clients, *Encounter's* subsidy was pure.

Kermode was nevertheless increasingly troubled. On 20 September he asked Lasky 'point blank' on the issue. Strenuous efforts were made to reassure him and to keep him from resigning. Kermode, like Spender, must at all costs be kept 'in the boat'. As he records in *Not Entitled*:

I had the memorably solemn word of Josselson: lunching at the Garrick, his London club, he had said in reply to my direct questions that there was no truth whatever in O'Brien's accusations, adding impressively, 'I am old enough to be your father, and I would no more lie to you than I would to my son.'

Spender had been receiving this kind of 'stroking' treatment for years.

Lasky meanwhile had gone off for the whole summer on a 'long trip' to South America. By boat. He might as well have been at the South Pole as far as his co-editor, Kermode, was concerned. Lasky could only be reached, at awkward times of day and night, by radio telephone. Being in sole charge at *Encounter* over summer 1966 was not a responsibility Kermode, only in his post four months, had either expected or contracted for. It was now odds-on that O'Brien would bring the fight from New York to Britain. What response should the magazine offer? On the crackling radio telephone, from somewhere in the Atlantic, Lasky instructed Kermode to fight.

In the event Kermode pursued two tracks. One was conciliatory, through the editor of the *New York Review of Books*, Robert Silvers, who was willing to mediate. An appropriate apology to O'Brien and some admission of the correctness of his aspersions on *Encounter*'s earlier funding would do it. But since Kermode still believed *Encounter* entirely innocent of any CIA connection, now or in the past, no satisfactory form of apology could ever be reached. 'I know what Jason [Epstein, another *NYRB* editor] says, but I have no reason to believe it's true,' Kermode told Silvers, whose efforts were doomed to failure.

The other track was legal and more aggressive. On Lasky's instruction Kermode consulted a QC, David Hurst, who gave him an 'exquisite little seminar' on libel law. Hurst assured Kermode that the journal could sue O'Brien in England on grounds of 'qualified privilege' – that is, if he uttered his libels on this side of the Atlantic. The quirk of 'qualified privilege' (Kermode never quite understood what the term meant) would allow them to bring a successful action without having to refute the *New York Times*'s 'false assertions'. They were not, of course, false. As Kermode later realized, Lasky had – deliberately or unwittingly – allowed him 'to misinform counsel'; itself a serious offence.

O'Brien was personally friendly with Karl Miller, literary editor of the *New Statesman*. Miller offered O'Brien space in his pages to reply to 'R''s attack (O'Brien had already responded to the piece, furiously, in the *Herald Tribune* – keeping the issue very much on the boil). Miller's motives were those of fairness and equity. O'Brien ought to be allowed to contest the kind of scurrilous allegations Rees had made.

A draft of O'Brien's retort was received by the *New Statesman*. Prudently, Miller inquired of his friend Kermode how *Encounter* would react when it was published. Kermode, still by himself, out on the limb where Lasky had left him, had to make an appallingly difficult decision. Giving Miller his *imprimatur* would be surrender. Despicable as he was, Rees must – out of loyalty – be backed up. Kermode decided that attack was the best defence. He phoned Miller to say that 'if they published a reply by O'Brien and if that reply contained (as in fact it did) a quotation of the *New York Times* statement about *Encounter* and the CIA, then *Encounter* would sue the *New Statesman*'. It was war. *Encounter* won the first battle. The *New Statesman* backed down.

Spender came back from America on another flying visit in mid-October 1966. As before, he received routine 'reassurances' from Josselson, whom he offered to visit in Geneva before returning to his duties in America. But 'Josselson was always too ill to see Stephen,' Natasha recalls, 'although he was seeing Lasky every weekend.' Then, 'late in 1966' (as Spender recalled in a letter of 11 August 1992), he took a taxi ride with Nicolas Nabokov in New York 'which alerted me to the possibility that I, with, more recently, Frank Kermode, had been lied to'. According to the apocryphal version of this conversation, spread by Mary McCarthy, Nabokov having dropped his bombshell jumped out of the taxi and Spender chose to ignore what he had been told. In fact 'Kermode and I immediately insisted on questioning Mike Josselson and Lasky together. This happened at the end of 1966. They convinced us that there was no truth in the rumours. Frank and I accepted their word.' This was again done over a Garrick meal.

On 19 November 1966, Isaiah Berlin (who had presumably been told of the taxi incident) wrote to Nabokov to say:

Dearest N., Stephen is being badly treated, I think, and the future of Encounter seems to me in danger – of course, I only know Stephen's end of the story, but it seems to me that awful things are going on. If what he fears happens, it would be a first-rate intellectual disaster. Yours, Isaiah

Berlin writes cautiously. But it is clear that he does not know what is 'going on'. And the 'what Stephen fears' is clearly some huge public scandal that will kill the magazine and indelibly taint its editors. The implication is − tell Spender (and through him the public) the truth. That truth would, however, remain elusive for at least a year more.

Stephen's friend Richard Wollheim was suggested as a possible editor for a relaunched *Encounter*. He was put off by Lasky's

amazing set of statements in which he said that there would be nothing easier than to open the books of *Encounter* and show that there was no CIA money in it at all, and then when Stephen suggested that would put an end to my worries said: 'But Stephen, do you think we should do that? Do you really think that when any Tom, Dick or Harry confronts us with a frivolous charge we should go down on our knees and show we are pure?'

'Dick' Wollheim was unimpressed.

Spender's last contribution to *Encounter* appeared in November 1966. Appropriately it is another elegy for Peter Watson − most honest of magazine proprietors: 'Isé: Voice from a Skull' (a much revised version of an earlier poem, published in 1962, 'Voice from a Tomb'). From the opening line, the poem was clearly conceived, some years previously, on a trip to Northern California:

> Here where the Pacific seems a pond,
> Winds like pocket-knives have carved out sandstone
> Islands to shapes of toys.

In this alien seascape, the poet suddenly hears the voice of his long-dead friend, and he recalls their pre-war trip to Switzerland, in 1939:

> In those gay sneering tones I knew −
> 'You were
> Once my companion on a journey
> The far side of the world, the Alps,
> Rock-leaded windows of the snow
> And glass of sky and ice and emerald grass.
> Blue, white and green were diamonded
> Upon my eyes, your seeing.
> Now

> I am drawn under in a sensual net,
> The earthiest of earth
> That tangles flesh and eyeballs, with
> Their visions glittering still. And you
> Lacking my eyes, your living seeing
> Turn like a shadow round the sunlit dial.'

It would be a finer valediction than the magazine deserved.

On 28 January 1967 Spender was finally installed at the Wesleyan Center for Advanced Studies in Connecticut. He intended to go later in the year to Chicago to take up the last semester of his three-year contract with Northwestern. His writing plans were in flux. He had begun the long haul of converting his Clark Lectures into what would eventually become *Love-Hate Relations*. As always, and even 3,000 miles away, the magazine preoccupied him. Kermode (not Lasky) kept him in touch with regular bulletins. The quarrel between *Encounter* and O'Brien might have fizzled out were it not for two things. This was 1967 – Vietnam was brewing up and there was strong sympathy with critics of American foreign policy and the CIA. Particularly on the streets of America, where opponents of the war were publicly burning their draft cards.

Second, O'Brien had been goaded to fury in December 1966 by what he took to be Lasky–Rees dirty tricks. To prosecute their counter-attack against O'Brien, they had, over the years, it was rumoured (with the aid of the CIA, it was further rumoured), assembled a 'thick dossier' of his alleged misdoings. These included, allegedly, financial misconduct 'both in Africa and in New York', when he was a UN servant. The whispers, lies and calumnies he heard were, O'Brien believed, planted. 'If I took them into court, all this would come out and I would be ruined, so in my own interest . . .' The conclusion was self-evident.

O'Brien was not a man easily intimidated. He kept up the pressure with demands for a published apology from *Encounter* for Rees's 'libel', with the implied threat of legal action if the magazine refused. At this stage the journal's editors could still have mollified O'Brien with a suit-able retraction and some mutually acceptable *amende*. Lasky, back from his South American travels, was obdurate. No retreat. To have apologized, of course, would have been tacitly to confirm the veracity of the *New York Times*'s 'false assertion'. As O'Brien later noted, 'one of the principals,

Lasky, already knew that the assertion which his lawyers stigmatized as false was completely true'.

All *Encounter*'s expensively laid defences were overturned when the wily O'Brien outflanked them by bringing suit against 'R''s libels not in England – where the attack was expected – but in his native Ireland. Irish law had no truck with the obfuscations of 'qualified privilege'. Nor was the Irish judiciary temperamentally sympathetic to British plaintiffs.

O'Brien versus *Encounter* was set for hearing in Dublin in February 1967. After various conciliatory overtures were turned down (for O'Brien it was war to the knife), the magazine's counsel let it be known that his clients would offer no defence, not regarding themselves bound to defend outside Great Britain. *Encounter* had no property to confiscate in Ireland. There would be no material loss, other than hefty legal costs. It would, of course, be a public relations disaster. Judgement was duly awarded against *Encounter* by default on 14 February 1967. A hearing to decide damages was set for 3 May. If those damages were substantial, as they most likely would be, a victorious O'Brien could be expected to bring the fight to England.

The final unravelling began in late February 1967. The editor of the muck-raking magazine *Ramparts* phoned Spender in California. They had, for a year, been investigating the government's Cold War cultural offensive. Their research had been carried on in the face of a barrage of dirty tricks by the CIA (operating illegally in the US). Their raking had come up with paydirt. Specifically, the fact that Michael Josselson and other managers had received money from the CIA which they then channelled through the Farfield Foundation to beneficiaries, including those at Panton House. *Encounter* had been, provably, on the CIA payroll. By the end of February *Ramparts* were ready to go into print in their April issue. The story would, of course, be picked up by the big US newspapers, who would run with it.

As journalists sadistically do, the editors of *Ramparts* phoned up their targeted victims for 'reactions' before going to press. Spender, Kristol and Lasky were called up, told the bad news, and asked what they felt about it. After this phone call in late February and some follow-up investigation Spender was – for the first time – wholly persuaded of the truth of the *New York Times*'s 'false assertions'. *Ramparts* had supplied irrefutable proofs that the CCF 'not only received channelled money from the CIA, it had also gone direct to the CIA for money, improvising the channels afterward'. With him at Wesleyan was another fellow at the Center for

Advanced Studies who had served in the Kennedy administration. He informed Stephen: 'of course it was a CIA operation – but you should not expect me to confirm that, or that I have spoken to you about it'. He further observed that it was CIA practice never to inform non-nationals about operations. Spender was, from Langley's point of view, an alien.

In mid-March there was a meeting of the directors of the Congress in Paris at which Lasky was present. Spender later learned, to his utter amazement, that Josselson had blandly admitted to his colleagues at this meeting that the account given by *Ramparts* was 'quite true'. This despite the fact that a few weeks earlier Josselson and Lasky had told Spender and Kermode that the charges were quite untrue. When *Ramparts* published its article in April, the story was picked up by the world press. *Encounter* was caught up in a mud storm. Josselson, as usual, wrote Spender a soothing letter. Things never looked *that* serious in orderly Geneva. All this US 'hysteria' would die down, Josselson prophesied. He blamed Jason Epstein and Dwight MacDonald for whipping things up. None the less, Josselson conceded – mysteriously – that '*some* of the manifestations of moral indignation are justified'. What could this mean? Spender and Kermode increasingly felt the magazine's trustees should be brought in.

A few days before, on 29 March 1967, Kermode had written to Lasky from Bristol effectively demanding that his fellow editor come clean: 'as recently as last week you were again willing to place me in a position of ignorantly defending *Encounter*, and yourself, against accusations which . . . are true.' Lasky was, as ever, disinclined to consign anything to paper. He came down to Gloucester to talk to Kermode in person in his country house. There followed a five-hour conversation between the co-editors as they walked 'round the garden and paddock'. As he later recalled, Kermode 'was never able to dislike this man, so vivid, so New York, so convinced, so clever'. But he could not but note 'that he preferred to discuss the matter orally, in a quiet garden'. It was evidently on this occasion that Lasky offered Kermode the preposterous explanation that yes, he did know about the CIA connection. But Josselson, fearing he was about to die in 1963, had vouchsafed it as a deathbed confession 'so that at least one trusted person should know, before he passed away'. Up to this point, Josselson had 'protected' his friend Mel from the burden of this awful knowledge. And Lasky had felt obliged similarly to protect *his* friend, Frank, 'from the knowledge that he himself had to bear'.

Kermode phoned Natasha after his conversation with Lasky, not knowing at the time where Spender was in America. Natasha immediately phoned her husband to report that Lasky had, effectively, confessed to Frank: 'there was a breach in the wall'. Spender was, by now, well beyond Josselson's power to soothe. Isaiah Berlin was appealed to in an effort to 'contain' him. In a letter of 8 April to Berlin, Josselson complained that Stephen in New York and Natasha in London were between them 'pouring oil on the flames'. 'I am genuinely fond of both of them,' he added, patronizingly. Berlin was disinclined to be co-opted. He was even fonder of the Spenders than Josselson and felt that he too had been deceived. He suggested, pointedly, that the CCF set up a public and fully confessional meeting 'to settle the moral, intellectual, and organizational future of *Encounter*'. If the CCF wanted the flames put out, they must do it honestly and openly.

Spender insisted that a trustees' meeting be called, immediately. They comprised Ed Shils (who had been given Josselson's place a couple of years before, by Josselson), Andrew Shonfield and Arthur Schlesinger (Victor Rothschild had retired after five years' quiescent service). There had never, as far as anyone knew, been a previous formal meeting of the *Encounter* trustees. They would not, it might be thought, be biased in favour of the complainants. Shils, the CCF's principal ideologue, had a chronically low opinion of Spender. On his side, Spender did not have a high opinion of Chicago sociologists.

After talking to Stephen, Natasha Spender confided her anxieties to Rees. At this point, the Welshman was shoulder to shoulder with the two English editors. A few hours after her conversation with Goronwy, however, she was phoned by Josselson – a very unusual event. He was 'very haranguing' and instructed her 'not to rock the boat'. He was only, he claimed, 'protecting' Stephen. 'What boat? . . . protect him from what?' she asked, adding: 'Frank and Stephen are in a different boat from Lasky who has deceived them.'

It was during this conversation that Natasha suggested an English trustee be appointed to balance the American majority of two on one. This led to the appointment of Sir William Hayter. Later Natasha realized how strange it was that Josselson could, apparently, decide who was or was not on the board of trustees (a body over which, having retired, he had, presumably, no authority). Boats came up again when Julius Fleischmann impudently suggested they might like to join him for a week's holiday on his yacht (the Spenders sent back a 'stinker' of a letter

to the invitation, 'and that was that'). After Josselson's phone call Natasha
Spender was sufficiently alarmed at the 'hornet's nest' awaiting Stephen
and Frank that she sought confidential legal advice, via their mutual
friend Annie Fleming, from Arnold Goodman for the forthcoming
meeting.

His five-hour conversation with Lasky in Bristol had not been, as
Kermode later recalled, 'rancorous'. But there was now no doubt in his
mind. He had been used – ruthlessly used. His legal advice was 'that I
could continue the present arrangement only at considerable hazard to
my reputation'. Not to mince words, he might jeopardize his academic
career. It was imperative to make some composition with O'Brien, lest
he hound the magazine and its individual editors through the British
courts for years to come. This was, in fact, precisely what the pugna-
cious Irishman intended to do. On learning of the *Ramparts* revelations,
O'Brien 'informed people whom I knew to be in touch with [the
managers of *Encounter*] that if they did not honour whatever award a
Dublin jury would make in my favour, I would immediately institute
proceedings against them in Britain'. One way or another, *Encounter*
would be made to pay. Instructions were issued to the magazine's lawyers.
An unreserved apology was issued, to be read out by *Encounter*'s counsel
in the Dublin court. Another apology was published in the magazine.
O'Brien was indemnified for his costs and the magazine undertook to
'pay an appropriate sum to a charity nominated by him'.

The trustees' meeting was scheduled for 20 April. Spender flew in
from America the day before. Natasha had arranged for Lord Goodman
to be on hand to advise them. After touching down, Stephen had only
hours to prepare for the meeting. Natasha picked him up at the airport
and whisked him back to Loudoun Road for a quick 'wash and brush
up' before going with Kermode to Goodman's office for a briefing. The
two editors prepared their formal statements, copies of which were sent
to Lasky who was meanwhile 'holed up', reportedly 'shaking like a leaf'.
The trustees' meeting took place in a private room at Scott's in Piccadilly.
During his presentation Lasky made what everyone later agreed were
'extremely personal and highly derogatory' remarks about Spender which
the trustees insisted should be struck from the record of the meeting (if
minutes were indeed kept they seem not to have survived). Lasky also
blurted out that 'Spender should come off his high horse'. His salary,
Spender was flabbergasted to hear, had been secretly paid by the British
Foreign Office for years – not, that is, from the British philanthropic

sources which Muggeridge had (allegedly) arranged, but from Whitehall. After this outburst Lasky declared he was willing to resign, and agreed to the publication of a statement drawn up by the trustees.

During this unpleasant meeting a way forward for *Encounter* was agreed ('a rather bitter and loathsome compromise', Spender called it). A statement would be published in the magazine; there would be a new financial arrangement and a complete break from the CCF. Kermode would carry on for two months as caretaker, until Spender was free of American commitments at the end of June. At that point, a purged and wholly independent *Encounter* might be relaunched. As they broke up for lunch, Spender phoned Natasha to report, jubilantly, 'total collapse of stout party'. They had won the day and saved the magazine.

What Lasky had said about the source of Spender's editorial salary over the years was deeply troubling. That evening, on 20 April, he phoned Muggeridge. 'You always said it came from Victor Rothschild, Alexander Korda, and the *Telegraph*,' he reminded his erstwhile friend. 'So I did, dear boy,' Muggeridge blandly replied, 'but I wouldn't bet your bottom dollar that's where it *really* came from.' It was a day in which amazement was piled on amazement. One of the American trustees, Arthur Schlesinger, came to dinner at Loudoun Road that same night. He confessed to the CIA connection 'in a very bland way'. Had they been less English and less well-mannered, Natasha Spender guesses, 'there might have been a terrible slanging match'. The revelation that 'I was implicated in receiving covert ('phoney') funds from the British Foreign Office, just as [Lasky] had been from the CIA' was, for Spender, the biggest bombshell of all. From the first, he had been lied to and used.

All plans for a 'sanitized' *Encounter* were confounded when, two days later, Lasky – who had clearly intimated his intention to resign – abruptly changed his mind. He was going to stay put. He informed the trustees, by letter, that 'for him to go now would be an admission of some kind of misdeed'. He had been in a 'stunned' condition when he offered to leave at the earlier meeting. Nor, for the same reason, would he consent to sign the statement drawn up for publication and agreed on by the trustees. Correspondence suggests that Ed Shils had been trying to find a berth for Lasky at the University of Chicago. In his present defiant mood Lasky would 'not be easy to move from *Encounter*', Sir William Hayter warned Kermode on 2 May. He would, of course, have been easier to move if Hayter himself had threatened resignation from the board of trustees, which he mysteriously declined to do, 'until the dust subsides'.

Even more astonishingly, Lasky was supported in his stubbornness by Cecil King, *Encounter's* paymaster. King wrote to Goodman and the trustees on 27 April 1967 to insist that 'Melvin Lasky's continued co-editorship and expertise are, of course, among the essentials if we are to preserve the success of *Encounter* as a publication'. As King put it, with lumbering platitude, in a subsequent press release, '*Encounter* without Lasky would be like Hamlet without the prince.' A draft announcement by Edward Shils, further supporting Lasky's continuance, was attached to King's letter. On 3 May the trustees' counter-proposal – that Shonfield edit the magazine – came to nothing. On the next day, 4 May, Kermode wrote to Hayter saying that he could not agree with King's assessment of Lasky's indispensability. If Mel remained he, Kermode, must resign.

Meanwhile, at a meeting in Paris, CCF officials voted to keep Josselson in post. Rees, who Kermode had earlier heard 'screaming abuse' at Lasky, also 'without explanation or apology . . . changed his mind' on the matter of resignation. He too would remain, even with Mel at the helm. Like Hayter, Arthur Schlesinger was another who declined to resign at this juncture – having earlier indicated his intention to do so. Much was evidently going on behind the scenes.

There was a second crunch meeting with the trustees on 5 May, after Spender had returned to Wesleyan. King presided. Hayter, Shonfield and Hugh Cudlipp (Cecil King's second in command at IPC) were in attendance. The Americans Shils and Schlesinger were absent. Kermode was present with Lord Goodman. Lasky was absent. As before, Spender was vilified behind his back in a last attempt to divide Kermode from him. King made threats against both men – 'Spender had better watch out. I own 180 newspapers.' The tycoon was, Goodman warned Kermode, 'a dangerous man to cross'. Lasky, it was agreed, would stay. After the meeting, Kermode phoned Natasha to report, bleakly, 'We've been shopped.'

Great pressure had again been put on Kermode to remain. He stood firm and presented his letter of resignation and a matching letter from Spender which he had in his pocket. The two men stood by the earlier joint statement of the trustees. Article 3 of the document read, damn-ingly: 'We believe that Mr Melvin Lasky has now admitted to us that he was informed at least as early as 1963 by the principals of CCF that the funds of this organization derive in whole or largely from the CIA.' As a conciliatory gesture, Kermode agreed not to issue any statement to the press until the CCF had prepared its simultaneous statement.

Spender, currently at Wesleyan, was kept abreast of all this by transatlantic phone-calls. He, like Frank, agreed to stay his hand. But, as far as he was concerned, his resignation was effective on 5 May 1967.

None the less, there remained slim, if diminishing, hope that the magazine might be saved. There were some significant changes of heart at the top; specifically a rift between Josselson and Lasky. On 6 May, Spender wrote to Natasha to say that:

Mike Josselson has told Irving that this is not the end for us, and he is still trying to get rid of Mel. He is stirring up the trustees, but I don't imagine this will really affect King, and I think it is too much to expect that Mike will really be able to use whatever his final weapon is against Mel. I have no doubt that all the Americans would like to see Mel go – but he has found a new protector, vast new funds, I suppose, so is likely to be able to have a run for his money. I find it a bit pessimistic.

Josselson, Spender said in another letter to Natasha, 'now hates his country'.

On the evening of 7 May Spender was phoned by the *New York Times*, who told him of a forthcoming article by Tom Braden (a known senior CIA operative) in the *Saturday Evening Post*. The next day the front page of the *Times* would report Braden's assertion that *Encounter* had been supported for years by the CIA and that one of the magazine editors was 'an agent in place'. Lasky had already pointed a finger at him, Spender, as being the guilty man, the *New York Times* reporter said.

In the circumstances, Spender was forced to make a difficult decision. He would go back on his undertaking to the trustees to wait. He would announce his resignation now. He gave the scoop to the *Times*'s Sylvan Fox and, on 8 May, the paper ran as a front-page lead story an article headed:'Spender quits *Encounter*: British Poet says Finding out about CIA Financing Led to his Leaving Magazine.' He 'was never able to confirm anything until a month ago', Spender told the paper, in the exclusive interview he gave them with the announcement of his resignation.

Josselson and Lasky were furious with Spender for 'sensationalizing' the affair. They had hoped that any resignations could be handled discreetly, with a minimum of fuss and publicity, until the *Encounter* affair slipped off the front pages, with Lasky still in office. Threats were made. Spender was ruthlessly blackguarded behind his back by the Americans.

Ed Shils wrote to Josselson in June to say he was sure that *Encounter*, under Lasky's editorship, could sort itself out, but for one thing: 'that unqualified coward and brute Spender might mess up. He has now persuaded the guileless Kermode to join him in his pogrom against Melvin. In this he is abetted by his distraught wife.' In addition to his other shortcomings, apparently, Stephen Spender was an anti-Semite determined to throw poor Jewish Lasky to his 'ravenous friends'.

Lasky himself wrote a vilifying article in the London *Observer*. Spender retaliated by warning in the *New York Times* on 27 June that if this assault on his reputation continued, he would sue *Encounter* and its officers for libel. Now that he had turned his back on the CCF, Spender could not but anticipate some dirty tricks campaign against him. When Natasha went with a friend, Bill McAllister ('something told me to take a witness'), to clear her husband's locked filing cabinet at Panton House, she found it had been rifled. 'We had a burglary,' they were airily informed by Lasky's secretary. One of the aftershocks, some years later, was the suspicion that at some point Margot Walmsley may have been involved in the clandestine cash arrangements. It was, in Natasha's words, 'totally flabbergasting: all of it'. As amazing was the cool response of their friend David Astor, with whom they had dined on innumerable occasions, who told Anthony Sampson: 'It's just the sort of thing the CIA *should* be doing.' It was a comment the Spenders would become wearily familiar with over the following years.

Everyone was suffering. On 18 May Diana Josselson wrote to tell Spender that Mike had collapsed from stress and overwork. 'The mess continues,' she said, 'it's like a Hydra.' The CCF was doomed. Josselson was, she said in another letter, 'killing himself over the Congress, but is more and more despairing about the possibility of saving it'. The Ford Foundation, its main financial backer, had indicated it would pull out. Under the strain Natasha Spender was obliged to postpone her final examinations at UCL until 1968.

Honourable to the end, Spender returned that portion of his salary which he felt was tainted. As he told Kermode:

We never really discussed what was said about me at the Cecil King meeting you attended [on 5 May], but you said that King's lawyers raised all the matters about the British Committee etc that had been raised before. I have not told any one else this, but I think I ought to tell you. I have repaid all the salary which had accrued to me at the time of your being here [Mas de St Jerome] last summer, and which dated for a year after March 1966 up to my resignation, and which I had, you will remember refused in March 1966 (after the *New York Times* articles about the CIA) and which then, after our deciding that *Encounter's* funds were fungible, I decided I could accept. I have paid as follows: $500 to Indian Famine Relief (by way of sending a cheque to the Congress), £580 (pounds) which I discovered the Congress still had as credit for my salary, which I have asked Josselson to give either to Famine Relief, or as a bourse to some Asian student. $200 to the Israel fund by way of Lord Goodman.

In this final phase of the wretched business Spender's overwhelming feeling was one of relief. As he told Nicolas Nabokov, with whom he had, despite all, retained good relations, on 21 July 1967, 'Damn the whole business. I must say I am enormously relieved to be out of it. It is like a new life.' To Kermode, on 3 June, he wrote, 'It is horrible having been entangled by all these liars.' The entanglement was now at an end. Later in the summer, on 4 August, he wrote, 'Funnily enough I have been writing poems. I think the release from *Encounter* has released me somehow.'

Encounter limped on until 1991. It was, at best, what Frank Kermode called a 'half life'. After June 1967, Spender never read the magazine again. Nor did he ever exchange a word with Melvin Lasky. Others joined the boycott, in disapproval of the way Spender and Kermode had been treated. Isaiah Berlin met Lasky only once more, unexpectedly, as they both arrived simultaneously at Goronwy Rees's deathbed. It was, for Spender, the personal treachery (and the bad manners) that most rankled. He told Josselson, on 18 August:

Alas, I have not got over my bitter feelings about Lasky! When I think that he sent his son to my son's school, his daughter to my daughter's, joined my clubs, and to do these things used my good offices without ever a word of thanks, or a word of apology for more recent events, it really is difficult to feel charitably about him.

Spender, despite everything, went out of his way to maintain friendly relations with Josselson, who he felt had been shabbily treated by his superiors. In Paris, in early October, Josselson was required to resign from the CCF, after seventeen years. He was replaced as President by Shepard Stone. Ed Shils remained on the new board of directors. Josselson apologized personally to the Spenders for the years of deception on one of their visits to Geneva, later in 1967. He was never a well man again. Melvin Lasky has never publicly explained his part in the *Encounter* affair.

Gradually, life returned to normal. On 16 June, Spender returned to England after his long American stint. There would be a visit in July from Auden, over from New York for the Poetry International Festival in London. Stephen would see little of him. He had arranged to teach a three-week creative writing summer school at New York State University, Oswego. On his return at the end of July the Spenders would go to Mas de St Jerome. There he would work on the text of his Mellon lectures. He had decided to speak on 'Painting and Literature'. Scholarship was a tremendous relief after what he had gone through in the previous twelve months. In September, he was off again to lecture in Italy. He contrived to squeeze in a visit with Natasha to Auden, at Kirchstetten.

Like an amputated limb, *Encounter* continued to ache. On 19 August, Spender had written to Kermode to say, 'I have long thought that the only effective answer to *Encounter* is to start a new magazine.' This 'Son of *Encounter*', or 'Counter-*Encounter*' project made some headway over the summer. Karl Miller, W. H. Auden, Isaiah Berlin, Stuart Hampshire and John Gross (who was willing to edit) were enthusiastic. There was a planning meeting at the Ritz in early August. Michael Astor or Lady Rothschild, it was hoped, might subsidize the venture. Allen Lane was later approached. Spender made a flying visit to New York, where Jason Epstein and Robert Silvers indicated friendly support. It was estimated that some £50,000 was needed to get the magazine off the ground. It would, Spender thought, achieve a circulation of 30,000 at a cover price of 5s. A press release was prepared, announcing plans for 'an independent English monthly'. It would have 'passionate convictions', Spender declared, and would aim to focus the imminent debate on the European Economic Community. Formal proposals were drawn up at Isaiah Berlin's flat in the Albany, on 10 September. In the short term the project came to nothing. Some years later it would flower as the *London Review of Books*.

Despite the traumatic events of 1967, Spender contrived to publish a mass of poetry – much of it never republished in volume form. The Autumn edition of *Transatlantic Review*, for example, published eight poems, illustrated by Patrick Procktor, concluding with the love lyric 'Present Absence', a good example of the poet's late style, combining what he called 'heartbreakingness and balm':

You slept so quiet at your end of the room, you seemed
A memory, your absence
I worked well, rising early, while you dreamed.
I thought your going would make only this difference –
A memory, your presence.
But now I am alone, I know a silence
That roars. Here solitude begins.

In December the American magazine *Shenandoah* published one of
the strongest of Spender's Auden poems, the anniversary piece 'Auden
aetat XX, LX'. It begins with the primal moment of their relationship:

You – the young bow-tyed near albino undergraduate
With rooms on Peck Quad (blinds drawn down at midday
To shut the sun out) – read your poems aloud . . .

Over the next three years, Spender – as he had promised – concentrated at last on his poetry, publishing in various places some fifty lyrics, most of which are excluded from the 1985 *Collected Poems*.

The year ended with a great domestic event, the marriage of Matthew and Maro on 13 December. The ceremony took place, as had Stephen's and Natasha's in 1941, at the St Pancras Registry Office. On their son's wedding, as the Inland Revenue allowed, the Spenders gave the couple £10,000 worth of pictures (including a Bacon, a Morandi and a Picasso). In April 1968 the couple decided to live in Tuscany, where Matthew followed his career as a sculptor and writer. The Spenders' daughter, Lizzie, had decided not to go to university. She would, for a while, work on an underground newspaper (as they were called in the 1960s), before eventually going to drama school. Stephen and Natasha spent the Christmas holidays, as before, at Mouton, with Baron Philippe and Pauline de Rothschild.

On Friday 12 January 1968 *The Times* and *Le Monde* published an open letter, addressed to 'the world press', from the Russian dissident scientist Pavel Litvinov, protesting the conduct of the Yuri Galanskov–Alex Ginsburg trial in Moscow at which the two writers received savage seven-year sentences. The Spenders, who saw *The Times* at breakfast, feared that no response would be made by Amnesty, or other well-meaning organizations, until after the weekend – by which time reprisals would be taken against the bravely outspoken Litvinov (he had demonstrated in Moscow, outside the courtroom).

As Spender recalls,

In order to make an immediate response, Natasha and I had spent two days telephoning to friends all over the world. After this we sent a telegram to Litvinov declaring that the signatories to the letter had read his appeal, admired his courage, sympathized with his cause and would do what they could to help. They were W. H. Auden, A. J. Ayer, C. M. Bowra, C. Day-Lewis, Stuart Hampshire, Jacquetta Hawkes, Julian Huxley, Mary McCarthy, Yehudi Menuhin, Henry Moore, Sonia Orwell, J. B. Priestley, Bertrand Russell, Paul Scofield, Stephen Spender, and Igor Stravinsky.

The telegram went out on Monday and was distributed to the world press. The signatories, as they said, 'are a group of friends, representing no organization'. The telegram was broadcast to the Soviet Union that evening by the Russian section of the BBC World Service, accompanied by a statement from Stravinsky (who was in hospital at the time). Litvinov did not receive the telegram – thanks to the efficiency of the Soviet bureau of censorship. Its contents were passed on to him by friendly foreign correspondents.

The publicity mobilized by the Spenders saved Litvinov from prison (although he was sent to Siberia, later in the year, for speaking out against the Red Army invasion of Czechoslovakia). A reply from the grateful Russian was smuggled out in August. Litvinov suggested in his letter that the Spenders might form 'an organization in England that would concern itself with making known the fate of victims of persecution and censorship – writers, scholars, artists, musicians. He emphasized that it should concern itself with cases not only in Russia but wherever they occurred in any part of the world.' This was the initial impulse for the magazine *Index on Censorship*, set up by David Astor, Stuart Hampshire, Spender and Edward Crankshaw in 1971. Litvinov, on his expulsion from the USSR, would become a patron of the magazine.

In March 1968 Spender gave six lectures for the Mellon Foundation at the National Gallery in Washington on the relationship between painting and literature. The occasion was prestigious and the subject he chose chimed well with that of his predecessor, Isaiah Berlin, who had given the series in 1965 on nineteenth-century Romanticism. Spender centred his series on the theme of twentieth-century modernism. The hero of the lectures is Baudelaire – a fellow poet with a lifelong passion for the visual arts and the first critic to use the term 'modernism'. The Frenchman was 'not just a critic, he was also a partisan, an advocate, a polemicist . . . he wanted an art which was a synthesis of past values with the heroism, beauty and squalor that characterized modern life'.

After the lectures concluded, in early April, the Spenders (including Lizzie) travelled on to Santa Barbara and then New York, before returning to Europe. As Stephen told Mike Josselson:

Everything here [in America] is a nightmare since the murder of Martin Luther King. One really begins to feel our world might be close to an end. It is only kept floating on dollars.

Politically 1968 was, above all, a year of international student revolt. Spender witnessed what were called 'the events' at first hand since he

happened to be in New York in April . . . when English friends [the economist Charles Gifford and his wife Lettie] asked me to look for their daughter [Mary] who was at Columbia University. Climbing through a window, I caught up with her in the President's office, which, together with other students, she was occupying. I became very interested in the students' revolt, which reminded me of ideological debates in my own youth, and I decided to write about it.

There followed a conversation on the issue, over breakfast in New York, with the publishers George Weidenfeld and Jason Epstein, of Random House. A contract was duly made for a work of reportage on the uprising of contemporary youth. The subject was topical and the advance was sufficient for Spender to travel to the hotspots of dissidence. The result was what the *TLS* reviewer would call 'the best book yet on student revolt'.

The Year of the Young Rebels, as it was melodramatically entitled, opens with a bang: 'On 23 April I went to the offices of *Rat* in East 20th Street' (entering, one assumes, through the door this time, not the window). The author met the underground magazine's editor, Jeffrey Shero. He would later meet Tom Hayden, the most thoughtful of the college radicals, and Mark Rudd, the firebrand advocate of physical force.

Spender concluded that the events at Columbia were, despite these young men's talent for PR, little more than a 'Happening' – something essentially theatrical and, in so far as it had a political dimension, to do with the specifically American issues of the draft and local university reform. Spender moved on to Paris, and its more cosmopolitan revolutionary atmosphere, on 24 May. Here he found himself trapped in the Sorbonne area for a month by the general strike which had paralysed the capital. The university was going mad in its 'explosion of talk' and the platitudes of *révolution permanente* (in fact, the uprising would last a mere three months – although it felt like eternity to the English observer). Revolution had its amenities. The young rebels, for whom everyone over the age of thirty looked the same, habitually mistook the snowy-haired Spender for their guru, Herbert Marcuse, and were inordinately deferential. And every evening, after spending the day with the young rebels, Spender would return to the apartment of his friends the Rothschilds, whose guest he was.

The Year of the Young Rebels offers a hilarious description of Jean-Paul Sartre at the Sorbonne, 20 May. On this occasion Spender and Mary McCarthy were moved from the speakers' stage on the grounds that 'Nous ne voulons pas des personnalités.' It made speaking difficult. All this nonsense was carried with great Gallic civility and respect for protocol. Spender declared the audience to be 'an irreproachable model of spontaneity and revolutionary manners'. It became less amusing when barricades were erected, cobblestones started flying and the Renault car workers expressed sympathy for their student comrades. De Gaulle cracked down savagely on *ce chie en lit* (this shit in the bed). From Paris Spender travelled on to Prague, to experience at first hand its short-lived spring and less romantic style of rebellion. He finished his fieldwork among the 'student theoreticians' of Berlin, where, in a sense, he had started as a young rebel himself, thirty-five years before.

Educationally the most interesting section of *The Year of the Young Rebels* is its conclusion, in which Spender pictures the university as an 'agora', or small republic. Unlike Plato's Republic, this utopia will not exile its poets, it will (as Shelley demanded) be legislated by them. Politically, Spender was opposed to unconstrained student power – although he approved of broader representation and access to the university apparatus. And, as he sagely warned the young: 'anything that is worth doing involves having to get old'.

Spender spent the summer of 1968 at Mas de St Jerome, working on the text of *The Year of the Young Rebels*, which was rushed out for publication by the end of the year. The house still lacked mains electricity and, in early August, their neighbour, Terence Kilmartin (literary editor of the *Observer* and, later, translator of Proust), 'hared up the hill' from his house to bring them a portable radio. On it they listened, hour after hour, to the news of the Soviet invasion of Czechoslovakia. It was the end of the student dream. *The Year of the Young Rebels* was published on Spender's sixtieth birthday and made him feel, as he told Mary McCarthy, '6,000 years old'. She, even more intrepid than he, had visited Hanoi that year – in defiance of American bombs. The book was applauded in the weeklies, left-wing and right-wing, as 'a healthy leaven in a soggily cynical world' (the *Listener*), 'idealistic' (the *Spectator*), possessed of a 'welcome coolness' (the *New Statesman*).

Spender's academic base for 1969 and 1970 was the University of Connecticut at Storrs. With both children now grown up it was easier for him and Natasha to spend longer periods away from home. His first stay in Storrs was from January to March 1969. Natasha (now graduated from UCL, and embarked on graduate work in the psychology of perception) was able to visit him for longish periods. His overseas life, always nomadic, was now more domestic. Over early 1969 the Spenders did an all-in exchange of house, car and pets with a Storrs family (the Goldstones) coming to London.

The small New England school had a number of attractions. Their friend Rex Warner was its resident writer. He and Stephen had been students together at Oxford. Warner was now reunited with his first wife, Frances, whom he had remarried after a complicated intervening love life. Although he was in the Classics Department, Spender observed that the 'social life of the English faculty' revolved around the convivial Rex. Spender claimed that Storrs 'was the most congenial English Faculty I was to know in all my years of teaching in America'. He became particularly friendly with the musicologist Petter Larsen. He, Warner and Larsen had lunch together every Tuesday. He also made friends with David Leeming in the English department, with whom he shared an office. Leeming would subsequently write a biographical study of Spender. Storrs was conveniently close to New York, and Auden. From Connecticut, Spender could keep in touch with the Buttingers (in Pennington, or their Manhattan apartment) and Isaiah Berlin and Stuart Hampshire, both currently teaching at Princeton. Auden was by now very cranky. On one occasion Warner and Spender called on him (by invitation) in Manhattan only for Warner to be met with the irritated remark: 'What on earth are *you* doing here? I've got *nothing* to give you.'

Warner and Spender were contemporaries and 'survivors' – giants of the interwar literary era: one a lyric poet, the other an expressionist novelist. The two writers co-taught courses and mounted a conference on 1930s literature, which attracted, among others, John Lehmann, Auden, Paul Goodman, Malcolm Cowley and Erskine Caldwell. The 1930s, Spender wrote in the *NYRB*, were 'sufficiently remote to be historical while simultaneously near enough to be discussed'. Spender also taught courses at Trinity College, Hartford, some thirty miles away, and gave the annual Wallace Stevens lecture in the great poet's home town. Spender had friends at Trinity: the art historians Michael Mahoney (whom he had got to know in Washington in 1965) and Rosamond Russell (sometime Paris editor of American *Vogue* and, before her divorce, known as Peggy Bernier), who launched her successful career as a lecturer on art at Hartford.

Spender celebrated his sixtieth birthday with a dinner party at Storrs, on 28 February. Auden sent off a birthday poem, which never arrived and is, presumably, still felicitating feebly in the dead letter office of the US Mails. Richard Ellmann came from Yale and Natasha flew in from London, bringing as her present the Henry Moore sketch 'a crowd of people looking at a tied-up object'.

Spender returned to London in June for the Poetry International Festival – since 1967 an annual event. Stephen and Natasha spent, as would be their pattern, the summer months at Mas de St Jerome – now fully habitable. There was lots of reading for him; ninety-eight novels, to be precise. He was one of the panel for the first Booker Prize. The award went, controversially, as always, to P. H. Newby. Spender took particular pleasure in the crustiness of his fellow panelist Rebecca West. Irritated by the explicit sex scenes in modern fiction, she declared: 'If I read again the line "he entered her" I shall stop reading. Are these women, or welcome mats?'

In November 1969, Auden made another trip to London. He gave a reading 'at some Bloomsbury church' (as Spender recalled; it was St George's). Afterwards, Tom Driberg took Natasha, Lizzie, Marianne Faithfull and Chris Jagger (brother of Mick) to supper. The conversation was memorable, and Spender commemorated it in one of the artfully prosaic 'diary poems' that he was experimenting with at the time. Auden described his famous daily routine:

> His talk
> Is concentrated 'I', 'I get up at eight;
> Then I have cawfee and rolls, then I do
> *The Times* Crossword, if I can get *The Times*.
> Then I go to the john, and then I work
> Until elevenses, when I have tea.'

And, so on, until:

> Then at nine bye-byes like mother taught me.
> Oh! the relief of getting between the sheets!

Marianne Faithfull talked about her suicide attempt. 'Naughty,' chuckled Auden, asking how many pills she took. Forty-two, the singer replied. 'I only take one,' said Wystan. As Spender later recalled to Reynolds Price, Auden denied that he had written the (much-circulated) scurrilous doggerel about fellatio 'The Platonic Blow', out of deference to the twenty-year-old Lizzie, and asked Stephen never to let her see the work. He did, however, ask Ms Faithfull if, when she secreted drugs, she 'packed them up your ass'. Spender was driven, unusually, to remonstrate:

> I say: 'You talk of nothing but yourself.'
> He looks full at me with a kind of sweetness
> And says: 'What else should I talk about then?
> What else do I know about?'

After Christmas, the Spenders went for what was now an annual reunion with Philippe and Pauline de Rothschild at Château Mouton in the Bordeaux country. The couple were in the throes of creating a Museum of Wine on their estate. Pauline's birthday was on 1 January and furnished a double occasion for celebration (she liked to give, rather than receive, presents on the day). The Spenders were among a number of favourite guests of the de Rothschilds: Balanchine, Sacheverell Sitwell, the poet Louis Aragon (now no longer a Communist, but ineffably bourgeois, and clad in impeccable Yves St Laurent suiting), Peggy and George Bernier (editors of *L'Œil*), the 'Bloomsberry' critic Raymond Mortimer, the American writers Glenway Westcott and Monroe Wheeler. Talents were displayed for the entertainment of the company. On one notably cosmopolitan occasion the Russian poet Mikhail Likachev declaimed Russian translations of English Elizabethan poetry, to be followed by Philippe reciting his translations of the same works into French, and Natasha reading the originals. The conversation, moving rapidly between French and English, was invariably good, the food and drink perfect. 'You couldn't drink wine when you got home,' Natasha remembers.

The 1970s: Grandparent, Not Yet GOM

Stephen Spender had all his life been a young man of letters – younger, that is, than his literary contemporaries: he had begun his career an apprentice to Auden, a 'pupil' of Isherwood's, a protégé of Eliot's, politely junior with writers like Graves and Sitwell, attentive to wiser heads, like William Plomer. In his sixties his old(er) friends began to drop away – particularly those whose lives were less orderly than his had become. Spender became expert in the sad art of the obituary. He none the less made important new friendships. Two (with Joseph Brodsky and Bryan Obst), were as important as any in his adult life. But with Auden, Eliot, C. Day-Lewis, MacNeice, Aldous and Julian Huxley, Peter Watson and Connolly gone, he felt his eminence to be somewhat lonely. He was the thirties survivor. With the statutory retirement age of sixty-five imminent, Spender embarked on what would be his third career. As with fire-fighting and UNESCO, his years as a salaried don, at University College London, were short. He would end his writing life as he had entered it, a freelance, and writing to the end. His time as a university teacher inspired his best critical writing since The Destructive Element. *After the trauma of the* Encounter *scandals, the 1970s were a relatively quiet decade for Spender. His children had grown up. His wife had survived a serious illness to take up* her *new career in higher education (she would keep her position at the RCA longer than he did his at UCL). Spender was, over these years of his early old age, increasingly honoured: as a man of letters, a patron and (through PEN and* Index on Censorship) *a protector of fellow authors. If some very high honours eluded him (the Nobel, the Oxford Professorship of Poetry), others came his way (the Queen's Medal for Poetry). Still others, the laureateship, for example, he had no appetite for. He remained England's best known, and most highly regarded, man of letters in America: a 'public intellectual'. He spent some four years of the decade in that country: lecturing, teaching, reading, contributing to opinion-forming journals, cultivating his extensive circle of friends. His interests ranged across more than literature: but his central loyalty was to modernism in literature and art, classicism in music, humane liberal values in life. As his seventies approached, the Spenders spent more time in France. The summers in Provence were relaxed but he did not otherwise notably slow down. Until his very last months of life, Spender never – as he often said in his journals – felt old; even if (as he also recorded in his journals) he might have looked it. The 1970s saw Spender's last major original volume of poetry* (The Generous Days). *Its reception again indicated the ambivalent regard in which some of his compatriots held him. He was respected for everything, it seemed, except what was most important to him. Privately, Spender's journals and some of his intimate letters dwell on mortality (particularly over the years 1973–4, which saw a holocaust of close friends). His poetry takes on a Sophoclean stoicism. Those who knew him personally testify that the gloom was reserved for his private moments. In conversation and society he was, as his wife recalls, 'wonderful to be with' and zestful for life (of which, as it happened, much remained).*

After their 1970 New Year celebrations with the de Rothschilds, the Spenders left Mouton for Florence to be present at the birth of their first grandchild, Saskia, on 2 January. Stephen commemorated grand-paternity with a diary poem:

> We looked at Matthew's child, our granddaughter,
> Through the glass screen, where eight babies
> Blazed like red candles on a table.

Matthew slyly asked one of the nuns, 'Is our baby a genius?' and 'started drawing Maro and her daughter', the poet recorded, 'nine hours after Saskia had been born'. The mother's labour ended, the father's started. According to Matthew, Spender 'didn't at first much like being a grand-father' – or, more precisely, finding himself old enough to qualify for the role. Who does? Over the following years he came to love his grand-daughters dearly.

When the academic term started towards the end of January, the Spenders returned to Storrs for the spring semester and a country-wide round of lecturing. Stephen had written to Michael Josselson, a couple of weeks earlier, with some interesting news:

I hope that this may be my last year of the American tours as there is just a possibility I might get a job at London University. I like America but year after year of trudging through the snow and attending dons' parties is a bit of an ordeal.

In Connecticut they had a different house this year, at Stonington (near his friend and fellow poet James Merrill, who arranged the accom-modation). Spender was again supplementing his earnings (and teaching load) with courses on modernism at nearby Trinity College. It meant an extra $3,000, on top of the $8,000 Storrs paid him. It was a good, if hardworking, arrangement. He could, at a pinch, squeeze all his Hartford teaching into a single day, if he taught till 10.30 p.m. It was then up to him to stay the night or drive back. He got on well with the Dean of Arts at Trinity, 'Bullet' Bob Fuller. Fuller promised to serve up for Spender's class 'the mixed-up imaginative kids you like' rather than 'football players with crew cuts'. Bullet Bob was as good as his word. Spender brought some of his 'long-haired, pot-smoking, gothic-looking students' to Storrs, scandalizing its sedate community.

On 28 February, Spender went to New York to celebrate his sixty-first birthday and Wystan's sixty-third. Stephen had his friend to himself; Wystan's partner, Chester Kallman, was in Greece. It inspired the mellow diary poem 'Auden at Milwaukee', a reminiscence on his friend's egotism:

> Dined with Auden. He'd been at Milwaukee
> Three days, talking to the students.
> 'They loved me. They were entranced.' His face lit up the scene.

Spender ruminates on precisely *what* those Milwaukee students adored in Auden:

> They see him as an object, artefact, that time
> Has ploughed criss-cross with all these lines
> Yet has a core within that purely burns.

It was the last time he would see Auden in America, or see Auden wholly happy.

In obituary retrospect Spender realized why this February 1970 occasion had struck him as so significant. Wystan had, at last, reconciled his public and private faces. For the rest of his life Spender would, like the poet's other close acquaintances, muse continually about the Auden enigma. Their mutual friend Jimmy Stern contended that Wystan – the most famous literary homosexual since Oscar Wilde – was 'not queer'. He had been 'turned' (more than once), Stern believed, by Christopher – a zealot who demanded 'total loyalty to the homosexual tribe'.

On 8 April, Spender received an honorary doctorate from Loyola University. Dr Spender was in Washington in May 1970, during the Cambodian bombing and the Kent State shootings, which convulsed the country and enraged its university community against Nixon – the president who encouraged the National Guard to fire on 'campus bums'. America's 'decade of agony' was reaching a climax. At a tea-party in the capital his hostess, Alice Longworth ('the legendary daughter of President

Theodore Roosevelt', and a close friend during his year as Poetry Consultant), was called away to answer a phone call from the White House.

She returned, after ten minutes on her hotline, 'rubbing her hands gleefully' to report:

> 'the new offensive
> Is going very well, yes excellently.
> They're rooting out the enemy from his hideouts
> And capturing his weapons. It will all be over
> Within eight weeks. Then, total victory!'
> 'They're killing them?' 'Deaths? Don't let's speak of deaths!'
> She looks all round the room, a little wildly.
> 'What is this silence?' Under your conversation
> I hear a silence – a terrible silence.

Ultima ratio regum, thought Spender. His war poems were all written.

The Spenders spent summer 1970, as was now habitual, in Mas de St Jerome. John Bayley and Iris Murdoch visited; as was also habitual. Provençal life was leisurely and civilized. But Spender could not but feel that – since *Encounter* – he had lost occupation. And he wanted something more intellectually stimulating than Storrs, congenial as it was, could offer. The job at London University, which he had mentioned to Josselson the previous December, eventually came through. For some time, Spender had enjoyed the friendliest relations with scholars who were recently installed at UCL. Frank Kermode had left Bristol and was now Lord Northcliffe Professor of English. Richard Wollheim was Grote Professor of Philosophy. Noël Annan – biographer of Leslie Stephen and a connoisseur of literary Bloomsbury – was Provost (i.e. president) of the college. Kermode had a mission for English at UCL. He wanted to dust off the subject by an injection of what was called 'theory'. But he also wanted to reconnect the department with the living world of London letters. To this end, he moved to appoint two poets – Grey Gowrie (a disciple of Lowell) and Stephen Spender. He would later appoint the novelist A. S. Byatt.

The announcement of Spender's appointment was made in March 1970. Richard Wollheim cannot recall any setpiece interview. He does recall that 'Frank [Kermode] and I had lunch with Stephen at the Garrick and put it to him. Then Frank put it to Noël', who went through the necessary formalities with CVs and committees. The appointment was approved. Spender was duly established at UCL with a personal chair in October 1970: the beginning of the English academic year. He was sixty-one years old. He had no degree, other than a string of honorary awards. He did, however, have experience in teaching English at the best institutions (all of them American, alas) in the English-speaking world. And he was a leading British writer. He gave his inaugural lecture, on 'Form and Pressure in English Poetry' on 22 October. William Plomer, sitting inscrutably in the front row, was pleasantly surprised at his friend's 'impressive energy and pace'.

The 'Godless Place in Gower Street' suited Spender, for much the same reason that its junior branch, University College School, had suited him forty years before. It was the least hidebound of institutions. There were no 'dons' parties'. Or dons, come to that; they were all 'university teachers'. The English department, the oldest in Britain, had tradition-ally close connections with London journalism (Spender's chair was, to Downing College's Scrutineers, a clear sign of imminent cultural apoc-alypse). UCL was indelibly 'liberal'. It was conveniently located in Bloomsbury, twenty minutes from Loudoun Road by public transport (Spender favoured the double-decker bus). The college was within walking distance of the Garrick, which was Spender's favourite club until it black-balled the provocative columnist, Bernard Levin, when he resigned. There were good restaurants in Charlotte Street (the College's own catering arrangements, as Annan invariably warned his friends, were squalid in the extreme). Spender liked to take students to lunch at the Anemos, a jolly, scruffy, and amazingly cheap Cypriot Greek taverna. Above all, UCL was somewhere that, as he liked to say, 'one could live one's values'.

Foster Court, which housed the English department, was a shabby converted mattress warehouse which had once belonged to the depart-ment store Maples. Spender had a tiny office on the second floor, distin-guished by a Hockney drawing of himself (Grey Gowrie also had a Hockney drawing of himself, in his neighbouring office). The English department boasted a one-to-one tutorial system. It suited Spender.

He got on well with his students: male and female. One, Richard Todd, who went on to an academic career, made himself some extra money checking the proofs of Spender's books in progress. Todd recalls a staff-student party at Loudoun Road in which, coming on a knot of his pupils happily puffing a gigantic joint (the fashion in the depart-ment was for spliffs the size of Cuban cigars), Spender politely declined a puff and benignly went on to see that other guests were being looked after. It was a matter of *politesse* to attend any party that any student was good enough to invite him to. He graced dwellings grottier than anything he had seen since Berlin in 1931.

Spender's closest friends in the department were Kermode, Gowrie and a young colleague, Keith Walker, whose musical tastes and sharp wit were congenial. Walker served as a guide for Spender through the thickets of the 'New Syllabus', 'Boards of Study', and such impenetrable mysteries as the 'flip flop option programme'. Spender never quite got the hang of the London federal system (on one occasion he addressed a letter to 'Royal Holloway Cottage'). Kermode's department was, however, refreshingly unstuffy. This was just as well, since administration was Professor Spender's Achilles heel. He would turn up to staff meetings with a vast Letts diary. The speculation among his colleagues was that he feared he would mislay anything smaller than a barn door. On one occasion, when 'student's progress' came up, he said – musingly – of a female pupil: 'I remember little about her, other than that when she leaves a fragrance of roses remains in the room.' There was a running joke in the department about who was taking down his notes from the boards and passing them on to Sotheby's. As a teacher, Spender was instrumental in introducing self-help essay-writing classes for the undergraduates (based on his creative writing methods).

As a visiting academic in America, Spender had been able to teach pretty much what he wanted; usually modernism, Henry James, or creative writing. As was everyone in the UCL department, he was obliged to mark tutorial essays on Spenser, Chaucer, Strindberg or even the poetry of Stephen Spender, if that was what the student elected to write on. It was a great strain. Natasha Spender (now a lecturer herself, at the Royal College of Art) recalls him staying up most of the night when one perverse undergraduate ordained a tutorial on Smollett.

Examining and setting finals papers were an annual trial. At such moments, he told the young American novelist David Plante, he was tempted to go into the department loo and scrawl 'Spender must go!' on the wall. He wrote in similarly jocular complaint to Reynolds Price (also a professor of English, at Duke):

This being a professor stuff really rather overwhelms me. I'm now having to set papers and can only think of questions like: a) Was Casaubon impotent? or b) Was Daniel Deronda circumcised?

In fact, over his six years at UCL Spender was a conscientious tutor, a stimulating lecturer and – most important – a productive scholar. Between 1969 and 1976, he turned out books on D. H. Lawrence, T. S. Eliot and W. H. Auden. During his tenure at UCL, he would also publish *Love-Hate Relations* (the revised text of his Clark Lectures).

In 1971, Spender brought out his first volume of new verse in England since *The Edge of Being* in 1949. It was not the 'long poem' he had been writing since 1957 (a small hump of which would break the waves with *Dolphins*, 1994), but a selection of what he considered his best lyrics and 'diary poems' over the preceding decades. *The Generous Days* represented poems 'worked over for 30 years'. None the less, he told Reynolds Price, 'they read, I think, very continuously and I am quite excited'. *The Generous Days* showcases his recent poem 'One More Botched New Beginning'. Endings are, however, the presiding mood of the collection. It is as if Spender anticipated, along with those comrades recently dead (MacNeice, Eliot, Ackerley, Leonard Woolf), the deaths soon to come: Day-Lewis in 1972, Auden, Elizabeth Bowen and Plomer in 1973, Connolly in 1974. Isherwood in 1986. Only the austere Edward Upward would outlive him.

The days celebrated in *The Generous Days* are yesterdays. The collection features a lament for (the still living) John Lehmann, 'Last Days', and poems in memory of Virginia Woolf and Peter Watson ('On the photograph of a friend, dead'):

> your ghost
> Emerged gelatinously from that tomb;
> Looking-glass, soot-faced, values all reversed
> The shadows brilliant and the lights one gloom.

The parade continues with 'Four Sketches for Herbert Read', who died in 1968, and an exequy for Matthew's luckless canary, Hector, slain a decade since by the family's Siamese cat.

After these mortuary reflections *The Generous Days* ends with an ambiguous image of youth and regeneration, 'Art Student'. Dated 'Connecticut, 1970', it immortalizes an undergraduate he had come to know in his Trinity creative writing class. The 'Art Student' is a modish child of the time:

With ginger hair dragged over fiery orange face,
Blue shirt, red scarf knotted round his neck
Blue jeans, soft leather Russian boots
Tied round with bands he ties and unties when
His feet are not spread sprawling on two tables –
Yawning, he reads his effort.

As this handsome oaf tells his instructor, 'He has only one subject – death – he don't know why.' But he embodies, of course, 'life'. He is an art student (not a 'lit major') and, as such he believes, 'Art's finished'. And yet, paradoxically, the image of the young man, for all his philistinism, exudes youth's vitality. The collection ends, poised between elegy for the dead and uneasy salutation for what, in 1932, Spender had called his 'young comrades' – the living.

Amazingly, the *Listener, Spectator* and *New Statesman* all ignored Spender's latest volume of poetry. The *TLS* (still, until 1973, anonymous) gave the volume to Anthony Thwaite (a champion of the 'Movement' and the man who had taken over Spender's vacated editorial chair at *Encounter*). Thwaite's review of *The Generous Days* was razor-edged. The journal gave the collection its full attention: 2,000 words and a portrait photograph. The piece came in very late in the year, establishing itself as the last word. Thwaite began with a retrospect of Spender, the public figure. Isherwood's 'truly weak man', and 'Stephen Savage' were haled out for whipping yet again. A belittling assessment followed. It was a consolation (and a confirmation of the more favourable judgements) that he was awarded the Queen's Medal for Poetry, later in 1971. Her Majesty was, apparently, relieved to know that unlike a previous recipient Spender enjoyed writing poetry. He no longer much enjoyed publishing it.

His best poems were as good as ever, if more chaste in style. Stravinsky died in 1971. Spender commemorated his friend's passing with a vignette poem, 'Late Stravinsky Listening to Late Beethoven'. The elegy begins with a conversational reminiscence by the composer's wife, Vera:

'At the end, he listened only to
Beethoven's last quartets.
Some we played so often
You could only hear the needle in the groove.'
She smiled,
Lightly touching her cheek.

They were, also, Spender's and Isaiah Berlin's favourite music. Stravinsky had composed his death as elegantly as his music.

On 15 October the magazine *Index on Censorship* was formally launched. It was supported by an independent charitable trust, Writers and Scholars International. An office had been set up at 35 Bow Street. The press conference announcing the new venture was addressed by Lord Gardiner, the Trust's first chairman, Spender and Michael Scammell, first editor of the quarterly magazine. The proclaimed aim was to 'monitor' censorship, internationally. It was a cause to which (via the Litvinov affair, two years earlier) Spender had devoted himself since the late 1920s, when he fled England to escape state oppression of literary freedom.

In the spring of 1972 after months of malaise Cecil Day-Lewis was terminally ill. He was to be the second member of MacSpaunday to go. Knowing that Wystan would later regret not having seen his old friend, but fearful that his brusque 'face up to it' attitude to death might be upsetting to Cecil, Jill Day-Lewis invited the Spenders to bring Wystan to visit without giving advance explanations. Initially Auden was testy at the prospect of driving to Greenwich, as he was to leave imminently for America. 'Damn, on my last day!' he exclaimed when Stephen told him of the invitation. It could have been awkward. In fact it was a gently affectionate meeting. Auden and Day-Lewis discussed with good-natured competitiveness from which cathedral pulpits they had preached and on which biblical texts. Cecil, though frail and resting on an air cushion, enjoyed the evening. Wystan, who had been jovial during the conversations, but silent on the long drive back through the summer traffic, said, quietly at last, to Stephen, 'I know, of course, that I'll never see him again.'

Day-Lewis had been Poet Laureate. Spender's name came up as an obvious successor. He did not want it. He did, however, lobby discreetly for Auden (tricky, given Wystan's American citizenship). The popular sentiment was behind the leader of the Movement school, Philip Larkin, who turned it down. The Queen's election eventually went to John Betjeman, of whom both Spender and Larkin approved.

It was arranged in summer 1972 that Auden would return to the UK to take up residence as an honorary fellow at his old college, Christ Church. An apartment was found for him in the converted Brewhouse, in the college grounds. He would, it was anticipated, enjoy a serene twilight as a GOM of English letters, as had Morgan Forster, at King's.

At the same period that Spender's oldest friend in poetry returned to England, after thirty years, he formed a rewarding new friendship with a young poet, Joseph Brodsky. The thirty-two-year-old Russian arrived in London in 1972 for the annual Poetry International Festival, now a regular summer event, half pop concert, half Glyndebourne. Brodsky, an exile from the Soviet Union, was on his way to the US, where he would settle and, eventually, win the Nobel Prize for Literature. Personally Spender came to love Brodsky. Brodsky's poetry was not, however, entirely to his taste. He found it, as he told Alan Ross, 'interesting in a *gritty* kind of way'.

Brodsky came to Britain with Auden, who had accompanied him from his transit centre in Vienna (Auden and his partner, Chester Kallman, had a house at nearby Kirchstetten). Over the previous few years, Spender had contrived to help Brodsky – a dissident always in hot water with the Soviet authorities – through PEN and the networks of *Index on Censorship*. The connection was made, initially, through the poet Anna Akhmatova, on one of her earlier visits to England to receive an honorary degree at Oxford. She was an intimate friend of Isaiah Berlin's, and a tireless supporter of Brodsky's genius.

As he came through the immigration inquisition in 1972, Brodsky found himself and Auden being met at the airport 'by a strikingly beautiful woman, tall and almost regal in her deportment'. Natasha drove them back from Heathrow. The Spenders had prepared rooms for both poets at Loudoun Road. Shortly after their arrival, Brodsky remembered, 'in walked a very tall, slightly stooped white-haired man with a gentle, almost apologetic smile on his face'. It was the Russian's first personal encounter with Spender. Stephen greeted Wystan. 'I don't remember the exact words,' Brodsky later recalled, 'but I remember being stunned by the beauty of their utterance. It felt as if all the nobility, civility, grace and detachment of the English language had suddenly filled the room.' Spender struck Brodsky as an 'old man' (he was sixty-three).

Over the next few days, Brodsky was 'mothered by the Spenders and by Wystan'. It was the beginning of a close relationship between the poets. Spender took the overwhelmed young Russian to the Café Royal, the House of Commons and the Garrick Club. He met Cyril Connolly, Angus Wilson, Sonia Orwell and various politicians. To Spender's gratification Brodsky put C. P. Snow down, peremptorily, when the sage of two cultures extolled 'the virtues and verities of Mikhail Sholokhov's prose'.

After his reading at the Poetry International event at the Festival Hall,

Brodsky travelled on to his new home in America (a teaching position
at Michigan). The Spenders retired to their second home in Provence
for the summer, and a procession of visitors. Their second granddaughter,
Cosima, was born on 24 August.

In February 1973, Auden was installed as a residential fellow at Oxford.
It should have been idyllic. In the event, leaving Manhattan proved disastrous. As Richard Davenport-Hines records:

Glaciers and fjords had all Auden's life been part of his poetic landscape, but
now, in his last year of life, he found himself in an Antarctic camp of his own
devising called the Christ Church Common Room. His meaningless drool was
usually excretory or sexual. 'Look here, if Auden wants to drink himself to
death, please could you ask him to do so in the Brewhouse and not in the
Common Room,' one senior colleague implored.

Spender, like other Oxford friends (Stuart Hampshire, Isaiah Berlin) was
distressed but impotent to intervene as Auden thrashed about in his final
agony.

   Spender had taken leave from the summer term at UCL to visit
Northwestern. Chicago was deadly this year, he told Keith Walker, and
he was feeling somewhat debilitated. There was nothing to do when
he was not teaching (his closest friend at Northwestern, Richard
Ellmann, had removed to Yale). Spender's routine in this empty place
was to get up at six, start work at seven, and 'work pretty continuously all day'. His lectures were on T. S. Eliot, and would form the
nucleus of the monograph on the poet he had been commissioned to
write for Frank Kermode's 'Modern Masters' series. The creative writing
class was 'absolute shit' – only two good students. The sixties were, it
seemed, all over. There was no 'rebellion', scarcely any signs of life. As
a temporarily dispirited Spender told Walker:

One feels incredibly cut off in this university where studies are pursued in a
listless kind of way, students only appear to think 'shall I ever get a job?' – there
is no social life (I keep on giving parties but practically no-one asks me back
or reacts in any way). I've made a great and revealing discovery about America:
that under all the activity, energy, excitement, there is an immense reverse force
of inertia, a kind of backwards pull as great as (much greater than) the forward
one. It is a country where people (like the students four years ago) are very

active for a time and then sink back into inactivity or just minding their own business or taking pot on the very faintest pretext that they are disillusioned.

The 'only thing' that kept him going was the festering drama of the Watergate scandal, unravelling day by day in Washington. He felt the American newspaper editors had been 'magnificent' in uncovering this corruption at the centre of the American system. It was in line with what he had experienced at *Encounter*.

Spender returned to the UK on 5 June. While he had been in America, his candidacy for the Professorship of Poetry at Oxford had been going forward. Roy Fuller's term was up. Spender would have been a natural successor to Fuller (one of his *Horizon* discoveries, thirty years before), Auden, Day-Lewis and Robert Graves. He was backed by Auden, and appointed Wystan and Isaiah Berlin as his campaign managers.

Nowadays the dreaming spires attracted more attention from Grub Street than they used to. It might, Spender thought, have been a mistake to let his name go forward in this new, media-conscious university world. He was sure he would lose 'to John Wain, who lives in Oxford and has a bicycle on which he pedals furiously'. Muhammad Ali (heavyweight boxing champion of the world) was another candidate: a 100–1 outsider. Spender and Wain were the front-runners. Spender, on Ladbroke's reckoning, was the favourite at 4–6 on (Wain was 4–1 against). The election was to be held on 26 May. The rule of the election was that only Oxford MAs could vote. It was a disadvantage that Spender would still be out of the country, unable to lobby for himself. The Wain supporters were active and mocked Spender as '"Stainless Splendour" – the establishment candidate'. Wain was the gritty man of the Oxonian people.

It was in the event a close-run thing. Wain won by 231 votes to Spender's 213 in a record post-war turnout. The bad news was communicated to Spender in America by Anthony Holden, then President of the Union, and a Spender supporter. He took it stoically, with the response 'Sic transit gloria'. The 1930s were truly over. The Movement had won. Some time, not too distant, its day too would pass.

He bounced back, as he always did. Even defeat had its funny side. On 29 May he wrote to Hamish Hamilton to say:

I just had an absurd telephone call from a journalist on the Chicago Herald Tribune. He said 'We've just heard what looks like a Goodbye Mr Chips story about you. We hear that you are a good gray kind old guy who's been narrowly defeated as Poetry Professor at Oxford University by a young whiz-kid type with a movie-star type name called John Wayne.'

Perhaps, in the larger scheme of things, the Poetry Professorship did not matter so much.

On 28 September Auden died after a poetry reading in Vienna. It occurred as the Spenders were making their way back by car from Mas de St Jerome. In Normandy they had picked up food for a dinner-party to celebrate their return to Loudoun Road. On getting back, they heard the grim news. The party was cancelled, and a series of memorials set in train in which, necessarily, Spender would play a leading part. It was some consolation that Auden had recently stayed at Loudoun Road. Natasha, even though Chester was the most difficult of guests, had extended the invitation to his partner; and was now glad for it. It was on this occasion that she observed what, in his last years, made Auden happy: small rituals of domestic life (she was particularly touched by Wystan's fussing, like a parent, over whether or not Chester had remembered where he had put his passport and could he find it again?).

The fact that Wystan had died alone in his room in Vienna was poignant. It was a city of huge significance to Spender, ever since 1935 – the year of Revolution, Muriel, and the 'Two Deaths' crisis with Tony. There were strange coincidences with the death of Peter Watson (even down to the suggestion of suicide, or foul play). Auden had died, alone, behind a locked hotel-room door, 'just hours before returning to Oxford, where in the preceding twelve months he had felt more miserable and rejected than at any time in his life'. The Spenders had feared that he might be murdered by one of the young men he casually consorted with, in the absence of Chester.

The first duty was to attend Auden's burial in Kirchstetten, Austria, where the poet had spent the most contented years of his life. Spender wrote a long and carefully composed epistolary elegy (and cast some flowers on the grave) for their comrade, Christopher, in California. Spender would compose out of this experience a fine sequence of poems, *Auden's Funeral*. It begins:

> One among friends who stood above your grave
> I cast a clod of earth from those heaped there
> Down on the great brass-handled coffin lid.

He imagined Wystan within ('Oh! the relief of getting between the sheets!'), 'Happy to be alone', at last. Spender did not get the poems drafted to his satisfaction until late 1976. The great difference between himself and Wystan, he noted in his journal, was that the other poet always knew when he began a poem that he would finish it. Stephen was less sure.

There were funerary addresses to be given over the next twelve months: at Christ Church Cathedral, at the Austrian Embassy, at Westminster Abbey (where Auden was installed in Poets' Corner), a celebratory reading at the Banqueting Hall (where Alec Guinness and Peggy Ashcroft read on behalf of the Apollo Society), and a ceremony at the American Academy. In his memorial address, at Oxford on 27 October, Spender juxtaposed two lapidary images: 'the tow-haired undergraduate poet with the abruptly turning head' and the 'famous poet with the face like a map of physical geography, crisscrossed and river-run and creased with lines'. Between these physiognomies was a lifetime's poetry.

Wystan, Spender observed, had good reason for being weary of the world.

He died a month ago now. How long it seems. In the course of these few weeks much has happened which makes me feel he may be glad to be rid of this world. One of his most persistent ideas was that one's physical disorders are reflections of the state of one's psyche, expressing itself in a psychosomatic language of spots and coughs and cancers, and unconsciously able to choose, I suppose, when to live and when to die. So I am hardly being superstitious in joking with him beyond the grave with the idea that his wise unconscious self chose a good day for dying, just before the most recent cacophonies of political jargon blaring destruction, which destroy the delicate reduced and human scale of language in which individuals are able to communicate in a civilized and affectionate way with one another.

It was the season of the three-day week, blackouts, and near insurrection in Britain, with the miners' strike. The oil shock had driven up inflation to double-digit levels. Everything was uncertain. Nineteen seventy-three was a dark winter.

In early 1974 there were changes at UCL. Frank Kermode went off to take up a position at Cambridge. His place was taken by Karl Miller. Miller, previously the editor of the *Listener*, was a congenial colleague for Spender. Both were veterans of the world of London journalism.

Saturnine by temperament, Miller was perennially puzzled by Spender's ineradicable good humour: 'Why do you always seem so serene and happy?' he asked. Spender could give no other reason than that he was. Miller confided to another of his colleagues, Stephen Fender (whose echoic name was the source of infinite confusion in the department), that, as an undergraduate studying under Leavis, he had been instructed to see Spender as the Great Satan. Now he was the friendly professor next door.

Love-Hate Relations was published in 1974 – infinitely revised from the Clark Lectures he had given in 1966. The book, originally called 'English Elegy, American Tragedy', had been under contract for ten years. Parts of it, he told the publisher, had been written twenty times or more. *Love-Hate Relations* came out, to Spender's relief and gratification, on Ascension Day, 23 May. By a nice irony there was a quarrel (love-hate indeed) with the American publisher, Random House, over 'territorial rights'. The book was warmly received. In the *Spectator* Denis Donoghue observed, correctly, that the book's many themes were held together 'however loosely by Mr Spender's sensibility'. Donald Davie, in the *New Statesman*, was considerably warmer:

I read this book with continued exclamations of gratified surprise and gratifi-cation . . . this is the product of the *poet* Stephen Spender. He has mastered the procedures of scholarship with a contemptuous ease and does not need to parade its credentials . . . sentence after sentence has the compacted substance of an aphorism.

In its review the *TLS* (now edited by John Gross) declared that '*Love-Hate Relations* is a good and stimulating book by a critic who has been writing excellent criticism for nearly 40 years.' This book, the paper concluded, spoke to the 1970s as *The Destructive Element* had spoken to the 1930s.

The voices of the thirties were, one by one, falling silent. In November, there was a seventieth birthday party for Cyril Connolly at the Savoy, given by the Glenconners. As Spender records, his friend went gallantly through the motions of being Connolly, dying beyond his means:

Cyril, who had interested himself tremendously in the menu, often visiting the chef to consult with him about it, was already ill. He ate very little of this feast. Neither – as he told me later – could he see the guests, who were as carefully chosen as the menu, for he was almost blind with cataracts. Cyril's exorbitant standards of hospitality outlived his own *gourmandise*.

The menu, over which he took immense pains, was his last publication.

Spender was asked, as Connolly faded in a Harley Street clinic, to write a memoir for the *TLS*. He rewrote it, at least six times, while his friend lingered on his deathbed ('I do not recommend dying,' Cyril wise-cracked). Spender's obituary stressed the gaiety Connolly brought into his friends' lives – sometimes without meaning to:

During the war, at a time when his love life was in disarray, he once said to me: 'I'll never believe in any woman again. I've been perfectly faithful to two women for five years, and now both of them have been unfaithful to me.' He certainly did not mean to be funny.

Spender composed a memorial poem, imagining Connolly (the most carnal of men) modulating from flesh into classic marble:

> This hews you to your statue:
> Flakes away the flesh
> Back to bone intellect:
> Lays bare the brow, pure semicircle,
> Star-striking dome –
> *sidera sublima vertice* –
> Proves finally the head was Roman.

In less poetic moments, he liked to imagine Connolly as a 'man in a diving bell': an impregnably armoured visitor to the rock pool of life. He gave the address at the memorial service – imagining a spectral Cyril introducing him: 'And now, Bishop Spender will say a few words.'

Spender went to Connolly's funeral, at Eastbourne on 2 December. He recorded the interment and breakfast in his journal:

We all stood round the flower-covered grave in the wet and cold, just a tarpaulin of some kind over the coffin. We drove with Alan and Jennifer Ross to a party at Deirdre Connolly's afterwards. Lots of champagne. Matthew Connolly [Cyril's infant son] was brought in and sat docilely on people's knees – the party acquired the normality of any champagne party.

Cyril would have approved of the 'lots of champagne'. Of the company, Stephen felt that Joan Leigh Fermor (one of Cyril's comrades from *Horizon* days) looked 'most stricken' and 'twenty years older'. Spender himself felt aged and oppressed. He wrote to Ted Hughes on 4 March:

My life has become quite intolerable with deadlines and obligations. Never being able to read a book I don't *have* to read is one of the worst things. I go on tour to America just to get a morning to myself, between engagements, in a motel or a DC10.

It was the second year in a row in which his most significant writing had been mortuary prose and verse. He wrote in his journal in November 1974:

Suddenly, it seems several of my generation have died, or been stricken with illness. The strangest thing is the feeling of being in a scratched vehicle. My friends' dying makes my legs ache . . . I find it more and more difficult to believe in personal immortality.

On 11 November Stephen dreamt of Wystan (miraculously immortal): 'He was very worried. He said because he had no pension. I said "But you must have at least $100,000". And he said, "Yes, well I must," and cheered up.' So, evidently, did the dreaming Stephen.

A diary entry for 19 November records an event which would later (long after he had forgotten it) return to haunt him:

A youth called Hugh David whom I met once after a reading at the National Book League rang me a few days ago and asked me to dinner [at the Post Office Tower]. He is very sensitive and refined. He looked nervous and said little. The meal was excellent. The tower restaurant turning round made me feel nervous.

Had he known he was dining with his future (unauthorized) biographer he might have felt doubly nervous as they gyrated around WC1. UCL finished its term in a whirl of parties, exams and departmental meetings which, unlike teaching, Spender found 'an utter waste of time'.

In mid-December the Spenders went to Mas de St Jerome and made a week's visit to Matthew, Maro and their two granddaughters in Tuscany.

Stephen craved light at this time of year. At this period, with both children grown up, he had a number of conversations with them about how he and Natasha had done as parents. Lizzie (currently between jobs and relationships and 'rather depressed') thought that perhaps her childhood, happy as it was, had lacked something in 'continuity'. Stephen resolved to spend more time with his children. He and Matthew began the process with a visit to Florence. Italy was a tonic. So much so that, as Spender reported, 'Natasha is hooked on the idea of us buying a house here [at San Sano] – which excites me too.' But he added, as reality broke in, 'we never will'.

In late December the Spenders left for a trip to Israel, with Noël and Gabriele Annan, Aline and Isaiah Berlin, and Stuart Hampshire. They were briefed before departure by the Israeli ambassador, who bluntly informed them that the Arabs wanted the total destruction of his country. It was hoped the distinguished visitors might do something to reverse the tide of anti-Zionist obloquy emanating from the UN.

The Middle East was still recovering from the Yom Kippur War, and Spender would write up his impressions for the *NYRB* (he had packed *The Prelude* – 'that spasmodically beautiful poem' – as his vacation reading). The English dignitaries had a memorable meeting with Teddy Kollek, the mayor of Jerusalem, who took them on a whirlwind tour of his city, enthusiastically showing off its conservation programmes. A succession of archbishops, local politicians and university professors were less memorable. On Christmas morning Stephen and Aline Berlin visited Herodium, the Fortress of Herod, near Bethlehem. They went on to the Dead Sea and Stephen vainly tried to picture the sins for which Sodom might have been destroyed (and New York perversely preserved).

Israel, Spender wryly thought, was more democratic than England. At least it did not have Harold Wilson to put up with. But the level of depression in the country was itself depressingly high. As the wife of the President, Ephraim Katzir, told them: 'the whole world seems to have turned against us'. A visit on 3 January 1975 to the Yad Vashem Holocaust Memorial Museum inspired solemn, but ultimately sceptical thoughts: 'are the Israelis right to insist so much on the horror of the Holocaust? There is, one may think, too much of the Wailing Wall about Israel.' Was not his own stress, in *Learning Laughter*, on the newborn vitality of the country healthier? The Spenders flew back on 7 January, in the company of many rabbis, for the start of the academic year at UCL two days later.

★

Spender was, after his friend's death, a main custodian of the reputation of Auden. Among many other events, he appeared in a BBC programme about Wystan at Oxford. He went with the cameras to the famous rooms in Peck Quad which 'looked much smaller than I had remembered – and shabbier'. Auden, peremptory to the end, had instructed his friends to destroy all his letters and that there should be no biography. He left his literary property to Chester Kallman, who drank himself to death, a year after his partner, surrounded (as Stephen grimly recorded) 'by alley cats and Greek boys'. He had liked Chester at his best, when he was warm, witty and genuinely talented. At his worst, he was a 'slob', ineffably 'camp' and incorrigibly self-indulgent. Stephen could never forget the tears running down Wystan's face, in Venice twenty years before, as he watched Chester chase off after some passing sailors. On reflection, Spender and Wystan's executor, the American scholar Edward Mendelson, decided that a memorial volume was essential to protect the poet from post-mortem vandalism.

Mendelson, a rising young professor, moved from Yale to Columbia in 1976. He had devoted himself to Auden scholarship and would, over the years, cultivate a warm friendship with Auden's closest friends. He recalls Spender at Yale, at parties to which 'the old Yalies didn't bother to turn up. Stephen would be standing among a group of undergraduates, fifty years his junior, completely relaxed and pleasantly drunk. I've never known anyone who showed less sense of place, anywhere.' In conversation with Auden, Mendelson observed, Spender was deferential, but any disagreement would be ended with Auden's conclusive: 'You, Stephen, will have the last word.' That last word, it seemed, would be a biography.

On his deathbed, T. S. Eliot had also requested of his young wife Valerie that there be no biography. Spender was, in January 1975, correcting the proofs of his monograph about Eliot for Frank Kermode's 'Modern Masters' series (published by Fontana). Spender tactfully introduced as much biography as he thought proper into his commentary (Mrs Eliot asked him to introduce less – particularly on the vexed issue of the poet's sexuality and first marriage). The book was vastly over-long for the series format (30,000 words were asked for, 70,000 were supplied). But it proved to be a bestseller. For many years it filled the gap left where the critical biography should have been.

At the end of January 1975, Spender had lunch with Harry Fainlight, one of the strange subplots to his London literary life. Fainlight was a 'gay, weird, Jewish, rather wonderful poet', prone through life to schizophrenia. As Natasha recalls, 'Stephen always had a particular sympathy for gifted people who were on the edge', and none was nearer the brink than Harry. Spender published some of his poems in *Encounter* in the 1950s and gave him the odd ('lifesaving') review to write. He was a character witness for the frequent occasions that Harry fell foul of the law. Fainlight made a name for himself at the June 1965 monster read-in at the Albert Hall, alongside the Beat heroes Ginsberg and Corso. In 1965, Fainlight published his major collection of verse, *Sussicran* ('Narcissus' backwards). It is dominated by obsessive poems about his father and solitary, masturbatory sex. He lived, as he gloomily punned, in 'the City of Dreadful Fainlight'.

When, as he did on 29 January 1975, Spender took Fainlight to lunch it made him think about what, after all, it was to be a poet. Was it to be a pinstriped, ultra-respectable professional man like Eliot or a madman like Harry? Spender concluded that:

On the whole, I hate the squalor of poets at poetry readings. I prefer the poets who are reticent, who wear the uniform of a kind of life which has some non-poetic status to those who will go back to their cellars and sup off their raw and bleeding metaphors. (But reading this I feel: 'How philistine!')

In the character of respectably suited man of letters Spender (somewhat reluctantly) accepted the presidency of the English Branch of PEN in February (with the proviso that it should be only a one-year stint) and, two years later in 1977 and more enthusiastically, the award of Companion of the Royal Society of Literature.

In between lectures and working stints in America, Spender and Mendelson discussed the Auden project. They were resolved to resist the publishers' and the public's appetite for 'scandal, gossip, etc.' While still in New York, on 18 April, Spender 'decided to resign at once from UCL'. This despite the fact that he had only one year to go before mandatory retirement and his pension. One reason for the peremptory decision was that the Auden biography would require two years of full-time effort. Giving up his chair meant hard work ahead. As he told Mike Josselson: 'I shall go on with writing – lecturing in America, etc. Perhaps live more in France. Economize. Everything seems to depend on my not getting quite gaga.'

He returned to London on 20 April, for what would now be his last term's work at UCL. He wrote his letter of resignation three days later. Annan, friendly and suave as ever, replied (after ascertaining that his friend did not want to be 'wooed' into staying) that he felt he was 'absolutely right in taking this step'. He thanked him for his 'valuable stay at the college'. Spender slipped out of Foster Court, at the end of the academic year, almost without anyone noticing (he took his Hockney, leaving a number of valuable pictures on the walls of his office in the safekeeping of the department for his successor, the novelist Dan Jacobson). He was awarded a modest golden handshake, in lieu of a pension. He invested it, with the proceeds from the sale of his Bomberg painting *The Fort*, in a flat for Lizzie, now at drama school.

He intended to be close to his children this summer. In early summer, he and Matthew had the first of their 'honeymoon' vacations together, in Venice. The initiative came from Maro, who felt that Stephen 'must get to know his son before he dies'. These vacations (there would be four or five of them over the next decade) were always constructed around a project – usually something art-historical. For Matthew, the 1975 Venice trip was a solution to what he ironically called 'my tackle your parent complex'. They saw sights and wandered around and gener-ally 'let off steam'. They studiously kept their conversation at the level of comradely intimacy. On one occasion, Matthew recalls, his father made as if to confess something but they both held back. It would be unfair to their wives, they felt, to talk too frankly. At Maussane in July Stephen and Natasha were joined by the Bayleys ('ideal guests . . . Iris was reading Plato. To them, this place is an enchantment and they fill it with their love').

The Wollheims visited Mas de St Jerome, as did Philippe de Rothschild and the Annans. There was good talk of the kind Spender relished and the occasional flash of comedy. The Provost of University College, as Spender told Keith Walker, came down one baking day in late August, to alarm the company by wearing only a '*cache sexe*' which graphically illustrated the 'difference between naked and stark naked'. Noël was, he decided, 'a character in an unwritten novel by E. M. Forster'. That summer Spender wrote, and sent to Alan Ross for publi-cation in the *London Magazine*, his ambitious poem 'To Become a Dumb Thing' with its yearning for the 'life of things'. But, the poet decides, he 'cannot throw aside Christian's burden / When he forsook wife and children'. He was committed to a life of work. Nor, on reflec-tion, did he regret it.

The Spenders returned to England on 30 August (ensuring themselves a tiring trip; it was the day when the whole French nation came
back from the summer holiday). A week later Spender flew to New
England, where, as in earlier years, he was contracted to teach at Storrs.
He described his daily routine to Keith Walker. He was teaching a
seminar on Auden, which was useful. And he was working on his 'Thirties
Book' (*The Thirties and After*, as it would be). But:

I am very dull here but I must say I never wake up in the morning without
thinking 'I don't have anything to do today except my own work', and that
really makes up for the fact of being exiled in Siberia (someone rang me from
New York today and told me Brodsky had been through and on hearing I was
here said 'poor Stephen in Storrs Connecticut' like one exile talking about
another). I am growing some moss I picked up off the bark of a tree in a wood
and am going to tame a mouse.

This mouseman of Storrs did not have a TV, or HiFi, 'because I think
they would be distracting. I am determined to be as miserable as
possible. Everyone here is very plain in a dogged agricultural kind of
way.' He did not miss UCL. New York, as always, lifted his spirits.
Driving back from the city with David Plante, the two friends became
so engrossed in discussing modernism that Stephen (at the wheel) went
100 miles past the Storrs turn-off. They might have forayed on to
Canada had not the younger man observed how beautiful the mountains around them were. 'Yes,' agreed Stephen, 'but we're not supposed
to be in the mountains.'

Spender was in New York, with Matthew and Maro, in mid-November
1975, before returning to the UK for Christmas. In late December he
and Natasha escaped from London's gloom for three weeks in Spain
with their friends the architect Jaime Palarde and his much-married wife
Janetta (one of 'Cyril's girls'). The Hispanist Gerald Brennan was a neighbour. Franco had died in December 1975: Stephen had never visited
(would never visit) the country while the Fascist dictator ruled. This
return to Spain, and the memories of forty years ago that it evoked, was
'rather marvellous', Natasha recalls. The Spenders left Marbella's orange
groves for London on 12 January 1976, to begin the first year of Stephen's
official 'retirement'. Whatever his reasons for leaving UCL, a sudden
access of personal wealth was not one of them. Nor was it his intention, in his remaining years, to cultivate his garden. He told one of the

students in the department, Theresa Wells ('with a sweet smile'): 'Natasha would like us to be a couple of little ducks bobbing on a Dutch canal. I don't think I could be a little duck.' He had, Reynolds Price joked, a 'restless gene' – as did all the Spenders.

Having given up his permanent teaching job (with its paid vacations and 'benefits'), Spender threw himself into a round of temporary teaching positions in American universities. The first of them was, again, at the institution where he had always felt easy, the University of Connecticut. While alone at Storrs (Natasha, now teaching psychology at the Royal College of Art, in London, was not with him), he had the news that their friend, Pauline de Rothschild, had died after 'a miserable winter following an operation for breast cancer'. Stephen had seen her, terminally ill, that winter, in Boston. He visited a distraught and bereaved Philippe in New York, where his friend told him, despairingly, 'I can see my way through till the Vendange this year but after October there's nothing but the abyss.' Increasingly Stephen saw himself as 'a survivor'. It was not easy to survive one's friends. He resolved to be at Mouton in October when the wine was pressed and Philippe faced his abyss.

In March 1976 Spender and Mendelson finally decided against doing a life of Auden (Spender substituted for his publisher, Random House, his autobiographical conspectus, *The Thirties and After*). They had come to the conclusion that Wystan's legacy would be better served by a monumental gathering, editing and scholarly reissue of his collected poetry and prose (a task which Mendelson scrupulously fulfilled over the following decades). According to Mendelson, 'we both felt we had different ways of proceeding'. There were, moreover, living parties who might be hurt by a frank biography. And anyway, 'we only did about two days work on the project'.

Having served his term in Connecticut, Spender travelled on for the ensuing summer semester to the University of Florida at Gainesville – one of the (increasingly few) American colleges where he had not hitherto hung his professorial shingle. His first impressions of the sunshine state were not cheerful. The university gave him an apartment nine storeys up a tower block, surrounded by 'yellowish jungly forest'. He wrote in mock despair to Keith Walker, from Gulag Gainesville, that 'being here is like being sent to a tropical Siberia, where you can't go into the countryside for all the snakes, nor swim in a lake for all the alligators, and where there are no exciting dissidents among your fellow exiles'.

Gainesville, he decided, was 'a non-place'. At least its nullity would give him peace to concentrate on his major creative effort over the next few years, a complete recasting of *Trial of a Judge* (renamed *The Corporal*). He had suddenly seen how the play (which had been with him now forty years) might be revised. 'Before I die,' he told Cuthbert Worsley, 'I would like to see an actable version of *Trial of a Judge*.' He saw how it might be done by folding into the characterization of the judge's son, Kolya, the character of his (Stephen's) dissolute 'boy' of 1932 – Georgi (in the 1938 version the judge is childless). In 1938, for a judge to have a male prostitute, drug-addict offspring would have seemed grotesque. But, in the mid-1970s, 'the events of the past years make such a situation quite feasible, almost a *sine qua non* of child-parent relations'. Rewriting and recasting the play would 'obsess' him (as he told many of his friends) for three and a half years. When finished, he regarded it as 'certainly my greatest effort'.

Despite expectation, Gainesville turned out to be a rewarding and rejuvenating experience. It was a good year to be in America. The bicentennial in June generated a communal cheer which soothed the aching wounds of Vietnam. The university, he discovered, had good taste in poetry instructors. Spender's predecessors included Richard Eberhart and Robert Dana. Spender admired and got on well with both of them (his only cavil was Dick Eberhart's 'obsessive' love of barbecued catfish, 'the only really nasty fish in Florida' as Spender thought).

The students Spender took over were not, he found, well read. The only poets they seemed to know were Bob Dylan and Rod McKuen. By the time he got into his teaching stride there were, he wryly estimated, 'about 30 drop outs and 6 really interested students'. But these half-dozen brands plucked from the fire (his 'Floridians', as he called them) made for what, in retrospect, Spender would see as a 'miraculous semester'. His pedagogic method was to have open, freewheeling discussion, in which students dissected each other's efforts, followed by intensely close tutorial commentary. With the outstanding student in his class, Anthony Lombardy, Spender would continue his tutorial discussions (by letter) for years after.

Spender returned from Gainesville to London in June for a coronation of sorts, with the National Portrait Gallery's exhibition of 'Young Writers of the Thirties'. It ran until November. Spender had been consulted on the show as early as the previous November, and had already expressed concern that the writers mainly to be featured were himself, Auden, Isherwood and Day-Lewis. It was, as Bernard Crick sourly described it in the *Listener*, 'the MacSpaunday Family Album'. Spender, anticipating this response, had also strongly urged (in vain) that due attention be given to John Cornford, Julian Bell, Ralph Fox, Christopher Caudwell – who were all killed in Spain. Even Roy Campbell, his old enemy, might have expected to get a look in. Even Connolly. The biggest omission was Orwell. Crick (Orwell's authorized biographer) assumed (wrongly) that the writer had been 'so rude to Spender and those he chose to call the "Nancy Boys of Literature" that perhaps they still don't want to include him'.

The exhibition drew largely on the collection of Humphrey Spender, Stephen's photographer brother. Humphrey, too, was disappointed. In *Gay News* (15 July) he complained 'that no specific mention has been made of openly gay authors'. Some of his photographs had been suppressed 'as not quite suitable'. The organizers (backed by Isherwood) had been 'insistent that homosexuality should not be mentioned'. A representative of the NPG defended the gallery: 'It was just thought to be heavy handed to go on about homosexuality and politics.'

Nineteen seventy-six marks a new phase in Spender's long and varied life. Technically it was his first year of retirement, although – as he had told Mike Josselson – it was his fate to keep his shoulder to the wheel until he was 'ga ga'. He could no more retire than Sisyphus. Nor, as it transpired, had he tired of life (as he had threatened to do, two years earlier, in the shadow of Auden's and Connolly's deaths). Gainesville, as he told Lombardy, represented 'a watershed of relationships which have brought me so much happiness'. It had helped bring him back.

Principal among these 'watershed' relationships was one with a young zoologist, Bryan Obst, who had audited Spender's summer 1976 poetry class at Gainesville. After his first seminar, Spender drove Obst home. He was mystified by the student's silence and his habit of fixing his eyes on the sky ('was he evangelical?' Spender wondered). He later realized it was the reflex of the trained ornithologist. Obst loved living things: if Spender ran over an armadillo (hard not to do in Florida), Bryan would be cast down for days.

The young man came from a German–Milwaukee blue-collar background (his father was, he told Stephen, as violently anti-Semitic as he was anti-Polish). On graduating in 1976, Obst – an earnest advocate of ecology – went into school-teaching in Dixie County, a few miles from the university, along the Sewanee River. Here he lived, in hippy simplicity, in a trailer with his dog Spot, 'who is very beautiful', writing in his spare time learned treatises on the tern and other sea birds.

Friends of Spender, such as Reynolds Price and Don Bachardy, recall finding Bryan simple and innocent ('wholemeal' is the word Price uses). Natasha found him interesting on the subject of ethology (in which they both had a professional interest). 'There was something self-sufficient about him,' she observed, 'that reminded me of Stephen's older brother Michael.' Lizzie found him wholly uninteresting. Obst himself was haunted by the sense that he was, in the eyes of Stephen's friends and family, 'unattractive and dim'. Spender entrusted some of Obst's letters to the care of Price. They reveal him to have been a young idealist of uncomplicated views and a natural 'loner' (as Stephen liked to call him), never happier than when he was in some frozen or jungle wilderness, looking at birds.

Spender wrote to Reynolds describing his complex affection for Obst:

I feel I ought not to love Bryan and yet his extraordinary gentleness, perceptiveness, and intelligence really made it impossible not to. If he had not had these qualities it would have been an 'affair'. But what it is really is a continuous hymn of gratitude that someone could have come to me in the way he did and that while changing and becoming independent and really doing marvellously in his world and life quite separate of mine, he is yet conscious of what we had and have in a way that remains true to my continuous consciousness of him.

He and Obst remained in touch by letter and occasional meetings in America until the younger man's death in 1991.

January 1977 was, as Spender told Price, 'a bit sad'. Natasha's eighty-six-year-old mother, who had often accompanied them on summer holidays to France, was dying of terminal cancer. Natasha, partly to spare her husband, took her mother to Italy for a last holiday with the great-grandchildren (Matthew's daughters). Stephen met up with them briefly there. The old lady died in April.

The summer opened with a 'blur' of visits to friends in Britain and France. By July Spender was at Mas de St Jerome, 'working against time to finish the play'. The play would rework many of Spender's early 1930s German experiences (it was, he told Ted Hughes, 'really about Hitler' – who, he confidently believed, was in Hell). Memories of Berlin were sharpened when the *New York Times* sent him there in early September to report on an exhibition of Weimar *Kunst*. It would mean writing 3,500 words in four days (and dictating them down a telephone to New York). An ordeal: but he was the best person to do it. Nineteen seventy-seven ended, as it had begun, with a 'big swing'. As retiring President of the English branch of PEN, Spender was sent on a tour of the Far East via Venice (where he met Brodsky – also on a great swing). Natasha came with him. They duly swung through Korea and Japan, on business, and Iran. For Stephen the end of the tour was a chance to reflect. In Iran, conducted by their and Lizzie's friend Cyrus Ghani (one of the Shah's lawyers), they undertook their most leisurely and pleasurable sight-seeing for years. Shiraz, Isfahan and Persepolis were 'a revelation'.

Spender was in Houston, Texas, in early March 1978 at a meeting of Poetry Consultants to the Library of Congress. His successor in Washington, James Dickey, was as usual 'throwing his weight about like Burt Reynolds', as Stephen told the other Reynolds (Price). Spender travelled on from Texas for another teaching stint at Storrs, now his normal academic base in the US. By May, he was in New York. Natasha would have joined him were they not, just at the moment, involved in expensive and extensive alterations to Loudoun Road (which they were still renting from the Eyre Estate). She remained in England to super-intend the work while Stephen lectured abroad to pay for it. The Spenders did manage, however, to get away for three weeks in June to Corfu, where they stayed with the Bayleys at the Glenconners' house at Rovinia, a 'beautiful place' by a little bay with a cave 'shaped like a tip-tilted cathedral window'. Spender painted (Bomberg-like land and seascapes) and began serious work on his 'homage' poem to Henry Moore, which would be published on the sculptor's eightieth birthday, two years later. After Corfu, the Spenders spent a month at Mas de St Jerome before returning to England in early August. Spender was still, as he told Reynolds Price, 'struggling (against many odds) to finish my play and having an awful time with it'.

His major literary effort in 1978 was, however, the publication of the semi-autobiographical, semi-documentary *The Thirties and After*. In his introduction the author records his original intention to produce 'a collection of essays'. But autobiography broke in. The best history of his time that he could write was a history of himself, built around his personal journals. This conviction is stated, most clearly, in the book's postscript:

I myself am, it is only too clear, an autobiographer. Autobiography provides the line of continuity in my work. I am not someone who can shed or disclaim his past. This is not merely an admission. It is something I have here tried to emphasize in presenting these records as a case history of the Thirties and after. I see pretty clearly that in this particular case – my own – of the self-discoverer, the ideological has been a trap into which I have too often fallen, and for which I have only saved myself by going back to my personal as distinct from my public life.

He now, at the age of sixty-nine, knew what he was: a self-explorer, a Columbus of himself.

Spender had engaged to teach a semester at Vanderbilt University in Tennessee in spring 1979. The stipend was a healthy $15,000. Early January found him in an unexpectedly snowbound Nashville. He was alone (Natasha had her own teaching obligations in London), tired, and he was beginning to dislike the classroom. As he told Anthony Lombardy:

the first few days of these teaching things are very trying. I get in a mood in which I feel very lonely (I have been quite alone sitting in a room in a horrible Holiday Inn for five days) but at the same time dread meeting the students, the faculty, the people at parties to meet me etc. I think this is definitely the last time I do this kind of thing.

He was momentarily amused by a mass redistribution of Gideon Bibles (after a perfunctory public blessing) in the Inn (inaptly named, Spender thought; he had never felt less the holidaymaker). This, he thought, was 'the kind of scene which gives one a sense of the foreignness of America'. At least he did not have to fear the oppression of faculty hospitality. He was left alone for three weeks in Nashville before anyone so much as invited him for a drink.

During his empty days in January he wrote letters, made long-distance telephone calls, read Ibsen (cover to cover), and worked on a review of David Jones's poetry. On 14 January he had a long dream about recently dead Cecil Day-Lewis, whose symbolism needed no psychoanalyst to decode:

In my dream I very much wanted to play Cecil a recording of a pianist (Clifford Curzon?) playing the 'Eroica' variations. I could anticipate the pleasure this would give him. But I could not find the record, though I had just been playing it before I saw him. Also there was no plug at the end of the wire connecting the gramophone with the wall plug. It was just a frayed end.

At Vanderbilt Spender was engaged to teach two courses: one on writing poetry, the other (a graduate class) on literature of the 1930s. His students were good, which bucked him up, as did a move from the Holiday Inn to a more congenial apartment. He eventually met and made friends with two couples. One was Robert Hunter and his wife, the other his former antagonist, the 'Movement' poet Donald Davie (author of 'Remembering the Thirties'), and his wife. By February, things were looking cheerful again.

Vanderbilt was harder work than many other places he had taught. He was grateful, in early February, for a short break in Philadelphia with the Irish-American collector and connoisseur of nineteenth-century French art, Henry McIlhenny. 'It was delightful,' Spender sighed in his diary, to be in a house 'with a really comfortable bed, servants, excellent food and Henry's exhilarating conversation and gossip.' And, he could have added, the company of an old friend, with congenial tastes in art, whom he had been visiting, on and off, in Ireland and the US, for twenty years. Spender was in Philadelphia not merely for the soft bed and the friendship but to give a reading. One of the poems he selected was 'The Pylons'. A feminist asked him, in the question session, why he hadn't written about 'nude giant *men* that have no secret'. It was a new world.

A few days later, on 7 February, Spender visited his old friend from Cincinnati, Allen Tate. It was the last time he would see him. Tate was on his death bed in hospital in Nashville. Spender was distressed both by the spectacle of his friend's terminal weakness and by his own weakness for making an excuse and leaving after only fifteen minutes. Two days later, in Gainesville, he learned of Tate's death. Anthony Lombardy phoned him with the news. Spender said 'he was glad, as [Allen] had absolutely nothing to live for'. He was meanwhile camping out in Gainesville in Obst's trailer, alongside the Sewanee River ('swampy', Spender thought). Bryan admired Stephen's new smile (Lizzie had persuaded him to have some dental work done). Stephen admired Bryan's new beard: 'with his pale green-grey shining eyes and dark brown hair, he looks more than ever like a portrait of a young Frenchman by Manet'. They managed a short trip to New Orleans.

Spender interrupted his time in America with a flying trip back to

London, via New York, for his seventieth birthday on 28 February. It was a major family event. The Matthew Spenders came from Italy. Natasha had organized a celebration at the Royal College of Art. Maro designed the birthday card; Lizzie baked the birthday cake. There were a hundred guests and Stephen, as guest of honour, was saluted with a Gabrieli fanfare sounded by four heralds from the Royal College of Music when he cut the cake. Philippe de Rothschild provided 100 bottles of Mouton Cadet claret. Over dinner, Stephen sat alongside Isaiah Berlin and his wife, Aline. There was another party the next day to finish up the excellent wine. Kingsley Amis was there, to confirm its excellence. William Empson, at whom Stephen had once thrown a glassful of wine, had his photograph taken with the guest of honour, now a friend again.

Four days later Spender was back in New York for ten days. His friends the art dealer Earl McGrath and his wife Camilla gave a second birthday party for him, in their mid-Manhattan apartment. Isherwood was there (and offended to be asked by the rock singer Peter Wolf, 'What part of England do you come from?' 'Santa Monica,' replied Isherwood coolly). Also present were the poet John Ashbery and the artist Larry Rivers (a friend from the 1950s). 'What's it like to be seventy?' Earl, who was a sprightly forty-eight, asked the guest of honour. 'It's exactly the same,' replied Spender. 'Every morning when I wake up I feel nineteen. Then I move this sad old body and I feel ninety.' He imagined his diary – this month packed with engagements every day – and over the page every day next month marked: 'dead, dead, dead'. Everyone laughed – not at what he was saying but the deliciously comic way he said it.

On 13 March Spender confirmed his status as a 'near celebrity' (a title bestowed, to its recipient's amusement, by an American immigration official) with an appearance on the Dick Cavett talk show. In New York he saw Jason Epstein, now chief editor at Random House, who proposed that 'we should renegotiate all my contracts so as to give me advances to free me from having to do things like Nashville'.

Things like Nashville could not, however, be put off this year. By 15 March Stephen was back teaching his seminars at Vanderbilt by day and working on *The Corporal* by night. On 1 April, when her Easter break started, Natasha flew over to join him. 'God knows what she'll do in Nashville,' Stephen wondered. The first thing she did, predictably, was to 'transform the apartment'. Spender had by now made a circle of friends on campus and the two of them enjoyed a social time, interrupted by the inevitable reading and lecturing trip through Indiana ('the most awful state in the Union') and Kentucky. They celebrated Natasha's sixtieth birthday in New Orleans.

Having wrapped up his teaching duties at Vanderbilt, Spender was back in England in late May. On 3 June he visited the eighty-year-old Henry Moore, who, he thought, 'has become an institution and thrives on it'. Spender now had ready for publication the poem, 'Sculptor and Statues: Homage to Henry Moore', on which he had been working for two years. It was designed to accompany a work on the sculptor's 'Stonehenge Series'. The poem's form is mimetic, following in its abrupt syntax the fall of chisel on stone:

> Hews
> Flakes from stone. Releases
> Imprisoned form
> His eyes presaged there. Quintessential
> Stoniness of Stone.
> Surfaces of light, radiant
> Altars of the sun, cut by the hand
> Of which the chisel is his pen
> In vibrant feathering strokes. These poems
> Of stone.

At the beginning of July Spender sent *The Corporal* to his agent, Ed Victor. He was beginning to have serious misgivings about the play. The National (currently in crisis, crippled by strikes) couldn't do it. Verse plays were out of fashion in the mid-1970s. Everyone who read it (including Harold Pinter, Joan Littlewood and Peggy Ashcroft) admired *The Corporal*, but producers were wary. The cultural situation was 'awful'. The Spenders spent the main part of July, as usual, in Mas de St Jerome with the Bayleys as house guests.

The Spenders returned to England in August. Towards the end of the month they motored up to visit their musician friend Gian Carlo Menotti at his magnificent Robert Adam house, in East Lothian. On the way they went past Skelgill. Natasha resourcefully (by asking 'a little old lady by the side of the road') located the farm, opposite 'Catbells', where Stephen had spent his memorable 'Wordsworthian' holiday, aged eight, in 1917. He had entirely forgotten spending another holiday there, in 1936, with Isaiah Berlin. His memory was not so much failing as becoming oddly patchy (fragmenting into 'spots of time', as Wordsworth would have said). His childhood recollections were intense enough to inspire the late poem, 'Worldsworth'.

In late September Spender had a joyous 'honeymoon' visit with Matthew to Venice. The mood was one of laddish camaraderie, in which the father was quite happy to play the clown:

I feel we are a comic duo, oversize the two of us. I with crumpled trousers, my legs like an elephant's, my face pushing fleshily through crevasses of red skin, my hair a windswept mass of white cotton and fluffed up round the sides like a mad ecclesiastic.

They saw 'quite a lot of old ladies' on this trip (i.e. Olga Rudge, Charlotte Bonham-Carter, Freya Stark) before driving back to Matthew's house and younger Spender womenfolk (Maro, Saskia, Cosima) in Tuscany. In his diary, Spender recalled Rudge ('almost Mrs Ezra Pound') rejoicing, a couple of years earlier, when she heard of Robert Lowell's death: 'the best thing that could have happened to him, after what he wrote about Ezra' (namely that the other poet had broadcast for the Fascists, which he had). Writing to Cuthbert Worsley, on 4 August, Stephen said that this week with Matthew in Venice 'was, I think, about the happiest in my life'.

Later in the month, a refreshed Spender made yet another short trip to New York (he was, at the time, doing a lot of work for the *Times*). From there he travelled on for an arduous series of teaching engagements at various campuses, beginning with a month in Virginia where his class comprised 'eleven poetesses'. He made up the apostolic twelve. He was, meanwhile, beginning to put down notes and ideas for his series of elegiac lyrics on 'Auden's funeral'. He suddenly realized, he wrote on 9 October, that like Yeats, whom he had been teaching, 'I am going to have a Final Phase.'

For some months, Spender had known that he would have a major medical examination and some treatment at the end of the year (for skin cancer – they were paying, as Humphrey ruefully complained, for all that 1930s German sun). 'I feel no dread,' he wrote in his journal on 10 October. He was, at the same period, increasingly convinced that 'I ought to write off my play.' If he did so, it would be 'three years in which I could have done a great deal else'.

At the beginning of December (in a prudent but not pessimistic spirit) he embarked on putting his literary remains in order. He wrote to tell Reynolds Price on 10 December that he had spent the last three days 'trying to tidy and file away all my papers'. It was an Augean task. He was meanwhile having a battery of 'medical checks on kidneys, bladder, etc.'. He was, he had been informed, 'all right. The specialist advised very strongly against my having an operation for a slight prostate condition.' So, he told Reynolds, 'we face 1980 undaunted'.

1980s: Retired, But Not Resigned

The 1980s began for Stephen Spender (as would the next decade) with a serious accident. He was in his seventies and now vulnerable to physical injury and ill health. But his life – after the necessary periods of recuperation – remained full, busy and productive. Teaching (at a variety of American institutions), lecturing (everywhere), and journalism (continuous) brought in income and kept his name known. His new agent, Ed Victor, helped consolidate his literary output. The result was a series of major books (collected poetry, journals, drama, and his first published novel since The Backward Son*). With Natasha's retirement from the Royal College of Art in 1984, the Spenders could spend more time in France. Stephen's life remained, as it had been from the 1950s, bi-continental; America and Britain were, culturally, home territory. He travelled farther afield, to China, with his artist friend David Hockney (it resulted in another book). Over the 1980s Stephen Spender's public fame grew, culminating in the award of a knighthood. As the decade advanced he was, however, exercised to protect his private life from a series of unwelcome biographical intrusions. The balance between public and private faces (as Auden called them) had never been more difficult. The Spenders' life, at Loudoun Road, at Mas de St Jerome, or in Manhattan, was comfortable and civilized. The Thatcher–Reagan years were less so, politically. Spender's liberalism was more challenged than at any period since the 1930s. Friendship remained a main source of pleasure in his life: and his friends, as ever, encompassed a remarkable range – from politicians, artists, men of letters, journalists, dons, to the students whom he befriended and (when they were talented) helped advance. Inevitably, given his time of life, there were personal losses: Isherwood, Henry Moore and Muriel Buttinger. As always, he demonstrated an ability to make rewarding new friendships (notably with Ted Hughes and Peter Ackroyd). His work for writers' causes and AIDS relief absorbed much of his time.*

The holiday interval from old to New Year, 1979–80, was passed, as in previous years, at Mouton. With the hostess, Pauline, gone, the Rothschild estate was 'a shadow of what it used to be twenty years ago', Spender ruefully thought. The inescapable TV news projected 'hideous' images of 'The Ayatollah in Iran, Russian tanks in Afghanistan', President Carter, the 'pale, grinning, innocuous boy' – so-called 'leader of the free world'. Spender consoled himself with the 'very good wines' (including a Mouton 1879) and Michael Holroyd's biography of Lytton Strachey. The vintages and literature of the past were more to his taste, just at the moment.

On 6 January the Spenders returned to London, and disaster. On the evening of the 14th an unexpected guest arrived at Loudoun Road. Spender went out to get some smoked salmon for supper. It was raining, dark, and the Finchley Road was busy with rush-hour traffic. Hurrying for a 13 bus on the other side of the road, Spender skidded off the pavement. He fell heavily and, 'incredibly', broke both quadricept tendons ('a cracking-whip-like sensation', his poet's mind coolly observed). It was an intimation of Henry James's 'distinguished thing', mortality. His 'whole life's achievement' flashed across his mind as he lay on the wet flags: 'a dozen jewels, perhaps, in a refuse dump of failures'.

He was carried into the shelter of Finchley Road tube station while helpful bystanders called for the ambulance which took him off to the Royal Free Hospital. Natasha arrived soon after. Over the next three months the hospital would become her second home. Initially the doctors assumed (in spite of the patient's insistent protests) that only one leg was injured. It was solidly encased in plaster while the tendon repaired itself. A week later the other leg was diagnosed as also broken. For eleven weeks, Spender was immobile and bedridden. At one point, to add to his woes, his eyesight failed and he contracted pneumonia. It was some comfort that after ten days he was moved to a private room. None the less, he could not but be gloomy. He hated illness. 'We worried about his morale,' Natasha Spender recalls. He was further demoralized and reduced to tears by news of the deaths of Michael Astor and Renée

Hampshire from cancer, while he was lying in hospital. Exactly above in the hospital lay another friend, Graham Sutherland, who was terminally ill. As Stephen lay, in enforced stillness, he summed up his life's achievement with the usual unwarranted self-deprecation: 'Everything I had done – or nearly everything – seemed a failure, not that of a person who does not use his talents, but worse, does not use them enough even to discover how much talent he has.'

Friends conspired to lift his spirits out of this trough. There was a constant 'picnics in the dorm' atmosphere. Peggy Ashcroft (who informed him, from personal experience, that the 'physio' would be 'absolutely excruciating', adding cheerfully, 'but it gets better') was 'wonderful'. So too was Isaiah Berlin ('he *loved* being in nursing homes'). Francis Bacon, Stuart Hampshire, Rosamond Lehmann, Juliette Huxley (who lived opposite), Sonia Orwell, laden with flowers and good stories, and John Golding were other morale-raising visitors. Sonia withheld the fact that she herself faced, in a few days, an operation for cancer. Brodsky flew in from America confirming his filial piety that 'Spender is my family.' Lizzie and Natasha, who was also teaching full-time, cooked for the patient. Philippe de Rothschild, from his apartment at the Albany, had his chef prepare delicacies. Annie Fleming sent caviare. Matthew came for a week from Tuscany and camped alongside his father's bedside. If he ever doubted he was loved, it was confirmed over these months.

Company made the affliction bearable. As Spender told Reynolds Price, two months into his treatment:

I haven't had pain, only a lot of discomforts most of which were due to the heavy plasters and all the horrors of not being able to get out of bed. There's also something very upsetting about losing the use of your legs. You begin to think of walking as miraculous like flying.

Price himself would, after undergoing treatment for cancer of the spine, find himself wheelchair-bound for life, four years later.

Spender had been contracted to teach at the University of Kentucky, at Louisville, for a month's teaching engagement from 28 March. His physicians thought that it would be a tonic – they 'absolutely pushed' Natasha on the matter. He would travel in a wheelchair (Natasha pushed). It was made easier by the fact that 1980 was America's 'year of the disabled' (the 'grinning boy', Jimmy Carter, had done at least one good thing). There were ramps, elevators, friendly WCs, and handholds everywhere.

In the last week of April the Spenders visited their friend, Henry McIlhenny, in Philadelphia. As (bad) luck would have it, he too was disabled, having broken his leg in a fall. He insisted that they stay at his house in Rittenhouse Square, greeting Stephen, his leg encased in plaster, with a cheery 'that makes two of us'.

The teaching at Kentucky was not arduous. Spender's classes 'consisted simply of students producing their poems' and a couple of lectures. After the first week, Natasha drove her husband up to the hills. Cooped up as he had been since January, the open countryside was 'like coming out of prison'. At the end of his time in Kentucky he was able to manage a few steps with the aid of sticks. Hardly 'flying', but Spender was mobile again. And his morale was raised with every footfall.

The Spenders returned to England in early May and squeezed in a trip to Mas de St Jerome. Stephen was by now 'much better at walking'. In June, back in London, they were visited by Isherwood and Don Bachardy at Loudoun Road, 'Christopher seeming scarcely altered from when I first knew him', Spender observed, but extravagantly American in his speech. The picture taken on this occasion shows a seated Spender looking, in his convalescence, decades older than his puckish Californian comrade (in fact the older man by seven years). Spender had just written a long piece on Christopher for the *NYRB*, touching on the vexatious topic of Herr Issyvoo's conversion to Vedanta. It was not to the subject's liking.

On 15 July the Spenders left for Taos and a ceremony to commemorate the fiftieth anniversary of D. H. Lawrence's death. The event had been arranged by the University of New Mexico (who were now custodians of the 'Lawrence Ranch'). Margaret Drabble was another invited English guest of honour and would become, on the trip, a close friend of the Spenders ('We liked her very much,' Stephen noted). Spender had been a Lawrentian since his schooldays. Homage apart, it was an opportunity to revisit the cabin where *World within World* had been written. Spender's legs (not yet fully recovered) ensured VIP treatment on the flight across to New Mexico. The grounds where he had written *World within World* were, Spender discovered, overgrown with trees – so much so as to be barely recognizable to him. Since 1948, Lawrence's ashes had been deposited at the ranch's phoenix-decorated chapel. The trio of Lawrentian guardian ladies (Frieda, Dorothy, Mabel) were long gone. The faithful Angelino had erected a plaque to his mate Frieda, alongside her more famous mate's resting-place. It was a solemn occasion, shot through with curious unsolemn moments. 'Bus-muddle' upset the programme. None of the English contingent were impressed by the troupe of Greek dancing girls, the constant thumping of a bearded drummer outside the shrine, the cascades of rose petals, or the film star Anne Baxter's (painful) recitation of Lawrence's poetry. The pelting rain did not help.

The Spenders called on the Buttingers in New York on their way back to England. By now, Spender's mood had risen as his mobility returned with the aid of sticks and 'physio'. While Natasha took Joe (whose wits were failing) off for a drive, Stephen settled down for a conversation with Muriel. He counted himself 'luckier than most of the world's population', he told her. She had not long to live and was asking all her old friends if they had enjoyed their lives. He had and still was.

All during that summer Spender's mood remained restless and strangely creative. On 4 September he had an anxiety dream of a transparently allegorical kind ('a strange nightmare', he called it):

I was made pope. I sat in a large waiting room preparatory to making my first sermon before millions of people. I had about two hours to prepare it. From numerous flunkeys, autograph hunters, etc. who kept on interrupting me while I tried to put my thoughts in order, I asked for paper on which I could write notes. They only brought me torn up sheets of newspaper covered with newsprint and impossible almost to write on. I scrawled a few notes between lines of typography and in looking over them my handwriting was illegible. I had a faint hope undermined by past experience of how this does not work, that when it came to making my sermon, my illegible handwriting might stimulate me to inspired improvisation. My sermon was intended to bring the full weight of starvation, preparations for atomic war all into the consciousness of people so that they would change the world. If I had armed myself with only a few telling examples and statistics I could do this. But I knew my sermon would be a humiliating failure.

For relaxation he was reading Iris Murdoch's latest novel, *Nuns and Soldiers*. The action is set in the Alpilles, around Mas de St Jerome. The novel (dedicated to the Spenders) was in part a guests' gesture of gratitude from John and Iris, who had spent numerous summer holidays with the Spenders. Stephen was impressed but not entirely won over by *Nuns and Soldiers*. Iris was, he concluded, 'extremely gifted yet doesn't seem quite a novelist'.

Spender had been deeply affected by the Brandt report, *North, South*. Commissioned by the UN, it starkly recorded the world's grossly inequitable distribution of wealth. The juxtapositions of first world prosperity and third world starvation troubled Spender's conscience. He experienced chronic guilt (as he always had) at the material comforts his class enjoyed, juxtaposed as those pleasures were with increasingly painful images of global exploitation and suffering.

He jotted his misgivings down, as a fractured poem, on 13 September:

> I'm eating steak
> In the corner of the room there's a glass faced box
> On which an ebony skinned child appears
> Stomach swollen, head a tarred skull from which eyes
> Stare at my steak
> I put my hands to hide it from him while
> I kiss my child so that he shall not see.

Increasingly Spender was preoccupied with 'the total inhumanity of the people in power'. He accepted they were not (all of them, at least) wicked. But what, then, were they? 'When I was young', he wrote later in the month:

I couldn't read history because I had absolutely no grasp of the motivations of rulers . . . I did not see that the world is run everywhere by a special race of monsters – those who understand the reality of having power.

September continued with its round of mild social pleasures and vexations. There was a burglary at Loudoun Road. The well at Mas de St Jerome ran dry. Another shaft would have to be bored. Cold northern mistral gave way, overnight, to hot and humid sirocco. Both were uncomfortable. To cap it all, their car (damaged on the trip over from England) was not ready for the planned visit to Philippe de Rothschild at Mouton, on 25 September. The repairs to the accident earlier in the month proved trickier than first expected. They decided to go by train. Then, when they phoned their friend Philippe, he airily instructed, 'Oh get an aeroplane and the firm will pay your fares.'

When they arrived the Spenders discovered that Rothschild had grandiose plans for the estate and a visitors' centre to enlarge the 'Museum of Wine' which, Spender perceived, was a monument for his friend's

dead wife Pauline. 'I sympathize very much,' he noted in his journal:
'This is how old age should be – megalomania expanding into eternity.
I thought of Yeats.' The visit to Mouton had moments of comedy. Beth
Chatto (whom the Spenders had introduced to their host) had been
invited to advise on gardens. Philippe, Natasha recalls, 'didn't know what
you were talking about when you used a word like ceanothus'. Chatto
reminded Spender 'very much of some undergraduette of Inez's generation'. Joan Littlewood – the founder of the People's Theatre in Stratford
East, and (improbably) Baron Philippe de Rothschild's close companion
– was also at Mouton. She and Philippe rowed madly. In bad moods
(frequent) she addressed him as 'you old reprobate', in good moods as
'Guv'. Spender mischievously pictured the diminutive impresario as a
poison dwarf, Mimi, in Wagner's *Ring*, or 'the mascot of a particularly
virile Highland regiment'. After a foot-stamping exchange between their
host and his theatrical friend, Spender inquired of Chatto how long she
was going to stay. 'If things go on like this, I leave tomorrow,' she replied,
wryly.

As usual, London meant dinner parties, concerts and public duties.
On 2 October Spender sacrificed an evening at the Royal Opera House
(*Siegfried*) to troop off to a poetry reading at St Paul's Church at
Hammersmith Broadway, with Laurie Lee and P. J. Kavanagh ('both un-
redeemed Georgian poets', Spender privately thought). He 'cursed whatever weakness it is that makes me accept such invitations'. The District
Line got him to the venue early and he passed the time with a nostalgic
walk round Brook Green, Hammersmith, 'where Inez and I used to live'
(and where, at nearby Queen Charlotte's Hospital, Lizzie had been born).
It had not changed much 'and brought back so many memories'. At this
reminiscential stage of his life, the past seemed like an adjoining room
into which one could simply open the door and go in: 'then one real-
izes the threshold is 45 years wide'.

Spender had arranged to spend another month or so in America, from
mid-October. His schedule would begin with readings in Toronto. After
three days in Canada he travelled south to Buffalo ('an extremely gloomy
place') on 22 October. His host was 'an enormous grave man with a
black beard, who never took off the trilby hat that he wore'. By 23
October Spender was in congenial New York, from where he travelled
on to a branch campus of the city university at Oneonta 'in a tiny plane
from a miniature airport beyond La Guardia'. There ensued the kind of
serial disaster he was accustomed to on his American trips and that he

invariably turned into hilarious, if self-mocking, stories for his friends. The event had begun well enough with a spell of blissful autumn weather. Spender was installed in a hotel room overlooking a colonial churchyard (Brodsky had stayed there, and had also been delighted with the view). His host tactfully left him alone ('which I was grateful for') and he worked in the solemn calm on the draft of his Oedipus plays, which the Oxford Playhouse had scheduled for the new year.

The reading itself went 'quite well'. Then things began to fall apart. Oneonta airport was socked in by bad weather. The tiny plane due to take him back to New York was indefinitely delayed, while storm clouds built up inexorably. After three hours waiting, Spender was agitated. He wanted to get back for the opening of Rodrigo Moynihan's exhibition and to give moral support to Rosamond Russell, who was due to lecture at the Met. He had known her since 1946 and had, over the years, encouraged her in her career as an art critic. He was also invited to join Russell, Jacqueline Onassis and her daughter Caroline, and Joe Alsop for dinner afterwards. 'I simply had to get there.'

The prospect of being kept overnight in Oneonta drove Spender to desperate remedies. He hired the town's sole taxi, and its octogenarian driver, to take him the 287 miles to New York. The subsequent trip was fraught with comic misadventure. The cab-driver insisted on stopping for a sandwich to fortify his ancient constitution. Spender had a hole in his trouser pocket which, for some time, he had been intending to do something about. Too late. Fifty miles down the turnpike, he discovered his wallet was lost. They returned to the ill-fated sandwich shop and retrieved it from their honest host.

At this point, 'everything became nightmarish'. The octogenarian driver declared he could go no further. His aged frame was unequal to the task – even with the meter running into three digits. Spender was obliged to hire another taxi, driven this time by 'an immense, gray-bearded black driver, who turned his car radio on to stations that had religious programmes'. Their sedate travel down the New York Thruway was punctuated by deep bass 'Praise the Lords', and 'Amens' from the front seat. Despite his theology, Spender drily recorded, 'he charged me $118 instead of the $100 he said he was going to charge'. Christian charity had its limits.

Spender got to the lecture by the skin of his teeth. At tea, after the event, he sat next to Jacqueline Onassis, whose face was 'a box-like enamelled mask, square almost, with large dark slits for eyes and a mouth a bit like the opening in a pillar box'. He asked the world's most famous widow what she considered her greatest achievement in life. Cool as always, she replied: 'I think it is that after going through a rather difficult time, I consider myself comparatively sane.' The answer made him feel somewhat contrite for asking the question. He was gratified to learn that 'I think continually' had been decided on as the celebratory reading for the opening of the Kennedy Library in Boston.

Spender was in New York for election day and Reagan's (truly depressing) victory on 4 November. After all these years there were many friends to see in the city and nearby Princeton. The most moving episode in this brief autumnal sojourn was a visit on 4 November to Vera Stravinsky in her Fifth Avenue apartment. She was talkative but confused by dementia. 'Here is Stephen,' announced her assistant:

Vera looked up at me in an unrecognizing way but seemed to realize I was a friend not a stranger. Her face, beautiful, soft and round, with the enormous brilliant eyes and the sumptuous Titian-like complexion, seemed to have shrunk: skin – red and white – drawn back like a scarf over the bone, wrinkled and heavily painted. She still smiled in her indulgent welcoming way.

She was not sure which city she was in. It was probably not Paris, she mused. Then she observed, 'I know so many languages – Let's see.' She reeled off four or five. 'Russian?' Spender interjected. 'No I don't know Russian,' she replied, suddenly attentive. 'No one anywhere knows Russian any more. It is not spoken,' she added firmly. The pathos of it overcame Spender. He 'stupidly allowed tears to trickle down my face' and remained silently weeping for the rest of the meeting.

Through Richard Sennett, Spender met Michel Foucault in New York. Spender was struck by the *philosophe*'s 'chalk white face, sparse black hair either side of a bald dome; the look of a waiter, or perhaps of a detective – Poirot – stark but anonymous'. They met at a 'very noisy French restaurant'. Foucault blandly informed Spender that the 'previous night he had gone to St Mark's Baths . . . had there had a blow job from a black, after which he had mingled with a crowd in Central Park, having given himself a shot of mescalin. He had a bad trip which made him completely blind for two hours.' The Frenchman was amusing company but, unsurprisingly, 'tired'.

On 9 November, Spender travelled on to more congenial Tulsa for a four-day trip. Here he was (over Thanksgiving) the guest of David Plante, with whom he had been friendly for some years. David's teaching was going well. 'He fairly glows in the atmosphere of praise and thanksgiving,' Spender noted goodnaturedly. Glowing even more brightly than Plante was the Australian feminist Germaine Greer (with whom David shared his office). She radiated a 'coarse vitality', Spender thought, and was – had he but known her fifty years before – 'a walking PYLON'. Germaine offered 'lively descriptions of walking through Central Park and many men emerging from the dark and flashing their dicks at her. She says she is too hefty to be mugged.'

Spender had arranged to end his tour in Los Angeles where, as he told Reynolds Price:

I shall spend three days with Bryan who is now being wildly happy as a graduate student with special honours at UCLA. It is really wonderful that he has got away from teaching school at Dixie County Florida and is now in one of the best departments for his subject in the country.

He flew back to the UK on 15 November. Bryan did not hang around to see him off ('farewells at airports are so sad'). The journey home was 'frightful'. Spender took two sleeping pills but could not sleep 'a wink'. His legs, still suffering, twitched uncontrollably. He was met in London by Natasha, who took him back to Loudoun Road, where he spent the next twenty-four hours 'either sleeping, or reading the Sunday newspapers – the same thing'.

Sonia Orwell died at the end of the year. The Spenders attended her funeral on 17 December at St Stephen's Church. Natasha had spent much time with her in her last month, as a tumour destroyed her brain. Stephen recalled, elegiacally, 'the "Venus of the Euston Road" of 1937 . . . with a round Renoir face, limpid eyes, cupid mouth, fair hair, a bit pale, perhaps'. Cyril Connolly had provided her 'intellectual ideal'. Then, typically, Spender recalled a good story about Sonia. In summer 1940 Dick Wyndham ('a man of notoriously sadistic character') pursued her until she threw herself into a pond to preserve her virtue. Peter Quennell dragged her out. 'Shivering, soaking and splashed with mud, she gasped, "It isn't his trying to rape me that I mind, but that he doesn't seem to realize what Cyril stands for."' Spender spent Christmas Eve writing up his journal, the fullest he had compiled for some years.

Over the next year (1981) Spender saw more of Isaiah and Aline Berlin than he had for some time. The two friends, having witnessed so much of life and twentieth-century history, discussed the future of the human race. Isaiah said 'he didn't mind very much about everything coming to an end'. Spender rejoined that he 'did care – meaning that what I cared about was the civilization the world produced'. Alfred Brendel, who was also present, said – to Spender's relief – that he too 'cared'.

In early 1981 Spender was collaborating with 'a young man who is writing a book about me'. The young man (Paul Binding) got well into his book but it was finally shelved – partly because of its subject's reservations about being lauded in print, even by a critic as perceptive as Binding. On another front, Spender was increasingly apprehensive of the invasions which he sensed were coming. When he looked around at what the vultures had done to his friends (particularly Wystan), he felt that 'The biographers have been second-rate diggers up of personal anecdotes so far, the scholars and research workers heavy-industry exegetes . . . one wishes one could escape from it all.' Escape was, alas, impossible. He would, however, fight back over the last fifteen years of his life. The 'second-raters' would get no easy victory over Spender.

Polite disinclination was his normal tactic. He was not worthy, he would imply – with a disarming display of self-mockery and an appeal to his correspondent's inherent decency. He replied in this vein to a would-be biographer on 22 May 1980:

I am very honoured by your wanting to write a life of me. But the fact is I regard my life as rather a failure in the only thing in which I wanted it to succeed. I have not written the books I ought to have written and I have written a lot of books I should not have written. My life as lived by me has been interesting to me but to write truthfully about it would probably cause much pain to people close to me – and I always feel that the feelings of the living are more important than the monuments of the dead.

His major literary enterprise at the moment was the translation of the *Oedipus* trilogy, for which he had a promise of performance at the Oxford Playhouse. This Sophoclean venture was one of those books that he felt he 'ought to write'. His interest in classic tragedy had been sharpened by his friendship with Nikos Stangos. The Spenders had first met the young Greek when he was serving on the diplomatic staff at his country's London embassy (following George Seferis there was something of a tradition of Greek poet-diplomatists). On the accession of the dictatorial Colonels, Stangos defected to take an editorial position with Penguin and then (more permanently) with the fine-art publisher Thames & Hudson in London. He and Spender later collaborated on translations and formed a close friendship (as did Spender with Stangos's partner, David Plante).

Spender wrote a sonnet commemorating his friendship with Nikos, built around the conceit of shared and not-shared language:

> When we talk, I imagine silence
> Beyond the multiplying words: as space
> Empty of all but ourselves face to face.

The poem (which was evidently written abroad) ends, strikingly,

> But far from you, willing you here with me,
> I write these words as flesh upon the page.

As always, he was translating from the German; a language which kept alive his connection with the energies of pre-war Hamburg and Berlin. He belonged, with Gaby Annan, Miriam Gross, George Weidenfeld, the poet Michael Hamburger, and the historians John Clive and Eric Hobsbawm, to an informal 'German Club'. Members would visit each other's houses, eat lunch (German dishes), and converse *auf Deutsch*: Spender fluently and incorrigibly ungrammatical, as ever, to the delight of his companions.

There were more workaday tasks to do. Money had to be earned. Spender was engaged to teach in Columbia, South Carolina, for a semester from the second week in January 1981. He was, before leaving London, preoccupied with his ritual New Year reflections. They tended towards the practical nowadays: 'Being nearly 72 makes me think how restless I am with time,' he noted. The time taken up in American classrooms was particularly burdensome. He was now a good seven years past retirement age – but labouring as hard and as productively as any mid-career academic.

When in America he habitually lived the life of a monk. And he resisted the monastic affliction of accidie by an effort of will. 'Waking up in the morning,' he recorded in his journal, 'I have the sense of an underlying depression like a large squid lying at the bottom of a tank, which if I don't act with resolution will come up from the depths and embrace me in its tentacles.' Reagan's inauguration, in January 1981, was not an event to vanquish large squids. Spender consoled himself, as usual, with books: in January his reading included Thackeray (disappointing), Curtius (brilliant as ever) and Day-Lewis (better than expected).

The end of his stint in South Carolina was enlivened by the arrival of Natasha, who came across for their fortieth wedding anniversary on 9 April. They celebrated privately; but, it being their 'Ruby', there was 'rather a lot of claret' consumed. After Columbia it was arranged that Spender would go on a journey to China, with David Hockney and Greg Evans. The trip had originally been planned for 1980, but was necessarily postponed because of Stephen's disaster salmon-hunting in the Finchley Road. A book (*China Diary*) was contracted for to pay for the journey. Stephen did the words, David the pictures. Amazingly, the publisher would pay Spender £10,000.

China Diary was, in terms of money, the most rewarding book of any that Spender published in his lifetime. It was equally rewarding as a celebration of boon companionship. The poet, the artist and the artist's assistant enjoyed each other immensely – more so, often, than the enigmatic country they were visiting. The three were nicely layered by age. Gregory Evans (destined to be the dedicatee of the book) was the youngest of the trio. In his twenties, it pleased Stephen to picture Greg as 'one of the group of young Florentine nobles standing in the foreground of Botticelli's *Adoration of the Magi*'. In manner, however, Evans was more the cool eighties Angeleno than a Renaissance golden youth. His ironic taciturnity was an antidote to his companions' pictorial and poetic flights.

At forty-four, Hockney was world-famous. Not, alas, among the billion residents of the world's most populous country. But American and British tourists immediately identified the flaxen-haired, owlishly horn-rimmed, colourfully togged artist, currently at the height of his international reputation. At seventy-two, Spender was the veteran. The first sketch of him in the book is ruefully described by its subject. The poet has been caught:

sitting in the transit lounge at Tokyo airport . . . looking saturated with exhaustion like a sponge with water. After living with myself for over seventy years I have, I suppose, a kind of serial image of myself though it is unlikely that one will recognize oneself in the final emanation of the series. The general impression I made in David's drawing was of bulbous obesity: bulbous cheeks, chins, limbs and fingers. Later drawings in wash or crayon confirmed an overall redness rendered sheep-like by the whitest of woollen hair. The eyes are veined pink by eye-strain. With the retina of one eye distorting lines it sees – or doesn't see into curves, and with knees creaking after an accident two years ago in which I severed the ligaments and had them sewn up – and with my considerable height and overall largeness I must have looked very much the odd man out compared with my two younger companions.

It was the portrait of the artist as an old but – as the journey progressed – still vitally engaged and energetic traveller.

What Spender composed for the journey, which lasted from 19 May to 11 June and covered some 3,000 land-miles, was less a journal (of the thoughtful kind which he kept for himself) than a diary for publication, comprising impressions of the day. They were necessarily superficial impressions. The rigid protocol of the official tourist office and their officious guide, Mr Lin, effectively kept China 'behind a pane of glass'.

There were, in fact, two Chinas. One, contemporary and loathsome to Spender (less to Hockney), was the 'Stalinist' China of Peking. The other, 'traditional' and more congenial, although no more penetrable, was the China of calligraphy schools, enamelling workshops and painting academies. They were also conducted through communes, universities and many museums. The visiting trio each had his camera. David's other vade-mecum was a sketchpad, Stephen's a notebook (as Greg noted, he bought and lost a straw hat every day, but he never mislaid his notebook).

The pervading tone of Spender's entries is one of polite, meticulously accurate bafflement. Particularly revealing is his reaction to a silk factory (in effect a worm farm) which they visited on 3 June:

As a boy I used to keep silkworms (to judge from the imagery in Yeats's 'Byzantium,' I suspect that he did too). These were obtained from a naturalist's shop near the British Museum. I kept them in a box with sides made of perforated zinc. When a chrysalis was formed I used to put it in a bowl of hot water and then pull the end of the thread till all the silk was unwound onto a card. I was pleased to discover that the silkworm chrysalises of Wusih are robbed of their precious silk in much the same way.

In the main, *China Diary* is a collection of exquisitely drawn, elegantly composed tourist postcards. The country, Spender concluded, was like one vast boy-scout camp, with Mao as its Baden-Powell. Greg, the most adventurous of the three, contrived to get away one evening and talk to students. He found them angry – very unlike boy scouts. One of them told him, 'In China, the old do not like the young.'

Spender gave himself the last word in *China Diary*. The book concludes with a conversation, on their return, dated 'Los Angeles, 9 January 1982'. The People's Republic of China was run by 'old men'; Hong Kong was run by the entrepreneurial young. 'Which do we prefer?' Spender asks. Yeats's Byzantium ('This is no country for old men / The young in one another's arms . . .') is again invoked. Nor is there much doubt which country Spender, old as he was, preferred. Not that Britain, in 1981, was at its best, racked as it was with race riots and Thatcherite conflict.

Spender flew to Williamsburg, Virginia, at the end of March 1982. There would be a month's teaching at William and Mary and the usual round of lecturing here, there and everywhere. His tour of duty was interrupted by what was at first suspected to be an unpassed kidney stone. It could have been something more serious. By courtesy of state-of-the-art American medical technology he had the unusual experience of viewing his entrails displayed on a hospital TV screen: 'I felt anything might appear,' he noted: 'the wreck of a ship sunk in the Armada, a shark, a coral branch attached to a drainpipe which proved to be cancer.' He was given the all clear. No cancer. Kidney stone it was. It would be removed on 20 June at King Edward's Hospital in London (Stephen was amused to think that, like Sam Pepys, he could keep it to show to his friends round the dinner table when conversation flagged).

While Spender was away, ships were indeed being sunk in the South Atlantic, where Mrs Thatcher had dispatched an English armada to reconquer the Falklands. The war ended in mid-June. Like many liberals, Spender had some uneasiness. War was so much messier, and less ideologically clear-cut, than it had been in 1936 and 1939. At this period of his life he was, gratefully, out of the political mêlée. He was concerned about the safety of British residents in the islands, and how they were to be rescued. But he also had doubts about the campaign which he confided to his journal: 'Why,' he asked, 'because Galtieri is a vile dictator should we send out young men to be shot to death and frozen to death drowning in those Antarctic waters?' Later he concluded, 'we should never have sent the Task Force'. He was disinclined, however, to make any public statement such as that of 'Authors take Sides' in the Spanish Civil War.

Spender received the good news at Christmas 1982 that the Oxford Playhouse had programmed his Oedipus plays for February. He had been working on his Sophocles translations 'on and off for almost two years' but, as he confided to Reynolds Price, 'funking the choruses'. He now must buckle down to doing them. It would occupy him for the best part of 1983. The verses required the exercise of dramatic imagination at the highest level. They are done in a chaste, late Spenderian mode; a style which suggests wisdom, exhaustion and contempt for the world:

> Whoever craves a longer life than his allotted span
> That man
> I count a fool.

His Uncle George Schuster, no fool, died in this year at the huge age of 101. Two years later Spender chose the Sophoclean choruses to end his *Collected Poems*.

Peter Ackroyd, who had helped winnow the drastically few poems which Spender allowed through into his (so-called) *Collected Poems: 1928–1985*, sent him a volume of Jeremy Prynne's notoriously impenetrable verse – 'a gift although I doubt it can be called a present', as the witty young writer said. Repugnant as he found much contemporary verse, Spender liked Ackroyd's post-modern novels – as did the critics and the awarders of British literary prizes. Peter did his friend the honour of including Fireman Spender in his 1982 novel *The Great Fire of London*.

With Auden gone, Ted Hughes would become Spender's closest poet friend. The seeds of the friendship had been planted by the meeting with the young poet and his young poet wife, Sylvia, at T. S. Eliot's dinner table in 1960. Much had happened since that evening: particularly to Hughes. Sylvia Plath had gassed herself, and so had his mistress Assia Wevill (together with the child she had by Hughes). The poet had been vilified and taunted – most cruelly by supporters of Plath, of whom there were more every year. Spender felt that the hounding was unfair. The two poets were united in their loathing of press invasion of the private lives of celebrated writers. In 1983, Spender agreed to join Hughes as a judge on Arvon writing centre competitions. It would mean weekend trips to Devon to meet with students and comment on their work.

Spring of 1983 was taken up with a hastily devised whirlwind tour of the United States to drum up funds for *Index*. The idea of the fund-raising trip originated with Spender. He was accompanied by 'friendly' Lois Sieff (widow of the Marks & Spencer chairman, J. Edward Sieff) and by Michael Scammell (*Index*'s editor). The trio were sent on their way with a letter of introduction to the rich people of America from the rich Englishman David Astor (one of the magazine's trustees), stating that 'the amount we are hoping to raise at any particular luncheon is in the region of $5,000 or $10,000'. The total aimed at was a massive £100,000.

Those zeroes were a forlorn hope. As Spender realized, they were three amateurs. A professional fundraiser informed them airily that 'no rich person was going to give us money unless doing so brought *him* something'. A 'Valkyrie blonde' who they thought might help told them 'you'd better make it snappy' (and did not help). *Index* had little to offer the putative rich American donor other than the heartfelt gratitude of persecuted writers, and that was not the 'something' looked for. Nor was the mood of the country propitious. America, as the *Index* trio discovered, was too engrossed in its own vast self (this was, after all, the '"Me" Decade') to worry its conscience about prisoners of conscience in 'Omsk, Bratislava, Krakow'. Lois complained that she felt like a good-cause prostitute. The word 'left', Spender discovered, was 'the reddest of flashing lights' to right-wing donors – and they were all right-wing. Americans with faces like 'split water melons' attacked them for being soft on South American leftist radicals. And, all considered, was there not something worthwhile in *Index*'s poverty? By rich American standards 'we are poor, and I think we are better for being poor'.

Spender had been visiting the USA now for almost forty years and had, in the distant past, had his difficulties with the Immigration and Naturalization Service. He was reminded of this fact when he arrived at New York immigration on 10 April. A brisk young official scrutinized the antique Spenderian visa, frowned, and went into the back office to consult with his superiors. He returned to say that Spender's documentation had 'something arcane from the past'; some 'special dots meaning socialist or some shit, we don't have that now'. Like socialism, Stephen Spender felt himself something 'arcane from the past'.

Spender, now seventy-four, could indulge one of the privileges of old age: unrestrained grumpiness. His journal of the New York trip is hilariously irritable. He had been commissioned by the glossy magazine *GEO* to do an interview with Henry Moore (for $2,000). They duly rejected

the piece ('not very interesting', in their high-handed editorial judgement), enclosing – for the spurned author's edification – a copy of *GEO*
featuring 'a lot of photographs of hideous centenarians'. Spender wrote
back saying:

Thank you for your kind suggestion that I should consider writing for you in
the future. Doubtless when I am as old and hideous as the centenarians who
fill up so much space in the particularly boring new number of *GEO* which
you enclosed, I shall take up this offer.

A few days later, being driven home after a tiring reading on Long
Island, his host's wife enraged him by asking a series of impertinent (as
he thought) questions about 'Woolf'. The luckless woman was, apparently, writing a thesis with some aggressive feminist angle. 'There was
so much Woolf this and Woolf that,' Spender records, 'that finally I got
annoyed and said, "Anyone who calls Woolf Woolf can't possibly understand Woolf." "Then what would you call her?" "Virginia Woolf."' Silence
ensued for the rest of the car journey.

Spender touched down in the UK on 6 May. Three days later he
attended a conference on T. S. Eliot at Canterbury. He was appalled by
the general 'twerpiness' and pomposity. All real connection with Tom had
been lost, he felt. Almost immediately he was again on his travels to Venice
and a PEN conference. In intervals from the conference activities he read
Muriel Gardiner's autobiographical *Code Name Mary* (1983). The Spenders
could claim to have been godparents of this interesting book, a memoir
of Muriel's heroism in pre-war Vienna. The background to its belated
publication was tangled and would involve Stephen in a running series
of quarrels between three of the most disputatious and formidable women
writers of the time: Lillian Hellman, Mary McCarthy and Martha Gellhorn.
The rows had begun, obscurely enough, on late-night TV, in January
1980, when talk-show host Dick Cavett provoked Mary McCarthy into
publicly indicting Hellman as an incorrigibly dishonest woman. McCarthy
clinched her point with the stinging wisecrack: 'Every word Lillian
Hellman writes is a lie, including "and" and "the".'

A furious Hellman brought a defamation suit for $2 million. She was
rich enough to hire lawyers capable of getting many pounds of flesh.
The event became a media circus. McCarthy's joke was too good not
to repeat (compounding the libel, as Hellman's lawyers might think),
and the catfight was fascinating. They were, of course, old cats: both

women were nearer eighty than seventy. But they still had sharp claws.

The source of the enmity could be traced back to their notorious new year's party, at Sarah Lawrence, in 1948, when the women had first crossed swords about which of them was the purer in pre-war Communism. As she prepared her defence, Mary consulted her old friend, Stephen. He and Natasha could, as it happened, supply her lawyers with some handy ammunition. There had, for years, been scepticism about the forty-seven-page 'Julia' story in Hellman's 1973 volume of autobiography, *Pentimento*. 'Julia' (a pseudonym, the reader apprehended) was, allegedly, an American friend of Lillian's – a psychiatrist, in Freud's city, Vienna. In the period 1934–7, this brave woman had saved many Jews and Socialists from the Fascists. And she recruited Hellman – as Hellman's autobiography recounted – to smuggle a large sum of money for the cause ($50,000) into Nazi Berlin. The heroic Julia later died: the heroic Lillian lived to tell her heroic friend's tale.

Pentimento went on to become a bestseller. The Julia episode was made into a film, *Julia*, in 1977, starring Jane Fonda and Vanessa Redgrave. Who was 'Julia'? It was clear to the Spenders that she must, of course, have been Muriel Gardiner. They had come to this conclusion a couple of years earlier. The problem was, Muriel Gardiner had never met Lillian Hellman: neither in Austria, Germany nor the USA. Gardiner had written to the author of *Pentimento* asking, bluntly, 'Am I Julia?' She received no answer. Hellman, it seemed, had coolly stolen Muriel Gardiner's life, without acknowledgement. McCarthy duly entered as one of the principal grounds of her legal defence 'the unbelievability of Julia'.

McCarthy's attempt to get her day in court was met with prevarication and deliberate running up of legal costs on Hellman's side (immensely the richer woman). For some years the Spenders had been encouraging their friend to publish the true account of her pre-war exploits in Vienna. She resolved to do so with her autobiography *Code Name Mary* (which, among other things, recounted in detail the love affair in Vienna of the young Stephen and Muriel in 1935). The book was published in May 1983. Its irrefutable account constituted, as Hellman's biographer attests, 'the severest blow to her beleaguered reputation'. Newspapers and magazines weighed in, overwhelmingly supporting Muriel Gardiner's account and implicitly accusing Hellman of fabrication. Hellman never publicly challenged Gardiner's version of events. Nor did she ever face McCarthy in court. Nor did she, or her supporters, or archivists in Vienna, produce a shred of evidence as to the historical existence of *her* Julia. The dispute was unsettled, and still bitterly seething, at the time of Lillian Hellman's death in 1984.

Spender's role in this had been to support two friends. Any satisfaction he may have felt was clouded by another, strangely linked, fracas. Martha Gellhorn, one of Ernest Hemingway's many wives and America's most admired woman journalist, had taken violent exception to another of Hellman's autobiographical volumes, *Scoundrel Time* (1976). Gellhorn was particularly vexed by Hellman's suggesting that, during the Spanish Civil War, she, Hellman, had been intimate enough to have good stories about the great literary bruiser, with whom Gellhorn *was* at the time intimate.

Gellhorn mounted her attack on Hellman's many 'apocryphisms' (lies, that is) in a 1981 article in the *Paris Review*. As a prelude to her main assault, she chose to open with a six-page denunciation of Stephen Spender's 'apocryphisms'. He too, allegedly, had been guilty of fibbing about her man. Spender initially provoked Gellhorn's ire with some throwaway remarks in an earlier interview in the previous issue of the *Paris Review*. The interview had taken place at Houston, on 13 May 1980, just after Spender had delivered the Rice University Commencement address. Peter Stitt, for the magazine, began by 'asking about some people you may have known'. Yeats and Dylan Thomas were duly reminisced about in Spender's customary friendly way. Then the interviewer asked: 'How well did you know Hemingway?'

Spender, who had clearly not prepared his answers, replied that 'I knew him during the Spanish Civil War.' Hemingway, he continued, 'often turned up in Valencia and Madrid and other places where I happened to be. We would go for walks together.' He then retailed various anecdotes – most of them recalled from *World within World*. One story added some garish details:

Another time, my first wife [Inez] and I met him and Marty Gellhorn in Paris. They invited us to lunch someplace where there were steaks and chips, things like that, but my wife ordered sweetbread. Also she wouldn't drink. So Hemingway said, 'Your wife is yellow. That's what she is, she's *yellow*. Marty was like that, and do you know what I did? Used to take her to the morgue in Madrid every morning before breakfast.' Well the morgue in Madrid before breakfast must have been something. Hemingway always said of me, 'You're OK. All that's wrong with you is you're too squeamish.'

The way Spender framed this might be taken to imply a warm and prolonged degree of intimacy between him and Ernest. Gellhorn furiously denied that any such intimacy happened. She strenuously contradicted that the four of them had ever had steak and chips together in Paris. Hemingway *never* took, or threatened to take her, to any morgue in Madrid or anywhere. 'It didn't happen,' she insisted, '*any of it.*'

Gellhorn demonstrated – by reference to Hemingway's movements – that he and Spender could never have met in Madrid, in July 1937, as Spender recalls in *World within World*. In that book Spender writes: 'One day in Madrid, Hemingway wistfully looking in Malraux's direction, said: "I wonder what Malraux did to get that tic? It must have been at well over ten thousand feet"' (in addition to being an author, the Frenchman was a pilot). This event cannot have happened – or, at least, not in Madrid in July 1937. The paths of Hemingway and Spender can only, Gellhorn demonstrated, have crossed for a mere seventy-two hours in Valencia when the American had much else on his plate. Hardly time enough for many 'walks'. Nor was Malraux there.

Spender responded with some asperity in the columns of the *Paris Review*. 'I am sorry,' he wrote, with heavy sarcasm, 'that Miss Gellhorn is having trouble with her memory; something that can happen at our age.' He insisted that the 1937 luncheon at the Paris brasserie *did* take place. Moreover, he could prove it did. The meal happened after a reading which he and Hemingway had given at Sylvia Beach's bookshop (commemorated by a photograph: proof positive. Muriel Gardiner also recalled the event). He was, he conceded, wrong in suggesting that Hemingway had been at the Madrid conference – probably the remark had been made by someone else or by the American on another occasion.

Gellhorn's swipes at Spender were secondary to her tooth-and-nail onslaught on Lillian Hellman. None the less, the episode 'fascinated' him. He pondered its implications in his journal. His memory (never good on dates, places, or times) had played him false. Was *anything* he recalled about Hemingway reliable? He was certain in his mind about the morgue business. But could he trust his mind (which had also been so sure about Malraux's tic)? There was no way after all these years of confirming or disconfirming the truth of the event. And what was it he remembered anyway? 'I don't really remember the original, I remember only these repeat performances going on in my mind. At least I think this is so.' In other words, he remembered memories. Or, he remembered the stories as they had been 'improved' by his retelling them over the years, accreting grace notes, embellishments and fabricated details. He was, it seemed, a poet, not a historian. Was the past (so real to him) ever recoverable? One could *see* it; but once it had passed, one could never revisit it: 'a great, if transparent, door slams,' he told himself, 'and one is shut off forever from the events behind it.' Shut off, but never free. And never entirely sure. But surer, of course, than those who had never been there.

In early June, Spender and Natasha went off for a fortnight's yacht trip along the Turkish coastline with Anne Cox Chambers. As their boat scudded along the waves, alongside Asia Minor, Spender, who had always loved seascapes, was enchanted by the sight of sportive dolphins following in their wake. They were, he thought, marine 'ideograms'. It inspired the title poem of his late collection, *Dolphins*:

> Happy, they leap
> Out of the surface
> Of waves reflecting
> The sun fragmented
> To broken glass
> By the stiff breeze
> Across our bows.

In early May, Spender had received an imposingly sealed letter. Would he accept a knighthood, the Queen's patronage secretary wished to know. After consultation with Natasha and some hesitation (it was, after all, at the recommendation of Mrs Thatcher, conqueror of the Falklands), he decided 'yes'. It was a club his friends thought he ought to belong to – as they (Isaiah, Stuart, 'K' (Kenneth Clark), Noël, Freddy) did. It would, he felt, be 'priggish not to take it'. On the eve of their return from Turkey the BBC announced the award.

The phone at Loudoun Road rang all day on 10 June, when the Honours List was published in *The Times*. Noël Annan wrote gracefully to complain that 'it would have been more appropriate had it been gazetted in the Diplomatic List as a KCMG; for you have been an ambassador for literature in general and English poetry in particular all your life'. Another friend, Mark Bonham Carter, wrote saying he was 'amazed that this deeply uncivilized government felt bound to dip its flag to a civilized man'.

Spender recorded his (inevitable) reservations about ennoblement in his *Journal*:

Although I've all too often said I would never accept this, when I got the letter I realized at once that I would do so, both for myself and for Natasha. There are those I respect for despising such things – they are the best. But there are many who don't despise them, and in their eyes this will be the equivalent of five or ten years taken off my age. Also there comes a time when one craves for recognition – not to be always at the mercy of the spite, malice, contempt – and perhaps even the just dismissal – of one's rivals.

Lizzie approved his decision. Matthew – ever the family puritan – did not.

The Spenders spent a quiet summer at Mas de St Jerome. As usual in these years, Iris Murdoch and John Bayley stayed with them. They had made their first visit in 1973. The two couples had, over the years, played parlour games in the long evenings in Provence. A favourite was what they called 'Quintonians' – that is, the most unlikely thing for anyone to say (the clear winner was, 'John Sparrow: "Helen Gardner is *marvellous* in bed"'). In the evenings they played Scrabble, which the Spenders liked to win (the Bayleys would be amused by the 'delight-fully cunning' look that came over their host's face during these post-prandial competitions). The four of them invented running narratives around the good-natured house cat, Daisy, and the omnipresent Bill the Lizard.

The Bayleys (as her novels attest) were inveterate swimmers. As Peter J. Conradi records, every day, 'Around 11.30 the Bayleys would go for a swim . . . they trooped down to reach an ever-changing, rapidly winding strip, the 16th century canal de Craponne.' Canal rather flatters the fast flowing, ditch-sized, ink-coloured stream, freezing cold in the shadow of the Alpilles. It cuts through long tunnels. In the novel set in the area (which Murdoch dedicated to the Spenders), *Nuns and Soldiers* (1980), the hero, Tim Reede, swims through one of these tunnels as (daringly) did his creator. 'The Bayleys,' Conradi records, 'relaxed Spender in a way that some of his worldlier friends did not.' After the novelist's harrowing death, from Alzheimer's, in 1999, Natasha wrote a memorial for her friend in the *Observer*. It drew tears from the widowed husband. He wrote, despairingly, 'Iris loved you and Stephen so much, and those visits, and the cats, and scrabble. All, all!'

The Spenders returned to London on 1 September. He would, in mid-October, make a trip to America, for the tenth anniversary of Auden's death. The memorial plaque was about to be laid. Bryan Obst was now in Alaska, Spender told Reynolds Price: 'he writes ecstatic letters about icebergs and stormy petrels and really seems to love Arctic or Antarctic wastes.' It was curious: 'However did I get to know this loner?' he asked himself. 'Perhaps because he *is* such a loner,' he concluded.

Spender had heard that Reynolds had contracted cancer of the spine. (Price narrates this horrible experience and the loss of the use of his legs in his invalid's autobiography, *A Whole New Life*.) Spender wrote on hearing early news of Reynolds's disaster. He had witnessed so many of his closest friends cut down – but none so young since the Second World War:

It's hateful to think of someone I first loved when he was young being really and seriously older than he was at our first meeting. Still less writing FINIS across his flesh (or with his penis in the snow). Personally – another family trait – I don't think I mind about dying, feeling that one dies every night anyway.

Initially Spender had intended to return from America in late November. But he stayed on to visit Reynolds in North Carolina in the first week in December. He brought with him a new-fangled present, a Sony Walkman (ironically, Reynolds Price, tragically unable to walk, would use it in his wheelchair). One of the bonds which had always joined them was a love of music.

Mr Spender returned to England where he had his 'dubbing of my Knighthood by the Queen' and arose Sir Stephen. Lizzie and Natasha accompanied England's newest literary knight to the palace. The ceremony was, he told Reynolds, 'as boring as Commencement – or any of those things – and of course I did not have those awful tail clothes you are supposed to get squashed into – which made Lizzie a bit ashamed of me'. They left the reception with David Sylvester (newly CBE) for a quiet celebratory drink.

Spender reacted with pleasure to the news, in 1984, that Ted Hughes had accepted the laureateship (a post Spender had never coveted), in succession to John Betjeman. Spender felt it would strengthen his friend in the combat against the 'Bacchantae' who would never forgive him, or stop tormenting his family, for Plath's 'murder'.

In April Spender undertook a short reading tour in America. In

Philadelphia (a city which always seemed to him 'like Edwardian England') he stayed with Henry McIlhenny (now disabled), and he visited the hugely successful Picasso exhibition at the Guggenheim in New York. He was buoyed up by the information that his agent, the indefatigable Ed Victor, had put together a three-book deal on his behalf with Faber: for a volume of his journals, for a volume of collected poems, and for the Oedipus plays.

As usual, nowadays, the Spenders spent a long relaxing summer at Mas de St Jerome. It was a relief for them both to get away from an England riven, almost to the point of civil war, by Arthur Scargill's strike action (a rebellion about which Spender had mixed feelings – were the miners, he wondered, worse off than those starving Ethiopians one saw pictures of?).

After twenty years, Spender had become addicted to the Provençal landscape with its 'honey coloured and rocky mountains, carved out, and indeed tortured, by the weather into smooth or lumpy, scrolled and scalloped, pillared sky-lines'. Natasha's English garden in Provence, beneath its wall of mountain, was flourishing. Spender painted a lot when they were in France ('if I'd stuck at it', he once wryly told Matthew, 'I'd be as rich as Francis'; then he giggled). More purposively he worked in his study, with its aspect on the Alpilles, on new and revised poems for the forthcoming collected volume which Faber had commissioned and were increasingly impatient for. He had privately promised himself to 'give up journalism'. Perhaps, he even thought, they might retire and live in Provence year-round.

Mas de St Jerome was very much Natasha's creation. Spender was candid on the subject to Reynolds: 'This place is marvellous, but a terrible worry which I could never have undertaken for *one day* without Natasha. It is kept together by her love and will power, and effective overdrive.' On 7 September, as they prepared to return to London, Spender regarded – in valedictory spirit – the view of the Alpilles from the front of the house: 'the rocks, in clear autumn air, like a pleated skirting drapery – the sculptured dresses of Greek goddesses on the Acropolis'.

There was a busy time ahead, he reminded himself: 'a lot of engagements in October, then November teaching at Brooklyn, then December perhaps here, then January [1985] to April in Atlanta Georgia. I don't see any break till next May.' He would earn $55,000 in those months – $25,000 in New York, $30,000 from Emory University, in Atlanta. The money was, as always, welcome. Stephen – unlike other university professors of his age – had no pension. Natasha had, this spring, retired from the Royal College of Art, which gave her an honorary fellowship in July. She was away for a few days for the ceremony, leaving Stephen alone and feeling 'haunted'. He realized that 'this whole house is kept together by her emotions running through it like the force of gravity without which it would collapse'.

Lizzie was with them over these last weeks in France, in a condition of 'arduous discontent', and between relationships. Why, Spender fretted, would his daughter not 'settle down'? (She would, five years later.) But for all her Spenderian restlessness, she remained 'genuinely sweeter and nicer than anyone else'. They had given him the greatest joy of his life but there was, he concluded, 'always an element of heartbreak in one's relations with one's own children'. He worked elements of this heart-break into his conception of Oedipus – a man both 'totally innocent' and 'totally guilty' of the ultimate familial crimes, parricide and incest. The paradox fascinated Spender.

Translating *Antigone* from the Greek (a language which he had painfully taught himself all those years ago as a sixth-former at University College School) induced a masochistic irritation with his lack of a proper grounding in the classics. 'How did I miss being educated?' he petu-lantly asked himself. 'I have thought a lot about this. The answer is that I was not clever enough – did not have the brains to get over neurosis.' But without the innocent, uneducated neurosis would he have ever been a poet? Was he actually uneducated? No and no.

Iris Murdoch and John Bayley visited, as usual, in July. At Mas de St Jerome other close friendships had to be kept up by letter. It distressed him that for many months he had heard nothing from Bryan Obst (was he still a friend?). 'I begin to have the complicated feelings that go with a friend not writing,' he recorded in mid-August. But he must not reproach him – Bryan was, after all, 'fifty years younger' (Stephen some-times liked to call him his 'grandson') and had, thanks to Stephen's efforts on his behalf, a full life nowadays. It transpired that the young man *had* written that summer, but his letter (from whatever frigid outpost this year's birdwatching had taken him) had gone astray. When he did get a letter, he discovered that the young ornithologist was 'having to share a bunk with a lady explorer which is far more frightening than the Moose, Polar Bears and Drunken Hippies in that region'. More seriously, Stephen worried about his young friend's fondness for singles bars and casual affairs. It was a bad time to be careless and gay.

The Spenders took a roundabout route home via Milan, where Spender and Joseph Brodsky ceremonially awarded a Guggenheim 'Montale' prize (a handy $5,000) to the poet Anthony Hecht, on 28 September. Matthew came up from Tuscany to see them in the North Italian city. His son, Spender noted, 'looks very *tall* (perhaps I have shrunk)'. Matthew's hair, Spender was amused to note, was also tall: 'tufted up in front like a duck's bottom'. Neither father nor son (who could now pass for brothers) had ever much cared about ornamenting their appearance. The three of them visited the Milanese galleries. 'Pictures,' Spender reminded himself, 'are nothing unless they become great experiences.' It infuriated him when they were nothing more than *décor touristique*, gallery fodder. So much so that he 'made a scene' when, in Milan's principal art museum, he came across a herd of American students stolidly chewing gum, like so many cattle with their cud, in front of a sublime Michelangelo *Pietà*. It was, Spender thought, an insult to things that he held sacred.

He remonstrated, loudly. Matthew, embarrassed by the fuss his father was kicking up, found a picture of absorbing interest at the other end of the gallery 'and looked as if he didn't belong to us'. Natasha loyally supported her husband in the face of the American class leader's philistine protests that his charges had a perfect right to be bored by Michelangelo. Afterwards, Spender realized that he had behaved 'very like my father, Harold Spender'. The students, probably, wondered 'who is that old idiot?' He recalled how he and Humphrey had giggled at their father's pomposity in the National Gallery, on those distant childhood Sunday excursions. Reflecting on the episode, he wrote in his journal: 'For a flash I see myself as him with his wrinkled forehead, white flowing hair, creased up eyes, stubborn nose, publicly impressive appearance, his moustache even.' Matthew's behaviour (scuttling away) was, Spender realized, 'exactly what I would have done with *my* father'. Life was strangely circular, if one lasted long enough to see the patterns.

On 1 October the Spenders drove back to England. Almost immediately, Spender was off again to Vienna for the annual Auden festival (he was seeing even more of his friend dead than in life, it seemed). He was down to lecture this year on the 'Young Auden' – very conscious that he himself was now the 'Old Spender'. As he talked to the audience he 'kept seeing a large face of Wystan grinning at me'. Friendly or mocking? Lennie Bernstein was at the event and there were 'many kissings and embracings'. There was also the inevitable wariness: 'When two old men meet after several years they look first to see how each has changed.'

Neither had decayed disastrously, it seemed. Vienna, however, was changed out of recognition from what he recalled in 1935, when he had first loved Muriel Gardiner and remained loyal to Tony Hyndman.

Spender and Peter Ackroyd were, over these months, making the final cut for the *Collected Poems*. It would be a very deep incision – bringing down the many hundreds of poems Spender had published over the last sixty years to a mere 100 or so. They spent an evening on 25 October discussing their selection at the Gay Hussar, in Soho. Ackroyd, Spender recorded, 'pressed me hard'. The young novelist asked particularly pointed questions about the thirties, and where Spender wanted the centre of the collection to be, historically. Despite the age difference, 'he talks to me like a contemporary', Spender was pleased to note. Between them, they resolved that the guiding principle of the collection should be 'clarity'. Spender was particularly exercised to remove the 'self-obsessed, solipsistic efforts'. He was also worried about including 'The Ambitious Son', which he now saw as a 'cruel merciless Oedipal poem against my father who died when I was, at the age of 16, at the stage of adolescent revolt against him'. His uncle, J. A. Spender, had read the poem, roused to terminal fury, on his deathbed and had cut his nephew out of his will. On reflection, Stephen kept the poem in.

All that year, Britain had been convulsed by strikes and civil strife, provoked by Mrs Thatcher's war to the death with the British unions and the drift of the Labour Party leftwards, under the hapless leadership (so called) of Michael Foot. The liberalism which Spender had believed in all his adult life no longer existed. The political world had, indeed, gone forward. But, it seemed, forward into a wilderness.

At the end of October, Spender was off again to New York, staying at Muriel Gardiner's new apartment in Manhattan, 155 West 68th Street. His teaching stint at the Brooklyn campus of CUNY began on 30 October. As it happened, Henry and Irina Moore were also in New York. Both, he noted, 'had the look of people being bombed out, the bomb being old age'. The sculptor would, in fact, live only two years more and was in a terminally depressed condition. His hands, denied the physical work of chisel on stone, fidgeted constantly. Moore had, however, been gratified immensely by President Mitterand, on a state visit to England, dropping by in his helicopter to award him the Légion d'honneur, before taking once more to the skies. 'I gave him a drawing,' Moore, momentarily happy, told the Spenders later that day, 'and he gave me a medal.' He had always been a sculptor of few words.

Spender's classes at CUNY went, as he cautiously felt, 'all right', although he was disconcerted when John Ashbery (an admirer and America's most advanced poet) burst into his seminars to 'audit the course'. It was also disconcerting (if gratifying) when over 100 people turned up at another so-called 'seminar', obliging him to give instead a three-hour lecture on 'metaphor'. Herbert Mitgang covered the event for the *New York Times* in rhapsodic terms:

For three hours, in the fastness of Flatbush at the end of line on the IRT No. 2, almost everything that really mattered in the world seemed to have taken place in the 16th and 17th centuries. Under the speaker's brilliant, diffident guidance, nothing appeared more significant than John Donne's seductive poetry and the nuances of Hamlet's character.

Since the publication of her book, *Code Name Mary*, and the controversy with Lillian Hellman, Muriel Gardiner had become famous as the 'real Julia'. A TV feature was being made, and Spender was recruited to be interviewed with her in Chicago in November. It was an uncomfortable experience. Spender found the piercing studio lights unbearable. Nor did he much like the piercing questioning about his and Muriel's long-ago love affair. It struck him as prurient, all this poking into their private lives. 'Why don't they ask us to take off our clothes,' he wondered sarcastically, 'and watch us make macabre love with our wrinkled old bodies?'

In other ways the reunion with Muriel (who did not have many months left to live) was a nostalgic experience. The old lovers had long conversations about 'old times'. Spender recalled, vividly, his first meeting with her, half a century ago, at Mlini – beautiful, worldly, accompanied by the three-year-old Connie and 'a rather steely fawn-eyed young man who passed as her cousin (actually he was her lover)'. Spender, of course, had been accompanied by a copper-haired young Tony Hyndman, who passed as his secretary. It brought to the surface other memories prudently suppressed in *World within World*'s account. 'One night in Vienna,' he remembered:

Muriel, Tony and I were sleeping side by side at the edge of a meadow, and – Tony falling into a deep sleep – I woke and started to feel her body. That was thrilling, but Tony's presence prevented us making love – a turning point I didn't turn. Then the jealousy of Tony, he and I going back to the Blockhaus while she was pursuing her medical studies in Vienna, our [Tony's and his] frightful rows, ending in violent love-making which seemed to make orgasm a climax of despair.

In early November, Spender squeezed in a trip to LA, *en route* to a reading in Houston. He found Christopher (although visibly ailing) 'very spry'. 'Don't be afraid of being eighty,' his old (in every sense) friend advised, chuckling. Bryan Obst drove down to see him at his hotel (the bizarrely named Shangri La) and the five of them (Chris, Don, Bryan, Bryan's 'grizzle-bearded, benign-looking' partner Bob, and Stephen) had a Japanese meal together. Bryan was now a rising star in his field. At his (very drunken) twenty-eighth birthday party he publicly thanked his friend and mentor. Without Stephen, he averred, he would still be a schoolteacher – or, God help him, a vet worming cats and dogs – in small-town Florida. The occasion was rendered less merry by the visible havoc that AIDS was wreaking among the West Coast gay community. Bryan, it seemed, was fatalistic. Spender was back in England and Mas de St Jerome at the end of December.

From January to April 1985 the Spenders were in Emory, the quiet but élite university in Atlanta, Georgia, where their Oxford friend Dick Ellmann now had a visiting professorship (one reason for his accepting the post was the care which the hospital at Emory could give his now wheelchair-bound wife, Mary; he himself would soon fall ill with motor neurone disease). The Spenders' friend from Mausanne, Anne Cox Chambers, also had a large mansion in Atlanta, which the Spenders often visited. Spring came early in the American south (the dogwood was out by March). Spender had a light teaching load but was fully occupied with the proofs and final corrections of his collected journals and his collected poems, both due for publication later in the year (Natasha recalls desperate journeys to the down-town post office, with parcels of proofs). The volumes would both be published by the same house, Faber, as would the text of his Oedipus plays. Spender had had some thoughts of changing allegiance but decided, in the event, that old loyalties mattered more than advances. His friend David Astor reassured him that 'you are obviously right to stick to Faber's'. The firm had also arranged, via Stephen's agent Ed Victor, to take over the rights to *World within World* from Hamish Hamilton and reissue it in paperback.

Both the *Journals* (which covered the years 1939–83) and the *Collected Poems: 1928–1985* represented a kind of Last Testament. John Goldsmith was recruited by Faber to edit the text of the *Journals*. Spender made some necessary deletions. They were relatively few. Like *World within World* (which they supplement) they surprise often by their frankness (especially in self-revelation) rather than any reticence. Like the *Journals*, the *Collected Poems* are arranged chronologically, with an overlaid thematic and loosely autobiographical structure, beginning with 'Preludes' and ending with 'Choruses from the Oedipus Trilogy'. The volume opened loyally (as did all such volumes) with the anthem to Marston, 'He will watch the hawk' and ended with Oedipus, blind, aged, but at last knowledgeable about the human condition. A highpoint in the collection is the 'Auden's Funeral' quintet, a deceptively limpid sonnet sequence which had, in fact, taken a Horatian nine years to complete. In his preface, Spender declared, bluntly: 'I now think that my best poems are those which are extremely clear and that, perhaps without my being fully aware of it, clarity has always been my aim. At any rate, the poems I have thrown out are those which seem to me confused or verbose.' Typically, this discarded segment amounted to over half of his life's poetic output.

It would be a good year for the Spenders, authorially and socially. There was, however, growing concern about the condition of Muriel Buttinger and Christopher Isherwood. Stephen sent his old friends xeroxed proofs of the *Journals* volume. Isherwood would, in fact, last longer than Muriel. In April, Spender was told she was in hospital with only a few days to live. He sent off a long telegram and was surprised when she phoned back right away from her hospital bed in New Jersey. It was early in the week. She would, she serenely informed Stephen, die by Friday 'the weekend at the latest'. She then, with manifestly sincere interest, asked about her godchild, Lizzie, Natasha and Stephen himself. As they were driving to Emory that week, Spender suggested to Natasha that he might dedicate the *Journals* to Muriel. Natasha agreed enthusiastically and instructed her husband to turn round, go home, and phone Muriel at once, to ask her permission. He did so, only to find that she had just (as she so calmly predicted) died. He made the dedication posthumously. The *Collected Poems* would be dedicated to Reynolds Price, who happily had survived his brush with cancer.

The Spenders, as usual, spent their summer at Mas de St Jerome. While they were in Provence the *Journals* and *Collected Poems* were published (in June) to generally favourable reviews. In the *Spectator* Elizabeth Jennings felt that 'Spender's warmth and passion really take fire in his love poems'; he was a poet 'prepared to display his own vulnerability'. In the *New*

Statesman Paul Binding was eulogistic about another segment of the collected verse. Spender, he maintained, had 'written the most emotionally moving and honest poems about the Spanish Civil War and has captured the besieged, bewildered, patriotic life of the English during that War in lyrics of a peculiarly concentrated clarity'. Ian Hamilton made a predictable and unnecessarily *ad hominem* assault in the *TLS*. Spender, he spitefully observed of the illustrations in the *Journals*, 'looked more attractively boyish than most of the boys, more shyly keen to please, more likely to drift off into some genuinely sweet poetic dream'. Alfred Kazin in the *New York Times* was, by contrast, judicious and approving. The *Journals*, Kazin perceived, were a chronicle of literary relationship – the invisible social networks on which great work is strung:

Shelley had never met Keats when he wrote *Adonais*. Keats was lucky. Mr Spender knew Auden and Auden knew Mr Spender and they both knew everybody else! But who, knowing anything about them at all, can read 'Auden's Funeral' without realizing that all this will go down in history as the great association that some English poets have made their history?

In the *Listener*, D. A. N. Jones thought, less portentously, that it was good to have the jokes 'because there are none in his poems'. Binding, who had been a boy in post-war Germany, thought the 'German Diary' (reprinted in the *Journals*) 'conveys a sense of the devastation and the displacement of that time and place better than anything else I have read except for the early novels of Heinrich Böll'.

There was praise enough to gratify Faber. Spender was – as always – deeply vexed by the harsh criticism his name in print always seemed to elicit in some quarters of literary London, used as he now was to shrugging it off. He confided his irritation to Reynolds Price:

I find the kind of sneering criticism which the English specialize in today very hard to take. One feels oneself being made a kind of scarecrow to one's friends. There was a really disgusting article in the *TLS* by a professional hatchet man called Ian Hamilton, which you may or may not have seen, saying among other things that Ian Hamilton did not understand why I was such an admiring friend of Auden since Auden never did anything in return for my friendship. Fortunately Brodsky saw this letter, and although he was about to have open heart surgery, wrote a letter which is really a masterpiece of indignation.

Along with Brodsky, other friends responded to the published volume with warmth. Noël Annan wrote to say that he had enjoyed the display of Stephen's private thoughts immensely, adding, however, the proviso: 'of course, someone of my generation would'. Ian Hamilton, Noël thought, was using Spender 'as shrapnel in the intergenerational war'. His friend should be 'too old and wise to worry about the bitches', he advised; 'what matters is that you have left a wonderful record of yourself'.

Isherwood died on 4 January 1986. Spender wrote a letter of condolence to Don Bachardy recalling that their friend had always been 'a force for love' – whether eros, agape or just thirties *Kameradschaft*. It was understandable, he said, that Don should have 'lost patience' with his partner during the harrowing last weeks (something about which the younger man felt horribly guilty). Christopher, who had once trained as a doctor, had a 'horror of hospital deaths' (as did Spender and Wystan) and was determined to die at home, hard as that might be on those who loved him.

Spender wrote Isherwood's obituary for the *Observer*. A month later he wrote a long prose appreciation which was never apparently published. In it Spender's mind turned to the period when he, Wystan and Christopher had been themselves young men. 'Auden's thirties was England,' he concluded: 'Isherwood's was Berlin. Mine was something in between.' And now, fifty years later, he was the survivor. The leftover fraction of 'We three'. It added to the sadness of the year that Henry Moore also died in August. Yet another appreciation and obituary notice were called for. There had been an awful casualty rate among friends over the last few years: Sam Barber (1981), John Betjeman, Robert Graves (1985) – and now Henry and Christopher. 'I have been feeling terribly old ever since my books were published,' he told Reynolds Price, 'all the reviews seem to concentrate on how *old* I am.'

That spring, Spender taught (in the capacity of 'distinguished writer') at Bard College, 100 miles from New York (close enough for reviving weekend visits). His mind was still preoccupied with dead comrades. He wrote a substantial article for the *New York Times* on 8 June called 'Writers of the Spanish Civil War'. Their role 'was not to be ideologists of propaganda, but to burn in the flame of Spain's martyrdom, producing from it a cry beyond politics'. The piece, incredibly, commemorated the fiftieth anniversary of the outbreak of the war.

On 24 February 1987 Spender wrote to Ted Hughes felicitating him on having won a lawsuit to protect his copyright in his dead wife's work. In August he wrote a similar letter to congratulate Jeffrey Archer on his victory against the *Star* (the victorious novelist modestly replied, 'I can only describe Mary as a "modern day Portia"'). Spender made this gesture of solidarity less out of admiration for Archer's amazingly bad novels than on the 'my enemy's enemy' principle. Anyone who could give the Fleet Street reptiles a bloody nose (half-a-million damages in Archer's case) was in his good books.

'I go to America for five weeks on February 26th,' Spender told Ted Hughes. The period before he left was, as usual, social. On 6 February Noël Annan wrote to thank the Spenders for an excellent dinner ('I owe at least one stone in weight to Natasha's cooking,' he complained, ruefully). The former Provost recalled that 'it was a good day when Frank called in on me at UCL and said "What would you think, if Spender were put forward for the vacant chair?"' Noël went on to reminisce about 'their time':

One of the good things about the maligned sixties was that it was in those days that one could make what only a few years before would have been considered in stuffy old England as a controversial appointment . . . and how odd it must seem to you when you look back at the Thirties to see yourself as the 'Grand Old Man of English Letters'!

Alas, England was stuffy again. And there were fewer old men, grand or otherwise, every year. In 1987 John Lehmann died: almost all the stalwarts of the *Horizon–Penguin New Writing* axis were now with O'Leary in the grave.

Spender ended the year with a teaching stint at Storrs where, as he told Reynolds, 'I have friends':

It is the kind of job they make very easy – no courses, but just having to attend classes of other teachers three times a week. They pay $30,000 and I really cannot afford to refuse as I owe in tax – I've suddenly discovered – £15,000 . . . Then in December I go to Los Angeles to see David Hockney's and Jonathan Miller's *Tristan* also, of course, to see Bryan whom UCLA likes so much they actually seem on the point of offering him a job there – against precedents, after he has done his Ph.D.

The university duly made Obst a tenured professor, at the precocious age of thirty, and set him up with a research grant of $150,000. Stephen wrote, jubilantly, to Reynolds:

It is rather amazing how my very poor friends (you and Bryan when I first knew each of you – David Plante) seem to have justified themselves – quite beyond, of course, my faith I had from the first penniless student day, in them.

Spender was, however, alarmed early in the year to learn that Bryan Obst and his partner Bob, radicalized by the AIDS awareness movement, had been involved in a violent confrontation with the LAPD (not, at this date, notably sensitive to gay protest). Both were beaten up and ended in hospital, with charges (for *their* alleged assaults) pending.

Spender was meanwhile working on the testament of his own radical homosexual era, *The Temple*. He recalls in a preface how he rediscovered the work:

Two years ago [i.e. 1985], John Fuller (whom I now thank) told me that during a visit he had made to the United States he had read in the Rare Books section of the Harry Ransom Research Center at the University of Texas the manuscript of a novel by me. It was called *The Temple*, and was dated 1929. I wrote at once to the Librarian for a Xerox of this. A few weeks later, a young lady appeared at my London house with a bundle under her arm, which contained a copy of the novel. I had completely forgotten that in 1962, during some financial crisis of the kind to which poets are liable, I had sold the manuscript to Texas.

Spender's agent, Ed Victor, encouraged him to rewrite the text with a 'double perspective': that of youth and age. As revised in the late 1980s, *The Temple* opens with an 'English Prelude' in which the hero, Paul Schoner, falls in love (at first sight, across the 'Univ' quad) with a fellow undergraduate, Marston. He composes poems for this hearty 'helmeted airman' (Freeman was a member of the university flying club). His love is not reciprocated. Paul meanwhile has come under the influence of the charismatic and eccentric poet Simon Wilmot (transparently Wystan) and Wilmot's friend, the 'novelist of tomorrow', William Bradshaw (Isherwood). In Simon's rooms at Peck, they persuade him that 'Germany's the only place for sex. England's no good.' This after the friendly intervention of the dean of New College, Dr Close (John Maud), who introduces him to Stockmann (Alport). The Hamburg visit (of 1929) ensues and with it Paul's new life as exile and poet. The volume ends with a reprinting of the poem 'In 1929'.

Even after the liberating legislation of 1967, publishing *The Temple*, with its frank descriptions of gay sex, represented a risk. Old prejudices die hard. And Spender was concerned that the candour of some of its scenes might cause some embarrassment to his family. He showed the proofs to Noël Annan, asking his advice. His friend, worldly as ever, replied with an unequivocal *nihil obstat*:

Your novel is marvellously authentic . . . Open, easy, free homosexual love between friends was, I suppose, not to be had in England in the twenties . . . What you describe in Germany is different. The conversations ring with truth . . . You obviously did not want Natasha to know when you gave me the book. I hope she is not unhappy about it. She shouldn't be. Those years are an essential part of you, long before you knew her, and they are part of the Stephen we all know and love. It shouldn't be suppressed.

In fact Spender and Natasha had already discussed the book (which she had read). She approved of its publication.

Other friends joined in praise of *The Temple*, and its openness about the complex sexual, social and political acts of rebellion that went into the making of a 1930s poet. Ackroyd pronounced 'the closing sequence and the poem that followed ['1929'] . . . are art of a high order'. Ted Hughes wrote to say he had read the novel in two sittings and concurred that 'the book is in some fashion a poem'. Spender appreciated the poet's compliment but felt that one day he must write a novel 'in which there is no Stephen'. *The Temple* was respectfully reviewed and sold through three reprintings – at home and abroad. On 27 June 1989, Spender wrote gleefully to Alan Ross:

no £50,000 advances for octogenarian writers, their life prospects being so futureless . . . Never mind. I just heard that the French edition of *Le Temple* sold 5,000 copies on the strength of the photograph of the boy on the cover – 'le plaisir sans risque de CEDA' (the French for Aids).

Spender was, over the early part of the year, preoccupied with his new verse play, *Creon*. It drew, as he told Ted Hughes, 'a good deal on my Oedipus trilogy but really re-doing the whole thing'. When finished

the play was going to be put on at the Haymarket, Leicester (John Dexter
directing), in spring. Then, to Spender's amazement, the company was
engaged to tour India later in the year, alternating his play with *Julius
Caesar*. His Creon, Spender told Ted Hughes, was a 'very politic villain':
more Cassius than Brutus.

The attacks on Hughes as a wife-, mistress- and child-murderer were
unrelenting. On 14 March Spender wrote, in sympathy:

Whenever I read things in the press about terribly painful things in your past
– my heart does go out to you. I am filled with disgust at the way people drag
you through this – disgust tempered by the feeling that they are ignorant,
unimaginative and above all, it seems, dangerously self-righteous and what the
Americans call judgemental. They don't seem at all to understand how difficult it is to live a positive and creative life as you do – not to realize that the
dead should not plague the living. Anyway I marvel always at your tremendous
courage and at the wide range of your activity which in my experience of it
has always been most generous and beneficial.

At Easter Spender and Matthew had undertaken the last of their
'honeymoons', after an exhibition of the young Spender's art in London
(he was immensely encouraged by Francis Bacon's approvingly buying
a bas-relief). Venice was this year so overrun with Japanese tourists they
resolved to go to the north of Italy and browse among the region's
Palladian architecture. But the weather turned bad, Spender found the
buildings hard work, so they cut the tour short and took themselves,
less high-mindedly, to Torri del Benaco – the fishing town on Lake
Garda where Matthew, thirty-seven years earlier, had first learned to love
Italy. They managed to find accommodation at their old hostelry, the
Gardesano – but a convention of gynaecologists forced them to share a
double room. Matthew met some of his childhood comrades of the
sword (one of them, Ugetto, he recognized from behind, walking down
the street, much to the middle-aged Italian's amazement). Three or four
times on this last trip Spender confided uneasily to his son, 'I don't want
to outlive my mind.' He did not, he affirmed, believe in an afterlife.

The Spenders spent (a hot) July in France where Natasha was beginning to lay down her garden. A new well, 109 metres deep, enabled her
to create an English oasis in Provence. Diviners had helped locate the
water (Iris Murdoch, no less, had helped divine an earlier source under
the arid soil). Over the autumn Spender and Natasha followed *Creon* on

its nine-week British Council-sponsored theatrical tour through the subcontinent. Literally an Indian summer. The play opened in Delhi, with Indira Gandhi in the audience. The Spenders followed it for six weeks around India. On one glorious leg of the journey, a holiday break, they travelled on a Maharajah's train – known as a 'palace on wheels' and 'very, very uncomfortable'.

Spender had two celebrations for his eightieth birthday, on 28 February 1989. The smaller was thrown by the children, the larger by Faber (who were, he felt, 'doing him proud'). The formal occasion, hosted by the publisher, took place at the Ivy. Stuart Hampshire had undertaken to make the celebratory speech. Before this could happen Anne Cox Chambers, sitting alongside Spender, noticed that he looked faint and suggested he sit outside in the air for a minute or so. He then collapsed. His initial reaction, on regaining consciousness, was that he had been summoned to some heavenly press conference – surrounded, as he later told Jeremy Treglown (editor of the *TLS*), 'by all those important literary people'. These immortals were soon replaced by two paramedics, one of whom (having ascertained the party's name) asked him: 'D'ya know where ya live, Steve?' ('Of course I do,' he replied testily.) He was taken off, with Natasha by his side, to University College Hospital. Hampshire gave the speech with the guest of honour absent and his friends nervously wondering how he was. These episodes were happening more frequently and caused Natasha (and his physicians) increasing concern.

On 5 March 1989 Spender wrote jauntily to Mary McCarthy, who had come to London for his Faber party. 'Being 80 was a great success,' he asserted, despite his mishap at the Ivy. He was:

too old to be envied, still alive to silence doubting whispers. Not yet dead enough for all too truthful obituaries written by jealous rivals in mid-life – all waiting for *the day* like time bombs. Still litigiously alive to stop biographies.

In May Spender threw his weight and prestige into the Aids Crisis Trust, an organization devised by Marguerite Littman. ACT had been founded in June 1987, with Elizabeth Taylor as its patron. It was launched with much fanfare and an auction of charitably donated gifts at Christie's which raised a monumental £250,000. 'Crisis' was no overstatement. Spender knew the havoc the epidemic was causing – particularly among America's youngest and brightest men. Spender had the idea for a book called *Hockney's Alphabet* to raise more money for the trust. Twenty-six poets and writers would create short compositions on each of the letters of the English alphabet. The resulting book would be illustrated by David Hockney and published (gratis) by Faber. Spender recruited Hughes to do 'S'. Others whom he prevailed on to contribute (free of charge) were Iris Murdoch, Norman Mailer, William Boyd, Doris Lessing, Arthur Miller, Anthony Burgess, Seamus Heaney and William Golding.

Spender was fit enough to give the centenary address for Robert Browning at Westminster Abbey on 19 December. None the less at this period and over the next few years his health began to fail in ways that his friends and family could not but notice. An intermittently heavy smoker in early life, he had long since given up the weed (although his and Eliot's poems on the joys of the cigarette were still on display at Loudoun Road). He no longer needed nicotine and vast supplies of coffee to write his poetry. Since 1980, he had not been able to walk as vigorously as he had in his younger days (his major form of exercise). The distant trauma of his childhood rheumatic fever had weakened his heart and was catching up with him. He was frequently faint and breathless nowadays. In 1983 he had radiotherapy (successful) for skin cancer. In Spender's last years he and Natasha would spend longer and more relaxed periods at Mas de St Jerome – ideally Easter to June; 'Stephen didn't like the *grande chaleur* of high summer,' his wife recalls. '*Still* ninety degrees,' he would inscribe, irritatedly, in the Mas de St Jerome log book, during hot spells.

The 1990s: 'Five years he shouldn't have had'

Stephen Spender's doctor consoled his widow with the words that her husband, thanks to her, 'had five years he shouldn't have had'. Despite injury and illness, they were happy years, marked by terminal mileposts: a golden wedding, a recent eightieth birthday, his daughter's wedding, honorary awards (typically for his work for fellow writers), the publication of a final and well-received volume of new poems. There were less welcome commemorations of his long life. He and Natasha (on his behalf) were vexed by intrusions from a succession of biographers, journalists and writers of romans-à-clef. There was, until his last hours, the familiar spite directed against him. Increasingly, too, he wondered about what literary legacy he would leave; specifically how posterity would judge his poetry. He died, as he wanted to, at home; among his family; 'suddenly'. The memorial service confirmed something he had always half-doubted, the esteem in which he was held – most of all by his fellow-writers.

On 15 February 1990 Don Bachardy wrote from California to say that Bryan Obst and his partner Bob were having 'problems'. Bryan was ill and cutting himself off from friends. He was, in fact, dying. As usual with this disease, it was a protracted business – the more wretched since Bryan was barely thirty years old and with a good career ahead of him. In his journal Spender later speculated that 'he got Aids because he identified with Aids'. Obst held on until autumn 1991. A memorial service was held at the Ornithological Institute of the University of Southern California. Bachardy attended. A medley of bird songs was played, in lieu of hymns. Spender could not attend. But he wrote a number of elegiac poems. The death of this young friend touched him as much as any, since Lolly. Obst's death made old friends even more important. On 29 May, Isaiah Berlin wrote to say:

Do write me or telephone me: we are both of a certain age, I can't wait too long, we must meet as frequently as possible, instead of being like that old gentleman who received a letter from an old friend and replied, 'I am so glad you are still alive, I rather thought we were both dead.'

Domestically the big event of 1990 for the Spenders was the marriage of Lizzie in July to the Australian stage performer Barry Humphries (known to the world as 'Edna Everage' and 'Sir Les Patterson'; less well known as a scholarly connoisseur of literature of the 1890s). Suitor and prospective father-in-law became fast friends. They all four holidayed together in Portugal, where Stephen revisited, after half a century, Cintra. Both men were amateur painters and lovers of classical music ('he was, after all, *German*', Humphries recalls). The younger man was amazed at how hard, in his eighties, his father-in-law worked. Among other friendly acts, the dandyish Humphries took it on himself to improve Spender's appearance (there was one glitch when the measurements sent to the Hong Kong tailor were mistranscribed as centimetres, not inches: Stephen emerged from his bedroom wearing what looked like Bermuda shorts. His smile, Humphries recalls, was serenely self-mocking). The bridegroom had, courteously, asked Stephen for permission to marry his daughter. It was as courteously granted. It would be a spectacular ceremony at Spoleto. Gian Carlo Menotti had given the couple his house in the town for the occasion and Humphries took over a whole hotel for the wedding guests. Menotti arranged a musical epithalamion.

The wedding coincided with a crisis in Spender's health. He collapsed at Mas de St Jerome shortly before the day of the ceremony. Natasha was unwilling to leave her sick husband. On the other hand, if neither parent were there it would blight the occasion for Lizzie. Stephen was adamant that the ceremony must not be postponed. Their neighbour in Maussane, Anne Cox Chambers, loaned her private plane to enable Natasha to make what was effectively a day trip to Spoleto. She left Provence in the morning and came back that evening (as Spender had prophetically said, seven years before, Anne was the most 'helpful' rich person he had ever met). Menotti stood in for Spender and gave Lizzie away.

It would be Spender's most serious health crisis since 1980. The symptoms were those of hernia and acute breathlessness. The local English doctor wrongly (and amazingly) diagnosed hay fever; something which could be rectified by bed rest and closed windows. Natasha consulted the French village doctor, who correctly perceived that the problem was Spender's chronically weakened heart and called in a cardiovascular expert from Arles. His prompt treatment, Natasha believed, saved her husband's life. It was, however, six weeks before he was strong enough to return to England. Spender survived this ordeal. Others of his friends did not survive. Rosamond Lehmann, Leonard Bernstein and A. J. P. Taylor all died in 1990.

Nineteen ninety-one was the year of Natasha's and Spender's golden wedding anniversary. Barry Humphries put together a 'Garland' of privately printed verses by distinguished poets. They included those like Ted Hughes whom Spender knew well and some well-wishing poets like Pete Morgan of whom he had never heard – but whose fraternal poetic tributes he was grateful to receive. The couple spent April to July at Mas de St Jerome. Stephen was still recovering his health. For the day of their anniversary, 10 April, Natasha bought a huge salmon trout for lunch in Tarascon market. That evening, with Anne Cox Chambers, they celebrated fifty years of love and companionship.

Aged eighty-two, Spender tired more easily nowadays and watched more TV than he ever had before. He wrote to Alan Ross on 6 February

1991, opening with one of their standing jokes about horses (Ross owned a racehorse and loved the turf: Spender liked to jest, 'I am my own race-horse,' with jokes about flogging dead quadrupeds):

One of my horses is a new crime series on the BBC called SPENDER which is the name of a detective. He seems to spend most of his time watching youths who turn out to be drug addicts, pee in men's rooms where they do most of their illicit business. He gets his kicks out of arresting them. It is quite well written and funny to those who share his name.

Angus Wilson died on 31 May. The Spenders had been closely involved with their friend's last years. In May 1985 they had loaned Angus and his loyal companion, Tony Garrett, Mas de St Jerome, thinking they were merely scouting the area. The Spenders were astonished to learn that the other couple (Wilson was by now seventy and ailing) had impulsively gone and bought a sixth-floor apartment in nearby St Rémy. After a promising start, the 'French Experiment' proved disastrous. Angus's physical and mental health broke down, as did his source of income. His derangements had their occasional comic side: on one occasion in France he solemnly complimented Stephen on his perfect command of Dutch. Angus's friends discovered that the Code Napoléon meant that Tony could not inherit the French property when Angus died. The wholly disoriented man was eventually carried back to a nursing home, at Pinford End, in Suffolk. Spender and Natasha visited him there.

Over the years Spender had been in intermittent correspondence with the poet and translator Michael Hamburger. The two men had met in Oxford, in 1942, when Hamburger was a student. Stephen had helped him through various crises and had himself been helped in his translations from the German (in 1951 the two men had embarked on a translation of Hoffmansthal's works, which eventually came to nothing). In the seventy or so surviving letters to Hamburger the older poet often writes about the condition of poetry. On 4 July 1991 he told Hamburger (smarting from being reviewed, as usual, as 'a non-English German construct'): 'the English poets form a quiet little mutual back-biting club'. The American poetry scene, by contrast, was dominated by 'paranoid megalomaniacs'. Spender saw himself, as usual, between these two worlds.

The great business of the summer and autumn was gathering in the contributions for *Hockney's Alphabet* and seeing the venture through the press. It was worryingly delayed (the editors had originally hoped to publish in autumn 1989). Contributors had to be bullied – the more difficult since they were some of the most eminent literary people of the age. Ted Hughes was among the laggards and Spender pestered him good-naturedly but unrelentingly. The Laureate, he jovially suggested, should look on the task as being like the commemoration of a '200-pound royal baby'. Ted Hughes eventually came out with a 'sinuous' S-poem. Faber and Spender arranged for de luxe printings of the book. There would be 350 autographed copies, to be sold at £1,000 apiece. Other volumes (signed by Hockney and Spender) would go for £250 – a snip for the well-heeled philanthropist. 'All the angels of light are needed now,' Spender told Ted Hughes. The volume was eventually printed in June. There was a black-tie Royal Gala Reception and Dinner (addressed by Elizabeth Taylor) on 6 November 1991 at the Banqueting House, Whitehall. Dignitaries attended *en masse*, as did many of the contributors, from Douglas Adams to Gore Vidal. Princess Margaret, the guest of honour, 'smoked throughout like a chimney'. It was, after all, an event to raise money for AIDS, not emphysema.

Nineteen ninety-two saw the climax of Spender's battles with his most pertinacious would-be biographer, Hugh David, whose *Spender: A Portrait with Background* came out this year with Heinemann. The background to the book was tangled. In November 1989, Spender had granted David (at the young writer's request) an interview. He was always forthcoming about such things. Spender understood that David was intending to write 'a general book about the thirties' and that it would be generally sympathetic to writers of the period (if not, necessarily, to himself). He had no recollection of having met his interviewer before (he had, in fact, in November 1974).

Spender was astonished on 25 February 1990 to read in the *Sunday Times* the announcement that Heinemann had commissioned what they called an 'authorized' biography of Sir Stephen Spender. The authorization had allegedly been given on the grounds that David 'was an ex-student of mine when I was professor at UCL'. No record of David's being registered at the college could be found (nor could anyone in the department remember him) and Spender firmly denied that he had ever given any such sanction to a biography.

Two days later, on 27 February, David's editor at Heinemann, Tom Weldon, sent Spender a copy of their author's proposal and outline.

Spender was appalled by its errors and the aspersions on his private life. He strongly advised the publisher to proceed no further. His anger was not mollified by a letter from David on 28 February arguing that 'unwittingly' Spender had given him permission. Of course, David assured his subject, he had 'no interest in muckraking'. Frank Kermode, who was shown the proposal, wrote to the publisher to deplore David's projected book and discourage its publication.

On 8 March Weldon replied, insisting that Heinemann's intention was not 'to taint [Spender's] reputation'. In the face of Spender's objections, David – it was now understood – had agreed to reform his approach and write a book about the period. That is, the 1930s book which Spender had originally understood the author intended to write. In view of the errors he had already seen, he remained suspicious of the author's accuracy and, on 13 March, refused David permission to quote from his published or unpublished sources. Spender understood that this would, effectively, suppress the project, which had already caused him much irritation.

There ensued a year and a half's silence. Then, in August 1992, Alan Ross (editor of the *London Magazine*) informed Spender that David's 'biography' was advertised for publication in Heinemann's autumn list. The publisher refused to let Spender or his solicitor see an early copy. Weldon was quoted in the press as saying, 'Why should I? We gave Spender numerous opportunities to have his say while the book was being written and he refused.' Spender contested this strenuously. Eventually, by means of a complaint to Reed International, Heinemann's parent company, Spender did, on the eve of publication, get sight of the 'portrait' of himself that was about to go on general sale.

He was outraged by what he read. The book was blemished with even more errors of fact than the proposal. David wrote from the general standpoint that Stephen Spender had been a lifelong traitor to the gay community. He was a snob. He was chronically spineless. Spender was inured to slanders against himself. But, in addition to its wrongness and inaccuracy, the book was, its subject felt, appallingly written. He described the awfulness of its style to Ted Hughes, on 22 August:

The (so called) biography is amazingly spiteful and vicious: and vulgar: written in the tone of voice of a skivvy . . . there really is an underclass of people who envy and hate us all. His general thesis is that I have never in my whole life sought for anything (apart from sex) except self-advancement . . . the

book is vilely written by a miserable creature who wrote a book on Fitzrovia
– he is called Hugh David. Myself I do not mind . . . but Natasha suffers
terribly.

'Of course,' he added, 'all this is nothing in comparison with what you
have gone through, which is one of the horrors of our unthinkably
destructive age.'

Spender and Natasha prepared for limited circulation a pamphlet,
Errors of Fact and Misreadings of Texts, which they deposited at the copyright libraries, 'for consultation only'. Spender wrote an article of
complaint in the *Observer*. For some time Natasha had been concerned
about misrepresentation which other of their friends had suffered at the
hands of biographers and investigative journalists; particularly in cases
where they had themselves vouchsafed information or unguardedly given
interviews. She published an article ('Private and Public Lives') in the
TLS on 9 October. She protested against the current vogue for 'Watergate
style investigations'. Biographies like David's were a kind of 'blackmail'.
She suggested that biographers should be bound, like house agents, solicitors or dentists, by a 'professional code of practice'.

David's biography was published in October 1992 to scathing reviews.
Robert Nye's dismissal, in the *Scotsman*, was headlined uncompromisingly 'A Book to be Ashamed of'. Hilary Spurling in the *Telegraph*
compared David to a street mugger. His book was 'prurient, patronizing,
absurd, lopsided'. Peter Ackroyd slated it in *The Times*. In the *Observer*,
Julian Symons rubbished it as 'a farrago of nonsense'. In the *TLS*, Peter
Parker denounced David's lack of research, his meretricious style, and
his innumerable mistakes, misrepresentations and misjudgements. The
book, Parker concluded, was 'worthless'. It was left to Matthew to lighten
what had been a very black episode. 'Aren't you lucky, Dad,' he told
Spender, 'that your biographer is such an idiot? Hugh David is a godsend
really.'

On 27 November the Society of Authors (under its chairman, Anthony
Sampson, who had been 'disgusted' by David's book) took up Natasha's
suggestion about a code of practice for biography. Heinemann's chief
executive, Richard Charkin, defended his firm and his author vigorously.
They had, Charkin pointed out, published Ian Hamilton's *In Search of
J. D. Salinger* (in the face of the American novelist's lawsuits) and Peter
Ackroyd's life of Eliot (in the face of the estate's obduracy). 'It did not
seem to us,' a defiant Charkin declared, 'that concerted pressure from

the literary world nor (later) press vilification of our author was sufficient reason to withdraw from our agreement with him.'

Spender and Ted Hughes continued the struggle. On 17 December,
Hughes suggested that the best remedy would be massed protest by
writers, so as to exert 'pack pressure on any publisher who did what
Heinemann did'. Fifty or so determined writers could, he thought, 'form
an effective superego for the literary world'. They only needed forty-
eight more. The Society of Authors continued discussions well into the
next year, but eventually the 'code of practice' proposal came to nothing.

The Hugh David business had impeded Spender's two works in
progress: the novel *Miss Pangbourne* (Miss Winifred Paine, that was) and
what John Bodley (an editor at Faber and longstanding friend) called
the 'real' (that is, comprehensive not selective) 'Collected Poems'. Natasha
was convinced that the strain of combating David had affected her
husband's health. There were, unhappily, further trials of the same kind
to come. In America in early 1993 a young American novelist, David
Leavitt, who was making a name in the new category of gay writing,
published a novel called *While England Sleeps*. Reviewing the American
edition in the *Washington Post* in September, Bernard Knox (a professor
of classics who had been in Spain at the same time as Spender, during
the war), pointed out that large chunks of Leavitt's novel were impudently lifted from *World within World* (which Knox had reviewed in 1951).
More specifically, the novelist had constructed his narrative around the
seventeen pages in the memoir devoted to Spender's relationship with
Jimmy Younger/Tony Hyndman. Knox passed on his review and a copy
of the book to Spender. The British author was appalled by Leavitt's
invention of sex scenes of 'pornographic' crudity. Worse still, the novel
was 'idle, slovenly, *dishonest*'. Paul Johnson, who was sent a pre-publica-
tion copy, described *While England Sleeps* as 'saturnine cannibalism'.

Leavitt's book was scheduled to be published in the UK by Penguin.
The novelist, when confronted with the accusation that he had filched
material from *World within World*, first denied that he had read Spender's
book then conceded some 'borrowing'. The American publishers, he
claimed (in a letter to the *Washington Post*), had forbidden him from
making the acknowledgement he first intended. Theft hardly described
it: in the *Guardian* (27 October 1993) Simon Tisdall called it 'book rape'.
Like other forms of rape, it was increasingly less tolerated in the 1990s.
World within World was not a work of fiction. Since 1988, British writers
had been granted what was loosely called a 'moral copyright' in their

work. This was seen, by the book trade, as a good test case for a new, and as yet legally undefined, category of literary ownership. It entailed something more extensive than the old 'Anglo-Saxon' idea that copyright inhered, essentially, in the work's 'form of words'. Moral copyright enlarged traditional property rights in creative material by asserting that the author could protect his ideas, his personal image and reputation, and – most importantly – his original intentions. Leavitt's treatment of *World within World* would have proved the perfect test case.

Faber (who now had the copyright of *World within World*) picked up the legal cost of opposing Leavitt, which ran into tens of thousands of pounds. They retained the services of the copyright lawyer Sam Sylvester. Affidavits were lodged in November 1993. Penguin initially indicated a wish to contest the matter, which seemed destined for the High Court of Justice, Chancery Division, where it would have made literary history.

Penguin agreed, in December 1994, by out-of-court settlement, to pay all legal costs and to pulp their edition. It would still have been possible to have pursued the case in court. The Spenders chose not to. Partly it was because his doctors and Natasha felt he would not be up to the physical ordeal; and partly because, having obliged Penguin to suppress the book, Spender was inclined to be magnanimous. Leavitt brought out a purged version of his novel (with a defiantly self-defensive foreword) in 1999.

Spender wrote a number of powerful articles, drawing on both the Hugh David and the David Leavitt experiences (and by implication the persecution visited on living friends like Hughes and dead friends like Eliot). In a piece for the *Evening Standard*, entitled 'Sex Secrets that Should Stay Private', he attacked the recent vogue for tell-all literary biographies. 'The idea that everything about oneself is destined to become public property is life-destroying,' he argued, 'to the extent that one's life is *one's own*, shared with a few others by the kind of respect which is another name for love.' Leavitt wrote an article for the *New York Times*, entitled provocatively, 'Did I Plagiarize his Life'. Spender retorted in the same newspaper with a piece entitled 'My Life is *Mine*, not David Leavitt's', making the point that it was the plagiarism of his work that he particularly objected to. Ted Hughes wrote congratulating him on his 'victory' over Leavitt but felt that these were 'hateful battlefields' on which a poet should not be forced to fight.

On 28 February 1994, Stephen Spender was eighty-five years old. A 'positively last appearance' party was thrown in his honour by Faber –

with whom his relationship reached back sixty years. 'The lyric poet of his generation' (as Eliot had called him) was, nowadays, beginning to feel out of it. On 8 March he wrote to the young novelist Alan Hollinghurst thanking him for a copy of his novel, *The Folding Star*. Spender wrote wryly about the energy of the current generation of British writers who chose to engage, as Hollinghurst did, with explicitly homosexual themes. The book was 'beautifully done', he said:

and gives very well the atmosphere of Bruges or wherever. I found it very difficult to understand the nature of the emotions involved in the relationships between the characters and how they could all be such sexual athletes – as though they were all football stars on one level of their lives. I think the difficulty in writing – or reading – about what people do in bed or in parks is that I (the reader, most readers?) have such limited standards of comparison with the sexual behaviour of other people. But I may be wrong and perhaps everyone knows what everyone does sexually nowadays.

In April, one of the 'Floridians', Tony Lombardy, wrote. He had not been told of Bryan Obst's death; he had, however, seen in print a poem of Stephen's which he guessed (correctly) was dedicated to Obst – 'Letter from an Ornithologist in Antarctica'. Spender wrote, elegiacally, about their dead friend, on 4 May:

I think it is quite true that I did change his life by making him like himself instead of being unhappy about himself. Also in a practical way of getting him out of teaching in that slum school on the Sewanee River, to UCLA where he did so marvellously. He became a very outgoing person, loved by all who worked with him. Incidentally, the poem you like, 'Letter from an Ornithologist' is almost word for word paraphrase of a letter from him.

The poem (subtitled 'Remembering SBO') was collected in *Dolphins*, Spender's last collection of verse, published by Faber in their spring 1994 list. It begins (in Obst's voice):

> Happy, you write, I am, happy to go alone
> On the cable chair from Palmer Station (where our base is)
> Across 'Hero Inlet' to 'Bonaparte Point'
> (Just a bare rock attached to a crumbling glacier!)
> Where at night I fumble stones for baby petrels

Until the cold has made my fingers freeze –
And I cannot tell the chicks apart from stones
Nor feel the cable well for my return.

On 14 April, the Spenders travelled to Florence, with Ed and Carol
Victor, to promote the Italian translation of *Dolphins*. David Leavitt (resident in the city on a fellowship in Italy) protested, vainly, to the British
Council at the visit of the suppressor of his book. After his PR duties
Stephen, serenely visiting the Bargello, recalled being at the museum
with his friend, William Plomer, in 1929. Such recollections were, increasingly, a source of joy to him. He returned to England via Matthew and
Maro's home in Avane, Tuscany, where there was some family fence-
mending to be done. He was 'very tired'. But he was stimulated enough
by the Italian trip to contemplate writing a new stage version of *Trial
of a Judge*, 'my best failure' – a typically Spenderian assessment. Matthew
drove his father to Rome and arranged the awkward business of wheel-
chairs, tips and embarkation at the airport. Remembering his son's
'sweetness', two days after his return on 21 April, Spender was moved
to tears.

He and Natasha spent the next few months in Mas de St Jerome. On
the first night their sleep was disturbed by three wild boars rooting in
the garden. Natasha at first thought it was 'Stephen snoring' – something that amused him next morning. Their French home had, in these
last years, become as dear to them as St John's Wood. Gardening was,
for Natasha, not merely the 'greatest pleasure in life', Stephen observed,
'but life itself'.

He settled down to the quiet Provençal rhythms, reading Gibbon,
writing poetry, reviewing the odd book, visiting or being visited. There
were, however, worrying health problems. He was increasingly troubled
by 'blackouts'. The term was not entirely accurate, since during these
episodes 'everything seems a kind of brilliant white'. They occurred regularly when he was being driven by car in bright sunlight and left memory
lapses in their wake. Fibrositis in his shoulder broke up his sleep at night
and, as he observed, 'I am notably more tired than I ever used to be.
Having a bath I sometimes feel I'll never be able to get out of it.' There
were other worries. Following various changes in tenancy law, the Eyre
Estate had doubled the rent on Loudoun Road. The couple had a grim,
but necessary, conversation about Natasha's finances 'if I die'.

Dolphins was very well received: by reviewers and by friends. Friends and family could, perhaps, understand the poems best. Many of them have private reference: most strikingly 'Her House', which opens:

> The city left behind them, they drove on
> Past factories, suburbs, farms.
>   She saw
> Suddenly, from a hill, the coast
> Outlined by surf, and rocks that seemed
> The shadows of the surf.
>   'My house!' she cried,
> Pointing in triumph where it stood
> High on a cliff above a bay.

The poem is based on something told him by Natasha long after the event. She had a vivid dream in early summer 1964, a couple of months before being diagnosed with cancer and at a period when she was (consciously) unaware of any problem with her health. In the dream she was driving with a friend, looking for a house. She recalled turning to her companion and saying: 'This is ridiculous, I have a beautiful house in England' (the Spenders had just bought Mas de St Jerome). The two women then found themselves outside a large building which Natasha 'half recognized' as a Leonard Cheshire home for the incurably ill. They were met by a man in a white coat who told them that the house was full up with patients. To which Natasha replied: 'Don't worry. I'll go and ask the borough council if I can live in a corner of it.' According to Natasha the premonition 'slightly infuriated me later, because I don't believe in the Freudian theory of dreams'.

The most substantial poems in *Dolphins* are 'A First War Childhood' and 'Worldsworth'. They deal with two of the primal experiences of Stephen's boyhood: the Zeppelin raid over Sheringham in 1916 and the family holiday in the Lake District the following year. They are small relics of the long autobiographical poem on which he had been working (but never completing) for thirty years. Ted Hughes thought 'Worldsworth' 'a clean, precise, concentrated evocation; in glassy miniature. Each precise particular like a rosary for remembering . . . Imagine a whole biography done like that!' That was precisely what Spender had once imagined. The poems are written in distilled form: unrhymed, imperfect lines composed mainly of monosyllables, varying in length from quadrisyllabic to octosyllabic:

> March 1916,
> The middle of a war
> – One night long
> As all my life –
> A child, I lay awake
> On my bed under
> The slant ceiling
> Of the attic of The Bluff,
> Our parents' house
> On the Norfolk coast.

Writing in the *TLS*, Julian Symons saluted Spender's 'ruthless' honesty and asked:

Who else would have cared to reprint between book covers forty years after the event the article he wrote for the *Daily Worker* on joining the Communist Party in 1937, with its general acceptance that the Party line was sacred and its belief in the official version at the first of the Moscow trials of dissidents? What other writer would, in 1951, have dared to write with candour about his earlier homosexuality, as Spender did in his memorable *World within World*?

He was, Symons concluded, 'an underrated poet'. Less seriously, but correctly, Fiona Pitt-Kethley observed that

as you read his poems, it is difficult to guess the age of the man behind; only the events covered give any inkling of this. *Dolphins* is the work of a man who is still developing, who still has much to say . . . he would have made a good poet laureate.

Too late now, alas, however young his poems sounded.

The Spenders spent the early summer, from May onwards, in Mas de St Jerome, where Stephen read Reynolds Price's invalid's testament, *A Whole New Life*. Reynolds's book was, Stephen thought, 'a masterpiece' (oddly enough it was a passion for Dante's *Vita Nuova* which had brought them together, in 1957). Spender had brought his own writing projects with him to France: *Miss Pangbourne* and *Trial of a Judge*. He also intended to write some new poems. Revisiting his novel-in-progress about Winifred Paine, he realized that it was, in fact, less about her than about his father, Harold.

The routine in Provence was as before. Stephen used the long hours of leisure to revisit his favourite classics (this year *Clarissa, Le Rouge et le Noir* and *The Brothers Karamazov*). Natasha gardened. They visited old friends in the area (notably the 'spirited millionairess' Anne Cox Chambers). On 24 May Rosamond Russell phoned from New York to say Jacqueline Onassis was dying. 'Although I only met her two or three times,' Stephen recorded in his diary, 'I lay awake praying for her.' He felt nowadays a kind of 'envy for the dead', whom he fancifully saw as occupying an 'upper house' while he was still in junior school.

The Spenders returned to England in early June – in time to see *The Rake's Progress* at Glyndebourne. The heat, even in England, bothered Stephen and brought on occasional fainting. He recorded, on 15 July, the 'rather depressing feeling at the end of my life – that I really have not done anything'. Had poetry been a 'false call'? He was, he concluded, 'depressed by my (comparatively speaking) lack of recognition'. Things looked up in late July with the arrival of Reynolds Price. He was appearing at the Festival Hall, for a 'Festival of American Southern Writers'. He arrived at Loudoun Road to be carried in his wheelchair to the garden. Stephen was moved by what he guessed (correctly) would be their last meeting.

While they holidayed in Italy, with Matthew and Maro, in August, a questionnaire (directed to the great and good) arrived from the *Guardian*. Father and son filled in the queries light-heartedly after lunch. 'What would you like to be remembered for?' the paper solemnly inquired. 'For loving my family and friends,' the poet replied. 'How would you like to die?' he was asked. 'Suddenly,' quipped Spender. Matthew held on to the document.

In October Spender visited America for a poetry reading, to coincide with the publication there of *Dolphins*. Since his collapse in France, in 1990, he always travelled with a doctor's letter on his person. It proved necessary when in New York, on his last evening in November, he slipped getting out of the taxi in 58th Street, on his way to a farewell meal with Earl and Camilla McGrath and Barbara Epstein. He blamed the 'particularly slippy rubber-soled shoes' he was wearing. It was raining. While they waited for the ambulance, McGrath got a chair and a glass of wine for him from the restaurant. Natasha held an umbrella over his head. Passers-by cheerily wished him good evening. An eminent English poet sitting in the drizzle on the sidewalk caused no stir – at least, not in Manhattan. Barbara Epstein called her physician, Stanley Mirsky, who correctly diagnosed the injury over the phone, gave first-aid instructions, and dispatched an ambulance (they were, initially, unwilling to go until Mirsky described Spender as a 'world-famous poet'). Meanwhile, Epstein recalls, he sat there quite serenely, 'like a god'. Or, perhaps, a world-famous poet.

Pavements were unlucky for him. This time he broke his hip. He was carried off to hospital in great pain. He passed out in the orthopaedic ward after an MRI and was transferred to Cardiology where, for a few minutes, his heart stopped. A pacemaker was subsequently installed as well as a 'new hip'. Matthew rushed to his bedside, as did Brodsky. The Russian (now a Nobel laureate) 'was marvellous'. 'Stephen is my family,' he told Matthew. Brodsky had himself survived three heart attacks, a bypass, and still over-indulged, heroically, in coffee, cigarettes and liquor. 'Your father's going to die,' he told Matthew, 'but it's irrelevant.' What he meant was that love mattered, not the count of years.

Stephen was heavily 'doped'. A routine was established around his hospital bed of which he was often only half conscious. Natasha took the 'morning shift' and retreated afterwards to a corner of the room. Brodsky would come (or telephone) and talk to him in the afternoon, when he was liveliest – about nineteenth-century fiction, poetry, Wystan, or literary gossip of the town. Matthew was meanwhile doing research in New York on the biography of his father-in-law, the artist Arshile Gorky. In the evening he would take over the family watch, and recount to his father what he had turned up that day until the patient 'flaked out and fell asleep'.

Spender was insured with BUPA for his hip operation and the installation of a pacemaker. But he was not covered for a private room. He detested sharing his sick quarters; more so since he was placed in a ward with a man who talked 'incessantly' about his heart attack. Friends (notably Drue Heinz) helped in getting him the privacy he needed for a quick recovery. Getting him back on his feet was, however, difficult. He had to be taught to walk again, as in 1990. But now he was weaker, and his heart was manifestly failing.

The British insurance company were at times less helpful than they might have been, and this added to the strain. None the less they provided first-class passage and a physician to accompany him on the plane – the aptly named Dr Angel, as Spender was delighted to discover. He had become, he ruefully noted, a 'package', to be posted home. This departure from JFK on 29 November would be his farewell to America – the country which, for almost fifty years, had been a second home. On arrival at his London home, Spender was so overcome that he burst into tears. Matthew set up a bed in the downstairs study at Loudoun Road. Sculptor that he was, he used his hammer to put in hand rails at strategic points. Spender would, in fact, be housebound if not entirely bedridden for a few weeks. Lizzie and Barry bought him a TV. There was a CD player in the room, a computer (which he had been using for some years), and many of his books. 'My capacity for being completely passive, letting things just happen to me pays off very well,' he noted in his journal. He recovered sufficiently to walk, but after a few steps was breathless. Dr Jarman gave him 'three months or six months' until recovery. 'I secretly resolved to make it three,' Spender wrote.

Mas de St Jerome was too far and too difficult a journey to contemplate in the near future. He seemed none the less, wrote John Bayley, to be somehow 'younger' in his terminal illness. As often happens, the child (the backward son, as he would say) protruded through the skin of the old man. Throughout 1994 he was still writing the odd piece for the journals. He did, for example, an article ('Silence Falls') for the relaunch of *Index*, a review (favourable) of Thom Gunn's collected poems for the *Spectator*. Late in the year he reviewed Kate Bucknell's edition of Auden's *Juvenilia* for the same journal. 'Somehow', he felt, this volume 'misses out the fun'. This was his last serious venture into higher journalism. There is a pleasing symmetry in the fact that his own (juvenile) foray into paid London journalism had been in the pages of the *Spectator*, sixty-five years before.

Gradually, in early 1995, Spender recovered – not to full health but back from the brink of death. In early February he recorded a month of 'bad nights'. But he was able to attend parties again, 'if I sit through them'. He visited the Poussin exhibition at the Royal Academy in a wheelchair. He should, perhaps, have stayed at home. Even at this venerable stage of his career, he remained a target for smart-young-men's barbs. In the *Spectator* Philip Hensher took it on himself to inform the magazine's readers that 'Spender, still among London's most desirable guests, has always been elevated by the company he keeps.' Stephen noted, stoically, in his journal: 'I feel people are already writing obituaries in which I am relegated to a position of inferiority to those friends. Well, that is not unjust.' It was unjust, but not worth the protest. What, he wondered, would he leave for posterity to admire? 'I don't want to be a writer of poems adding up to some total which is an *œuvre*. I want a few poems to survive and some memoir of *myself* as distinct from any group.'

During the early spring days he worked on *Miss Pangbourne*. Barry Humphries arranged to have it typed up by his secretary, as the manuscript came in. The novel was, Spender felt, the fruit of 'hard-won memories'. Composition, as always, was a restless business for him. But writing eased the 'panic' that sometimes consumed him. Always in his writing he had, he felt, sought for the 'beyond'. But now '"beyond" seems to mean only two things – the death of friends and my own death'. As he wrote about the past, Spender ruminated on his life: 'I definitely do enjoy living,' he concluded, 'only recently have I become conscious of myself as an old person or body.' The days passed easily, but he 'hated and dreaded the night'. Sleep was only possible with pills.

On 18 February a book about English Communism gave him nightmares about being back in Spain. On other occasions he dreamed, fitfully, about Obst and other dead friends (some of whom appeared mysteriously 'sexy'). The past was now as real as the present. In March he resolved to read the whole of Proust again. Not that the present could be entirely avoided. On 7 March he woke at three in the morning when 'it suddenly struck me, as though out of the blue, that we have very little money – only £350 from the *Sunday Telegraph* for reviewing Ted Hughes'.

On 9 March, Spender wrote to Tony Lombardy that 'At the end of my life I feel that my wife and children have been the greatest happiness to me. We have been extraordinarily lucky in having children.' Of their friend and fellow 'Floridian', Bryan Obst, he wrote: 'I still think of him every day of my life as though we are still sharing the same interests, the same jokes.' On 17 March, Stephen Spender was awarded a gold pen by PEN for his work, over the decades, for fellow writers. Three days later he went to dinner at the Isaiah Berlins, at the Albany, where he enjoyed conversation with James Fenton, 'a large slightly fleshy man, a good conversationalist'. They took to each other – it was the last important new friendship he would make. Spender toyed with the idea of sending Fenton (later a Professor of Poetry at Oxford) his poems: 'but it is probably too late to think of such things'. (Actually he and Fenton would, on 26 April, give a reading together on Shakespeare's birthday at the Tricycle Club, Kilburn; it was, Natasha recalls, one of the happiest public events of his last months.) On 10 March Spender's sleep was ruined on learning, from Matthew, that a revised edition of David Leavitt's novel was coming out in America. He was strong enough ten days later to attend a debate at the National Portrait Gallery on classical versus popular music. There was little question where his sentiments lay.

None the less he found David Bowie friendly and 'intelligent'. Spender was finding music nowadays 'a terrible devourer of time'. He had little of it to waste: even on Beethoven.

By the end of March Spender could hold his own at the Cranium Club and on 9 April he spent a convivial evening with Barry and Lizzie, celebrating their wedding anniversary. He was taking a constitutional walk, daily, around the square of streets surrounding Loudoun Road. Despite his access of energy, he and Natasha decided against France just yet. Apart from anything else, he thought, he could not write *Miss Pangbourne* there. He was engrossed in the book. His recollection of the past was, he observed, sounder than his short-term memory.

On 5 June he was in hospital again. His room overlooked Lord's cricket ground. It was 'wasted on you', Alan Ross said with mock bitterness (the editor of the *London Magazine* was passionate about the game). Stephen found the experience less stressful than last time. In bed he read Margaret Drabble's life of Angus Wilson. The long relationship between the novelist and his partner, Tony Garrett, was, he thought, 'a triumph of the homo-sexual get-together'. He was back in the last week of June. Matthew came over from Italy. It was, Stephen thought, a 'haunting' – like meeting his earlier self: Matthew looked so much like the young Stephen. In early July, a party was given in his honour by Drue Heinz at Berkeley Square. Many of his old friends attended. The last entry in his journal is for 6 July. It was a nagging worry – less for himself than for Natasha: 'the fact is I need about £10,000 a year more than my income of the same amount'.

Spender was, at last, given the all-clear from his doctors to go to Mas de St Jerome later in the summer. Karl Miller visited Loudoun Road on Friday 14 July, for tea. He found Stephen lucid and cheerful, 'but lacking his usual force, somehow'. The following day the Spenders went for an impromptu lunch with the Annans and some other friends. Spender was in good form. As he and Natasha got out of the car, he threw his walking stick on to the back seat with the remark, 'I don't need that any more.' At table the conversation turned to the recent film about Carrington. Spender had not seen it, but he was inspired to recall some good stories about Bloomsbury, including one about visiting Ham Spray that Natasha had never heard before (she phoned Frances Partridge the following day to check if the story were true; it was).

That Saturday evening there was to be a 'house cooling party' thrown by Margaret Drabble and Michael Holroyd. The two writers, though married, had lived and worked in separate domestic establishments for several years. They were now moving in together at his house in Notting Hill. The Spenders had intended to drive across London to attend. On the steps down from the front door at Loudoun Road, however, Stephen suddenly halted and told Natasha, 'I can't go.' They went back inside and he lay down on the chaise-longue in the front room study.

Although two parties in one day were too much for him, he did not regard himself as in any sense a housebound invalid. He was due to record a selection of his poetry for Penguin's CD series the following Monday. Two days later, on Wednesday, he was scheduled to go down and give a speech at Oxford, to commemorate the centenary of Robert Graves's birth. Although the *Observer* was not taken at Loudoun Road, Spender had written for it for years and still occasionally contributed. The issue for Sunday 16 July featured, in its magazine section, a lead review by Peter Conrad of *Between Friends* – a selection of correspondence between Hannah Arendt and Mary McCarthy. Both women had been friends of Spender. Conrad's review is particularly sharp about Spender. He wrote:

McCarthy's political interventions were stagier. After a trip to Hanoi [during the Vietnam War] she proposed a return visit with 'a delegation of notables', including Stephen Spender, who would serve as hostages to Nixon's bombers. The North Vietnamese unsurprisingly dismissed this nutty notion. McCarthy the novelist adored anecdotes, while Arendt the philosopher took a longer, loftier view. When Auden proposed to Arendt in drunken desperation McCarthy blamed Spender's pimping: 'It's typical of a homosexual, I mean Spender, to have been married for 20 years and to know so little about marriage.'

Thus the last words about Spender during his lifetime were a snide characterization of himself as a nut, a pimp, a homosexual, and a woefully imperceptive husband. The unfairness of it still has the power to jolt the reader.

On his desk this Sunday was the much scored-over manuscript of his Winifred Paine novel, *Miss Pangbourne*. He was also making notes for his lecture on Robert Graves from recent biographies of the poet, who had died in 1985. Natasha popped her head into his study around eleven o'clock. He was, Stephen told her, amazed at the 'childlike' aspect of Graves. The man seemed so 'gullible'. And then, he laughed. Perhaps, he slyly suggested, Graves's gullibility '*was all an act*'. These were his last recorded words.

An hour or so later, Natasha called up (the dining-room was in the basement) to say lunch was ready. There was no reply. She went upstairs and found him collapsed by the front door. By a terrible coincidence, the telephone at Loudoun Road chose this moment not to work. Having called 999 she could not get it out of its 'alarm mode' and back to a normal connection. The desperate woman was obliged to leave the body of her unconscious husband and rush into the street outside. Mrs Solomon (the pianist's widow) across the street tried to call Dr Jarman. Natasha tried to flag down passing cars. Most 'whizzed by'. Eventually a friendly young lady stopped and came in to help. She it was who finally summoned the emergency services on her mobile phone.

The ambulance took Stephen and Natasha to St Mary's, Paddington. He had suffered, the doctors reported, a massive heart attack and was probably beyond resuscitation when his wife found him. His pacemaker was still beating. Dr Jarman consoled Natasha, now a widow, by saying that 'he had five years he shouldn't have had' – and would not have had, but for her care. Natasha rang her son from the hospital.

Philip Spender (their nephew) was called and took her home. Matthew and Maro flew over from Italy that evening. A friend spent the night with Natasha. Lizzie was, that evening, attending a performance of Verdi's *Requiem* in the main square at Spoleto. Natasha told her to stay to hear it: 'It's a wonderful work,' she explained, 'it will help you.' Gian Carlo Menotti arranged for the performance to be dedicated to the memory of Stephen Spender.

Friends of many years came to the funeral later that week, on Friday 21 July. When he arrived at Heathrow on 20 July, the immigration official asked Joseph Brodsky: 'Business or pleasure?' 'What do you call a funeral?' the Russian smartly retorted. Natasha met him with the sad words: 'Of all the people he was the unlikeliest to die.' Brodsky couldn't eat. Only whisky helped him. He wrote up his impressions in his journal:

On account of my Russianness, Natasha arranges for me to see Stephen in an open coffin. He looks severe and settled for whatever it is ahead. I kiss him on his brow, saying, 'Thank you for everything. Say hello to Wystan and my parents. Farewell.' I remember his legs, in the hospital, protruding from the gown: bruised with burst blood vessels – exactly like my father's, who was older than Stephen by six years . . . Now Matthew screws the bolts into the coffin lid. He fights tears, but they are winning. One can't help him; nor do I think one should. This is a son's job.

Brodsky thought the funeral 'as beautiful as such an affair can be'. The St Mary's Paddington churchyard was sunlit, a Haydn and Schubert quartet were played. Stuart Hampshire gave the address. After the service there were drinks in the garden at Loudoun Road in the bright sun, 'the sky a solid blue slate'. Everyone agreed 'it was the end of an era'. The event, with its muted good form and restraint, struck the Russian as strange: 'The whole thing looks like a garden party. Perhaps this is the way the English keep their real sentiments in check.'

After the funeral, Isaiah Berlin (another Russian) apologized for not having written to Natasha. It was not that he did not feel – he felt too strongly. On 1 August Isaiah composed a long letter to his widowed friend. In it he said:

I cannot even now bring myself to realize that I shall not see him again. His face, his figure, his voice, haunt me, and will I expect haunt me till my dying day. I have never loved any friend more – nor respected, nor been happier to be his friend.

After he had returned to Italy, Matthew faxed his mother the question- naire he and Stephen had light-heartedly filled in the year before. 'How would you like to die?' 'Suddenly.' That wish had been fulfilled.

The obituaries were warm and appreciative – more so than much that had been written about him during his life. That originally drafted by Wystan, in *The Times*, would have meant most to him, had he been able to read it. There was a 'Service of Thanksgiving' on 20 March 1996 at St Martin's in the Fields, Trafalgar Square (Natasha thought this church was the 'right dimension'; the Abbey would have been too large). Matthew chose and read the lesson from Ecclesiastes. Harold Pinter read 'Worldsworth'. Richard Wollheim did the eulogy, saluting his friend as 'a champion of intellectual freedom'. Stephen had known many truly great men of his time. Ted Hughes (who had helped Natasha devise the literary part of the programme) read the well-known poem about the truly great. Other poems (including one of Stephen's elegies for Bryan Obst) were read by James Fenton, Jill Balcon and Barry Humphries. There was a Bach cantata sung by Emma Kirkby; the Sorrell Quartet played Beethoven and Haydn, which Stephen himself had indicated he wanted.

Spender's last publication (in life) came out in the *London Magazine* in July – a poem called 'Timothy Corsellis'. It begins:

No gift this Christmas, Timothy Corsellis,
– Transport Transatlantic pilot –
Could equal this, your poem that reached me
Here, but with news that you were dead –
Shot down or lost mid-ocean . . . drowned . . .

Spender gives the background to this cryptic elegy in *World within World*. Corsellis was a young Battle of Britain pilot whom he had met through *Horizon*. Corsellis had protested on being switched from fighters to bombers 'on the grounds that he wished only to fight against destruction, not to destroy'. He was punitively shifted to transport command, and died in a flying accident (like Michael). At a period when everything was changing in his life, Spender had spent a day with the young airman. 'All I remember of that day,' he recalls:

was meeting Corsellis in a bar off Piccadilly where he sat talking to a platinum blonde . . . Some years later I came upon a poem by him addressed to myself, in an anthology of war poets, in which he described our meeting. It concluded with the words: 'Now I see you much as I am.' I was moved by reading this, and I have in my notebooks numerous sketches for a poem in which I endeavoured to thank Corsellis. But I never succeeded in writing anything which seemed adequate.

Now, at last, he had.

Sources

STEPHEN SPENDER: PRINCIPAL WORKS

Nine Experiments, London, privately printed, 1928

Twenty Poems, Oxford, Blackwell, 1930

Poems, 1933, London, Faber, 1933

Vienna, London, Faber, 1934

The Destructive Element, London, Jonathan Cape, 1935

The Burning Cactus, London, Faber, 1936

Forward from Liberalism, London, Gollancz, 1937

Trial of a Judge, London, Faber, 1938

The Still Centre, London, Faber, 1939

The Backward Son, London, Hogarth, 1940

Ruins and Visions, London, Faber, 1942

Life and the Poet, London, Secker & Warburg, 1942

Spiritual Exercises, London, privately printed, 1943

Citizens in War – and After, London, Harrap, 1945

European Witness, London, Hamish Hamilton, 1946

Poems of Dedication, London, Faber, 1947

The Edge of Being, London, Faber, 1949

World within World, London, Hamish Hamilton, 1951

Learning Laughter, London, Weidenfeld & Nicolson, 1952

The Creative Element, London, Hamish Hamilton, 1953

Collected Poems, 1928–1953, London, Faber, 1955

The Making of a Poem, London, Hamish Hamilton, 1956

Engaged in Writing, London, Hamish Hamilton, 1958

The Struggle of the Modern, London, Hamish Hamilton, 1963

The Year of the Young Rebels, London, Weidenfeld and Nicolson, 1968

The Generous Days, London, Faber, 1971

Love-Hate Relations, London, Hamish Hamilton, 1974

Eliot, London, Fontana, 1975

W. H. Auden: A Tribute, London, Weidenfeld & Nicolson, 1975

The Thirties and After, New York, Random House, 1978

China Diary (with David Hockney), London, Thames & Hudson, 1982

Journals, 1939–1983, London, Faber, 1985

Collected Poems, 1928–1985, London, Faber, 1985
The Temple, London, Faber, 1988
Dolphins, London, Faber, 1994
Collected Poems, London, Faber, 2004

Details of works by other authors mentioned in the text can be found
in the Notes.

A Note on Primary Sources

There are three main deposits of Stephen Spender's literary remains. The
Stephen Spender Archive, currently administered by the author's estate,
contains the largest body of Spender's incoming and outgoing correspondence, literary manuscripts, business papers, photographs and various
ancillary materials (including the bulk of Stephen Spender's library). The
SSA is supplemented by the twenty-volume Xerox archive of Spender's
journalism and occasional writing (a second copy of this archive is
deposited in the British Library, with a searchable digitized catalogue).
Where not otherwise indicated in the notes, the location may be assumed
to be the SSA.

There are two other main deposits. The Bancroft Library at the
University of California, Berkeley, has the manuscripts of those journals
and diaries not held by the SSA (the Bancroft has most of them up to
the year 1984). The Bancroft also has many of the letters from other
authors to Spender (Edwin Muir, Herbert Read, Robert Graves, for
example). It also holds many of the author's working notebooks.

The Harry Ransom Research Center at the University of Texas,
Austin, has many of Spender's literary manuscripts and the bulk of his
business correspondence with his literary agents. The HRC also holds
the letters of John Lehmann.

Smaller collections are in the Berg Collection in the New York Public
Library (notably Spender's correspondence with Virginia Woolf and
material relating to the Group Theatre); Sussex University Library (which
has correspondence with Virginia and Leonard Woolf); Durham
University Library (which has William Plomer's papers); the Brotherton
Library at the University of Leeds (which has the Alan Ross and Michael
Hamburger correspondence with Spender); the Bodleian Library (which
has Spender's correspondence with Isaiah Berlin, with his grandmother

Hilda Schuster, and Philip Toynbee's unpublished diaries); University College London (which has Spender's correspondence with George Orwell); the McFarlin Library at the University of Oklahoma, Tulsa (which has Cyril Connolly's papers); the Henry E. Huntington Library (which has Christopher Isherwood's papers); the Woodson Center at Rice University (which has Julian Huxley's papers); Boston University Library (which has the *Encounter* archive); the University of Chicago Library (which has the Congress of Cultural Freedom papers); the University of Bristol Library (which has Spender's correspondence with the firm of Hamish Hamilton); the Archive of the British International Brigade Association (which has correspondence relating to Spender's activities on behalf of Tony Hyndman during the Spanish Civil War); Princeton University Library (which has those Lehmann family papers not in the HRC); the Sarah Lawrence College Library (which contains material relevant to Spender's teaching there and correspondence with Harold Taylor). Other collections of Spender's material (or material related to him) may be located through the National Register of Archives website.

Spender's correspondence with Faber (through his agent A. D. Peters) is available at the HRC. Northwestern University's Charles Deering McCormick Library has much of Spender's correspondence with T. S. Eliot. Spender's correspondence with Ted Hughes is held in Emory University's Woodruff Library.

The largest private collection of Stephen Spender's correspondence and literary papers is held by his friend of many years, Reynolds Price. It is deposited (under restriction) at Duke University Library. An important and remarkably interactive archive containing letters between all the principals in the break-up of Spender's first marriage with Inez Pearn is held in the archive of the Watkinson Library, Trinity College, Hartford. The owner is David Elliott, the son of Inez Spender's closest friend at the time.

Keith Walker and Tony Lombardy have private collections of their correspondence with Spender which they have kindly made available, as did Stephen's nephew Philip Spender. I am grateful for many helpful pieces of information and letters from, among others: Alan Hollinghurst, Jeremy Treglown, Gerard Boyce, Laurie Bates, and Paul Binding.

For the purpose of this biography interviews were conducted over the period 1998–2003. Humphrey and Christine Spender (whose accounts are drawn on heavily in the first sections of the narrative), Natasha Spender and her children, Matthew and Lizzie, and Lizzie's husband, Barry

Humphries, have supplied invaluable material. Other interviewees include: Frances Partridge, Alan Ross, Dan Jacobson, Elizabeth Longford, Janet Adam Smith, Stuart Hampshire, Reynolds Price, Gabriel Carritt, Don Bachardy, John Heath Stubbs, Anthony Sampson, John Craxton, Karl Miller, Frank Kermode, John Gross, David Sylvester, Sally Graves, Nancy Coldstream, Patrick Leigh Fermor, Sir John Margetson, Clissold Tuey, Gian Carlo Menotti, David Plante, Ed Mendelson, Edward Upward, David Gascoyne, Richard Felstead, Richard Wollheim, Patrick Woodcock, George Weidenfeld, Robert Silvers, Earl McGrath, Arthur Schlesinger, Jeremy Hutchinson, Barbara Epstein. Where recorded, tapes of the interviews have been deposited with the SSA.

Notes

The notes do not always directly identify the location of unpublished material. Anyone wanting this information (where I can supply it) is invited to apply to j.sutherland@ucl.ac.uk.

The following abbreviations are used in the endnotes.

BL	Bancroft Library
CI	Christopher Isherwood
CK	Christopher Isherwood, *Christopher and his Kind*, New York, 1976, repr. 1977
ES	Edith Sitwell
GC	Gabriel Carritt
HEH	Henry E. Huntington Library
HN	Harold Nicolson
HR	Herbert Read
HRC	Harry Ransom Research Center, University of Texas
HS	Hilda Schuster
IB	Isaiah Berlin
JFK	Frank Kermode
JL	John Lehmann
Jrnls	*Stephen Spender, Journals, 1939–1983*, ed. John Goldsmith, London, 1985, repr. 1992
LC	*Letters to Christopher*, ed. Lee Bartlett, Santa Barbara, California, 1980
MJ	Mike Josselson
NS	Natasha Spender
RP	Reynolds Price
SS	Stephen Spender
SSA	Stephen Spender Archive
TH	Ted Hughes
TSE	T.S. Eliot
VSW	Vita Sackville-West
WP	William Plomer
WWW	Stephen Spender, *World within World*, London, 1951

Ambitious Son, Failed Father: 1909–30

p. 8   *'A born hostess . . . devoted public worker'*: J. A. Spender, *Life, Journalism and Politics*, London, 1927, 2 vols, p. 3.

'*Writing came to us as naturally as walking*': E. H. Spender, *The Fire of Life*, London, 1926, p. 8.

'*For twenty years . . . a wide circle of friends*': J. A. Spender, *Life, Journalism and Politics*, p. 3.

'*the whole bent of his mind was literary*': ibid., p. 2.

p. 9   '*I wondered . . . set foot in Balliol again*': ibid., p. 16

p. 10   *if Harold had a fault it was 'impulsiveness'*: these comments are taken from newspaper reviews on Harold Spender's death in April 1926.

p. 11   '*Fleet Street . . . despised our degrees*': E. H. Spender, *The Fire of Life*, p. 18.

'*Passmore Edwards . . . we parted company*': ibid., p. 26.

pp. 12–13   '*we constantly met . . . or Italy*': from Smith's obituary on Spender in the *Daily Telegraph*, April 1926.

p. 14   '*I had no sleep for a week . . . from fourteen to twelve*': E. H. Spender, *The Fire of Life*, p. 77.

p. 16   '*practically sentenced . . . death from the start*': ibid., p. 110.

p. 17   '*That we [the children] . . . began to feel Jewish*': SS, *WWW*, p. 13.

The marriage settlement . . . eighteen pages: the document is in the possession of Philip Spender.

p. 18   '*My mother . . . like a minute church*': *WWW*, p. 2.

p. 19   '*We don't want politicians . . . who really know the poor*': Harold Spender, *The Arena*, London, 1906, p. 52.

'*These were the great days . . . the smoky underground*': E. H. Spender, *The Fire of Life*, p. 180. The underground was smoky because, until the early twentieth century, the pre-electric metropolitan line still used steam engines.

p. 20   '*I remember . . . some Venetian beauty*': *WWW*, p. 5.

p. 21   '*perpetually grieving over I know not what*': ibid., p. 324.

p. 23   '*My childhood . . . a white cat, can't you see that?*': ibid., p. 323.

'*an old man . . . Charles Darwin*': ibid., p. 325.

p. 24   '*related a story . . . he always did*': ibid., p. 46.

p. 25   '*One morning . . . reverted to the Neanderthal*': ibid., p. 44.

p. 26   '*you'll be hanged if you kill her*': this is from an unpublished memoir of Sheringham life composed by Christine Spender, now in the possession of Philip Spender.

p. 27   *'have unseeing, rhetorical faces . . . gives him back his body'*: WWW,
            p. 315.

p. 28   *'My father . . . parrot my father owned when he was a boy'*: ibid.,
            p. 324.
            'with whom I used to fight . . . my whole body': ibid.

p. 30   *'My father did not . . . "The Prime Minister"'*: ibid., pp. 82–3.

p. 32   *'It is no exaggeration . . . everything to rhetorical abstraction'*: ibid.,
            p. 7.

p. 33   *'On the guidance of their . . . Harold'*: undated letter, presumably
            around 1922, in the possession of Christine Spender.
            'She was hysterical . . . an air of tragic disapproval': WWW, p. 4.

p. 35   *'With so much sorrow . . . joy this coming year'*: Violet's poems are
            taken from her privately printed collection (1922), *The Path to
            Caister*.

p. 36   *'I remember the rainy lakeside days . . . enjewelled caskets'*: WWW,
            p. 87.
            'The countryside . . . Poems of Wordsworth to my mother': ibid.

p. 37   *'Left Sheringham at 8:13 . . . in his pocket'*: Violet's diary of this holiday
            is in the possession of Philip Spender.

p. 39   *'when I was nine . . . boarding school'*: WWW, p. 326.

p. 41   *'On my second morning . . . a strong impression on me'*: ibid., p. 330.

p. 42   *'You may go on . . . the happiest time of your life'*: ibid., p. 334.

p. 44   his later essay, *'Day Boy'*: 'Day Boy' was published in the collection
            The Old School, ed. Graham Greene, London, 1934, pp. 185–98.

pp. 45-6   *'One day . . . that would doubtless fall on me'*: 'Day Boy', pp. 187–8.

p. 46   *'Tell them . . . a very happy life'*: WWW, p. 336.

pp. 46-7   *'I remember . . . we were all he had'*: ibid., pp. 5–6.

p. 47   *'A few days after . . . watched me from the grave'*: ibid., p. 6.

pp. 48-9   *'After the death of my mother . . . for ever changed'*: ibid., p. 90.

p. 50   *'character changed . . . and ask for leave'*: ibid., p. 7.

p. 51   *'My father . . . any of the boys [at University College School] using it'*:
            'Day Boy', p. 194.
            'the daily bristly kiss . . . as was possible': ibid.

p. 52   *'The revenge we took . . . hasten to correct it'*: ibid., p. 196.
            'on a 31 bus . . . out of the workhouse': WWW, p. 3.

p. 54   *'In our house at Frognal . . . should be held sacred'*: ibid., p. 76.
            'used, when my father was away . . . performances of Shakespeare': ibid.,
            p. 10.

p. 55   *'What I enjoyed most at UCS . . . Free Trade'*: 'Day Boy', p. 196.

pp. 55–6	'Their amusement . . . the end of adolescence for me': ibid.
p. 57	'He was a member . . . aesthetically avant garde': SS, *The Thirties and After*, London, 1978, p. 14.
	'I had the most tormented adolescence . . . revolved on a spit': the manuscript of 'Mr Branch', incomplete, is in the SSA.
p. 58	'At the end of my time . . . the snobbish environment of Oxford': 'Day Boy', p. 192.
	'were brought down . . . Vote for Daddy': WWW, p. 7.
p. 59	'On this walk . . . childish and profitless game': ibid., p. 89.
p. 61	'My father's dying . . . gently wiped his mouth': ibid., p. 18.
pp. 61–2	'I took the train home . . . he was shocked': ibid., p. 19.
p. 63	'The smell of the hot oil . . . extraordinary motion': this letter is in the possession of Philip Spender.
p. 64	His grandmother . . . her diary: Mrs Schuster's diaries are in the possession of the family.
p. 67	'Winifred smoked . . . syphilis, etc., these days': these comments are from a memorandum supplied by Humphrey Spender.
	'My sister and I . . . perhaps rather dangerous': WWW, p. 27.
p. 69	'By sending me to Nantes . . . a great many years': ibid., p. 30.
	'In spite of the expensiveness . . . the middle of the town!': [July 1927].
p. 70	'When I was nine . . . I started to do so with men': SS, *The Burning Cactus*, London, 1936, p. 255.
	'What distressed me most . . . my relationship with her [had] weakened': WWW, p. 31.
p. 71	'homosexuality and "intelligence" . . . took to drink': Jon Stallworthy, *Louis MacNeice*, London, 1995, p. 108.
p. 72	'On fine days . . . down on it read poetry': WWW, p. 31.
p. 73	'he was grandly told . . . to make up the deficit': Michael Ignatieff, *Isaiah Berlin: A Life*, London, 1998, repr. 2000, p. 58.
	'I was little bit overwhelmed': this and other quotations are from an interview recorded with GC in 1999.
p. 74	'We're just piddling undergraduates . . . he might despise me': WWW, p. 41.
p. 77	'it influenced my life . . . present also in my poetry': ibid., p. 67.
	'I don't . . . complementary to it': SS to GC, August 1930.
pp. 77–8	'I do not feel . . . interested to follow your work': *The English Auden*, ed. Edward Mendelson, London, 1977, repr. 1986, p. xiii.
p. 79	'he asked me . . . one poem in three weeks': WWW, p. 52.
pp. 79–80	'After I had known him . . . his icy voice': ibid.

p. 80   '*A few weeks . . . His name was Stephen Savage*': Christopher Isherwood,
             Lions and Shadows, London, 1938, p. 173.

p. 82   '*There are four or five friends . . . which may be taken up by the others*':
             SS to JL, 12 July 1931.
             '*I am very fond of my friend . . . and perhaps obscurantist*': SS to HN
             and VSW, 'September 1930', SSA.

p. 83   '*at the end . . . written four hundred sonnets*': *WWW*, p. 98.

p. 84   '*Despite the TLS . . . snobbery about looks*': SS to Humphrey Carpenter,
             8 May 1980.
             '*were in editions . . . in Auden's or my handwriting*': SS, *The Author*,
             Winter 1990, pp. 127–7.

p. 85   *Auden's sarcasms . . . 'a little man*': see *Jrnls*, p. 365.

p. 86   '*Spencer, son of a High Court Judge . . . obscene figures in pencil*':
             Stallworthy, *Louis MacNeice*, p. 126.
             '*was the nearest . . . his own limelight*': Louis MacNeice, *The Strings
             are False*, ed. E. R. Dodds, London, 1965, p. 113.

p. 87   '*I can't remember . . . rather in awe of him*': Elizabeth Longford,
             recorded interview in December 2000.

p. 88   '*There is a sort of impenetrability . . . J. A. Spender*': J. A. Spender to
             HS, 1 May 1929.
             '*very keen that I should go . . . all right*': SS to HS, [May 1929].

p. 89   '*Berlin meant boys*': *CK*, p. 2.
             '*take at face value . . . well, simply – for sex*': Norman Page, *Auden
             and Isherwood: The Berlin Years*, London, 1998, p. 3.

p. 90   '*The sun . . . like kings among their courtiers*': *WWW*, p. 107.
             '*he couldn't relax sexually . . . working-class foreigner*': Page, *Auden and
             Isherwood*, p. 36.
             '*sex with the working class . . . contact with the working class*': ibid.
             '*Wherever he was . . . the trenches*': LC, p. 9.

p. 91   '*The novel is getting on slowly . . . Very sporadically*': SS to HN and
             VSW, [September 1930].

p. 92   '*Cape wrote saying . . . for a year or two*': SS to CI, [Spring 1930].

pp. 92–3   '*The point about The Temple . . . wealth, work and happiness*': SS to
             CI, *LC*, pp. 69–70.

p. 93   '*I have started sketching . . . possible in our time*': SS to CI, *LC*,
             p. 72.

p. 94   '*I wrote it . . . in a Revolution*': SS to HS, [May 1930]. Spender sent
             a copy to E. R. Curtius at the same time.
             '*hoped to marry . . . if you see her*': SS to CI, *LC*, p. 36.

p. 95   *'Everything became politics'*: SS made this observation in the 1987 preface to *The Temple*.

                 'My first impression of Stephen': IB to NS, 1 August 1995.

p. 96   *'He was extremely . . . his great charm'*: ibid.

                 'like a muscular owl': CK, p. 104.

p. 97   *'one of the most beautiful women of her generation'*: WWW, p. 143.

                 'I am producing . . . for a few days': SS to HS, 29 May 1930.

p. 98   *Frances Partridge . . . the handsome young undergraduate*: interview, 2000.

                 'I can understand . . . "being a poet"': WWW, p. 146.

p. 99   *'saying that he knew . . . laugh whenever I think of them'*: SS to GC, 9 August 1930.

                 A pseudonym . . . for Richard Crossman: see Anthony Howard's 1999 'new biography' of Crossman.

pp. 99-100   *'I have spent . . . I'm absolutely pure'*: SS to CI, *LC*, p. 37.

p. 100   *'Before he went down . . . valuable by the author'*: IB to NS, 1 August 1995.

p. 101   *'It is no use . . . I care really for nothing but that'*: SS to HS, [August 1930].

                 'This is chiefly a letter of condolence . . . Johnny Freeman, and Isaiah Berlin': SS to GC, 5 October 1930.

The 1930s

p. 105   *'the queen adored by queers'*: SS to GC, 12 November 1936.

                 'wide staring eyes . . . wearing crowns flying over them': unpublished entry, journal 1982.

                 'an intelligent young man . . . whom we both liked': *Harold Nicolson: Diaries and Letters: 1930–1939*, ed. Nigel Nicolson, London, 1966, p. 50.

p. 106   *'not even the puppies and kittens are virgins'*: SS, *The Temple*, London, 1988, p. 185.

                 Soon afterwards . . . became occasional lovers: See Richard Davenport-Hines, *Auden*, London, 1995, pp. 53–5.

                 the 'Spender bequest' . . . 'did not like the idea': communicated to the author by Robert Fraser, from an interview with SS in 1994.

pp. 106–7   *'He lived very poorly . . . long ago ruined his'*: WWW, p. 121.

p. 108   *'There were buildings . . . camping, all were accepted'*: ibid., p. 108.

                 'real values . . . fucking, money, and religion': Peter F. Alexander, *William Plomer: A Biography*, London, 1987, p. 178.

p. 109   'would have been almost impossible . . . at least very unlikely': ibid.,
                p. 180.
                'I could never face . . . "intellectual equal"': SS to JL, 11 February 1932.
                'little chum': SS to CI, [August 1931], HEH.
                'I was 20 . . . Whitman's idea of camaraderie': Jrnls, p. 26.
                'the best film I have ever seen': SS to JL, 1 February 1932.
                'a tremendous sense of relief . . . Oxford and home': Page, *Auden and
                Isherwood*, p. 46.
                Innocentia Strasse . . . were 'adequate': SS to GC, 9 August 1930.

p. 110   'swimming in the Alster . . . sun, water, friendship': WWW, p. 107.
                'I started the poem . . . It was very funny': SS to HN and VSW,
                [August 1930].
                'I am always writing . . . the very thought of them': SS to VSW, 16
                September 1930.
                'I remember . . . I hope it is': CK, p. 43.

p. 111   he wrote to Isaiah . . . 'incredibly amusing': SS to IB, 5 August
                1930.
                'I took him down to St Pauli . . . isn't a gentleman': SS to IB, 5 August
                1930.

pp. 111–12   'Erich [Alport] I do not like . . . as I hoped it would be': SS to GC,
                [August 1930].

p. 112   'go on the streets' . . . as a male prostitute: SS to HN and VSW, 21
                August 1930.
                'Now I look back . . . a kind of mutual exploitation': WWW, p. 117.

p. 113   'a young Jewish girl . . . a young fox': CK, p. 63.
                'I am in the middle . . . but easier to get on with': SS to IB, 5 August
                1930.
                'trying for something new . . . achieved the ludicrous': SS to HN and
                VSW, 16 September 1930.

p. 114   'a child of the sun . . . run a factory': E. R. Curtius to SS, 3 August
                1929.
                'a very beautiful and intelligent woman': SS to GC, 23 November 1930.
                a suppressed passage in the 1939 Journal: the manuscript journal is in
                the BL.

p. 115   'an orgasm of work': SS to WP, 1 December 1930.

p. 117   'I have lived now . . . in that direction': SS to GC, 8 December 1930,
                SSA.
                'My dear Richard . . . incapable of sin': the manuscript of the story
                is in the SSA.

| p. 118 | 'Stephen Spender did most . . . But I am tired of saying what is so obvious to me': Ignatieff, *Isaiah Berlin*, pp. 52–3. |

'Stephen Spender did most . . . But I am tired of saying what is so obvious to me': Ignatieff, *Isaiah Berlin*, pp. 52–3.

'One [cannot] buy . . . Kurfürstendamm': SS to IB, [December 1930].

pp. 118-19   'she is really a very sweet girl': see *CK*, pp. 63–4.

p. 119   'that absolute lunatic . . . beaming, beaming, beaming': Rosamond Lehmann to Dadie Rylands, 29 December 1930, reference supplied by Selina Hastings.

'The moment I met him . . . makes lovemaking impossible': SS's recollections of JL in 1930–31 are in an unpublished section of his 1982 Journal, held in the BL.

p. 120   'How nice that will be! . . . got to be swum': *LC*, p. 38.

p. 121   'which I did not like at first . . . enthusiastic about': SS to VSW, 15 December 1930.

'you must remember . . . the whole Push that we are in': SS to JL, 18 February 1931.

p. 122   'Berlin was an immensely alive . . . Die Bürgschaft by Kurt Weill': *New York Times*, 30 October 1977.

p. 123   'hypnotic fascination of Christopher's life there': Page, *Auden and Isherwood*, p. 46.

'enjoyed preaching Lane-Layard . . . bend even lower': *CK*, pp. 53–5.

'the gushings of concert audiences . . . the Nazi attitude: ibid., p. 64.

'living precariously . . . being with Isherwood': *WWW*, p. 127.

pp. 123-4   'Most of my life . . . having boys myself': SS to GC, 10 March 1931.

p. 124   'smell of hopeless decay . . . cardboard box': *WWW*, p. 122. The following descriptions of Berlin and Isherwood in Berlin are from the same section of *WWW*.

'We are not amused . . . I have read this week': SS to VSW, 16 October 1930.

p. 125   'I don't think . . . for about three years': SS to JL, 18 February 1931.

p. 126   'Our house is about . . . singing in the branches': SS to VSW, 23 May 1931.

'Stephen, in the middle . . . standing in a hole': *CK*, p. 82.

'are lying in the sun . . . the pier for boys': SS to JL, 15 June 1931.

p. 127   'whatever happens to this novel . . . at all events': SS to HN and VSW, 29 June 1931, SSA.

'so excited . . . difficult to sleep': SS to WP, 6 July 1931.

'I can't face . . . quite alone': SS to JL, 2 July 1931.

p. 128   'like a day of public mourning': SS to JL, 25 July 1931.

'All in all . . . wasn't a success': *CK*, p. 82.

The American writer and musician . . . for his 'Sally': Page, *Auden and Isherwood*, pp. 48–9.

p. 129   'Salzburg in political terms . . . in the Europe of the 1930s': Ignatieff, *Isaiah Berlin*, p. 54.

             'a very nice schoolboy from Hamburg': SS to JL, 25 July 1931.

p. 129-30   'Cape do not dare . . . like that would stand by it?': SS to JL, 18 August 1931.

p. 130   'a very threatening letter': SS to JL, 1 August 1931.

p. 130-31   'there is no reason . . . the duty of the poet': SS to JL, 18 September 1931.

p. 131   'miniature sensitive beauty . . . Gandhi': *WWW*, p. 133.

             'I think we have all . . . the Communist Party': SS to JL, 26 August 1931.

             'almost exclusively . . . young communists': SS to VSW, 2 December 1931.

p. 132   'He must have wanted . . . truly considerate of him': CK, p. 85.

             who were the 'young poets' to watch at the university: from an interview with Janet Adam-Smith in 2001.

             ready for his 'London phase': SS to JL, 12 August 1931.

p. 133   'I think it is better if we don't all live . . . the trouble at Ruegen': CK, p. 82.

             'sad . . . as I was wanting to learn portrait photography': SS to JL, 11 January 1932.

p. 134   'I cannot be responsible for waifs and strays': SS to JL, 26 January 1932. Other quotations on this page are from the same letter.

p. 135   'and the necessities . . . a month's overdraft': SS to JL, 11 January 1932.

             'Miss Adam Smith or any other . . . tries to sell him poetry': SS to JL, 20 February 1932.

p. 136   'For some reason . . . anxious I shouldn't come': SS to JL, 9 March 1932.

             'I would come home except . . . as a warning': SS to WP, 6 March 1932.

p. 137   'hated having Stephen . . . "I am a camera" in those days': CK, p. 93.

             'Half my income goes to 10 Frognal': SS to JL, 8 May 1932.

p. 138   'in order to save money as it is very cheap': SS to JL, 29 April 1932.

             'I have no idea . . . what I shall do': SS to JL, 13 May 1932.

p. 139   'an elegant, distinguished, dark-eyed young man': see *WWW*, p. 131 and CK, pp. 65–7 for the powerful effect Israel had on the young Englishmen.

p. 139   *'perhaps my manhood?'*: SS to WP, 27 July 1932.

p. 140   *'plumper and much more attractive'*: SS to JL, 12 August 1932.

           the *'obstreperous' Georgi was also proving difficult*: SS to JL, 27 September 1932.

p. 141   *'a memory of my own . . . intolerably indiscreet, etc.'*: CK, pp. 106–7.

p. 143   *'I do not think . . . I tried to be fair'*: WWW, p. 170.

           'The young man . . . in contrast to his heavy lips': SS, *The Burning Cactus*, p. 154.

p. 144   *'as nurse and hand-holder . . . peculiarly well suited'*: SS to WP, 26 October 1932.

           'It really is . . . no wonder he has got ill now': SS to JL, 26 October 1932.

           Stephen took Hellmut away from Barcelona: the following description of the excursion is taken from SS's journal, unpublished, in the BL. Several trial versions exist. It is supplemented by a letter, SS to JL, 22 November 1932.

p. 145   *'if I wanted to meet anyone at all decent'*: SS to WP, 21 November 1932.

           The parting was bad-tempered: for Hellmut's later career, see Christopher Isherwood, *Lost Years: A Memoir 1945–1951*, ed. Katherine Bucknell, London, 2000, p. 126.

p. 146   *'macabre' feats of drunkenness*: LC, p. 53. This section of the letters, centred on January 1933, has extensive description of Kirk's outrages.

           'I am going to try . . . abroad in May': LC, p. 56.

p. 147   *'portentous tripe – what idiot wrote it?'*: CI to SS, 20 January 1933.

p. 148   *'incredibly, as it seems to me . . . "weighed on his spirits"'*: SS to JL, [January] 1933.

p. 149   *'From now on . . . at least a year I hope'*: SS to IB, 1 March 1933.

           'The problem, in removing a tapeworm . . . Can this be it?!!!': CK, p. 121.

p. 150   *which left him . . . 'trembling with joy'*: LC, p. 61.

           'Tony Hyndman came . . . which often astonished me': WWW, p. 175.

pp. 150-51 *'His appearance was attractive . . . the curtain went up, for me'*: CK, p. 222. For details about Hyndman's past, I am indebted to Richard Felstead, and his research on Welsh volunteers in the Spanish Civil War. For details on Hyndman later in life see Alan Strahan's 2004 biography of Michael Redgrave and Isherwood's *Lost Years*, pp. 113–15 and 145.

p. 153   '*to some people called the Berensons . . . would swim in*': SS to IB, 25
             May 1933.
             '*I get thinner . . . a bloody nuisance*': SS to Rosamond Lehmann,
             [May] 1933.
             '*As the result of this . . . more difficult than most people do*': SS to JL,
             27 May 1933.
             '*I want to read all the epic works I can*': SS to WP, 27 June 1933.

p. 154   '*It's impossible to write about him . . . different from me as he is*': SS to
             Rosamond Lehmann, 13 June 1933.
             '*Quite early in our relationship . . . I can't bear it*': *WWW*, p. 175.

p. 155   '*I would love to stay on . . . which may or may not be cured*': SS to IB,
             15 June 1933.
             '*he's a nice poetic youth . . . the Lilies of the Valley*': Virginia Woolf to
             Quentin Bell, 31 December 1933.

p. 156   '*Along the banks . . . were a Turkish bath*': *WWW*, p. 149.

p. 157   '*I do so hate the clique . . . tittle-tattle criticism*': SS to HR, [December]
             1933.
             '*difficult for a writer . . . the field far away*': a retrospective quotation,
             November 1982, in SS's journal, BL.
             '*It seems to us . . . the "diary"*': TSE to SS, 13 January 1934.
             '*The ship continues to sink . . . earn money*': *LC*, 63.

p. 158   '*The writing of the 1920s . . . fascism, approaching war*': *WWW*, p. 139.
             '*I never lost my awe*': ibid., p. 166.

p. 159   '*she always had the air . . . to her ear again*': ibid., p. 161.
             '*the appearance of an overgrown . . . blind gaze*': ibid., p. 163.
             '*I seem to have reached a stage . . . melting pot*': SS to HR, [February]
             1934.

p. 160   '*We seem . . . the final circle of the whirlpool*': CI to SS, 7 August 1934.
             '*Shyah and I each . . . is very comfortable*': SS to HS, 8 April 1934.

p. 161   '*a perfectly preserved town*': SS to WP, 14 April 1934.
             '*a little village . . . under the trees*': *WWW*, p. 193.
             '*crystal . . . the atmosphere timeless*': SS to HR, 11 April 1934.

p. 162   '*lovely spring flowers . . . touch with civilization*': SS to WP, 15 April
             1934.
             '*I really may be able to pay off my overdraft*': SS to HS, 5 May 1934.

p. 164   '*I had selected this spot . . . suggested a graceful animal*': this descrip-
             tion of the lovers' first meeting is taken from Muriel Gardiner,
             Code Name Mary, New Haven, 1983, pp. 46–7.
             '*her profile, as she looked . . . suffered at some time*': *WWW*, p. 193.

'certainly a James character': SS to WP, 19 June 1934.

p. 165   *'Vienna . . . even when one is in the street'*: SS to HS, 14 June 1934.

'Stephen was perfectly open . . . less difficult than one might expect': Gardiner, *Code Name Mary*, p. 54. The following poem was sent to WP on 10 August.

p. 166   *'it has not made . . . relationship with Tony'*: *LC*, p. 67.

'All these days . . . keeping me from Muriel': *WWW*, p. 197.

'dangers seem to be averted . . . holding me together': SS to WP, 19 June 1934.

p. 167   *'I read a lot of documents . . . gave me the idea'*: SS to HS, 14 June 1934.

'I can't help wishing . . . murder seems to breed murder': SS to HS, 27 June 1934.

'which will mean a lot of typing': SS to WP, 10 August 1934.

pp. 168-9   *'By the way, almost . . . just makes me sick'*: *LC*, p. 66. The full text, quoted here, is in HEH.

pp. 169-70   *'I shall be very glad . . . the whole thing as a journey'*: SS to Tony Hyndman, 5 October 1934.

p. 170   *'when we are quite alone together'*: SS to WP, 3 July 1934.

'we are going to settle . . . abroad till 1936': SS to Lincoln Kirstein, 16 August 1934.

p. 174   *'Don't worry about your work . . . damage your reputation'*: TSE to SS, 10 December 1934.

'two or three a week', *he told Christopher*: *LC*, p. 69.

'rather fun' . . . one's travel plans: SS to WP, 11 January 1935.

p. 175   *'My money affairs . . . permit it'*: SS to WP, [January] 1935.

'Then she would come in . . . like fire against her cheeks': *WWW*, p. 198.

'her black hair . . . her firm breasts': SS, *The Burning Cactus*, p. 17.

p. 176   *'ambivalence . . . like a sword'*: *WWW*, pp. 196–200; Gardiner, *Code Name Mary*, pp. 66–72.

p. 177   *'war is inevitable'*: *LC*, p. 75.

'The strings were left dangling . . . to warn artists': SS to WP, 18 April 1935.

'We hardly ever see her': SS to WP, 18 April 1935.

p. 179   *'shameful . . . proper meaning of the word'*: HR to SS, 6 July 1935.

'It is unbelievably . . . contrast with Eliot': HR to SS, 10 May 1935.

'really quite favourable': SS to HS, 12 May 1935.

the 'extraordinary' wisdom' of the book: HR to SS, 16 May 1935.

'*your remarkable faculty for accurate generalization*': Cecil Day-Lewis to SS, 21 April 1935.

'*first option*' . . . *prose or poetry*: TSE to SS, 9 May 1935.

'*I really must write much better*': SS to WP, 22 May 1935.

p. 180   '*to learn German really well*': LC, p. 75.

'*He is going back to London . . . I want to be alone*': SS to WP, 31 July 1935.

p. 181   '*amazingly quiet . . . Wystan a lot*': SS to WP, 31 July 1935.

'*Of course I understand . . . for that matter is Tony*': SS to JL, 19 July 1935.

p. 182   '*in the company . . . the profundity of his remarks*': Lyndall Gordon, *Eliot's New Life*, London, 1988, pp. 162–3.

'*one those awful moods . . . my work*': LC, p. 80.

'*going through a crisis . . . self dissatisfaction*': SS to HR, 18 October, 1935.

p. 183   '*Brian wants to go to Portugal . . . come with us*': CK, p. 217.

p. 184   *On 10 December . . . bound for Rio via Lisbon*: the following account of the Cintra venture is drawn, substantially, from the Cintra diary – held in the BL – supplemented by Humphrey Spender's addenda. CI offers an account of the episode in *CK*, pp. 218–50.

pp. 184–5   '*And the cares . . . write about things terrifically*': CK, pp. 224–5.

p. 186   '*in order that I may . . . write about Hitler*': SS to Lincoln Kirstein, 8 January 1936.

p. 188   '*the entire fixture . . . embarrassingly in the buttocks*': CK, p. 232.

'*the longest spell of rain . . . Lisbon earthquake*': SS to Elizabeth Bowen, 19 April 1936.

'*suitable for 8-year-olds*': SS to HR, 20 June 1936.

p. 189   '*our attempt at living together . . . tacitly dropped*': CK, p. 234.

'*a bloody German-Italo-Hispano-Fascist Colony*': SS to Lincoln Kirstein, 8 November 1936.

'*for two thousand years*': SS to WP, 26 March 1936.

too '*deliberately descriptive*': HR to SS, 21 April 1936.

'*even more characterless than Berlin*': SS to HS, 18 March 1936.

'*modern poet . . . extremely beautiful*': SS to WP, 3 April 1936.

p. 190   '*that none of his servants . . . heard of Homer*': LC, p. 116.

p. 191   '*the best of the publishing rackets*': SS to Cecil Day-Lewis, 20 February 1936.

'*a lot of people . . . by uncle Alfred*': SS to HS, 23 June 1936.

'*has changed and strengthened . . . to work*': SS to JL, 14 July 1936.

p. 192   *'I would acquire a mask . . . freeze into my little group'*: SS to WP, 3 April 1936.

                      'I think the Spanish business . . . disaster to date': SS to Lincoln Kirstein, 8 November 1936.

                      'You don't, I feel . . . freely enough': HR to SS, 13 November 1936.

p. 193   *'is by far the most interesting . . . scared of it'*: CI to SS, 12 May 1936.

p. 194   *'I decided I must separate from Tony'*: WWW, p. 204.

p. 195   *'not quite big enough for Stephen'*: MacNeice, *The Strings are False*, pp. 166–7.

                      'I received a cheque . . . which also resembled Herbert's': WWW, p. 204.

                      'a small flat . . . comes up to town': SS to Lincoln Kirstein, 8 November 1936.

                      'I had sought out . . . poets, artists, left-wing layabouts': T. C. Worsley, *Fellow Travellers*, London, 1971, p. 15.

p. 197   *'semi-deified' status . . . 'the hall would be packed'*: *Observer*, 20 June 1976.

                      wonder at his 'extreme beauty': from an interview with Sally Graves, 2001.

                      'an oval, child-like face . . . an Eton crop': WWW, p. 204.

p. 198   *'Stephen has just left . . . Inez Perne'*: Rosamond Lehmann to JL, 12 October 1936. Reference supplied by Selina Hastings.

                      'the famous Inez': the following account of the intricate love manoeuvrings of Toynbee, Spender, Inez et al. is taken from Philip Toynbee's unpublished diary for 1936.

p. 199   *'made her the success of my party . . . in the afternoon I proposed to her'*: WWW, p. 205.

p. 200   *'Poor Tony' . . . Stephen's marriage was 'absurd'*: CI to SS, 25 November 1936; Isherwood, *Lost Years*, p. 114.

p. 201   *'attractive, with the look . . . entirely devoid of emotional content'*: Rosamond Lehmann to JL, 1 December 1936. Reference supplied by Selina Hastings.

                      'I'm just not capable . . . build up a satisfactory life together': LC, p. 126.

p. 202   *'I did not completely . . . Part of my mind stood aside'*: WWW, p. 207.

                      'like the masked . . . all in black': SS to Elizabeth Bowen, 7 December 1936.

                      'we don't intend . . . shit and morning sickness don't': SS to Rayner Heppenstall, 20 December 1936.

p. 203   *'Freddy is an absolute Italian . . . suitable for even a temporary flutter'*: IB to Elizabeth Bowen, July 1937.

pp. 203-4   '*We walked slowly along . . . fatal to hang around*': this and other details are from Tony Hyndman's autobiographical chapter in *The Distant Drum*, ed. Philip Toynbee (London, 1976).

p. 204   '*Tony will tell you . . . my only intimate friend in London*': SS to CI, 20 December 1936.

'*Let's see if . . . Inez would come too*': CI to SS, 23 December 1936.

p. 205   '*awful business . . . undermines everything*': LC, p. 130.

p. 206   '*Perhaps [Tony] ought . . . a really high class tart*': Worsley, *Fellow Travellers*, pp. 68–9.

p. 207   '*Since I wrote these . . . it must be legalized*': SS, *Forward from Liberalism*, London, 1937, p. 288.

p. 208   '*Pollitt was willing . . . when I joined*': WWW, p. 211.

p. 209   '*Shortly after Tony's departure . . . the Italians in the Mediterranean*': ibid., p. 214.

'*It is really the least . . . friends of mine are doing*': SS to HS, 5 January 1937.

p. 210   '*He was in constant conflict . . . caught out in them*': Worsley, *Fellow Travellers*, p. 54.

'*preoccupied with Tony*': WWW, p. 216.

p. 212   '*In future the C.P. are going . . . to cross for a long time*': SS to WP, 10 February 1937.

p. 213   *Both were shattered*: a good account of Tony Hyndman's front-line experience is given by Robert Stradling in his *History and Legend*, Cardiff, 2002.

p. 214   *At tea with the Woolves . . . regret his marriage to her*: The Diary of Virginia Woolf, ed. Anne Olivier Bell, London, 1984, 18 February 1937, p. 56.

p. 215   '*You must get me out of here*': WWW, p. 221.

'*no one, or almost no one . . . from the Brigade*': SS to WP, 2 April 1937.

p. 217   '*positively praying . . . hit an Arab*': WWW, p. 223.

'*At the Casa de la Cultura . . . where the journalists lunched*': ibid., p. 225.

p. 218   '*you ought, as a communist . . . disciplined by us*': SS to WP, 2 April 1937.

p. 219   *famous as the resort of 'spies and harlots*': Stradling, *History and Legend*, p. 86.

'*to prevent Tony being killed . . . bullying of the commissars*': SS to WP, 2 April 1937.

'*We would go on walks together . . . yeller*': *The Paris Review*, Winter-Spring, 1980.

pp. 219-20   '*My Dear Stephen . . . But do come if you can*': Tony Hyndman to SS, 17 March 1937.

p. 221   '*until right at the end . . . "in the mud"'*: SS to WP, 12 April 1937.

p. 222   '*is that politicians are detestable . . . cannot get away*': SS to Virginia Woolf, 2 April 1937.

p. 223   '*This, according to other prisoners . . . rid of undesirables*': *WWW*, p. 238.

'*he failed abysmally . . . become a dangerous embarrassment*': James K. Hopkins, *Into the Heart of the Fire*, Stanford, 1998, p. 261.

p. 224   '*Tony Hyndman . . . whole British battalion put together*': Stradling, *History and Legend*, p. 44.

p. 226   '*amused himself by explaining . . . mountain district*': *WWW*, p. 238.

p. 227   '*Her extensory smiling mouth . . . highly convenient from her point of view*': ibid., p. 245.

'*an irritated idealist . . . a wounded feeling*': Claire Harmon, *Sylvia Townsend Warner*, London, 1995, p. 162.

'*Will you please stop sending . . . rub it in good and hard*': *The Collected Essays, Journalism and Letters of George Orwell: An Age Like This, 1920–1940*, eds. Ian Angus and Sonia Orwell, London, 1968, p. 668.

p. 228   '*breaks in our married life*': SS to CI, 18 May 1938.

p. 229   '*I might still become . . . others had done*': *WWW*, p. 255.

in the bottom right-hand corner: interview with Nancy Coldstream, 2000.

p. 230   '*that it would be a good thing . . . dependent on my resources*': SS to Tony Hyndman, [November 1937].

p. 231   '*smash your friends . . . to pieces*': *WWW*, p. 248.

'*passionately about Republican Spain . . . brilliant stuff*': personal communication, 2002.

'*History . . . 'And history took him out again*': Samuel Hynes, *The Auden Generation*, London, 1976, p. 263.

p. 233   '*a grey mountaineer . . . substitute for sex*': *Jrnls*, p. 441.

'*I have to speak . . . about Spain*': SS to J. B. Leishman, 26 October 1937.

p. 235   '*a moving play . . . brilliancy of the others*': *Diary*, 22 March 1938.

p. 236   '*is really a very upsetting experience*': SS to WP, 24 March 1938.

'*one after one . . . Marx and Marx*': MacNeice, *The Strings are False*, p. 168.

p. 237   *'the best food in Switzerland . . . buffets of railways stations'*: Michael Shelden, *Friends of Promise*, London, 1989, p. 32. Shelden gives the fullest account of Watson and the founding of *Horizon*.

p. 238   *'I have inflicted an injury . . . one's attention to the fact'*: SS to CI, 18 May 1938.

p. 240   *through Mary Elliott, her best friend at school*: I am indebted to Mary Elliott's son, David Elliott, who drew my attention to the run of correspondence dealing with the break-up of the Spenders' marriage.

p. 241   *'because I was told . . . would never leave me'*: SS to Mary Elliott, 17 October 1938.

p. 242   *'entirely on account of . . . count as one of my follies'*: SS to CI, 23 August 1938.

pp. 243–4   *'not altogether surprised . . . urgent cases from Germany'*: Muriel Gardiner to SS, 30 January 1938.

p. 245   *'you have kept your integrity . . . genitals, entrails'*: CI to SS, 8 July 1938.

p. 247   *'her face became distorted . . . across the room'*: *WWW*, pp. 258–9.

            'I've got to go away with Inez . . . going to be!': SS to Mary Elliott, 31 August 1938.

p. 248   *'Dear Stephen, If I saw you now . . . both be profoundly dissatisfied'*: Inez Spender to SS, 24 July 1938.

            'lovely time in Wales . . . a chest of drawers': Charles Madge to Mary Elliott, 25 July 1938.

p. 249   *'At the moment I feel rather shattered . . . Inez cannot live with me'*: SS to Mary Elliott, 31 July 1938.

            'there can be no question . . . I don't cheat and lie': SS to Mary Elliott, 31 August 1938.

p. 250   *'We have been married . . . try and forget her'*: SS to Mary Elliott, 31 August 1938.

            'full of regret and bitterness': *The Diary of Virginia Woolf*, 11 September 1939, p. 236.

p. 251   *'run away . . . with my work'*: LC, p. 164.

            'I feel that I ought to be doing . . . unknown poets': LC, p. 188.

            'A loose jointed mind . . . I forget': *The Diary of Virginia Woolf*, 24 September 1939, p. 238.

p. 252   *'Everything I read in the papers . . . about her'*: suppressed passage in *September Journal*, 3 September 1938.

            'a crook . . . Wykehamist flattery': SS to HR, 30 October 1938.

            'Inez seems so far away . . . all the same they hurt him': suppressed

passage in *September Journal*. So too is the subsequent conversation with Connolly and the meeting with Inez in London.

p. 253   '*It's all right . . . rather hopeless rivalry to me*': SS to Mary Elliott, 3 October 1938.

p. 254   '*her habit of keeping . . . Cockteasing*': suppressed passage in *September Journal*.

p. 255   '*I did not suggest . . . object to being divorced*': SS to Mary Elliott, 18 December 1938.

p. 257   '*Peter asked me specifically . . . to help Peter carry on*': Shelden, *Friends of Promise*, p. 31.

pp. 257–8   '*I know he is my enemy . . . years of extravagant self-deception*': Adrian Wright, *John Lehmann: A Pagan Adventure*, London, 1998, p. 101. Wright gives the fullest account of JL's activities at this period.

p. 258   '*I'm not officially connected . . . in the blackout*': SS to WP, 19 October 1938.
'*You are quite right . . . disturbs me very much*': SS to Cyril Connolly, 9 May 1935.

The 1940s: An Englishman Again

p. 263   '*He paints all day . . . also wise I think*': SS to Mary Elliott, 25 January 1940. An account of this episode in Wales is given by William Feaver, in *Guardian Weekend*, 6 September 2003.

p. 264   '*wild and amusing conversation*': Corin Redgrave, *Michael Redgrave: My Father*, London, 1995, p. 95. A fuller account of this period of Redgrave's life, and his association with Hyndman, is given by Alan Strahan in his 2004 biography.

p. 265   '*it will be better . . . worst six months of my life*': SS to Mary Elliott, 15 February 1940.
'*very naked . . . write from my heart*': SS to JL, [November] 1939.
'*Lolly can live only . . . nearly crazy*': SS to Mary Elliott, 15 February 1940.
'*apparently disconnected activities . . . made it more bearable*': WWW, p. 232.

p. 268   '*if you are bored . . . down and see you*': W. J. West, *Orwell: the Lost Writings*, London, 1988, p. 243.

p. 269   '*I have known since about 1931 . . . the future must be catastrophic*': Bernard Crick, *George Orwell: A Life* London, 1981.

'Peter Watson paid . . . that concerned Horizon': *Jrnls*, p. 57.

'by himself on a bicycle . . . afternoon rowing': Shelden, *Friends of Promise*, p. 55.

'such an entirely good . . . love being with him': SS to Mary Elliott, [June] 1940.

p. 270   'one of the meanest things I have heard of': SS to Mary Elliott, 30 October 1940.

'is a sad business . . . more grown up way': SS to Mary Elliott, 9 December 1940.

p. 271   'Thinking of the war . . . seemed in England during the war': SS, *The Thirties and After*, p. 91.

p. 273   'a struggling actor and schoolteacher': Shelden, *Friends of Promise*, p. 69.

p. 275   'I am not a good teacher . . . no poetry in it': SS to JL, 18 October, 2 November 1940.

p. 276   'I think it is better . . . the idea of our marrying': SS to Mary Elliott, 3 February 1941.

pp. 278–9   'in the summer of 1940 . . . worth noticing': *WWW*, p. 284.

pp. 279–80   'by a drinks party . . . later to marry my brother Michael': *Jrnls*, p. 57.

p. 280   'I am very thrilled . . . a revolutionary effect on me': SS to JH, 2 April 1941.

p. 281   'If God so wishes . . . before being called up': SS to JH, 29 July 1941.

p. 283   'but my life seems . . . the British Lion, I suppose': SS to WP, 23 November 1941.

'I hid for half an hour . . . sweet scents': *WWW*, p. 267.

p. 284   'Perhaps the war . . . brings him to his senses': *New Statesman*, 4 April 1942.

p. 285   'cleaning up lavatories . . . could put poetry to': this, and other description of his life as a fireman, is from an unpublished journal Spender kept. The ms. is now at the BL. Parts of the 'Fireman's Journal' were integrated into *WWW*.

pp. 285-6   'Vulnerability, closeness . . . drama of the station': SS, *Citizens in War – and After*, London, 1945, p. 6.

p. 287   'parallels with the ideal . . . Abbey of Thélème': *WWW*, p. 279.

p. 288   'Connolly did not really regret . . . pushed the magazine too far into politics': Shelden, *Friends of Promise*: p. 94.

'A group of ordinary firemen . . . and many other subjects': *WWW*, p. 305.

p. 289   'as a result of all this . . . so much hard work to do at the piano': Robert Graves to SS, [July] 1942, [January] 1943.

p. 291   'in constant communication . . . the unexperienced landscape for the first time': SS, *Life and the Poet*, London, 1942, pp. 66-7.

pp. 292-3   '*Michael Jones [was] killed . . . was that we should create*': WWW, p. 266.

p. 294   '*The fact is . . . so many directions*': SS to ES, 21 March, 23 April 1943.

p. 295   '*The idea of expanding . . . his wife, and Cecil [Day-Lewis]*': Sean Day-Lewis, *C. Day-Lewis: An English Literary Life*, London, 1980, p. 149.
'*was like that of a train . . . to the rails*': SS, *The Thirties and After*, p. 97.

p. 296   '*I looked out of the window . . . visioning of Botticelli*': WWW, p. 308.
'*almost worth it to have produced such a poem*': 9 March 1944.
'*a relief . . . a wonderfully calming effect*': SS to ES, 28 February 1944.

p. 297   '*Morgan Forster always . . . "how abominably vulgar I am"*': unpublished fragmentary diary entry, SSA.

p. 298   '*appallingly sad . . . which other people have amassed*': SS to ES, 8 August, 4 September 1944.

pp. 298-9   '*When I went into the Board Room . . . therefore I was not suitable for this work*': SS to JH, 4 December 1944.

p. 299   '*one candle burning . . . dark cathedral*': SS, *The Thirties and After*, p. 97.

p. 300   '*Riding on top of a bus . . . earth to heaven*': ibid., pp. 97–8.

p. 302   '*was to go to Bonn . . . Curtius*': *Jrnls*, p. 59.

p. 304   '*As he passed the frontier*': the following description of Spender's German tour of duty, and his spells of furlough in France, is taken from the following sources: SS, *European Witness*, London, 1946; 'Rhineland Journal', *Horizon,* December 1945, and Spender's manuscript diary, held in the BL. An edited form of the last is printed in *Jrnls* as 'German Diary: 1945'. The frank comments on Curtius were largely purged from *European Witness*.

p. 306   *his undergraduate novel, 'Instead of Death'*: the typescript of this unpublished novel (parts of which resurface in the published version of *The Temple*) is held in the SSA.

p. 311   '*He could not, of course . . . T. S. Eliot and others*': *Jrnls*, pp. 59–60.

p. 312   '*disturbed by . . . has put himself in the wrong*': Eliot's letter, which dates clearly from early January 1946, was passed on to me in transcript by Jason Harding.
'*but I felt . . . could not be unforgiven*': *Jrnls*, p. 166.

p. 313   '*charming, bearing no grudges . . . All was forgiven*': unpublished journal entry, April 1985.

'*I'm going to write . . . things imaginable*': SS to John Hayward, 6 February 1946.

p. 314   '*Stephen was always looking . . . Stuart Hampshire recalls*: interview, 1999.

p. 317   *To Spender's rage . . . for financial gain*: the episode is covered from Campbell's angle in Peter F. Alexander, *Roy Campbell: A Critical Biography*, London, 1982, p. 209.

p. 318   '*we should raise such a stink . . . a calumniator*': Cecil Day-Lewis to SS, 7 June 1946.

'*Tom Eliot is not blameless here*': SS deposited all the relevant correspondence from which I quote at the HRC.

'*it will be the first . . . "witness" volumes*': Hamish Hamilton to SS, 4 March 1946.

p. 319   '*provided the occasion . . . accept the Ten Commandments*': *Jrnls*, p. 93.

p. 320   '*Sam always liked Stephen . . . fifty years later*': interview with Gian Carlo Menotti, 2002.

pp. 321-2 *Isherwood . . . overcoats through the performance*: Isherwood, *Lost Years*, p. 102.

p. 322   '*How can one write . . . there will be the words*': unpublished journal, SSA.

'*the best thing you have ever done . . . of being a father??)*': CI to SS, 23 November 1946.

p. 323   '*I feel sure . . . provided she'll like me!*': CI to SS, 9 February 1947.

p. 326   '*When UNESCO moved to Paris . . . the secretariat of UNESCO*': *Jrnls*, p. 93.

pp. 326–7 '*When I met . . . taken over Scotland Yard*': *The God that Failed*, ed. R. Crossman, London, 1950, p. 264.

p. 327   '*was in a state . . . any of his books before*': Hamish Hamilton to SS, 13 August 1947.

'*in this worst of provincial . . . any intellectual life at all*': *The Collected Letters of Dylan Thomas*, ed. Paul Ferris, London, 1986, p. 100.

'*Spender raised more lovely . . . dared to hope*': ibid., p. 456.

p. 328   '*We don't want . . . "a certain habit"*': *Selected Letters of Edith Sitwell*, ed. Richard Greene, London, 2001, p. 144.

p. 329   '*including Mary McCarthy . . . Randall Jarrell, poet and critic*': *Jrnls*, p. 84.

'*a tremendous thing for her*': SS to Harold Taylor, 16 June 1947.

p. 330   '*I try to comfort myself . . . for poetry out there*': *Selected Letters of Edith Sitwell*, p. 151.

'*spent the morning . . . absolutely staggering*': SS's account of his introduction to America is taken from letters to his wife. Her first-hand
recollections of their first time together in America are also drawn on.

pp. 333–4 '*comfortably but not elaborately furnished*': Harold Taylor to SS, [June]
1947.

p. 336 '*red-handed in a brainwashing job*': Carol Gelderman, *Mary McCarthy:
A Life*, New York, 1991, p. 138.

to humiliate and '*red-bait me*': Lillian Hellman to SS, 1 September
1983.

'*Outside teaching spoiled . . . where one can sit occasionally and write
poetry*': SS to Cyril Connolly, 18 March, 5 August 1948.

p. 338 '*Lawrence took Brett . . . Sartre's Huis Clos*': unpublished journal entry,
1948.

p. 339 *Doubtless they inspired four poems*: SS wrote his own account of the
transcontinental Buick trip in 'On the Road with Lennie', *The
Times*, 3 November 1990.

p. 340 '*We are a perfect . . . three Graces to have been*': SS to Dorothy Brett,
1 June 1948.

p. 341 '*Stephen has arrived . . . a sort of divine gift*': William Goyen to Dorothy
Brett, 25 September 1948.

'*oh, so dull! . . . awake at night thinking about it*': SS to Dorothy Brett,
3 October, 14 October 1948.

pp. 341–2 '*Here I am on this train . . . always like to be with them*': SS to Dorothy
Brett, [October] 1948.

p. 342 '*It will be very nice . . . have stayed in America*': SS to Dorothy Brett,
8 December 1948.

pp. 342–3 '*was conceived . . . know what it's all about*': *The God that Failed*, p. 2.

p. 343 '*explicitly conceived as anti-Communist propaganda*': David Cesarani,
The Afterlife of Arthur Koestler, London, 1999.

'*My duty is . . . the only solution of the world's problems*': *The God that
Failed*, p. 272.

'*Last night . . . an honest £1*': this letter is with the other Roy
Campbell material which SS deposited in the HRC. Bernard
Bergonzi communicated his recollection personally.

p. 344 '*Everywhere this week . . . talk of Communism*': *Jrnls*, p. 99. Other
quotations that follow are from the same section of the published
journals.

p. 345 '*rather excessively pretty*': SS to Dorothy Brett, 15 September 1949.

'*Though Auden, Spender, MacNeice and I . . . together in one room*':

C. Day-Lewis, *The Buried Day*, London, 1960. Ed Mendelson's correction is by personal letter.

p. 346   *'busted the hell out of . . . designed by Michelangelo'*: William Goyen to Dorothy Brett, 20 January, 4 January 1950.

p. 347   *'make as much of a row as I can'*: SS to Harold Taylor, 23 October 1949.

p. 348   *'not to run the gauntlet . . . ever again'*: the resolution was made in his unpublished journal, January 1950.

The 1950s: Middle Years, Mid-Atlantic

p. 351   *'I can work all day'*: SS to Dorothy Brett, 27 June 1950.
'slept little . . . so that I can hardly sleep': unpublished journal entries. Subsequent unreferenced quotations, covering SS's research visit to Europe, are from the same source.

p. 353   *'Finally, Koestler screeched away . . . too bad it was your wedding night'*: Cesarani, *The Afterlife of Arthur Koestler*, p. 349.

p. 354   *'It's* terrific *having a daughter . . . down for Sarah Lawrence?'*: SS to Harold Taylor, 19 June 1950.
'We were all so . . . coitus interruptus': SS to Harold Taylor, 6 August 1950.
approved the idea of a *'ten year break'*: Geoffrey Faber to SS, 18 September 1950.

p. 355   *'Our life . . . despite debts, etc.'*: SS to Dorothy Brett, 5 November 1950.
'weighs about two tons . . . December': SS to Harold Taylor, 23 December 1950.
'indulging myself by putting . . . if not a Shaw': SS to John Hayward, 28 December 1950.

p. 356   *'Secret CIA funding . . . Royal Society of the Arts in London'*: Stephen Dorrill, *Inside the Covert World of Her Majesty's Secret Intelligence Service*, New York, 2000. Other authoritative accounts of the foundation and the funding of what eventually became *Encounter* are given by Frances Stonor Saunders, *Who Paid the Piper?* (in the US, *The Cultural Cold War*), New York and London, 1999, and Neil Berry, *Articles of Faith*, London, 2002.
is to humanize . . . the rest of the world': *New York Times*, 17 November 1950.

p. 357	*'wonderful . . . this highly autobiographical time'*: CI to SS, 13 September 1950.
	'calculation and coldness of heart': W. H. Auden to SS, 20 June 1951. I take the quotation from David Leeming, *Stephen Spender: A Life in Modernism*, New York, 1999, p. 178.
	typically Connollyan compliment: Connolly's review was published in the *Sunday Times*, 8 April 1951.
p. 358	*'We have an entire wing . . . with visiting poets'*: SS to John Hayward, 12 June 1951.
p. 359	*'the predicament of a generation'*: *Jrnls*, p. 95.
	'Blunt, Burgess and MacLean . . . manage other people': ibid., p. 442.
p. 360	*'The combination . . . one cannot be certain'*: Davenport-Hines, *Auden*, p. 275–6.
p. 361	*'appalled and frightfully sorry'*: John Lehmann, *The Ample Proposition*, London, 1996, p. 479.
	'definitely considers . . . a triangle, perhaps': recorded by SS in an unpublished diary entry, 1982.
p. 362	*'Because you aren't . . . he said you were'*: *Jrnls*, p. 105. The following remarks on age are unpublished. The comments on Britten's *Billy Budd* are on p. 106.
p. 364	*'The idea of going to Greece . . . a turning point in my work and my life'*: SS to Ronald Bottrall, [February] 1952.
	Spender left in early March for two months: the following narrative of the trip to Israel draws on *Learning Laughter* and the notebook-journal SS compiled for the book.
p. 365	*On his return from Israel . . . Modern Arts' in Paris*: the festival is fully described in Saunders, *Who Paid the Piper?*, pp. 113–28.
p. 366	*Spender was invited . . . the Elliston Professorship at the University of Cincinnati*: a full description of the chair's history, conditions of tenure, and the university is given by Bevis Hillier in the second volume of his biography of John Betjeman, *New Fame, New Love*, London, 2002.
p. 367	*'never to run the gauntlet of publishing a volume of poems again'*: the resolution is reiterated in *Jrnls*, p. 113.
	Spender's voluminous FBI file: I am grateful to Matthew Spender for sight of this much-blacked-out document.
p. 369	*'I had the strong impression . . . the young man's mercy'*: *Jrnls*, p. 118. This section draws on the published journal, unpublished passages, and NS's recollections. The founding of *Encounter* draws on Neil

Berry's account in *Articles of Faith*. The relevant documents and manuscripts are in the *Encounter* archive at Boston University.

p. 370 *'fantastically complicated British tax situation'*: Irving Kristol to Mel Lasky, 23 December 1958.

p. 371 *He was chronically suspicious . . . 'American auspices' of the magazine*: TSE to SS, 20 October 1953.

p. 372 *Spender thought . . . 'rather obvious anti-communism'*: SS to A. Korda, 5 November 1953.

'musty odor' in 'Spender's part of the magazine': N. Glazer to Irving Kristol, 30 December 1953.

'obvious defect . . . uncritical of the American situation': from an interview with Robert Silvers, 2003.

p. 373 *'The political atmosphere emitted . . . your present co-editor remains'*: E. M. Forster to SS, 9 March 1954.

'Irving Kristol fascinates . . . one over-worked secretary': unpublished entry. The following Swanage entries are also unpublished.

p. 375 *'I myself see things . . . the instrument of what I am'*: journal entry published in *Encounter*, January 1956.

p. 376 *'impossible to work with him . . . if it is made by his colleague'*: SS to MJ, 10 July 1954(?).

p. 377 *His first impression of the country was stark*: the account of the travels to Australia and India are taken from the published *Jrnls*.

'playing five concertos . . . till midnight': SS to ES, 22 September 1954.

p. 379 *There survives a series of letters*: held in the SSA. For details of Tony Hyndman's last years in Cardiff I am indebted to Richard Felstead.

p. 381 *On his part . . . towards his new employers*: Saunders, *Who Paid the Piper?*, p. 310.

'There was a lunch-hour patrol . . . a dawn watch': Frank McShane, *The Life of Raymond Chandler*, New York, 1976, p. 234.

p. 382 *'things I do . . . larger place in my life'*: *Jrnls*, p. 146. The following account of Matthew's injury is on p. 148.

'the great centre of hallucinations': journal entry published in *Encounter*, August 1956.

p. 383 *'is Wordsworth's whole sentient . . . a part of being'*: unpublished journal entry, 6 August 1955.

The encounter ended amicably, if awkwardly: the encounter is described at length in *Jrnls*, pp. 162–6.

p. 384 *The 'glittering . . . false teeth'*: journal entry published in *Encounter*, December 1955.

'*the first of its kind . . . and Western European intellectuals*': *Jrnls*, p. 130.
'*If we refuse . . . likely to become a* déluge': SS to MJ, undated from Venice.

'*the kind of horrified satisfaction . . . I am here*': journal entry in *Encounter*, September 1956. The subsequent description is from this source.

p. 386   '*Introductions which attempt . . . are always tiresome*': *New Statesman*, 7 July 1956.

'*young instructors . . . complaints about their boredom*': *New York Times*, 10 January 1957.

p. 387   '*he said that he did not like . . . Kruschev very sympathetic*': from an unpublished account of the dinner conversation which SS prepared.

'*It got no further than a pub in Knightsbridge*': from an interview with Anthony Sampson, 2002. The following account of SS's movements and events in his life is taken from the published and unpublished journal entries of the period.

p. 390   '*George Weidenfeld . . . agency money in Encounter*': said during an interview in 2003.

The upheaval dwarfed the Suez crisis: *Jrnls*, pp. 179–81. The subsequent account of SS's physical condition is from an unpublished entry. The account of the meeting of Eliot and Stravinsky is in *Jrnls*, pp. 183–4, supplemented by NS's recollections.

p. 393   '*liked the stories very much . . . bash it through*': SS to RP, 9 December 1956, 22 January 1957.

'*the house is golden when you are here*': SS to RP, 22 January 1957.

p. 394   '*every relationship with a man . . . has broken down*': SS to RP, 29 April 1957.

The austere Edward Upward . . . own such a vehicle: interview with Edward Upward, 2000.

p. 395   '*to re-read and I hope rewrite*': SS to RP, 22 January 1957.

'*all my red corpuscles . . . empty old trash can*': SS to RP, 9 February 1957.

p. 396   '*He said . . . Better put it on Stephen's plate*': from SS's unpublished journal account of the holiday.

'*Poor Natasha . . . while I was away*': SS to RP, 29 April 1957.

p. 397   '*his whole body tubular . . . botched inspired look*': SS to RP, 7 May 1957.

'*I hated every moment of it . . . the pants off Robert*': SS to RP, 20 June 1957.

p. 398   '*when word went round . . . asked for our autograph*': Margaret Drabble,

Angus Wilson, London, 1997, p. 234. Drabble gives a lively account of this episode. The following quotation about being interviewed twelve hours a day is in a letter from SS to Nicolas Nabokov, 9 September 1957.

p. 400   '*charming and detached*': Nicolas Nabokov gives an account of the composition and production of *Rasputin's End* in his autobiography, *Bagazh*, New York, 1975. SS's corresponding account is given in *Jrnls*, pp. 185–6.

'*pub-crawled a bit . . . young San Francisco poets*': *Jrnls*, p. 187. The following account of SS's second trip to Japan draws on the same source, supplemented by unpublished entries.

p. 401   '*an illegitimate son . . . throw yourself over a cliff*': SS to RP, 18 May 1958.

'*Met at station . . . best way of retrieving it*': *Jrnls*, p. 193.

p. 402   '*at that appalling place . . . unseeable and inaudible*': SS to RP, 11 September 1958.

p. 403   '*helps pay for the Jag*': SS to RP, 27 November 1958.

'*There was a sort of anarchism . . . the head of a university*': Jenny Rees, *Looking for Mr Nobody: The Secret Life of Goronwy Rees*, London, 2000, p. 179.

'*grateful to me for ever and ever*': ibid., 210.

p. 405   '*which will be . . . worse and worse in America*': SS to RP, 3 July 1959.

p. 406   '*How can you bear it? . . . you're unique*': unpublished entry, from SS's 1959 journal.

'*The idea that . . . any review I've ever read*': SS to RP, 30 July 1959.

p. 407   '*smelled like cushions . . . talcum powder*': SS to RP, 9 October 1959.

p. 408   '*the trouble about it is . . . lifted me out of the world of the John Wains*': SS to RP, 7 December 1959.

The 1960s: Young Rebels and Old Rebel

p. 411   '*quite strange and original*': SS to RP, 30 March 1960.

Spender spent two weeks in Moscow in early 1960: this episode follows that given in *Jrnls*, with supplementary material from NS.

p. 413   '*I'd probably end up . . . the other side was Dad*': SS to RP, 30 March 1960.

'*live in a surprisingly . . . lean, vibrant, talkative*': Sylvia Plath, *Letters Home: Correspondence, 1950–1963*, London, 1975, p. 380.

'*Natasha was not offered . . . for us both to go*': SS to RP, 13 May 1960.

p. 414 '*200% Jewish . . . as quickly as possible*': SS to RP, 29 June 1960.

'*in a financial mess again*': SS to RP, 16 August 1960.

'*sound on Lawrence*': from an interview with Jeremy Hutchinson, 2003.

'*It was slightly absurd . . . purest book ever written*': SS to RP, 18 November 1960.

p. 415 '*The Spender matter . . . his insincerity and characterlessness?*': *Who Paid the Piper?*, p. 372. The original is in the HRC.

p. 416 '*bringing up both my children in the same house*': unpublished 1960 journal entry.

'*I accepted because . . . pleased and excited for years*': SS to RP, 'January' 1961. The following account draws, largely, on NS's recollections, and SS's unpublished journal for 1961.

p. 417 '*bothers me a great deal . . . impossible to deal with*': SS to RP, 7 April 1961.

p. 419 '*All Matthew does . . . the facts of life*': drawn, as is other descriptive material at this period, from SS's unpublished 1961 journal. The remark about Matthew in the next sentence is from a letter, SS to Ruth Witt Diamant, 20 July 1961.

p. 420 '*three dark smelly rooms . . . I have had anywhere*': SS to RP, 9 March 1962.

'*I can earn £2,000 in a week . . . writing that matters*': SS to A. D. Peters, 2 May 1962.

'*Dad, if I get a scholarship . . . nothing but write poetry?*': *Jrnls*, p. 227. Other description in this section (such as the first meeting with Murdoch) draws on unpublished 1962 journal entries.

p. 421 '*Everyone I have ever met . . . staying with us*': SS to RP, 6 June 1962.

p. 422 '*I write poetry for some time . . . to finish anything*': *Jrnls*, p. 232. The previous quotation is from an unpublished entry.

'*it would have been no loss . . . strangled at birth*': ibid., p. 251. The account also draws on unpublished entries in the 1962 journal.

p. 423 '*that it will be reviewed by my arch-enemy, Alvarez*': SS to Hamish Hamilton, 14 February 1963.

'*I thought how little . . . all seemed scruffy*': *Jrnls*, p. 253.

p. 425 *a 'farewell gesture*': Saunders, *Who Paid the Piper?*, p. 375. I draw on Frances Stonor Saunders's account, the file of material assembled by JFK which contains originals and copies of correspondence, and relevant clippings from journals and newspapers on the *Encounter* crises in 1963 and 1966–7.

p. 426   'perhaps the most controversial . . . uncontroversially': Robert Silvers, interview, 2003.

p. 427   'It is a marvellous part . . . help me get some lectures': SS to RP, 12 May 1963.
           'will need all my 1964 dollars': SS to MJ, 17 September 1963.
           'something about having . . . always horrifies me': SS to RP, 11 June 1963.

p. 428   'is the uneasy feeling . . . that I do not know about': SS to MJ, [September] 1963.

p. 429   'Stephen, I think . . . what's going on': Saunders, *Who Paid the Piper?*, p. 377.
           'just a matter of money . . . instead of Castro': SS to MJ, 15 March 1964.

p. 430   'We have not changed . . . thought of as Cold War': SS to MJ, 22 September 1964.

p. 431   'I lead a terribly austere . . . ought to learn myself': SS to RP, 7 May 1964.

p. 432   'The next months . . . a bit anxious for us': SS to RP, 6 October 1964.
           'some permanent arrangement here': Richard Ellmann to SS, 12 November 1964.

p. 433   'if you really want to do this . . . not irrevocable': IB to SS, 2 June 1965.
           'I hope you will feel . . . with English writers': SS to MJ, 18 May 1964.
           'unable to resist the call of the first siren': Saunders, *Who Paid the Piper?*, p. 372.

p. 434   'writing editor . . . editing editor': ML to JFK, 16 September 1964.
           'I have real hopes of Kermode': SS to MJ, 26 December 1964.

p. 435   'feeling rather scared . . . glass walled office': SS to RP, [September] 1964.
           'like the hoof of an elephant': the account of SS in Washington draws on *Jrnls*, SS's unpublished journal for these two years, and the recollections of NS.

p. 436   'I don't really care . . . too political for me': SS to MJ, 19 October 1964.

p. 437   'like everyone else I put you in touch with': SS to JFK, 3 June 1967.

p. 438   'in some ways a barely credible . . . delayed and uneasy': Frank Kermode, *Not Entitled*, London, 1996, p. 225.
           'living in Gloucestershire . . . content of the magazine': ibid., p. 228.

p. 440 '*old Stalinists*': MJ to SS, 18 May 1966.

 '*to go through . . . keep such funds out*': SS to Mary McCarthy, 22 October 1966.

p. 441 '*I still don't quite . . . got into print*': Kermode, *Not Entitled*, p. 232.

 '*sultry badlands*': SS to RP, 27 June 1966.

p. 443 '*I had the memorably solemn . . . I would to my son'*'': Kermode, *Not Entitled*, pp. 234–5.

 '*exquisite little seminar*': ibid., p. 233.

p. 444 '*Kermode and I immediately . . . accepted their word*': SS to Carol Brightman, 11 August 1992.

p. 445 '*amazing set of statements . . . and show we are pure?*': personal communication, Richard Wollheim, 2003. See also Saunders, *Who Paid the Piper?*, p. 469.

p. 448 '*some of the manifestations . . . are justified*': MJ to SS, 9 April 1967.

 '*was never able . . . so clever*': Kermode, *Not Entitled*, p. 235.

 '*from the knowledge that he himself had to bear*': SS to MJ, 29 March 1967.

p. 451 '*I was implicated in receiving . . . had been from the CIA*': SS to Nicolas Nabokov, 21 July 1967.

pp. 454–5 '*We never really discussed . . . by way of Lord Goodman*': SS to JFK, 7 September 1967.

p. 458 '*In order to make an immediate response . . . Igor Stravinsky*': *Jrnls*, p. 258.

p. 459 '*Everything here . . . kept floating on dollars*': SS to MJ, 9 April 1968.

 '*happened to be in New York . . . decided to write about it*': *Jrnls*, p. 258.

p. 460 '*an irreproachable model . . . revolutionary manners*': SS, *The Year of the Young Rebels*, London, 1968, p. 49.

 '*anything that is worth doing involves having to get old*': *NYRB*, 11 July 1968.

p. 461 '*6,000 years old*': SS to Mary McCarthy, 2 May 1969.

p. 462 '*sufficiently remote to be historical . . . to be discussed*': *NYRB*, 25 September 1969.

p. 463 '*I only take one,*' said Wystan: *Jrnls*, pp. 269–70.

The 1970s: Grandparent, Not Yet GOM

p. 467 '*Is our baby a genius . . . after Saskia had been born*': entries in unpublished 1970 journal.

'*I hope that this may be . . . a bit of an ordeal*': SS to MJ, 22 December 1969.

p. 468   '*long-haired, pot-smoking, gothic-looking students*': Leeming, *Stephen Spender*, p. xi.

'*Dined with Auden . . . a core within him that purely burns*': *Jrnls*, pp. 272–3.

p. 469   '"*the new offensive . . . a terrible silence*': ibid., pp. 273–4.

'*Frank [Kermode] and I . . . put it to Noël*': interview with Richard Wollheim, 2002.

p. 470   '*impressive energy and pace*': WP to JL, 1 November 1969.

p. 471   '*This being a professor . . . Daniel Deronda circumcised?*': SS to RP, 14 January 1973. Spender's irreverent comments to David Plante are from an interview, 2003.

p. 474   *In spring 1972 . . . I shall never see him again*': account taken (as is much else in this section) from the recollections of NS.

p. 475   '*interesting in a* gritty *kind of way*': SS to Alan Ross, 2 June 1975.

'*by a strikingly beautiful woman, tall and almost regal in her deportment*': J. Brodsky, *New Yorker*, 8 January 1966. The subsequent description of Brodsky's encounter with C. P. Snow draws on SS's unpublished journal.

p. 476   '*Glaciers and fjords . . . one senior colleague implored*': Davenport-Hines, *Auden*, p. 339.

pp. 476–7   '*One feels incredibly cut off . . . that they are disillusioned*': SS to Keith Walker, 5 May 1973.

p. 480   '*Why do you always seem so serene and happy?*': *Jrnls*, p. 289.

'*I read this book . . . compacted substance of an aphorism*': *New Statesman*, 7 June 1974.

pp. 480–81 '*Cyril, who had interested . . . outlived his* gourmandise': *Jrnls*, p. 277.

p. 481   '*During the war . . . certainly did not mean to be funny*': SS, *The Thirties and After*, p. 221.

'*We all stood round . . . normality of any champagne party*': *Jrnls*, p. 281.

p. 482   '*Suddenly, it seems . . . in personal immortality*': this, and following quotations and descriptions, are taken from the unprinted portions of SS's 1974 journal. The account of the trip to Israel is largely taken from *Jrnls*, supplemented by the recollections of NS.

p. 484   '*the old Yalies . . . less sense of place, anywhere*': interview with Ed Mendelson, 2003.

p. 485   '*On the whole, I hate . . . "How philistine"*': *Jrnls*, p. 292.

'*I shall go on with writing . . . getting quite gaga*': SS to MJ, [April] 1975.

p. 487   *'I am very dull here . . . going to tame a mouse'*: SS to Keith Walker, 6 September 1975.

p. 488   *'I can see my way through . . . nothing but the abyss'*: *Jrnls*, p. 315.

            'being here is like . . . dissidents among your fellow exiles': SS to Keith Walker, 14 April 1976.

p. 489   *'Before I die . . . actable version of Trial of a Judge'*: SS to Cuthbert Worsley, 4 August 1975.

            'the events of the the past years . . . child-parent relations': *Jrnls*, p. 363.

            'certainly my greatest effort': SS to Alan Ross, 8 July 1979.

p. 490   *'a watershed . . . brought me so much happiness'*: SS to Tony Lombardy, 30 July 1979.

p. 491   *'who is very beautiful'*: SS to RP, 19 March 1977.

            'I feel I ought not to love Bryan . . . my continuous consciousness of him': SS to RP, 12 March 1978.

            'working against time to finish the play': SS to Tony Lombardy, 7 August 1977.

p. 493   *'the first few days . . . the last time I do this kind of thing'*: SS to Tony Lombardy, 9 January 1978.

            'the kind of scene which . . . the foreignness of America': *Jrnls*, p. 328.

pp. 493–4   *'In my dream . . . It was just a frayed end'*: ibid., p. 334.

p. 494   *'It was delightful . . . exhilarating conversation and gossip'*: ibid., p. 338.

p. 495   *'What's it like to be seventy'*: interview with E. McGrath, 2003. The account of this period of SS's life is supplemented from his unpublished journals for 1978 and 1979.

p. 497   *'I feel we are a comic duo . . . like a mad ecclesiastic'*: *Jrnls*, p. 373.

            'I am going to have a Final Phase': ibid., p. 378.

The 1980s: Retired But Not Resigned

p. 501   *'a shadow of what . . . twenty years ago'*: *Jrnls*, p. 397.

            'a dozen jewels . . . dump of failures': ibid.

p. 502   *'Everything I had done . . . much talent he has'*: ibid., p. 401.

            'I haven't had pain . . . miraculous like flying': SS to RP, 8 March 1980.

p. 503   *'consisted simply of students producing their poems'*: *Jrnls*, p. 401.

            'Christopher seeming scarcely . . . knew him': ibid., p. 402.

p. 504   *'luckier than most of the world's population'*: ibid., p. 404.

            'I was made pope . . . a humiliating failure': unpublished journal entry. The following comments on Murdoch are from *Jrnls*, p. 404.

p. 505   *'I'm eating steak . . . the reality of having power'*: unpublished journal
             entry. The following account of the visit to Mouton draws on *Jrnls*,
             1980, and unpublished material in the same source, as does the
             subsequent account of SS's reading at Hammersmith on 2 October
             1980; his journey from Oneonta to New York later in the month;
             his visit to Vera Stravinsky and others in New York in early November
             and his visit to Tulsa.

p. 509   *'I shall spend . . . the best departments for his subject in the country'*: SS
             to RP, [November] 1980. The subsequent account of SS's depar-
             ture from the US and arrival in the UK is from *Jrnls*, pp. 424–5,
             and unpublished entries in the journal.
             'It isn't his trying to rape me . . . what Cyril stands for': *Jrnls*, p. 435.

p. 510   *'he didn't mind . . . he too 'cared''*: ibid., p. 431.
             'a young man . . . escape from it all': ibid., p. 432.
             'I am very honoured . . . monuments of the dead': SS to unknown
             correspondent, 22 May 1980.

pp. 511–12   *'Being nearly 72 . . . embrace me in its tentacles'*: *Jrnls*, pp. 436–8.

pp. 512–13   *'sitting in the transit lounge . . . my two younger companions'*: SS, *China
             Diary*, pp. 10–11.

p. 513   *'As a boy . . . precious silk in much the same way'*: ibid.

p. 514   *'I felt anything . . . proved to be cancer'*: *Jrnls*, p. 441. Subsequent comments
             about the Falklands War draw on unpublished entries in the 1982
             journal.

p. 515   *'on and off for almost . . . funking the choruses'*: SS to RP, 27 February
             1983.

pp. 515–16   *Spring of 1983 . . . drum up funds for* Index: the following account
             of Spender's movements and activities in the first half of 1983 draws
             on *Jrnls* and unpublished entries from the same source.

p. 517   *'Thank you for your . . . shall take up this offer'*: *Jrnls*, p. 467.

p. 518   *'the severest blow to her beleaguered reputation'*: William Wright, *Lillian
             Hellman*, New York, 1986, p. 403.

p. 519   *'Another time . . . you're too squeamish'*: *Paris Review*, Winter 1980,
             p. 123.

p. 520   *'"I wonder what Malraux . . . ten thousand feet"'*: *WWW*, p. 239.
             'I don't really remember . . . think this is so': *Jrnls*, p. 426.

p. 522   *'Although I've all too often . . . of one's rivals'*: ibid., p. 481. The previous
             letters of congratulation were penned on 10 June 1983.
             'Around 11.30 . . . canal de Craponne': Peter J. Conradi, *Iris Murdoch:
             A Life*, London, 2001, p. 562.

'*Iris loved you . . . All, all*': John Bayley to NS, [February] 1999.

p. 523 '*he writes ecstatic letters . . . made Lizzie a bit ashamed of me*': SS to RP, 14 September, 'October' 1983.

p. 524 '*honey coloured and rocky mountains . . . pillared sky-lines*': the following account of SS's movements and thoughts in 1984 draws on the unpublished journal for that year, supplemented by recollections by NS and Matthew Spender.

'*This place is marvellous . . . and effective overdrive*': SS to RP, 14 September 1984.

p. 525 '*having to share . . . Drunken Hippies in that region*': SS to RP, 22 June 1984.

p. 528 '*For three hours . . . the nuances of Hamlet's character*': New York Times, 20 November 1984.

p. 529 '*you are obviously right to stick to Faber's*': David Astor to SS, 18 February 1985. The account of SS's movements and thoughts in 1985 draws on the unpublished journal for that year.

p. 531 '*Shelley had never met . . . English poets have made their history?*': New York Times, 26 January 1986.

'*I find the kind of sneering criticism . . . really a masterpiece of indignation*': SS to RP, 2 January 1986.

p. 532 '*of course, someone . . . a wonderful record of yourself*': Noël Annan to SS, 11 January 1986.

'*lost patience . . . horror of hospital deaths*': SS to Don Bachardy, 22 January 1986.

'*I have been feeling . . . how old I am*': SS to RP, 14 February 1986.

p. 533 '*I have friends . . . after he has done his Ph.D.*': SS to RP, 23 May 1986.

p. 534 '*It is rather amazing . . . penniless student day, in them*': SS to RP, [July] 1988.

p. 535 '*Your novel is marvellously . . . It shouldn't be suppressed*': Noël Annan to SS, 11 February 1987.

'*the closing sequence . . . art of a high order*': Peter Ackroyd to SS, 20 February 1988.

'*the book is in some fashion a poem*': TH to SS, 1 March 1988.

p. 536 *At Easter Spender and Matthew . . . believe in an afterlife*: the account of the last 'honeymoon' draws on interviews with Matthew and SS's unpublished journal for 1988.

The 1990s: 'Five years he shouldn't have had'

p. 541   *'he got Aids because he identified with Aids'*: unpublished journal entry, February 1995. The account of Obst's funeral draws on an interview with Don Bachardy, 2002.

Suitor and prospective father-in-law became fast friends: the subsequent account draws on interviews and conversations with Barry Humphries, 2002 and 2003.

p. 544   *'200-pound royal baby . . . the angels of light are needed now'*: SS to TH, 12 December 1989, 4 October 1991.

p. 546   *'Aren't you lucky, Dad . . . a godsend really'*: SS to TH, 11 October 1992.

p. 547   *'real . . . "Collected Poems"'*: John Bodley to SS, 3 February 1995. SS's unpublished journals over these years are preoccupied with these disputes – which, privately, he accepted stoically.

p. 548   *'My Life is Mine, not David Leavitt's'*: *Evening Standard*, 6 March 1994.

'hateful battlefields': TH to SS, 1 February 1994.

p. 549   *'and gives very well . . . everyone does sexually nowadays'*: I am grateful to Alan Hollinghurst for showing me this letter.

p. 550   *On 14 April . . . moved to tears*: this account, and those following, draw on the unpublished journals which SS kept, almost to the day of his death, supplemented by the recollections of NS.

p. 551   *'a clean, precise, concentrated . . . done like that!'*: TH to SS, 1 February 1994.

p. 552   *'Who else would have cared . . . his memorable* World within World*?'*: *TLS*, 18 February 1994. Pitt-Kethley's comments are from the *Guardian*, 24 February 1994.

p. 554   *Stephen was heavily 'doped' . . . 'flaked out and fell asleep'*: this account is taken from recollections of NS and Matthew Spender, as is much else in the description of SS's last days.

p. 555   *'Spender, still among . . . the company he keeps'*: *Spectator*, 10 February 1995.

p. 557   *Karl Miller . . . for tea*: the following is taken from conversation with Karl Miller, supplemented by NS's recollections.

p. 559   *'On account of my Russianness . . . their real sentiments in check'*: *New Yorker*, 8 January 1996.

p. 561   *'was meeting Corsellis . . . which seemed adequate'*: *WWW*, p. 292. The poem was published in *London Magazine*, June–July, 1995.

Acknowledgements

My main debt in writing this biography is to Lady Spender. She authorized the book and allowed unfettered access to her husband's literary and personal papers, the bulk of which are in the estate's private keeping. She has also contributed, often in the spirit of a co-author, to the writing of the work. At no point has she imposed restraint on the biographer – although more often than I care to acknowledge she has pointed out errors of fact, scholarship, interpretation or emphasis, which I have gladly corrected (those that remain are my own).

I am indebted to other members of Stephen Spender's family. Humphrey and Christine Spender offered information about their brother's life and personal background which only they were in a position to supply. Younger members of the family – Stephen Spender's nephew, Philip, his children Matthew and Lizzie, and his son-in-law Barry Humphries – have been generous with time, reminiscences, and (where they survive) literary documents.

Stephen Spender's surviving friends have been cooperative and helpful in practical ways. Frank Kermode, Stuart Hampshire, Richard Wollheim and Karl Miller spent many hours talking to me and more hours reading my typescript. One of Stephen's closest American friends, Reynolds Price, not only gave me days of his time (and read the typescript) but also allowed me access to his unrivalled collection of correspondence with Stephen Spender. Without him, I could not have written this biography as I wished to. And it has been a privilege to come to know him.

Ed Mendelson, a model of scholarship for all those working on the Auden Generation, was extraordinarily helpful (and tactful in his corrections). Other scholars working in adjacent biographical areas – Selina Hastings, Peter Conradi, Henry Hardy and Peter Parker – have helped me more than, I regret, I have been able to help them.

A number of Stephen Spender's friends – Anthony Lombardy, Gabriel Carritt and Keith Walker – allowed me to see his correspondence with them. David Elliott wrote, unsolicited, alerting me to the illuminating run of correspondence generated by the break-up of Spender's first marriage which he owns. I have listed these, and other resources, made available to me in the *Note on Primary Sources*, pp. 563–5. I wish to express my gratitude here.

Natasha Spender and I were the recipients of a fellowship from the Harry Ransom Center, and the British Academy underwrote the compilation of a xerox archive of Spender's journalism and prose writings (expertly assembled by Ann Totterdell).

The principal justification for this biography is the publications – and particularly the poetry – which Spender produced over his long writing career. It is particularly gratifying that Faber are publishing, at the time that this biography will appear, what Spender's friend and editor, John Bodley, liked to call the 'real' *Collected Poems* (edited by Michael Brett). John Bodley, and Spender's editor, Ed Victor, have worked hard and successfully to keep their author in print and his critical reputation high. I would like to thank my own agent, Victoria Hobbs (and her predecessor, Alexandra Pringle), and my editor at Viking Penguin, Mary Mount.

Faber, who have been vigilant stewards of Spender's published work for three-quarters of a century, have been generous in the matter of permissions, for which I am grateful, as I am for permission to quote from the following holders of copyright: Jason Toynbee, John Bayley, Diana Josselson, Valerie Eliot, Gabriele Annan, Carol Hughes, Peter Ackroyd, Jill Day-Lewis, David Elliott, Lady Berlin. T.S. Eliot's texts are the copyright of Mrs Valerie Eliot. They are quoted by permission of the Estate and Faber & Faber Ltd. Quotations from letters written by Isaiah Berlin © The Isaiah Berlin Literary Trust 2004 are published by permission of the Trustees. Humphrey Spender has supplied many of the photographs gathered in this book.

If, by oversight, any estate, or holder of copyright, has been overlooked, I request them to contact me, or the publisher.

Index

Huxley, Juliette, 502

Hyndman, Tony ('Tommy', 'Jimmy
Younger'), 293, 528–529; origins and
background, 150–52; travels and
settles in London with Stephen,
152–7; 'secretary', 157; overwhelmed
by Venice, 161; appendicitis, and
operation in Vienna, 164–5; recovery,
166–7; returns to England, 168; difficulties with Stephen, 180–81; residence in Cintra, 183–9; dedicatee of
The Burning Cactus, 192; joins
Communist Party, 194; break with
Stephen, 194–5; moves in with
Cuthbert Worsley, 195; reaction to
Stephen's first marriage, 201–2; joins
the International Brigade, 203–4;
leaves for Spain, 204–5; problems in
the International Brigade, 211; fights
at Jarama, 213; breaks down, is
arrested, and induces Stephen to
rescue him, 216–20; returns to
England, 224–5; post-war difficulties
and 'dependence' on Stephen,
230–31; assists Muriel Gardiner, 231;
at loose end in England, 238–9;
employed by John Lehmann, 242;
and Stephen's divorce, 255; joins
Horizon, 257; relationship with
Michael Redgrave, 263–4, 277;
invites Natasha Litvin to party,
where she meets Stephen, 273; post-
war affair with Christopher
Isherwood, 323; as 'Jimmy Younger',
357; difficulties in later life, 378–9;
death, 379

Hynes, Samuel, 231–2

I am a Camera, 107

Idelma (Loncrini, servant), 358

Ignatieff, Michael, 118, 129

Iliffe, James, 269

Index on Censorship, 2, 407, 458–9, 474,
516, 555

Inverchapel, Archie, 334

Isherwood, Christopher, 192–3, 228,
236, 245, 468, 495, 503, 529; first

meeting with Stephen, 80; relationship with Auden, 83; enthusiasm for
Germany, 89; austerity of life there,
90; sexual philosophy, 90–91; distaste
for England, 91; *Berlin Stories*, 92,
111; in Berlin, 106–7, 110–11;
Stephen joins him in Berlin, 122–3;
dominates Stephen, 123–4; at Insel
Ruegen, 126–8; meets Forster, 128;
Hogarth Press accepts *The Memorial*,
131–2; excludes Stephen from
Mohrinsee, 136; relationship with
Heinz Neddermeyer, 136, 138–9;
estrangement from Stephen, 140–41;
accepts dedication of *Poems, 1933*,
158; dubious opinion of *Vienna*, 173;
is reassured by Stephen as to his
sexual preference, 180; residence in
Cintra, 183–9; on Stephen's marriage
to Inez, 200–201; leaves for America,
243; strained relationship over
Horizon, 265–6; post war visit to
London, 320; post-war affair with
Tony Hyndman, 323; death of, 530,
532

Israel, Wilfrid ('Bernard Landauer'),
139

Jacobson, Dan, 486

Jagger, Chris, 462

James, Henry, 9, 15, 126, 161, 179, 501

Janin, René, 159

Jarman, Dr, 555, 559

Jarrell, Randall, 329, 334

Jaspers, Karl, 319

Jay, Douglas, 87

Jeffries, Cynthia, 353

Jennings, Elizabeth, 530

Jennings, Humphrey, 240

Johnson, Lyndon B. (President), 435–6

Johnson, Paul, 547

Jones, Alan Pryce, 385

Jones, D.A.N, 531

Jones, Michael, 292–3

Josselson, Diana, 454

Josselson, Michael, 356, 369–70, 376, 415,
417, 424–5, 427, 429–30, 432–3, 436,